Philosophy of Beauty

Philosophy of Beauty

Francis J. Kovach

UNIVERSITY OF OKLAHOMA PRESS
NORMAN

By FRANCIS J. KOVACH
Die Aesthetik des Thomas von Aquin-eine genetische and systemtische
   Analyse (Berlin, 1961)
Philosophy of Beauty (Norman, 1974)

The paper in this book meets the guidelines for permanence and durability of the Committee on Production Guidelines for Book Longevity of the Council on Library Resources, Inc. ∞

Library of Congress Cataloging in Publication Data

Kovach, Francis Joseph.
    Philosophy of beauty.
    Bibliography: p. 318
    ISBN 978-0-8061-1363-0 (Paper)
    1. Aesthetics.   I. Title.
BH39.K65   III.8'5   73–19389

Copyright 1974 by the University of Oklahoma Press, Norman, Publishing Division of the University. Paperback published 1976.

All rights reserved. No part of this publication may be reproduced, stored in a retrieval system, or transmitted, in any form or by any means, electronic, mechanical, photocopying, recording, or otherwise--except as permitted under Section 107 or 108 of the United States Copyright Act--without the prior written permission of the University of Oklahoma Press.

*To my beloved wife and children, who are all,
I know, lovers of beauty.*

Preface

THIS BOOK grew out of my gradual realization over the years that, at the present, aesthetic objectivism is being challenged from every direction and thus is on the defensive; and that the precious heritage and the admirable wisdom of the aesthetic objectivists of the past, especially those in the Middle Ages, are virtually forgotten.

This twofold realization has determined this work, as it gradually took shape, in three fundamental respects: first, that the historical material constitutes a considerable portion, if not the larger part of the work; second, that the work is argumentative both positively and negatively; and third—and this, perhaps, is the most important—that my main purpose has been not novelty or originality of thought but the truth about beauty, at least as I see it on the basis of epistemological (although not naïve) realism. Indeed, if I have regrets in retrospection, it is not that the doctrinal material is not more original, but that perhaps I could have argued for an objectivist philosophy of beauty with greater eloquence and efficiency.

In connection with the argumentative character of this work, I wish to point out that I do not consider all the arguments herein to be of equal probative force. Some arguments, like those concerning the extramentality and transcendentality of beauty, are conclusive in my opinion; whereas the argumentation in the various phases of establishing the three analytic principles of beauty is not meant to be more than persuasive. Why, then, have I included such arguments? Because I wholeheartedly agree on this issue with one of the greatest figures in the history of philosophy, St. Thomas Aquinas—who pointed out that a reasonable opinion based on good but not decisive reasons is better than no opinion or, I may add, a pathetically apologetic *Ignoramus et ignorabimus* to a question.

Speaking of its form, this book is so written that it can be used as a textbook by both undergraduate and graduate students; and I hope that it will serve also as source material on some segments of the history of aesthetics which are presently rather ignored, e.g., the patristic, the medieval scholastic, and the nineteenth-century German aesthetic literature. Undergraduate students using this book may largely ignore the footnotes and even some chapters or articles. Graduate students should be interested in all the chapters and a considerable amount of footnoted material. Experts in metaphysical aesthetics and the history of aesthetics may find certain topics, such as the transcendentality and division of beauty and the metaphysics of ugliness, as well as the footnotes to be of professional interest.

Throughout the years of my research for this book, I had the opportunity to use, on ancient and medieval aesthetics, the libraries of the University of Oklahoma, The Saint Paul Seminary in St. Paul, Minnesota, St. Benedict's College in Atchison, Kansas, Villanova University in Villanova, Pennsylvania, and the Thomas Institute in Cologne, Germany; and, on modern European and American aesthetics, also the libraries of the University of California in Los Angeles and the California State College in San Diego. I take this opportunity to thank these institutions for all the courtesies, both professional and personal, I received from their personnel.

I was able to borrow numerous books from libraries throughout the country by means of the interlibrary loan services of the University of Oklahoma. Also, I received financial aid for research trips from the Faculty Research Committee of this same university, and the Administration and the Department of Philosophy of the University of Oklahoma obliged me by granting clerical help. For all these generosities I wish to express my sincere thanks and appreciation.

I am also obliged for various reasons to a number of individuals in connection with this work. Among them are Mrs. Elizabeth M. Cowan and Mrs. Patricia Parkhurst, who typed the manuscript; Mr. Louis Parkhurst, who originally compiled the Index of Names; my wife, Elizabeth, and Mr. Joseph L. Pappin, who so kindly assisted me in the proofreading; and Mr. Curtis L. Hancock, who carefully read the finished manuscript. Most of all, however, I owe a very special gratitude to Professor R. E. McCall of the Catholic University of America, Washington, D. C., and the late Professor Paul Wilpert of the University of Cologne, who were, many years ago, among the first to encourage me to write a realistic and systematic philosophy of beauty; to Professor Emeritus Béla von Brandenstein of the University of Saarbruecken, Germany, and Professor Josef de Vries of *Berchmanskolleg* in Pullach at Munich, who in their unique ways inspired me to write such an aesthetics; and to Professor Joseph Owens of the Pontifical Institute of Mediaeval Studies, Toronto, and Professor John M. Quinn of Biscayne College, Miami, Florida, for their helpful suggestions on an elusive metaphysical issue I discuss in this book.

In concluding my reflections on the genesis of this work, all I can ultimately hope is that the intellectual, moral, and technical assistance and the work of research and metaphysical speculation that was given and went into this book will not have been in vain; that at least some of the readers will feel somewhat illumined about the history of aesthetics, or will receive some insight into the perennial metaphysical mysteries of beauty.

F.J.K.

Norman, Oklahoma
March 7, 1974

Table of Contents

Preface   *Page vii*

PART ONE: Aesthetics in General

Chapter I: The Etymological Definition of Aesthetics   5
- Article 1: "Aesthetics" and A. G. Baumgarten   5
- Article 2: Reasons for the Name "Aesthetics"   7
- Article 3: Evaluation of the Name "Aesthetics"   8

Chapter II: The Essential Definition of Aesthetics   11
- Article 1: Difficulties of Finding the Essential Definition   11
- Article 2: The Essential Definition of Aesthetics   21

Chapter III: Division of Aesthetics   32
- Article 1: Division of Speculative Aesthetics   33
- Article 2: Division of Practical Aesthetics and Auxiliary Sciences   38

PART TWO: Philosophy of Beauty

Section One: The Existence of Beauty   51

Chapter IV: Direct Argument for Aesthetic Objectivism   55
- Article 1: Outline of the Argument   55
- Article 2: Details of the Objectivist Argument   56
- Article 3: Clarification of the Objectivist Position   62

Chapter V: Evaluation of Aesthetic Subjectivism   65
- Article 1: Apparent and Implicit Real Aesthetic Subjectivism   65
- Article 2: Metaphysical, Cosmological, and Negative Psychological Aesthetic Subjectivism   73
- Article 3: Aesthetic Associationism and Relationism   93

Chapter VI: Reasons for Aesthetic Disagreement   101
- Article 1: Reasons for Apparent Disagreement   105
- Article 2: Partly Subjective Reasons for Real Disagreement   107
- Article 3: Completely Subjective Reasons for Real Disagreement   118

Section Two: The Essence of Beauty — 137

Chapter VII: Historical Review of Positions on the Essence of Beauty — 138
- Article 1: Skeptic Views on Beauty — 140
- Article 2: Subjectivist and Idealist Views on Beauty — 149
- Article 3: Realistic Definitions of Beauty — 156

Chapter VIII: The Aesthetic Method — 166
- Article 1: Aesthetic Methods — 167
- Article 2: The Aesthetic Method To Be Used — 176

Chapter IX: The Essential Definition of Beauty — 184
- Article 1: Presentation of the Essential Definition — 184
- Article 2: Demonstration of the Essential Definition — 193

Section Three: Consequences of the Essence of Beauty — 215

Chapter X: Division of Beauty — 217
- Article 1: Historical Consideration — 217
- Article 2: Doctrinal Consideration — 229

Chapter XI: Extension and Privation of Beauty — 236
- Article 1: The Transcendentality of Beauty — 236
- Article 2: Ugliness — 250

Chapter XII: The Aesthetic Experience — 265
- Article 1: A Historical Review — 265
- Article 2: The Structure and Components of the Aesthetic Experience — 290

Bibliography — 318

Index of Names — 338

Index of Topics — 345

Philosophy of Beauty

Part One: Aesthetics in General

EVERY SCIENCE, to be properly understood, requires definition and divison. Aesthetics is no exception to this. Therefore, the first objective for us is to define and divide aesthetics itself.

One can define a thing in several ways which can be reduced to two groups: essential and non-essential definitions. Of these, it has been more or less traditional in realistic philosophy to use two definitions concerning any given science, namely, an essential and an etymological definition. The latter of these two explains the name of the science in question; the former, the very nature of that science.

As far as aesthetics is concerned, neither the etymological nor the essential definition is a simple matter, although for different reasons. The etymological definition is not a simple task because the literary meaning of the name "aesthetics" does not simply refer to what we would expect, or what we generally mean, by the name today. The essential definition, on the other hand, is not a simple task for a number of reasons that are partly historical, partly epistemological.

Due to all these circumstances, the introductory part of this book will comprise three chapters: one on the etymological definitions; another on the essential definition; and a third on the division of aesthetics in such a way that, within each chapter, the various aspects of the question will be treated in separate articles.

CHAPTER I

The Etymological Definition of Aesthetics

ONE OF THE NUMEROUS PARADOXES surrounding aesthetics is the fact that, in one way, aesthetics is among the oldest sciences; in another way, it is a relatively new science.

Aesthetics is one of the oldest sciences in the sense that there has been aesthetic speculation going on in the Western World, beginning in Greece, from as early a time as the sixth century B.C. throughout ancient, medieval, and modern times at least in connection with and occasioned by other sciences, like philosophy, mathematics, theology, and psychology. Thus, we know from Aristoxenus, a disciple of Aristotle, that the early Pythagoreans recognized and, consequently, practiced the purification of the soul by music;[1] and, from Porphyry, that Heraclitus already had an insight into the omnipresence or transcendentality of beauty.[2] Other thinkers occasionally touching on questions of aesthetics in ancient times are Plato, Aristotle, Philo of Alexandria, Cicero, Plotinus, Augustine, Dionysius the Areopagite, etc.; in medieval times, Alexander of Hales, John of la Rochelle, Thomas of York, Bonaventure, Albert the Great, Thomas Aquinas, and Dionysius the Carthusian, etc.; in modern times, from Descartes and J. Addison on, virtually all rationalists and empiricists, then Kant, Hegel, Schopenhauer, Nietzsche, Tolstoi, Santayana, and Croce to such contemporaries as Maritain, Sartre, H. Read, and Thomas Munro.

On the other hand, as an independent, sovereign science, aesthetics is relatively young: scarcely more than two hundred years old.

ARTICLE I: *"Aesthetics" and A. G. Baumgarten*

1. The one who made aesthetics an independent science was Alexander Gottlieb Baumgarten (1714-1762), the most significant disciple of the rationalist Christian Wolff. This he accomplished with his work, *Aesthetica*, published in 1750, and complemented by a second volume in 1758.[1] The title of

---

[1] Fragment 279 in G. S. Kirk and J. E. Raven, *The Presocratic Philosophers* (New York: Cambridge University Press, 1963), p. 229.

[2] Fragment 209; *ibid.*, p. 193.

[1] *Aesthetica scripsit Alexander Gottlieb Baumgarten.* (Francofurti cis Viadrum: Joannes Christianus Kleyb, 1750. Reprographic reprint: Hildesheim: G. Olms, 1961.) It was followed by *Aestheticorum pars altera* (Francofurti cis Viadrum: J. C. Kleyb, 1758). The *Aesthetica* is an extension of what Baumgarten, in his doctoral dissertation entitled *Meditationes philosophicae de nonnullis ad poema pertinentibus* (Halle: J. H. Grunertus, 1735; English tr., *Reflections on Poetry*, ed. K. Aschenbrenner and W. B. Holther, Berkeley: University of California Press, 1954), called "philosophical

the former work has become the name of the new science of aesthetics. Baumgarten used this name in this sense first in his doctoral dissertation of 1735.[2] Characteristically enough, this meaning of the name was so novel that it probably would not have survived had it not been for the fact that Kant, who in his *Critique of Pure Reason* had criticized the very idea of an independent science of beauty,[3] and used the term "aesthetic" still in the old, literary sense,[4] eventually changed his mind,[5] and adopted the name in the novel, Baumgartenean meaning in his *Critique of Judgement*.[6]

2. What, then, is aesthetics according to the name as coined by Baumgarten? Or, to put it in another way, what is the etymological definition of aesthetics?

Αἰσθάνομαι is a verb that in classic Greek meant "to perceive or apprehend through the senses";[7] αἴσθησις, a noun, meaning sensory perception;[8] and finally, αἰσθητικός, an adjective, signifying "pertaining to sense perception," or "that which is perceivable." From this it follows that the Baumgarten-given name αἰσθητική or (*scientia*) *aesthetica*, means "science dealing with sense perception." This is explicitly confirmed by Baumgarten himself both in his *Aesthetica* and his *Metaphysica*.[9]

Comparing this etymology with the names of some other sciences, like biology ("science of life"), physics ("science of nature"), or anthropology

---

poetics" (philosophia poetica; *Meditationes*, § 9; *transl. cit.*, p. 39). At the same time, the *Aesthetica* was also the realization of what Baumgarten envisioned in his doctoral work as a possible task of philosophical aesthetics, which task he expressed as follows: "[We] have no doubt that there could be available a science which might direct the lower cognitive faculty in knowing things sensately." (*Meditationes*, § 115; *transl. cit.*, p. 78.)

[2] Baumgarten, *Meditationes*, § 116; *transl. cit.*, p. 78.

[3] In a footnote to the very first paragraph of the *Critique of Pure Reason*, Kant speaks of Baumgarten's "abortive attempt" (*eine verfehlte Hoffnung*) "to bring the critical treatment of the beautiful under rational principles." (A 21. English translation by Norman Kemp Smith. London: Macmillan, 1963, p. 66.)

[4] *Critique of Pure Reason*, I, Part I: "Transcendental Aesthetic" (*Die transzendentale Asthetik*) A 19 = B 33. "The science of all principles of a priori sensibility I call *transcendental aesthetics*." (*Ibid.*, A. 21 = B 35)

[5] Kant did so step by step. First, in April of 1787, he inserted certain adjectives in the footnote on Baumgarten (mentioned in note 6 above) in the second edition of the *Critique of Pure Reason*. Two months, later, June 25, he expressed his intention to Christian G. Schütz to investigate the principles of a critique of taste. (*Werke*, Berlin: B. Cassirer, 1922, vol. IX, 329.) The fruit of this investigation was his *Critique of Judgment*, the first part of which deals with aesthetic judgment.

[6] "Der Kritik der Urteilskraft Erster Teil, Kritik der ästhetischen Urteilskraft."

[7] This verb is first to be found in Herodotus, III, 87. Cf. Plato, *Theaet.* 185 and Aristotle, *De an.* II, 5, 417a 10–14.

[8] To be found, e.g., in Plato, *Phaed.* 111b, and Aristotle, *De an.* II, 5, 416b 33.

[9] In his *Aesthetica*, he writes: "Aesthetica . . . est scientia cognitionis sensitivae." (§ 1. Cf. *ibid.*, § 14.) In the earlier *Metaphysica* (first edition, Halae Magdeburgical: C. H. Hemmerde, 1739), we find this: "Scientia sensitive cognoscendi et proponendi est aesthetica (die Wissenschaft des Schömen)." (§ 533, *ed. cit.*, p. 124.) See the same also in George F. Meier's *Anfangsgründe aller schönen Wissenschaften*, §§ 2 and 5. (Halle im Magdeburgischen: Carl Hermann Hemmerde, 1748), 3, 8, and 9.

("science of man"), the difference between these sciences and that of aesthetics is quite obvious. For, while the names of these listed sciences express exactly what we generally mean by them, the name "aesthetics" as "the science of sense perception" means something totally different from what people nowadays generally mean by aesthetics.

What, then, is the meaning of this Baumgartenean etymology, and why did he give this apparently irrelevant name to our science?

ARTICLE 2: *Reasons for the Name "Aesthetics"*

There are two answers required by the above questions: one, explaining what Baumgarten had in mind in giving the name "aesthetics" to our science; and two, explaining why he had what he had in mind. Thus, the first answer is doctrinal; the second, historical.

1. According to Baumgarten, aesthetics is a science whose subject, beauty, is a perfection of things that delights only inasmuch as it has become sensorily perceived. For it is not the intellect through which we can come to know and enjoy beauty, but rather through the senses; not through clear concepts, but through confused sensory images.[1]

Without asking, at this point, to what extent this view on the knowability of beauty is true, let us ask instead another relevant question: How did Baumgarten come to hold this view? This question is the more intriguing since Baumgarten was a rationalist, like Descartes or Spinoza, and the rationalists generally shared the aesthetic views of ancient and medieval philosophies, beginning with Plato and Aristotle—such as, the objective reality of beauty, and beauty being the proper object of the rational intellect—a position that is the contrary opposite of Baumgarten's above-expressed view.

2. It is a common doctrine of major ancient and medieval thinkers[2] that beauty is only intellectually knowable. Descartes, the father of modern phi-

---

[1] "Repraesentationes distinctae . . . non sunt sensitivae ergo nec poeticae." (*Meditationes philosophicae*, § 14.) "Quum clarae repraesentationes sint poeticae, . . . iam distinctae non sunt . . . ergo confusae." (*Ibid*., § 15. Cf. also § 115.) "[In] omni sensatione connexa cum senso, seu eo, quod sentitur, singula repraesentantur, at non clare . . . Ergo in omni sensatione est aliquid obscuri." (*Metaphysica*, § 544; *ed. cit.*, p. 127) Cf. *Aesthetica*, §§ 15–16.

[2] The basic reason to them was this reasoning: Beauty is order or unity in variety. But order or unity in variety is the proper object of the intellect and, as such, knowable only to the intellect. Therefore, beauty is knowable only through the intellect. For Plato, see *Hipp. mai*. 299e–300b. For Aristotle, compare *Met*. VIII, 9, 1032a 24 and *Phys*. 252a 12 with *Poet*. VII, 4, 1450b 34–39. For Plotinus, see *Enn*. I, 6, 3, and also texts dealing with beauty as form (VI, 7, 12; 37; VI, 9, 1; etc.) Cicero is quite explicit on this issue: "Itaque eorum ipsorum, quae adspectu sentiuntur, nullum aliud animal pulchritudinem, venustatem, convenientiam partium sentit." (*De off*. I, 4, 14.) In Augustine, *De ver. rel*. 30, 55 (Migne, *Patrologia Latina*, henceforth *PL*, 34, 146) is the relevant text. Aquinas states his position this way: Unde cum cetera animalia non delectantur in sensibilibus nisi per ordinem ad cibos et venerea, solus homo delectatur in ipsa pulchritudine sensibilium secundum seipsam. (*Summa theol*. I, q. 91, c. 3, ad 3.) Cf., apprehensio sensitiva non se extendit ad hoc quod cognoscere possit proportionem unius ad alteram, sed hoc est proprium rationis. (*Ibid.*, II–II, q. 58, c. 4.)

losophy, went along with this view. But, influenced by Spinoza's much-emphasized division of knowledge that opposes sensory and rational knowledge as being inferior and superior, and confused and clear, respectively, Leibniz eventually took the position that musical beauty is born in the subconscious mind, and is knowable and enjoyable only through "confused perception."[3] This unexpected turn in rationalist thinking about beauty influenced Christian Wolff and, after him, Baumgarten himself. Baumgarten simply extended what Leibniz said of music to beauty in general, and came to hold the following views. No beauty is rationally knowable. Instead, beauty is knowable only through confused knowledge, i.e., sensory images, whereas essences are rationally knowable through clear concepts. But concepts are the subject of logic. Therefore, if there is a science professionally dealing with beauty at all, then that science must be distinct from and precisely the contrary opposite of logic.

There is only one more historical fact to be added to this genesis of Baumgarten's theory of the independent science of aesthetics. Christian Wolff, Baumgarten's master, in his division of sciences made logic *the* propaedeutic science, and failed to make room for a science opposite to logic and dealing with beauty. Thus, Baumgarten, having recognized the need for an independent science of beauty and also its character opposite to logic, needed to make only a small change in the Wolffian division of sciences, namely, dividing propaedeutic science into logic, as the science of suprasensory knowledge, and his own aesthetics, as the science of sensory knowledge, that is, a knowledge whose proper object is beauty.[4]

ARTICLE 3: *Evaluation of the Name "Aesthetics"*

The name "aesthetics" can be evaluated in two ways: absolutely, in itself, and relatively, in comparison to other conceivable names that might be given to our science.

1. One thing is certain about the name Baumgarten gave to our science. If it is true that beauty is the proper object of the senses, then the etymological definition of aesthetics as the science of sense perception does make sense. For

[3] "Musica est exercitium arithmetica occulta nescientis se numerare animi. Multa enim facit in perceptionibus confusis seu insensibilibus quae distincta apperceptione notare nequit . . . Anima igitur, etsi se numerare non sentiat, sentit tamen huius numerationis insensibilis effectum, seu voluptatem in consonantiis . . . Ex multis enim congruentiis insensibilibus oritur voluptas." Leibniz, *Opera mathematica*, No. 79: Epistolae tres ad Christianum Goldbachium, Epistola II, n. 4. *Opera omnia*, ed. L. Dutens (Geneva: Fratres de Tournes, 1768), III, 437.

[4] "Sunt erga νοητά cognoscenda facultate superiore obiectum logices, αἰσθητὰ ἐπιστήμης αἰσθητικῆς sive aestheticae." (Baumgarten, *Meditationes philosophicae*, § 116.) In doing so, Baumgarten followed, at least materially, Giambattista B. Vico, who in his *Scienza Nuova* distinguished between "poetic" and "intellectual logic." (See B. Croce, *The Philosophy of Giambattista Vico*, chap. 4, R. G. Collingwood, tr., London: H. Latimer, 1913, pp. 46 ff.; and *Aesthetic*, tr. Douglas Ainslie, New York: The Noonday Press, 1956, pp. 220 ff.)

then aesthetics is the science of sense perception in as much as sense perception is the sole and proper source of knowing beauty.

But is it true that beauty is sensorily knowable? Without trying to anticipate the analysis of the relevant doctrinal question that will emerge in the last chapter of this book, in the context of the philosophy of beauty, we can easily recognize from our own experiences with beauty that one does, indeed, need his senses, such as his sight or hearing, in order to come to recognize and to enjoy the beauty of material things.

Thus Baumgarten's etymological definition of aesthetics is correct insofar as sensory perception is the necessary condition of aesthetic experience.

However, it is equally clear that beauty is not the sole object of sense perception, since beauty is only one among many aspects in material things. Furthermore, as will be demonstrated, sense perception alone is not sufficient for the recognition and the subsequent enjoyment of beauty. Instead, sense perception merely presents the image to the mind, and it is ultimately the mind, the intellect, that intuitively recognizes and, consequently, enjoys the beauty of the perceived object. This is to say that sense perception is truly a necessary condition, but not the only condition, of aesthetic experience.

In this light, then, the Baumgartenean name given to our science makes some sense, but by no means complete sense. For, if one wants to name a science after the faculties that per se recognize the proper object of that science, then he ought to list both (or all) such faculties and not only one of them, and the essentially less important one at that. Using Baumgarten's logic, our science should thereby be called not only the science of sense perception but also that of intellectual intuition.

From all this it follows that Baumgarten's etymological definition of aesthetics is not only indirect, naming not the subject of the science in question but rather a faculty through which that subject is knowable, but also incomplete, since naming only one of the two faculties necessary for our knowing and enjoying beauty.

2. By way of a relative evaluation, we may ask, especially in the light of the absolute evaluation, this question: Is not there a better name conceivable for our science?

The answer to this particular question is definitely affirmative. For, insofar as aesthetics is a science somehow related to or professionally interested in beauty or "aesthetic value," the most appropriate name for it would be *callology*. For κάλλος meaning beauty, and λόγος meaning science, "callology" means exactly and literally "the science of beauty." As a matter of fact, A. Rosmini used this name for "the science of beauty in general." The neo-scholastic J. Jungmann used the corresponding adjective, "calleologic" (*kalleologisch*), referring to non-artistic beauty, to distinguish it from "aesthetic" (*asthetisch*), which refers to artistic beauty;[1] and a former president of Princeton, James McCosh, explicitly suggested the name "calleology" for aesthetics in the last century.[2]

There are also other names that either had been actually used by some authors or could possibly be used instead of "aesthetics." For instance, St. Augustine used the term "philocaly" (*philocalia*),[3] that is similar to the universally accepted term, "philosophy,"[4] and Lepore reports[5] that some have used even such terms as "calleoaesthetics" (*calleoaesthetica*) and "calleophily" (*calleophilia*) to designate aesthetics.

Of these possible names, "calleoaesthetics" is awkward and, while an improvement over "aesthetics," it shares the basic weakness of "aesthetics"; "philocaly," meaning "love of beauty," is much better and, as a matter of fact, as expressive as the name "philosophy" ("love of wisdom"); but the best of all is the properly descriptive "callology" or "calleology."

However, one ought to take the following facts into consideration before even thinking of changing the name "aesthetics." First of all, a name or an etymological definition need not signify or refer to the essence of the thing in question; instead, it is enough if it expresses something significant or characteristic about the thing. As a matter of fact, this is the case with the names of many ancient sciences, such as "logic," "metaphysics," and "ethics." Secondly, even if a name or an etymological definition always or necessarily expressed the essence of the designated thing, the fact remains that the rather poor name "aesthetics" has been adopted, and is in use today in all modern languages. Adding to this another fact, namely, that novel terms have very seldom succeeded in replacing widespread, commonly used old terms, we must recognize that even the best replacement of the term "aesthetics" would have little or no chance of being universally adopted.

---

[1] A. Rosmini-Serbati, *Sistema philosofico* (Torino: Unione tipografico, 1886), § 210. See J. Jungmann, *Ästhetik* (Freiburg in Breisgau: Herder, 1884), 167n., 325.

[2] J. McCosh, *The Emotions* (New York: C. Scribner's Sons, 1880), 148f. Interestingly enough, McCosh himself retained the term "aesthetics" despite his suggestion of a better name. See, e.g., his *Psychology, The Motive Powers* (New York: C. Scribner's Sons, 1887), Bk. II, chap. 3.

[3] "Quid est enim Philosophia? Amor sapientiae. Quid Philocalia? Amor pulchritudinis." Augustine, *Contra Academicos*, II, 3, 7 (PL 32, 922). See also *Retract.* I, 1, 3 (PL 32, 586). However, it was not Augustine who coined this term. For φιλοκαλία occurs as early as in Diodorus of Sicily, I, 51 (Loeb-edition, n. 2); and φιλοκαλεῖν is to be found in Thucydides, *Hist.* II, 40, *princ.*; whereas the grammatically similar φιλογύνειδ occurs in Cicero, *Tuscul. disp.* IV, 11, 25.

[4] Φιλία means love; κάλλος, beauty; and σοφία, wisdom. Thus, "philocaly" means "love of beauty"; and "philosophy," "love of wisdom."

[5] G. Lepore, O.S.A., *Lectiones Aestheticae* (Viterbii: Agnesotti 1905), 10.

Chapter II

The Essential Definition of Aesthetics

HAVING SEEN the etymological definition of aesthetics, it is only natural that the next question should be concerned with the essential definition of aesthetics.

Essential definition in general is the explanation of the very nature of the thing in question. Thus, looking for the essential definition of aesthetics, what we really want to determine is the nature of aesthetics as a science.

Since this task is difficult, and even more difficult than the question of the etymological definition, we shall begin with the consideration of the difficulties involved in finding the essential definition of aesthetics. This consideration will, at the same time, prepare the mind for the topic of chapter 3, namely, the division of aesthetics.

ARTICLE 1: *Difficulties of Finding the Essential Definition*

There are at least two different kinds of difficulties involved in the essential definition of aesthetics: one, concerned with the vast scope of the field; and two, concerned with the considerable differences in the treatment given to aesthetics throughout history. Let us take up each of these difficulties separately.

1. The first difficulty can be summed up this way. If too many and too different areas of knowledge are considered to be one generic field, then that generic field becomes very difficult to define. But, as a matter of fact, there are many considerably different specific areas of knowledge that are all considered to belong to the field of aesthetics. Therefore, it is very difficult to define the generic field of aesthetics.

There are two ways of proving the minor premise in this syllogism. One is in the light of the attendance of international congresses of aesthetics; the other is by pointing out the large number of specific areas in which aesthetics has been cultivated in ancient, medieval, and modern history.

Those who attended at least one or two international congresses of aesthetics in recent years[1] know from personal experience how many different areas of specialization the active members of such congresses represented. One could find among them scientists and philosophers, theologians and technicians, historians and creative artists. Or to be more specific, some members were specialists in psychological, physical, and sociological aesthetics; others,

---

[1] The last three international congresses of aesthetics prior to the one held in Bucharest, 1973, were the fourth, held in Athens, Greece, 1960; the fifth, in Amsterdam, Holland, 1964; and the sixth, in Uppsala-Stockholm, Sweden, 1968.

in metaphysical and cosmological aesthetics as well as the philosophy of literature, music, painting, sculpture, architecture, etc. Again others represented liturgical, dogmatic, and moral theological aesthetics; some were literary, music, theater, and film critics, or teachers of such fields of technological aesthetics as those of music, painting, literature, and architecture. Some of them were art historians or historians of aesthetics, or teachers of history of art and aesthetics; others were specialists in therapeutic aesthetics or art pedagogy, while several of them were even architects, composers, poets, and painters, etc. Upon seeing a gathering of representatives of so many different areas of specialization, one can easily begin to wonder what, if anything, ties all those areas together in such a way as to produce some common interest among the congress members.

The second way of showing that there has been so much variety within the so-called generic field of aesthetics as to render aesthetics difficult to define is by considering the history of aesthetics. The entire pre-socratic period, with its generally aesthetic outlook on this world as a beautiful order ($\kappa \acute{o} \sigma \mu o s$) represents the first contributions to the general area of cosmological aesthetics. In addition to this, however, the Pythagoreans, Plato, and Aristotle make observations in the field of psychological aesthetics, for instance, about such things as catharsis.[2] Next to mention are Heraclitus, Anaxagoras, Socrates, and Plato as the first contributors to metaphysical aesthetics.[3] Also, following the principles of the Pythagoreans, Plato and Aristotle make remarks pertaining to mathematical and geometrical aesthetics.[4] Socrates, Plato, and Aristotle begin the cultivation of the field of ethical aesthetics by stressing the beauty of virtue in general or certain virtues in particular,[5] a trend that was continued by Philo of Alexandria,[6] the Stoics,[7] and Plotinus.[8]

---

[2] Pythagoras, in Cramer, *An. Par.* I, 172; Iamblichus, *Vita Pythagorae*, 110; and Porphyry, *Vita Pythagorae*, 30 (all three in G. S. Kirk and J. E. Raven, *op. cit.*, p. 229, n. 4.); Plato, *Rep.* III 399e, 401d–403c; *Tim.* 47cd; *Laws*, VII, 812; Aristotle, *Poet.* 17, 1455b 15; *Pol.* VIII, 7, 1341b 35–40; *Problemata*, X, 52 and XIX; etc.

[3] For Heraclitus ("To god, all things are beautiful"), see *Porphyry, In Iliadem* 4, 4; for Anaxagoras ("The divine intellect arranged all things"), Simplicius, *Phys.* 164, 24 and 156, 13; for Socrates ("Everything is good and beautiful"), Xenophon, *Memor.* III, 8, 5 and 7; for Plato, on the identity of goodness and beauty, *Lysis* 216d, *Symp.* 201c, and *Tim.* 87c; on absolute Beauty, *Symp.* 210e–211b; on the transcendentality of beauty, *Tim.* 53b; and on the principles of beauty, *Phileb.* 64e.

[4] On geometric beauty, see Pythagoras in *Diog. Laert.* VIII, 1, Loeb-ed. n. 35; Plato, *Phileb.* 51c; and Aristotle, *Post. an.* I, 7, 75b 17–20; *Problem.* XVI, 10, 915a 35f. On mathematical beauty, see Aristotle, *Met.* XIII, 3, 1078a 32–b 6. Cf. also Philo of Alexandria, *De congressu quaerendae eruditionis gratia*, Loeb-ed. 14, 75.

[5] For Socrates' disciple, Anthisthenes, see *Diog. Laert.* VI, 1, 12; for Plato, *Rep.* IV, 444e; for Aristotle, *Nic. Eth.* I, 8, 1099a 17–30; *Eudem. Eth.* VIII, 3, 1248b 20ff.; 1249a 12–15; *Polit.*, VII, 1, 1323b 10–12.

[6] Philo, *Legum allegoria*, I, 17, 57f.; II, 20, 81; *De posteritate Caini*, 39, 133; *Quod Deus immutabilis sit*, 19, 89; *De ebrietate*, 29, 112; *De sobrietate*, 13, 62 and 68; *Quis rerum divinarum heres*, 1, 4; *De vita Mosis*, II, 27, 139f.; etc.

Plato, Aristotle, and Aristoxenus are the first great contributors to musical aesthetics.[9] Plato's *Ion* and Aristotle's *Poetics* are the first independent works on the philosophy of poetry that, together with passages in some other works by Aristotle,[10] are among the first contributions to the history of art. The *Poetics* is significant also insofar as it displays a turn of interest toward a more scientific approach to aesthetics, a turn that was continued in several related fields such as the science of poetic aesthetics, by Longinus, Horace, and Demetrius;[11] musical aesthetics, by Aristoxenus; pictorial and sculptural aesthetics, by Xenocrates of Sikyon (fl 280 B.C.), Antigonos of Karystos, M. T. Cicero, M. T. Varro, Cornelius Nepos, the Elder Pliny, etc.; and architectural aesthetics, by Vitruvius and St. Augustine.[12]

To all these specific areas Philo of Alexandria adds, with a few oblique remarks and implication,[13] the chronologically first species of theological aesthetics, viz., angelological aesthetics. He is followed eventually by the church fathers and the medieval schoolmen in this field[14] as well as in a long

[7] On Zeno, see *Diog. Laert.*, VII, 1, Loeb-ed., nn. 23, 99, 100 and 130; on Chrysippus, *ibid.*, VII, 7. n. 202; for Cicero, *De off.*, II, 10, 37; *Tusc. disp.* I, 28, 70; *De finibus bonorum et malorum*, I, 13, 42; IV, 15, 42; and *Epist. ad Fam.* 9, 14; for L. A. Seneca, *Dial. moral. De consolatione* (Loeb-ed. vol. XII), 16, 4; *De beneficiis*, IV, 22, 2; *Epistulae morales ad Lucilium*, epistulae 66, 6 and 67, 16; and for Epictetus, *Discourses*, II, 5, 5; IV, 3, 3; V, 10; V, 12, 1; 75.

[8] Plotinus, *Enn.* I, 4, 4; II, 9, 15-17; VI, 3, 17; 7, 30; 9, 1; etc.

[9] Plato, *Laches*, 188d; *Rep.* III, 397bc; 399f.; *Laws*, VII, 700; 812d; etc. Aristotle, *Pol.* VIII, 5, 1340a 40-b 5; 6, 1341a 17-b 8; 7, 1342a 27-b 18; *Problem.* XIX, 10 and 35, etc. For Aristoxenus, see *The Harmonies of Aristoxenus*, ed. H. S. Macran (Oxford University Press, 1902). Later contributors are Plotinus (e.g., *Enn.* V, 2, 9), Augustine (*De musica*), Boethius (*De institutione musicae*); John Cotton (*De musica*); etc.

[10] *Eth. Nic.* VI, 6, 1141a 9-11; *Top.* VI, 2, 140a 21ff.; *Met.* II, 1, 993b 14f. Eventually, Aristotle was followed by the author of the first extant book on art history, the *Historia Naturalis*, *viz.*, the Elder Pliny, who utilized such earlier historians of art as Xenocrates of Sikyon (a disciple of both Plato and Aristotle), Antigonos of Karystos, Duris of Samos, Heliodorus of Athens, M. T. Varro, Cornelius Nepos, and others. In the Renaissance, L. B. Alberti and G. Vasari stand out in the field; whereas in the eighteenth century, J. J. Winckelmann rekindles the interest in the history of art.

[11] Longinus (Dionysius?), *On the Sublime*; Horace, *Ars poetica*; and Demetrius, *On Style*.

[12] Vitruvius, *De architectura*; St. Augustine, *De ordine*, II (*PL* 32, 994ff.).

[13] Philo, *De Cherubim* (Loeb-edition) 8, 25-26; 9, 27-29; to be read in the light of 25, 86.

[14] E.g., John Chrysostom, *In Epist. II. ad Corinthios*, hom. 7, n. 7 (Migne, *Patrologia Graeca*, henceforth: *PG*, 61, 454); Augustine, *In Psalm.* 44, 3, 7 (*PL* 36, 498); *De Scriptur.*, sermo 19, 5 (*PL* 38, 136); Boethius, *De fidei Christianae complexio* (*PL* 64, 1334 B); Dionysius the Areopagite, *De div. nom.*, 4, 22, 210f. (*PG* 3, 724 B); *De coelesti heirarchia*, 7, 2; 7, 1, (*PG* 208 C; 205 C); Bonaventure, *In II. Sententiarum*, d. 9, a. 1, q. 6, ad opp. 3; d. 9, a. 1, q. 1, 4a and *ibid.*, q. 8, concl. (Quaracchi, 1885, vol. II, 252, 242, and 255b); *Sermones de assumptione B. Virginis Mariae*, sermo 1 (IX, 689a); Albert, *Summa theologiae*, II, tr. 10, q. 39, m. 1, a. 1, p. 2, q. 2, 7a and ad 7 (ed. S.C.A. Borgnet, *Opera omnia*, vol. 32, Paris: L. Vivés, 1895, pp. 437f.); *In Dion. De caelesti hierarchia*, VII, 5, 2, ad 3 and expos. text. (XIV, 173f.); *De pulchro* (in Martin Grabmann, "Des Ulrich Engelberti von Strassburg O. Pr. (+1277) Abhandlung De pulchro," *Sitzungsberichte der Bayerischen Akademie der Wissenschaften, Philosophisch-philologische und historische Klasse*, Jahrgang 1925, 5. Abhandlung; München: Verlag der Bayer. Akademie der Wissenschaften, 1926, p. 77, line 2); Thomas Aquinas, *In II. Sententiarum*, d. 9, q. 1, a. 5, sed contra 2a; d. 6, q. 1, a. 1, sed contra; *De div. nom.* 4, 18, ed. C.

series of other, novel areas within theological aesthetics, such as moral theological aesthetics,[15] trinitarian aesthetics,[16] Christological aesthetics,[17] eschatological aesthetics,[18] charismatic aesthetics (aesthetics of grace),[19] Mariological aesthetics,[20] ecclesiological aesthetics[21] (all these six being species of dogmatic theological aesthetics), and even logical aesthetics.[22]

Pera (Taurini: Marietti, 1950) n. 525; 1, 2, 44; 4, 12, 457; *De veritate*, q. 8, a. 7, tertium item, 1a; *Summa contra gentiles*, III, c. 80, n. 2551; *In Iob*, 40, 1; *De malo*, q. 16, a. 2, ad 13; *De substantiis separatis*, art. 19; Dionysius the Carthusian, *De venustate mundi et pulchritudine Dei*, art. 15-16 and 22 (*Opera omnia*, vol. 34, Tornaci: Cartusiae S. M. de Pratis, 1901) 241B; 241C-242C; 243B; 248D. Dionysius the Carthusian treats pneumatological aesthetics separately from angelological aesthetics: *ibid.*, art. 15, 17, 20, 22; pp. 241, 242f.; 245AB; 248C.

[15] E.g., Clement of Alexandria, *Paedagogus*, II, 12 (*PG* 8, 544 BC); Origen, *De orat.* 17 (*PG* 11, 472 BC); Gregory Nazianzen, *Orat.* 18, 8 (*PG* 35, 993 BC); Ambrose, *De Isaac et an.*, 8, 78 (*PL* 14, 558); Augustine, *Epist.* 120, 4, 20 (*PL* 33, 462); *In Psalm.* 64, 8 (*PL* 36, 780); Albert, *In III. Sent.* 32 E, 2, ad q. (XXVIII, 600 f.); *Ethica*, IV, 2, 3 (VII, 299); Aquinas, *In IV. Sent.* 33, 3, 3. 1a; *In Rom.* 13: 12, 3; *S. theol.* II–II, 129, 4, ad 3; 141, 2, ad 3; 145, 1 and 2; 180, 2, ad 3; and on specific virtues, *In I. Sent.* 46, 1, 4,1a; *In II. Sent.* 42, 1, 5, ad 4; *In IV. Sent.* 17, 1, 1, sol. 3; 18, 2, 2, 1a; 49, 5, 3, sol. 1, ad 3; *In Is.* 26; *In Psalm* 44:2; *S. theol.* I, 96, 3; II–II, 141, 2, 3a and ad 3; 2, 8, ad 1; 142, 4; 143, 1; 152, 5. Dionysius the Cartusian, *op. cit.*, art. 4 and 17; pp. 230 C, 242 A and D.

[16] E.g., Hilary, *De Trin.* II, 1 (*PL* 10, 51); Augustine, *De Trin.* VI, 10 (*PL* 42, 931); *De doctr. Christ.* I, 5, 5 (*PL* 34, 21); Thomas, *In I. Sent.* 31, 2, 1, sol; *S. theol.* I, 39, 8; Dionysius the Carthusian, *op. cit.*, art. 23-24, pp. 249-250; etc.

[17] E.g., Clement of Alexandria, *Paed.* III, 1 (*PG* 8, 556c-560a); cap. 3, *passim*; Basil, *In Ps.* 44, 5 (*PG* 29, 400); Augustine, *In Ps.* 44, 3, 7 (*PL* 36, 498); Albert, *S. theol.* I, 12, 50, q. 1, intr. (I, 518); Bonaventure, *Breviloquium*, VII, 7, 5 (V, 290); *Lignum vitae*, III, 9, 35 (VIII, 81); *Vitis mystica*, c. 5, nn. 1, 3, 7; c. 16, n. 1. (VIII, 168f.; 171, 182); Ulrich Engelbert of Strasbourg, *De pulchro*, ed. cit., p. 84, lines 6 and 9-14; Thomas, *In Ps.* 44, 2; *In Is.* 53 and 63; *In Salut. Angel.*, exp., *Opuscula theologica*, II, ed. R. M. Spiazzi (Taurini: Marietti, 1954), n. 1126; *Resp. ad Ioan. Verc. de art. CVIII*, q. 57; etc.

[18] E.g., Bonaventure, *Lignum vitae*, 3, 9, 35 (VIII, 81); Thomas, *S. theol.* III, 54, 4, ad 1 and 2; *In III. Sent.* 21, 2, 4, sol. 3, ad 2; *In IV. Sent.* 17, 1, 1, sol. 3; 44, 2, 4, 3a; 49, 5, 4, sol. 3; *In ev. Ioan.* 20: 2, 6; *In Hebr.* 1: 1, 5; *In Is.* 32f. Ulrich Engelbert of Strasbourg, *De pulchro*, ed. cit., p. 84, lines 7, 13-14; Dionysius the Carthusian, *op. cit.*, art. 18 and 20, pp. 243D, 245D; etc.

[19] E.g., Bonaventure, *In II. Sent.* 5, 3, 1 resp.; 29, 1, 1, ad 5; 29, 2, 2, ad 2-3 (2, 155a; 696b; 704a); Thomas, *In II. Sent.* 27, 1, 4, sol; *In IV. Sent.* 1, 1, 2, 1a; 16, 2, 1, sol. 2 ad 3; 16, 2, 2, sol. 4 ad 1; *De malo*, 4, 2, 17a; *In Ps.* 21: 12; *S. theol.* I–II, 109, 7; 112, 4; II–II, 152, 5, 1a; 168, 1, 1a; *In Symb. Ap.*, art. 4; Ulrich Engelbert, *De pulchro*, ed. cit., p. 84, lines 6 and 8-9; Fr. Eustachius, O. F. M., *Comm. in P. Lombardi Sentent.*, Cod. Scaff. I, 158, fol. 56r, in Padova, Biblioteca Antoniana (quoted in M. Grabmann, "Des Ulrich Engelberti von Strassburg O. Pr. Abhandlung *De pulchro*," ed. cit., p. 47); Dionysius the Carthusian, *op. cit.*, art. 17, 18, 22, pp. 242D, 243f., 248D.

[20] E. g., Albert, *De laud. B. M. Virginis*, V: *De pulchritudine Mariae* (36, 273-319); Thomas, *In III. Sent.* 1, 2, sol. 1, ad 4; *In Salut. Ang., Opusc. theol.* II, ed. cit., n. 1115; *In Is.* cc. 11, 16, 40; *In Matth.* 12: 4; *In ev. Ioan.* 15: 7, 2; *In Psalm* 17: 18; and 44; Giovanni Balbi of Genova, O. P., *Tractatus de splendore vultus B. Mariae Virginis*, in *Dialogus de quaestionibus animae ad spiritum* (Cod. Vat. lat. 1308-09); Jacob of Voragine, O. P., *Mariale*, P, cc. 1-2: *Pulchritudo Mariae* (Cod. B2 1219, Florence, Bibliot, nazion., fol. 124r-126v)—both referred to in M. Grabmann, "Des Ulrich Engelberti von Strassburg, O. Pr. (+ 1277) Abhandlung *De pulchro*," ed. cit., p. 17; etc.

[21] E.g., Bonaventure, *Brevil.* prol. 3, 3 (V, 205a); Thomas, *S. theol.* I–II 112, 4; II–II 183, 2, sed contra and corpus; 183, 3; 184, 4; *In I. Sent.* Prol.; *In IV. Sent.* 15, 3, 1, sol. 4, ad 1; 24, 1, 1, sol. 1; *In I. Cor.* 12: 1, 1; *Cat. aur. in Matth.* 4: 2; etc.

[22] E.g., Albert, *Phys.*, Iv, 1, 8, B (III, 254); *In Dion. De eccl. hier.* V, 11, exp. text. A (XIV,

In the light of this large number of special fields touched upon before the dawn of the Renaissance, it is no wonder that the subsequent few centuries produced no new field of aesthetics at all. Instead, they deepened, enlarged, and enriched the various branches of aesthetics that emerged in ancient and medieval times. This holds true most obviously for the philosophy of poetry[23] and psychological aesthetics,[24] and, to a lesser extent, also for other branches, like mathematical aesthetics,[25] musical aesthetics,[26] pictorial aesthetics,[27] and the history of art.[28] This, however, does not mean that modern philosophy has made no other contribution to aesthetics. For, after Baumgarten systematically treated the sovereign science of aesthetics, a number of new fields came into existence in the two centuries or so that elapsed since the publication of his *Aesthetica*. The first among these novel areas of thought is the generic field that may most appropriately be called general philosophy of fine art.[29]

One hundred years later, under the leadership of A. Comte, sociological aesthetics as such was born,[30] to be followed soon by a whole series of novel species of both philosophic and scientific aesthetics. Among the novel and systematically treated branches of philosophic aesthetics, we find the philoso-

704); Thomas, *Quodlib*. XII, 22, 1c; *In IV. Phys*. 5, 447; *In Psalm* 44, 2; *S. theol*. II–II, 180, 2, 3a; *S. contra gent*. III, 80; ed. C. Pera (Taurini: Marietti, 1961) nn. 2548–2550; *Comp. theol*. I, 2, in *Opuscula theol*. I, ed. R. A. Verardo (Taurini: Marietti, 1954), n. 239; etc.

[23] From the fourteenth to the eighteenth century, there are such significant and influential promoters of the philosophy of poetry as G. Boccaccio, L. Castelvetro (1570), P. Corneille (1660), L. A. Muratori (1706), A. Pope (1709), E. B. de Condillac (1716), G. B. Vico (1721), A. G. Baumgarten (1735), Abbé Batteux (1746), Dr. Samuel Johnson (1755), and G. E. Lessing (1766).

[24] Among the eighteenth-century representatives of psychological aesthetics, we find Lord Shaftesbury (1709), J. Addison (1711), F. Hutcheson (1725), D. Hume and R. Price (1758), A. Gerard and Jean d'Alembert (1759), Lord Kames (Henry Home) (1761), Kant (1764), D. Diderot (1765), Dr. Thomas Reid (1785), A. Alison (1790), W. von Humboldt (1798), etc.

[25] Piero della Francesca, *De prospectiva pingendi* (c. 1482; Parma, Bibliotheca Palatina, Codex 1576; recent ed. by G. N. Fasola, Florence: Vallecchi. 1942); Luca Pacioli (*De divina proportione*, Venice, 1509); John Ruskin (1900), etc.

[26] E.g., Descartes (*Compendium musicae* of 1618), Leibniz (1712), James Harris (1775), E. Hanslick (1854), H. Spencer (1857), G. Engel (1884), H. Riemann (1887) and C. Lalo (1908).

[27] Among the promoters of pictorial aesthetics, one finds L. B. Alberti (1435), A. Dürer (1500), G. P. Lomazzo (1584), L'Abbé Dubos (1719), W. Hogarth (1753), Sir J. Reynolds (1759), J. J. Winckelmann (1765), K. Fiedler (1887), etc.

[28] The author of the first systematic work on the history of art is J. J. Winckelmann (*Geschichte der Kunst des Althertums*, 1764). Outstanding nineteenth-century art historians are R. Zimmermann (1858), R. H. Lotze (1868), K. Schnaase (1862), E. von Hartmann, H. von Stein (1886), etc.

[29] In the first 100 years of its existence, more or less systematic and comprehensive works on the philosophy of fine arts were written or published. Among them, in addition to Baumgarten's, are those by G. F. Meier (1748), M. Mendelssohn (1761), J. G. Sulzer (1771), J. A. Eberhard (1783), J. J. Eschenburg (1783), J. G. Herder (1790), I. Kant (1790), F. W. Schelling (1802), F. Ast (1805), Hegel (1835), F. T. Vischer (1857), etc.

[30] H. A. Taine (1865), P. J. Proudhon (1865), J. M. Guyau (1889), E. Grosse (1894), J. M. Baldwin (1895), F. H. Giddings (1896), M. Nordau (1897), G. Sorel (1901) and C. Lalo (1921) are some of its more significant early contributors.

phy of natural beauty,[31] the philosophy of physical beauty,[32] botanical aesthetics,[33] zoological aesthetics,[34] the philosophy of social beauty,[35] the philosophy of historical beauty,[36] general psychological aesthetics,[37] special psychological aesthetics,[38] cultural aesthetics,[39] etc. Among the novel branches of scientific aesthetics, especially physical and psychological aesthetics came into vogue. The former included such areas as optical aesthetics (physical aesthetics of light, color, and form)[40] and acoustical aesthetics (physical aesthetics of tones).[41] The latter, i.e., psychological aesthetics, included such branches as general psychological aesthetics,[42] physiological aesthetics of tones,[43] psychological aesthetics of light, color, and form,[44] etc. The twentieth century merely continued to add new fields and new approaches to the generic field of aesthetics. Among them are the aesthetics of symbols,[45] therapeutic aesthetics,[46] philosophy of the history of aesthetics, general and special psychoanalytic aesthetics, phenomenological aesthetics, art appreciation, etc.

2. The second difficulty with defining aesthetics has to do not so much with the scope as with the approach to and the treatment of aesthetics. The argument can be formulated in the following syllogistic manner. If, in the various periods of history, a certain field of knowledge has received not only considerably different but even contrarily opposed approaches, treatments, and considerations in terms of its subject, principles, and relation to other fields, then one can scarcely speak of it as a single definite science and one will find it extremely difficult to define its essence. This is exactly the case with the field of aesthetics. Therefore, aesthetics can be defined in its essence only with grave difficulty. To prove the minor premise, let us briefly compare ancient and medieval with modern and contemporary aesthetics in three major respects.

[31] E.g., Hegel (1818), F. T. Vischer (1847), R. Zimmermann (1865), A. Tari (1884), and M. Schasler (1886).
[32] E.g., F. T. Vischer (1847), R. Vischer (1873).
[33] E.g., F. T. Bratranek (1853) and M. Schasler (1886).
[34] E.g., A. Tari (1884) and M. Schasler (1886).
[35] E.g., R. Zimmermann (1865) and M. Schasler (1886).
[36] E.g., F. T. Vischer (1847). See also sociological aesthetics in n. 30 above.
[37] E.g., H. Spencer (1855), H. Lotze (1868), H. Siebeck (1875), G. T. Fechner (1876), A. Biese (1890), K. Groos and M. Diez (1892), P. Stern (1898), K. Lange (1901), Th. Lipps (1903), J. Volkelt (1905), etc.
[38] E.g., J. F. Herbart (1813), C. Stumpf (1883).
[39] E.g., M. Carrière (1863), C. Merz (1890), M. Dessoir (1906), C. Lalo (1933), etc.
[40] E.g., F. G. Roeber (1862), G. T. Fechner (1876).
[41] E.g., H. L. F. Helmholtz, D. C. Miller and George W. Stewart, all of the later 19th century.
[42] E.g., Grant Allen (1877), G. Hirt (1885), F. Galton (1896), etc.
[43] E.g., H. L. F. Helmholtz (1863), relying on such earlier sources as J. P. Rameau (1721), G. Tartini (1751), and J. d'Alembert (1762).
[44] E.g., R. Vischer (1873) and Theodor Lipps (1891).
[45] E. Cassirer (1923), C. Ogden, I. A. Richards, J. Wood (all in 1925), E. Panofsky (1939), S. Langer (1942), etc. One of their early forerunners is J. Volkelt (1876)
[46] E.g., H. Shaefer-Simmern (1948), M. Neumberg (1955), D. Blair, B. Y. Mair, P. Wortis, etc.

The first significant difference between premodern and modern aesthetics lies in the respective treatments aesthetics received before and after the birth of modern philosophy. While ancient and medieval aesthetics were undifferentiated from other fields, and were treated unsystematically, modern and contemporary aesthetics, beginning with A. G. Baumgarten, are clearly differentiated from other fields of knowledge and are being treated systematically. The general context in which aesthetics received scant and only occasional attention by the pre-socratics, was cosmology. In Socrates, Plato, Aristotle, and Plotinus, it was metaphysics and ethics; in the church fathers, it was dogmatic or moral theology; in the medieval schoolmen, metaphysics and theology.[47] Works of exclusively, predominantly, or considerably aesthetic character, like Aristotle's *Poetics*, Longinus' *On the Sublime*, Pseudo-Dionysius' *On the Divine Names*, Albert's theological work on Mary's beauty, or Dionysius the Carthusian's theological treatment of the beauty of the world and God, are extremely rare up to the eighteenth century; whereas, especially from the nineteenth century on, aesthetics has received separate, extensive, and systematic treatments.

The second major difference is, perhaps, the most basic of all. It consists in this, that ancient and medieval thinkers mentioning or writing on aesthetics, with possibly the sole exception of Pyrrhon of Elis (c. 360–270 B.C.),[47a] were all epistemological realists and aesthetic objectivists, whereas a considerable portion of modern and contemporary philosophers and aestheticians are skeptics and, consequently, aesthetic subjectivists. Such ancient and medieval giants as Plato, Aristotle, Plotinus, Augustine, Albert, Bonaventure, and Thomas Aquinas all trusted their senses and reason and thus took the existence of beauty for granted, never (or scarcely ever) trying to offer any proof for it. This attitude suddenly disappeared at the dawn of modern thought, in the pantheist Spinoza (1677) and certain British and German aestheticians of the eighteenth century, like F. Hutcheson (1725), D. Hume (1757), Lord Kames (Henry Home, 1762), I. Kant (1790,) A. Alison (1790), R. P. Knight (1805), *et al.*, followed by an uninterrupted line of European and American aestheticians in the nineteenth and twentieth centuries, because all of them doubted or denied the objective reality of beauty on such grounds as aesthetic disagreement among critics and laymen concerning the beauty of artworks. Thereby there are, on the one hand, aestheticians believing in the existence of beauty and considering aesthetics a real science and, on the other hand,

---

[47] One of the outstanding aestheticians of the Middle Ages, Thomas Aquinas, for instance, touches on questions of beauty in connection with such dogmatic theological questions as the Son in the Trinity, the creation of the world, the resurrection of the body, and grace; and such moral theological questions as virtue in general, the various cardinal virtues, sin, etc. (For details, see F. J. Kovach, *Die Aesthetik des Thomas von Aquin*, Berlin: W. de Gruyter, 1961, p. 38, n. 5.)

[47a] Diogenes Laertius, IX, 11, 83 (Loeb-edition, II, 494).

aestheticians believing in no existent beauty outside the mind and considering aesthetics an ideal science.

The third and most complex major difference between premodern and modern aesthetics concerns the treatment of beauty before and after the dawn of modern aesthetics. For in ancient and medieval aesthetics, beauty is the central aesthetic value and a generic notion in reference to which all other aesthetic notions were being defined.[48] Longinus, for instance, defines the sublime as being really identical with the beautiful;[49] St. Augustine understands the gracious, the specious, and the suitable (*decus, species, aptum*) in terms of or in their relation to beauty;[50] Alexander of Hales explains the suitable (*aptum*) in its similarity to the beautiful;[51] Albert the Great does so with some half a dozen aesthetic notions;[52] and Thomas Aquinas, with at least ten such notions.[53]

In modern times, however, the situation begins to change step by step. The first step in this gradual and lengthy process consists in this, that the beautiful and the sublime are being mentioned and analyzed together, and beauty loses thereby its central significance. Edmund Burke's explicitly stated reason for treating these two notions separately is what he considers their radical difference, even opposition, in contrast to their similarity or genus-species relation in the minds of premodern thinkers.[54] Half a century later, Dugald

[48] This explains why a work like Aristotle's *Poetics*, as it concentrates on tragedy, or Longinus' *On the Sublime* (3rd c.), Augustine's lost *De pulchro et apto* (4th c.), and Matteo Pelligrini's treatise on the comic (*Delle Acutezze, che altrimenti spiriti, vivezze, e concetti si appellano trattato*; Genova and Bolognia: Clementi Ferroni, 1639) are extremely rare before the eighteenth century.

[49] Longinus, *On the Sublime*, VII, 4.

[50] E.g., Augustine, *Conf.* IV, 13, 20; IV, 15, 24 (*PL* 32, 701; 703); *Epist. 138 ad Marcellin*, n. 5 (*PL* 33, 527).

[51] Alexander of Hales, *Summa theol.* II, s. 1, i. 1, tr. 2, q. 3, c. 2 (Quaracchi, II, 100b, n. 76).

[52] For *decus* and *decorum* in reference to beauty, see Albert, *Summa theol.* II, 11, 62, 1, sol. (*ed. cit.* 31, 597); *Opusc. de pulchro*, q. 2. sol.; (reprinted in *S. Thomae Aquinatis Opuscula philosophica et theologica*; ed. M. de Maria, Tiferni Tiberni, 1886, Opusculum 38, p. 556); for *ornatum, Sum. theol.* II, 11, 62, 1, sol. (31, 597); *In IV. Sent.* 24 B 7, resp. (30, 405); *Sum. de Creat.* I, 4, 71, 2, resp. and ad 1 and 2 (34, 727-29); *Sum. theol.* II, 11, 57, 1, ad 3, 4 (31, 578); for *formositas, Eth.* IV, 2, 1 (7, 295f); and for *speciositas* and *venustas, In I. Sent.* 31 F 6, 3a (26, 108). Albert's disciple, Ulrich of Strasbourg discusses the relations of *formositas, honestas, decor*, and *aptum* to beauty. (*De pulchro, ed. cit.*, pp. 78-80.)

[53] Aquinas refers all the following notions to beauty: *decus* (*Sum. theol.* II-II, 145, 2; 152, 5; *In Is.* 53; *In Ps.* 25, 5; *In IV. Sent.* 4, 1, 3, V, 2a; 16, 2, 2, IV, ad 1; 33, 3, 3, 1a); *ornatum* (*In II. Sent.* prol.; *In I. Tim.* 3: 2, L. 1; *In IV. Sent.* 49, 4, 2, ad 1); *formositas* (*De pot.* 4, 2c; *In Psalm.* 26, 3); *venustas* (*In Is.* prooem.); *gratiosum* (*In Psalm* 44, 2; 44, 8); *species* (*In Is.* 53); *speciosum* (*In Job*, 42, 1; *In Thren.* 2, 2; *In Jer.* 11, 3; *In Psalm* 44, 2); *suave* (*In X. Eth.* L. 6, ed. R. M. Spiazzi. Taurini: Marietti, 1964, n. 2028); and *nobilitas* (*In Gal.* 2: 6, L. 2).

[54] In the preface to the first edition of *A Philosophical Enquiry into the Origin of our Ideas of the Sublime and Beautiful*, E. Burke makes the following statement: "He [sc. the author himself] observed that the ideas of the sublime and beautiful were frequently confused; and that both were indiscriminately applied to things greatly differing, and sometimes of natures directly opposite. Even Longinus ... has comprehended things extremely repugnant to each other, under one common name of the *Sublime*. The abuse of the word *Beauty*, has been still more general." (Ed. J. T. Boulton; London: Routledge and K. Paul; New York: Columbia University Press, 1958; p. 1.)

Stewart expresses a very similar opinion on this issue.[55] And neither of them stands isolated in this view. Before Burke, for instance, J. Addison already speaks of the sublime ("the great") and the beautiful together with the novel ("the uncommon");[56] and after him, Alexander Gerard,[57] Hugh Blair,[58] Thomas Reid,[59] A. Alison,[60] and I. Kant[61] (to mention only a few) all treat both the sublime and the beautiful.[62]

The next step is taken by Lord Kames (1761), who differentiates between the grandeur and the sublime, and by Thomas Reid, who does the same for different reasons (1785).[63] Thereby, there is now a trichotomy in place of a dichotomy of aesthetic values, viz., that of the sublime and the beautiful. As the next phase in this development, the picturesque, that is merely the species of the beautiful to the mind of William Gilpin,[64] is being added to the old pair of the beautiful and the sublime in the philosophy of Sir Uvedale Price,[65] whereby the aesthetic trichotomy becomes explicit. This view was represented later on by several other aestheticians, like Dugald Stewart[66] and John G. Macvicar,[67] whereas it underwent partial changes, e.g., in the thought of George Ramsay[68] who replaced the picturesque with the ludicrous.

But Lord Kames, together with M. Mendelssohn (1761), becomes the

[55] D. Stewart, *Philosophical Essays*, part II, Essay First: "On the Beautiful"; Essay Second: "On the Sublime," in *The Collected Works of D. Stewart*, ed. Sir Wm. Hamilton (Edinburgh: Thomas Constable and Co.; London: Hamilton, Adams, and Co., 1855), V, 189-274, 275-329.

[56] J. Addison, *The Pleasures of Imagination*; in *The Spectator*, No. 412, June 23, 1712.

[57] A. Gerard declared, "Beautiful objects are of different kinds [sc. from the sublime], and produce pleasure by means of different principles of human nature." *An Essay on Taste*, I, 3. First edition (London: A. Millar; Edinburgh: A. Kincaid and J. Bell, 1759), 31. Third edition (Edinburgh: J. Bell, and W. Creech, 1780), 29.

[58] H. Blair, *Lectures on Rhetoric and Belles Lettres* (London: W. Sharpe and Son, 1820), Lectures 3 to 5.

[59] Reid, *Essays on the Intellectual Powers of Man*, VIII, 2. Ed. Sir Wm. Hamilton (Edinburgh: Maclachlan and Stewart, 1863), I, 493a.

[60] A. Alison, *Essays on the Nature and Principles of Taste*. Ed. A. Mills (New York: Harper and Brothers, 1858), throughout Essays I and II.

[61] Kant, *Beobachtungen über das Gefühl des Schönen und Erhabenen* (Königsberg, 1764); and *Kritik der Urteilskraft*, §§ 23-29.

[62] Later authors treating of this dichotomy between the beautiful and the sublime include D. Stewart (1810), Sir William Hamilton (1830), and virtually every significant German aesthetician after Kant, for about a century.

[63] Lord Kames, *Elements of Criticism*, ed. R. Boyd (New York: A. S. Barnes, 1855), 129f.; and Thomas Reid, *op. cit.*, VIII, 3; *ed. cit.*, I, 498a.

[64] Gilpin, *Three Essays: On Picturesque Beauty* (London: T. Cadell, W. Davies, 1808), I, p. II.

[65] U. Price, *An Essay on the Picturesque, as Compared with the Sublime and the Beautiful* (London: Hereford, 1794). This work was followed by another, *A Dialogue on the Distinct Characters of the Picturesque and the Beautiful* (London: Hereford, 1801).

[66] D. Stewart, *Philosophical Essays*, 1810. *Collected Works*, V (Edinburgh: Th. Constable; London: Hamilton, Adams, 1855).

[67] J. G. Macvicar, *On the Beautiful, the Picturesque, the Sublime* (London: Scott, Webster, and Geary, 1837).

[68] G. Ramsay, *Analysis and Theory of the Emotions, with Dissertations on Beauty, Sublimity, and the Ludicrous* (London: Longmans, 1848).

source of an even more radical innovation, that of aesthetic pluralism. For Mendelssohn discusses five values: the beautiful, the sublime, the naïve, the dignified, and the gracious; and Lord Kames, in addition to the triad of beauty, grandeur, and sublimity, such notions also as risibility, congruity, propriety, dignity, and grace. Ten years after Kames, in 1771, J. G. Sulzer surpasses both of them in aesthetic pluralism by treating alphabetically all conceivable aesthetic notions in his celebrated aesthetic encyclopedia.[69] A few decades later, F. Schiller follows in his footsteps by writing essays on the tragic, the graceful, the dignified, the trivial, the pleasant, the pathetic, the sentimental, the sublime, etc. Similar plurality is to be found in other authors, like Richard Payne Knight[70] and Hegel.[71]

A further development may seem to be small; yet, it is great in its consequences. While ancient and medieval philosophy throughout and even modern thought for a long time considered ugliness the lack or privation of beauty, under the impact of German idealism, and especially dialectics, some aestheticians began to soften this privative opposition between beauty and ugliness. In 1797, F. Schlegel attributes some aesthetic significance to the piquant, the striking, the daring, the cruel, and even to the ugly. K. W. Solger adopts this view (1819) in dialectical terms, as a "positive negation." Ch. H. Weisse, in the Hegelian spirit, goes along with this idea, and considers ugliness as leading, through the dialectics of beauty, from the sublime to the comic (1830). Somewhat later, in 1853, J. K. F. Rosenkranz publishes the first *Aesthetics of the Ugly*, offering an elaborate dialectical and hierarchical system of the ugly from the common to the satanic, and characterizing the ugly as creating a synthesis with the beautiful in the comic. Finally, sixteen years later, M. Schasler goes so far as to claim that the ugly enters into all beauty, a view shared later by Eduard von Hartmann.[72] Thereby, ugliness took its place among the aesthetic values, be it considered by contemporary aestheticians as a negative aesthetic value, as by Harold N. Lee,[73] or even a positive

[69] J. G. Sulzer, *Allgemeine Theorie der schönen Künste* (Leipzig: Weidmann, 1792).

[70] Besides the trichotomy of the beautiful, the sublime, and the picturesque, R. P. Knight considers also such notions as the grotesque, the sculpturesque, the pathetic, the tragic, the comic, the tragi-comic, the ridiculous, and the ludicrous as well as dignity and elegance. *An Analytical Enquiry into the Principles of Taste* (London: T. Payne, and J. White, 1808), *passim*.

[71] The aesthetic notions discussed by Hegel in his Berlin lectures of 1818, and in his *Vorlesungen über die Ästhetik* posthumously published (ed. Heinrich Gustav Hotho; Berlin, 1835) include the beautiful, the sublime, the tragic, the pathetic, the comic, the ironic, the satirical, the romantic, the phantastic, etc.

[72] M. Schasler, *Kritische Geschichte der Aesthetik, Grundlegung für die Aesthetik als Philosophie des Schönen und der Kunst* (Berlin: Nicolai, 1872) 1035–37. E. von Hartmann, *Ästhetik*, I: *Die deutsche Ästhetik seit Kant* (Leipzig: W. Friedrich, 1886), 377.

[73] Harold N. Lee speaks of ugliness as a negative aesthetic value in *Perception and Aesthetic Value* (New York: Prentice-Hall, 1938), 98, 185ff. On "negative aesthetic value," see also M. Damjanovich, "Das Problem des Hässlichen in der Ästhetik," in *Actes du IV. Congrés International* (Athens, Greece, 1960), 454–57.

[74] G. Santayana, *The Sense of Beauty*, § 3 (New York: Dover, 1955), 25.

value, as by George Santayana,[74] or "aesthetically excellent," as by B. Bosanquet.[75] With this last phase, the modern development in the treatment of beauty is completed in such a way that the present treatment is the exact opposite of the premodern treatment: beauty is not only dethroned but even made co-equal with its own privation.[76]

In the light of all these differences, it is indeed difficult to see what is common to all the areas and treatments of aesthetics that are to be found throughout history.

ARTICLE 2: *The Essential Definition of Aesthetics*

An indication of the vastness of the field of aesthetics, and one of the clearest signs of the confusion due to the difficulties in defining aesthetics is the great variety of definitions given to the science. A little sampling of this divergence in definitions will constitute the first part of this article, whereas our own definition, the second part.

1. Perhaps the most basic of all the differences among the definitions of aesthetics is that, while many authors do define aesthetics in their works on their own, others merely state the historical development of thought about the nature of aesthetics, without giving any definition of it. To do so in an encyclopedia is more or less proper and understandable;[1] but in one's own work on aesthetics, it is simply a sign of positivism.[2]

The next difference concerns the scope of aesthetics, and lies in the fact that some aestheticians use only certain remote genera in the definition of aesthetics—thereby apparently indicating their own uncertainty about the specific nature of aesthetics as a science—whereas others use some kind of proximate genus. Among the employed remote genera one finds "knowledge," "branch of knowledge," "general theory," "study," "systematic training," and "science (in the broad sense)."[3] Furthermore, of those who define aesthetics as a

---

[75] B. Bosanquet, *Three Lectures on Aesthetic*, III; ed. R. Ross (Indianapolis: The Bobbs-Merrill Co., 1963), 50 f.

[76] Fortunately, this development affected only some rather than all aestheticians. For instance, while the above described development took place from Addison to Rosenkranz, a long line of French and German aestheticians retained the traditional view that beauty is the central idea of aesthetics. Among them are J. P. de Crousaz (1712), Père André (1741), A. C. Quatremère de Quincey (1805), V. Cousin (1813), Th. Jouffroy (1843), A. Pictet (1856), and J. C. Lévêque (1862), on the one hand, and J. J. Winckelmann (1764), F. Schlegel (1794), W. Humboldt (1795), F. Bouterwek (1806), J. F. Herbart (1813), G. W. F. Hegel (1818), K. C. F. Krause (1828), C. H. Weisse (1830), and R. H. Lotze (1848), on the other hand.

[1] E.g., the articles on "Aesthetics" by James Sully in the 11th edition of the *Encyclopedia Britannica* (1910), I, 277a; and by M. Beardsley in the *New Catholic Encyclopedia* (New York: McGraw-Hill, 1967), I, 160 f.

[2] E.g., Torrossian, *A Guide to Aesthetics* (Stanford University Press, Stanford, California, 1937), 2; Susanne K. Langer, *Feeling and Form* (New York: C. Scribner's Sons, 1953), 12; Thomas Munro, *Toward Science in Aesthetics* (Indianapolis: The Bobbs-Merrill Co., 1956), 134; etc.

[3] "Knowledge": K. E. Gilbert, art. "Aesthetics," in the *Dictionary of World Literature*, ed. J. T. Shipley (Paterson, N. J.: Littlefield and Adams, 1960), 3; "branch of knowledge"; D. W. Prall,

"science (in the broad sense)," some do not specify any further. Those who do specify further, however, specify it as being either philosophic, scientific, and historical,[4] or philosophic and scientific,[5] or merely philosophic,[6] or else merely scientific (a natural science),[7] or, more specifically, psychological.[8]

Turning next from the scope to the subject of aesthetics, we find an even greater variety of opinions. First of all, according to some authors, aesthetics is an ideal science, since its subject is some mental (ideal) being(s).[9] Others define our science as if its subject were partly mental, partly real.[10] Most aestheticians, however, define aesthetics as having some real being for its subject. But even they differ on details. For some list beauty and ugliness as the subject of aesthetics;[11] others, beauty and art;[12] or beauty, art, and taste;[13] or beauty, art, and aesthetic value;[14] or just aesthetic value in general;[15] or beauty only,[16] or art,[17] or "mainly art,"[18] or "arts and related types of be-

---

Aesthetic Analysis (New York: T. Y. Crowell, 1936; Apollo-edition, 1967), 5; "general theory": G. Calugero, "Estetica," in the *Encyclopedia Italiana* (1932) XIV, 402; "study": J. L. Jarrett, *The Quest for Beauty* (Englewood Cliffs, N. J.: Prentice-Hall, 1957), 2; R. M. Ogden, *The Psychology of Art* (New York: C. Scribner's Sons, 1938), 3; and Carl Lemcke, *Populäre Aesthetik* (Leipzig: E. A. Seemann, 1879), 1; "systematic training": G. Gietmann, art. "Aesthetics," in *Catholic Encyclopedia* (New York: The Gilmary Society, 1913), I, 174b; and "science (in the broad sense)": J. Jungmann, *Ästhetik*, p. 15; and L. Tolstoi, *What Is Art?*, A. Maude, tr. (New York: Oxford University Press, 1962), 138.

[4] E.g., N. Wiener, "Aesthetics," *Encyclopedia Americana* (1963) V, 198; A. Torossian, *ibid.*
[5] E.g., Thomas Munro, *ibid.*; Gietmann, *ibid.*
[6] E.g., Max Diez, *Allgemeine Ästhetik* (Berlin-Leipzig: Göschen, 1912), 5; S. K. Langer, *Feeling and Form*, p. 12; N. Hartmann, *Ästhetik* (Berlin: W. de Gruyter, 1953), 1; H. N. Lee, *Perception and Aesthetic Value*, p. 98; H. Osborn *Aesthetics and Criticism* (New York: Philosophical Library, 1955), 24.
[7] E.g., H. R. Marshall, *Aesthetic Principles* (New York: Macmillan, 1895), 2.
[8] E.g., Theodor Lipps, *Ästhetik: Psychologie des Schönen und der Kunst* (Hamburg-Leipzig: L. Voss, 1903), I, 1; Karl Groos, *Der ästhetische Genuss* (Giessen: J. Ricker, 1902), 1; J. Volkelt, *System der Ästhetik*, I: *Grundlegung der Ästhetik* (München: C. H. Beck, 1927), 3, 5.
[9] "Aesthetics is the branch of philosophy that is concerned with the analysis of concepts and the solution of problems that arise when one contemplates aesthetic objects." John Hospers, art. "Aesthetics" in the *Encyclopedia of Philosophy* (1967), I, 35. "Aesthetics is that branch of philosophy whose function is to investigate what is meant to be asserted when we write or talk correctly about beauty." H. Osborne, *ibid.*
[10] E.g., "The science of aesthetics . . . is an effort to obtain a clear general idea of beautiful objects, our judgments upon them . . . ." DeWitt H. Parker, *The Principles of Aesthetics* (New York: Appleton, Century, Crofts, 1946), 2. Cf. also G. Gietmann, *ibid.*
[11] E.g., Lemcke and D. W. Prall, *ibid.*; H. S. Langfeld, *The Aesthetic Attitude* (New York: Harcourt, Brace, 1920), 34; and Vernon Lee–C. Anstruther-Thomson, *Beauty and Ugliness and Other Studies in Psychological Aesthetics* (London–New York: J. Lane, 1912), 80f., 111. Cf. the compromise view on this issue taken by James L. Jarrett, *op. cit.*, p. 2.
[12] E.g., N. Wiener and Gietmenn, *ibid.*; and R. Bayer, art. "Esthétique," in *Grand Larousse Encyclopédique*, ed. H. Laminault (Paris, 1961), XIV, 715.
[13] E.g., R. M. Ogden, *ibid.*
[14] E.g., J. L. Jarrett, *op. cit.*, p. 2.
[15] E.g., H. N. Lee, *op. cit.*, p. 98.
[16] E.g., A. G. Baumgarten, G. F. Meier, H. R. Marshall, L. Tolstoi, M. Diez, DeWitt H. Parker, S. K. Langer, and K. E. Gilbert (the last six all *ibid.*).

havior and experience" (a view representing a transition from the objective to the subjective realm),[19] or aesthetic experience in general,[20] or only aesthetic perception,[21] or aesthetic delight alone,[22] or else aesthetic delight and artistic creation.[23]

Finally, aestheticians disagree with each other on the overall character of the science of aesthetics. Most of them maintain that aesthetics is a theoretical (speculative) science;[24] others claim it to be practical (normative);[25] and again others hold that aesthetics is both theoretical and practical, both speculative and normative.[26]

2. In the light of all this variety of thought in defining aesthetics, what can be truthfully and properly said to be the essential definition of aesthetics?

One thing is certain: aesthetics is not just one science. The vastness of scope and the gradual birth of the various specific areas within it have made this quite clear. Consequently, aesthetics must be, at least initially, defined as a broad, generic field of scientific knowledge. Only in connection with the division of aesthetics into its many specific areas can the various specific branches of it be defined one by one.

Let us then say that aesthetics is a generic field of many specific sciences, all dealing in some manner with beautiful things.

In this essential definition, each phrase needs some explanation. The first of them, "generic field of many specific sciences" points out an analogy between philosophy and aesthetics in the broad sense. For philosophy as such is not one specific science but rather a generic field consisting of a number of specific sciences, such as cosmology, psychology, metaphysics, and ethics in

---

[17] E.g., K. W. F. Solger, *Vorlesungen über Ästhetik*, ed. K. W. L. Heyse (Leipzig: F. A. Brockhaus, 1829), 1; B. Croce, *Estetica*; M. Beardsley, *Aesthetics* (New York: Harcourt, Brace and World, 1958), 3; R. Lechner, *The Aesthetic Experience* (Chicago: H. Regnery, 1953), 66; E. Gilson, *Painting and Reality* (Cleveland, New York: The World Publishing Co., 1959), 126; V. Tejera, *Art and Human Intelligence* (New York: Appleton, Century, Crofts, 1965), 10; etc.

[18] E.g., A. G. Lehmann, *The Symbolist Aesthetic in France 1885–1895* (Oxford: B. Blackwell, 1950), 3. Cf. Peter Koestenbaum, *Philosophy: A General Introduction* (New York: American Book Co., 1968), 83.

[19] E.g., Thomas Munro, *op. cit.*, p. 134.

[20] E.g., E. F. Carritt, *An Introduction to Aesthetics* (London: Hutchinson's University Library, No. 26, 1949), 17; also, J. Volkelt, and H. N. Lee, both *ibid.*

[21] E.g., G. Santayana, *The Sense of Beauty* § 1, p. 15; and M. Diez, *ibid.*

[22] E.g., Grant Allen, *Physiological Aesthetics* (London: H. S. King, 1877), 1; F. Schleiermacher, *Ästhetik*, ed. R. Odebrecht (Berlin and Leipzig: W. de Gruyter, 1931), 3; C. Adam, art. "Esthétique," in *La Grand Encyclopédie*, XVI, 406.

[23] E.g., Karl Groos, *ibid.*; A. Torossian, *op. cit.*, pp. 1–3.

[24] E.g., H. Osborne, *ibid.*; D. W. Prall, *Aesthetic Analysis*, p. 31; Jarrett, *op. cit.*, p. 8; Thomas Munro, *op. cit.*, p. 316.

[25] E.g., Baumgarten, *Aesthetica*, §§ 1 and 13; G. F. Meier, *op. cit.* §§ 2 and 5, pp. 3 and 9; C. Hermann, *Die Ästhetik in ihrer Geschichte und als wissenschaftliches System* (Leipzig: Fr. Fleischer, 1876); J. Jungmann, *op. cit.*, p. 15; n. 10; J. K. Feibleman, *Aesthetics* (New York: Duell, Sloan, and Pearce, 1949), 292.

[26] E.g., A. G. Lehmann, *op. cit.*, p. 7; V. Tejera, *op. cit.*, pp. 8, 10.

such a way that these specific sciences include both theoretical or speculative and practical branches. Similarly, the generic field of human knowledge called "aesthetics" includes, as shall be seen in the next chapter, many, more or less specific, sciences of which some are speculative, others practical.

The next phrase, "dealing" refers to the subject of aesthetics, that is, a definite field of human knowledge considered from a specific point of view. "All dealing" expresses the truth that all specific sciences within aesthetics have the same general subject. The phrase "beautiful things" specifies the subject common to all the specific sciences within the genus "aesthetics"; and, within this phrase, "beautiful" means that which, in sole virtue of a knowledge of it rather than of its usefulness, delights its knower.

Finally, the phrase, "in some manner" is supposed to signify that, although all specific areas of aesthetics have beautiful things for their subject, not all of them are concerned with beautiful things in the same manner. To understand this statement, one must know that the "subject" of any science is a logical composite that means two things: a subject matter and an object matter. Subject matter is a given field or area or "object" of human knowledge, with definite limits, as organism is to biology; man, to education; or triangle, to trigonometry. Object matter, on the other hand, is an aspect in the subject matter of a given science, or a particular point of view from which one approaches and professionally investigates the subject matter of the science. Thus, organism is the subject matter of biology, and its empirical knowability is its object matter; man is the subject matter of education, and man's capacity for being educated, i.e., mentally and/or morally perfected, is its object matter.

Now, the phrase "in some manner" in the above definition of aesthetics indicates two basic versions of the treatment the various branches of aesthetics may give to beautiful things. For some branches of aesthetics consider various kinds of beautiful things, like natural or artistic, pictorial or poetic objects, in such a way that the things are the subject matter, and their beauty is the object matter of those branches of aesthetics. On the other hand, in many other areas of aesthetics, certain kinds of beautiful things are the subject matter, and some additional aspect in them are the object matter. For instance, the philosophy of art has the artwork, the work of fine art, for its subject matter; and the beauty of that artwork, artistic beauty, for its object matter. In contrast, in the field of the so-called therapeutic aesthetics, the beautiful work of art is the subject matter, and its quieting, healing power over the emotionally disturbed child or adult is the object matter. In brief, then, aesthetics is that generic area of human knowledge within which the beauty of certain things is either the object matter or (a part of) the subject matter of the various specific aesthetic sciences. As a matter of fact, as will be seen in the next chapter, the speculative branches of aesthetics use beauty as their object matter, whereas the practical branches and the auxiliary (related) sciences employ beauty as (a part of) their subject matter.

3. No single explanation of anything is so complete and perfect as to render any further question or objection superfluous or impossible. For this reason, it is proper at this point to consider some foreseeable questions about or objections to the above essential definition of aesthetics.

The first objection is this: The essence of anything is something definite, specific, and necessary, whereas the above definition of aesthetics, although allegedly essential, is unspecific, loose, and admits of certain alternatives. Therefore, the above definition is not essential.

The reply is easy and brief: it has been stated that aesthetics is not one specific science but rather a vast, generic area within which there are many, more or less specific, sciences. But a generic nature necessitates only a generic rather than a specific essential definition. Therefore, the generic nature of aesthetics demands only a generically essential definition, and the above given definition is precisely such.

A second objection is incomparably more complex both in its premises and its conclusions or implications: By virtue of its subject, aesthetics must deal with works of fine arts. But the works of some fine arts necessarily include some element of ugliness, whereas modern and, especially, contemporary art works employ ugliness with an ever-increasing frequency and intensity. Therefore, by virtue of its own subject, aesthetics must treat of ugliness as well as beauty and, as such, ought to be defined as the generic science of beautiful *and ugly* things. However, in the above definition, there is no mention of ugliness, but only of beauty. Consequently, the above definition of aesthetics is incomplete or defective.

In reply, we may say the following: The premises are true, but the stated conclusion does not follow. Both parts of this answer demand some explanation.

The premise of the objection includes a doctrinal and an historical part. The former claims that some kinds of artwork necessarily employ an element of ugliness. Now, the tragedy certainly does so, since the greatest tragedies in Greek, French, English, and German literature are full of horrifying, if not repulsive, deeds and characters. Moreover, as Aristotle correctly remarked, an element of the comic is ugliness.[27] However, while this first part of the premise is no more than a doctrinal matter, the second and historical component of the premise is a matter of fact. Whereas the medieval painting and sculpture employed almost exclusively religious, holy and, consequently, delightful or beautiful objects and topics, Renaissance art became increasingly secular and

---

[27] "Comedy . . . is an imitation of the more base . . . in respect of that part of the ugly which is ludicrous" (Aristotle, *Poet.* 5, 1448a 33–36). The nineteenth-century Hegelian aestheticians in Germany (Solger, Weisse, Rosenkranz, Schasler, etc.) merely gave a novel, dialectical formulation to this view.

humanistic (man-centered). As a consequence of this trend, human life and the world began to be represented more and more realistically. Concretely this meant a more and more frequent and a more and more intensive employment of the ugly in the form of the bizarre, the rustic, the horrible, the bawdy or sexually vulgar, the strongly repulsive or obscene, and the perverse.

At the end of this development some painters solemnly renounced beauty and aesthetics and proclaimed themselves to glorify the ugly, carefully avoiding anything beautiful and habitually seeking out and emphasizing the ugliness of things and objects. Something similar holds true not only for a rather closely related fine art, namely, sculpture, but also for such an area of fine arts as music. Operatic music is a classic manifestation of this long, gradual, and profound change from the clarity and intelligibility of the simple and delightful monotonal bel-canto style, through the increasingly more complex harmonies and chromatic melodies as well as ambiguous, vague tonality, to such final stages as bitonality, polytonality, and atonality in the twentieth-century operas. A parallel change in the librettos indicates the equally vast changes in poetry (novel, drama, etc.), as the overwhelmingly naïve, simple, and sentimental topics and plots gradually turned into the wildly passionate plots and characters of the grand and veristic operas and, in the twentieth century, into the plots and characters of all kinds of sexual perversion (promiscuity, Lesbianism, necrophilia, bacchanalia, etc.) whose nerve-shattering character is matched only by the frightening dissonances and cacaphonies of the operas. Countless similar developments in other areas of music and the rest of the fine arts could be listed as further corroborations of the historical premise concerning the ever-increasing employment of ugliness in modern fine arts.

Can one from this premise jump to the conclusion that aesthetics is a science professionally concerned with ugliness as well as beauty? Correspondingly, is there a need properly to correct the above definition of aesthetics? The answer to both questions is negative, and it is so on the basis of the following considerations. Ugliness is either apparent or real. The former is the seeming absence of beauty, and means therefore unrecognized beauty. As will be shown later, there are many possible reasons why one would fail to recognize the beauty of an object and judge it, consequently, to be ugly. Real ugliness, on the other hand, is the ugliness that is not merely apparent but truly predicable of an object on the basis that it lacks beauty or, at least, that its beauty is defective or impaired. This latter type of ugliness is, conceivably, either total or partial. Total ugliness, by definition, is the total absence of beauty or the absence of all beauty from a thing or object. Partial ugliness is predicable of things that, as Plato puts it,[28] are beautiful in one part or one respect, and lack

---

[28] Plato, *Symp.* 211 ab. Parallel texts to this: Dionysius the Areopagite, *De div. nom.* chap. 4 n. 7, § 137 (*PG* 3, 704 A); and Aquinas, *De div. nom.* 4, 5, 345.

beauty in another part or another respect. Moreover, partial ugliness may be considered in one of two ways: absolutely or in itself, and relatively or with regard either to other beautiful parts of the thing or to the whole of the thing.

Why or how is this division of ugliness relevant to the present objection? Because it enables us to consider all the possible alternative ways in which something called an artwork can be ugly.

Let us suppose, first, that the ugliness of an artwork is only apparent. In that case, the artwork is really beautiful. Consequently, even though aesthetics may consider that artwork, there is no reason why one should define aesthetics as the science of the beautiful *and the ugly*. Next, let us suppose that an artwork is totally ugly. In that case, if such is possible at all, the work is by definition outside the realm of the works of fine arts and, consequently, need not be professionally considered by the aesthetic philosopher or scientist as a source of information about the proximate or ultimate principles of beauty. Therefore, such cases do not compel us to insert "ugliness" as a second subject into the essential definition of aesthetics. Let us suppose next that an artwork is partly ugly. (If a modern artwork is not merely apparently ugly, then it is in most cases partly ugly either insofar as some of its integral parts are beautiful, and others are not; or else inasmuch as its topic or subject matter, or some characters or scenes in it, are ugly—since they are repulsive—whereas the mode of presentation of such a topic or subject matter is beautiful.) Now, the partly ugly is actually partly beautiful (or of a kind of beauty, i.e., partial beauty). But the partly beautiful certainly does not demand that ugliness be included in the very definition of aesthetics as one of its formal objects.

However, somebody may insist at this point that aesthetics must face such basic questions as what is ugliness or why ugliness is being used so much and so often in modern art. The answer to this insistence is found in any realistic metaphysics, like the Aristotelian or Thomistic one. According to them, every science naturally deals with the privative opposite of its subject,[29] as metaphysics does with non-being;[30] or ethics, with moral evil;[31] or aesthetics, with ugliness. But, since the negative member of a privative opposition (ugliness, evil, falsity) is intelligible only through its positive counter-part, and never vice versa,[32] any investigation of a privation is necessarily carried out in the light of the perfection of which it is the opposite. Therefore although it is perfectly true that the aesthetician must find some explanation for the em-

---

[29] Aristotle, *Met* XI, 1, 1059a 22f.; 3, 1061 a 13–15; *Post. an.* I, 7, 75b 13. Thomas, *In VIII. Phys.* L. 2; ed. P. M. Maggiolo (Taurini: Marietti, 1954) n. 977. *In I. Post. an.* L. 15; ed. R. M. Spiazzi (Taurini: Marietti, 1964), n. 133

[30] Aristotle, *Met.*, IV, 2, 1003b 4–10; Thomas, *In IV. Met.* L. 1; ed. M. R. Cathala (Taurini: Marietti, 1964), nn. 539 f.; *In II. Periherm.* L. 1; ed. R. M. Spiazzi (Taurini: Marietti, 1964), n. 207.

[31] E.g., Aristotle, *Eth.* Nic. II, 6; IV, 11 and 14; Thomas, *In II. Eth.* L. 7; ed. R. M. Spiazzi (Taurini: Marietti, 1964), n. 329; *In. IV. Eth.* 13, 801–12; 16, 850–53; etc.

[32] Aristotle, *Top.* VI, 9, 147b 4–25.

ployment by modern art of ugliness, he will find the answer precisely in terms of beauty. For he may point out, as one possible reason for using ugliness in an artwork, the truth that the beauty of a thing becomes even more conspicuous if contrasted with an ugly thing;[33] or that even the ugliest object can be represented by the artist in a very beautiful manner;[34] or that ugliness may even contribute to the beauty of the whole;[35] and consequently, the proper manner of contemplating modern artworks employing ugliness, and artworks in general, is to consider them as wholes while considering their (ugly) parts never in themselves, absolutely, but rather in their relation to the other (beautiful) parts as well as to the whole.[36]

Thus, although the aestheticians must answer questions concerning ugliness,[37] ugliness is not a second subject to aesthetics but rather a subordinate issue in connection with beauty. The above definition can, thereby, stand as it is, despite the enormously increased use of ugliness in modern art.

The third objection is also historical in its basis, but less complex in its solution. It runs like this. There are many great artworks that are anything but beautiful. But aesthetics must professionally concern itself, among other things, with great works of art. Therefore, aesthetics must professionally consider things other than beautiful, and ought, thereby, be defined not merely as the science of beautiful things but also as the science of sublime, picturesque, gracious, bizarre, etc., things.

The major premise of this objection has been held true by many aestheti-

---

[33] Cf., Aristotle, *Rhet.* III, 2, 1405a 12–13; Augustine, *De civ. Dei*, XI, 18; 23, 1 (*PL* 41, 332; 336); *De ordine*, I, 7, 18 (*PL* 32, 986); Alexander of Hales, *Summa theologica*, II, p. 1, i. 1, tr. 2, q. 3, c. 6, contra la (II, n. 82, p. 104a); Albert, *Summa theol.*, II, 11, 62, 2, 4, (XXXII, 601 f.) and *Compendium theologiae veritatis*, II, 65 (XXXIV, 87); Aquinas, *Summa theol.* II–II, 144, 3, ad 4; Ulrich of Strasbourg, *De pulchro* (*ed. cit.*, p. 78, lines 30 f.); Dionysius the Cartusian, *op. cit.*, art. 8 and 9, pp. 233 D and 235 D.

[34] E.g., "Aliqua imago dicitur esse pulchra, si perfecte raepraesentat rem, quamvis turpem" (Thomas, *Summ. theol.* I, 39, 8c.; see also *Quaest. quodlibetales*, XII, 22, 1.); "dicitur imago diaboli pulchra, quando bene repraesentat foeditatem diaboli" (Bonaventure, *In I. Sent.* d. 31, p. 11, a.1, q.3, ad 2. I, 544b); "Possunt turpia pulcre cogitari, ut talia" (Baumgarten, *Aesthetica*, § 18; *ed. cit.*, p. 8).

[35] E.g., Augustine, *De civ. Dei*, XI, 23, 1; XII, 4 (*PL* 41, 336; 351 f.); J. Dewey, *Art As Experience*, ch. 9 (New York: G. P. Putnam's Sons, 1958), 204n.

[36] E.g., Plotinus, *Enn.* III, 23; Augustine, *De civ. Dei*, XVI, 8, 2 (*PL* 41, 480); *De vera religione*, 40, 76 (*PL* 34, 156); Bonaventure, *Breviloquium*, prolog. 2, 4 (V, 204b); *In II. Sent.* d. 32, a. 3, q. 2, sol. opp. 5 (II, 774b).

[37] There are also other questions related to ugliness which the aesthetician can answer by means of the above-given division of ugliness. Such is the question concerning the most common errors which people are prone to commit in judging ugliness. These errors are three in number: (1) the confusion of apparent with real ugliness (the negative subjective reaction of the beholder with the ugliness of the beheld object); (2) the confusion of partial with total ugliness (e.g., when rejecting the entire play or film because of some morally objectionable words, scenes, characters, or other details in the play or film); and (3) the failure to consider the ugly parts of the beheld object relatively rather than absolutely (e.g. a morally objectionable scene as being the key to the climax of a drama).

cians, beginning with the eighteenth-century Joseph Addison down to contemporaries. Monroe C. Beardsley, for instance, writes in his *Aesthetics*, "If the word 'beauty' has any clear and restricted meaning, it does not apply, I suppose, to *Oedipus Rex*, to *The Magic Mountain*, to *King Lear*, to parts of Bartók's piano concertos, to some paintings of Rubens and Tintoretto, much less the Grünewald *Crucifixion*. . . . These works may be powerful, grand terrible, yes—but not beautiful."[88]

In reply to this objection, one must simply point out that "beauty" can be used in the broad as well as the strict sense. In the latter sense, beautiful is anything that simply and solely delights by the knowledge of it; in the former sense, the beautiful is anything that both delights and causes some other, mostly unpleasant, emotion in the beholder's mind. For instance, certain songs by Schubert, some paintings by Renoir, Mozart's *Magic Flute*, etc., can profoundly delight the beholder without eliciting any other emotional reaction in him; but the above-listed tragedies cause both delight and pain; a stormy sea both pleasure and horror, etc. Everything depends, then, on the way one uses the term "beauty" or "beautiful."

Speaking in the strict sense, Beardsley is right, and so is the entire objection against our definition of aesthetics. If, however, one uses these terms in the broad sense, as is the case with the essential definition in question, then Beardsley is wrong in the above quoted text, and so is the entire argument against our definition. In other words, if the proposed additional aesthetic values were not reducible to beauty as their common genus, the objection would be well taken, and the above definition of aesthetics should be extended so as to include them explicitly. But as many aestheticians, among them even some eighteenth-century British,[89] explicitly admitted, all the conceivable specific aesthetic values are reducible to the notion of beauty taken in the broad, generic sense. Thus, pure beauty merely delights; the sublime delights and awes; the tragic delights and saddens; the comic delights and makes one laugh; etc. Therefore, despite the partial truth of the major premise of the objection, there is no need to add any further aesthetic value to our definition of aesthetics, just as there is no need to add ugliness to it.

A fourth objection may attack our definition of aesthetics from a different angle, but basically for the same reason: an alleged narrowness of the subject of aesthetics. This argument can be formulated the following way. There are things, other than those of natural or artistic beauty, that, when known, delight by themselves. But, according to everybody's admission, aesthetics is professionally concerned with all things that cause delight in such a way.

---

[88] M. C. Beardsley, *Aesthetics*, p. 509.

[89] E.g., Thomas Reid, *Essays on the Intellectual Powers of Man*, Essay VIII, ch. 2, *ed. cit.*, I, 493a. Cf. also R. P. Knight, *op. cit.*, II, 2, 20 f., 23, 25, 27 (*ed. cit.*, pp. 72f., 151, 153, 156); and Dugald Stewart, *Philosophical Essays, ed. cit.*, p. 234.

Therefore, aesthetics is professionally concerned with things other than those of natural or artistic beauty. Therefore, the essential definition of beauty must include those other things, too, as the subject of aesthetics. But all things of natural and artistic beauty as well as those that delight man by themselves have precisely this much in common, that they all delight by the mere knowledge the beholder acquires of them, rather than by virtue of their usefulness of any kind; and the value by which all these things delight by themselves is universally called in contemporary philosophy "aesthetic value." Therefore, the essential definition should include "aesthetic value" rather than the narrower notion of "beauty" as the subject of aesthetics. Consequently, the above proposed definition of aesthetics is unsatisfactory.

In answer to this argument, one may readily concede two things: one, that "aesthetic value" is a much more commonly used term nowadays than "beauty"; and two, that some aestheticians do consider "aesthetic value" to be broader than "beauty" is. Thomas Munro, for instance, asserts that aesthetics "is now commonly conceived as the subject which . . . considers the aesthetic experience of nature and of other types of object in addition to works of art . . ."[40] However, the majority's use of a term, being a matter of free decision, unlike truth, alone does not render its use in the essential definition of aesthetics right or more correct than another term, like "beauty." Besides, if the "beautiful" is taken in the broad sense, it does properly cover everything that the term "the aesthetic" does. Moreover, the use of the term "aesthetic" or "the aesthetic" in the definition of aesthetics, as the subject of this science, renders the definition embarrasingly circular: "aesthetics is the science of the aesthetic." Of course, those who prefer this formula to the "old fashioned" phrase, "aesthetics is the science of the beautiful," will assure their readers that there is nothing logically wrong with this begging of the question. J. L. Jarrett, for instance, having stated that "Aesthetics is the study of the aesthetic," hastens to add immediately, "This sounds like a trick." Then he endeavors to assure us that "it would be no bad definition of "economics" to speak of it as the study of the economic."[41] Of course, there is nothing wrong with it except that it does not explain the definitum, and is, for this reason, not a definition. For, to argue further, as Jarrett does, "But everyone knows what *that* (sc. the word "aesthetic") means," does not eliminate or remove the circularity of his definition. In brief, then, one still has to offer a convincing reason why the term "the beautiful" should be replaced by "the aesthetic" in the above given definition of aesthetics.

Finally, one may even try the following objection against the offered definition of our science. This definition speaks of the beautiful as if it were something real, objective, existent. But beauty is only in the mind (or eye)

[40] Munro, *op. cit.*, p. 134. Cf. also J. L. Jarrett, *op. cit.*, p. 3.
[41] J. L. Jarrett, *op. cit.*, p. 2.

of the beholder. Therefore, the suggested definition in question is erroneous.

Now, this line of argument touches not on a preliminary or introductory question of aesthetics but rather on one that will be our first major problem in the philosophy of beauty, whereas we ought first to tackle one more introductory question, viz., the division of aesthetics. Therefore, in order not to anticipate the proper, systematic treatment of the question of the existence of beauty, it should suffice here to point out that the view expressed in the minor of the objection is that of aesthetic subjectivism—a view that will be proved erroneous. Therefore this, just as all the previous objections, fails to necessitate any change in the essential definition of aesthetics, viz., that aesthetics is a generic field of many specific sciences, all dealing in some manner with beautiful things.

With this in mind, we may turn now to the question of the division of aesthetics.

Chapter III
Division of Aesthetics

THERE ARE TWO REASONS other than the customary logical one for discussing the division of aesthetics after a chapter on the definition of aesthetics. One of them is historical in nature; the other, methodological.

The historical reason consists in the fact that relatively few authors on aesthetics touch on the question of the division, and even if they do so, they offer a list of some significant branches in a more or less arbitrary manner rather than give a systematic division of all (or all conceivable or known) genera, species, and subspecies of the vast field called aesthetics.

The methodological reason for taking up the division of aesthetics right after the chapter on the definition of this science is that our understanding of the various areas and branches of aesthetics is not satisfactory merely on the basis of the generic essential definition offered in the previous chapter. Instead, we need an essential definition for each specific science within the realm of aesthetics. But this is possible only on the basis of and in connection with a detailed division of the generic field itself.

If one takes aesthetics in the broadest possible sense, aesthetics includes two large areas of scientific knowledge: that of speculative aesthetics, and that of practical aesthetics. The former, as any speculative science, is knowledge sought for its own sake rather than for the sake of its usefulness in action; the latter, as any practical science, is knowledge that, by its very nature, aids human action and is, therefore, sought not for its own sake but for the sake of action which it may direct. It should be noted here that this differentiation of speculative and practical aesthetics is not supposed to deny the possible usefulness of speculative aesthetics. For every knowledge, the speculative as well as the practical, can be useful, at least per accident. In other words, practical and useful knowledge or science are not contrarily opposed; only the practical and the speculative are so opposed.

To these two vast realms of speculative and practical aesthetics, a third one may be added, from without: the related or auxiliary sciences of aesthetics. These comprise specific sciences that are not under the genus aesthetics but under other genera of speculative sciences, viz., history and philosophy. Yet, their subject naturally complements the specific knowledge that one may acquire about beauty by studying aesthetics. Thus, these sciences are truly related and auxiliary to aesthetics.

Altogether, then, three large areas ought to be investigated, or at least divided and, in their species, defined. Since of these three, speculative aesthetics is the vastest and most complex, article 1 will deal with the division of speculative aesthetics, whereas in article 2 the division of practical aesthetics and the auxiliary sciences will be discussed.

ARTICLE 1: *Division of Speculative Aesthetics*

All sciences, except one, use human reason relying on the data of the senses as their sole source. The only exception to this is what is traditionally called theology. Theology uses two sources, of which the primary is faith in a so-called divine revelation, whereas the secondary is the same as the sole source of all the other sciences: reason relying on the senses.

On the other hand, sciences differ both in method and in specific professional interest. For all sciences are interested in the causes or principles of the empirical facts they investigate, but not all sciences are professionally interested in, or aim at, explaining the same kinds of causes. Similarly, all sciences have a certain method they primarily use, but not all sciences use the same method as their primary way of reasoning. Those using primarily the inductive method aim at finding the direct or proximate causes of the facts in question; those using deduction as their primary method endeavor to find the ultimate principles or causes of the empirical facts.

On the basis of these twofold divisions, one can easily discover three large areas within the genus of speculative aesthetics: philosophic, scientific, and theological aesthetics. The first two differ from the third as all sciences other than theology do from theology itself; and the first differs from the second as the deductive sciences, interested in ultimate causes or principles, do from the individual sciences seeking the proximate causes or principles of empirical facts.

Let us consider these three vast genera of speculative aesthetics one by one.

1. *Philosophic aesthetics* is the generic science that deals with the ultimate principles or causes of the beauty of things. In this science, the things that are beautiful constitute the subject matter; their beauty, the object matter.

The philosopher can do one of two things about beauty. He can investigate the ultimate principles or causes of the beauty of all things or only of some things. Accordingly, philosophic aesthetics can conveniently be divided into general and special philosophic aesthetics. The former may properly be called metaphysical aesthetics (since it is metaphysics that deals with anything and everything that exists at all), or simply philosophy of beauty; the latter includes a number of specific and analogous branches, of which each has its own name.

Metaphysical aesthetics or the philosophy of beauty is the science that deals with the ultimate principles or causes of the beauty of everything beautiful; or, the philosophic science of beauty in general or beauty as such. Its primary concern is to determine what principles, i.e., parts, components, or factors, render anything and everything that is beautiful at all beautiful. Its subject matter is being in general, the Aristotelian "being as being"; its object matter, the beauty of being in general.

Special philosophic aesthetics is a generic science of many species all investigating the ultimate principles or causes of the beauty of the various genera of beings. From this it immediately follows that special philosophic aesthetics comprises two analogous genera, namely, the philosophic aesthetics of real beings, and the philosophic aesthetics of mental beings.

Taking up, first, the philosophic aesthetics of real beings, one can differentiate between the following branches within it: theistic aesthetics, pneumatological aesthetics, cosmological aesthetics, philosophy of natural beauty, and philosophy of artistic beauty (or, simply, art). The first of these is the philosophic science investigating the existence, essence, and properties of divine beauty (in as much as it is rationally knowable). The second does the same with the beauty of purely spiritual substances. The third inquires about the ultimate principles or causes of the beauty of matter as matter. The fourth concerns itself with corporeal beauty only in as much as it is sensorily knowable, i.e., with the beauty of sensory accidents. The fifth and last endeavors to determine the ultimate principles or causes of the beauty of the works of fine arts.

Of these five branches of special philosophic aesthetics, cosmological aesthetics and the philosophy of natural beauty may be reduced to one discipline, the philosophy of material beauty. As such, it serves as the foundation of metaphysical aesthetics or the philosophy of beauty in general, since the knowledge of the material being is prior to the knowledge of being. Thus, the main outlines of the philosophy of material beauty constitutes an integral part of the philosophy of being in general. So does, strictly speaking, theistic aesthetics. For God, at least in realistic metaphysics, is the cause of being, and any treatment of God is thereby an integral part of metaphysics in general. Furthermore, pneumatological aesthetics ($pneuma$ = spirit) is metaphysically possible only for those few who hold certain arguments from the perfection of the created world for the existence of immaterial substances to be conclusive, or else for those who are willing to philosophize about the beauty of spiritual substances under the condition that such beings might not exist at all.

All this leaves us with only two significant, since irreducible, and ever-intriguing, branches of philosophic aesthetics, viz., the philosophy of beauty (= metaphysical aesthetics) and the philosophy of (fine) art, the former being general philosophic aesthetics; the latter, one branch of special philosophic aesthetics.

Turning now specifically to the philosophy of art, its division is determined by the analogy of this science to philosophic aesthetics in general, on the one hand, and by the division of the fine arts, on the other hand. Accordingly, then, the philosophy of art can be divided into general and special philosophy of art. General philosophy of art is the science that investigates the ultimate principles or causes of the beauty of the works of the fine arts. In it, the work of fine art is the subject matter, and the beauty of the artwork, the object matter. Thereby, general philosophic aesthetics, just as all the branches of the special philosophy of art, is as much a speculative branch of aesthetics as the philosophy of beauty itself is. Special philosophy of art, on the other hand, is a generic field composed of a number of more or less specific sciences treating philosophically the beauty of the various kinds of fine artworks. Thus, the special philosophy of art includes, first of all, the philosophy of creative and the philosophy of reproductive fine arts.

Moreover, both genera comprise a philosophy of liberal fine arts and a philosophy of mechanical fine arts, and they do so in such a way that within each of these four genera, there will be two or more specific sciences. Under the philosophy of the mechanical creative fine arts, there are the philosophy of pictorial arts (painting, drawing) and the philosophy of sculpture. Under the philosophy of the liberal creative fine arts, we find the philosophy of poetry, musical composition, and choreography. Under the philosophy of the liberal reproductive fine arts, three specific sciences are included: the philosophy of stage directing, conducting, and dance directing. Finally, under the philosophy of the mechanical reproductive fine arts, one finds these sciences: the philosophy of reciting and acting; that of singing and playing music; that of dancing; and that of film.

This long list of the species of the genus "philosophy of art" is still not complete. For each of these many species can be conceived as a genus that can be further divided and subdivided. To use only one example, the philosophy of poetry can be divided into general and special philosophy of poetry in such a way that special philosophy of poetry itself includes the philosophy of epic poetry, lyric poetry, and dramatic poetry, with each of the three being capable of further differentiation.

All these branches of philosophic aesthetics deal with the beauty of real being. There is, however, a second genus of philosophic aesthetics, that dealing philosophically with the beauty of mental beings. It includes logical aesthetics, dealing with the beauty of concepts and their composites, and mathematical aesthetics, dealing with the beauty of numeric relations (arithmetico-algebraic aesthetics) and the beauty of geometric elements (geometrical aesthetics).

2. *Scientific aesthetics* is a generic science that is composed of numerous, more or less specific sciences, all dealing in some manner with the proximate principles or causes of the beauty of material things.

Its generic subject matter is material being; its generic object matter, the beauty of material being considered in its proximate principles or causes. Thereby, the difference between scientific and philosophic aesthetics is quite clearly twofold. The first difference is partial and a matter of scope; the second, total, and a matter of consideration. For, while the scope of philosophic aesthetics is unlimited in so far as general philosophic aesthetics deals with beauty in general, the scope of scientific aesthetics is considerably limited, since confined to material beings only. Secondly, while philosophic aesthetics concerns itself with the ultimate principles or causes of its subject matter, scientific aesthetics, due to its primarily inductive method, confines itself to the direct, proximate principles or causes of material beauty. This latter difference means concretely that, while the philosopher inquires about the components of beauty as such or material beauty as such, i.e., what makes anything beautiful necessarily beautiful or any material thing necessarily beautiful, the scientist asks himself much more specific and different questions, such as what components of beauty can be *empirically* found in minerals, plants, animals, or given artworks.

According to these differences in nature, the main division is also different in scientific and philosophic aesthetics. For, being interested not in supreme genera but in proximate genera and species of material beauty, and investigating them in a predominantly empirical manner, scientific aesthetics is divided not into general and special scientific aesthetics but, instead, into objective and subjective scientific aesthetics. The specific reason for this twofold division is that there are two basic manners in which material beauty can be considered: absolutely, in itself and irrespective of man as its cause or beholder, and relatively, in its relation to man as its maker and/or beholder.

Within this main distinction, however, the divisions of both objective and subjective scientific aesthetics are analogously identical. For, whether one considers material beauty absolutely, or in its relation to man, material beauty has the same levels and realms. Therefore, both objective and subjective scientific aesthetics comprises the following species: physical, chemical, biological (i.e., botanical and zoological), psychological, and sociological aesthetics.

Objective physical aesthetics deals with the proximate principles of the beauty of the most universal components or aspects of the material world. They are visible, on the one hand (light and color, shape and structure, motion and rest); and auditory (tones), on the other hand. Thus, objective physical aesthetics includes optical, spatial, dynamic, and tonal aesthetics. The next genus, objective chemical aesthetics, considers the proximate chemical components of material beauty, namely, atoms, molecules, and crystallic structures. Objective biological aesthetics is professionally concerned with the biological principles and the organic unity of plants (botanical aesthetics) and brutes (zoological aesthetics), considered both statically (structurally) and dynamically (functionally). Objective psychological aesthetics is the science investigating the proximate principles or causes of human beauty insofar as it is directly knowable, i.e., the beauty of the human body (structurally and functionally) and the external expressions of the beauty of the human mind.

Finally, sociological aesthetics is the science that treats of the proximate principles or causes of the structural and functional beauty of human society, i.e., the institutions, cultures, and subcultures, on the one hand, and the life or behavior or functioning of these structural components, on the other. To all these comes as an analogous genus a sixth branch that investigates the proximate principles not of the beauty of natural things but that of manmade, artificial things, namely, the artworks. This is the objective science of art (meaning artwork).

Opposite to these six genera of objective scientific aesthetics, there are the same number of analogous genera of subjective scientific aesthetics. Of these six, however, the first five are normally treated as one formal science, with physical aesthetics dominating them and, thereby, its proper name is the psychology of physical beauty. Opposed to it is the subjective science of art (artwork), or the psychological aesthetics of art, or, even more briefly, the psychology of art. What the psychology of physical beauty and the psychology of art have in common is this: they both investigate the nature of the knowledge and/or delight caused, at the level of physiology (biology), or psychology, by the various components of material beauty (natural or artistic). There is, however, one significant difference between the two. The psychology of physical beauty deals only with the psychological effects of natural beauty upon man as a beholder (since man is never the cause of this beauty), whereas the psychology of art is the science that deals not only with the effects of the beautiful artwork in the beholder but also with the psychological process of artistic creation (since man is both the maker and the beholder of this beauty). Of all the branches of scientific aesthetics, those dealing with art and, especially, the psychology of art, are extremely widespread and popular at the present.

3. *Theological Aesthetics* is the third of the three main genera of speculative aesthetics. It is the science that professionally investigates the beauty of things that are knowable only by faith. Its subject matter, then, is things that are knowable not by reason but only by faith; its object matter is the beauty of these things insofar as it is knowable either exclusively by faith or, secondarily, also by reason.

Since the primary source of this kind of aesthetics, just as of theology in general, is faith, and since faith varies with individuals and societies, there are, in terms of subject matter, as many kinds of theological aesthetics as there are faiths (religions). In regard to its subject matter, one can speak of both Christian and non-Christian theological aesthetics, each of the two groups having various kinds. Of all of them, however, the early and medieval Christian theological aesthetics is the most developed.

The main division of medieval Christian theological aesthetics is twofold, and includes dogmatic and moral theological aesthetics. The former deals with the beauty of only theologically known beings or institutions; the latter, with the beauty of the so-called theological virtues. Dogmatic theological aesthetics comprises, thereby, the following branches: trinitarian, Christological, Mariological, charismatic, eschatological, and ecclesiological aesthetics. Trinitarian aesthetics investigates the beauty of the triune God; Christological aesthetics, the beauty of Christ according to his human nature; Mariological aesthetics, the corporeal and spiritual beauty of Mary; charismatic aesthetics, the material beauty of divine grace in general, and of sacramental grace in particular; eschatological aesthetics, the beauty of the resurrected human body; and ecclesiological aesthetics, the beauty of the Church with respect to its inner structure and external hierarchy.

Moral theological aesthetics is the theological science concerned with the beauty of theological virtue in general, and the various theological virtues in particular. As such, it is the theological counterpart of moral philosophic aesthetics that, in turn, is only conceivably an integral part of the philosophy of natural beauty in general, and the philosophy of human beauty in particular.

With this list of the divisions of philosophic, scientific and theological aesthetics we have more or less exhausted the realm of speculative aesthetics and, consequently, can turn now to the division of practical aesthetics.

ARTICLE 2: *Division of Practical Aesthetics and Auxiliary Sciences*

1. *Practical aesthetics* is a generic field of knowledge comprising a number of specific sciences all concerned with practical knowledge about beautiful things. Practical knowledge, in turn, is by its nature directed toward action.

The specific sciences in question include technological aesthetics and art appreciation in such a way that three additional branches are somehow integral parts of technological aesthetics, viz., art pedagogy, therapeutic art pedagogy, and liturgical aesthetics; and there must be added a field that is more a kind of mental operation, a process, rather than a science, art criticism in the strict, proper sense.

The generic reason for these three sciences and the intellectual operation of art criticism is the fact that man can do three things with beautiful objects: he can either make them for one purpose or another, or behold and appreciate them, or else help others to behold and appreciate them. Now, in technological aesthetics one learns the first of these three roles; in art appreciation, the second; and in art criticism, he does the third. Despite these specific differences, however, all three have beautiful things for their subject matter (or object), whereas some practical aspect in the beautiful things is their object matter (or purpose). Let us take up these sciences one by one.

Technological aesthetics is the science of making beautiful things (works of fine art) in the proper, prudential manner. Its subject matter is the individual beautiful work to be made; its object matter, the prudential mode of making such a work. The principles of the proper mode of making are determined by the nature of the material (or material cause) out of which the individual artwork is to be made (e.g., wood, marble, clay, etc. in case of sculpture). And since all the conceivable materials or art media are material beings which, in turn, are the subject of physics and chemistry, technological aesthetics is a science that, in respect to its object matter, is dependent upon the principles of physics and chemistry. On the other hand, inasmuch as it deals with the making of precisely beautiful things, technological aesthetics depends in its subject matter upon the principles of the philosophy and science of beauty and art. Thereby, this practical science is subordinate to several and quite heterogeneous superior sciences that are all speculative. Moreover, precisely because the artistic medium is physically and/or chemically so much different in the various kinds of fine arts, and even within any one species of fine arts (as clay, bronze, wood, marble, and iron are within sculpture), it is completely unfeasible to expound something like a general technological aesthetics. This is to say that the only division (in terms of its object matter) of technological aesthetics is a list rather than a true division, predetermined by the various species of the fine arts and, within each one of them, by the variety of the materials that can be used in the making of the artwork. There are pictorial, sculptural, poetic, musical, choreographic, theatrical, etc., technological aesthetics and, within them, significantly different branches according to the artistic materials to be used.

Before turning to art appreciation, three sciences related to technological aesthetics ought to be discussed. First is art pedagogy; second, therapeutic art pedagogy or, simply, therapeutic aesthetics; and third, liturgical aesthetics.

Art pedagogy (or pedagogy of technological aesthetics) is a science twice removed from speculative aesthetics, for it is the science of the prudential mode of teaching technological aesthetics. In other words, it is professionally concerned with teaching somebody the proper, effective manner of teaching somebody else how to make works of arts properly. Thus, a book is on art pedagogy insofar as it systematically expounds and describes the proper way of teaching, let us say, singing or playing a musical instrument in school or to individual students of music. The subject matter of art pedagogy is the making of a beautiful thing; its object matter, the prudential mode of teaching the making of beautiful things (artworks). However, this subject matter of art pedagogy is the subject of technological aesthetics, as it itself is composed of a subject matter and an object matter. The remote subject matter of art pedagogy is the beautiful thing; its proximate subject matter is the proper making of beautiful things; and its object matter, the proper (mode of) teaching how to make an artwork or beautiful thing properly. Furthermore, since the prudential manner of teaching anything is determined by scientific psychology, the science of human behavior; art pedagogy depends materially on the philosophy and science of beauty and art, on the one hand, and physics and chemistry, on the other; and, formally, on the principles of psychology. Also, since the principles of proper teaching are generically the same in respect to any field to be taught, the division of art pedagogy is determined only by its subject matter, i.e., technological aesthetics. Accordingly, then, art pedagogy can be divided into the art pedagogy of drawing, painting, sculpting, acting, singing, playing music, dancing, etc., with a rich variety of subdivisions within any one of these specific branches (such as teaching the use of water color or oil painting, portrait painting, or landscape painting).

Therapeutic art pedagogy, a recent branch of art pedagogy in general, is a science of the prudential mode of teaching the making of artwork to emotionally disturbed or mentally ill children or adults as a therapeutic treatment. While its generic relation to technological aesthetics and its division are similar to those of general art pedagogy, there is one significant difference. General art pedagogy is determined by the principles of general psychology; therapeutic art pedagogy, by the principles of the specific science of pathological psychology.

Liturgical aesthetics (not to be confused with the aesthetics of liturgy) is a science that can be defined as one of the usefulness of art to religion in general and to worship in particular. Its subject matter is the beautiful thing, the work of art; its object matter, the prudential making of the beautiful thing so as to render it useful for religion and worship. From this characterization, it is obvious that liturgical aesthetics as a practical science is to the speculative science of theological aesthetics as the practical science of technological aesthetics is to the speculative sciences called the philosophy and the science of beauty and art. The scope of its subject matter is at least coextensive with the scope of fine art, since every species of fine art can be used in some manner in religious life and worship. There are even works of the so-called applied or decorative arts and mixed arts (e.g., architecture, gold smithery) that can be useful to religion and worship if properly made. The range of the object matter, viz., the religious suitability, of liturgical aesthetics comprises a generic or intrinsic and a specific or extrinsic factor. The former lies in the generic nature of the artwork, whereby it is capable of being used in liturgy in such a way as to promote religious feelings or facilitate religious ceremonies prior to and irrespective of any authoritative religious norm or code. The latter component, the specific suitability, is posterior to and determined by specific prescriptions or codes within any given religion. In other words, generic suitability flows from and is determined by the artistic-aesthetic nature of an artwork, whereas specific suitability determines the individual nature of the artwork, as the liturgical notion of worship limits, for instance, the interior architectonic of a church building. As far as its division is concerned, liturgical aesthetics can be divided both according to its subject matter and its object matter. In the former way, liturgical aesthetics is general and special; in the latter way, liturgical aesthetics can be of as many kinds as there are religions, the principles of which guide liturgical aesthetics, and specify its branches.

Art appreciation is unrelated both to technological aesthetics and to the above listed three practical sciences. For, as stated above, technological and liturgical aesthetics are concerned with the making of certain beautiful things; and art pedagogy and therapeutic art pedagogy deal with the proper teaching of how to make beautiful things. In contrast, art appreciation has nothing to do either directly or indirectly with the making of any kind of beautiful things, or with the proper teaching of any practical science of aesthetics. Nor is art appreciation strictly speaking one science, due to the lack of unity of its subject. Instead, it is conceived as a science that outlines the history of art with special emphasis on great artists, artworks, and art styles, by using as a guide for evaluation the philosophy and the science of art and, for presentation, the science of psychology; and all this for the purpose of rendering the owner of this selected knowledge intellectually prepared and willingly inclined and desirous to have personal aesthetic experiences with artworks.

The complex character of art appreciation as a quasi-science is obvious, both in terms of its subject and in terms of aims. For, first of all, the remote subject matter is art history in general; the proximate subject matter is material selected from art history by the aid of the philosophy and science of art; and the object matter is the attractiveness of this material and its presentation, the latter being aided by the principles of psychology, so that the material presented in this manner can motivate the student to seek aesthetic experiences with artworks on his own. Secondly, art appreciation is complex also in terms of its two goals. For its proximate goal, in the order of formal causality, is the imparting of a psychologically impressive knowledge about fine art; and the remote (or ultimate) goal, in the order of efficient causality, is the learner's activity of seeking firsthand knowledge and delight in artworks. In regard to its subject matter and its proximate goal, art appreciation is materially speculative. However, in respect to its object matter and remote (ultimate) end, art appreciation is quite obviously a formally practical (quasi-) science, that is, a knowledge which, by its nature, aims at and is directive of action.

Moreover, in terms of its subject matter, art appreciation can be divided into general and special art appreciation; and the latter, either into the generic appreciation of the visual arts or the creative mechanical arts (drawing, painting, and sculpture), the creative liberal arts (poetry, musical composition, and choreography), the reproductive mechanical arts (theatrical arts, singing and playing music, dancing, and film), or else directly into the specific appreciation of poetry, music, dance, painting, sculpture, architecture, acting, singing, playing music, dancing, etc.

In addition to all these listed branches, there is one more field of practical aesthetics that must be discussed here. It might be called, despite its special

Anglo-American connotation, *art criticism*. Taking it historically, art criticism has come to mean, misleadingly enough, the philosophy and/or science of art. In this sense, it is a formal science that does not concern us here, since under the names "philosophy" and "science of art" it has been discussed among the speculative branches of aesthetics. Among the fields of practical aesthetics, however, art criticism has a considerably different meaning, viz., one that is its primary and etymological meaning. For "criticism," primarily, means the act of criticizing or critical judgment; and, secondarily, the habit or intellectual power of properly judging or evaluating the beauties and faults of the works of art in general or of, say, literature in particular.

Taking it in the last listed senses, art criticism is clearly neither speculative nor a science but only a mental act or process, or the literary expression of a mental act or process, whereby the aesthetic value of one or more artworks or the aesthetic achievements of one or more artists is argumentatively determined. The subject matter of art criticism, taken in this particular sense, is the artwork itself that is being aesthetically evaluated; its object matter is the beauty (aesthetic value) of the artwork; and the formal process of art appreciation is the act of aesthetic judgment passed on an artwork, based on personal aesthetic experience and proved by means of certain principles of the philosophy and/or science of beauty and art as well as history, for the purpose of inducing the potential beholder actually to behold or not to behold the artwork in question. With respect to any one individual artwork, art criticism comprises three acts: the act of personal beholding, the act of aesthetic judgment, and the act of aesthetic reasoning whereby the art critic shows that his personal judgment does follow, in regard to beauty, from principles of the philosophy and/or science of beauty and art and, in regard to originality, from the history of art. That art criticism in its written form, but so understood, is listed here among the practical branches of aesthetics is due to its purpose. For it is obvious that, unlike the historian, the art critic writes down his aesthetic judgment and the speculative reasons for it not for his own sake but for the sake of others in the hope that his reasoned judgment will influence potential beholders to act or not to act; i.e., to go or not to go to behold the artwork in question. The beneficiary of art criticism is thereby the average man, to be motivated positively or negatively by the written criticism which he may read or hear about. Consequently, if everyone could properly enjoy and appreciate all true works of art, and reject all alleged works of art, then art criticism would completely lose its *raison d'être*.

Art criticism can be divided according to both its subject matter and its object matter. According to the former, in turn, both a "qualitative" and a quantitative division is possible. Qualitatively (using this term somewhat loosely), art criticism can be divided into as many fields as fine art itself, on the basis of the works of fine art that are its subject matter. In this way, there are literary criticism, music criticism, pictorial criticism, film criticism, dance criticism, etc. Quantitatively, art criticism can be divided into two kinds: one, concerning itself with individual works of art; and two, concerning itself with a group of artworks selected under some formal aspect, such as works of a certain phase in the development of one given artist, or works of a certain kind or genre by the same artist, or the works of a group of artists belonging to the same school, style, etc.

According to the object matter, i.e., the specific mode of criticism, one can loosely speak of scholarly and journalistic art criticism, thereby indicating between these two groups and within each of these two groups a difference of degree ranging from art criticism of highest scholarship, exactness, thoroughness, and objectivity in judging the artworks aesthetically and proving those judgments according to sound, objective principles to the brief, incomplete, and often quite superficial book, music, theater, and film critiques which are written for local newspapers and contain only or mostly subjective reactions to the artworks in question. As to its relation to some aesthetic and non-aesthetic sciences, art criticism must be clearly differentiated from the history of art according to its subject matter, and from moral philosophy according to its object matter. For, insofar as the sole subject matter of art criticism is the work of fine art, the sole task of the art critic is to consider nothing but the artwork itself, while leaving all other informations disregarded, whereas the art historian is naturally concerned with data both about the artists and their works. Concretely, this means that such factors as the intentions of the creative artist or his personality (as possibly expressed in the artwork) must not be the criteria of the value judgment which the art critic passes on the artwork, although the art historian may validly consider such aspects.

Hence the only legitimate analogy between art criticism and art history is to be found in their common interest in the aesthetic value and the originality of the artwork. In regard to aesthetic value, both the art critic and the art historian use the principles of the philosophy and the science of beauty and art; in regard to the aspect of originality, the art critic uses the history of art as the proper source of this information. In regard to its object matter, art criticism differs by its nature from moral philosophy. For this reason, the art critic should never act, although erroneously he often does, like a moralist. Concretely, this means that while the task of the art critic is the evaluation of the aesthetic value and the extent of originality in a work of fine art, it is never his but the moralist's task to pass a moral judgment on any artwork. To predict what possible or probable effects a work may have on children, adolescents, or even adults, is clearly neither a question of beauty or ugliness nor a question of originality or unoriginality but the sovereign problem of moral goodness or evilness. Since the art historian is professionally concerned with both the artist and the artwork, and since the intentions of the artist have a great influence on the ultimate formation of the artwork, the art historian and the moralist do have some common interest in the morality of the artwork, but the art critic has no such interest unless he arbitrarily assumes the role of the art historian and/or moralist.[1]

2. *Auxiliary science* in general, although considered in itself a science in its own right, considered relatively is useful to another science to which it is auxiliary. To aesthetics and, more specifically, to philosophic aesthetics, any science is useful or auxiliary that utilizes the principles of a generically different, non-aesthetic science in such a way that beauty or art is its subject matter in some manner.

Some of these auxiliary sciences are philosophic; others, nonphilosophic. The former include at least the philosophy of the history of art; the latter, two sciences: the history of aesthetics and the history of art. Since the philosophic auxiliary science has a historical auxiliary science for its subject matter, we shall discuss the historical auxiliary sciences before the philosophy of the history of art.

History of aesthetics as a name can be used both generically and specifically. Generically, it means the history of both philosophic and scientific aesthetics; specifically, it signifies only the history of philosophic aesthetics.[2] Taking this name in the specific sense here, we may define the history of aesthetics as the science of the chronological and causal relations of important philosophic theories concerning beauty and art. The subject matter of this science is the various significant philosophic theories of beauty and art; its object matter, the chronological sequence in which these theories have been expounded, and the causal order of theories influencing others and influenced by others.

According to its subject matter, or scope, the history of aesthetics is twofold: general and special. The former deals with all significant theories of beauty and art in general; the latter, with some significant theories of beauty and art in general or with all significant theories of beauty and art in particular. From this definition of special history of aesthetics, it follows that, according to its subject matter, special history of aesthetics can be divided in a quasi-qualitative as well as a quantitative manner. In the former way, the special history of

---

[1] Since, despite the formal distinction between beauty and moral goodness, it is easy, although erroneous, to conclude from some moral defect to aesthetic defects in the artwork; many unfair judgments could have been avoided by art critics in the past, and could be avoided by them in the future if they only realized the limitations of their field and the difference of aesthetics from moral philosophy. Besides, to ignore this distinction between the proper tasks of the art critic and the moralist is, on the part of the art critic, a matter of fairness to the moralist and a safeguard of the sovereignty and purity of art criticism. For, if the art critic passes moral judgment on an artwork, he goes beyond his professional competence and, in turn, makes it impossible for him to object to the moralist's passing aesthetic judgments on artworks without being inconsistent.

[2] The textbooks on the history of aesthetics do not generally make any such distinction, mainly because the two fields are intrinsically correlated, and the history of scientific aesthetics is much younger than the history of aesthetics.

aesthetics deals either with one doctrinal aspect of the entire field of general philosophic aesthetics, or with the history of any one of the branches of the special philosophy of art, such as the history of the philosophy of poetry, music, painting, sculpture, or architecture. In the latter, quantitative manner, the special history of aesthetics is the history of any one integral part of the general history of aesthetics selected on a chronological or geographical basis of varying scope.[3]

According to its object matter, the history of aesthetics, as any history, is twofold: descriptive and critical. The descriptive history of aesthetics is concerned only with chronological and causal relations standing between the various aesthetic theories. The critical version of the history of aesthetics, on the other hand, superimposes on the chronological and causal order a third order, the logical order, and investigates both the inner consistency and the truth-value of the various aesthetic theories. This distinction holds true, of course, for general as well as special history of aesthetics. In regard to its relation to history in general, the history of aesthetics is under the ultimate genus of history; under the intermediate genera (in a descending order) of special history, the special history of thinking (cultural history, with the special histories of doing and making as its two co-species) and the special history of speculative, deductive thinking (or sciences) etc.; and the proximate genus of the history of metaphysics.

The second historical auxiliary science to aesthetics is the *history of art*. It is the science that deals with the chronological and causal relations of significant artists and artworks. The subject matter of this science is artists and artworks selected on the basis of a more or less objective judgment passed on their aesthetic significance. The object matter of this history is the chronological sequence and the causal relations of the subject matter. Causal relations mean here the positive or negative influence any chronologically prior artist exerted by his works on any chronologically posterior artist, on the one hand; and the influence of heredity and individual, social, and subcultural environment, viz., biological factors as well as economic, social, political, moral, and religious circumstances influencing the artist.

The history of art is divisible into general and special history. The general history of art deals with all significant artists and artworks of all nations throughout history, limited only by the author's judgment on their significance

[3] Most works on the special history of aesthetics combine the limitations of chronology and geography in such a way as to cover only one integral part of the general history of aesthetics as limited on both chronological and geographical grounds, or only one part of the history of the philosophy of any one fine art taken on a chronological and/or geographical basis, or else on both and some additional grounds. As these limitations increase in number and scope, works on the history of aesthetics approach the character of monographs, as when discussing and comparing the aesthetic theories of only two or three thinkers; or such works actually are formal monographs treating any one aesthetic theory systematically and/or genetically and/or historically (as to its sources), and ranging in thoroughness from voluminous works to brief articles.

and his intentions concerning the length of his work. Special history of art is the science of any integral part of the general history of art. Quantitatively, this can mean any one part of the history of all arts as limited either chronologically or geographically or stylistically;[4] quasi-qualitatively, this can mean the entire history of any one fine art, such as the history of poetry (or literature), music, choreography and dance, painting, sculpture, architecture,, or theatrical arts. All these divisions are, of course, divisions of the history of art according to its subject matter. But the history of art can be divided also according to its object matter. In this respect, art history is either purely descriptive, considering artists and artworks only in terms of chronological and causal relations; or else critical, considering the artists and their artworks chronologically and causally, and their artworks also from the aesthetic point of view, i.e., critically evaluating their relative greatness. Both the former and the latter utilize the principles of the philosophy and/or science of beauty and art; but while the former does so only in the original selection of artists and artworks to be included; the latter does so also in the explicit characterization and evaluation of their aesthetic greatness.

Turning now to the second group of philosophic kind of auxiliary sciences, one must be discussed, and another may be mentioned. The *philosophy of the history of art* is the science of the ultimate principles or causes of the variety and gradual development of fine arts and art styles throughout history. The remote subject matter is the artists and artworks with all their variety in style; the proximate subject matter is the gradual development of their variety; the object matter, the ultimate reasons (principles, causes) of the gradual development of their stylistic variety in precisely that order or sequence in which this variety has developed. In terms of the subject matter, this science is historical, that of the history of art; but in terms of its object matter, this science is philosophic in its nature. Moreover, due to the fact that the object matter of the philosophy of the history of art is the *entire* gradual development of artistic styles throughout history, this science is unique in the sense that it cannot be divided either into general and special philosophy of the history of art or into any other parts. For the explanation of the whole can be only one explanation. The only conceivable, but not actually expounded, division of it is quasi-qualitative, i.e., one into the philosophies of the history of the various specific branches of fine art. It is, however, highly questionable that there are any ultimate, genuinely philosophic principles involved in the development of such contingent things as the beginnings of the styles within the various species of fine arts.

At least by virtue of an analogy to the philosophy of the history of art, one

[4] On a *chronological* basis, this means the history of ancient and/or medieval and/or modern and/or contemporary artists and artworks; or the history of all arts within a century, period, etc. On a *geographical* basis, this means the history of Western or Eastern arts, or of one or more continents or countries or of parts of a country. On a *stylistic* basis, this means the history of all arts within one or more than one stylistic period.

can conceive a second philosophic auxiliary science to aesthetics. It may be called the philosophy of the history of aesthetics. If expounded, it would be the science that discusses or searches for the ultimate principles or causes of the development of the various aesthetic theories throughout history in the sequence in which they actually came into being. Thus, its remote subject matter would be the various aesthetic theories; the proximate subject matter, the chronological sequence in which they were expounded; and the object matter the philosophic reasons for the chronological sequence in which the aesthetic theories have been expounded. However, since this sequence seems to be totally accidental, this science appears to be entirely hypothetical in character.

Part Two: Philosophy of Beauty

THE PHILOSOPHY OF BEAUTY or metaphysical aesthetics is, in one respect, as unique a science as its genus, metaphysics itself. For, as Aristotle and Aquinas correctly pointed out,[1] all sciences other than metaphysics take the existence of their subject for granted, whereas metaphysics concerns itself precisely with everything existing ("being as being"[2]). Indeed, which textbook on biology starts out with raising the question whether or not there are living beings? Or which work on medicine begins by asking whether there are sick people at all? And which book on physics treats first the question of the existence of the material world? What they all do, instead, is to postulate as evident the existence of their subject. But the situation is radically different with the philosophy of beauty. For while all ancient and medieval philosophers simply postulated the existence of beauty, just as the scholars in all non-metaphysical fields do so with their own subjects, Spinoza in the seventeenth century and some eighteenth-century British empiricists began the modern trend either to deny or, at least, to question the extramental, objective reality of beauty. There is, therefore, an obvious need today to discuss the problem of the existence of beauty in the philosophy of beauty.

However, the existence of beauty is obviously not the only question to be dealt with in the philosophy of beauty. As any philosophic science, the philosophy of beauty must also discuss the essence and the properties or necessary qualities of beauty. The reason for this is the following. The various inductive, empirical sciences concern themselves only with the directly observable aspects and qualities of their subject and their proximate principles or causes. Thus, the philosophic science of beauty must face the question of what beauty essentially is. Moreover, once this question of the essence of beauty is settled, the philosopher of beauty must also ask himself the question what qualities or truths, if any, necessarily follow from the essence of beauty. Hence there are three basic issues to cover in the philosophic science of beauty: the existence, the essence, and the properties or the implications of the essence of beauty.

As to the sequence in which these three questions must properly be discussed, we can argue this way. In order to know what follows from a certain thing, such as the essence of beauty, one must obviously know first that essence. Consequently, the analysis of the essence of beauty must precede the analysis of the

---

[1] Aristotle, *Post. an.* I, 10, 76b 3-11; *Met.* VI, 1, 1025b 9-19; Thomas, *In I. Post.* an. 18, 157f.; 2, 17; *In VI. Met.* 1, 1147; 1151.

[2] Aristotle, *Met. IV*, 1, 1003a 20; VI, 1, 1026a 31; Thomas, *In IV. Met.* 1, 530; *In VI. Met.* 1, 1170; *In XII. Met.* 1, 2419. See also Albert, *Met.* I, tr. 1, c. 2; ed. B. Geyer (Münster, 1960), I, 4b.

properties of beauty. On the other hand, unless beauty exists, there is nothing to analyze but only to conceive in an arbitrary manner. Consequently, the question of the existence of beauty naturally precedes the question concerning the essence of beauty. It follows, then, that the philosophy of beauty must deal with the following three questions in precisely the following sequence: first, the existence of beauty; second, the essence of beauty; and third, the properties or the implications of the essence of beauty.

Section One: The Existence of Beauty

THE QUESTION OF THE EXISTENCE OF BEAUTY is simply the question of whether or not beauty exists in existent things themselves as their objective quality rather than merely in the mind. This realization already indicates that all the aesthetic theories concerned with the existence of beauty can be reduced to two basically different views: those holding that (some) beauty does exist outside and independent of the mind in existent things, and those maintaining that no beauty exists in such a manner, but only in the mind. The former theories comprise the position called aesthetic objectivism; the latter theories, the position called aesthetic subjectivism. However, while there is only one way of recognizing and admitting the objective, extramental reality of beauty, there are many specific ways in which one may hold the intramentality or subjectivity of beauty. This circumstance necessitates a division of the major versions of aesthetic subjectivism ever expounded.

Aesthetic subjectivism is either apparent or real. Apparent aesthetic subjectivism is a philosophic theory that seems to deny the extramental reality of beauty while implicitly admitting the same. This is accomplished by its representatives in the following manner. On the one hand, they seem to deny the objective reality of beauty by defining it as being mere pleasure in the beholder; on the other hand, they imply the objective reality of beauty through speaking of objective qualities in things as being the sources or causes of the aesthetic delight engendered in the beholder's mind. This is being done apparently, among others, by Santayana. For he declares, first of all, that "beauty is pleasure regarded as the quality of a thing," or "pleasure objectified," hence, generally an "emotion."[1] This, of course, would make him an aesthetic subjectivist. But, on the other hand, he speaks among the "materials of beauty" of such things as the "exquisite and continuous gradation in pitch," the frequency of sounds as the "simple physical basis" of the "pleasantness of sounds," the "brilliancy" of "colours of the sunset" that attract attention, and the "softness and illusiveness" of sensuous materials from which garments, buildings, and poems derive their subordinate beauty, the form of a circle which is "beautiful in its purity and simplicity," and "flowing and graceful curves"[2] as well as of faces that are "in reality fair or ugly," a "distinct quality" and "singular beauty" of straight lines, and the "charm of symmetry" as a "kind of unity in variety."[3] He even explains how the above mentioned objective qualities of things are physiologi-

---

[1] G. Santayana, *The Sense of Beauty*. § 11 (New York: Dover, 1955), 49, 52.
[2] *Op. cit.*, §§ 16, 17, 18, 21, 22; pp. 69f., 75, 77, 89, 90.
[3] *Op. cit.*, §§ 19, 22, 23; pp. 83f., 91, 95.

cally apt to elicit pleasure in the beholder. "Flowing and graceful curves," for instance, produce a "natural and rhythmic set of movements in the optic muscles"; symmetry balances "the tensions of eye"; and the "beauty of form appeals to an aesthetic nature" being unlike a "formless stimulus."[4] While his definition has a subjectivist character, all his talk about the above listed "materials" of beauty as the ground, the source, or the cause of the pleasure that he calls beauty has an objectivist character.

Real aesthetic subjectivism differs from its apparent version insofar as it is the philosophic position that truly denies the extramental, objective reality of beauty. According to the ways of denying the objective reality of beauty, aesthetic subjectivism has two kinds: an implicit and an explicit. Implicit aesthetic subjectivism merely implies the non-objectivity of beauty; explicit aesthetic subjectivism explicitly maintains the non-objectivity of beauty.

Implicit aesthetic subjectivism is represented by the aesthetic relativists. Aesthetic relativism is the philosophic position holding explicitly the individual and/or social variableness of beauty and, thereby, implying the intramentality of beauty. As such, it stresses that the recognition and appreciation of beauty varies with and depends completely upon the individuals or the different historical periods and the different societies. The relativist implies that all this would not be so if beauty were an objective quality of things as the objectivists claim. Sir Joshua Reynolds, for instance, puts this position in the following way, "I have no doubt but, that if we were more used to deformity than beauty, deformity would then lose the idea that is now annexed to it, and take that of beauty; as if the whole world should agree that *yes* and *no* should change their meaning, *yes* would then deny, and *no* would affirm."[5]

Explicit aesthetic subjectivism is the philosophic position that explicitly denies the extramentality of beauty, and explicitly identifies beauty with something other than an objective quality—enabling the thing possessing it to elicit cognitive delight in the beholder. Expressions of the explicit denial of the extramentality of beauty can be found, among others, in Kant and Croce. The former remarked, for instance, that every beholder spoke "of the beautiful as if beauty were a characteristic of the object," "as if it were a property of things"; that "beauty, without a reference to the feeling of the subject, is nothing by itself"; and that from the aesthetic judgment, "This flower is beautiful," it does not follow that "beauty is to be regarded as a property of the flower itself."[6] Similarly, B. Croce asserted, "the beautiful is not a physical fact; it does not

---

[4] *Op. cit.*, §§ 21, 22, 23; pp. 90, 91, 96.

[5] Essay in *The Idler*, No. 82, November 10, 1759; in *The British Classics*, vol. 24 (London: W. Suttaby, 1810), 112. Cf. Descartes' letter to Père Mersenne of March 18, 1630, in *Descartes, Oeuvres et lettres; Bibliothèque de la Pléiade*, vol. 40 (Paris: Gallimard, 1953), 924–25.

[6] Kant, *Critique of Judgment*, §§ 6, 7, 9, 72. English tr. J. H. Berard (London: Macmillan, 1914) 56, 58, 65, 154.

belong to things."[7] Explicit aesthetic subjectivism, in turn, has (at least) three versions according to the nature of the principles or facts on the basis of which it denies the objective reality of beauty. Accordingly, one can speak of metaphysical, cosmological, and psychological aesthetic subjectivism. The first of these three was first expounded by Spinoza,[8] to be followed by others, like Lord Francis Jeffrey. The cosmological version of explicit aesthetic subjectivism is advocated by all those who accept the Lockean distinction between the primary and the secondary qualities of material beings. The psychological version, finally, rests its case completely on the psychological fact of aesthetic disagreement among beholders and art critics.

The psychological version of explicit aesthetic subjectivism is itself divisible into two kinds: a negative, and a constructive or positive. The former confines itself to denying the objective reality of beauty on the basis of aesthetic disagreement, without explaining how we form the notion of beauty in our minds, despite the non-existence of beauty. The latter endeavors to account for the origin of this notion in terms of associations. Thus, Lord Jeffrey declares, "Beauty is not an inherent property or quality of objects at all, but the result of the accidental relations in which they may stand to our experience of pleasures and emotions; and does not depend upon any particular configuration . . . but merely upon the associations" by which the "inherent, and otherwise indifferent qualities . . . recall to the mind emotions of a pleasurable or interesting description."[9] Then everything we call beautiful is beautiful only on the basis of its "accidental power of reminding us of other emotions."[10] Correspondingly, our aesthetic interest in material objects "arises, in every case, not from any physical qualities they may possess, but from their association with some idea of emotion."[11] It is clear that this version of aesthetic subjectivism is properly called aesthetic associationism.

In addition to the two main genera of views on the existence of beauty, viz., aesthetic objectivism and subjectivism, there is a supposedly sophisticated third view that is claimed to be neither that of aesthetic objectivism nor that of aesthetic subjectivism but a combination or compromise of the two. This theory may appropriately be called aesthetic relationism. It is the philosophic position holding that beauty is neither in the object, nor in the subject, but in the meeting of the two. This is erroneously attributed by Leonard Callahan to no earlier

---

[7] B. Croce, *Aesthetic, ed. cit.*, p. 97.

[8] Spinoza, *Ethics*, part 1, appendix.

[9] F. Jeffrey, "Beauty"; reprinted in *Contributions to the Edinburgh Review* (London: Longman, Brown, Green, and Longmans, 1855), 4-5.

[10] *Op. cit.*, p. 5a. Cf. also, "If things are not beautiful in themselves, but only as they serve to suggest interesting conceptions to the mind, then every thing which does in point of fact suggest such a conception to any individual, is beautiful to that individual." (*Ibid.*, p. 34 b).

[11] *Op. cit.*, p. 33b.

thinker than Aquinas,[12] and truly represents the position of the neothomist Maurice de Wulf.[13] However, Lord Kames seems definitely to be an early advocate of this idea when he states, "Beauty, therefore, which for its existence depends on the percipient as much as on the object perceived, cannot be an inherent property in either."[14] A contemporary relationist, J. L. Jarrett, formulates this view as follows: "for beauty to be present something is required of both object and subject: the object must be right—right for some person; and the subject must be ready—ready for engaging this object. Then beauty emerges in the relation between the two."[15]

The question is now, which of the two basic positions is right: aesthetic obectivism or subjectivism? And if the former, what should we think of the various versions of aesthetic subjectivism listed above? In chapter 4, we shall discuss the direct argument for aesthetic objectivism; in chapter 5 we shall indirectly argue for aesthetic objectivism by critically evaluating the various kinds of aesthetic subjectivism; and in the third chapter of the present section (chap. 6), we shall treat of aesthetic subjectivism indirectly, by showing that there is a sufficient psychological explanation for aesthetic disagreement even if beauty is extramental and, thus, there is no need to try to explain that disagreement in terms of aesthetic subjectivism.

[12] "We may state his [sc. Aquinas'] theory in brief as follows: Beauty is not a simple but a complex notion; not an absolute, but a relative conception. In its entirety it exists neither as a physical nor as a psychical fact; it is neither wholly in the object, nor wholly in the subject, but the result of an intimate connection of both object and subject." Leonard Callahan, *A Theory of Esthetic According to the Principles of St. Thomas Aquinas* (Washington, D. C.: The Catholic University of America Press, 1927; 2nd ed., 1947), 29. This is a good characterization of the relationist notion of beauty, but it is not Aquinas' own. Nor did William of Auvergne hold that "beauty is born of the meeting of an object, considered in its appropriate structure, with our soul," as the English translation of Edgar De Bruyne's *L'Esthétique du moyen age* (Louvain: L'Institute Superieur de Philosophie, 1947; tr. by Eileen B. Hennessy under the title *The Esthetics of the Middle Ages*, New York: Frederick Ungar, 1969, p. 88) puts it on the basis of the following, possibly misinterpreted text: Pulchrum visu dicimus quod natum est per se ipsum placere spectantibus et delectare secundum visum. (William of Auvergne, *De bono et malo*. Oxford, Balliol College Ms. 207, fol. 206v. Ed. J. Reginald O'Donnell. *Mediaeval Studies*, 8, Toronto: Pontifical Institute, 1946, p. 268.) The best proof for the justification of this criticism is William's own words: delectatio ex aspectu pulchritudinis visibilis sit in visu exteriori et ex coniunctione eorum invicem (*op. cit.*, B 216r; *ed. cit.*, p. 297); which is to say that aesthetic delight, not beauty itself, originates from the union or meeting of the beautiful object and the external senses.

[13] "I hope to show that the truth lies between the two extremes; that . . . artistic beauty implies both technical and objective elements on the part of he work, and impression on the part of the observer; so that beauty is the result born of an intimate correlation of the two." Maurice De Wulf, *Art and Beauty*. Tr. M. G. Udell (St. Louis, Mo.: Herder, 1950), 40.

[14] Lord Kames, *Elements of Criticism, ed. cit.*, p. 116.

[15] J. L. Jarrett, *op. cit.*, p. 34.

Chapter IV

Direct Argument for Aesthetic Objectivism

SPEAKING OF THE FACT that, while in the past the subjectivist was forced to assume the burden of proof, presently the objectivist has been put on the defense, Hunter Mead remarks in his *An Introduction to Aesthetics* that, "to argue that 'beauty' or 'aesthetic significance' has an existence in the universe as real as 'matter' or energy' requires considerable intellectual courage at the present time."[1] However, there seems to be reason to believe that all that one needs to uphold the objectivist position is to listen to his sound reason while relying on empirical data—a requirement that holds true for realistic versus skeptic philosophy in general.

What, then, is the empirical fact from which one can reason out the objective, extramental reality of beauty? It is what we may term the "positive aesthetic fact" versus a certain "negative aesthetic fact," the latter being a fact that has been used as the point of departure by a large majority of the representatives of aesthetic subjectivism. The positive aesthetic fact is aesthetic delight being experienced by people while beholding certain objects. The negative aesthetic fact is the aesthetic disagreement among people throughout history on whether or not certain things are beautiful.

Let us now use the positive aesthetic fact for investigation, and discuss the negative aesthetic fact in connection with the evaluation of the subjectivist theories.

ARTICLE 1: *Outline of the Argument*

The entire argument for aesthetic objectivism may be summed up this way.

Occasionally, some people, while beholding certain objects experience delight. The total experience of the beholder of such objects includes both knowledge and delight in such a way that both of them occur in the beholder. But that which occurs, begins, or becomes has a cause other than itself. Therefore, the knowledge as well as the delight of the beholder has a cause other than itself. The question, then, is merely this: what is the cause of the aesthetic knowledge, and what is the cause of the aesthetic delight? Taking up, first, the latter question, we may argue thus. Every delight is caused, as experience shows, by some sort of possession. But possession can be only threefold: physical, mental, and moral. And of these three, neither physical nor moral possession cause the delight in the beholder. Therefore, the cause of aesthetic delight is mental possession, i.e., the possession of aesthetic knowledge. But what is the cause of aesthetic knowledge? Absolutely speaking, knowledge is caused either by the

[1] H. Mead, *Introduction to Aesthetics*, chap. 10 (New York: The Ronald Press Co., 1950), 160.

knower himself or something other than the knower, i.e., an external object. But there are both negative and positive reasons to say that the knowledge which the beholder comes to have, while perceiving an object, does not come from the beholder himself. From this it follows that the knowledge of the beholder, that causes the delight in him, comes from something other than himself, i.e., the object which he beholds. Therefore, the object he beholds is a thing which, when known, delights the beholder. But that which, when known, delights has always been called the beautiful. Therefore, the object which the beholder sees and/or hears is beautiful. But a thing is beautiful by virtue of the fact that it possesses beauty. Therefore, the object the beholder sees and/or hears has beauty. Consequently, at least some beauty exists in certain objects, extramentally, rather than merely in the mind, or, in other words, some beauty is an objective quality of things. This is exactly what aesthetic objectivism maintains. Therefore, aesthetic objectivism is a theory conforming to facts.

Evidently, in the bare outline of the objectivist argument, many points need clarification, and many others, proof. To clear up and to prove these points is our next task.

ARTICLE 2: *Details of the Objectivist Argument*

1. The entire argument rests on an empirical fact knowable to anybody and known to many. It is this: Occasionally, while seeing and/or hearing certain objects, some people experience delight.

This fact is called the "positive aesthetic fact." The reason for calling it "positive" is that the experience of such a delight is truly enriching. The reason why this delightful experience is called aesthetic is that it is not brought about by, and has nothing to do with, the usefulness of the thing beheld. The positive aesthetic fact has two limitations: in terms of scope and in terms of frequency. For nobody would seriously claim that *every time* we see and/or hear something, we experience this disinterested delight; nor would anyone seriously maintain that *everybody* who sees and/or hears a certain object or certain objects will experience aesthetic delight. On the other hand, it is a matter of common experience that *some* people at *some* times do experience such a delight while beholding *certain* objects. Thus, the point of departure in the argument for the objective, extramental existence of beauty is an incontestable empirical fact. Incontestable, of course, only for and by the epistemological realist; whereas the rationalist skeptic may question the reliableness of the senses through which we know of this fact. But, then, who can or should want to argue with one who ignores facts for the sake of a theory?

It is the task of the philosopher, upon being given a fact, to analyze that fact in order to explain it in terms of some ultimate principles or causes. Thus, being given the above mentioned and described positive aesthetic fact, the philosopher must analyze it. In doing so, he will soon realize (if in no other way than at least by reflection upon his own aesthetic experiences) that there are two basic elements or components in aesthetic experience, and two modalities of these two basic components. The two basic elements are cognitive and appetitive, respectively, i.e., the knowledge and the delight of the beholder. For, while beholding certain objects, the person experiences some knowledge as well as some delight in himself. On the other hand, the other two components are the modalities of the two basic components, namely, the contingency of the beholder's knowledge and the contingency of his delight. This is to say that the beholder, upon reflection, can recognize not only that he, precisely as a beholder, possesses certain knowledge and delight, but also that this knowledge and this delight began in him, and that they began in him exactly when he began to behold the object.

The realization through self-reflection of the contingency of the knowledge and the delight of the beholder gives rise to a philosophic question: What is the cause of this knowledge and delight? The reason for this question is the following line of reasoning. According to the self-conciousness of the beholder, both his knowledge and his delight began in him. But anything that begins to be comes either from nothing or from something; and if from something, either from itself or from something other than itself. But no thing can come from nothing since to come from nothing is a contradiction. For, if a thing came from nothing, that from which it came would be both nothing (according to the supposition), and something (i.e., the source of a being); and to be both something and nothing is a contradiction. Nor can anything come from itself since this, too, involves a contradiction. For, if a thing came from itself or were produced by itself, then that thing would exist before it exists in order to bring itself into existence (since that which does not exist cannot do anything). Therefore, anything that begins to be comes from or is caused by something other than itself, which is called efficient cause. (This conclusion is what is called the principle of causality.)

Of course, there are those who say with a great pride of sophistication, "Since Hume, you cannot take the principle of causality seriously anymore!" But this is skeptic talk again, the end of any philosophizing; and why should not one take this evident principle seriously if its chief rejector in modern philosophy, Hume himself, took it so seriously that he endeavored to explain the cause of the almost universal acceptance of the principle of causality? But more important than this is the fact that the principle of causality passes the Humean test of analyticity, being demonstrably a derivatively analytic proposition.

The positive aesthetic fact and the principle of causality compel us, then, to raise two questions: What causes the beholder's knowledge which he is aware of, and what causes the delight which he is equally conscious of? For methodological reasons, let us take up the latter question first.

2. Experience teaches us that any and every kind of delight is caused by some

kind of possession. This is why delight has often been defined as the resting of the will in the possession of the good desired.[1] Now, the possession of the good can be as manifold as is the power or potency of possessing a good. In regard to man, this means that possession is twofold: physical (material) and superphysical (immaterial); and the latter, again, of two kinds: cognitive or mental and moral.[2] The reason for this is that man has a body and mind, and with the latter he can do two uniquely human acts: knowing and willing. Accordingly, man can possess something, first of all, materially. This is achieved either by physical contact, as when we hold or touch something in our hands, or else by physical union, as when we eat or drink something. For, once we consume some food or drink, it is ours; and inasmuch as we hold or touch something, we consider it our own—at least for the duration of holding or touching it. Secondly, man may possess something mentally, viz., by knowing it. For what we know is, at least mentally, ours. Thirdly, man can possess something morally, in terms of ownership. For we are said to own a thing if we can do with it what we want.

This division of the modes of possession is complete, since, besides the body and the mind, there is no third essential part in man; and, besides the intellect and the will, there is no additional rational power in man. From this completeness it follows, then, that the aesthetic delight which the beholder experiences in himself must be caused by one of the above listed three kinds of possession: physical, mental, and moral.

Now, the delight of the beholder is obviously not caused by physical possession. For, first of all, there is no physical union taking place in aesthetic experience between the beholder and the beheld object, and there cannot even be any such union. (This is why eating or drinking as such is not an aesthetic experience, although such circumstances as the table setting, the silverware, etc. may per accident cause some such experience.) Secondly, the delight of the beholder is not due to physical possession because, as a rule, the beholder does not touch the object he beholds (except in extremely rare cases, as when one wants to know better the surface of a statue, and touches it). As a matter of fact, even if he wanted to, the beholder could not touch the object in many cases (any kind of music, singing, poetry, etc.), and if he did, it would not contribute to his aesthetic experience in any way, but might detract from it (as when he touched an actor or dancer).

Nor is the delight of the beholder caused by moral possession. For, generally, the beholder does not own the object he beholds: the scenery, the artwork, etc.

---

[1] Cf., Delectatio est quies appetitus in re delectante, qua quis per operationem potitur. Aquinas, *In X. Eth.* L. 6 (ed. R. M. Spiazzi, Taurini: Marietti, 1964), n. 2038. Cf. *In III. Eth.* 20, 618; *In X. Eth.* 8, 2052; and *Summa theol.*, I-II, 33, 2 and 3.

[2] Cf. Aristotle, *Cat.* 15, 15b 17-30; *Met.* V, 23, 1023a 8-23; and Thomas, *Summa theol.*, I-II, 32, 1, ad 1; II-II, 32, 3c; *De ver.* 25, 1c.

As a matter of fact, some artworks cannot be owned at all, like the dramas of Euripides, the symphonies of Beethoven, or the choreography of the *Sylvia* ballet. If someone objected that, at least occasionally, the beholder actually owns the artwork which he beholds, either as its personal proprietor or its legal custodian, (as the *Kurfürst* of Liechtenstein or the curator of the Metropolitan Museum of Art), then the reply is that one can be delighted *as a beholder* in either one of these two ways: merely as a beholder, or both as a beholder and a user or owner of the thing beheld. But the delight of him who is both the owner (or user) and the beholder of an object is itself twofold: both utilitarian (pragmatistic) and aesthetic (non-utilitarian), and we are talking here only about the former and not the latter type of beholder.

Summing up, then, if there are only three kinds of possession that can cause delight in the beholder, and if neither physical nor moral possession causes that delight, then the delight must be caused by mental possession. This is to say that the beholder experiences non-utilitarian or disinterested delight while beholding an object only inasmuch as he comes to have some knowledge that delights him. Thereby, we have found the answer to one of the two questions raised about the positive aesthetic fact in the light of the principle of causality, and the answer is this: the delight of the beholder is caused by knowledge—the knowledge which the beholder came to have while beholding the object. Thus, we must face next the question: What causes the beholder's knowledge that, in turn, causes the delight in him?

3. We may begin our reflections over the present question by realizing that any knowledge has only two possible sources: the knower himself or something other than and outside the knower. When, for example, one person meets another the first time in his life, he comes to know the other in such a way that the other person presents himself to his senses, and the first person's knowledge of the second comes from the second, that is, from without. On the other hand, when a creative artist suddenly conceives in his mind the artwork he will later realize in physical matter, as when Michelangelo conceived the *Pietà*, that artistic-creative knowledge stems from the artist himself—comes from within rather than from without. Thereby, the question is this: does the knowledge which the beholder comes to have while seeing or hearing an object, come from the beholder himself, i.e., from within, or from the object which he beholds, i.e., from without.

Of course, to the beholder's mind, this is not a question at all. For, according to his self-consciousness, he receives the delightful knowledge from the thing which he beholds; he takes in that knowledge; he is only its receiver. To the beholder, this settles the issue completely. But, of course, this is not so with every aesthetician. For this reason let us turn to two formal arguments in defense of what the beholder accepts on the basis of his self-consciousness. One of these arguments is indirect, proving the opposite proposition to be false; the other argument is direct, aiming to prove that the aesthetic knowledge comes from the object which the beholder sees or hears.

The indirect argument runs like this. If the knowledge that causes the delight in the beholder came from within the beholder's own mind, as the creative idea does from the artist's mind, then the beholder would be aware of it, just as the creative artist is perfectly well aware of *his* conceiving the idea of an artwork, and even of the very moment *when* it suddenly emerged in his mind. Diaries, personal letters, and autobiographic writings of creative artists can only confirm this statement.[8] But, as a matter of fact, no beholder as a beholder is aware of any such thing. If the beholder is aware of anything in regard to the origin of his delightful knowledge, it is that this knowledge came from the object which he beheld. Therefore, the knowledge that delights the beholder does not come from within, that is, from his own mind. Hence, it must come from without, namely, from the object that he sees and/or hears.

We have also a direct argument for the same conclusion. It is a commonly known fact that, in order to have aesthetic experience in general, and aesthetic delight in particular, three conditions must be fulfilled by any one person. These conditions are as follows: (1) the presence of certain objects; (2) the possession of the organ of vision and/or hearing; and (3) the actual functioning of the eye and/or ear. That the presence of certain objects is needed for aesthetic experience can be seen from the fact that one must see not just anything but something like the Cologne Cathedral, Renoir's *Bathers* in the Philadelphia Museum of Art, or the King Lake (*Königsee*) in Bavaria rather than a New York tenement house, a dirty sheet of paper, or a burned-down tree somewhere in California, in order to be delighted. Similarly, one must hear not just anybody but rather one like Caruso, Marian Anderson, or Shaliapin in order to enjoy what he hears. It is precisely for this necessary condition of aesthetic experience that we go to concert halls, art museums, opera houses, galleries, theaters, cathedrals, and movie-houses when we want to have aesthetic experience and aesthetically to enjoy ourselves. Similarly, we all know that we need eyes to see and ears to hear for aesthetic enjoyment, because he who was born blind will never enjoy anything visible, and he who was born deaf will never be delighted by even the greatest music ever written. And thirdly, it is

[8] For a confirmation of this statement, see, for instance, what W. A. Mozart, L. von Beethoven, D. H. Lawrence, Mary Wigman, John Dryden, Jean Cocteau, S. T. Coleridge, A. E. Housman, Amy Lowell, Stephen Spender, Brewster Ghiselin, Dorothy Caufield, Henry Miller, and Thomas Wolfe (all these in *The Creative Process*, ed. Brewster Ghiselin, New York: The New American Library, 1964, pp. 44f.; 51; 69–72; 78–80; 81f.; 85, 90f.; 110f.; 119; 127; 169f.; 183; and 187), as well as Aaron Copland (*Music and Imagination*, The Charles Eliot Norton Lectures; New York: The New American Library, 1952, pp. 51 and 56f.) have to say about this question. To quote here only one, Mozart wrote his father about a concert, "I then played . . . a fugue in C minor and then all of a sudden a magnificent sonata in C major, out of my head, and a Rondo to finish up with." *The Letters of Mozart and His Family*, Letter No. 228b of 1777. E. Anderson, tr. (London: Macmillan, 1938), II, 498.

also empirically known that the mere presence of the greatest artwork and the possession of the organ of vision or hearing do not suffice in themselves unless one actually uses his eye and/or ear. Close your eyes while standing before Rubens' *The Last Judgment* in Munich's *Alte Pinakothek*, and you will experience no enjoyment at all. Open your eyes, and you will have one of the greatest experiences with pictorial art. Shut your eyes again, and, unless you remember what you saw before, the pleasure will disappear together with the mental image of the painting. Continuing, then, the syllogism, we may say: all these three necessary conditions show one thing, and one thing only: that the knowledge of the beholder which causes the delight in him comes not from his own mind but from the object he beholds with his eye and/or ear. For we need to see or hear certain objects because we cannot at our pleasure, whenever we like to have aesthetic enjoyment, create (conceive) delectable ideas all by ourselves in our own minds. And we need the eye and the ear, and must also use them for the same reason: because we need to see the products of nature and the fine arts in order to acquire from them delightful knowledge in our minds.

From all this we can conclude that the knowledge which causes the delight in the beholder comes not from the beholder's own mind; instead, it is caused by the object that he beholds. It is only at this moment that we realize formally that the relation between the seeing and/or hearing of a certain object and the delight the beholder experiences in his mind is not merely one of simultaneity (chronological) but also one between cause and effect (causal): the object of contemplation being the cause of aesthetic knowledge, just as the aesthetic knowledge is the cause of the aesthetic delight.

To arrive at the final conclusion, only two more syllogisms are needed. The object beheld, we have seen, is the cause of the delightful knowledge in the mind of the beholder. But that which when known delights is precisely what is traditionally called beautiful.[4] Therefore, the beheld object, that causes aesthetically delightful knowledge in the beholder, is beautiful; or to put it in another way, there are beautiful things in this world which, when beheld, delight us. But a thing is beautiful by virtue of the fact that it has beauty.[5] Therefore, there is beauty in at least some objects or things; beauty is an objective quality of things; and beauty has not only an intramental and subjective but also an extramental and objective existence. This is exactly the position held by the aesthetic objectivist.[6] Consequently, aesthetic objectivism is a true theory.

[4] For some historical details on this question, see chapter 7, article 1, nn. 28–34, and chapter 12, article 1, nn. 28–30.

[5] (Pulchrum) dicitur hoc quod participat pulchritudinem. Thomas, *De div. nom.* 4, 5, 337. Cf. Plato, *Phaed.* 100c.

[6] Concerning the fine arts, S. T. Coleridge expresses this position as follows: "The Apollo Belvedere is not beautiful because it pleases, but it pleases us because it is beautiful." *On the Princi-*

ARTICLE 3: *Clarification of the Objectivist Position*

One may react to this objectivist argument either favorably or unfavorably. In the latter case, one may either find some objections to it, or even misunderstand its conclusion at least partly. Let us, therefore, consider first some foreseeable objections to the above detailed objectivist argument, and attempt also to iron out the possible misunderstandings.

1. If somebody thinks to find some weaknesses in the objectivist argument, he will most probably raise one or both of the following two objections to it.

Objection one: This argument completely fails to take into consideration that the beauty of the beheld object is not the only possible or probable cause of the beholder's delight. For the prejudice of the beholder toward the beheld object can also delight the beholder. It is commonly known for instance, that the creative artist loves his own work precisely because it is his, hence, with an understandable prejudice analogous to the mother's pride in and love for her child, both being apt to cause non-aesthetic delight. In this light, the objectivist argument seems simply to be a fallacy of *non sequitur*.

Objection two: The above objectivist argument considers only the positive aesthetic fact, which tends to support the objectivist's case. It neglects to take into consideration an equally frequent and well-known *negative* aesthetic fact, namely, that people disagree on whether a certain object is or is not beautiful. This neglect makes the objectivist argument vitally vulnerable. For if there were beauty in a given object, all people beholding it would agree rather than disagree on its beauty. Therefore, the objectivist conclusion of the above argument is, at least, highly questionable.

Of these two objections, the second will be taken up and answered quite extensively in chapter 6. Thus, here it will suffice to answer the first objection.

We may begin our reply to the first objection by conceding its premise: there is, indeed, such a thing as emotional prejudice, and its object actually tends to delight the beholder quite independent of its beauty. However, as to the anti-objectivist conclusion deduced from this premise, one can point out the following facts.

While favorable prejudice does lead to non-aesthetic delight in the beholder, just as some other factors do, like ownership, usefulness, etc., the converse is certainly false, viz., that whenever a beholder is pleased by whatever object he beholds, his delight is caused always and solely by his favorable prejudice about

---

ples of Genial Criticism; Essay 2, in *Biographia literaria* (Oxford: Clarendon Press, 1907), II, 224. For amazing parallel passages to this text in ancient literature, see Augustine (Et prius quaeram, utrum [ista] ideo pulchra sint, quia delectant, an ideo delectant, quia pulchra sunt. Hic mihi sine dubitatione respondebitur, ideo delectare, quia pulchra sunt; *De ver. rel*, 32, 59; PL 34, 148); Boethius (*De cons. phil*. II, 5, 134; PL 63, 692 A–693 A); and Aquinas (Non enim ideo aliquid est pulchrum quia nos illud amamus, sed quia est pulchrum et bonum, ideo amatur a nobis; *De div. nom*. 4, 10, 439).

the beheld object. For, apart from such non-aesthetic causes as ownership and usefulness, a person beholds, more often than not, objects which neither he nor any of his relatives or friends have made, and which he has never known before, so that there is absolutely no reason for any kind of favorable prejudice. Thus, the objectivist argument is still valid.

Secondly, even if favorable prejudice does influence the beholder, in most cases that favorable prejudice is not the sole cause but rather the "co-cause" of the beholder's delight in such a way that his prejudice simply deepens or enhances the degree or intensity of his aesthetic delight. The beauty of the beheld object is thus still the basic explanation of the beholder's delight as its primary cause, whereas the favorable prejudice is a quantitative modifier of that delight. Thereby, the objectivist conclusion of the above discussed argument is not weakened by these cases of the beholder's delight at all.

Moreover, upon reflection, most delighted beholders can realize rather easily when their delight is genuinely aesthetic, due to the beauty of the beheld object, and when it is caused, either solely or together with the beauty of the beheld object, by their own prejudices. If, for instance, a composer listens to his own work, and finds it more delightful than a similar work by another composer, it will not take much reflection on his part (provided he does give any thought to it) to realize that he is naturally prejudiced about his own work. For this reason the beholder himself has a chance, too, to recognize that, while in some cases his delight is due mainly (or solely) to favorable prejudice, in other cases his delight can have only one cause: the beauty of the object which he beholds.

Summing up: this objection does not invalidate the objectivist argument at all. Its only significance is a warning to the beholder not to take, without reflection on the circumstances, every delight which he experiences while beholding an object to be the only possible objectively proportionate sign of the beauty of the beheld object.

2. The objectivist argument, which we discussed above, is often misunderstood by people in general and by the subjectivists in particular. For from the fact that the aesthetic objectivist holds beauty to be extramental, some people conclude that aesthetic objectivism denies the intramentality of beauty in every form. This idea, of course, is totally wrong.

To eliminate any misunderstanding, it seems necessary to make clear two separate things about beauty: one, what the objectivist does assert about it; and two, what the objectivist does not deny about it.

a. First of all, the aesthetic objectivist asserts the following propositions to be true:

(1) Primarily or basically, beauty is an objective quality of things; that is,
(2) Beauty exists in things independent of the mind's consideration; and,
(3) Some beauty, the beauty of natural things, can exist in such a way that

nobody ever comes to know or enjoy it; other beauty, the beauty of artworks, can exist in such a way that, with the exception of its artist maker, nobody ever comes to know it or enjoy it.

b. On the other hand, in virtue of these assertions, the aesthetic objectivist does not deny or intend to deny the following:

(1) That secondarily and derivatively, that is, in addition to its being primarily and basically in things or objects—beauty can be also in the mind insofar as somebody recognizes it in an object. As a matter of fact, the beauty of many objects (natural things and artworks) is actually known to people, and is, thereby, in their minds. Such a known beauty exists in two ways simultaneously: independently, in the thing; and dependent on the thing, in somebody's mind; furthermore,

(2) That, apart from any objective beauty (beauty in objects), some beauty is only in the mind; such as in the mind of the creative artist, in the form of an artistic idea; or in the mind of the average person with some imagination, in the form of imagined beauty. But some beauty, although in the mind, is thought to be also outside and independent of the mind, viz., in a thing.

c. What, however, the aesthetic objectivist does actually and categorically deny is the following:

(1) That all beauty is only, exclusively, and totally in the mind;

(2) That all beauty is nothing but an idea or pleasure in the mind; and,

(3) That the perception of material beings is merely the occasion for, rather than the true cause of, aesthetic delight.

To find out why the objectivist denies the above three propositions, we must turn now to the evaluation of the various versions of aesthetic subjectivism.

Chapter V
Evaluation of Aesthetic Subjectivism

HAVING ESTABLISHED THE OBJECTIVE, extramental reality of beauty by a direct argument, and having thereby taken sides with aesthetic objectivism, we must now face and critically evaluate the opposite theory, aesthetic subjectivism. To avoid any false generalization, we shall criticize each and every specific version of subjectivism separately: apparent and implicit real aesthetic subjectivism in article 1; of the explicit types of real aesthetic subjectivism, the metaphysical, the cosmological and the negative psychological version in article 2; and aesthetic associationism and relationism in article 3.

ARTICLE 1: *Apparent and Implicit Real Aesthetic Subjectivism*

A. Apparent Aesthetic Subjectivism

To properly evaluate apparent aesthetic subjectivism, we must first compare it with aesthetic objectivism.

1. Looking for any similarities between them, one finds, first of all, that both the objectivist and the apparent subjectivist talk about three related topics: one, certain objective qualities in the things we behold; two, aesthetic delight which we experience upon beholding things of such objective qualities; and three, a causal relation between the first two things, so that the objective qualities are the causes, and aesthetic delight is their effect. To prove this threefold topical similarity between the objectivists and the apparent subjectivists, let us compare the statements or teachings on these three issues by St. Thomas, one of the greatest objectivists of all times, with statements or teachings on the same topics by Hume, one of the best known and most influential subjectivists.

Thomas lists three analytic principles and one synthetic principle of beauty, all being in the aesthetic object.[1] Of the analytic principles, the one next to integrity is due proportion or convenience: "Everything is beautiful inasmuch as ... it has due proportion."[2] Hume seems to echo this view when remarking, "The most vulgar ballads are not entirely destitute of harmony or nature."[3] About the third analytic principle Aquinas has this to say, "We call a man

[1] Nam ad pulchritudinem tria requiruntur. Primus quidem, integritas sive perfectio ... Et debita proportio sive consonantia. Et iterum claritas. (Thomas, *Summa theol.* I, 39, 8, c. Cf., *In I. Sent*, 31, 2, 1, sol.) Order-texts in Thomas are: *Contra impugnantes cultum Dei et religionem*, II, 6, 5, ad 9 (*ed. cit.* of Thomas' *Opuscula theologica*, II), n. 339; *Summa contra gent.* III, 71, 2469; *Summa theol.* I–II, 49, 4c.; etc.

[2] Thomas, *De div. nom.*, 4, 5, 339. Cf. *ibid.*, nn. 340, 349; 4, 6, 365; 22, 572; 589; *Summa contra gent.* III, 139, 3142; *Summa theol.* I, 5, 4, ad 1; I–II, 145, 2c; etc.

[3] D. Hume, "Of the Standard of Taste" (1757), in *Essays, Moral, Political, and Literary*; *The Philosophical Works of David Hume*, ed. T. H. Green and T. H. Grose (London: Longmans, Green, 1898), I, 276.

handsome ... because he has a bright and shining color," and, "Every being is called beautiful inasmuch as it has clarity of its own kind."[4] Hume apparently shares this view, for he remarks, "The coarsest daubing contains a certain lustre of colors and exactness of imitation, which are so far beauties, and would affect the mind of a peasant or Indian with the highest admiration."[5] The synthetic principle of beauty prompts Thomas to these remarks, "The highest beauty would be taken away from things if the order of distinct and unequal parts were removed from them," and, "beauty consist in the commensuration of plurality."[6] Hume supports him in this respect, too: "In all the nobler productions of genius, there is a mutual relation and correspondence of parts"; and, speaking of the need for practicing aesthetic judgments, he points out that, at the first perusal of any piece, "the relation of the parts is not discerned: the true characters of style are little distinguished," and that "where good sense is wanting, he (the beholder) is not qualified to discern the beauties of design and reasoning, which are the highest and most excellent."[7] Turning next to the topic of aesthetic experience in general and aesthetic delight in particular, Thomas makes both general statements, like "the beauty of creatures allures the minds of men" or "we call beautiful that the very apprehension of which pleases," and also specific remarks, like "Women take delight in the beauty of men" or "No man falls in love with a woman unless he was, first, delighted by her beauty."[8] Correspondingly, Hume speaks of the aesthetic sentiment as arising from the aesthetic object's "operation upon the organs of the mind"; of "a species of beauty which, as it is florid and superficial, pleases at first"; and of the experienced beholder, who "perceives the beauties and defects of each part" in the object, and whose aesthetic feeling "becomes more exact and nice."[9] Finally, Aquinas treats also of certain objective qualities in things as they cause aesthetic delight in the beholder. In one such text, he argues: "If I ought to speak about fornication, and some beautiful modes of presentation occur to me, I am delighted by them." In another passage, having stated that both internal and external beauty consist of some kind of order, he remarks that "both kinds of beauty delight man, and are desirable to him."[10] Quite analogous are the words of Hume about this topic: "It must be allowed that there are certain qualities in objects which are fitted by nature to produce

---

[4] Both are in Thomas, *De div. nom.*, 4, 5, 339. Cf. also, *ibid.*, n. 349; 4, 6, 360; *Summa theol.* II–II, 145, 2, 2a and corpus; etc.

[5] Hume, *ibid.*

[6] Thomas, *S. contra gent.* III, 71, 2469; *S. theol.* I–II, 49, 4c.

[7] Hume, *ibid.*, pp. 277; 275; 278.

[8] Thomas, *S. contra gent.* II, 2, 861; *S. theol.* I–II, 27, 1, ad 3; *In Isai.* 3, 3; and *In IX. Eth.* 5, 1824. Cf. *De regno*, II, 4; *In I. Eth.* 13, 161; etc.

[9] Hume, "The Sceptic," *ed. cit.*, p. 218; and "Of the Standard of Taste," *ibid.*, p. 275.

[10] Thomas, *Contra impugnantes*, II. 6, 5, ad 9; *ed. cit.*, n. 339. Cf. *De regno*, II, 4; and *Quaest. quodlibetales*, XII, 22, 1c.

those particular feelings," that is, the aesthetic "sentiment, internal or external"; and he adds, "Now, as these qualities may be found in a small degree, or may be mixed and confounded with each other, it often happens that the taste is not affected with such minute qualities."[11]

2. Turning, next, from the similarities to the dissimilarities between objectivism and this version of subjectivism, we find two significant differences. One of them concerns the presence or absence of beauty in objects; the other, beauty as it is considered a cause or an effect. For concrete instances, let us go back to Thomas and Hume. The former calls beauty "some kind of quality" of the object, that is the cause of aesthetic delight.[12] The latter categorically denies that beauty is an objective quality by stating that it is "certain that beauty and deformity, more than sweet and bitter, are not qualities in objects . . .," and defines beauty to be, instead, the effect of certain objective qualities: "Beauty is not a quality of the circle . . . . It is only the effect which that figure produces upon a mind, whose particular fabric or structure renders it susceptible of such sentiments."[13]

3. From this twofold comparison, the true nature of apparent aesthetic objectivism is quite clear: In terms of the three similarities, this version of subjectivism explicitly agrees with the objectivist view, openly admitting the existence of certain objective qualities by which objects with such qualities can cause aesthetic pleasure. In this respect, then, the aesthetic objectivist can have no quarrel with this kind of subjectivist. On the other hand, the above listed two differences show with equal clarity that the subjectivist in question deviates from the objectivist only in terminology or, more specifically, in the use of the term "beauty." For, while the objectivist applies this term to those objective qualities that cause aesthetic delight, the subjectivist in question applies the same term to the *effect* of such objective qualities, viz., to aesthetic delight. This terminology is unusual, arbitrary, contrary to a usage that spans history from the earliest times of human culture to the 18th century, and, for this reason, strongly misleading.[14] Yet, despite all these well-based objections to this subjectivist usage of the term "beauty," this version of aesthetic subjectivism does not amount to a doctrinal difference from or opposition to aesthetic objectivism.

It may be noted here that Sir William Hamilton, the editor of the works of Thomas Reid, obliquely contends in an editorial remark on Reid's refutation of aesthetic subjectivism that the subjectivist denial of the objective reality of

---

[11] Hume, "Of the Standard of Taste," *ed. cit.*, p. 273 includes both texts.

[12] Sed nitor animae est quaedam qualitas, sicut pulchritudo corporis. (Thomas, *S. theol.* I–II, 110, 2, sed contra.) For the tenet that beauty is the cause of aesthetic delight, see, e.g. *S. theol.* I, 5, 4, ad 1; and I–II, 27, 1, ad 3.

[13] Hume, "Of the Standard of Taste" and "The Sceptic"; *ed. cit.*, pp. 273 and 219, respectively.

[14] Cf. Thomas Reid's remark on Locke's "secondary qualities" as being "not so much an error in judgment as an abuse of words." (*Essays on the Intellectual Powers of Man*, VIII, 4; *ed. cit.*, I, 499b.)

beauty is only Reid's own fiction;[15] and Walter John Hipple, Jr., concurs with Hamilton by saying that Reid interprets aesthetic subjectivism in a way in which "no one ever held" it.[16] In reply, we may say this: *If* this contention be true, our above-given distinction between apparent and real aesthetic subjectivism is superfluous, and the objectivist has no quarrel with any subjectivist, because such an aesthetic subjectivism is simply a misleadingly formulated and ill-concealed aesthetic objectivism.

B. Aesthetic Relativism

Aesthetic relativism, insofar as it is implicit subjectivism, puts the emphasis not on the negative aesthetic fact, namely, disagreement on the aesthetic value of an object, but on the reason of this fact, viz., the intrinsic changeableness of taste. It holds that aesthetic taste changes and varies not only with individuals but also with different societies and in different historical periods. As a consequence of this, the same object, let us say, an artwork, may be appreciated by one society or in one period, and rejected by another society or in another period; or, it may be appreciated by one society or in one period for one reason, and by another society or in another period for another, considerably different, if not contradictory, reason.

1. By way of a positive evaluation, one may readily concede the above outlined variableness of social taste as being basically an historical fact. However, some qualifications and interpretations are here in order about the changeable social taste and its relevance to the objectivity or non-objectivity of beauty. One necessary qualification is this: the relativist generally tends to exaggerate the variableness of social taste. The best proof for this is the fact that some artworks have always been appreciated throughout the centuries, in all civilized societies, despite the changes in aesthetic attitudes, preconceptions, or preferences in those periods and societies. The skeptic Hume himself readily admits, and even emphasizes this fact: "The same Homer who pleased at Athens and Rome two thousand years ago, is still admired at Paris and at London. All the changes of climate, government, religion, and language, have not been able to obscure his glory." The second important qualification to make is this: however much social or individual taste may be changeable, aesthetic taste is to some extent always dependent upon the objective qualities and value of the aesthetic object. Even this is confirmed by Hume when he declares that, if someone is "a real genius, the longer his works endure, and the more wide they are spread, the more sincere is the admiration which he meets" and, conversely, "authority or prejudice may give a temporary vogue to a bad poet or orator; but his reputation will never be durable or general. When his compositions are examined by

---

[15] Reid, *An Inquiry into the Human Mind on the Principles of Common Sense*, VII, editor's note; *ed. cit.*, I, 205 b–206 a.

[16] W. J. Hipple, *The Beautiful, the Sublime and the Picturesque in Eighteenth-Century British Aesthetic Theory* (Carbondale: The Southern Illinois University Press, 1957), 150.

posterity or by foreigners, the enchantment is dissipated, and his faults appear in their true colors." From all this the great skeptic and "subjectivist" concludes to this: "It appears, then, that amidst all the variety and caprice of taste, there are certain general principles of approbation or blame, whose influence a careful eye may trace in all operations of the mind."[17]

But even if the relativists did not exaggerate the changeableness of taste or its dependence on the objective qualities of the aesthetic objct, they would still owe the objectivist an argument conclusively establishing the implied intramentality of beauty. For the fact remains that at least occasionally some people who have no reason to be favorably prejudiced do experience disinterested, aesthetic delight upon beholding certain objects. But we have seen that this could never possibly happen to an unprejudiced beholder without the observed object being beautiful. That the same beauty is recognized, enjoyed, and admired by one individual in one society or period, but not by another individual in the same or in another society and/or period is, thus, not an implicit refutation of the objective reality of that beauty but only the confirmation of this, that for someone actually to have aesthetic experience two conditions must be fulfilled: the observed object must be beautiful, and the beholder must have the capacity and be properly disposed to take in and to enjoy the beauty that is there. The societies and the historical periods, then, which reject artworks appreciated by other societies or in other periods prove not what the relativist implies, namely, the subjectivity of beauty, but only one thing: some societies or periods are incapable or unwilling or unprepared for recognizing and taking delight in the beauties which other people do notice, enjoy, and admire.

Thereby, to conclude with the relativist from the variableness of social taste to the intramentality of beauty is simply the fallacy of *non sequitur*. For further and more specific evaluation of relativism, let us turn now to the theory of Sir Joshua Reynolds and of a contemporary relativist, George Boas.

2. Sir Reynolds' central doctrine, as expressed in *The Idler*, 1759, is that what we consider to be the most beautiful form is simply "the most general (i.e., most frequent) form of nature," that is, the form which we are most used to: "We have no criterion of form by which to determine our judgment (sc. on the beauty of form)," except the frequency of form in nature, our custom or familiarity with the frequent form, and the pleasure consequent upon our custom.[18] For, as the frequency of a form causes habit, habit in turn "causes our delight taken in the general forms of nature; and the relativistic doctrine derived in regard to beauty itself is the already quoted proposition that, if deformity were more frequent and, consequently, we were more used to it than to

[17] Hume, "Of the Standard of Taste," *ed. cit.*, p. 271.
[18] Essay in *The Idler*, No. 82, November 10, 1759; *ed. cit.*, pp. 111 f. This conclusion is supported by three concrete examples (*ibid.*, p. 110). On the other hand, the author speaks of custom and pleasure as subjective criteria of beauty on pages 113 and 112, respectively; and of the objective criterion of frequency, on p. 112.

beauty, we would consider it to be beauty, and vice versa."[19] All this means that beauty is nothing absolute; but rather something dependent on chance frequency and the degree of our familiarity with that frequency.[20]

What is undoubtedly true, since empirically known, in this intriguing theory is the following: one, that in every species a certain form is most frequent (and this is what we consider to be the characteristic form of the species); two, that frequency leads to habit; and three, that what we are used to is, as such, although only within certain limits, pleasurable. From this, however, it does not follow that beauty completely depends on frequency or, as Reynolds puts it, that "the most beautiful is the most general form of nature." This proposition can be maintained only for the following reasons: In every natural species there is a most common form, which is obviously the characteristic form of the species. The most common or frequent form is that most familiar to us and, consequently, the one that pleases us most. And that which pleases us most is the one we call the most beautiful. Therefore, within every natural species, the most common form is the most beautiful and, conversely, the most beautiful form is the most common form. Now, there are two kinds of defects in this argument: defects of formal and of material logic. The formal defect is that of invalid conversion. For from the fact that the most common form is the most beautiful, the proposition, "The most beautiful is the most common" follows no more validly than from the proposition, "Every creative artist is human," follows the other proposition, "Every human being is a creative artist." The material defects are psychological and cosmological. The psychological defect in the above reasoning lies in the fact that there is only a limited connection between the frequency and pleasurableness of an object. For, while we may be more pleased by a form which we have seen more frequently, we also may reject a form as displeasing if seen by us too frequently. Another psychological defect of this theory is that, even if the connection between the frequency and the pleasurableness were not limited, this connection is of a generic and not of a specifically aesthetic nature. This means that the pleasurableness of the familiar (since frequently experienced) object is due not only to the aesthetic but also to any kind of non-aesthetic value of the object as well as to the fact that man need not make any great effort to recognize the frequent and familiar value of an object.

On the other hand, the cosmological defect of Reynolds' theory consists in this, that there is no necessary connection between the frequency and the

[19] *Op. cit.*, p. 112.
[20] In the Third Discourse of 1770, Sir Reynolds seems to have given up his relativist view when he states that "in every particular species there are various central forms, which are ... undeniably beautiful." (*Discourses on Art*, New York: Crowell-Collier, 1961, p. 47.) However, in a letter to J. Beattie, Reynolds repeats his contention expressed in 1759 in *The Idler*, that we are more accustomed to beauty than to ugliness or deformity. (*Letters of Sir Joshua Reynolds*, No. 61, London, March 31, 1782; ed. Frederick W. Hilles, Cambridge University Press, 1929, pp. 92-93.)

beauty of any individual either within its own species or in reference to any given species. That the frequency of a form within a species has nothing to do with the beauty of the form follows from two facts. One is that, strictly speaking, the most beautiful form is the rarest within any given species; the other is, that the form of an individual can be more beautiful precisely insofar as it conforms less to the form of the species, hence, to the most frequent individual forms within a given species. That the frequency of a form irrespective of any given species has nothing to do with the beauty of that form can also be seen from two facts. One is that the form of one species can be aesthetically more pleasing than the form of another species even though individuals of the two species are equally familiar to a person—that is, such individuals are experienced by somebody with equal frequency. The other fact, even more detrimental to Reynolds' theory, is that the form of an individual of a rare or seldom-seen species can be more pleasing than the form of an individual of a well-known, since frequently experienced, species.

Turning next to the corollaries Reynolds derives from the above invalid conclusion, the following can be remarked. First of all, to say that there is no objective criterion of the beauty of form except the frequency of form is as unproved as the above-discussed conclusion from which it has been deduced. What if somebody proves that there are certain objective qualities or principles in everything that cognitively delights (as we shall attempt to do in the next chapter)? At any rate, not knowing any objective criterion of beauty does not necessarily mean that there is no such criterion.

As to the concrete cases which Sir Reynolds lists, all that can be said is that they can*not* be "easily granted." Why would not for instance, a person who has seen only one individual of any animal species, enjoy the orderliness of such an animal individual; and why would he not be displeased, even repulsed, let us say, by the lack of the symmetry of its shape or the lack of proportion of its limbs, even if he never saw that kind of animal before? Similarly, why could the man born blind, having recovered his sight, not take delight in the body of the most beautiful woman about whom our author is talking? Would not the proportion, the symmetry, and the spatial arrangement of the parts of the body of the most attractive woman please him, and the lack of these objective qualities in the most deformed woman displease him, even pain him, although he has never seen any woman before? Thus, all that Sir Reynolds may truthfully say about the person who saw only one individual animal of its species is that this person could not possibly determine whether the animal conformed to the general characteristics of its species. But this is a question of zoology, and not of aesthetics.

Similarly, it is possible that both the European and the Ethiopean will prefer the color and the shape of his own race simply because each one of them is more used to his own race. But, as pointed out above, one race may still have aesthetically superior features irrespective of whether or not they are recognized and enjoyed by individuals of another race.

Finally, a few words about the allegation that if deformity were more frequent we would consider it beautiful. If, through some catastrophe, every man became disfigured, it is true that eventually they would become somewhat more used to it and less repulsed by it. But Reynolds failed to prove that such unfortunate people would be unable to recognize and enjoy the symmetry of the body and the proportion of its parts if they saw such in somebody. For this reason, Reynolds' relativism is unproved, arbitrary, and unconvincing.

3. While Reynolds concentrates on the individual in his theory, George Boas places society in the center of his relativism. In his theory, we find both negative and positive components. The former are these: one, there is no beauty value in artworks; two, there is no absolute criterion of beauty usable in aesthetic judgments of artworks. He put the latter this way: "There is no a priori method—except that of fiat—of determining which of the many values are properly 'aesthetic.' "[21] The two positive doctrines concern the actual admiration of the great artworks throughout the various historical periods. Boas contends that this almost continuous or universal admiration of artworks is due to two circumstances: one, that people of various societies or periods admired the artworks either for different reasons (one period extolling the work for one reason; the other period, for another reason), or else even for contradictory reasons (one period admiring an artwork for the opposite reason for which another period admired it).[22]

His denial that there is any a priori method or principle of judging the aesthetic values of artworks places Boas right on the side of Sir Reynolds; and thus the criticism concerning the latter's tenet applies also to Boas. One additional point must be made, nevertheless. Having already categorically denied the presence of any beauty in the works of fine arts, it is superfluous on his part to explicitly deny also any aprioristic method or criterion of finding aesthetic values in the artwork. How could there be any method or criterion for finding the non-existent?

Turning to his positive assertions, we can find several weaknesses in them. First of all, Boas' long list of historical data concern only one great artwork, the *Mona Lisa*. One may reasonably assume that he chose this artwork as an example because it showed quite well, better than others, the changing considerations and interpretations which an artwork may receive throughout history. But this circumstance indicates that the *Mona Lisa* is atypical rather than typical in this respect. Boas himself realizes this weakness since he draws out his final conclusion only conditionally, "If this instance is typical."[23] Thereby,

[21] G. Boas, "The Mona Lisa in the History of Taste," *Journal of the History of Ideas*, I, 2 (April 1940) 207.
[22] *Op. cit.*, p. 224.
[23] *Op. cit.*, p. 224.

the foundations of his relativism are as arbitrary as his choice of a great artwork, and are, at best, as hypothetical as the typicalness of his choice itself.

Even if his choice in question is typical for the fate of all great artworks, Boas' theory is not free of difficulties. To see the truth of this, one must realize, first of all, that the entire essay attempts to show in a typically relativistic manner that the customary objectivist argument for the objectivity of beauty taken from the admiration and appreciation which some artworks have received throughout history does not prove anything. The reason given is this: those artworks did not remain the same throughout the centuries; instead, they changed "their nature," became different works, and failed thereby to "withstand the test of time." In reply, we may grant the various considerations and interpretations, and yet must disagree with Boas on this issue for several reasons. One reason is that the dictum, "a given work of art in different periods has essentially different content" is true only in the order of knowledge but not in the order of being. This is to say that what all this contention amounts to is that people in different periods or societies may get considerably, even radically different pictures from the same artwork, whereas the artwork itself remains, of course, basically unchanged with all its inherent aesthetic qualities. Thereby his own argument is already seriously weakened, since Boas wants us to believe that, due to the different interpretations and considerations on the part of art critics and beholders, the artworks themselves lose their identity and fail to survive, so that the objectivist cannot argue anymore that some artworks have always been appreciated. Furthermore, the more Boas stresses the variety of considerations and interpretations, the more he reveals to the mind the inexhaustible inner richness or wealth of the great artworks whereby they can be the sources of so many different interpretations and considerations; and in this inner wealth and richness, the aesthetic element is obviously predominant. If this were not so, one and the same artwork could not possibly please so many different beholders and art critics in so many different periods and societies. In this light, Boas' argument is not so much deflated as turned against him, and favors aesthetic objectivism.

ARTICLE 2: *Metaphysical, Cosmological, and Negative Psychological Aesthetic Subjectivism*

Explicit aesthetic subjectivism categorically rejects the objective, extramental reality of beauty on the basis of some fact or principle that seems to the subjectivist to be irreconcilable with the objectivity of beauty. These facts or principles are either metaphysical, cosmological, or psychological. Accordingly, we can speak of metaphysical, cosmological, and psychological aesthetic subjectivism.

A. Metaphysical Aesthetic Subjectivism

1. Metaphysical subjectivism, the chronologically first of all versions of

subjectivism, was held first by Baruch Spinoza for the following reasons. There is, he maintained, no teleology among finite beings, and he offered three proofs for this. Firstly, he argued, God acts and everything finite comes about from Him with absolute necessity,[1] and this necessity excludes any finality.[2] Secondly, the direct effects of God have been proved to be more perfect than the indirect effects;[3] but, if the direct effects were for the sake of indirect effects, the former would be less perfect. Thirdly, and above all, if God acted purposively, He lacked something, and that is a contradiction.[4] Therefore, any talk about teleology in this world is, on the part of theologians, nothing but a reduction of events or facts to ignorance;[5] and, on the part of people in general, a matter of false analogy: men think of themselves as free agents acting purposively; therefore, analogously, they tend to consider everything in nature teleologically, i.e., as if God had made everything for the sake of man.[6] Concrete consequences of this false analogy are such notions as "goodness, badness, order, confusion, warmth, cold, beauty, deformity, and so on." Thus, for instance, "Everything which conduces to health and the worship of God they have called good.... When phenomena are of such a kind, that the impression they make on our senses requires little effort of imagination, and can consequently be easily remembered, we say that they are well-ordered; if the contrary, that they are ill-ordered or confused."[7] Then he goes on to say, "The other abstract notions are nothing but modes of imagining.... For instance, if the motion whose objects we communicate to our nerves be conducive to health, the objects causing it are styled beautiful; if a contrary motion be excited, they are styled ugly."[8]

2. Considering these doctrines critically, it is obvious that, if the premises can be refuted, the subjectivist conclusion concerning order and beauty will be disproved also. Now, as to the first argument against teleology in nature, Spinoza does not clarify how necessity excludes purposiveness. For one may maintain that God does everything necessarily for a purpose. If Spinoza objected to this by saying it is contradictory to say that God acts for an end since it would mean that He lacks something, then this would be Spinoza's third argument. Moreover, the metaphysician may seriously question Spinoza's very premise of God acting "externally" with necessity. For, if everything comes from God, as Spinoza himself admits, and if one kind of creature, man, acts freely in the psychological sense, God would be inferior to His own creature

[1] *Ethics*, props. 16–17, 29, 32, and 33.
[2] *Ibid.*, Appendix to Part I; in *Philosophy of Benedict de Spinoza*, tr. R. H. M. Elwas (New York: Tudor, 1934), 73.
[3] *Op. cit.*, props, 21–23.
[4] *Op. cit.*, Appendix, *ed. cit.*, p. 73.
[5] *Op. cit.*, p. 74
[6] *Op. cit.*, p. 71 f.
[7] *Op. cit.*, p. 75.
[8] *Op. cit.*, p. 76.

unless He too acts freely *ad extra*—freely not only in the Spinozean, deterministic but also in the psychological sense; nor would there be an explanation for the causal origin of human freedom unless God Himself is also free. This is, of course, not to deny that, precisely because of His infinite perfection, God does certain things necessarily, such as know and love Himself; but these are immanent rather than quasi-transient activities, really identical with His absolutely necessary essence.

Turning to the second argument, it can be objected that the contradiction can be avoided by proper distinctions. The direct effects of God may be more perfect in terms of their origin, i.e., in the order of efficient causality; the indirect effects, more perfect in terms of their character as ends, i.e., in the order of final causality. This argument then is inconclusive.

Finally, the third argument can be encountered in several ways. One is by making the following distinction: God acts or creates the world for a reason, but not for an end that He lacks. For the divine reason of creation may be said to be God's love for the creature in general and for man in particular; whereas if He acted for an end, He would, indeed, not be infinite. Now, acting out of love as a reason or motive, God can so arrange human nature and everything in this world that man be capable of attaining somehow the end of creation and his own ultimate end, God Himself.[9] But, if this is so, teleology in creation is not a mere fiction or a matter of misapplied analogy; instead, there is actually teleology in creation. Another way of attacking this third argument against the possibility of teleology in the created world is to point out that to make the world purposive is more perfect than to make it or leave it without any purpose. But, according to Spinoza's own admission, God makes everything in the most perfect manner.[10] Therefore, teleology in this world is the demand of God's own infinite perfection rather than a "human figment." Moreover, all three arguments for the impossibility of teleology and, through it, for the fictitiousness of basic human concepts, among them order and, through it, beauty, rest on the existence of God as an infinitely perfect being that always acts necessarily. But this metaphysical premise is shared by few thinkers: certainly not by the materialists and atheists; nor by the Humean or Kantian agnostics, because to them, God's existence is simply indemonstrable; nor by the modern thinkers who speak of an imperfect or relatively perfect God only; not even by the metaphysical and epistemological realists, like Augustine or Aquinas or Maritain, because they uniformly hold the existence of God Who, by virtue of His infinity, is the *free* cause of creation. Therefore, from the viewpoint of all these philosophies, Spinoza arbitrarily or wrongly attached the question of cosmic teleology to the problem of the exist-

---

[9] This is what Spinoza refers to as "the object of assimilation." (*Ibid.*, p. 73.)
[10] "I have shown that everything in nature proceeds ... with the utmost perfection." (*Ibid.*, p. 73.)

ence and nature of God. Furthermore, if something so universal (although not without exception) and so basically empirical as finality, goodness, order, and beauty in this world is declared to be mere figment or wishful thinking on the part of mankind, it will not suffice to label any teleological interpretation simply as "reduction to ignorance." Indeed, much more specific refutations would be needed for Spinoza in order to avoid having this label backfire against him. Finally, the specific notion of beauty being merely a human invention to express something conducive to health is a complete and fatal confusion of the good or useful with the beautiful on Spinoza's part, and fails to recognize the so widely-known and empirically so well-founded disinterested character of beauty. For that which is conducive to health is the least disinterested of all pleasurable things.

3. This much will suffice for disposing of Spinoza's metaphysical reason for aesthetic subjectivism. However, there is a second metaphysical reason used by some aestheticians against objectivism. Unless there are some common objective qualities to be found in *all* those things which we call beautiful, beauty is nothing but a name or, at best, something in man's imagination. But, as a matter of fact, there are many things, all called beautiful, which have quite obviously no single common quality. Therefore, beauty is only a name or a figment of our imagination.

This argument is to be found, among others, in Lord Francis Jeffrey's essay on beauty. He starts out by pointing to the "prodigious and almost infinite variety of things to which this property of beauty is ascribed; and the impossibility of imagining any one inherent quality which can belong to them all, and yet at the same time possess so much unity as to pass universally by the same name." Looking, for instance, at the snow and a piece of chalk, we immediately notice their common quality of whiteness. "But is this felt, or could it even be intelligibly asserted, with regard to the quality of beauty?" Next, he turns to concrete examples to support this view. "Take even a limited and specific sort of beauty—for instance, the beauty of form. The form of a fine tree is beautiful, and the form of a fine woman, and the form of a column, and a vase, and a chandelier. Yet how can it be said that the form of a woman has anything in common with that of a tree or a temple? Or to which of the senses by which forms are distinguished can it be supposed to appear that they have any resemblance or affinity?" Lord Jeffrey winds up his argument by remarking that this inquiry becomes considerably more difficult once we realize that beauty is referred not only to forms or colors but also to sounds, and even to sentiments and ideas, and "intellectual and moral existence."[11]

4. What is there to say to this objection to aesthetic objectivism? Lord Jeffrey tries himself to answer his own question by stating that all these things listed above have at least agreeableness in common. But then he immediately and

---

[11] Lord Jeffrey, *ed. cit.*, pp. 2b–3a.

triumphantly rebuts this reply by pointing out that, according to the thinking of the aesthetic objectivist, the agreeableness of objects depends on their beauty, and not vice versa.[12] This rebuttal is, of course, not completely justified. For the objectivist, who might offer this Jeffreyan solution, could further argue that those things which have similar effects must have some similar quality common to them, and even if we do not know what this quality specifically consists of, it is precisely the objective beauty in them. For that by which a thing is cognitively delightful is, according to an almost universal agreement and philosophic tradition, beauty itself.

Another attempted solution of this metaphysical difficulty is to be found in the *Philosophical Essays* by Dugald Stewart. He suggests forgetting about the "scholastic" tendency to consider the various meanings of a word as if they were necessarily the species of a common genus, and consequently, to look always for common aspects in all the individuals to which a generic term is applied. Instead, he offers a theory of language on his own. According to this, several objects may be denoted by the same term despite the fact that no quality is common to them all, simply because the first has one thing in common with the second; the second, another thing in common with a third; the third again another thing in common with the fourth; and so on.[13]

Clearly, Dugald Stewart's theory is a sign of how serious he thought this line of objection was to the traditional, objectivist notion of beauty. However, one must recognize that the mere fact that one cannot find any common quality or qualities in the things we call beautiful is not yet a proof in itself for beauty not being an objective quality at all; instead, it may possibly be the sign only of his inability to go far enough in the realm of abstraction to find the generically and/or analogously common qualities in all the objects that are called beautiful. As a matter of fact, one can easily find common objective qualities in the very things which Lord Jeffrey lists as *lacking* any common qualities. To take them up one by one, isn't it obvious that the form of a woman, of a tree, and of a temple may all have symmetry, i.e., an inverted similarity of the spatial arrangement of parts along a dividing line? Comparing next forms and colors, or colors and sounds, isn't there such a thing possible in them as proportion or harmony? Moreover, is it not possible to extend, analogously, these terms to poems and novels and dances and moral characters? Thereby, the second metaphysical argument collapses both at the level of facts and of possibilities.

B. Cosmological Aesthetic Subjectivism

1. The cosmologically founded version of aesthetic subjectivism is rooted in the philosophy of John Locke with respect to his distinction of the so-called

[12] *Ibid.*, p. 3a–b.
[13] Dugald Stewart, *Philosophical Essays*, II, 1, 1, 1, *ed. cit.*, V, 193–96. A similar theory concerning the notion "artwork" was expounded, under Wittgenstein's influence, by Paul Ziff in "The Task of Defining A Work of Art," *The Philosophical Review*, LXII (January 1953) 58–78.

primary and secondary qualities. The theory rests on the observation that some qualities are "utterly inseparable from the body," whereas others "in truth are nothing in the objects themselves, but powers to produce various sensations in us by their primary qualities."[14] The former comprise solidity, extension, figure, motion or rest, and numbers; the latter, color, sound, taste, smell, etc. Correspondingly, the ideas of the former are resemblances; those of the latter, that are produced in us by the former, are not resemblances.[15] This theory spread so fast that a number of eighteenth-century British and non-British aestheticians took it as a matter of fact and drew out its subjectivistic, aesthetic implications.

Lord Kames, for instance, declared in 1761, "The distinction between primary and secondary qualities in matter, seems now fully established .... Color, which appears to the eye as spread upon a substance, has no existence but in the mind of the spectator .... This distinction suggests a curious inquiry, whether beauty be a primary or only a secondary quality of objects?" He gives the answer immediately and unhesitatingly. "The question is easily determined with respect to the beauty of color; for, if color be a secondary quality, existing nowhere but in the mind of the spectator, its beauty must exist there also." Then he proceeds to extend the same conclusion to "the beauty of utility" and, on the basis of some relationist argumentation, even to the beauty of regularity (form). Thereafter, he makes two remarks. One is, that it is a witty poetic observation "that beauty is not in the person beloved, but in the lover's eye"; the other is a self-contended self-appraisal: "This reasoning is solid."[16] Almost three decades later, Kant raised the same question, and arrived at a somewhat less dogmatic conclusion than Lord Kames. For Kant declares that vision and hearing produce "a peculiar sensation ... of which we cannot strictly decide whether it is based on sense or reflection .... That is, we cannot say with certainty whether colours or tones (sounds) are merely pleasant sensations or whether they form in themselves a beautiful play of sensations, and as such bring with them in aesthetic judgment a satisfaction in their form." However, Kant seems to be inclined toward a more objectivistic view, explaining delightful tones either "as the beautiful play of sensations (of hearing), or else as a play of pleasant sensations."[17] The contemporary Hunter Mead, on the other hand, returns to the radical subjectivist view of Lord Kames when he declares, "Of course, if we insist that only primary qualities can be considered truly 'objective' (in the sense of being independent of all observers), then there can be no objective aesthetic values of any kind."[18]

What can we say to this cosmological position?

[14] J. Locke, *An Essay Concerning Human Understanding*, II, 8, 9–10, 14.
[15] *Ibid.*, n. 15.
[16] The last sentence is in Lord Kames' *Elements of Criticism*, chap. 3, n. 190; the previous ones, *ibid.*, n. 189; *ed. cit.*, pp. 115f.
[17] Kant, *Critique of Judgment*, § 51, n. 3.
[18] H. Mead, *op. cit.*, p. 164.

The Lockean epistemology is either true or false. If it is true, the beauty of color and tone is not an objective quality of things, but the beauty of form is. For inasmuch as something, like form, is real, so is its beauty. Consequently, even if the Lockean epistemology is correct, there is still some objective beauty left in this world, namely, the beauty of form, and aesthetic subjectivism is, thereby, not universally true. On the other hand, if the Lockean position is false, not only is the beauty of form objective but also that of color and tone. Thus, the question facing us is really this: is the Lockean theory distinguishing between primary and secondary qualities right or wrong?

One may begin this inquiry into Locke's distinction of material qualities by realizing a number of relevant facts. One is that Locke's epistemology is skeptic insofar as it accepts the testimony of some senses but not of others, or some data of a certain sense but not other data. Another relevant truth is that, even though the problem of epistemological realism *versus* skepticism is basically a matter of personal choice (since neither view can formally be proved or refuted without begging the question of the reliableness of the senses), epistemological realism has the enormous advantage over skepticism that it has a powerful ally, sensory evidence, on its side. For the so-called secondary qualities are sensorily as evident as the so-called primary qualities. Consequently, the burden of proof rests not on the realist (who needs no proof, since proof is a means to certitude which certitude he has through sensory evidence even in regard to colors and sounds), but on the Lockean skeptic. On what grounds can Locke maintain, contrary to the evidence of the senses, that, while the primary qualities are objective, the secondary ones are not?

Locke has only one such basis: The "utter inseparableness from the body" of the primary qualities,[19] in contrast with an alleged separableness of the so-called secondary qualities. Against this argument, one can ask Locke with Berkeley (without accepting the immaterialism of the latter) this simple question: "But do not colours appear to the eye as co-existing in the same place with extension and figure?"[20] This is to say that, as long as Locke stresses that one can never see any material object without or in separation from qualities like figure and size, one can point out the same thing about color, too. Should a Lockean epistemologist reply to this that one can imagine a body without color but not without any shape or size, the answer is twofold. Firstly, it *is* possible to imagine a colored object without any specific shape or size; secondly, what counts really is not what one can imagine but rather what is the case in reality; and the case is simply that we never see things without any color.

Thereby the Lockean epistemologist may be forced slightly to change his argument by saying that, while the secondary qualities do easily change under

---

[19] Locke, *ibid.*, II, 8, 9.
[20] G. Berkeley, *Three Dialogues Between Hylas and Philonous* (Cleveland-New York: The World Publishing Company, 1963), 186.

various conditions, the primary qualities do not do so. To this Berkeley retorts that "upon approaching a distant object, . . . size and figure . . . are in a continual change."[21] The skeptic opponent may, of course, hesitate to concede this at least about shape. However, is it not true that the shape that we perceive at any given moment depends on the direction from which we approach and consider the object? Distance and direction then render size and shape, respectively, as variable as, for instance, light does colors. Moreover, it can also be argued that the formal and precise manner in which we perceive shapes and sizes is through colors. For we know where one thing terminates, and the next begins, by seeing that one color ceases and another color begins at a certain point or, rather, line or area. Therefore, if form and size are objective qualities, so is color, through which form and size are generally known. Furthermore, it is one thing on Locke's part to declare that the secondary qualities "depend on those primary qualities";[22] but it is another thing actually to account for each specific secondary quality in terms of specific primary qualities. For instance, which quality or qualities cause color? If any of them did, it should be true that whenever size and/or figure and/or texture change in a material being, and/or whenever a material being begins or ceases to move, it also changes its color; but this is obviously not the case. Thus, the only "dependence" Locke may claim is that, as long as a body has, let us say, figure and size, it has color. But, unfortunately for him, the converse is also true: as long as a body has color, it has also figure and size. From this it follows that the only thing Locke can truthfully assert is a mutual dependence or interdependence of primary and secondary qualities, and this fact favors epistemological realism, but not his skeptic distinction between primary and secondary qualities.

2. Some, like Lord Kames and Hunter Mead, seem to have avoided this final conclusion favoring aesthetic objectivism, by denying the conclusion of the first original alternative, i.e., that the beauty of form is an objective quality if form itself is such. However, Hunter Mead holds this view without reason or explanation. He simply authoritatively declares, "if we insist that only primary qualities can be considered truly 'objective' (in the sense of being independent of all observers), then there can be no objective aesthetic values of any kind."[23] This conclusion, of course, simply does not follow with respect to the beauty of form, unless form is also listed, in an un-Lockean manner, as a secondary quality. Lord Kames, on the other hand, rejects the objectivist argument in question, viz., "If regularity be a primary quality, why not also its beauty?" by declaring, "That this is not a good inference, will appear from considering that beauty, in its very conception, refers to a percipient."[24] As he continues this

---

[21] *Op. cit.*, p. 185.
[22] Locke, *op. cit.*, II, 8, 14.
[23] H. Mead, *op. cit.*, p. 164.
[24] Lord Kames, *ed. cit.*, p. 116.

argumentation, he turns out to defend the position which we earlier called aesthetic relationism. For this reason, we shall consider and evaluate it separately. Apart from this reason, the above anti-Lockean conclusion remains unrefuted. This, in turn, means that there are in things two kinds of visible beauty, namely, that of form and that of color. But what can be said about audible beauty, the beauty of tones? Is it objective, as the objectivist maintains; or subjective, as Locke claims it to be?

3. Basically, the situation is analogous with sounds as with colors. For we are no less clearly aware of perceiving sounds than of perceiving colors or forms. Therefore, in the question of audible beauty, too, the powerful ally called sense evidence is on the side of the realist, leaving the Lockean skeptic with the burden of proving his position. But, as a matter of fact, Locke has no better arguments or reasons for the subjectivity of sound than for the alleged subjectivity of color. To this somebody may say, it is possible to differentiate between the objective aspect of tones, namely, the vibrations of material particles, and its subjective correlatives, the auditory sensations. In reply, the objectivist can point out two facts. One of them is that anyone making this distinction postulates that there is nothing more objective about sounds or tones than vibrations of material particles, and this is begging the question (for it argues with what it should prove to be true). Natural sciences, like physics, are professionally interested only in the measurable aspects of the material world. The other truth is that, even if this distinction were correct rather than the fallacy of begging the question, it is still evident that the orderly vibrations of tones are themselves rooted in certain objective qualities of things, which qualities are, even according to Locke, primary qualities, such as solidity or density, texture, size, and shape; whereas the vibrations themselves are orderly primary qualities (Locke's "motion") which, when perceived, cause delight in the beholder. But that which, when known, delights is, by definition, beautiful. Therefore, tones, precisely as physical vibrations, are objectively beautiful.

The objective reality of both visible and audible beauty or the beauty of form, color, and tone, is thereby upheld against cosmological aesthetic subjectivism. Thus, it is time now to turn our attention to what we previously called negative psychological aesthetice subjectivism.

C. Negative Psychological Aesthetic Subjectivism

1. It is virtually the trademark of psychological aesthetic subjectivism to base all its contentions in the spirit of Pyrrhonism[24a] on the negative aesthetic fact, namely, aesthetic disagreement. This fact of disagreement involves three factors. One is the well-known disagreement among art critics on whether or not a

[24a] A part of Sextus Empiricus' argument against the teachableness of the corporeal being is that the corporeal being cannot be sensory "since then it ought to be equally apparent to all men and be pre-evident." (*Adv. Math.* I, 3, 27; Loeb-ed. IV, 16.)

certain object is beautiful. Another factor is an equally well-known disagreement among amateur beholders on the same question. The third and less well-known factor is this, that any one individual may pass on an object a positive aesthetic judgment now, and a negative aesthetic judgment at a later time, or vice versa. Stolnitz puts this as follows: "Now there is one fact which is invariably cited to disprove objectivism. You can probably guess what it is. It is the fact that men do not agree about the goodness or badness of works of art. If beauty is "out there" in the object, then why do we not all find it there?"[25] Hunter Mead goes into greater details about this disagreement: "The first argument against the claimed objectivity of aesthetic value is the notorious disagreement, not only among laymen but also among expert critics, concerning works of art. . . . Third, there is a similar lack of agreement regarding natural beauty, both in itself and in its relation to art. In the fourth place, there is the impressive fact that an individual's aesthetic evaluations usually change as his experience in the field increases, or perhaps as he matures intellectually and emotionally."[26]

This threefold fact is used by the subjectivist as the basis of the following argument against aesthetic objectivism: If beauty were an objective quality of things, there would be an agreement rather than a disagreement on the beauty of things. But there is a disagreement rather than an agreement on this question. Therefore, beauty is not an objective quality of things; instead, beauty is only in the mind. To find out whether this is a fair representation of the foundations of aesthetic subjectivism of the psychological kind, let us listen to some of the representatives of this position.

Spinoza, the first modern subjectivist, clearly admits the fact of disagreement: "What seems good to one seems bad to another; what seems well ordered to one seems confused to another; what is pleasing to one displeases another, and so on."[27]

Hume goes a step further when he connects the subjectivist position with this disagreement: "Beauty is no quality in things themselves: it exists merely in the mind which contemplates them; and each mind perceives a different beauty. One person may even perceive deformity, where another is sensible of beauty."[28]

Lord Jeffrey takes the third step when he uses the negative aesthetic fact argumentatively against the aesthetic objectivist. For he lists as "the first, and perhaps the most considerable" objection "against the notion of beauty being a simple sensation," viz., against objectivism, "the want of agreement as to the presence and existence of beauty in particular objects." Then he proceeds to

[25] Jerome Stolnitz, *Aesthetics and Philosophy of Art Criticism*. (Boston: Houghton Mifflin, 1960) 392.
[26] H. Mead, *op. cit.*, p. 160 f.
[27] Spinoza, *Ethics*, Appendix to Part One, *ed. cit.*, p. 76.
[28] Hume, "Of the Standard of Taste," *op. cit.*, p. 268f.

argue this way: "Where one man sees light, all men who have eyes see light also. All men allow grass to be green, and sugar to be sweet, and ice to be cold .... With respect to beauty, however, it is obvious, at first sight, that the case is entirely different. One man sees it perpetually, where to another it is quite invisible, or even where its reverse seems to be conspicuous."[29] Now, "if beauty were a real and independent quality, it seems impossible that it should be distinctly and clearly felt by one set of persons, where another set, altogether as sensitive, could see nothing but its opposite."[30] For, "(if) external objects were sublime and beautiful in themselves, it is plain, that they would appear equally so to those who were acquainted with their origin, and to those to whom it was unknown."[31]

Contemporary authors argue the same way. Curt J. Ducasse, for instance, has this to say: "One of the most notorious facts about beauty is its variability. One man finds beauty where another finds none; and, indeed, one man may judge drab today what yesterday he judged beautiful, or beautiful today what tomorrow he will find drab or even perhaps ugly .... Probably it is this variability with person, time, and context that, as much as anything else, has raised the question as to whether beauty is objective or subjective."[32] The naturalist Thomas Munro, another leading figure in the field, feels so assured about the subjectivist implication of the negative aesthetic fact that he attacks an objectivist's position as "the old and obsolete conception of aesthetics" precisely on grounds of aesthetic disagreement: "Of course, not everyone feels such an object to be beautiful, and some feel other things to be beautiful; but this does not worry the self-assured dogmatist."[33] Another prominent aesthetician, Monroe C. Beardsley, speaks in a more subdued tone but not less categorically: "Of course, the Beauty Theory has difficulty in explaining why there is so much variability in the apprehension of beauty."[34] One could go on indefinitely citing additional evidence for the issue; but the heretofore listed sources will certainly suffice to demonstrate the stress which the subjectivists lay upon the negative aesthetic fact.

What can the objectivist say to this argumentation? He can, of course, make several points against it, but one thing he should never do: try to deny the disagreement in question, or even to belittle the extent or significance of it. No philosophic position can possibly benefit from denying facts. For resorting to such dubious methods to defend aesthetic objectivism is contrary to the very nature and the natural purpose of philosophy, a science that is professionally

[29] Lord Jeffrey, *op. cit.*, p. 2a.
[30] *Op. cit.*, p. 18b.
[31] *Op. cit.*, p. 19b.
[32] C. J. Ducasse, *Art, the Critics, and You* (Indianapolis–New York: The Bobbs-Merrill Co., 1955), 87f.
[33] Thomas Munro, *op. cit.*, p. 270.
[34] M. C. Beardsley, *Aesthetics*, p. 509.

concerned with the ultimate explanations (rather than denial) of facts about reality. Let us discuss the arguments against psychological aesthetic subjectivism, proceeding from the relatively weakest or persuasive argument to the strongest and conclusive or peremptoric argument.

2. An argument of authority may be construed against this version of aesthetic subjectivism this way: If disagreement were a natural and necessary sign of the subjectivity of beauty, the premodern philosophers most certainly would have recognized it as such. But, while they were aware of the fact of aesthetic disagreement, they did not recognize it as the natural and necessary sign of the subjectivity of beauty. Therefore, disagreement in itself is not a natural or necessary sign of the subjectivity of beauty and, consequently, psychological aesthetic subjectivism is an erroneous theory. In support of the major premise one can point out two relevant facts. One is the long list of first-class thinkers from Plato to Aquinas who, together with many other, less outstanding philosophers, all belonged to ancient or medieval philosophy. In light of their number and greatness, it is inconceivable that the allegedly obvious, since natural, implication of the fact of aesthetic disagreement, provided it was known to them, should have remained unrecognized by all of them over a period of some twenty-four centuries. In support of the minor premise, two things must be proved: one, that ancient and medieval thinkers were actually aware of the fact of aesthetic disagreement; and two, that, despite this awareness, they did not become subjectivists but remained, instead, firm believers of the extramental, objective reality of beauty.

For the fact that ancient and medieval thinkers actually knew about aesthetic disagreement, one can quote such individuals as Heraclitus, Plato, Aristotle, Plotinus, Dionysius the Areopagite, and St. Thomas. Heraclitus made a remark to the effect that people disagree on what is beautiful although to God everything is beautiful.[35] Plato's statement on this issue is much stronger, for he emphasizes that there is nothing about which there is more disagreement and dispute among people than about beautiful things.[36] Aristotle obviously shared this view for he declared, "Things often appear to be beautiful to some and the contrary to others."[37] Plotinus, too, talks in a similar vein: "Things sometimes appear beautiful, sometimes not."[38] Finally, paraphrasing a passage in Plato's *Symposium*, both Dionysius the Areopagite and St. Thomas assert that every beauty in this world is subject to possible disagreement.[39]

---

[35] Fragment 102 in H. Diels, *Die Fragmente der Vorsokratiker* (Berlin: Weidmann, 1922), I, 98.
[36] Plato, *Hipp. mai.* 294 cd.
[37] Aristotle, *Met.* XI, 6, 1062b 19. Cf., *ibid.*, 1063a 1–6; *Nic. Eth.* X, 5, 1176a 11–12; VII, 14, 1153b 31 f.
[38] Plotinus, *Enn.* I. 6, 1. English tr. S. MacKenna (London: Faber and Faber, 1956), 56.
[39] Plato's *Symp.* 211a is being paraphrased by Dionysius the Areopagite, *De div. nom.* 4, 7 (*PG* 3, 701D) and by Aquinas in his commentary on Dionysius' *De div. nom.* (4, 5, 345f.). For Aquinas' view on this question, see also *In X. Eth.* 8, 2060 and *In VII. Eth.* 13, 1510.

On the other hand, these same philosophers as well as others were firm believers in the objective reality of beauty. Thus, the very same fragment in which Heraclitus declares that people disagree on the beauty of things is evidently objectivistic insofar as it also states that, to God, viz., in reality, all things are beautiful. Similarly, we know that Empedocles was aware of the fact that order and beauty were present in nature.[40] Plato also talks like an aesthetic objectivist whenever he declares that all things are beautiful as well as good; that all things are beautiful by participating in Beauty itself; and that all things that are good are also beautiful.[41] Aristotle clearly implies the objective reality of beauty when he lists the kinds and the principal forms or principles in virtue of which the beautiful is beautiful.[42] After Aristotle, similarly objectivistic about beauty are Plotinus, Augustine, Boethius, Bonaventure, Albert, and Thomas, to mention only a few.[43] Having thus demonstrated the premises of the syllogism in question to be true, the conclusion, that is detrimental to psychological aesthetic subjectivism, is true in proportion to the enormous authority of all the major figures of ancient and medieval philosophy.

3. The second argument against psychological aesthetic subjectivism can be taken at the practical level from universal human activities. If beauty were merely subjective, as the subjectivists claim, all the characteristic activities of artists, beholders, and even of women (insofar as they are themselves aesthetic objects) would be superfluous and, hence, unreasonable and wrong. But it is inconceivable that all artists, all beholders, and even all women as aesthetic objects could be wrong throughout history, with only the relatively few aesthetic subjectivists being right. Consequently, beauty is not merely subjective, and psychological aesthetic subjectivism is wrong.

Which are the characteristic activities of the artists, the beholders, and of women as aesthetic objects that would be superfluous and, hence, unreasonable and wrong if aesthetic subjectivism were right? First of all, the practice and training of all creative and reproductive artists that last for years and years, and go on to some extent throughout their lives. For why should actors, singers, musicians, conductors, and dancers as well as painters, sculptors, writers, composers, and choreographers work for years trying to acquire the necessary technique and to develop their artistic talents if their works—be they the per-

---

[40] This Empedocles fragment is in Aristotle's *Met.* I, 4, 984b 34–985a 1.

[41] (a) Plato, *Hipp. mai.* 289d; *Tim.* 53b; (b) *Hipp. mai.* 287c; 289d; 292d; and (c) *Lysis* 216d and *Tim.* 87c.

[42] Aristotle, *Poet.* 7, 1450b 34–37; *Met.* XIII, 3, 1078a 33–1078b 2. Cf. also *Met.* XIV, 4, 1091a 30–32; *Poet.* 6, 1450b 2; 7, 1451a 11–13; etc.

[43] Plotinus, *Enn.* I, 6, 1 and 2; I, 6, 5 and 6; VI, 3, 11; Augustine, *De ver. rel.* 32, 59 (*PL* 34, 148); *De civ. Dei*, XXII, 19 (*PL* 41, 780–83); Boethius, *De cons. phil.* II, 5, § 133 (*PL* 63, 691 B); Bonaventure, *Itiner.* II, 10; I, 14 (V, 302b, 299a); *De triplici via*, 3, 7, 12 (VIII, 17b); Albert, *Sum. theol.* I, 6, 26, 1, 2, 3, sol.; II, 11, 62, 1, sed c. 2a and ad 1; II, 11, 62, 2, 4, sol. (31, 242; 32, 596f.; 601f.); Thomas, *De div. nom.* 4, 10, 439; *In Matth.* 3, 1; *In I. Pol.* L. 3; ed. R. M. Spiazzi (Taurini: Marietti, 1951), n. 73; *In IX. Eth.* 14, 1944; *De malo* 2, 4, ad 7.

formances of plays, compositions or dances or else paintings, statues, plays, or musical choreographic compositions—have no beauty at all, and cannot have any, hence, there is no chance at all ever to produce more beautiful works through practice or training? Thus, in the light of subjectivism, everybody engaged in the training and preparation of artists, teachers, and students as well, is only wasting his or her time and energy. Secondly and similarly, all the endeavor, work, time, energy, and money spent by women for self-beautification with the purpose of pleasing men would also be futile, as futile as their innate, universal desire to please men at all. Thirdly, all the visits by hopeful beholders of artworks to art galleries, art museums, exhibitions, opera houses, stage and movie theaters, and concert halls would also be superfluous—time, energy, and money wasted on as unreasonable efforts—as the efforts of people who, to the subjectivist's mind, naïvely go to see allegedly beautiful scenery all over the world. Who is going to believe all this? The creative artist? The reproductive artist? Women? Enthusiasts of art or nature? Indeed, aesthetic subjectivism in general strains credibility.

Furthermore, what psychological aesthetic subjectivism specifically suggests is that artistic training, production, and reproduction, as well as visits to art museums, theaters, and scenic places in nature are all superfluous. Instead, it sugggests that one try simply to imagine something aesthetically as delightful as the performance of Beethoven's *Emperor Concerto*, a Verdi opera, a Bolshoi ballet, and a film directed by Ingmar Bergman or Elia Kazan, or the sight of a Rodin statue or a Rubens painting. Is this suggestion impossible? Unreasonable? Wrong? Then so is aesthetic subjectivism in general and psychological aesthetic subjectivism in particular.

4. This argument showing how much aesthetic subjectivism is contrary to universal human tendencies and activities receives further support from aesthetic subjectivists themselves through their manner of speaking about beauty. For virtually all subjectivists seem to forget occasionally their denial of objective beauty, and speak of beauty as any aesthetic objectivist would. Lord Kames, for instance, writes, "Viewing a fine garden, I perceive it to be beautiful or agreeable; and I consider the beauty or agreeableness as belonging to the object, or as one of its qualities. When I turn my attention from the garden to what passes in my mind, I am conscious of a pleasant emotion of which the garden is the cause.... In a word, agreeable and disagreeable are qualities of the objects we perceive; pleasant and painful are qualities of the emotions we feel: the former qualities are perceived as adhering to objects; the latter are felt as existing within us."[44] Does this not sound like a classic text of aesthetic objectivism? And this is not the only such text in the quoted author's work. For he also states that "the emotion produced by an agreeable object is invariably pleasant"; that "the agreeableness denominated *beauty* belongs to objects of sight"; that beauty,

[44] Lord Kames, *op. cit.*, p. 72.

a quality so remarkable in visible objects, lends its name to express everything that is eminently agreeable"; that "considering, attentively, the beauty of visible objects, we discover two kinds"; that "when these two beauties coincide in any object, it appears delightful"; that "intrinsic beauty ... cannot be handled distinctly without being analyzed into its constituent parts"; that "the beauty of figure" arises "from regularity, uniformity, proportion, order, and simplicity"; etc., and he states all these only a few pages before he declares that beauty "cannot be an inherent property in either" the object or the percipient.[45]

For those who might think that this inconsistency is an isolated instance involving a third-rate aesthetician, let us consider a few passages from no less a thinker than Kant himself. He remarks that "colours and tone cannot be reckoned as mere sensations, but as the formal determination of the unity of a manifold of sensations, and thus as beauties in themselves"; that "ornaments ... which augment the satisfaction of taste, do so only by their form .... But if the ornament does not itself consist in beautiful form, it ... injures genuine beauty"; that "flowers are free natural beauties .... Many birds ... and many sea shells are beauties in themselves ... So also delineations *à la grecque*, ... are free beauties"; that "human beauty (i.e., of a man, a woman, or a child), the beauty of a horse or a building ... is therefore adherent beauty"; that "we must seek a ground external to ourselves for the Beautiful of nature; but seek it for the Sublime merely in ourselves"; that "the beautiful requires the representation of a certain quality of the Object"; that "we can thus, in respect of the Beautiful in nature, suggest many questions ... e.g., to explain why nature has scattered abroad beauty with such profusion"; that, in aesthetical judgments, we "feel with pleasure the mental state produced by the representation"; and that "the beautiful formations in the kingdom or organised nature speak loudly for the realism of the aesthetical purposiveness of nature ... Flowers, blossoms, even the shapes of entire plants; ... the charming variety so satisfying to the eye and the harmonious arrangements of colours."[46]

To use, finally, also a contemporary example, John Dewey writes, "In the presence of a landscape, a poem or a picture that lays hold of us with immediate poignancy, we are moved to murmur or to exclaim, 'How beautiful!' The ejaculation is a just tribute to the capacity of the object to arouse admiration that approaches worship." However, one sentence later, he declares, "Unfortunately, it (*sc.* beauty) has been hardened into a peculiar object ... and the concept of beauty as an essence of intuition has resulted."[47]

5. Closely connected with the above argument is a second one, also at the

---

[45] *Op. cit.*, pp. 72, 108, 109, 110, 112, 116. See also, pp. 131 f., 136, 149, 151, 186, 268f.; 273, etc.

[46] Kant, *Critique of Judgment*, §§ 14, 16, 23, 29, 30, 39, 58; *ed. cit.*, pp. 74, 76, 81, 82, 104, 133, 150f.; 169, 243.

[47] J. Dewey, *Art as Experience*, p. 129f.

practical level, that runs like this: Any theory that obviously and deliberately ignores evident facts must be judged to be wrong. Aesthetic subjectivism in general, including its psychological version, ignores evident facts connected with the production of works of fine art as well as the enjoyment of artistic and natural beauty. Therefore, aesthetic subjectivism, including its psychological version, must be judged to be wrong.

But what are those above-mentioned facts that are being ignored? The ignored fact connected with the production of works of fine arts is the evident and joyous self-realization of the artist that he is actually producing something beautiful. Every creative and reproductive artist has, at least occasionally, such an experience. (As a matter of fact, even the opposite type of experience, the frustration of the artist which he feels over his failure to produce a truly beautiful work is, in a way, indirectly, a proof for this.) Correspondingly, the ignored facts connected with the beholder are of two kinds. One of them concerns the conditions of experiencing delight; the other, the aesthetic delight itself. For it is commonly known from experience that, unless one has eyes and/or ears that function well, here and now, and unless certain objects are presented to him, he will not experience the delight of the beholder. Similarly, everyone who has ever beheld natural objects, like a Norwegian fjord, or a sunset in Arizona, or the Matterhorn in Switzerland; or artworks like the interior of the Cologne Cathedral, the exterior of the Reims Cathedral, the performance of a mass by Palestrina or Bach, or the opera *Boris Godunov*, or *Fidelio*, will know from personal experience that that beauty was really "out there"; that he "took it in," received it passively; and that it filled his mind and caused an emotional storm in his heart. As a matter of fact, no speculative argument for the objective reality of beauty can ever be so powerful and coercingly convincing as a soul-shattering aesthetic experience is to a beholder. (This is why a person with such previous experiences will never understand the aesthetic skeptic hammering on the question, "But how do we know that there is beauty out there, in things?") Nevertheless, the fact that the beholder is sometimes overwhelmed by the beauty of an object is completely ignored by the aesthetic subjectivist.

6. It must be pointed out here that it is entirely possible for the subjectivist to fence off the last two arguments simply by declaring that the subjectivist does not deny any of the above listed facts, such as, that the presence to the beholder of certain objects is needed for aesthetic delight, and that, consequently, the training, preparation, and efforts of the artists and the visiting of certain places of the world by beholders, etc., are not futile at all. At the root of this statement there may be the subjectivist's realization that there cannot be any aesthetic delight unless, as Kant puts it, there is some basis for it in the object or, as Santayana puts it, there are some materials of beauty or, as Dewey puts it and many others, there is a capacity or power in the object to delight the beholder. But what is this basis or the material in the object? It can be only some objective,

visible, or audible feature or quality that gives the object the capacity or power to delight the beholder. For if it were not objective or actual, it could not actually enable the object to please: that which is not existent or not really present cannot do anything. Similarly, if that quality were not actually visible and/or audible, it could not possibly render the object visibly and/or audibly pleasing. The great skeptic subjectivist, Hume, admits all this unwittingly in these words: "Though it be certain that beauty and deformity ... are not qualities in objects, ... it must be allowed, that there are certain qualities in objects which are fitted by nature to produce those particular feelings."[48] But that objective quality through which an object, when seen and/or heard, delights its knower is what is traditionally called beauty.

Therefore, if the aesthetic subjectivist wants to evade the thrust of the above two arguments, that is, the charges of unreasonableness and ignoring of facts, he is forced into an objectivist position. Or, to put this in another way, the subjectivist has only these two alternatives: deserve the above discussed grave charges, or use a defense that is implicitly objectivist.

7. After one argument of authority and two practical arguments, let us take up now some arguments at the speculative level, leaving the decisive argument last. The first specific argument is methodological, and can be formulated as follows. If there are two intrinsically or causally related facts to explain, then one must not deny the necessary condition of one fact in order to account for the other. The reason for this: the denial of facts or their necessary conditions for the sake of a theory is contrary to the very nature and purpose of philosophy as a science explaining certain facts.

When the subjectivist denies the objective reality of beauty to explain the fact of aesthetic disagreement, he denies the necessary condition and the only sufficient explanation of the positive aesthetic fact for the sake of explaining the negative aesthetic fact. In doing so, the aesthetic subjectivist acts like an atheist who denies God's existence to account for the presence of evil in this world. For in this latter case, too, there are two causally related facts to be explained: the existence of the contingent or changing world, and the presence of evil in the world. Now, inasmuch as the classic theist can validly demonstrate the existence of God, an all-perfect and necessary being, as the necessary condition of the world, nobody must deny God's existence only to account for why there is evil in the world. Instead, while the positive fact of the existence of the contingent world demands a proportionately positive explanation, and that is given by the existence of God, the negative fact of the privation of goodness in the world demands a proportionately negative fact as its necessary condition, and that is the inability of the finite being to be perfect according to its nature both in itself and in its relation to other beings.

[48] Hume, "Of the Standard of Taste," *ed. cit.*, p. 273. Cf. *ibid.*, pp. 271, 275, 277.

With respect to our present question, all this means that the positive aesthetic fact demands a positive fact as its cause and explanation, viz., the existence of objective beauty in things, whereas the negative aesthetic fact demands some negative cause or explanation that does not interfere with the explanation of the positive aesthetic fact. But the subjectivist's denial of the existence of some extramental beauty does ignore and interfere with the only sufficient explanation of the positive aesthetic fact. Therefore, the subjectivist position is methodologically wrong, and contrary to the nature and the end of philosophy as a science.

8. The main argument against psychological aesthetic subjectivism must consider the following reasoning: If something is an objective quality of things, it is recognized by all men, i.e., there is a universal agreement on it. But the beauty of things is not recognized by all men, i.e., there is no universal agreement on it. Consequently, beauty is not an objective quality of things.

Evaluating this conditional syllogism, we may say the following: (1) Formally, the syllogism is valid, with the minor destroying the consequent. (2) Materially, however, while the minor premise is true, since a well-known fact, the major premise is false. (3) Therefore, the conclusion is false, too, and so is psychological aesthetic subjectivism resting on this conclusion.

Proof for the falsity of the major premise:

(1) There is no universal but only a partial agreement on Locke's so-called primary qualities—just as there is about the so-called secondary qualities. For Locke's list of the primary qualities comprises solidity, extension, figure, motion, rest, and number, and there is a generic but no specific agreement on them among men. Everybody agrees that bodies have some solidity, extension, and figure, that they may be in motion or at rest, and that there is a certain multitude of them in existence. But people disagree specifically on all of these qualities of things. For what may seem soft to one may seem solid to another; what may seem big to one may seem small to another; what may seem to be in motion to one may seem to be at rest to another (if the latter is himself in motion); what may seem to be many to one may seem few to another; and even the same figure may seem different to different people if viewed from different angles. There is then no universal agreement on Locke's primary qualities considered specifically, contrary to the allegation of the major premise in question.

(2) Moreover, there is no universal but only a partial agreement on qualities which are undoubtedly objective. The same person may be judged to be sane by one physician, and insane, by another, while, evidently, a person cannot be both simultaneously. Similarly, the same person may be judged to need penicillin by one physician, and not to need it by another physician, while, obviously, he cannot both need it and not need it simultaneously; instead, he may live or die according to which medical opinion prevails. Also, most

people know that one should not touch an electric wire carrying a high voltage of electricity, while a primitive man may not believe this, touch the wire, and die as a result; a circumstance showing that, despite the disagreement, electricity is an objective quality of things.

(3) Finally, there is not even a universal but only a partial agreement on the very qualities which psychological aesthetic subjectivists themselves list as being objective and universally agreed upon. Lord Jeffrey, for example, argues for universal agreement being the criterion of objectivity in this amazing manner: "Where one man sees light, all men who have eyes see light also. All men allow grass to be green, and sugar to be sweet, and ice to be cold; and the unavoidable inference from any apparent disagreement in such matters necessarily is, that the party is insane, or entirely destitute of the sense or organ concerned in the perception. With regard to beauty, however, it is obvious, at first sight, that the case is entirely different."[49] Now, who does not know that the green of the grass looks different in certain (red and blue) artificial light or at dusk to all people; or that sugar does taste bitter after having tasted something much more sweet, and ice does not seem cold after one has touched a much colder object; whereas light as such is not visible to anybody, and the degrees of light are matters of opinion or vision? Therefore, the major premise in question does not hold true even for cases cited by the users of this subjectivist criterion.

Having proved that the subjectivist criterion for the objectivity of qualities is wrong in the major premise of the subjectivist argument, the question arises why this subjectivist premise is false. The premise in question recognizes only one of the two objective requirements of true knowledge, the object; and fails to recognize the other necessary requirement, the subject's capacity of recognizing the object as it is. Indeed, there can be no knowledge unless there is something knowable in the object, such as a quality of it; nor can there be any knowledge unless there is also someone who has the capacity to cognize that quality of the object as it is. Conversely, the disagreement may be due either to the fact that a certain quality is not in the object observed but only in the observer's mind, or else to the fact that some people can recognize the quality in the object, others cannot.

This answer to our question is, incidentally, not of one epistemological school of thought, that of realism, but rather one that is recognized even by skeptics. Hume, for example, made this crucial statement while discussing the ontological status of beauty: "this sentiment (*sc.* of aesthetic delight) must depend upon the particular fabric or structure of the mind, which enables such particular forms to operate in such a particular manner . . . . Vary the structure of the mind or inward organs, the sentiment no longer follows, though the form remains the same. The sentiment being different from the

---

[49] Lord Jeffrey, *art. cit.*, p. 2a.

object, and arising its operation upon the organs of the mind, an alteration upon the latter must vary the effect; nor can the same object, presented to a mind totally different, produce the same sentiment."[50]

The recognition of the epistemological reason why the major premise of the subjectivist argument is false is also of further help to us. For once we realize that disagreement may be due to either one of two reasons, viz., the objectivity of a quality, or the incapacity of the subject to recognize the objective quality, we can argue this way: Of the two necessary conditions of universal agreement on a quality, only one is listed in the subjectivist premise, namely, the objectivity of the quality; the other condition, the capacity of all men to recognize that objective quality, is left unmentioned. In other words, instead of two necessary conditions, only one is listed in the antecedent of the major premise. For this reason, the consequent does not follow from the antecedent. This circumstance renders the entire syllogism of the psychological aesthetic subjectivist a fallacy of *non sequitur*, comparable to the following argumentation: If my friend is at home, he will answer the phone; but he does not answer the phone; therefore, he is not at home. (He may be at home, but he may not have heard the phone ringing. Thus, the premise should run like this: If my friend is at home, *and* if he hears the phone ringing, he will answer it.) It is this logical classification of the subjectivist argument that necessitates the entire chapter right after the present one.

9. The argument of the psychological aesthetic subjectivist is not only fallacy of *non sequitur*, but also reducible to the absurd. This can be proved by construing a syllogism analogous to the one of the psychological aesthetic subjectivist: "If something is objective, there is universal agreement on it. But, as a matter of fact, there has never been any universal agreement on anything among philosophers, for the following reasons: That which is sensorily knowable can be doubted by the rationalist skeptic (as multitude was by Parmenides, or material being by Berkeley); that which is rationally knowable can be doubted by the empiricist skeptic (as the principle of causality was by Algazel and Hume, or as substance was by Hume and Kant); moreover, for any agreement, an object and a knower are needed, and knowledge must be possible, and all three were denied by Gorgias. Therefore, nothing is objective." But, evidently, this is a nihilistic position and, as such, totally absurd. Therefore, the original consequent does not truly follow from the antecedent, namely, that objectivity ensures universal agreement. Consequently, psychological aesthetic subjectivism rests on an argument that is reducible to the absurd.

Having established that psychological aesthetic subjectivism is a fallacy

---

[50] Hume, "The Sceptic," *ed. cit.*, p. 218.

of *non sequitur* reducible to the absurd, it seems that those who deem aesthetic subjectivism to be irrefutable, are wrong.[51]

ARTICLE 3: *Aesthetic Associationism and Relationism*

A. Aesthetic Associationism

Of all the explicit aesthetic subjectivist theories, there is only one kind that deals not only with the question why beauty is not an objective quality of things but also with what beauty actually is and how it originates in the mind. This theory is *associationism* and we shall consider it here as expounded by Lord Francis Jeffrey.

Jeffrey's reasons for rejecting aesthetic objectivism are two: the lack of universal agreement on beauty and what he calls the impossibility of finding common qualities in the things which we call beautiful. Having listed his reasons for denying the objective reality of beauty, he proceeds to construe a positive theory of what beauty is, and concludes that beauty is simply the power of certain objects to elicit aesthetic delight by reminding us, through associations, of previously experienced delightful objects. For instance, even though "the countenance of a young and beautiful woman" is "the most beautiful object in nature," a very little reflection can convince us, says Jeffrey, that "what we admire is not a combination of forms and colours . . . but a collection of signs and tokens of certain mental feelings and affections, which are universally recognized as the proper objects of love and sympathy," namely, youth and health in the first place, and "innocence, gaity, sensibility, intelligence, delicacy, or vivacity" in the second place.[1] When asked, why the association of these qualities should elicit aesthetic pleasure in us, Lord Jeffrey's reply consists in "the great principle of sympathy with human feelings," i.e., in "the indisputable fact, that we are pleased with the direct contemplation of human comfort, ingenuity, and fortune."[2]

In evaluating this theory, we can concede some minor points in it. One is that all men are pleased by "the direct contemplation of human comfort, ingenuity, and fortune." This is true because it merely expresses that that which is good delights—a principle recognized as evident by the ancient Greeks. Another point we can concede is that there is no reason for insisting on three basic aesthetic values, namely, the sublime, the beautiful, and the picturesque, since other values may equally be added to this arbitrary list insofar as other kinds of objects also elicit specifically different emotional

---

[51] Cf. C. E. M. Joad, "The Objectivity of Beauty"; reproduced in *The Problems of Aesthetics*, ed. E. Vivas and M. Krieger (New York: Holt, Rinehart, Winston, 1962), 465; and J. Stolnitz, who quotes Joad. (*Op. cit.*, pp. 412f.)

[1] Jeffrey, *art. cit.*, p. 15b.

[2] *Op. cit.*, p. 26b.

responses, whereas all three of them are generically similar.[3] The third point we can admit to be true is that from this theory it logically follows that "all tastes are equally just and true, insofar as concerns the individual whose taste is in question"[4]—a view shared by some contemporary subjectivists, too, like Curt J. Ducasse ("But, like the fact or dislike it, there is a realm where each individual is absolute monarch though of himself alone, and that is the realm of aesthetic values").[5] But this is already the end of agreement between the associationist and the objectivist view.

By way of negative criticism we say this: Jeffrey's theory is superfluous; dogmatically postulated; offers either some arbitrary and awkward explanations or no explanation at all for certain aesthetic facts; and fails to explain the central question connected with aesthetic experience.

First of all, why is Jeffrey's theory superfluous? It is superfluous because neither one of the two reasons why he rejected the objective reality of beauty stands up against the objectivist criticism. For, on the one hand, aesthetic disagreement does not invalidate the objectivist argument for the extramental reality of beauty; nor is, as will be demonstrated in the next chapter, the intramentality of beauty the only or even the better or simpler explanation of aesthetic disagreement. On the other hand, despite all the variety of things that are called beautiful, it is possible to find some common qualities or principles in them. Thus there is no need for the associationist (or any other) version of aesthetic subjectivism.

Secondly, why should we say that Jeffrey's theory is dogmatically postulated? For two reasons: it is not supported by self-consciousness and it either ignores or contradicts certain facts connected with self-consciousness.

This theory is not supported by self-consciousness insofar as we are generally aware of our associating one thing with another, at least subsequently and upon reflection; but, generally or as a rule, one can take aesthetic delight in a beheld object without being aware of any association that he may have with other things. This is especially obvious in cases of beholding utterly novel aesthetic objects, abstract paintings or statues, and sheer ornamental designs. Moreover, Jeffrey's associationism ignores or contradicts data of self-consciousness. For, led or forced by the evidence of the senses and aesthetic intuition as the object of the beholder's self-consciousness, the beholder cannot help, as Jeffrey himself admits it, invariably ascribing beauty to the contemplated object. But this means that self-consciousness tells the beholder not that beauty is only a matter of association but that beauty is in the contemplated object.

Thirdly, on what basis may we assert that Jeffrey's associationism offers

---

[3] *Op. cit.*, p. 34b. For this question, see chap. 10, articles 1 and 2.
[4] *Op. cit.*, p. 35a.
[5] Curt J. Ducasse, *The Philosophy of Art* (New York: Lincoln Mac Veagh, 1929), 288.

quite arbitrary or awkward explanations for certain facts concerning aesthetic experience? When Jeffrey states that the face of a young and beautiful woman strikes us not with its beauty but through associations with youth, innocence, delicacy, vivacity, etc., he seems to maintain an absurdity. First, one must see a young and beautiful woman to learn what youth, innocence, delicacy, vivacity, etc., are; then, having acquired these delightful ideas and upon seeing the same or similar woman at a later time, the same beholder will associate her features with these delightful ideas that will then elicit aesthetic delight in him.

One cannot help responding to this "explanation" of how we come to have aesthetic experience with a very simple and pertinent further question: Why is it that anything of "human comfort, ingenuity, and fortune," like youth, delicacy, etc., delights us in a *non-aesthetic* manner while observed directly and originally; but, when the same thing comes to one's mind by way of associating it with a directly observed object, it causes *aesthetic* delight in the same beholder?

Lord Jeffrey has only two alternative courses to follow. One is the road of evasiveness, viz., that of denying that there is any formal difference between the agreeable or good and the beautiful, or between the agreeably and the aesthetically delightful, thereby, precluding the need to answer this delicate question. The other road is that of directly answering the above question. Being probably reluctant to do the former, Jeffrey takes the latter road, and attempts to answer our question which he rephrases this way: "Why should beauty in all cases affect us in a way so different from the love or compassion of which it is said to be merely the reflection?"[6]

His reply is multiple. The first reason he gives for the difference between the two kinds of emotional responses is that aesthetic delight is "reflected from material objects, and not directly excited by their natural sources," like moonlight vs. sunlight. The second reason given is that aesthetic delight is caused "pure" or free of unpleasant factors accompanying the things that cause non-aesthetic responses. The third reason listed is the transitoriness or lesser depth of aesthetic delight as opposed to those emotions of which it is a "shadow and a representative." Fourthly, "the perception of beauty implies a certain exercise of the imagination, that is not required in the case of direct emotion." Fifthly and finally, aesthetic emotion always involves, besides associations, some direct perception rendering it more lively, and imparting to it "some share of its own reality."[7]

Now, as to reason five, as everybody knows from personal experience, the agreeable emotions are themselves due to "real and direct perceptions," just as are the aesthetic emotions. Thus, this reason represents no real difference

[6] Lord Jeffrey, *art. cit.*, p. 24a.
[7] *Op. cit.*, p. 24a–25a.

between the two types of delights at all. Similarly, as to reason four, Lord Jeffrey fails to convince us that, as a matter of fact, imagination is not involved at all or cannot be involved in the perception of objects causing non-aesthetic sentiments. Instead, he even begs the question on this point: first he *declares* that beauty is due to associations; and then he *explains* the difference between aesthetic and non-aesthetic emotion by pointing out that, in perceiving objects that cause aesthetic delight, "it is evident that our fancy is kindled by a sudden flash or recollection."[8] As to the remaining reasons listed, it seems that the "reflected" character and the greater transitoriness of aesthetic delight (reasons one and three) cancel out its purity and greater liveliness (reasons two and five, respectively). Thereby, the fivefold answer is actually no answer at all, and leaves Jeffrey's associationism unexplained on the central issue.

The fourth and final, if not crowning, weakness in Jeffrey's theory consists in its inability to explain the central question connected with aesthetic experience, namely, where we obtain our notion of beauty. For objects causing agreeable sensations are agreeable, not beautiful, according to his own doctrine; and the things which have the power of reminding us of those agreeable objects remind us so, again according to his own theory,[9] on the basis of some similarity. But that which is similar to an agreeable thing is itself agreeable in some manner, but not beautiful. Consequently, all we seem to be able to derive from our associations is an indirect experience of the agreeable, but not of the beautiful. Unless he identifies the agreeable with the beautiful, which he evidently does not want to do (this is why he listed five alleged differences between the emotions of the two kinds), Lord Jeffrey fails to explain the very notion of beauty or, rather, its psychological and epistemological origin, just as he fails to explain the ontological basis of aesthetic delight. This much should suffice as a criticism of Jeffrey's theory.

B. Aesthetic Relationism

1. Let us finally evaluate the position that we have called aesthetic relationism. J. L. Jarrett has already been quoted as its representative. We may add to that also the characterization of relationism offered by another advocate of this theory, just to make sure that its tenets are properly understood. H. S. Langfeld writes in *The Aesthetic Attitude*: "(Beauty) is neither totally dependent upon the person who experiences, nor upon the thing experienced; it is neither subjective nor objective, neither the result of purely intellectual activity, nor a value inherent in the object, but a relation between two variables —the human organism and the object.... What has been termed beauty does not exist when there is no organism to experience it...."[10]

---

[8] *Op. cit.*, p. 25a.
[9] See the three bases of associations on p. 15a.
[10] Herbert Sidney Langfeld, *The Aesthetic Attitude*, p. 108.

What does this theory consist of? What is it supposed to accomplish? The answers to these questions can be summed up as follows. Aesthetic relationism has a negative or destructive and a positive or constructive part. For, first of all, the aesthetic relationist claims to deny both the objectivity and the subjectivity of beauty, and, thereby, to differentiate himself from both the aesthetic subjectivist and the objectivist. Secondly, the aesthetic relationist endeavors to find and construe a compromise between the subjectivist and the objectivist position. Langfeld indicates this intention when he states, "Philosophy must decide whether beauty is subjective, that is merely a creation of the observer—something entirely mental, or whether it is objective, and as such an intrinsic characteristic of the object. . . . It must also consider whether these are the only possibilities."[11] Jarrett is even more to the point when observing, "Each of these three theories, Subjectivism, Cultural Relativism, and Objectivism, is rooted in a fact, and each of these facts is an important part of the whole truth of the matter. It will be well to make a fresh display of these facts in order to determine whether they cannot all be accommodated within a unified, coherent theory."[12]

How then does the relationist go about reducing the opposite aesthetic views to a unified theory? Jarrett answers the question in these words, "Beauty belongs to this picture for those who can be 'nourished' by it. For me, the picture has beauty, that is, the picture being what it is and I being what I am, when we are brought into relation, my experience (feelings, etc.) is such that I attribute to the picture the power, the capacity, to do this to me." In other words, "the object must be right . . . ; and the subject must be ready . . . . Then beauty emerges in the relation between the two."[13] What is this relation, as Langfeld puts it, "between two variables, the human organism and the object"?[14] This is the most crucial and the most difficult part of the entire relationist position. However, both authors heretofore quoted give enough clues as to realize that what they have in mind while speaking about this "relation" between the aesthetic object and subject is actually the mental recognition of the aesthetic object by the subject, the beholder, i.e., the "event" of aesthetic experience. Langfeld indicates this by remarking that beauty, as the relation between the two variables, is "just as real as an experience of color or sound. What has been termed beauty does not exist when there is no organism to experience it."[15] Thus, beauty, to his mind, is the actual experience of the "right" object by the "ready" subject. Jarrett confirms this analysis "very concretely" as follows: "[Here] is a picture on the wall. I insist that the picture is beautiful, and the question is, where is its presumed beauty? The

[11] *Op. cit.*, p. 15.
[12] Jarrett, *op. cit.*, p. 31.
[13] *Op. cit.*, p. 34.
[14] Langfeld, *op. cit.*, p. 108.
[15] *Ibid.*

answer is that its beauty belongs to it—beauty is a quality of the picture. What? In independence of the observer? No, not at all: in dependence on the observer. How can this be? Roughly, in the way that the nourishing character of milk is dependent upon the digestive system of an organism."[16] While then "objective beauty" is compared by Langfeld with color and sound (which are supposedly "real" only for the duration of our seeing and hearing it, respectively), the same is compared by Jarrett with milk that is actually nourishing only if and when actually consumed by the organism.

What can we say about this theory? This theory can be criticized in two ways: one, as it talks about "suitable object" and "ready subject"; and two, as it speaks of beauty consisting "in the relation" of such an object and subject.

2. Evaluating relationism in the former way, we may reason as follows.

Aesthetic relationism is right insofar as it speaks of two necessary factors, variables, or conditions, at least in reference to aesthetic experience; but it is wrong and inconsistent as it attributes those two necessary conditions to the existence of beauty itself.

Aesthetic relationism is right in speaking of a suitable object and a ready subject as being the necessary conditions of aesthetic experience. For, evidently, there will never be any aesthetic experience unless there is an object capable of delighting a person, and also a subject capable of recognizing that object and of being delighted by it. If this were all the relationists are saying, the objectivist would have no quarrel with them, and no reason to disagree with them. However, the fact is that what they rightly say is true only of aesthetic experience, but false of the ontological status of beauty. For, clearly, the only difference in this case between actually experienced and unexperienced beauty is this: the latter can, but does not delight; the former both can and does delight. But to say that, up to the moment of beholding it, the object has no beauty at all is to say either that the act of beholding renders the beheld object beautiful, or that the object does delight while being beheld although it cannot delight (since, without beauty, a thing cannot cause aesthetic delight); and both are patently absurd. If a thing is able to do something, it will or will not do so; but if a thing actually does something, as the aesthetic object does delight the beholder, then that thing is also able to do so. It is for this reason that C. I. Lewis, the "objective relativist,"[17] defines aesthetic value as a property of an object that represents the capacity of that object to cause delightful experience in someone.[18]

Interestingly enough, Jarrett seems to agree. For, adopting C. I. Lewis' terminology[19] on the various kinds of value, and thus defining intrinsic value

[16] Jarrett, op. cit., p. 38.
[17] An expression used by Stolnitz, op. cit., pp. 421-23.
[18] C. I. Lewis, An Analysis of Knowledge and Valuation (La Salle, Illinois: Open Court, 1946) 458.
[19] Lewis, op. cit., pp. 386f., 391f., 432-34.

as pleasurable experience, and inherent value as the objective property and capacity of a thing" to afford intrinsic value", i.e., pleasurable experience,[20] Jarrett declares: "Our aim ... is to come up with an explanation that will do justice" to all three aesthetic views: subjectivism, relativism, and objectivism. "If, now, beauty is seen to be an inherent value, our problem will have been solved." At this point and on this issue, no objectivist would object to Jarrett. But then a few lines later he falls back into the relationist framework of thinking and speaking when declaring that beauty belongs to an object "in dependence on the observer."[21] What he and any aesthetician should say instead is this:

On the basis of the positive aesthetic fact, beauty is and must be recognized as being an objective quality which, when becoming known to the beholder, delights. However, while being *objectively* actual, beauty is *subjectively potential* while unrecognized and unenjoyed, and it becomes *subjectively actual* only the moment that it is recognized and enjoyed by somebody.

Now, if the relationist formally denies beauty to be objectively actual in things and objects, he is wrong in the light of the objectivist argument we used in chapter 4. On the other hand, if he merely wants to state the actually recognized and enjoyed beauty to be actual beauty, then

(a) *at best*, he is using a misleading, arbitrary terminology (in order to stress that, in vain is there beauty in a thing, it will not become known and enjoyed unless the subject is psychologically fit to recognize and enjoy it); yet, it is his privilege to use such a terminology, and he himself is merely another *apparent* aesthetic subjectivist; whereas

(b) *at worst*, the relationist confuses the objectively existent beauty with its knowability that depends and is contingent upon the suitability of the subject, and this is a fatal confusion.

3. Next, evaluating aesthetic relationism in terms of its contention that beauty is born "in the meeting" of a "suitable object" and a "ready subject," or that beauty consists "in the relation" of a suitable object and a ready subject,[22] we can argue in the following manner.

If beauty is or is born in the meeting of two things, or consists in the relation of two things, then we can rightly ask *where* beauty is born when a certain object and a certain subject meet or create a relation between themselves. The answer can be only this: Beauty is born either nowhere or somewhere; and if somewhere, it is born either in the object, or in the subject, or in both, or outside both.

To say that beauty is born nowhere is to say that no beauty is born at all, that is, there is no beauty that becomes known; and that contradicts the cos-

---

[20] Jarrett, *op. cit.*, p. 32f.
[21] Both texts, *ibid.*, p. 33.
[22] Langfeld, *ibid.*, p. 108; Jarrett, *ibid.*, p. 34; Callahan, *op. cit.*, p. 29; De Wulf, *op. cit.*, p. 40.

mological fact that every material being is somewhere, and also the psychological fact that the beholder does experience beauty.

On the other hand, to say that beauty is born in the object is objectively false since knowledge does not change the thing known; whereas, apart from this falsity, the statement formally expresses aesthetic objectivism.

Moreover, to say that beauty is born in the subject is aesthetic subjectivism open to the general criticism of the same, and aesthetic relationism is not a compromise position as claimed by its advocates.

Furthermore, to say that beauty is born in both the object and the subject is a position open to all the criticism of the previous two alternatives listed above.

Finally, to say that beauty is born outside the object and the subject, "in between them," means either that no aesthetic knowledge and delight originates at all, and that is contrary to facts; or that this aesthetic knowledge and delight are outside the mind of the beholder, and that is patently absurd; or else that the aesthetic knowledge and delight are in the mind of something other than man, and this too contradicts the testimony of the beholder's self-consciousness.

Therefore, aesthetic relationism is either contrary to facts, or a kind of aesthetic objectivism, or a kind of aesthetic subjectivism.

If aesthetic relationism contradicts facts, it is to be rejected; and if it is some kind of aesthetic subjectivism, it is open to all the criticism given aesthetic subjectivism above. But if it is an ill-disguised kind of aesthetic objectivism, we have no basic quarrel with it.[23]

[23] An excellent confirmation of this view comes from M. De Wulf who, having stated that neither ancient objectivism nor modern subjectivism is right since "the truth lies between the two," presents in his chapter "Return to Objectivism" some "direct proofs of the objectivity of the Beautiful." (*Op. cit.*, pp. 40, 176.)

Chapter VI
Reasons for Aesthetic Disagreement

IN CHAPTER 4 we argued for aesthetic objectivism. In Chapter 5 we argued against aesthetic subjectivism. There is one more thing to do before the problem of the existence of beauty can be considered completed. This is to discuss a question that is in favor of aesthetic objectivism and against aesthetic subjectivism, although it seems to favor aesthetic subjectivism. This question concerns the reasons why there is aesthetic disagreement among men.

How can the question of the reasons for aesthetic disagreement work in favor of aesthetic objectivism? By finding psychological and/or metaphysical reasons for aesthetic disagreement which completely explain the disagreement without needing to resort to the radical subjectivist supposition of the subjectivity of beauty. How can, on the other hand, this question work against aesthetic subjectivism? By pointing out that, since psychological and other reasons perfectly and naturally explain the fact of aesthetic disagreement, the subjectivist explanation, the subjectivity of beauty, is clearly not the only explanation of the disgreement but rather an explanation that does not necessarily follow from the fact of disagreement and that is much more radical than the simple and plausible explanation offered by the aesthetic objectivist. Hence, inasmuch as one should always follow the principle of economy, i.e., prefer the simpler and more plausible explanation, the radical subjectivist explanation, that is so much contrary to everyone's self-consciousness and universal human tendencies, ought to be rejected.

Then which are the true reasons for aesthetic disagreement? Generally, they are psychological or subjective reasons rooted in the nature of man, the subject of aesthetic experience; some others are also objective, as they are rooted not only in human nature but also in the nature of the aesthetic object or something related to it.

Let us first give the complete division of these reasons; and, subsequently, let us discuss those reasons one by one. The reasons for aesthetic disagreement can be divided into reasons for apparent and real disagreement.

I. REASONS FOR APPARENT DISAGREEMENT

These reasons are facts explaining why people often *seem* to disagree in their aesthetic judgments or views without really holding opposite opinions on any one given aesthetic object. These reasons can be divided as follows.

A. Various Uses of Aesthetic Terms

1. Various Uses of the Term "Beautiful"

a. Analogous Uses of the Term "Beautiful." These are uses of the term "beautiful" in partly different meanings. Such are:

(1) Use of the term "beautiful" in a broad and a strict sense, namely, as meaning "beautiful with or without defect" and "beautiful without any defect" (Reason One).

(2) Use of the term "beautiful" in senses differing in degree, namely, as meaning "beautiful to any extent" and "considerably beautiful" (Reason Two).

b. Equivocal Use of the Term "Beautiful." This is the use of the term "beautiful" in two entirely different senses, namely, "aesthetically valuable" and "pleasing to me" (Reason Three).

c. Subjective Use of the Term "Beautiful." This is the term "beautiful" as meaning only "pleasing to me" or "delightful to me" (Reason Four).

2. Analogous Use of the Term "Ugly." This is the use of the term "ugly" in partly different senses, viz., "not beautiful at all" and "not beautiful enough" (Reason Five).

B. Different Considerations of the Aesthetic Object

This means the consideration given by one beholder to one part or aspect of the aesthetic object, and the consideration given by another beholder to another part or aspect of the same aesthetic object. (Reason Six).

II. Reasons for Real Disagreement

These reasons are facts explaining why people often actually or truly disagree on the beauty of any one given object in such a manner that some of them do find it beautiful, others do not. The reasons for real disagreement are basically twofold: partly subjective and completely subjective reasons.

A. Partly Subjective Reasons: Defects

These are reasons which are rooted partly in the aesthetic object or something pertaining to it, and partly in the aesthetic subject, the individual beholder. Insofar as they are rooted in the aesthetic object, these reasons are objective; insofar as they are rooted in the aesthetic subject, these reasons are subjective. The double foundation of these reasons is such that the objective basis is prior to and more fundamental than the subjective basis.

There are many generically and specifically different kinds of partly subjective reasons. Yet, they all have this much in common: they all consist of some kind of objective defect that confuses or misleads beholders. This is to say that these reasons represent some imperfection or limitation in the aesthetic object or in something related to it, which imperfections or limitations, in some manner, render some beholders incapable of properly recognizing and enjoying the beauty which is there in such objects.

These partly subjective reasons can be divided according to the generic and specific nature of the defects which these reasons objectively represent, namely, aesthetic and non-aesthetic defects.

1. Aesthetic Defects as Reasons for Disagreement

Aesthetic defects are defects in the beauty or in the environment of the aesthetic object which detract somehow from the beauty of the aesthetic object as it is being contemplated. These defects, when noticed by some beholders, render those beholders unable to enjoy properly the aesthetic object in which or in whose environment the defect is found.

a. Aesthetic Defects in the Aesthetic Object. These are simply the limitations or the finiteness of the beauty in every being of this world. Insofar as every being in this world is essentially finite, it is only natural and inevitable that its beauty should also be finite. This natural aesthetic limitation becomes the objective basis of aesthetic disagreement in one of two ways: when considered absolutely, or when considered relatively.

(1) Aesthetic Defects in Objects Considered Absolutely. These defects can cause disagreement among beholders in one of these four manners, dependent on the individual beholder:

(*a*) By virtue of excessive familiarity with the limited beauty (Reason Seven);

(*b*) By virtue of the novelty (lack of familiarity) with the limited beauty (Reason Eight);

(*c*) By virtue of some wrong consideration given to the limited beauty (Reason Nine);

(*d*) By virtue of aesthetic ignorance overlooking the ugliness of the aesthetic object (Reason Ten).

(2) Aesthetic Defects in Objects Considered Relatively. These defects are rooted in a certain aesthetic hierarchy which one finds among the material beings, especially the natural things. This hierarchy causes some beholders to compare more beautiful with less beautiful aesthetic objects while beholding an aesthetic object and, thereby, to disagree with those who do not do so. The aesthetic hierarchy itself, causing disagreements, is twofold:

(*a*) Hierarchy between species of aesthetic objects (Reason 11); and

(*b*) Hierarchy among the individuals within any given species of aesthetic objects (Reason 12).

b. Aesthetic Defect in the Environment of Aesthetic Objects. This aesthetic defect is the unsuitability or disproportion of the environment to the specific or individual character of the beauty of the object under contemplation (Reason 13).

2. Non-Aesthetic Defects of Aesthetic Objects

These are defects that affect something other than the beauty of the aesthetic object. They can be threefold:

a. Defects in the Non-Aesthetic Qualities of the Aesthetic Object: These are:
    (1) Lack of suitable size in the visible aesthetic object (Reason 14).
    (2) Lack of suitable volume in the audible aesthetic object (Reason 15).
b. Defects in the Objective Circumstances of the Aesthetic Object. These are:
    (1) Lack of suitable distance of the aesthetic object (Reason 16).
    (2) Lack of suitable light for the aesthetic object (Reason 17).
c. Defects in the Proportion between the Aesthetic Object and the Mental Capacity of the Beholder. These may be due to at least three objective qualities:
    (1) Large size (Reason 18).
    (2) Extreme length (Reason 19).
    (3) Complexity of aesthetic order (Reason 20).

B. *Completely Subjective Reasons: Individual Differences*

These are reasons explaining aesthetic disagreement among men, in complete disregard of the aesthetic object. Since aesthetic experience involves only the object and the subject of aesthetic knowledge and delight, these reasons, by definition, are rooted in the individual differences that can be found in people acting as beholders.

These individual differences render some people unable to recognize either the aesthetic defect (ugliness) in certain objects, or the beauty of certain objects. Accordingly, one can divide these inabilities in the following way.

1. Inability to Recognize Aesthetic Defects

This inability can be at least threefold according to its specific causes to be found in the individual. For this inability can be due to either one of these facts about the beholder:

a. His favorable prejudice toward the aesthetic object (Reason 21).

b. Pleasant associations (Reason 22).

2. Inability to Recognize Beauty

This generic reason for aesthetic disagreement can be divided according to its duration into two groups. For some inabilities to recognize beauty affect a person only here and now; others, over a long period of time, perhaps even for a lifetime.

a. Temporary Inabilities. These aesthetic inabilities can be divided according to the level of human life at which they are caused by various factors.

    (1) Inabilities at the Sensory Level. These may be due to any one of these factors of sensory life:

        (*a*) Malfunction of sense organs (Reason 23);

        (*b*) Ill-feeling or pain (Reason 24); and

        (*c*) Disproportionate mood (Reason 25).

    (2) Inabilities at the Rational Level. These may be due to:

(*a*) Inattention (lack of attention) (Reason 26); or
(*b*) Distraction (Reason 27).

 b. Habitual Inabilities. These can be divided on the same basis as the above listed temporary inabilities.

(1) Inabilities at the Sensory Level. They can be caused by at least five different factors:

(*a*) Malfunction of the sense organs (Reason 28);
(*b*) Unpleasant associations (Reason 29);
(*c*) Lack of aesthetic distance (Reason 30);
(*d*) Emotional prejudice toward the aesthetic object (Reason 31); and
(*e*) Unsuitable temperament (Reason 32).

(2) Inabilities at the Rational Level. They, too, can be caused by any number of factors, such as:

(*a*) Aesthetic habits (taste) (Reason 33);
(*b*) Mental unpreparedness (Reason 34);
(*c*) Habitual expectations (Reason 35); and
(*d*) Individual standards (Reason 36).

Let us discuss now all these thirty-six reasons for aesthetic disagreement in three distinct articles.

ARTICLE 1: *Reasons for Apparent Disagreement*

1. The first of these reasons can bring about an aesthetic disagreement in this manner. Suppose one art critic takes the crucial aesthetic term "beautiful" in the strict sense, i.e., as meaning "aesthetically perfect or great, without any (noticeable) defect," whereas another art critic takes the same term in the broad sense, i.e., as meaning simply, "aesthetically valuable with or without some imperfection." (This is not an unreasonable supposition since, as Hume pointed out, "when critics come to particulars, . . . unanimity vanishes, and it is found, that they had affixed a very different meaning to their expressions,"[1] and it is confirmed by the well-known disagreement between E. Burke and Dugald Stewart that rested on the fact that the former considered an object beautiful only if it was smooth; the latter, even if it was rough, jagged, or angular.[2]) Let us further suppose that both of the art critics in question consider the same artwork and that this artwork has some noticeable defect or defects. All this being so, the first art critic will obviously judge that artwork *not* to be beautiful; the second art critic, to be beautiful.

This seems, of course, to be a case of aesthetic disagreement, but it is not

---

[1] Hume, "Of the Standard of Taste, *ed. cit.*, p. 266.
[2] E. Burke, *op. cit.*, §§ 14 and 27; and D. Stewart, *Philosophical Essays*, Part 2, Essay I, part 1, ch. 4; *ed. cit.*, V, 219–24. For Rodin's broad and strict use of the term "beauty," see Louis W. Flaccus, *The Spirit and Substance of Art* (New York: F. S. Crofts, 1926), 10.

really, since both notice the beauty of the artwork, and both recognize also that its beauty has some defect. The difference lies, thereby, not in the judgments they pass on the artwork but in the verbal expression of their judgments.

2. *Reason 2* is very similar to Reason 1. To understand it, let us suppose that two people behold the same aesthetic object; while, however, one of them is willing to call an object beautiful as long as there is the slightest degree or trace of beauty in it, the other will call beautiful only objects which are considerably beautiful, that is, beautiful above a certain minimal or average level.[3] Let us further suppose that the object which both of these persons behold is only slightly rather than considerably beautiful, and that both recognize it as such. All this being so, the former beholder will call it beautiful, but the latter will not.

Thereby the two will seem to disagree, although in reality both agree that the object is only slightly beautiful.

3. The understanding of *Reason 3* necessitates the following suppositions. Of two beholders considering the same object, one uses the term "beautiful" in the objectivist sense ("aesthetically valuable"); the other, in the subjectivist sense ("pleasing to me").[4] Furthermore, the former beholder does find the object beautiful, whereas the latter is not pleased by it. All this being so, the former beholder will say, "This is beautiful"; the latter, "This is not beautiful"; and yet, they do not really disagree. For only the former passed an aesthetic judgment on the object; the latter did not. The latter merely reported that he did not experience any aesthetic delight while beholding the object in question. He may even concede explicitly that the object *may* be beautiful despite the fact that he failed to take delight in it.

4. *Reason 4* can happen under the following conditions. Two people behold the same object; only one of them is pleased by it for some reason; and both use the term "beautiful" in the subjectivist sense, as meaning that the object is pleasing to them.[5] If all this is realized in a given case, the former beholder will say, "This is beautiful" (meaning, "This object is pleasing me"); the other, "This is not beautiful" (meaning, "This object is not pleasing me" or "displeases me");[6] and yet, they do not disagree on the beauty of the object, since they talk about and report only their own reactions to the object.

5. *Reason 5* consists of a situation in which a certain aesthetic object is beheld by two persons who both recognize it as being slightly beautiful; yet, one of them uses the term "ugly" in the strict sense, as meaning "not beautiful

---

[3] Cf. John Rickaby, *General Metaphysics* (London and New York: Longmans, Green, 1902), 151.

[4] Cf., "It is customary to make distinction between what is good and what we like." C. E. Joad, "The Objectivity of Beauty"; *ed. cit.*, p. 464. For the same two meanings see also M. C. Beardsley, *op. cit.*, p. 506.

[5] Cf., Ducasse, *Philosophy of Art*, chap. 15, §§ 10, 11, pp. 284, 286.

[6] Cf., "An order is called bad when the order itself is less well maintained." St. Augustine, *De natura boni*, c. 23 (PL 42, 548). Cf. Plato, *Protag.* 346d.

at all," whereas the other uses it more loosely, as meaning "not beautiful enough (to please me)."[7] In this situation, the former will judge the object by saying, "This is not ugly"; the latter, "This is ugly." Thereby, they will appear to disagree although, in fact, both express the same thing, viz., "This is somewhat beautiful," only in different ways. This kind of apparent aesthetic disagreement is, incidentally, rather frequent. Many of us gradually become more and more sophisticated and demanding and, thereby, unwilling to call a thing beautiful unless its beauty is considerable, conspicuous, or striking.

6. *Reason 6* represents a radically different situation. It has nothing to do with the use of aesthetic terms in different meanings. Instead, it consists in the fact that of two art critics or beholders each may behold and evaluate the same artwork (or object), but each one does so by considering a different part or aspect of it. Under these circumstances, it can happen that one of them finds one part or aspect of that artwork or object beautiful; the other one finds another part or aspect ugly. Carroll C. Pratt, for example, points out, "One listener may be impressed by the gorgeous rhythms and melodies of Gershwin while another is depressed by the stodgy and unimaginative use of the bass and the sameness of style."[8] Similarly, one art critic may praise the novel, imaginative style of an artwork, while another may blame the artist for the unoriginal, often-used idea or subject matter, etc. in the same artwork. This way the two beholders seemingly disagree, but they do not really, since they do not talk about the same part or aspect of the artwork.

ARTICLE 2: *Partly Subjective Reasons for Real Disagreement*

A. Aesthetic Defects

The first among the seven reasons of real aesthetic disagreement, that are rooted in some aesthetic defect, is excessive familiarity with the aesthetic object.

1. *Reason 7* refers to the following situation. Out of two persons who behold the same aesthetic object, one has seen or heard a given aesthetic object previously only a few times, if ever; another person has perceived it too often, and is consequently very familiar with it to the point of being indifferent about it or bored by it. Natives of such cities as Rome, Florence, Paris, Toledo, Cologne, or London, for instance, generally do not pay too much, if any, attention to the glorious architectural and sculptural works of their cities simply because

---

[7] Cf. Bartók's evaluation of a few compositions by an amateur composer: "Regrettably enough, on the basis of the compositions sent to me, I cannot say anything favorable. These are completely primitive things, in which one cannot detect any trace of talent." Letter to John Kemény, Budapest, December 30, 1920; in *Bartók Béla Levelei* (Letters of Béla Bartók), part III, no. 36. Ed. J. Demény (Budapest, Zenemükiadó Vállalat, 1955, 378. Cf. also letter no. 38, p. 379; and Bernard C. Heyl, *New Bearings in Esthetics and Art Criticism* (Yale University Press, 1943), 98, n. 8.

[8] C. C. Pratt, "The Stability of Aesthetic Judgments," *The Journal of Aesthetics and Art Criticism*, XV/1 (September 1956), 9. Cf. E. I. Watkin, *A Philosophy of Form*, II, 4 (London: Sheed and Ward, 1950), 328.

they have seen those art treasures much too often and, thereby, have exhausted the delightfulness of their beauties.

As a matter of fact, there is no such artwork or natural scenery so gorgeous that it cannot become unexciting or even boring after one beholds it too often in a short period of time. Aristotle was already aware of this: "Some things delight us when they are new; but later do so less ... for at first the mind is in a state of stimulation ... but afterwards ... the pleasure ... is dulled."[1] St. Augustine endorses this statement in a more concrete manner when remarking that we may pass by certain beautiful places in a city or in the country without any delight after having seen those places too often.[2] Modern aestheticians merely echo their views. Lord Kames, for instance, points out that "custom, after a longer familiarity, makes it (*sc.* the aesthetic object) again disagreeable."[3] Kant makes this incidental remark: "Marsden in his description of Sumatra makes the remark that the free beauties of nature surround the spectator everywhere and thus lose their attraction for him."[4] And Thomas Brown asks rhetorically, "Who that is not absolutely deaf, could sit for a whole day in a music room, if the same air, without any variations, were begun again in the very instant of its last note?"[5] From all this it follows that, if two persons behold the same object, one of whom is excessively familiar with that object and the other not, the former will not find it beautiful, but the latter will, and thereby they will truly disagree.

2. *Reason 8* for aesthetic disagreement is the contrary opposite of Reason 7. While in the above-discussed case disagreement is due to excessive familiarity with the object of limited beauty as it leads to indifference or boredom, in the present case some beholder is not familiar at all with the aesthetic object; instead, the object is completely new to him. This being so, there is a good chance that this beholder will be affected by the power of novelty, that is, he will be inclined to leave the defects of the aesthetic object unnoticed just because he is overwhelmed by the novelty of that object. Ancient philosophers[6] were as well aware of this effect of novel beauty upon the beholders as were modern aestheticians. J. Addison, for instance, stated, "Every thing that is new or

---

[1] Aristotle, *Eth. Nic.* X, 4, 1175a 6–9; *transl. cit.*, pp. 1099f.

[2] Augustine, *De catechizandis rudibus*, 12, 17 (PL 40, 324). Cf. *De utilitate credendi*, 16, 34 (PL 42, 90); and Aquinas, *In X. Eth.* 6, 2034f.; *S. theol.* I–II, 42, 5c.

[3] Lord Kames, *ed. cit.*, chap. 14, n. 333, p. 219.

[4] Kant, *Critique of Judgment*, § 22; *ed. cit.*, p. 99. The text which Kant mentions is, according to the Bernard edition (p. 99), William Marsden, *The History of Sumatra* (London, 1783), 113; and this text seems to be on page 139 of the reprint of the third edition of Marsden's work (Kuala Lumpur–New York: Oxford University Press, 1966).

[5] Thomas Brown, *Lectures on the Philosophy of the Human Mind*, II, lecture 53 (Hallowell: Glazier, Masters, and Smith, 1842), 14. Cf. Henry J. Koren, *An Introduction to the Science of Metaphysics* (St. Louis: B. Herder, 1955), 100.

[6] E.g., Aristotle, *Eth. Nic.* X, 4, 1175a 6–8 (although in *Problem.* XIX, 5 and 40, 918a 3–9 and 921a 32–38, familiarity is treated as being advantageous to aesthetic delight); Cicero, *De nat. deorum*, II, 53, 131; Plotinus, *Enn.* V, 1, 1.

uncommon raises a Pleasure in the Imagination";[7] and Lord Kames maintained, "Of all the circumstances that raise emotions, not excepting beauty, nor even greatness, novelty has the most powerful influence."[8] How, then, does the novelty of the aesthetic object or the utter unfamiliarity of the beholder with the aesthetic object result in aesthetic disagreement? Very simply this way: as long as one beholder is completely unfamiliar with an object of defective beauty, he will not notice its defects; whereas one who is familiar with the object, and is thus not overwhelmed by it, will probably notice the aesthetic defects in it. Thereby the two are likely to disagree, just as Oscar Wilde stated it: "Diversity of opinion about a work of art shows that the work is new."[9]

3. A wrong consideration of limited beauty as *Reason 9* for aesthetic disagreement can be explained as follows. Every aesthetic object, whether a natural thing or a work of fine art, must be considered as a whole, and every part or aspect of it in its relation to the other parts or aspects as well as to the whole. Bonaventure puts this truth in the following way: "Nobody can see the beauty of a poem unless he considers the entire poem";[10] and Augustine warns, "It is clear to a learned man that what displeases in a portion displeases for no other reason than because the whole, with which that portion harmonizes wonderfully, is not seen."[11] He who forgets or ignores this or he who does not realize this considers the aesthetic object in the wrong way. "He who blames the whole," remarks Plotinus, "on grounds of its parts, blames it unreasonably."[12]

There are two consequences of this mistake: one is cognitive; the other, appetitive. The former consists in such a person's failure to recognize the object in its aesthetic order, i.e., beauty. The latter consequence flows from the former; he who fails to intuit the beauty of an object will also fail to enjoy it. The question is now, why should anybody fail to consider an aesthetic object properly? Objectively, because some beautiful works, especially novels, plays, paintings, and statues, "contain elements that, taken in isolation, are hideous";[13] subjectively, because he who does not consider the whole of the aesthetic object will easily let his attention be directed to such a defect in that object, and this circumstance hinders him from noticing and enjoying the other parts or aspects of the object which are actually beautiful. Henry Koren puts this as follows: "If an object lacks a perfection, is *mutilated*, man's attention is more or less irresistibly drawn towards this defect, and as a result the intellect cannot

[7] J. Addison, *The Spectator*, No. 412, June 23, 1712.
[8] Lord Kames, *op. cit.*, chap. 6, n. 237, p. 152.
[9] O. Wilde, *The Picture of Dorian Grey*, preface.
[10] Bonaventure, *Brevil.*, prol. 2, 4 (V, 204b), Cf., *In II. Sent.* d. 32, a. 3, q. 2, ad 5 (II, 774b).
[11] Augustine, *De ord.* II, 49, 51 (*PL* 32, 1019). Cf. *De civ. Dei*, XII, 4; XVI, 8, 2 (*PL* 41, 352, 486).
[12] Plotinus, *Enn.* III, 2, 3.
[13] S. K. Langer, *Feeling and Form* (New York: C. Scribners' Sons, 1953), 396.

come to rest in the contemplation of the perfections that remain in the object."[14]

How is all this relevant to real aesthetic disagreement? By the simple fact that, whether or not it is wrong, some people will always consider the ugly parts or aspects of an aesthetic object in isolation from the others and the whole, will thereby fail to recognize and enjoy its beauty, and will, ultimately, disagree with those who consider that object properly. Does this kind of disagreement happen seldom or often?

Since it is very natural for man to look for beauty everywhere, especially in a work of fine art, and since an ugly part is quite conspicuous if found where we look for beauty, this kind of aesthetic disagreement happens quite often. It may happen, for instance, every time that some people enter the Delphi Museum to see the famous *Charioteer* from which no less important and conspicuous a part than the left arm is missing. But this aesthetic disagreement comes about most frequently whenever some people find the subject matter, or some parts of the art medium, or even the artist himself objectionable, especially on moral grounds. Tatian, the second-century church father, objected for instance to the fact that many of the Greek works of art were "devoted to worthless objects ... For Selanion [cast a statue] of Sappho the courtezan, and Nancydes one of Erinna the Lesbian .... This Sappho is a lewd, lovesick female, and sings her own wantonness .... Euthycrates cast a brazen statue of Panteuchis, who was pregnant by a whoremonger ... I condemn Pythagoras, too, who made a figure of Europe on the bull .... Is it not shameful that fratricide is honoured by you who look on the statues of Polynices and Eteocles ... What care I ... to gape with wonder at the art of Callistratus, or to fix my gaze on the Neaera of Calliades? For she was a courtezan, Lais was a prostitute, and Turnus made her a monument of prostitution. Why are you not ashamed of the fornication of Hephaestion, even though Philo has represented him very artistically?"[15] Should somebody think that this sort of thing could happen only in ancient times, he may be reminded of such facts as the public rejection of Manet's *Luncheon on the Grass*[16] in 1865, or Tolstoi's judgment of Shakespeare's *King Lear* as a "wicked and vicious play,"[17] and of ballet as being simply "a lewd performance" in which "half-naked women make voluptuous movements, twisting themselves into various sensual wreathings,"[18] or the attack of Gaston Calmette, the editor of *Le Figaro* on the performance in Paris, 1912, of the ballet, *The Afternoon of A Faun*, choreographed by Vaslav Nijinsky, one of its scenes appearing morally

---

[14] Koren, *op. cit.*, pp. 99f.
[15] Tatian, *Address to the Greeks*, chaps. 33f. Tr. J. E. Ryland, in *The Ante-Nicene Fathers*, II: *Fathers of the Second Century* (New York: C. Scribners' Sons, 1926.) 78f.
[16] *Dejeuner sur l'herbe*. Louvre, Paris.
[17] C. E. M. Joad, *Guide to Philosophy* (New York: Dover, 1936), 336.
[18] Tolstoi, *What Is Art?*, ed. cit., p. 79.

objectionable, and only August Rodin coming to its defense,[19] or the recent film, *Who's Afraid of Virginia Wolff?*, starring Elizabeth Taylor and Richard Burton, in which some movie-goers noticed hardly anything except some four-letter words. The worst aspect of this kind of aesthetic disagreement, however, is that, since it is based on ignorance and prejudice, it will probably keep on plaguing artists, artworks, and beholders unless people take heed of St. Thomas' reminder that a picture can properly be called beautiful even if it represents a very ugly object, provided, it represents that object beautifully.[20]

4. *Reason 10* is an inability to recognize beauty due to the aesthetic ignorance of the beholder. This holds true for everyone who is ignorant about certain aesthetic requirements in the various kinds of fine arts. For such a person may not notice that a given artwork actually violates aesthetic principles, whereas he may notice the beauty which is present in that artwork despite the fact that it is limited because of the violation of an aesthetic principle. This case is obviously the contrary opposite of Reason 9: while some beholders improperly consider the aesthetic object insofar as they concentrate on the *ugly* parts or aspects of the artwork, those with whom we are presently concerned wrongly consider the artwork inasmuch as they notice only the *beautiful* parts or aspects of the artwork while, out of ignorance, they fail to recognize the ugly parts or defective aspects of it.[21] Aquinas has an interesting observation that has a bearing on this matter. He says, "Because of ignorance ... People ... have given divine worship ... to certain creatures on account of their beauty."[22] Apart from the question whether or not this is true of the history of religions, Thomas accurately diagnoses here the above-described aesthetic ignorance. For if someone who knows or believes that God is infinitely perfect, recognized the finiteness of the beauty of a thing, he would realize that the beautiful thing could not possibly be divine. The implication of all this is clear: aesthetic ignorance can lead to aesthetic disagreement. He who is not aesthetically ignorant will notice the defect which the ignorant fails to notice, and thereby he will reject the same aesthetic object which the ignorant hails as beautiful. This can be the case with the musical arrangement of a poetic work. The poem may be beautiful; the arrangement as a musical composition may be quite powerful and melodic; yet, the melody may ignore the linguistic demands of the words with respect to the length of the syllables, etc. This being so, one who does not realize that the music must follow the character of the text set to music may be so much delighted by the music or the text or both taken separately that he never becomes aware of the above-mentioned discrepancy, even though a better trained person becomes immediately aware of it and may reject the whole work for that reason.

[19] Grace Robert, *The Borzoi Book of Ballets* (New York: A. A. Knopf, 1949), 20f.
[20] St. Thomas, *S. theol.* I, 39, 8c. Cf. *Quodlib.* XII, 22, 1c.
[21] Cf. Ralph B. Perry, *General Theory of Value* (New York: Longmans, Green, 1926), 639.
[22] Thomas, *S. theol.* II–II, 94, 4c.

5. About *Reason 11* of aesthetic disagreement, rooted in the aesthetic hierarchy of species and mental comparison, the following must be said. It is both a fairly common philosophic doctrine[23] and a very obvious and conspicuous fact that there is an aesthetic hierarchy among the genera and species of natural things. This is to say that some genera or species of natural objects are more beautiful than others. Few people would doubt, for example, that a piece of crystal or diamond is more beautiful than a piece of sand stone or coal; that the orchid is more beautiful than the dandelion; the peacock, than the sparrow; the horse, than the donkey; and man, than the horse. This being the case in all three kingdoms of natural things as well as in the field of fine arts, whenever a person beholds any kind of thing, he will invariably compare it in his mind with other kinds of things (of the same genus) previously beheld and, unless the present object is at least as beautiful as those which he experienced before, he will reject that object as non-beautiful. This fact was known to many early thinkers. According to Heraclitus, for instance, "the most beautiful of apes is ugly compared with the human race."[24] Similarly, Plato affirmed that "the most beautiful maiden is ugly in comparison with the race of gods,"[25] whereas Plotinus and Augustine stated the same thing about the ape with respect to man.[26] Indeed, he who has developed the custom of enjoying majestic symphonies will find operettas, like those of Offenbach, too light and simple to be enjoyable to him; and he who has often listened to polyphonic church music by Palestrina or Bach, as performed by first-class, professional choruses and orchestras, will find little if any pleasure in hearing simple church hymns sung by enthusiastic but untrained amateurs.

Why is this fact, which we may term aesthetic sophistication, a reason for real aesthetic disagreement? Because the aesthetically sophisticated, i.e., he who has experienced many different kinds of very beautiful things will very likely reject as non-beautiful many of the things which an unsophisticated, aesthetically less demanding person simply accepts as beautiful, and thereby the situation of disagreement is given.

6. *Reason 12* is analogous to the previous reason. Philosophers, like the average beholder himself, have long been aware of the fact that certain individuals within any given species or class of things, whether natural or artificial, are more beautiful than others. Epictetus maintained, for example, that "in

---

[23] E.g., Aristotle(?), *Problem.* X, 52, 896b 12–13; Augustine, *De ver. rel.* 36, 67; 41, 77; *De nat. boni*, cc. 5, 15; *Conf.* XII, 28, 39 (*PL* 34, 152, 157; 42, 553, 555; 32, 842); Albert, *S. theol.* II, 11, 62, 2, ad q.2 (32, 603); Thomas, *In Symb. Ap.*, art. 1, 878; *De div. nom.* 4, 5, 339; 345; 349; *In II. Sent.* 34, 1, 1, sol.; *Comp. theol.* c. 102, n. 201; *De malo*, 2, 9c; John Ruskin, *Modern Painters*, I, sect. 1, ch. 6, § 6 (New York: Merrill and Baker, n.d.), 28; etc.

[24] In Plato, *Hipp. mai.* 289a. Cf. *ibid.*, 289b.

[25] Plato, *Hipp. mai.* 289b.

[26] Plotinus, *Enn.* VI, 3, 11; Augustine, *De nat. boni*, c. 14 (*PL* 42, 555). Cf. also *Conf.* XII, 2, 2; 6, 6 (*PL* 32, 827, 828).

every class of creatures nature produces some outstanding individual,"[27] and Plato pointed out that individual bees differ in beauty.[28] This is the objective basis of the psychological fact that the more and the more beautiful individuals a given person saw in any given species or class of things, the more likely he would compare the presently-beheld individual with those individuals of the same species which (individuals) he experienced before, and the more likely he would reject it as not beautiful just because it did not measure up to those objects which he had experienced and enjoyed in the past. Hume was fully aware of this fact, for he wrote, "[a] great inferiority of beauty gives pain to a person conversant in the highest excellence of the kind, and is for that reason pronounced a deformity."[29] Indeed, he who admired the beauty of mountain lakes, like Königsee in the Bavarian Alps, the Vierwaldstätter Sea in the Swiss Alps at Lucern, or Jerry Lake in the Grand Teton National Park of Wyoming, because they are surrounded not only with forests but also with high mountains with snowcovered peaks, will find it difficult to enjoy the lakes of flatlands, like those in Oklahoma, Minnesota, or Ontario, as long as he keeps on comparing the former with the latter. Similarly, he who was profoundly touched by the Gothic cathedrals of Reims, Cologne, Chartres, or Toledo, will hardly be capable of subsequently enjoying third-rate Gothic imitations in towns and cities anywhere. He who has listened to the Berlin or New York Philharmonics under the baton of a Toscanini or Bruno Walter; he who has watched Galli-Curci, Gigli, Shaliapin or Maria Callas sing operas; Nijinsky or Anna Pavlova dance classic ballets; Yehudi Menuhin or Jascha Heifetz play Beethoven, Brahms, or Tchaikovsky violin concertos; will most probably reject the same works being conducted, performed, and played, respectively, by student artists at a small country college. In contrast, those who never have had any great previous experiences with such things, may naturally enjoy almost anything, even slightly beautiful. Thereby, the situation of aesthetic disagreement has arisen.

7. The situation constituting *Reason 13* for aesthetic disagreement is the following. It is a well-known fact that an object may be very beautiful and yet may happen to be in an environment that is aesthetically quite disproportionate. As a consequence of this, such an object may look less beautiful or even ugly when considered in the light of or in reference to its disproportionate environment. Heraclitus' way of putting this was that "the most beautiful of pots is ugly when grouped together with maidens."[30] Plato declared that even a beautiful stone can look ugly if it is out of place in respect to its surroundings, and

---

[27] *Discourses of Epictetus*, III, 1.
[28] Plato, *Meno* 72b.
[29] Hume, "Of the Standard of Taste," ed. cit., p. 276. Cf., Augustine, *Conf.* XII, 6, 6 (*PL* 32, 828).
[30] In Plato, *Hipp. mai.* 289a.

that "gold and ivory ... when they are appropriate, render things beautiful; and when they are not appropriate, ugly."[81] Aquinas, on his part, points out that "the home of a lord looks better in the city than in the country."[82] Lord Kames even goes so far as to admit that "a thing beautiful itself, may, with relation to other things, produce the strongest sense of incongruity," and, as examples for both suitable and unsuitable environment, he cites the following: "Every ornament upon a shield should relate to war; and Virgil, with great judgment, confines the carvings upon the shield of Aeneas to the military history of the Romans: that beauty is overlooked by Homer, for the bulk of the sculpture upon the shield of Achilles is of the arts of peace in general, and of joy and fertility in particular."[83] As a matter of fact, it is not difficult to find many examples for both suitable and unsuitable environment of beautiful things. Both the Strasbourg cathedral and St. Patrick's in New York are, for instance, in themselves beautiful Gothic artworks. While, however, the former is in a very suitable environment, on the top of a hill, and much higher than anything nearby, the latter is completely dwarfed and frustrated in its tendency to rise to lofty heights by the skyscrapers across from it and nearby. Similarly, one may have a very beautiful French provincial livingroom set and also an exquisite Spanish livingroom table; yet, it would look very strange, to say the least, if he placed that table so as to be surrounded by the French provincial chairs and sofa. Also, it would be an aesthetic monstrosity to fill a high-Gothic cathedral with baroque statues or, even worse, baroque paintings.

If two beholders viewed this kind of stylistic mixture: one who considers the unsuitable parts in relation to each other, and another person who considers the parts of different styles unrelated to each other; then the former beholder would be aesthetically highly displeased by that "composition," and the latter would be pleased by the components. Thereby, a classic case of aesthetic disagreement would arise.

B. Non-Aesthetic Defects

1. There are altogether seven non-aesthetic defects in or connected with the aesthetic object that can be reasons for real aesthetic disagreement. Of these the first three, listed as *Reasons 14, 15,* and 16 for aesthetic disagreement have a common analogous basis, viz., that every human sense, such as vision and

---

[81] Plato, *Hipp. mai.* 290cd. Cf. Plotinus, *Enn.* I, 6, 5.

[82] Thomas, *In Psalm.* 18, 3. Cf. also *De div. nom.* 4, 2, 301, and the Basil-quotation in *Cat. aur. in Lucam*, 3, 3. William of Auvergne complements this example taken from the world of art by stressing the ugliness of the eye that, although beautiful in itself, is in the place of the ear or in the middle of someone's face. (*Op. cit.*, Oxford Balliol 287, fol. 2v; Balliol 207, fol. 206vb; *ed. cit.*, p. 245.) G. E. Mueller unwittingly wrote a striking paraphrase to this observation by remarking that the ugly is "a beauty in a wrong place." "Style," *The Journal of Aesthetics and Art Criticism*, I, 2/3 (Fall, 1941), 121.

[83] Lord Kames, *op. cit.*, chap. 10, nn. 285, 288; pp. 186, 187.

hearing, is "a certain ratio."[34] This is to say, the sense "takes delight in proportioned objects as they are similar to it,"[35] whereas it is displeased or even pained by objects of disproportioned size and volume, i.e., objects lacking proportion to the eye or ear. Augustine refers to this fact when he states, "We do not like listening to whisper."[36] Thus, an object that is too small in size, even though beautiful in itself, may not be recognized as beautiful by some people: "Beauty is ... impossible," remarks Aristotle, "... in a very minute creature, since our perception becomes indistinct as it arises in an almost imperceivable length of time."[37] Similarly, even a very beautiful tone or voice, if too soft, like the pianissimos in certain musical compositions; or if too loud, as Wagner's music is often accused to be, may not please some listeners, because they cannot hear it without undue effort or because they are hurt by its excessive volume.[38] At the same time some people, who have better vision, may have no difficulty in clearly seeing the small-sized aesthetic object, like the miniature portrait medallions so popular in certain European countries in the seventeenth and eighteenth centuries, or the miniature book illustrations in Persia and India. Likewise, some listeners who have better hearing or who are less sensitive to loud sounds may find very soft or very loud music quite enjoyable. In both kinds of cases, those whose sense organs are more or less sensitive, will tend to disagree with those whose vision and/or hearing is less perfect (or more sensitive).

2. Closely related, since of the same physiological basis as Reasons 14 and 15, is the case of *Reason 16* for aesthetic disagreement, namely, lack of suitable distance. Since our vision and hearing demand a proportionate object, any object which, although of moderate size or volume, is perceived from too great a distance, can fail to be perceived distinctly enough so as to please the beholder with its beauty.[39] Both ancient and modern aestheticians have recognized this fact. Plotinus, for instance, stated that colors "seen from a distance are faint";[40] and Kant remarked that "beautiful objects are to be distinguished from beautiful views of objects (which often on account of their distance cannot be clearly recognized)."[41] Now if one observer contemplates an aesthetic object from the proper distance, whereas another observer does so from too far away (or even

---

[34] Aristotle, *De an.* II, 12, 424a 28. For the same on hearing, see *ibid.*, III, 2, 426a 29f. Cf., Thomas, *In II. De an.* 24, 555; and *In III. De an.* 2, 598.
[35] Thomas, *S. theol.* I, 5, 4, ad 1. Cf. Bonaventure, *Itin.* II, 5(V, 300b, 301a).
[36] Augustine, *De mus.* VI, 13, 38 (*PL* 32, 1184).
[37] Aristotle, *Poet.* VII, 4, 1450b 36–39. See also Witelo, *Perspectiva*, IV, 150 (4) in Clemens Baeumker, *Witelo, ein Philosoph und Naturforscher des XIII. Jahrhunderts* (Münster: Aschendorffscher Verlag, 1908), 176f.
[38] Cf. Thomas, *In II. De an.* L. 21; ed. A. M. Pirotta (Taurini: Marietti, 1959), n. 509. For a visual example, see Witelo, *op. cit.* IV, 150 (2); *ed. cit.*, p. 176.
[39] Cf. Thomas, *In III. De an.* 6, 663.
[40] Plotinus, *Enn.* II, 8, 1.
[41] Kant, *Critique of Judgment*, § 22, *ed. cit.*, p. 100.

from too close a range), the former will enjoy what the latter fails to enjoy, and thus the two will probably disagree on the beauty of that object.

3. Lack of proportionate amount of light, as *Reason 17* for aesthetic disagreement, is partly related to the above-discussed three reasons. For, as is commonly known, there is no vision possible without light; on the other hand, on the basis of the above discussed physiological principle of proportionality, it is not enough simply to have light; but it is also necessary that we should have a proportionate amount of light by which to see the object we want or need to see. "We do not want to see objects which are too obscure" (Augustine),[42] just as we do not want to see them in glaring light. Michelangelo confirms this in an interesting letter to Benvenuto Cellini, the great sculptor: "Messer Buido Altoviti took me to see his bust in bronze . . . I liked it very much, but I was sorry to see it exhibited in a bad light. If it had proper lighting, one would really see what a beautiful piece of work it is."[43] Some beholders may not be so perceptive or fortunate as Michelangelo was with that Cellini-made bust; in a poor light they may not notice the beauty of an artwork or a natural scene at all. This may be quite true of many of the visitors to such great museums of art as the Prado or those in Florence, where the lighting is quite inadequate (unlike such art museums as the *Alte Pinakothek* in Munich, the Art-Historical Museum of Vienna, or the Glyptothek in Copenhagen). As a consequence of this, those who see a beautiful place or artwork in poor light and, therefore, fail to enjoy it or enjoy it only a little will inevitably disagree with those people who are fortunate enough to see the same place or artwork in the proper light. C. I. Lewis has implied a second way, opposite to the one above in which Michelangelo became involved, in which poor light may lead to aesthetic disagreement: "We may momentarily like a picture because it is hung in a poor light which obscures its bad drawing or its crude colors. In so liking it, we may be as mistaken about the objective value of it as about the relation of its lines or the quality of its coloring."[44] For, if the same picture is beheld by one in good light, he may easily discover its defects in drawing and coloring, and thus disagree with the one who saw the painting in a poor light.

A similar situation may arise conversely, with some people beholding the aesthetic object in glaring, excessive light; others, in the proper light. When, for instance, the ballet, *Concerto in E Minor*, (music by Chopin, choreography by Bronislava Nijinska) was performed by Olga Slawska and the *corps de ballet* of the Polish Ballet at the Hall of Music, World's Fair Grounds, New York, in 1939, it was favorably received neither by the critics nor by the general audiences. One of the obvious reasons for this was an overlarge auditorium,

[42] Augustine, *De mus.* VI, 13, 38 (PL 32, 1184). See also Witelo, *op. cit.*, IV, 150 (1); *ed. cit.*, p. 176.

[43] Rome, 1552. English translation in *I, Michelangelo, Sculptor*, Irving and Jean Stone eds. (New York: The New American Library, 1964), 205.

[44] C. I. Lewis, *op. cit.*, p. 411.

causing disproportionate distance from the stage; and another reason was that the stage had footlights so high that they hid the feet of the dancers. A revised version of this ballet, performed at the Metropolitan in 1942, that did not suffer from these visual defects, was highly praised.[45] Evidently both too little and too much light can lead to aesthetic disagreement among critics and laymen, as well.

4. Another partly objective and partly subjective reason for aesthetic disagreement consists generically in some disproportion between the aesthetic object and the mental capacity of the person trying to behold and enjoy it, this disproportion being due not to the inferiority of the person involved but rather to some excess in the objective qualities of the aesthetic object.

Reason 18 specifically involves the excessive size or the unusually large number of parts of the aesthetic object that renders the average beholder unable to see all the details of it simultaneously. Thereby, he will see only parts and their beauty, but not the whole object and its beauty. An interesting instance of this fact is asserted by Carl Lemcke, namely, that we shudder at the sight of a moving centipede because we cannot see the motion of its numerous legs as an orderly whole.[46] This disproportion is the drawback of some very high or very bulky architectural works, and even with some paintings that are so long that one has to walk along them to see them in their entirety.

Reason 19 is an analogate of the one just mentioned. It consists in a disproportion between object and beholder due to the extreme length of the former. Obviously some novels, plays, operas, etc., are so lengthy that they violate the principle of mental proportionality expressed by Aristotle this way: "A beautiful whole ... must be of ... a length to be kept in the memory."[47] Thereby, the average beholder will indeed fail to keep in mind all the parts of such lengthy objects, and will not be able to see or enjoy them as wholes but only parts of them.

Similar is the case with *Reason 20*. Some aesthetic objects represent such a complex order that they transcend the mental capacity of the average beholder; thus, he will be unable to take delight in them. Shaftesbury, speaking of certain things "which the vulgar understand not," mentions "in music the chromatic kind," and "a skilful mixture of dissonances" as instances of rather complex aesthetic orders.[48] Bernard Bosanquet's opinion is very similar to Shaftesbury's, namely, that in music "the failure of appreciation is often simply the inability to follow a construction which possesses intricacy beyond a certain degree."[49]

---

[45] Grace Robert, *op. cit.*, p. 80.
[46] C. Lemcke, *op. cit.*, p. 52.
[47] Aristotle, *Poet.* VII, 4, 1451a 1–6. Cf. Thomas, *De ver.* 26, 5c.
[48] Lord Shaftesbury, "The Moralist," part III, section 2, in *Characteristics*, II, ed. J. M. Robertson (Indianapolis: The Bobbs-Merrill Co., 1964), 130.
[49] B. Bosanquet, *Three Lectures on Aesthetics*, p. 47.

Indeed, there are musical compositions, old and new, that go far beyond the intelligibility by the average listener, such as some baroque polyphonic music employing eight, twelve, sixteen, or even more parts, or the rebellion scene in D. Milhaud's opera, *Cristopher Colombo*, employing seven different keys simultaneously.

How do extraordinarily large size, extreme length, and too great complexity of order lead to aesthetic disagreement? By the simple fact that some, namely, some extraordinary, beholders may comprehend and follow objects despite their extraordinary size, length, or complexity and, for this reason, they will disagree with the average people who cannot grasp and enjoy such objects.

ARTICLE 3: *Completely Subjective Reasons for Real Disagreement*

Of the completely subjective reasons for real aesthetic disagreement, let us discuss first the two individual inabilities to recognize aesthetic defects. Next, we will take up the temporary inabilities and, finally, the habitual inabilities to recognize beauty as being reasons for real aesthetic disagreement.

A. Inabilities to Recognize Aesthetic Defects

1. *Reason 21* for aesthetic disagreement represents the following situation. There is an aesthetic object with more or less obvious aesthetic defects. On the other hand, there is a beholder who is emotionally involved either with the aesthetic object itself or with the maker of the artwork in question. His imagination will beautify and glorify the object in question, and, consequently, he will tend to overlook the defects of the aesthetic object or to overestimate its actual beauty.

Ancient thinkers and aestheticians, like Epicurus, Horace, Cicero, Quintilian, and St. Jerome noticed this fact.[1] In the Middle Ages Aquinas expressed the same fact in more generic terms: "Predisposed by passion, a person judges something to be convenient and good—a thing which he would not judge so without passion," and, "To the lover, the things he loves seem to be better."[2] Virgil C. Aldrich speaks of this in the following way: "[You] fall in love with things and find them beautiful."[3] But it is Thomas Brown who expresses this truth in concrete terms by remarking, "The hill and the waterfall may be pleasing to every eye; but how doubly beautiful do they seem to the very heart of the expatriated Swiss who almost looks as he gazes on them, for the cottage

---

[1] Epicurus, *Fragments*, fragment 61 (*The Stoic and Epicurean Philosophers. The Complete Extant Writings of Epicurus, Epictetus, Lucretius, Marcus Aurelius*. Ed. Whitney J. Oatis. New York: The Modern Library, 1940, p. 43). Q. Horatius Flaccus, *Satirarum* I, 3, 38–40 (amatorem quod amicae—Turpia decipiunt caecum vitia, aut etiam ipsa haec—Delectant). M. T. Cicero, *De nat. deorum*, I, 28, 79. M. F. Quintilian, *Institutio oratoria*, VI, 2, 6. St. Jerome (Hieronymus), *Commentarius in Osee*, lib. III, prooem. ("amantium caeca iudicia sunt"; *PL* 25, 905 A). Cf. Thomas, *S. theol.* I–II, 27, 2, ad 2; 9, 2c.

[2] Thomas, *S. theol.* I–II, 10, 3c; 44, 2c.

[3] V. C. Aldrich, *Philosophy of Art* (Englewood Cliffs, N. Y.: Prentice Hall, 1963), 100.

of his house, half-gleaming through the spray, as if they were the very hill and the waterfall which had been the haunt of his youth."[4]

The classic instance of this favorable emotional prejudice is the mother to whom her child looks quite beautiful just because he is her child, even though he is actually not too beautiful. Other instances of this situation are the friends and relatives of an artist who find his music, singing, composition, painting, or film performance extremely beautiful and delightful despite certain flaws in his work, or simply, anyone who is somewhat familiar with an aesthetic object.[5] It is very easy to see how this emotional prejudice can be the source of aesthetic disagreement among people. For, just because it is through the imagination that the emotionally involved person tends to overlook aesthetic defects and to overestimate the beauty that is in the object, those whose emotions do not activate their imagination to do a "decorating job" will fail to take delight in the aesthetically defective object or to estimate it as highly as the emotionally prejudiced beholders do. For this reason the prejudiced and the unprejudiced beholders are prone to disagree.

2. *Reason 22* for aesthetic disagreement is somewhat similar to the one discussed above. While in the above situation it is love that activates the imagination to make one see an object as more beautiful than it is or to have its defects unnoticed, in the situation in question it is something in the aesthetic object itself that triggers the beautifying activity of the imagination. This something is any aspect or quality of the aesthetic object that may elicit pleasant associations in a given beholder; such as warm childhood memories in connection with the countryside one revisits and beholds again after many years of absence; or the memories of wonderful childhood Christmas seasons upon hearing the Christmas carols usually sung in that area; or the memories one may recall about a certain country which he visited in the past, upon hearing folk tunes of that country being played or sung. Undoubtedly the same countryside may not at all impress one who has no ties to it; the Christmas carols of one land do not sound so sweet and charming in the ears of a foreigner who has no memories of that land; and nobody finds the national music of a country so touchingly and heart-rendingly beautiful as one who used to live in that country but was forced to leave it. Thus in all these and similar instances aesthetic disagreement between those who have pleasant associations with an aesthetic object and those who do not have them is more or less inevitable.

B. Temporary Inabilities to Recognize Beauty

Let us first discuss the three temporary inabilities at the sensory level to recognize beauty.

1. The psychological background to *Reason 23* (just as to *Reason 28*, an

---

[4] Thomas Brown, *op. cit.*, lecture 55 (II, 33).
[5] E. H. Griggs, *The Philosophy of Art* (New York: B. W. Huebsch, 1913), 292.

habitual inability) is concisely summed up by Thomas in the following passage: "We should further understand that delight is engendered by the apprehension of a suitable good. Thus sight rejoices in beautiful colors, and taste in sweet savors. But this delight of the senses can be prevented if the organ is indisposed; the same light that is charming to healthy eyes is annoying to sore eyes."[6] This idea is complemented by Richard Payne Knight when he points out that "there are persons whose eyes have naturally a sort of morbid irritability which renders those degrees of light and modification of colour which are merely sufficient to be pleasant to others, quite painful to them."[7] What is the aesthetic significance of this fact? Simply, those who do not suffer from either temporary or chronic malfunction or disease of the eye or the ear will take delight in seeing or hearing the same object which will be painful to a person suffering from some such malfunction or disease. As Augustine put it, the "very light which is so pleasant to them, disagrees with and hurts weak eyes."[8] In this manner, the situation of aesthetic disagreement is given.

2. Closely similar to these two is another reason for aesthetic disagreement (*Reason 24*). The generic psychological background to this is expressed by Aquinas as follows: "Physical pain strongly attracts the attention of the mind ... For this reason, if the pain is intensive, man is prevented from perceiving anything else."[9] Indeed, anyone who is sick or ill and anyone who suffers from any kind of pain may become unable to concentrate on the aesthetic object and, thereby, to enjoy its beauty; or, to use Thomas' words again, "bodily pain interferes more with contemplation, that requires total quiet, than the pain of the mind does."[10] Therefore, whenever two people are confronted with the same aesthetic object in such a way that one is in pain and the other is not, the latter will be able to enjoy that object, whereas the former probably will not; thus, the two will probably disagree on its beauty.

3. Disproportionate mood, as *Reason 25* for aesthetic disagreement, can be explained in the following manner. Whether or not it is due to the fact that the prevalent mood demands so much attention to its proportionate object that it prevents us from concentrating on other objects,[11] it is an empirical fact that, while being in a gay mood, we simply cannot enjoy and appreciate an aesthetic object that is apt to engender sad emotions in us, and vice versa. Archibald Alison states this truth in these words: "To a man under some present impression of joy, we should not venture to appeal with regard to the Beauty of any

[6] Thomas, *Compendium theologiae*, part 1, ch. 165; tr. Cyril Vollert, *Compendium of Theology by St. Thomas Aquinas* (St. Louis: B. Herder, 1952), 176. Cf. *De sensu et sensato*, I, 17. Shortsightedness as an habitual inability is listed among reasons for aesthetic disagreement called "error" in Witelo, *op. cit.*, IV, 150 (8); *ed. cit.*, p. 177.

[7] R. P. Knight, *An Analytical Inquiry into the Principles of Taste*, I, 5, 10; *ed. cit.*, p. 64.

[8] Augustine, *De civ. Dei*, XII, 4 (PL 41, 352).

[9] Thomas, *S. theol.* I–II, 37, 1c.

[10] *Ibid.*, art. 1, ad 3.

[11] Thomas, *In III. Eth.* 22, 637; *S. theol.* I–II, 39, 3, ad 3; 33, 3, ad 2.

melancholy or pathetic composition; to a man under the dominion of sorrow, we should much less presume to present even the most beautiful composition, which contained only images of joy."[12] Spinoza touches on the same truth more concretely when stating that "music is good for him that is melancholy; bad for him that mourns."[13] In fact, as we know from our own experience, even if the greatest orchestra played the most beautiful of all *requiems*, let us say, that by Mozart or Verdi or Brahms, to a happy bride, she might be unable to enjoy it. Conversely, it would be futile to play the records of such compositions as Franz Liszt's *Second Hungarian Rhapsody* or Brahms' *Hungarian Dances* for someone who is saddened by the death of a beloved one; for he would be annoyed rather than delighted by those or similar works. Similarly, he who is depressed will not be the proper beholder of a comedy; and he who is happy may reject even a great tragedy performed in the theater. From this it follows that whenever two persons of opposite sentiments or moods listen to gay or sad music, or read a novel or watch the performance of a play that is comical or tragically sad in its generic character, one of the two persons will take delight in that artwork, whereas the other will most probably be displeased by it, and thus the two will most likely disagree on the beauty of that artwork.

4. The next two reasons for aesthetic disagreement, *Reasons 26 and 27*, both being inabilities at the *rational* level to recognize beauty, are closely related, and work in an almost identical manner. For inattention here means simply the lack of attention necessary for the recognition and the enjoyment of beauty, whereas distraction is the lack of attention with respect to an aesthetic object due to the fact that one's attention is concentrated on another object.

Both inattention and distraction are possible sources of aesthetic disagreement for the same two psychological reasons. One of these reasons is that generally there is no aesthetic knowledge or enjoyment possible without considerable concentration on the beautiful object. "A perfect serenity of the mind," observes Hume, "a recollection of thought, a due attention to the object; if any of these circumstances be wanting, ... we shall be unable to judge of the catholic and universal beauty."[14] The correlated second reason, on the other hand, is that, while we concentrate on one object, we cannot concentrate also on another. "In the works of the soul," remarks Aquinas, "certain attention is required which, while being strongly turned to one object, cannot strongly be turned to another."[15]

Every time that one does not pay enough attention to an aesthetic object, he will derive little, if any, delight from it. This is why those who employ what is

---

[12] A. Alison, *op. cit.*, Essay I, ch. 2, section 2; ed. Abraham Mills (New York: Harper and Brothers, 1858), 80.
[13] Spinoza, *Ethics*, part IV, preface; *ed. cit.*, p. 191.
[14] Hume, "Of the Standard of Taste," *ed. cit.*, p. 271.
[15] Thomas, *S. theol.* I–II, 77, 1c. Cf., *ibid.*, 4, 1, ad 3.

called "background music" may have their nerves soothed by it, but will only occasionally, for fleeting moments, notice and enjoy its beauty. Similarly, every time that one's attention is preoccupied with and distracted by an object, aesthetic or non-aesthetic, he will either take little notice or will fail to notice at all another object's beauty physically present to him. One such distraction may be sorrow;[16] another, pleasure: "Corporeal pleasures interfere with the use of the intellect in three ways. First of all, by virtue of distraction. For ... we attend much to those things in which we take delight, and whenever our attention is directed strongly to one thing, it is either weakened concerning other things or totally diverted from them."[17] Those, for instance, who go to an opera house to see the newest trends in the ladies' fashion, and keep on focusing their opera glasses throughout the performance on the fur coats and gowns worn by the ladies, will experience very little aesthetic delight stemming from the opera, although they may enjoy the evening otherwise.

Applying all this to our topic of aesthetic disagreement, we may conclude: those who do not pay enough attention to or are distracted from an aesthetic object will find little enjoyment in the beauty of that object, and will consequently tend to disagree with those persons who do pay sufficient attention to that aesthetic object.

C. Habitual Inabilities to Recognize Beauty

Let us treat first the *sensory* kinds of habitual inabilities to recognize beauty. Since, from the aesthetic point of view, it makes little difference whether the malfunction of a sense organ is temporary or chronic (habitual), and since we already discussed above (in connection with *Reason 23*) how such a malfunction can lead to aesthetic disagreement, we can omit here the discussion of *Reason 28*, and begin immediately with *Reason 29*, i.e., unpleasant associations as causing aesthetic disagreement.

1. As is well known, association is an act mentally connecting the presently beheld object with something else previously experienced. In terms of its basis, association can be objective or subjective, that is, based upon and caused by some actual similarity or causal relation between two things, or based upon and due to some accidental connection in space and/or time in which two things were experienced by a person. Both types of association can play some aesthetic role in respect to the recognition and appreciation of beauty.

The objective type of association that is based on objective similarity can play the role of preventing virtually everybody from properly enjoying and appreciating the beauty of certain things, due to one of two possible facts. One of these facts is the possibility that a given thing resembles an ugly, unpleasant, or harmful thing. Snakes, roaches, spiders, and other such things, for example,

[16] Cf. Thomas, *In III. Eth.* 22, 637.
[17] Thomas, *S. theol.* I–II, 33, 3c.

have their own beauty, but they almost invariably remind us of danger, poison, illness, suffering, or even death and, for this reason, only a few people are capable of recognizing their beauty. That the almost universal aesthetic rejection of such things is due to unpleasant association can be best illustrated by the fact that those people, mostly scientists and their assistants, who are professionally concerned with things like those listed above, and who succeed in considering such things objectively, without any unpleasant association, do actually find those things beautiful. Herbert Ellsworth Cory, who was a scientist before becoming a philosopher of beauty, confirmed this fact in the following words: "If I look at a dead, rotting body as a human body—which it is not—I do not find it beautiful. But I learned a long time ago in the laboratories of the Johns Hopkins University, to discern in the chemical changes of physiological disintegration, in the wonderful purifying work of the saprophytic bacteria, the emergence of a multitude of simple but unimpeachably beautiful entities."[18]

The other fact that can cause objective and more or less universal association and, through it, hindrance to recognizing the beauty of a thing is that an object may resemble a much more beautiful thing, but not in respect to beauty; and therefore its inferior beauty will appear as ugliness in the light of the great or greater beauty of the thing associated with it. Cicero quotes Ennius as one who had already realized that the ape, precisely because it resembles man so much, appears to us as the ugliest of all beasts.[19] The nineteenth-century art critic, Sully-Prudhomme, concurs with Ennius completely: "To know really whether there are ugly monkeys we should consult a monkey; for the beauty we unconsciously look for, and certainly do not find, in the monkey, is the beauty of the human form; and when we declare the monkey ugly, what we really mean is that it would be ugly if it were a human being; which is undeniable."[20]

Neither one of these two versions of objective association can cause much aesthetic disagreement because both are more or less universal, affecting virtually everybody's imagination. However, the situation is different with subjective associations. Their basis is nothing intrinsic to things or naturally connected with things, as similarity or causality is, but rather a merely incidental spatial or chronological connection. On account of this not only is it true that, as F. Hutcheson put it, "many don't admire what is beautiful,"[21] but also that many people disagree with others on the beauty of certain things. This latter aesthetic role of subjective associations can come about as follows. It sometimes

[18] H. E. Cory, *The Significance of Beauty in Nature and Art* (Milwaukee: Bruce, 1947), 180f.
[19] Cicero, *De nat. deor.* I, 35, 97.
[20] R. F. Sully-Prudhomme, *L'Expression dans le beaux arts*, quoted in Desiré F. F. J. Mercier, *A Manual of Modern Scholastic Philosophy*, I: *General Metaphysics*; T. L. and S. A. Parker, trs. (St. Louis: B. Herder, 1932), 595.
[21] F. Hutcheson, *Enquiry into the Original of Our Ideas of Beauty and Virtue*, treatise 1, sect. 6. (London: Ware, Knapton, Longman, 1753), 71–84.

just so happens that a person receives some bad news or experiences something very painful or unpleasant while beholding an aesthetic object. As a result of this, he may subsequently for a long time associate that beautiful object with that painful event or experience and, thereby, remain completely unable to enjoy that object. Instead, he will find it unpleasant or even repulsive.[22] A very sad but excellent example of this condition is that late professor at a state university who loved to listen to Beethoven's works, but suddenly came to hate one of his symphonies because while listening to it he was notified of the sudden and tragic death of his wife. Descartes must have had this sort of association in mind when stating, "What makes one dance, makes another weep, because esthetic preference depends much on casual association."[23]

Since this kind of connection between the aesthetic object and the unpleasant thing associated with it has nothing to do with the objective nature or qualities of the beautiful thing, and consequently the association is confined completely to individual persons, it is easy to see how a person with such completely subjective associations is very likely to disagree on the beauty of certain objects with other beholders not suffering from unpleasant associations.

2. Closely connected with this reason for aesthetic disagreement, if not simply a species or border case of it, is *Reason 30*, namely, what we may term lack of psychical distance. The classic author on the topic of psychical distance, Edward Bullough, characterizes this notion by describing how it can be brought about: "[This distance] is obtained by separating the object and its appeal from one's own self, by putting it out of gear with practical needs and ends."[24] Psychical distance is thus a requirement of the enjoyableness of the aesthetic object, affecting both the aesthetic object (negatively), and the aesthetic subject, the beholder (positively). It demands of the aesthetic object to be removed from or to be outside the realm of the beholder's practical considerations and uses. At the same time, it demands of the aesthetic subject to be ready for, interested in, and personally concerned with the aesthetic object. The result of this double requirement is what Bullough calls the "antinomy of Distance": the need for distance without too much of it (or else the aesthetic object will be completely removed from the personal concern of the beholder), and the need for personal concern without destroying the distance (or else the aesthetic object will be considered practically and pragmatically by the beholder); or, in brief, "the utmost decrease of Distance without its disappearance."[25]

Now, since we are interested presently in the completely subjective reasons

---

[22] Cf. Aquinas, *S. theol.* I–II, 77, 1c; and *De ver.* 26, 4, ad 7.

[23] Descartes, Letter to Père Mersenne of March 18, 1630; in *Oeuvres et Lettres, ed. cit.*, p. 925.

[24] E. Bullough, "'Psychical Distance' As a Factor in Art and An Esthetic Principle," in *A Modern Book of Esthetics*, ed. Melvin Rader (New York: Henry Holt, 1952), 405.

[25] *Op. cit.*, pp. 407 and 409, respectively.

for aesthetic disagreement, we need to consider here only the case in which the aesthetic subject fails to conform on his part to the antinomy of psychical distance. Every time a beholder gives up this psychical distance from the aesthetic object for some reason rooted in himself or in his life, that is, every time he considers that beautiful object in a practical-utilitarian rather than a merely intellectual-speculative manner, that beholder may become very emotional about the aesthetic object, perhaps more emotional than another beholder who retains the psychical distance; yet, he will not experience any aesthetic delight. What happens in such a case is that, as Georg Mehlis put it, "beauty is destroyed by non-observance of distance."[26]

Bullough describes such a case as follows: "Suppose a man who believes that he has cause to be jealous about his wife, witnesses a performance of Othello. He will the more perfectly appreciate the situation, conduct and character of Othello, the more exactly his feelings and experiences of Othello coincide with his own—at least he *ought* to on the above principle of concordance. In point of fact, he will probably do anything but appreciate the play. In reality, the concordance will merely render him acutely conscious of his own jealousy; by a sudden reversal of perspective he will no longer see Othello apparently betrayed by Desdemona, but himself in an analogous situation with his own wife. This reversal of perspective is the consequence of the loss of Distance."[27] Many other examples can be cited for the need of psychical distance to have aesthetic experience. Anyone, for instance, who personally suffered in World War II may find it difficult to enjoy a film about the war, even if it has a great screenplay, cast, director, and photographer. Similarly, any novel, film, or drama dealing with the tragic fate of a great person, like the Columbia-film, *The Cardinal* (1963, starring Tom Tryon, and produced and directed by Otto Preminger), will be difficult to enjoy for him to whom that tragic fate is not a matter of objective history merely but mainly a painful past event personally experienced.

The relevance of all this to aesthetic disagreement is quite clear. Take two observers of the same aesthetic object, and suppose that one of them maintains the necessary psychical distance for aesthetic enjoyment, while the other does not. In that case, the former will enjoy the aesthetic object, while the latter will not, and thus the two will disagree on the beauty of the object which they both beheld.

3. *Reason 31* for aesthetic disagreement is analogous to Reason 21. The identical aspect in both is the emotional prejudice that favorably predisposes the beholder. The difference between the two reasons, however, is equally obvious. For in Reason 21, the aesthetic object is defectively beautiful, and this defect is

---

[26] G. Mehlis, "The Aesthetic Problem of Distance," in *Reflections on Art*, ed. Susan K. Langer (New York: Oxford University Press, 1961), 83.
[27] Bullough, *art. cit.*, p. 408.

overlooked by the prejudiced beholder; in the present reason, on the other hand, the aesthetic object does not have any imperfections to be overlooked. Instead, the only requirement is to have a person who is emotionally prejudiced, either favorably or unfavorably. For, as Thomas Aquinas put it, the sense appetite (one's emotionality) "very powerfully predisposes man in such a way that something will appear to him this way or that way;"[28] and, as Hume expressed himself on this question, the art critic "must preserve his mind free from all prejudice, and allow nothing to enter into his consideration, but the very object which is submitted to his examination."[29]

Should prejudice enter into a beholder's consideration, one of these three things can happen: (1) Whenever some unprejudiced and some favorably prejudiced persons view an aesthetic object, the latter will find it *more* beautiful than the former. Thus, of a team of dancers, all performing the same dance, for instance, a naturally prejudiced group of beholders, like parents, relatives, or friends, will find their child, relative, or friend performs more beautifully than the others. (2) Whenever some unprejudiced and some unfavorably prejudiced persons behold the same beautiful object, the latter will find it *less* beautiful than the former. Finally, (3) Whenever some favorably prejudiced and some unfavorably prejudiced people consider the same aesthetic object, the former will find it *more* beautiful than the latter, or they alone will find it beautiful. Reason 31 can thus account for aesthetic disagreement in three different ways.

4. *Reason 32* for aesthetic disagreement involves unsuitable temperament as its principle. Whatever the specific disagreements about temperament in premodern psychology, the following points seem to be certain. Firstly, temperament is a relatively permanent factor of the personality and strongly influences human behavior. Secondly, there are contrary opposites in temperament with respect to the speed or facility and the duration of physical and/or emotional reaction to motivations. Thirdly, and most important to us here, the contrarily opposite reactions due to temperament include positive and negative or favorable and unfavorable emotional and intellectual reactions to aesthetic objects. The reason for this last fact is obvious: there is favorable reaction to an aesthetic object only if there is similarity between the specific nature of that object and of the temperament of the beholder. "A young man," observed Hume, "whose passions are warm, will be more sensibly touched with amorous and tender images, than a man more advanced in years . . . . At twenty, Ovid may be the favorite author, Horace at forty, and perhaps Tacitus at fifty . . . . We choose our favorite author as we do our friend, from a conformity of humor and disposition."[30]

---

[28] Thomas, *S. theol.* I–II, 9, 2, ad 2.
[29] Hume, "Of the Standard of Taste," *ed. cit.*, p. 276.
[30] Hume, *op. cit.*, p. 281.

Indeed, a melancholic person will very likely prefer Chopin's nocturnes and etudes to his mazurkas and polonaises, whereas a person of sanguine temperament will prefer mazurkas and polonaises. Similarly, the melancholic person will probably favor romantic music, like Schumann's, Mendelssohn's or Grieg's piano compositions or songs, and operas like Bellini's *Norma*, Wagner's *Lohengrin*, and Puccinis's *La Bohème* and *Madame Butterfly*, while a sanguine person will rather listen to compositions by Liszt, Berlioz, Maurice Ravel, or Bartók, and to operas like Verdi's *Aida*, Bizet's *Carmen*, and Leoncavallo's *Pagliacci*. One may even suspect that a choleric will love such works as Beethoven's *Fidelio*, Wagner's *Meistersinger*, Mussorgsky's *Boris Godunov*, and some Stravinsky, rather than the favorites of the melancholic.

Now, all that is needed for aesthetic disagreement is to have people with different temperaments listen to music suiting only one kind of temperament. For instance, if a sanguine or a choleric and a melancholic listen to romantic-sentimental music, the former will reject it while the latter will love it; or if a sanguine and a melancholic listen to powerful, robust, wild, and barbaric music, the melancholic will reject it while the sanguine or the choleric will enjoy it extremely. Temperament unsuitable to the aesthetic object can, thus, truly cause aesthetic disagreement.

Turning our attention finally to the inabilities at the *rational* level to recognize beauty, we must consider four reasons for real aesthetic disagreement.

5. One of the greatest and most frequent reasons for aesthetic disagreement is *Reason 33*, which is aesthetic taste. By aesthetic taste we mean the capacity for easily and clearly recognizing and enjoying, that is, appreciating, beauty in things. Taste is thus a genuine habit of the intellect based upon education (learning) and practice ((experience). It is based on education or learning insofar as the first step toward having aesthetic taste is to learn about beauty and beautiful things: their principles and properties, their characteristics and kinds. Thereby the human mind acquires the necessary foundation on which it can rely every time it encounters a beautiful thing. But taste is also based on practice or experience, because theoretical knowledge about beauty and beautiful things is not enough, although altogether indispensable. One must also be repeatedly forced in concrete situations to lean back on that theoretical knowledge in recognizing and properly appreciating the beauty of the encountered object. "For 'tis not instantly we acquire the sense," warns Lord Shaftesbury, "by which these beauties are discoverable."[31] If a person is allowed, observes Hume, "to acquire experience ... he not only perceives the beauties and defects of each part, but marks the distinguishing species of each quality, and assigns it suitable praise or blame. A clear and distinct sentiment attends him through the whole survey of the objects; and he discerns that very degree

---

[31] Lord Shaftesbury, "The Moralist," part 3, sect. 2; in *Characteristics*, II, *ed. cit.*, p. 129.

and kind of approbation or displeasure which each part is naturally fitted to produce."[32]

Before going on in the analysis of aesthetic taste, we can already see how this taste can lead to aesthetic disagreement between the aesthetically uneducated and the aesthetically educated. For, evidently, the aesthetically uneducated cannot and, consequently, does not recognize the beauty which is there in the object, and is discernible only to the one who has developed aesthetic taste. Plato's words are relevant here, stating that ignorance which prevails among men results in all the contention and fighting between individuals as well as between States.[33] Sir Joshua Reynolds is even more to the point: "The higher efforts of those arts, we know by experience, do not affect minds wholly uncultivated."[34] In his own way, Ralph Barton Perry echoes in this respect both Plato and Reynolds.[35] The chance of aesthetic disagreement between the aesthetically educated and uneducated becomes even greater in a case in which the beauty of an object is minimal or in a mixed rather than pure state. As the aesthetic qualities in objects, "which are fitted by nature" to produce aesthetic delight, "may be found in a small degree," remarks Hume, "or may be mixed and confounded with each other, it often happens that the taste is not affected with such minute qualities, or is not able to distinguish all the particular flavors, amidst the disorder in which they are presented."[36] Hugo von Hofmannsthal expresses this truth in the following manner: "The pure poetic content of a work of art, the real meaning it contains is never understood at first. What is understood is only that which needs no understanding, the obvious, plain anecdote: Tosca, Madam Butterfly, and the like."[37] It is for these reasons that the greatest German poet, Goethe, who probably enjoyed more recognition in his lifetime than any other poet in his country, complained to Schiller, "[how] many can see a work of art as such and how many can comprehend it?"[38]

Therefore, if both a person with aesthetic taste and another lacking such taste view the same aesthetic object, there is a good chance that the former will find it beautiful and will enjoy it, whereas the latter will do neither: a clear-cut case of aesthetic disagreement.

---

[32] Hume, "Of the Standard of Taste," *ed. cit.*, p. 275.

[33] Plato, *Hipp. mai.* 294d.

[34] Sir J. Reynolds, *Discourses on Art*, Discourse 13. Ed. R. Lavine (New York: Crowell-Collier, 1966), 204. Cf. Augustine, *De doctrina Christ.*, IV, 6, 10 (PL 34, 93).

[35] R. B. Perry, *General Theory of Value*, § 255, (London: Longmans, Green, 1926), 639. Cf. also Augustine, *De doctr. Christ.*, IV, 7, 20 (PL 34, 98).

[36] Hume, "Of the Standard of Taste," *ed. cit.*, p. 273.

[37] H. V. Hofmannsthal, Letter to Richard Strauss, July 23, 1911; in *A Working Friendship, The Correspondence between Richard Strauss and Hugo von Hofmannsthal*, tr. H. Hammelmann and E. Osers (New York: Ransom House, 1961), 98.

[38] J. W. Goethe, Letter to Schiller, Weimar, July 7, 1796, in *Letters from Goethe*, letter 262; tr. M. Herzfeld, C. M. Sym (Edinburgh University Press, 1957), 245.

This role of creating aesthetic disagreement between the educated and the uneducated is, however, only one of the two roles which aesthetic taste can play. For while a person's theoretical education in beauty, as his mental preparation for easily recognizing and enjoying beauty, can be quite broad, his actual practice, his concrete encounters with beautiful things, which is the second and equally important component of the process of developing aesthetic taste, is almost invariably limited to certain types or kinds of beautiful things, such as to one or two fields of the fine arts and, even within them, to one or two styles or genres only. As Lord Kames puts it, "our ideas of beauty are modified by the differences of instruction or education;"[39] and as J. Stolnitz expresses it, "No man can be completely catholic in his tastes. We respond to some things but not to others. The emotional capacities and 'turn of mind' which enable us to respond to one kind of art, keeps us from appreciating another kind.... When ... men have the taste required to appreciate one style or school of art, they must often pay the price of being insensitive to other styles."[40] Having listened, for instance, for years to classical music, one will develop an extreme sensitivity for discerning and enjoying classical music. At the same time, however, precisely because while listening constantly to classical music he had no chance or only little chance to listen to jazz music, he will be virtually insensitive to and ignorant about jazz music and its unique beauties. Thereby, the acquisition of taste becomes a matter of familiarity with one kind of things, accompanied by unfamiliarity with other kinds of things, and this itself, as we have seen, constitutes a reason for aesthetic disagreement.[41]

From what has been said here about the natural limitations of aesthetic taste, it follows that these undesirable aspects of aesthetic taste cannot be avoided simply by realizing them. "It is plainly an error," Hume tells us, "in a critic to confine his approbation to one species or style of writing, and condemn all the rest. But it is almost impossible not to feel a predilection for that which suits our particular turn and disposition. Such preferences are innocent and unavoidable."[42]

The relevance of this feature of aesthetic taste to our over-all topic is evident: aesthetic taste can create disagreement not only between him who has taste and the one who lacks it, but also between aesthetically well-educated people who have learned to easily discern and properly appreciate beauty. The specific reason for this second type of aesthetic disagreement caused by taste is the fact that everyone develops his taste through something analogous to what modern psychology calls *channelization*. If two people develop aesthetic taste,

---

[39] Lord Kames, *op. cit.*, chap. 3, part 2; *ed. cit.*, p. 126.
[40] J. Stolnitz, *op. cit.*, p. 429.
[41] Cf., Augustine, *De civ. Dei*, XV, 16, 2 (*PL* 41, 458); Thomas, *In II. Met.* 5,333; and Sir J. Reynolds, *Discourses on Art*, Disc. 8; *ed. cit.*, pp. 141, 130.
[42] Hume, "Of the Standard of Taste," *ed. cit.*, p. 281.

there is a good chance that one of them will do so by being often exposed to one kind of beauty, with the result that he will prefer that kind; whereas the other will develop his taste by often encountering another type of beauty, with the result that he will prefer that kind to any other. The end result is that what one of them loves as beautiful will be rejected by the other as non-beautiful, and vice versa. The situation of aesthetic disagreement is thereby inevitable.

Various authors give various examples or instances of differences in taste. "One person," writes Hume, "is more pleased with the sublime, another with the tender, a third with raillery.... Simplicity is affected by one: ornament by another. Comedy, tragedy, satire, odes, have each its partisans, who prefer that particular species of writing, and condemn all the rest."[43] Bernard Bosanquet also uses literary instances: "Aristotle speaks in a most suggestive phrase, of the 'weakness of the spectators,'[44] which shrinks from the essence of tragedy. In other words, the capacity to endure and enjoy feeling at high tension is somewhat rare"; and again, "It is a remarkable and rather startling fact that there are genuine lovers of beauty, well equipped in scholarship, who cannot really enjoy Aristophanes, or Rabelais, or the Falstaff scenes in Shakespeare. This is again, I venture to think, a 'weakness of the spectator.' "[45] Jarrett writes along similar lines: "There are some who cannot enjoy the lusty, bawdy, profane humor of a Rabelais. Some are repelled, or at least easily discouraged by complex structures such as those of Bartók, and much other 'modern art'.... What for some persons is difficult beauty is, for others, ugliness."[46]

One concrete and very early historical instance of differences in taste is indicated by Diogenes Laertius between Croesus, the rich king and lover of jewels, and Solon, the wise man who preferred "cocks and pheasants and peacocks, because they shine in natural colors that are ten thousand times more beautiful."[47] William Hazlitt, the art critic, speaks of the dispute between the admirers of Homer and Virgil as one that "has never been settled, and never will: for there will always be minds to whom the excellences of Virgil will be more congenial, and therefore more objects of admiration and delight than those of Homer, and vice versa."[48] Jerome Stolnitz mentions a fairly recent instance of difference in aesthetic taste between aesthetically well-educated persons: "To those who know the writings of both E. M. Forster and James Joyce, it will be easily understandable why Forster, as he tells us, does not like

---

[43] Hume, *ibid*. A very similar passage on the same topic can be found in John Cotton's *De musica* (late 12th century), cap. 16 (*PL* 150, 1413 B–C).

[44] Aristotle, *Poet*. XIII, 7, 1453a 34.

[45] B. Bosanquet, *Three Lectures on Aesthetic*, Lecture 3; *ed. cit.*, pp. 48, 49.

[46] James L. Jarrett, *op. cit.*, p. 37.

[47] *Diog. Laert*. I, 2, 51.

[48] W. Hazlitt, "On Criticism"; in *The Complete Works of William Hazlitt*, VIII, ed. P. P. Howe (London: J. M. Dent, 1931), 222f.

Joyce's *Ulysses*. The world depicted by Joyce is teeming, vulgar, and sprawling . . . [whereas] Forster has shown himself to be . . . a man of fastidious refinement and gentility."⁴⁹ Finally, let us hear the amazing confession of the poet Coventry Patmore: "The partiality and limitation of my appreciation of art often surprises myself. I have the most acute delight in some of the best music, but it seems a mere accident. Most of Beethoven, for example, seems to me to be simply noise."⁵⁰

In brief, aesthetic taste may produce aesthetic disagreement between two groups of people and in two ways: between those who have taste and those who do not, and also between those who have different tastes, and between either two groups. This disagreement may result either in one rejecting what the other holds beautiful, or in one holding an object much more beautiful than the other.

6. *Reason 34* for aesthetic disagreement may seem to be simply a component of the just-discussed taste: mental and/or emotional maturity (preparedness) vs. immaturity (unpreparedness). Indeed, the two reasons are closely connected and definitely similar. For taste grows as a person gradually, slowly sheds his mental and emotional immaturity, and reaches instead the maturity which is indispensable for the proper appreciation of certain genres of artworks. This maturation is analogous to the one of which, surprisingly enough, Aquinas remarked, "Jerome says that 'a young boy' is not delighted upon seeing a woman."⁵¹ Apart from the similarity in their gradual development, mental and emotional maturity, or preparedness, and aesthetic taste are also closely connected. For this maturity promotes the working of aesthetic taste. However, maturity and taste also differ from each other, as any two things do of which either one can be reached or developed without the other. Indeed, maturity can be reached without the development of aesthetic taste, and vice versa. The consequence of this fact is that unless a person is mentally and emotionally mature enough, he cannot possibly enjoy certain types of artistic beauty. Plotinus' following words have definite relevance to this fact: "The perception of beauty and the awe and the stirring of passion towards it are for those in some degree knowing and awakened."⁵² S. K. Langer comes right to the point when stating that "the conception of beauty as the expressiveness of a form explains why beauty may go unperceived where, none the less, it exists, why maturity enables us to appreciate what was once too strange, or too unpleasant in some way, or perhaps too enigmatic, to elicit our response to it as an expressive form."⁵³

⁴⁹ Stolnitz, *op. cit.*, p. 418.
⁵⁰ Letter to G. M. Hopkins, in *Further Letters of G. M. Hopkins Including His Correspondence with Coventry Patmore*; ed. C. C. Abbott (London: Oxford University Press, 1938), 207.
⁵¹ Thomas, *S. theol.* I–II, 142, 2, 1a.
⁵² Plotinus, *Enn.* V, 5, 12; *ed. cit.*, p. 412.
⁵³ S. K. Langer, *Problems of Art* (New York: C. Scribners' Sons, 1957), 119f.

A concrete example illustrating how much we must be mentally and emotionally mature to appreciate certain art forms is furnished by the Irish poet Coventry Patmore, when he writes to G. M. Hopkins, "It was twenty years before I could learn to see anything in Wordsworth's sonnet to the River Duddon."[54] David Hume, too, hints at the element of maturity as a necessary condition of aesthetic enjoyment of certain artworks when he observes that, while, at twenty, Ovid may be the favorite author, Horace will be such probably at forty, and Tacitus, perhaps, at fifty.[55]

The picture is thus complete. Mental and emotional immaturity vs. maturity is a possible reason for aesthetic disagreement in the following manner. If a certain kind of aesthetic object is viewed by both a mature and an immature person, i. e., by one who is well prepared for that kind of object and by another who is ill prepared for it, then the former probably will appreciate it, whereas the latter will not. Thereby, the two will disagree on the beauty of that aesthetic object demanding maturity.

7. Of habitual expectation, as *Reason 35* for aesthetic disagreement, the following can be said. This reason for aesthetic disagreement, which stands close to, or is a special case of aesthetic taste at the practical level, is the habitual expectation, in potential beholders of artworks or artists, of the fulfillment of some more or less reasonable requirements. This is to say that, unless an artwork or a performing artist conforms to one's expectations either in general or in a particular manner or aspect, that artwork or the performance of that artist will be rejected rather than enjoyed and appreciated by persons with such expectations.[56]

If, for instance, somebody has the image of a tragic actor about a certain artist, then he may expect of him to appear always and only in tragedies. Thus, should that actor ever appear in a comedy, the beholder in question is likely to reject that role and, with it, the entire play, perhaps even before he has had a chance to see it performed. This seems to be at least one of the reasons why many actors and actresses desperately try to avoid being type-cast in certain roles. For once an actor or actress is type-cast by the general public, the public will be prone to reject him or her playing a different type of role because, by playing a different role, he or she will fail to conform or live up to the expectations of the public. In a similar manner, once certain forms of artistic species or practices connected with certain artistic species become commonly known and accepted, the public accustomed to those forms or practices will probably reject an individual artwork failing to comply with those forms or practices.

Should, for example, the story be true, then the great *Don Giovanni* opera

---

[54] *Further Letters of G. M. Hopkins*, Letter No. 87E; *ed. cit.*, p. 207.
[55] Hume, "Of the Standard of Taste," *ed. cit.*, p. 281.
[56] Cf. Aquinas, *S. theol.* II–II, 144, 3, ad 4.

might have been rejected by the general public in Prague had Mozart not written hastily, the day before the first performance (October 29, 1787), an overture to it, just because the people in that city were used to having overtures in operas, and thus expected of every opera to begin with an overture. A concrete instance of rejection by one critic because of habitual expectation was the American debut at the Metropolitan, on April 12, 1916, of the ballet, *Le Spectre de la Rose* (music by C. M. von Weber, choreography by Michel Fokin; story inspired by a poem of Théophile Gautier), with Thamar Karsavina and Vaslav Nijinsky. The reason for rejection was that the great Nijinsky seemed to that art critic to dance in an effeminate manner, dancing, among other things, on the toes—a practice in which, generally, only female dancers used to indulge.[57]

It is easy to see how such expectations can lead to aesthetic disagreement. All that is needed for such a disagreement is two beholders: one, with certain expectations concerning the artist and/or the artwork; the other, without such expectations. For, unless the artist and/or the artwork conforms to those expectations, the former beholder will tend to reject the artwork, while the latter beholder will rather tend to accept it.

8. *Reason 36*, the last of the above listed reasons for aesthetic disagreement, complements at the theoretical level the reason just discussed. This reason is individual standards set up and applied to individual artworks by individual art critics. To understand this reason for aesthetic disagreement, one must bear in mind that the formal evaluation of an artwork requires of the art critic certain more or less universal principles of beauty to be used as premises in the demonstrations of the aesthetic value or disvalue of a work of fine art. These principles are either directly or indirectly aesthetic in nature, representing direct or formal and indirect or material requirements of beauty. One formal requirement on which some art critics or aestheticians such as Ernest Ansermet, the famous Swiss conductor in the late 1930's, insist is that music be melodic—a requirement which precludes, among others, atonal music, like Arnold Schönberg's twelve-tone music. Another such requirement is that ballet employ only non-classical music as an accompaniment.

One concrete instance of insisting on the latter principle involved the ballet *Chorearteum*, choreographed by Leonide Massine, and first performed by the Ballet Russe in London, October 4, 1933, causing bitter complaints among art critics about the "wickedness" of dancing to Johannes Brahms' *Fourth Symphony*, with only Ernest Newman defending it in the *London Sunday Times*.[58]

A historical instance of insisting that no opera music should be used for performing a ballet involved N. Rimsky-Korsakov's opera, *Le Coq d'Or*, first per-

[57] Critical appraisal in the *New York Times*, April 13, 1916. See, G. Robert, *op. cit.*, p. 303.
[58] G. Robert, *op. cit.*, p. 74.

formed as a straight ballet rather than an opera at the Metropolitan on October 23, 1937. Its first performance caused musicologists to decry it as "the vandalism of reducing an opera to an orchestral suit," while only O. Downes was defending it.[59]

Among the material requirements insisted upon by art critics, we find those of G. M. Hopkins, who rejected Robert Bridge's *Ulysses* for lack of honesty, arguing this way: "I cannot take heathen gods in earnest; and want of earnest I take to be the deepest fault a work of art can have. It does not strike at first, but it withers them in the end."[60] Leo Tolstoi expressed another material requirement of the aesthetic value of artworks when he categorically rejected ballet in general because of the partial nudity of its dancers: "The ballet, in which half-naked women make voluptuous movements, twisting themselves into various sensual writhings, is simply a lewd performance."[61] Tolstoi set up also another and, if possible, even more astounding artistic requirement, namely, the artwork's obligatory appeal to religious and social-humanistic feelings, thereby implying that no work is to be considered a true artwork unless it represents such an appeal: " 'What! the *Ninth Symphony* not a good work of art!' I hear exclaimed by indignant voices. And I reply: Most certainly it is not. All that I have written I have written with the sole purpose of finding a clear and reasonable criterion by which to judge the merits of works of art. And this criterion, coinciding with the indications of plain and sane sense, indubitably shows me that that symphony of Beethoven's is not a good work of art.... Beethoven's *Ninth Symphony* is considered a great work of art. To verify its claim to be such I must first ask myself whether this work transmits the highest religious feeling? I reply in the negative, since music in itself cannot transmit those feelings; and therefore I ask myself next: Since this work does not belong to the highest kind of religious art, has it the other characteristic of the good art of our time—the quality of uniting all men in one common feeling—does it rank as Christian universal art? And again I have no option but to reply in the negative.... And therefore, whether I like it or not I am compelled to conclude that this work belongs to the rank of bad art."[62] While Cardinal Newman's view on the primary role of the fine arts being religious in nature[63] definitely favors Tolstoi, it is interesting to see J. P. Sartre sharply attack Nobel Prize winner Francois Mauriac ("God is not an artist. Neither is M. Mauriac"[64]) on the quasi-theological grounds that Mauriac

---

[59] *Op. cit.*, p. 100.
[60] Letter to C. Patmore, Dublin, April 4, 1885, in *Further Letters of G. M. Hopkins*, p. 212.
[61] Tolstoi, *op. cit.*, p. 79.
[62] Tolstoi, *op. cit.*, pp. 248f.
[63] J. H. Cardinal Newman, *The Idea of A University*, Part I, Discourse IV, n. 5 (Garden City, New York: Doubleday, 1959), 110.
[64] J. P. Sartre, "Francois Mauriac and Freedom," in *Literary Essays* (New York: Philosophical Library, 1957), 14, 15, 16, 23.

writes his novels pretending to be omniscient, and considers his characters "*sub specie aeternitatis.*"

Anybody can easily see how all these examples are relevant to our present topic of aesthetic disagreement. For every time an art critic sets up an arbitrary requirement of aesthetic value, he will probably reject the artwork which another art critic, who is not blinded and misled by any arbitrary requirement, will appreciate; and thereby the two will genuinely disagree on the beauty of that artwork.

In retrospect and summary, we may say the following. All the above listed and discussed reasons for aesthetic disagreement show that aesthetic subjectivism has a weak case not only because of the criticism offered in the previous chapter but also on the grounds that its principal argument, aesthetic disagreement, if real rather than apparent, can be explained through more than two dozen psychological circumstances rooted in human personality, and thus the subjectivist explanation of aesthetic disagreement is far from being the only explanation.

More specifically, of the thirty reasons for real aesthetic disagreement, at least one, the thirtieth reason, viz., arbitrary standards of beauty, involves art critics in explaining the disagreement in question, whereas the rest are reasons involving just any beholder, professional or amateur. Regarding the same reasons from the viewpoint of the specific nature of the opposition standing between the aesthetic judgments of the disagreeing parties, some above listed and discussed reasons account for contradictory opposition (e.g., "This is beautiful" vs. "This is not beautiful"), such as reasons 7, 8, 11, 12, 14–20, and 26–28; other reasons, for partial contrary opposition (e.g., "This is a little beautiful" vs. "This is a little ugly"), such as reasons 9, 10, 13, 25, and 32; or for complete contrary opposition ("This is beautiful" vs. "This is ugly"), such as reasons 9, 10, 24, and 25.

Most important of all, however, is the fact that some of the above listed and discussed reasons for aesthetic disagreement are quite frequent; others, rare. For instance, of the six reasons of apparent aesthetic disagreement, the first two and the fifth are quite frequent; the others, rare. Similarly, of all the thirty reasons of real aesthetic disagreement, reasons 9, 11, 12, 29, and 33 are quite frequent; reasons 18, 19, 23, 24, 28, 30, 31, and 35, quite rare.

Before ending this discussion on the various psychological reasons of aesthetic disagreement, let us face briefly an objection aimed at not merely weakening but totally destroying the value of this chapter's service to aesthetic objectivism. This objection comes in an implied manner from Curt John Ducasse. He states, "It is of course quite possible that two persons, or two million, should have similar tastes, i.e., should happen alike to find pleasure in a given food or wine, or to obtain pleasurable feelings in contemplating aesthetically a given picture, melody, etc. But such community in the experience of pleasure . . . leaves wholly untouched the . . . bare fact that other persons—whether many, few, or only one—find not pleasure but displeasure in the very same objects."[65] From this statement, the following argument may be construed against the leading idea of the present chapter: Both aesthetic agreement and disagreement show only one thing, viz., that a certain number of persons have a similar inner constitution. But if so, aesthetic agreement does not indicate the objective reality of beauty directly; nor does aesthetic disagreement do so, indirectly.

To this argument, this reply can be given. It is perfectly true and also the underlying idea of this entire chapter that only those who are similar in their psychological make-up or individuality will enjoy the beauty of a certain object, just as those who fail to do so are, probably, also similar to each other in that one respect. However, the point here is not similarity among the enjoyers or the non-enjoyers of a certain beauty, nor the number of similar people, but rather the fact that if, in an aesthetic object, there were no definite objective qualities suitable to one group and unsuitable to another group of people, then the former group would have nothing to be delighted by, and the latter group, nothing to be displeased by and nothing on which to disagree with the former group of persons. On the other hand, inasmuch as, and only inasmuch as, there is beauty in an object, will those whose constitutions conform to it be able to take delight in that object, and will actually do so, whereas those whose constitutions do not conform to the beauty of the object will be unable to take delight in that aesthetic object, and will actually be displeased or left unaffected by it. Thus the objection fails both to demolish the direct argument for aesthetic objectivism offered in chapter 4 and to destroy or even to lessen the value of the indirect argument for aesthetic objectivism contained in the present chapter.

[65] C. J. Ducasse, *The Philosophy of Art*, chap. 15, § 11; p. 286.

Section Two: The Essence of Beauty

HAVING ESTABLISHED the extramental objective reality, that is, the existence, of beauty, the next question is: If beauty exists, what is it? This is the question of the essence of beauty.

The question of the essence of a thing can be answered only by an essential definition of that thing. Thus, the ultimate task facing us in this section is clearly a discussion of the essential definition of beauty—a task requiring a separate chapter. However, before this task can be accomplished there are two other related topics to be discussed.

First of all, there is a need for an historical review of the various attempts made heretofore at defining the elusive nature of beauty. This will be done in the first chapter of the present section by a rather complex division of the various positions ever taken on the question of defining beauty. This chapter, in turn, will inevitably make one wonder whether beauty can ever be defined correctly. Assuming, for the time being, that this can be done, the next question is how this is to be accomplished, or what is the suitable method which, when employed, can lead to the desired essential definition of beauty. Therefore the proper method of defining beauty will be the topic of the second chapter in this section. Only after these two chapters will an essential definition be offered and defended in the light of the methodological steps suggested in the preceding chapter.

Chapter VII
Historical Review of Positions on the Essence of Beauty

NOBODY CAN REASONABLY EXPECT to succeed in tackling a difficult problem unless he is well aware of the obstacles involved in solving that problem. For the philosopher of beauty this means that he must be well aware of the extreme elusiveness of beauty before he even begins to treat the problem of the essence of beauty. The obvious reason for the need to realize the proverbial elusiveness of beauty is that whatever is very elusive to the mind tends to defy any attempt to define it essentially. From this it immediately follows that one has good reasons to wonder whether he will be able to succeed in finding the essential definition of beauty, and what method he must use in order to have any reasonable hope for success at all. Let us, therefore, first discuss briefly the elusiveness of beauty that constitutes an epistemological paradox about beauty.

That beauty is an elusive quality whereby it is difficult to grasp its nature has been known throughout history. This fact was probably first expressed by Plato. For, in the *Major Hippias*, after several futile attempts to define beauty, he has Socrates pronounce the truth of the old proverb, "Beautiful things are difficult [sc. to understand]" (χαλεπὰ τὰ καλά).[1] This truth was also explicitly recognized by modern and contemporary thinkers. In the eighteenth century J. J. Winckelmann complained this way: "Beauty is one of the greatest secrets of nature, the effect of which we all see and feel, but a universal and clear notion of its essence belongs to the undiscovered truths."[2] Similarly, the great schoolman of the nineteenth century, J. J. Urráburu, called the task of discursively grasping the nature of beauty "difficult and rough";[3] and the contemporary C. N. Bittle had this to say about the issue: "Beauty is a most elusive quality. Its nature is so tenuous that it always seems to escape in the very moment of its capture. There is hardly a term in any language which is used more and abused more than 'beauty.' "[4]

But in what way is this elusiveness an epistemological paradox? It is again Plato who gives us the answer in two texts, one in the *Lysis*; the other in the *Greater Hippias*. In the former dialogue, Plato calls beauty a "soft, smooth, and slippery thing," that "easily slips in and permeates our souls."[5] In the

[1] Plato, *Hipp. mai.*, 304e.
[2] J. J. Winckelmann, *Geschichte der Kunst des Alterthums* (Leipzig: Dürr, 1882), 105.
[3] (Quod) omnes audito nomine pulchritudinis sentiunt atque intelligunt, id verbis explicare, opus arduum est et salebrosum. J. J. Urráburu, *Ontologia* (Vallisoleti: Cuesta, Lutetia Parisiorum: Lethielleux, et Romae: F. Melandri, 1891), 517.
[4] C. N. Bittle, *The Domain of Being, Ontology*, (Milwaukee: Bruce, 1939), 206.
[5] Plato, *Lysis*, 216d; tr. B. Jowett, in *The Dialogues of Plato* (New York: Random House, 1937), I, 45.

Greater Hippias, on the other hand, as already seen, he emphasizes the difficulty involved in formally grasping the nature of beauty. Putting these two texts together, we learn from Plato the following paradox: beauty can easily, effortlessly be recognized in aesthetic experience, since this is a matter of intuition; and yet, it is very difficult to reason out its essence.

But how do we know that Plato or the modern aestheticians are right in asserting this epistemological paradox about beauty, and how can it be shown specifically that beauty is truly so elusive as asserted?

There are, we can reply, at least three sets of historical facts that clearly show this elusiveness: one, the relatively late interest in defining beauty; two, the relatively rare attempts in ancient philosophy to define beauty; and three, and above all, the enormous variety of positions on the essence of beauty. Let us take up each of these facts one by one.

To appreciate the first historical argument for the elusiveness of beauty, it must be pointed out that there are three kinds of persons connected with beauty: the artist, who makes it; the beholder, who enjoys it; and the aesthetician, who reasons about it. Now, it is a well known fact that there had been artists at work as early in pre-historic times as in the upper paleolithic period. The sculptural works, like the Venus of Willendorf and Lespugue; the bas-reliefs, like the Laussel Venus and the paintings on the cave walls at Lascaux, all these being of the Aurignacian culture; furthermore, the wall paintings at Niaux or Font-de-Gaume, and the clay models at Tuc d'Audoubert, all of the generic Magdalenian culture; also, the paintings at Altamira and the Spanish Levant: these are only a few instances of the works of pre-historic artists thousands, if not tens of thousands, of years ago. These artworks also testify, of course, to pre-historic man's aesthetic interest in and appreciation of nature. In contrast with this amazingly early appearance of making and enjoying beauty, philosophizing about beauty began thousands of years later; even hundreds of years after Homer, Hesiod, and the earliest cosmologists. For Socrates is known to have been the first to offer some universal standard or principle of beauty.[6]

The other set of historical facts obviously indicates an ever-human reluctance to analyze and define beauty and, through it, the elusiveness of beauty. From the earliest beginning of Greek philosophy to the beginning of medieval philosophy, that is, in fourteen centuries, of all the Greek and Roman thinkers, there were probably less than a dozen who took the trouble or had the mental boldness to offer an essential definition of beauty. Among them are Plato, Aristotle, Epictetus, Cicero, Philo of Alexandria, Vitruvius, Plotinus, Augustine, and Dionysius the Areopagite. This is, indeed, a very brief list of thinkers.

If somebody is not impressed with these historical facts indicating the elusive-

---

[6] Xenophon, *Memorabilia*, III, 8, 4 and 7.

ness of beauty, then he must turn his attention to the almost endless variety of views on and definitions of the essence of beauty that philosophers and aestheticians held or offered throughout history, from Plato down to American contemporaries.

Since it is hardly possible or necessary to mention all the singular positions ever taken on the definableness of beauty or all the essential definitions ever offered of beauty, in the next three articles the reader will be offered a fair idea of the variety of these views and definitions, enumerated or mentioned in a highly complex logical division.

Of the three articles, the first will list numerous skeptic views on the knowability of the essence of beauty; the second will treat, of the non-skeptic views, some subjectivist and idealist definitions of beauty; and the third article will list numerous realistic definitions of the essence of beauty.[7]

ARTICLE I. *Skeptic Views on Beauty*

As shown in the previous section, one can do basically no more than one of two things about the existence or extramental reality of beauty: accept it or reject it. In a similar manner, one can do basically only one of two things concerning the question of the essence of beauty: he can be either skeptical or non-skeptical about the possibility of defining it. Of these two fundamental positions, the former will be divided and subdivided in the present article.

1. First of all, the skeptic positions can be divided into objectively and subjectively skeptic positions. The former are actually skeptic; the latter seem to their holders to be skeptic, but in reality they are not skeptic positions.

The objectively skeptic views, in turn, can be divided into explicitly and implicitly skeptic views. The holders of the former views unequivocally express their skepticism about the possibility of finding the essential definition of beauty. The holders of the latter views do not do so; instead, their skepticism is implied by and can be seen from what they actually say about the definableness of beauty.

The explicit skeptic views themselves can conveniently be divided into immoderate and moderate skeptic views. Immoderate are the skeptic views that categorically deny the possibility of finding the essential definition of beauty; moderate skeptic views, on the other hand, are those which do not categorically deny this possibility.

The immoderate skeptic views are themselves twofold: those generically and those specifically denying the possibility of finding the essence of beauty.

2. An immoderate and explicit skeptic view which generically denies the possibility that man could ever recognize the essence of beauty is one like

---

[7] Apart from its greater scope and details, this proposed division of theories to be followed in the next chapter happens to be strikingly similar to Jared S. Moore's in "Beauty as Harmony," *The Journal of Aesthetics and Art Criticism*, II, 1, (Winter 1942–43), 40–50.

that of the nihilist Gorgias of Leontini. For, by denying, as he did in his *On the Non-Being or Nature*, the very possibility of all knowledge, he thereby obviously denied also the possibility of knowing the essence of beauty.

While the ancient Gorgias' position is generically immoderate and explicit, one finds a number of modern and contemporary aestheticians whose positions are specifically immoderate and explicit in their skepticism. The first among them is Albrecht Dürer, who confesses not only his own ignorance about beauty ("I know not certainly what the ultimate measure of true beauty is, and cannot describe it aright . . ."), but also categorically asserts man's inability to comprehend the essence of beauty ("I believe that no man liveth who can grasp the whole beauty of the meanest living creature . . . . I grant indeed that one man will conceive and make a more beautiful figure and will explain the natural cause of its beauty more reasonably, than another but not to such an extent that there could not be anything more beautiful. For so fair a conception ariseth not in the mind of man; God alone knoweth such.").[1] George W. Samson, another skeptic, considers the entire inquiry into the nature of beauty irrational.[2] Similarly, J. Sully opines that any metaphysical investigation of the principles of beauty is useless. For, to him, the properties of fine art are "innumerable, and can only be subsumed under some such conception as pleasurability"; and, "This conception obviously excludes all hypotheses of some one eternally fixed quality of art, some essence of Beauty."[3] Lucy Crane, on her part, thinks that no "universal formula" could be found for the beautiful.[4] Thomas Munro agrees with all such views when writing, "Aesthetics is still commonly regarded in the traditional way as 'the branch of philosophy dealing with beauty.' This definition . . . directs the aesthetician's quest . . . toward a conceptual will-o'-the-wisp, an abstraction whose meaning is endlessly debatable and ambiguous so that he never can be sure that he has found his quarry or is looking at it. Hence he may cover countless pages with fruitless debate over the proper definition of beauty."[5] Stolnitz expresses this same view as follows: "It is most unlikely that we can find any set of specific properties which always occur along with beauty. Considering the history of taste, and the great number of artistic traditions and styles, we can even say that it is impossible for all practical purposes, to find any such properties."[6]

3. Turning next to the moderate skeptic views explicitly expressed, we find

[1] *Literary Remains of Albrecht Dürer*, ed. W. M. Conway (Cambridge: University Press, 1889), 224f.

[2] G. W. Samson, *Elements of Art Criticism*, I, chap. 1, section 4 (Philadelphia: J. B. Lippincott, 1867), 32f., 37.

[3] J. Sully, "On the Possibility of A Science of Aesthetics," in *Sensation and Intuition, Studies in Psychology and Aesthetics* (London: Henry S. King, 1874), 342, 341.

[4] L. Crane, *Art and the Formation of Taste*, chap. 4 (Boston and New York: Educational Publishing Co., 1889), 104.

[5] Munro, *op. cit.*, p. 154.

[6] J. Stolnitz, *op. cit.*, p. 401.

them doing something less than denying categorically any chance man may have to determine correctly the essence of beauty. Instead, these views do one of at least these two things: admit not to know what beauty is, or unsuccessfully try to find the essence of beauty. One type of the former position is represented by those who simply assert that nobody knows the essence of beauty. Among them is Tolstoi, claiming that "the question, What is beauty?, remains to this day quite unsolved."[7] Thomas Reid represents the second type of the former position by stressing only his own inability to find the essence of beauty: "Beauty is found in things so various and so different in nature, that it is difficult to say wherein it consists, or what these can be common to all the objects in which it is found . . . I am indeed unable to conceive any quality in all the different things that are called beautiful, that is the same in them all."[8] Since holding that something is unknown is a less radical position than asserting the unknowability of something, Tolstoi's and Reid's positions are clearly moderately skeptic. So is also William Gilpin's, but for different reasons. For, although not inquiring directly into the "general sources" of beauty, Gilpin obliquely investigates the nature of the beautiful and the picturesque relatively, taking up several explanations for their differences, but finally he gives it up as an impossible task: "Thus failed, should we in the true spirit of inquiry, persist; or honestly give up the cause and own we cannot search out the source of this difference? I am afraid this is the truth, whatever airs of dogmatizing we may assume, inquiries into principles rarely end in satisfaction."[9] Since this author attempted or pretended to attempt to find the answer to his question, he seems to be one degree less skeptic than Tolstoi or Reid.

4. The implicitness of skeptic positions on defining beauty is manifested in at least three ways: by never taking sides with any specific position; by expressing the hope that beauty will be defined some day; and, most frequently, by offering some sort of non-essential definition of beauty.

Among those who never express any opinion about which kind of position on the definition of beauty or which kind of definition of beauty is right and which wrong is, for example, M. C. Beardsley, although in his *Aesthetics* he treats the various views on the question of the essence of beauty at great length. A similar method is being used by J. Stolnitz who, in his *Aesthetics and Philosophy of Art Criticism*, confines himself to listing the pros and cons with respect to each one of the various schools of thought.

Another version of implicit skepticism is to be found in James McCosh's *Psychology*, in which, having listed three genera of theories concerning the essence of beauty, he makes the following remark: "I confidently cherish the

---

[7] L. Tolstoi, *op. cit.*, p. 86.

[8] Reid, *Essays on the Intellectual Powers of Man*, Essay VIII, chap. 4: "Of Beauty"; *ed. cit.*, I, 498.

[9] W. Gilpin, *Three Essays: On Picturesque Beauty; On Picturesque Travel; and On Sketching Landscape.*; *ed. cit.*, I, 4, 30. Cf., *ibid.*, p. 33.

belief that sooner or later we may have a mathematical expression of the laws of form discerned as beautiful,"[10]—a statement clearly implying that he does not think that beauty has, up to date, properly been defined by anyone.

The third version of implicit skepticism about the possibility of an essential definition of beauty, namely, offering some nonessential definition instead of an essential one, has so many alternatives that we must deal with them separately and at considerable length.

The various non-essential definitions offered in place of an essential definition can be divided, first of all, into logically incorrect and logically correct definitions. The former, although themselves of a considerable number of kinds, all have one thing in common, namely, that they all violate in some manner the logical rules of definition and, as such, are more skeptic than the logically correct non-essential definitions of beauty.

5. Among the logically incorrect non-essential definitions of beauty, we find quite a number of types.

One such definition is a nominal definition. Thomas Munro suggests, for instance, "The only short, simple, correct answer to the question 'what is beauty?' is to say, 'beauty is many different things, not yet well understood, to which the name "beauty" has been applied.' "[11]

Some aestheticians have been satisfied with metaphorical definitions. The historian William Knight quotes, for example, J. W. Goethe as remarking in his *Wilhelm Meister*, "Beauty is inexplicable: it is a hovering, floating, and glittering shadow, whose outline eludes the grasp of definition," and also Ludwig Tieck as describing beauty as "a unique ray out of the celestial brightness."[12] Needless to say, neither one of these "definitions" is worth more from the logical point of view than its poetic beauty.

Not much higher in perfection or usefulness than metaphorical definition is the negative definition. Anton Raphael Mengs (1728–79), a pupil of J. J. Winckelmann, for example, defined beauty as being the opposite to ugliness ("La bellezza è l'opposito della brutezza"), and Sir Charles Bell not only quotes this definition in his work but also adopts it from Mengs, whereas Winckelmann confines himself to stating that it was easier to say what beauty is not than what it is.[13] D. W. Prall moves along similar lines when writing that if aesthetics were limited to investigating the notion of beauty, then "Beauty would be at most what is not aesthetically unsatisfactory."[14] Jonas

---

[10] J. McCosh, *Psychology, The Motive Powers*, p. 136.

[11] Munro, *op. cit.*, p. 265. See also pp. 262–301.

[12] W. Knight, *The Philosophy of the Beautiful, I: Its History* (London: J. Murray, 1903), 60, 67.

[13] J. J. Winckelmann (*op. cit.*, p. 105) quotes this negative definition from A. R. Mengs, *Über Schönheit und guten Geschmack in der Malerei*, III, 1. See Sir Charles Bell, *The Anatomy and Philosophy of Expression as Connected with the Fine Arts* (London: J. Murray, 1844), 21–22.

[14] D. W. Prall, *Aesthetic Analysis*, p. 3.

Cohn's definition also bears the character of negativity as it equates beauty with a conflictless modification of the aesthetic.[15]

6. Sometimes the violation of the rules of logic lies not in the chosen species of the definition of beauty but in the obscurity of it. Fully realizing that, out of context, any proposition is less clear or more obscure than in context, one may still not be unfair to the author, Harold Osborne, when quoting his following definition as an instance of obscure definition: "Beauty itself is simply the extension of that principle of emergent perceptual configuration immediately apprehensible by unreflective intuition . . ."[16]

Very similar is a definition that lacks clarity on account of the vagueness of the genus ascribed to beauty. Michelangelo, for example, defined beauty as "the purgation of superfluities."[17] Obviously, this statement would be enlightening to us only if we were told what the thing is in reference to which the purged things are superfluous. Nor does one learn much more about the essence of beauty by such statements as this by Horatio Greenough: "I define beauty as the promise of function."[18]

7. An additional violation of the rules of logic is committed by definitions of beauty that are more universal than the definitum and, thus, are not convertible with it. Let us take, for example, the following three definitions. According to Van Meter Ames, "Beauty is value contemplated"; according to Max Schoen, "Let us for the sake of simplicity . . . call whatever positive value a critic finds in a work of art 'beauty' "; and, according to Charles W. Cooper, "Beauty is a positive value regarded as inherent."[19] It is easy to see that, while all these assertions may be true of beauty, they are not convertible with beauty since things other than beauty may also be said to be values described in these definitions.

A curiously incorrect non-essential definition of beauty is of the *idem per idem* type, using a synonym of the definitum. Such seems to be the case at least objectively (although not subjectively, according to the intentions and notions of the authors), with the definitions offered by S. Alexander and William David Ross. The former writes, "Beauty is the expression not of any and every feeling but specifically of the aesthetic feeling."[20] The latter declares, Beauty is not a form of intrinsic value, but only the power in an object of

---

[15] Cohn, *Allgemeine Aesthetik*, II, 4, 2 (Leipzig: W. Engelmann, 1901), 168.

[16] H. Osborne, *Theory of Beauty* (London: Routledge and Kegan Paul, 1952), 122.

[17] See, R. W. Emerson, *Conduct of Life*, Essay VIII: "Beauty" (Boston: New York: Houghton Mifflin, 1904), 294.

[18] Harold A. Small, ed., *Form and Function, Remarks on Art by Horatio Greenough* (Berkeley: University of California Press, 1947), 71. See also p. 76.

[19] Van Meter Ames, *Introduction to Beauty* (New York: Harper, 1931), 5, 171, 204. Max Schoen, *The Enjoyment of the Arts* (New York: Philosophical Library, 1944), 312. C. W. Cooper, *The Arts and Humanity* (New York: Philosophical Library, 1952), 82.

[20] S. Alexander, *Beauty and Other Forms of Value* (London: Macmillan, 1933), 132.

evoking something that has value, the aesthetic experience."[21] Now, what Alexander seems to be saying is that beauty is the expression of the feeling about beauty; and what W. D. Ross seems to be saying is simply that beauty is the power of evoking experience with beauty; and, thereby, neither definition is anything more than circular.

Finally, there is a curiously defective sort of definition, which is, in reality, not a definition at all but a division used as and used in place of a definition. The historically first instance of this is to be found in Plato's *Major Hippias*. Socrates asks the young and self-assured Hippias the great and fundamental question, "What is beauty?"; to which Hippias replies by telling Socrates that "a beautiful maiden is beauty," not seeing the difference between "What is beauty?" and "What things are beautiful?"[22] This error is repeated by Père André who, in answering his own question, "What is beauty?"divides beauty into divine, natural, and artificial beauty.[23]

8. Taking up next the logically correct non-essential definitions of beauty, whereby the skepticism of the authors is implied, we find at least three species among them. They are: definition by accident, definition by efficient cause, and definition by effect.

Definition by accident can be found, for instance, in Père Buffier, who wrote the following: "What is termed beautiful, or beauty, seems to me to consist in that which is at the same time the most common and most rare in things of the same species."[24] Now, it should be obvious that the relative frequency of occurrence with regard to any kind of being is merely a matter of discrete quantity, hence, an accident rather than anything the being in question itself is. Similarly, when Michelangelo observed that beauty was "the mirrored image of God,"[25] he simply expressed of beauty its qualitative relation of similarity, and that is as much an accident as quantity is.

Definition by efficient cause has been employed by all those who, instead

---

[21] W. D. Ross, *The Right and the Good* (Oxford: Clarendon Press, 1930), 70. However, this defect is corrected in a paraphrase of this definition on page 127.

[22] Plato, *Hipp. mai.*, 286d–287e.

[23] Père (Le P. Yves) André, *Essai sur le Beau*, Discourse 1 (Paris: H. L. Guérin et J. Guérin, 1770), 4–6. It must be pointed out here that one is not guilty of this kind of erroneous definition of beauty if he does what Hippias does in Plato's dialogue *after* he actually defined beauty in some proper manner. Thus, Gustav E. Mueller is somewhat unfairly quoted by Isabel C. Hungerland (review of G. E. Mueller's *The World as Spectacle*, New York: Philosophical Library, 1944 in *The Journal of Aesthetics and Art Criticism*, IV, 4, June 1946, p. 251) as identifying beauty with "the living universe as one spectacle" (Mueller, *op. cit.*, p. 115). For, before he made this statement, Mueller had already defined beauty as the "dialectical unity of the one and the many" in a previous context (*ibid.*, p. 103).

[24] Père Claude Buffier, *Traité des Vérités premières et de la source de nos jugements*, part I, ch. 13, § 94 (Paris: V. Monge, 1724); English tr., *First Truths, and the Origin of Our Opinions* (London: J. Johnson, 1780), 66.

[25] Michelangelo, "To Cavalieri" (1536–42); quoted in Sir A. Blunt, *Artistic Theory in Italy 1450–1600* (Oxford: Clarendon, 1962), 69, n. 2.

of telling what beauty is, express what causes or produces beauty. Among them we find the aestheticians advocating the idea that some impulse or instinct causes man to make artworks. For instance, Schiller writes in his aesthetic letters that beauty is "the common object of both impulses (sc. the sense impulse and the form impulse), that is to say of the play impulse."[26] While Schiller named man as the efficient cause of beauty, W. Barns claimed both God and man to be this cause by stating that "the beautiful in Nature is the unmarred result of God's first creative or forming will, and the beautiful in Art is the result of unmistaken working of man in accordance with the beautiful in Nature."[27]

A third and very large group of thinkers employ definition by effect in their implicitly skeptic characterization of beauty. However, while the generic character of these definitions is one by effect, there is an amazing variety of specific versions to be found among them.

9. The basic formula of the definition by effect of beauty, according to classical and especially medieval tradition, is this: The beautiful is that which, when it becomes known, delights.[28] It is easy to see that this basic formula consists of two parts, the first being the cognitive element, viz., knowledge; the second, the appetitive element, viz., delight. Richard Payne Knight puts it

[26] F. Schiller, *On the Aesthetic Education of Man*, letter 15; tr. Reginald Snell (New Haven: Yale University Press, 1954), 77.

[27] W. Barns, "Thoughts on Beauty and Art," in *Macmillan's Magazine*, ed. D. Masson (London: Macmillan, June 1861), 126.

[28] Thomas Gallus Vercellensis: (Anima) circa summe pulchrum delectatur per cognitionem; *In Canticum Canticorum* of 1224; ed. Pez, *Thesaurus anecdotorum novissimus*, II, 1, (Aug. Vindel., 1724), col. 503–690; quoted in E. De Bruyne, *Études d'Esthétique Médiévale* (Brugge, Belgium: De Tempel, 1946), III, 59, and referred to in M. T. D'Alverny, "Le second Commentaire du Thomas Gallus, abbé de Verceil, sur le Cantique des Cantiques," *Archives d'Histoire doctrinale et litteraire du Moyen Age*, XIII (1942), 392, n. 8. William of Auvergne: Pulchrum visu dicimus quod natum est per seipsum placere spectantibus et delectare secundum visum; *De bono et malo*, Codex Balliol 207, fol. 206v (ed. cit., p. 268). Thomas Aquinas: pulchra enim dicuntur quae visa placent; *S. theol*. I, 5, 4, ad 1; and pulchrum autem dicatur id cuius ipsa apprehensio placet (*ibid*., I–II, 27, 1, ad 3). See this same definition or some paraphrase of it also in Aquinas' disciple, Dionysius the Carthusian, *op. cit.*, art. 1 (*ed. cit.*, p. 227 B); Cardinal Cajetan, *Commentaria*, II. ad *S. Thomae Summam theologiam*, I–II, q. 27, a. 1, ad 3 (Leonine-edition of *Opera omnia S. Thomae Aquinatis*, VI, 192); D. Petavius, *De Deo Deique proprietatibus*, in *Dogmata theologica*, I, l. 6, c. 8, n. IX; ed. J. B. Fournialis (Paris: L. Vivès, 1865), 347; F. Suarez, *Disputationes metaphysicae*, disp. 10, sec. 2, n. 1; *Opera omnia*, vol. 25 (Paris: L. Vivès, 1861), 337b; John of St. Thomas, *Cursus Philosophicus Thomisticus*, III: *Naturalis philosophia*, pars IV, q. 4, a. 2, tertio arguitur; ed. B. Reiser (Taurini: Marietti, 1948), 120a; etc. For formulations of this definitions see, e.g., Cicero, *De off*. I, 28, 98; Plotinus, *Enn*. I, 6, 2; V, 5, 12; Proclus, *Commentarium in Platonis Alcibiadem priorem*, n. 221 (*Proclus: Alcibiades I, A Translation and Commentary*, by William O'Neill, The Hague: M. Nijhoff, 1965), 146; and Augustine, *De civ. Dei*, XXII, 24, 4 (*PL* 41, 791) and *De ordine*, II, 12, 35 (*PL* 32, 1011). For modern restatements of this definition, see, e.g., Thomas Hobbes, *De homine*, c. 11, n. 5 in *Opera philosophica*, II, ed. G. Molesworth (London: J. Bohn, 1839), 97; G. Berkeley, *Alciphron*, dial. III, 8; in *The Works of G. Berkeley*, III, ed. T. E. Jessop (London: Thomas Nelson and Sons, 1950), 123; E. Burke, *op. cit.*, I, 9; A. G. Baumgarten, *Metaphysica*, § 662 (*ed. cit.*, p. 171); and J. Ruskin, *The True and the Beautiful in Nature, Art, Morals, and Religion*, selected by L. C. Tuthill (New York: Merrill and Zatzer, 1886), 3.

this way: "The word Beauty is a general term of approbation ... applied indiscriminately to almost everything that is pleasing, either to the sense, the imagination, or the understanding."[29] This definition makes it clear that, firstly, beauty delights and that, secondly, this delight is due to some kind of knowledge. G. E. Moore is briefer and, if possible, even clearer: "It appears probable that the beautiful should be defined as that of which the admiring contemplation is good in itself."[30]

Now, if there are going to be some variations on this basic formula of the definition by effect of beauty, they may either increase the number of its components, or decrease them, or weaken or understate at least one of the two components. Sir George Stewart Mackenzie does the former, adding one more note to perceptive pleasurableness: "[Beauty in a particular high degree and Beautiful are] the sign by which we express the consciousness of pleasurable effects following the perception of certain qualities in objects."[31] Others keep the classic dualism of the formula, but understate either the cognitive or the appetitive part or both parts of it. Curt J. Ducasse writes, for example, "Beauty ... is ... a capacity—the capacity some things have of causing pleasure in some contemplative beholders of them,"[32] and, thereby, he does not make clear that contemplative knowledge causes the delight in question. On the other hand, Eric Newton understates the pleasing effect of bauty: "Beauty is that aspect of phenomena which, when perceived by the senses and thence referred to the contemplative faculty of the perceiver, has the power to evoke responses drawn from his accumulated experience."[33] The third alternative seems to be the case with the definition of F. W. Ruckstull, rendering both the cognitive and the appetitive component merely implicit: "Objective beauty appeals principally to the Eyes ...; semiobjective beauty, ... to the eyes and partly to the Ears, and partly to the mind; subjective beauty appeals to the Mind alone."[34]

The third generic alternative of reducing the two components in the definition by effect of beauty consists in eliminating either the factor of pleasure or that of knowledge. Franz Hemsterhuis, a Dutch disciple of A. G. Baumgarten, does the former when defining beauty as that (quality?) in the object which elicits the largest number of ideas within the shortest time in the intellect.[35] Similarly, in his analysis of the aesthetic experience, D. W. Gotschalk

[29] R. P. Knight, *op. cit.*, p. 9.
[30] G. E. Moore, *Principia Ethica* (Cambridge University Press, 1962), 201.
[31] G. S. Mackenzie, *Essay on some subjects connected with Taste* (Edinburgh: Oliphant, Waugh, and Innes, 1817), 39.
[32] C. J. Ducasse, *Art, The Critics, and You*, p. 91.
[33] E. Newton, *The Meaning of Beauty* (Penguin Books, 1962), 212.
[34] F. W. Ruckstull, *Great Works of Art* (Garden City, N. Y.: Garden City Publishing Company, 1925), 98.
[35] F. Hemsterhuis, "Alexis," in *Philosophische Schriften*, II, ed. Julius Hilss (Karlsruhe und Leipzig: Dreililien Verlag, 1912), 272. Cf. p. 275.

comes to such conclusions as "Aesthetic experience, then, is intuitive perception or attention directed simply toward the full apprehension of the intrinsic perceptual being and value of the object of perception," and, "aesthetic experience is simply alert perception allowed intrinsic scope."[36]

Others, on the other hand, oppress the cognitive factor completely, while either keeping the pleasure factor explicit or weakening it somehow. Elizabeth Schneider chooses the former alternative by defining beauty "provisionally" as "that which produces or tends to produce in the beholder, under favorable conditions of mood and attention, an aesthetic response," and characterizing that response as one that "derives from feeling rather than from thinking."[37] Others have chosen the second alternative: ignoring the cognitive factor and weakening the component of delight. Stephen C. Pepper wrote, for instance, "We shall call a thing beautiful in the broadest aesthetic sense if it is simply something liked for itself."[38] Similarly, together with other followers of the theory of empathy (Theodor Lipps, Sourian, etc.), Vernon Lee characterizes the beautiful as anything that causes in us dynamical responses which are "favourable to our existence," and which we then attribute to the thing as its beauty.[39] Max J. Friedländer accomplishes the understating of the second factor by narrowing the delightfulness of beauty to vision: "We call beautiful that which pleases the eye."[40]

Even more radical than these authors are those who leave the cognitive component unmentioned, and are quite vague about the other component to the point of transforming it into another factor. Grant Allen, for instance, declares, "The aesthetically beautiful is that which affords the Maximum of Stimulation with the Minimum of Fatigue or Waste";[41] and Charles H. Caffin uses this formula: "In a general way that which for the time being satisfies some craving of our nature, seems to us to be beautiful."[42]

Finally, let us quote a definition by effect of beauty in which there seems to be no trace either of the cognitive or of the appetitive component. Such is F. Ram's, in whose opinion "those qualities of body and mind which have tended in the environment of a race to the production of the largest number of descendants constitute Beauty among that race,"[43] and also Ethel D. Puf-

---

[36] D. W. Gotshalk, *Art and the Social Order* (New York: Dover, 1962), 17, 20.

[37] E. Schneider, *Aesthetic Motive* (New York: Macmillan, 1939), 29, 34.

[38] S. C. Pepper, *Principles of Art Appreciation* (New York: Harcourt, Brace, 1949), 12.

[39] V. Lee, C. Anstruther-Thomson, *op. cit.*, p. 21.

[40] M. J. Friedländer, *On Art and Connoisseurship* (Boston: Beacon Press, 1960), 87.

[41] G. Allen, *op. cit.*, p. 39.

[42] C. H. Caffin, *Art for Life's Sake* (Chicago: Prang, 1913), 90. See also *Art Today*, ed. R. Faulkner, E. Ziegfeld, G. Hill (New York: H. Holt, 1959), 526.

[43] F. Ram, "Beauty in the eyes of an evolutionist," in *The Journal of Science* (London: Horse-Shoe Court, Ludgate Hill, February and March, 1882), 78.

fer's: "The beautiful object possesses those qualities which bring the personality into a state of unity and self-completeness."[44]

Before turning to other skeptic definitions, the following question must be raised: Should the use of the definition by effect of beauty always be considered as a sign of aesthetic skepticism? The answer to this question is a categorical *No*. Indeed, some of the greatest epistemological realists described beauty in terms of its effects. Thus, whether or not the employment of the definition by effect of beauty is a sign of skepticism depends, in case of the absence of any explicit statement, on whether or not this is the only kind of definition of beauty which any given author offers. This is to say that, if the definition by effect is the only type of definition given in a work, the author is or appears to be a skeptic in this matter; if there are other and logically better definitions (one by property or essence) also offered in the work, the author is clearly non-skeptic.

10. The listing of the various types of skeptic definitions may properly be ended by mentioning a view which connects the heretofore listed skeptic positions with the non-skeptic ones. It is the rather unique position taken by a few persons like Edward Howard Griggs and John Bascom. Griggs lists three objective principles, "in the nature of beauty," just as any objectivist thinker would. Yet, he adds to this objectivist theory the following unexpected remark: "Thus it is possible to show the elements of beauty and the conditions of our appreciation of it, but beauty itself remains undefined."[45] Similarly, John J. Bascom asserts that, since beauty is a simple, primary quality, analysis cannot resolve it into more basic components; yet he proceeds to list three conditions or principles of beauty, namely, expression, unity, and truth.[46] Now, by virtue of their listing the objective principles of beauty, these authors, if considered objectively, are undoubtedly non-skeptic thinkers. Yet, in virtue of their above quoted remarks, they are subjectively, according to their own ideas and convictions, skeptic thinkers. For this reason they differ from all the authors of all the other above-quoted definitions as the subjectively or apparently skeptic does from the objectively or actually skeptic. Being, however, objectively non-skeptic, they lead us over to the advocates of non-skeptic theories of beauty to be discussed in the next articles.

ARTICLE 2: *Subjectivist and Idealist Views on Beauty*

1. All the non-skeptic views are epistemologically realistic. An epistemologically realistic position is thus one that expresses the thinker's conviction that it is possible to define beauty essentially.

---

[44] E. D. Puffer, *The Psychology of Beauty* (Boston: Houghton Mifflin, 1905), 49.

[45] E. H. Griggs, *The Philosophy of Art*, pp. 294–99. Cf. also, p. 292.

[46] J. Bascom, *Aesthetics, or the Science of Beauty*, Lectures 1–5, (New York: G. P. Putnam, 1881), 8, 11–12, 14–76.

If there are many kinds or versions of skeptic views, then there are incomparably more kinds or versions of epistemologically realistic definitions. Due to the variety of such definitions, the question of how to divide them is very difficult. There have been many attempts made at the division of the realist definitions. One relatively recent and well-known attempt is to be found in *The Foundations of Aesthetics* by I. A. Richards, C. K. Ogden, and James Wood, listing sixteen different definitions, reduced to three generic groups.[1] Another attempt can be found in the *Dictionary of World Literature*,[2] reducing the various definitions to four classes, viz., those considering beauty as essence, as relation, as cause, and as effect. A third attempt is much older, contained in James McCosh's *The Emotions*. It divides the various aesthetic theories into idealistic, objectivistic, and subjectivistic views.[3] Of these three listed attempts, the first two, unlike the third, are rather arbitrary and haphazard divisions, whereas they are much more detailed and comprehensive than the third one. This circumstance may give us already a hint as to the necessary requirements of any division of the realistic definitions of beauty: such a division must obviously be both comprehensive or reasonably detailed as well as systematic both in its general framework and its details. On this basis, we may venture to offer the following over-all division of non-skeptic or epistemologically realistic views.

First, all non-skeptic definitions may be divided into subjectivist and objectivist definitions: the former including all definitions that reduce beauty to something intramental; and the latter, to something extramental. The objectivist definitions, in turn, may conveniently be divided into idealistic and (metaphysically) realistic definitions. The former are characterized by the assertion that some idea, constituting or contributing to beauty, exists outside the mind; the latter, that beauty is a quality of things that exists in things independent of the mind's consideration.

For methodological reasons, the subjectivist and the idealist views will be discussed in the present article; the realistic definitions, in the next.

2. As already stated, all the subjectivist definitions have this in common: they all express the intramental nature of beauty, that is, the fact that beauty is something to be found only in the human mind.

Now, the subjectivist definitions can be divided, first of all, into really and apparently subjectivist definitions. The former assert the non-objectivity of beauty without adding anything that might indicate the opposite. The latter

---

[1] Richards, Ogden, Wood, *The Foundations of Aesthetics* (New York: Lear, 1925), 20–21. See the same 16 definitions in C. K. Ogden, I. A. Richards, *The Meaning of Meaning*, (New York: Harcourt, Brace, 1952), 142f.; and in C. W. Cooper, *op. cit.*, pp. 69–73.

[2] *Dictionary of World Literature*, ed. J. T. Shipley (Paterson, N. J.: Littlefield, Adams, 1960), 36–38.

[3] J. McCosh, *The Emotions*, pp. 148–53.

express the non-objectivity of beauty in such a way as to indicate also the opposite, namely, the objectivity of beauty.

Taking up first the actually subjectivist definitions, we find that they can further be divided into completely and partly subjectivist definitions. The former express that beauty is intramental in every respect; the latter, that beauty is partly extramental and partly intramental.

The completely subjectivist definitions themselves are manifold: cognitive, emotional, and mixed. The cognitive type of completely subjectivist definition makes beauty a mental picture which, when superimposed on the image of the perceived thing, delights the knower. This is the theory of Benedetto Croce, as he remarks, "it seems now both permissible and advisable to define beauty as successful expression, or rather, as expression and nothing more, because expression when it is not successful is not expression."[4] In explaining this theory, Croce further states that "the beautiful is not a physical fact; it does not belong to things, but to the activity of man, to spiritual energy"; and, "nature is beautiful only for him who contemplates her with the eye of the artist; . . . without the aid of the imagination, no part of nature is beautiful."[5] This expression, as the addition by the imagination to the perceived image is, thus, an "internal fact" to which, as to a content, an extrinsic, material, physical "form" may accidentally be added by the artist.[6] All this makes it quite clear that, to Croce, beauty is indeed nothing but an internal picture or vision of man's cognitive power, and that this theory is unmistakenly intellectualistic.

3. Much more widespread and popular is the voluntarist or hedonist version of completely subjectivist definition of beauty, according to which beauty is simply pleasure.

Among the subjectivists who so define beauty, some simply state that beauty is pleasure; others add to this that beauty is pleasure objectified. Henry Rutgers Marshall and Richard Müller-Freienfels belong to the former group,[7] whereas among those who define beauty as pleasure objectified, we find, besides G. Santayana and J. Dewey,[8] both earlier and more recent aestheticians. Dr. Thomas Brown, for example, writes thus: "Beauty, I have said, is necessarily an emotion that is pleasing, and it is an emotion which we diffuse, and combine with our conception of the object that may have excited it. These two circumstances, the pleasing nature of the emotion itself, and the identification of it with the object that excites it, are essential to it."[9] Charles W. Cooper, on the

[4] B. Croce, *Aesthetic*, p. 79.
[5] *Op. cit.*, pp. 97, 99.
[6] *Op. cit.*, p. 98.
[7] H. R. Marshall, *The Beautiful* (London: Macmillan, 1924), 78 and 60f., respectively. R. Müller-Freienfels, *Psychologie der Kunst*, I: *Allgemeine Grundlegung und Psychologie der Kunstgeniessens* (Leipzig-Berlin: R. G. Teubner, 1922), 222, 233.
[8] Santayana, *op. cit.*, § 11. J. Dewey, *Art as Experience*, p. 248.
[9] Thomas Brown, *Lectures on the Philosophy of the Human Mind*, Lecture 53; *ed. cit.*, II, 19. See also p. 20; and Lecture 54, in II, 21.

other hand, puts the same definition this way: "Beauty is a positive value regarded as inherent."[10]

A third basic version of completely subjective definition of beauty is more sophisticated than either of the other two, and identifies beauty with a complex subjective experience called synaesthesis which is said to include both "equilibrium" and "harmony." This view is described in *The Foundations of Aesthetics* by I. A. Richards, C. K. Ogden, and James Wood.[11]

4. In contrast with the completely subjectivist definitions, there are those which are only partly subjectivist. These are the definitions of the relationists, who hold that beauty is neither in the object, nor in the subject, but in the meeting of the two. Such are, as discussed previously, the definitions of Lord Kames, Maurice de Wulf, J. L. Jarrett, and others. However, since aesthetic relationism is at least objectively, although not according to intention, a sort of aesthetic objectivism, relationist definitions lead us directly to the least radical of all subjectivist definitions of beauty, those of apparent aesthetic subjectivism.

Robert Morris Ogden, for instance, authored this curious definition: "Beauty is the experience we enjoy and value when a figure-ground pattern engages our interest by its own attractions and in its own right."[12] This definition quite clearly begins as a subjectivist one, stating beauty to be an enjoyable experience. However, when it proceeds to name the "own attractions" of certain patterns as the cause of this enjoyable experience, it suddenly turns into an objectivist definition. Similar seems to be the case with certain statements made by Aram Torossian. For, on the one hand, he declares that the "beautiful" or the "ugly" "never characterizes definitely the qualities of an object," and thereby he talks like a subjectivist. On the other hand, he remarks also in the immediately preceding proposition that "the statement, 'That is beautiful,' in the aesthetic sense is a general remark implying our satisfaction for the successful expression of the values or for the values themselves in the perceived object,"[13] and this sounds very much like the talk of the objectivist.

With the apparent subjectivist definitions, we have come quite close to the definitions of the aesthetic objectivists. Let us, therefore, take up and divide next the first main genus of objectivism, viz., the idealist definitions of beauty.

5. All idealist definitions agree on at least one thing, namely, that some kind of idea constitutes beauty in some manner.

This characterization indicates a twofold variety of idealist views: one, with respect to the specific nature of the idea in question; and another, with respect to the manner in which the idea constitutes beauty.

With regard to the nature of the idea in question, there are two funda-

---

[10] C. W. Cooper, *op. cit.*, p. 82.
[11] Chap. XIV: "Synaesthesis"; *ed. cit.*, pp. 72–88.
[12] R. M. Ogden, *op. cit.*, p. 19.
[13] A. Torossian, *op. cit.*, p. 29.

mentally different versions of idealist views on beauty: the transcendent or superhuman, and the immanent or human.

The transcendent or superhuman version of aesthetic idealism considers the idea that constitutes beauty to be outside, above, and beyond the human mind, that is, a kind of infinite, divine, or absolute Idea; the immanent or human version of aesthetic idealism considers the idea constituting beauty to be in the human mind.

The transcendental version of aesthetic idealism is itself twofold, according to whether the divine or absolute Idea is held to be immutable or mutable.

Beauty is held to be an immutable, divine Idea by Plato: "It is an everlasting loveliness which neither comes nor goes, which neither flowers nor fades, for such beauty is the same on every hand, the same then as now, here and there, this way as that way, the same to every worshipper as it is to every other."[14] Others consider beauty to be a divine or absolute Idea that undergoes an immanent or transient process of self-development.

Within this general framework of thought, the definitions of the various German idealists and their disciples seem, at first sight, to be very similar, if not identical. They all express that beauty is the Idea as it shines through matter, thereby materially conforming to the theory of Plotinus. Thus, F. W. J. Schelling defines beauty as the finite representation of the Infinite;[15] Hegel, as the sensory shining or manifestation of the Idea;[16] A. Schopenhauer, as the representation by the manifold, definite, and distinct form of the Idea;[17] K. W. F. Solger, as "an idea placed into matter" or "An appearance in which the Idea lies";[18] Theodore S. Jouffroy, as the expression of the Invisible by the natural signs manifesting it;[19] F. T. Vischer, as "the idea in the form of finite appearance";[20] A. C. Bradley, as "the image of the total presence of the Infinite within any limits it may choose to assume," hence, "the image of its immanence";[21] etc.

However, upon closer examination, the various idealist views, especially those of the German idealists, show variety in at least two respects: firstly, in terms of the successive stages in the self-development of the Idea; and secondly,

---

[14] Plato, *Symp.* 211a. Tr. Michael Joyce, in *The Collected Dialogues of Plato*, ed. E. Hamilton, H. Cairns, Bollingen Series LXXI (New York: Pantheon Books, 1961), 562.

[15] Schelling, *System des transcendentalen Idealismus*, VI, 2; in *Sämtliche Werke*, III (Stuttgart, Augsburg: J. G. Cotta, 1858), 620. Cf. *Philosophie der Kunst*, I, 3, 65; *ed. cit.*, V, 461, 468f.

[16] Hegel, *Vorlesungen über die Ästhetik*, part 1, chap. 1, § 3; in *Sämtliche Werke*, Jubiläumsausgabe, XII (Stuttgart: Fr. Frommans, 1927), 160.

[17] A. Schopenhauer, *The World as Will and Idea* (1818), I, 3, §§ 39, 41.

[18] K. F. Solger, *Vorlesungen über Ästhetik*, pp. 4, 127.

[19] T. S. Jouffroy, *Cours d'Esthétique*, ed. Damiron (Paris: Librairie de L. Hachette, 1843), 243.

[20] F. T. Vischer, *Ästhetik, oder Wissenschaft des Schönen.* I: *Die Metaphysik des Schönen*, § 14. Ed. Robert Vischer (München: Meyer und Jessen, 1922), 52.

[21] A. C. Bradley, "The Sublime," in *Oxford Lectures on Poetry* (London: Macmillan, 1926), 62.

in terms of the necessity or contingency of a union between the Idea and matter in constituting beauty.

6. With respect to the successive stages of the inner development of the Idea, one finds five different versions of theories among the German idealists, as they describe the Idea as manifesting itself in the form of beauty or art, truth or philosophy, and goodness or religion. For, according to Schelling, art succeeds both philosophy and religion, being the identity of the two; according to Hegel, the Absolute Spirit reaches first the stage of art (artistic beauty) before reaching the stages of religion and philosophy; according to Christian Weisse, the stage of art follows that of philosophy and precedes that of religion; according to F. T. Vischer, art follows religion, and precedes philosophy; and, finally, according to Wirth, the stages of religion and philosophy preceded art.[22]

The other way of classifying the German idealist views is that according to the mode or manner in which beauty involves, besides the Idea, matter itself. One of the two positions is, to use Eduard von Hartmann's terminology, that of "abstract idealism"; the other, that of "concrete idealism."

According to abstract idealism, beauty is essentially the Idea, a suprasensory element, in an accidental union with matter as the sensory element of it. According to concrete idealism, on the other hand, beauty is the essential union of Idea and matter, of the suprasensory and the sensory element. The former view is represented, among others, by F. W. J. Schelling, A. Schopenhauer, K. C. F. Krause, K. W. F. Solger, C. H. Weisse, and H. Lotze; the latter view, among others, by Hegel, K. F. E. Trahndorff, F. E. D. Schleiermacher, M. Deutinger, H. C. Oersted, F. T. Vischer, A. Zeising, Meising, M. Carrière, M. Schasler, and E. von Hartmann.[23]

7. Opposed to all versions of transcendental idealism is immanent aesthetic idealism. This is the generic position holding that beauty is the expression of something human in matter. There are two classes of this position: one, that does not specify the object of aesthetic expression; and another that does specify it.

Among the representatives of the former version of immanent idealism we find, for instance, Bernard Bosanquet, who defines beauty as that "which has characteristic or individual expressiveness for sense-perception or imagination, subject to the conditions of general or abstract expressiveness in the same medium";[24] and L. A. Reid, who declares simply, "Beauty is the absolute ideal of perfect expressiveness."[25]

Those who do specify the object of aesthetic expression comprise three

[22] See F. T. Vischer, *op. cit.*, part I, Introduction, § 5; *ed. cit.*, pp. 21–24.

[23] See E. von Hartmann, *Die deutsche Ästhetik seit Kant* (Leipzig: W. Freidrich, 1886), 357–62; and *Die Philosophie des Schönen* (Leipzig: H. Haacke, 1890), 463f.

[24] B. Bosanquet, *A History of Aesthetic* (Cleveland, New York: The World Publishing Company, 1961), 5. Cf. *Three Lectures on Aesthetic*, p. 33.

[25] L. A. Reid, *A Study in Aesthetics* (London: George Allen and Unwin, 1931), 218.

groups: one, that is intellectualist; another that is emotionalist; and a third that is vitalist.

The intellectualist version of immanent aesthetic idealism holds beauty to be the expression of human ideas. F. Schleiermacher, for instance, defines the beautiful as "that which conforms in reality to the Ideal," whereas "the Ideal means the basic type of the play of imagination."[26] Similarly, Vincenzo Gioberti defines beauty as "the individual union of an intelligible type with an imaginative element called into being by the acts of aesthetic imagination," the intelligible element being its form, and the imaginative element, its matter.[27] Leopold Eidlitz echoes both: "The nature of beauty is to be found in the successful expression of an idea in matter."[28] W. T. Stace puts this idea the following way: "[Beauty] is the fusion of an intellectual content, consisting of empirical non-perceptual concepts, with a perceptual field, in such manner that the intellectual content and the perceptual field are indistinguishable from one another; and in such manner as to constitute the revelation of an aspect of reality."[29]

Some authors go so far in this direction as to specify the human idea of which beauty is an expression. Bertram Morris, for instance, thinks that "purpose" is such an idea: "We may define beauty as the expression of a purpose in a sensuous medium."[30]

The second specific group of human idealists specifying the object of aesthetic expression define beauty as an expression of a human emotion or feeling. E. F. Carritt is one of the advocates of this view: "The beauty we ascribe to sensible objects is really their expressiveness of some feeling—of fear, of confidence, of joy in life, of longing for death...."[31]

A third specific group of human idealists specifying the object of aesthetic expression side neither with those holding that beauty is the expression of human ideas nor with those maintaining that beauty is the expression of human feelings. Instead, they prefer to think that beauty expresses human life in general, or anything about it. Harold Osborne, for instance, speaking of the theory of aesthetic expressionism, remarks, "On this view beauty in a work of art is defined in terms of expression: any work of art is beautiful in accordance with the adequacy with which it communicates the inner life or experience of the Artist...."[32]

[26] F. Schleiermacher, *Aesthetik*, p. 101.
[27] V. Gioberti, "Il Bello," cap. 1, in *Scritti scelti*; *Classici Italiani*, 85 (Torino: Temporelli, 1966), 214.
[28] L. Eidlitz, *The Nature and Function of Art, more especially of Architecture* (London: Sampson Low, Marston, Searle and Rivington, 1881), 186.
[29] W. T. Stace, *The Meaning of Beauty*, chap. 3 (London: G. Richards, H. Toulmin, 1929), 43.
[30] B. Morris, *The Aesthetic Process* (Evanston: Northwestern University, 1943), 52.
[31] E. F. Carritt, *An Introduction to Aesthetics*, p. 50. Cf. also his *The Theory of Beauty* (New York: Macmillan, 1914), 286f.
[32] H. Osborne, *Aesthetics and Criticism*, p. 141.

Those who disagree with both the subjectivist and all idealist views on beauty are the aesthetic realists. Let us, therefore, complete our investigation of the variety of views on beauty by finding out the disagreement prevailing among the aesthetic realists.

ARTICLE 3: *Realistic Definitions of Beauty*

1. Realistic definition is one that implies or presupposes the objective, extramental existence of beauty.

The enormous variety of this kind of definition may be divided into three large genera, listing first the definitions which are farthest removed from the proper definition of the essence of beauty and, successively, those which come closer and closer to a proper essential definition of beauty.

The first genus of realistic definitions is that which may be called transcendentalist; the second, formalist; the third, totalist.

The first of the three genera includes all definitions that express the nature of beauty in terms of or in reference to notions which in ancient and medieval philosophies had been considered to be transcendental, i.e., transcending all genera of being since predicable of all genera of being. The second genus of definitions identifies the nature of beauty only with the forms of the beautiful things. The third genus of definitions includes all the definitions that identify beauty with the totality, rather than with only the form, of the beautiful thing.

Of these three genera, the first seems to be the least proper type since, instead of specifically differentiating beauty from everything else, it tends generically to identify or connect beauty with other transcendentals. The second genus seems to be more correct or perfect than the first insofar as it actually specifies beauty in its nature; yet, it also seems to be less correct than the third genus, because it arbitrarily excludes certain contributing principles (matter, content) from the inner constitution of beauty.

Let us discuss these three genera of realistic definitions of beauty in the above-mentioned sequence.

2. The transcendentalist type of definitions of beauty can be divided into pure and mixed types of definitions. The former include nothing but an identification with or a reference to a transcendental concept; the latter add some non-transcendental to the transcendental notion.

The purely transcendentalist definitions of beauty can be of three kinds: those relating beauty to (or identifying it with) truth, goodness, or both truth and goodness.

Of these three, the most frequently employed version is the first, connecting beauty with truth in some manner. Lord Shaftesbury wrote, for instance, that "all beauty is truth";[1] Pierre Nicole, that "Truth is the source of beauty";[2] and

---

[1] Lord Shaftesbury, "Freedom of Wit and Humor," part 4, section 3; in *Characteristics*, treatise 2, *ed. cit.*, p. 94.

Nicolas Boileau, that nothing is beautiful that is not true.[3] On the other hand, Jules E. N. Lachelier maintained conversely that "the only stable truth which is worthy of this name is beauty."[4]

Others, like J. Jungmann,[5] define beauty as being goodness of some kind or in some manner. This is, as a matter of fact, the oldest version of all transcendentalist views, going back as far as Plato's identification of goodness and beauty[6] on the one hand, and to Albert's and Thomas' merely logical distinction of the two,[7] on the other hand.

A third version of transcendentalist definitions identifies beauty with both truth and goodness, or relates beauty to the other two. One advocate of this view is R. W. Emerson who stated, "Truth, and goodness, and beauty, are but different faces of the same All."[8]

Different from all these three kinds is the transcendentalist definition that adds another notion to that of truth and/or goodness as constituting the essence of beauty. Thus, Rodolphe Töpffer asserted that beauty was the splendor of truth,[9] whereas Albert J. Steiss wrote, in a less specific manner, that "Beauty is the special quality of concentrated truth."[10] T. Pesch, on the other hand, added splendor to three transcendental concepts in his definition of beauty, declaring that beauty is the splendor of unity, truth, and goodness.[11]

3. The second genus of realistic definitions is formalistic. This view is hardly more than a century old, although it seems to be rooted in Plotinus's theory that all beauty was due to the splendor of (substantial) form shining through and organizing the darkness of matter.[12]

Of the modern thinkers, Kant lent his authority to this view by defining beauty as "the form of the purposiveness of an object, inasmuch as this form is

---

[2] Pierre Nicole, *An Essay on True and Apparent Beauty in Which from Settled Principles is Rendered the Grounds for Choosing and Rejecting Epigrams.* Tr. J. V. Cunningham. The Augustan Reprint Society, No. 24 (Los Angeles: University of California, 1950), 12.

[3] N. Boileau, *L'Art Poétique*, I, 37f.; II, 45–57; III, 29–37, 47–50, 124–34, 160–76, 360–72, 411–78; IV, 230–35; etc.

[4] "(Et) que la seule vérité solide et digne de ce nom, c'est la beauté." J. E. N. Lachelier, *Du fondement de l'induction*, I, 6; in *Oeuvres* (Paris: F. Alcan, 1933), I, 78. *The Philosophy of Jules Lachelier*, tr. E. G. Ballard (The Hague: M. Nijhoff, 1960), 46.

[5] J. Jungmann, *op. cit.*, p. 149.

[6] Plato, *Lysis*, 216d; *Tim.* 87c; and 53b.

[7] Albert, *Opusc. de pulchro*, q. 11, *ed. cit.*, pp. 580f.; *S. theol.* I, 6, 26, 1, 2, 3; II, 11, 62, 1, sol; *S. de bono* I, 2, 2, sol. 8, 9 (*ed. cit.*, p. 27). Thomas, *In Dion. De div. nom.* 4, 5, 356; *S. theol.* I, 5, 4, ad 1; I–II, 27, 1, ad 3.

[8] Address I, chapter 3: "Beauty"; in R. W. Emerson, *Nature* (Boston, New York: Houghton Mifflin, 1903), 24.

[9] R. Töpffer, *Réflexions et Menus-Propos d'un Peintre Genevois, ou Essai sur le Beau dans les arts* (Paris: Hachette, 1872), 395, 397.

[10] A. J. Steiss, "Outline of A Philosophy of Art," *The Thomist*, II, 1 (January 1940), 29. Cf. *ibid.*, p. 47.

[11] T. Pesch, *Ontologia* (Freiburg in Breisgau: B. Herder, 1919), 144.

[12] Plotinus, *Enn.* Vi, 7, 22; 9, 1; 6, 1; etc.

perceived in the object without any presentation of a purpose."[13] In his footsteps, J. F. Herbart founded an entire school of aesthetic formalism. Among the twentieth-century advocates of this theory, holding that beauty is expressive or significant form, we find Roger Fry, Clive Bell, E. I. Watkin, Susan K. Langer,[14] and many others.

Some formalists give a slight twist to this theory. D. Petavius, for instance, declares in a rather Platonistic manner that the beauty of a being is due to the fact that it exactly corresponds to its archetype or specific form,[15] which means, in effect, that beauty is the form of the individual conforming to (and thereby expressive of) the form of the species.

Petavius' theory excellently shows how close the formalistic definitions of beauty stand to the definitions of the transcendent idealists as well as the intellectualist type of humanistic idealists, which were discussed in the previous article. Their difference is actually scarcely more than that of emphasis. For the idealists put the stress on the transcendent or immanent idea or its equivalent; the formalists, on the form of the beautiful object. Thus to the former beauty is the transcendent idea or the human idea, emotion, etc., manifested in the beautiful thing; to the latter beauty is the form manifesting or expressing the idea, emotion, etc. This intimate closeness of the two types of theories explains also the historically common roots of these theories.

4. In contrast with the formalists, most aesthetic realists hold that beauty involves not merely the form but the total reality of the beautiful individual, be it a natural thing or a work of art. Thus, the originally Herbartian Hermann G. Siebeck declared that things are beautiful due to content and form rather than form alone;[16] and before him, Cornelius W. Opzoomer had expressed similar ideas quite explicitly.[17]

What universally characterizes the totalistic realists is that they all define beauty in terms of one or more principles constituting beauty, either without or with some specific difference added to that principle or those principles listed. Due to the incredible variety of their views, the handiest basis of division appears to be the number of principles listed by them as constituting the essence of beauty.

Taking up immediately the definitions that employ one single principle of beauty, we may divide them, first of all, into those identifying beauty with

---

[13] Kant, *Critique of Judgement*, § 15.

[14] R. Fry, *Vision and Design* (New York: Brentano, 1925), 302. C. Bell, *Art* (New York: G. P. Putnam's Sons, 1958), 17. E. I. Watkin, *op. cit.*, p. 319. Susan K. Langer, *Philosophy in A New Key* (New York: The New American Library, 1962), 178, 119. S. K. Langer, *Problems of Art*, p. 109.

[15] D. Petavius, *op. cit.*, p. 347.

[16] H. Siebeck, *Das Wesen der aesthetischen Anschauung, Psychologische Untersuchungen zur Theorie des Schoenen und der Kunst*, Kap. 8 (Berlin: Ferdinand Dümmler, 1875), 125–31.

[17] C. W. Opzoomer, *Het Wezen der Kennis, een Leesboek der Logika*, part I, § 12 (Amsterdam: J. H. Gebhard, 1867), 77–82.

order (or any one of its synonyms) and those identifying beauty with something other than order.

The chronologically first theory identifying beauty with one principle other than order is that of Socrates, who asserts the beautiful to be the useful.[18] In the nineteenth century, James Ferguson held this view in relation to the arts.[19] Epictetus, G. F. Meier, A. R. Mengs, Tolstoi and T. C. Terberg identify beauty with perfection or specific perfection.[20] Robert Grosseteste defines beauty simply as consonance (*concordia, convenientia, consonantia*).[21] Further views include that of George Berkeley, holding that beauty consists "in a certain symmetry or proportion";[22] that of Diderot[23] and J. F. Herbart,[24] identifying beauty with relation; that of Henry Howard, making proportion the "essential element" of beauty;[25] and that of Avary W. Holmes-Forbes, considering "the quality of suggestiveness" to be "the objective element of beauty."[26]

In addition to all these views, there is a rather strange and definitely unique theory operating with only one principle of beauty. This is the theory of *gyneism*, holding that the only and universal principle of beauty is woman. Among its advocates we find Ernst Platner, who proclaimed that all beauty stems from and has as its center the female form; Benjamin W. Haydon, who taught that the beautiful "has its origin altogether in woman," with "the face and form of woman" being "the base of all beauty morally or by form," so that anything is beautiful in proportion to its similarity to female beauty; Samuel Tyler, who declared, "What I mean by the Beautiful, is whatever, in the material world produces impressions within us analogous to those awakened by our intercourse with woman. In fact, ... I make woman the spiritual dispenser of beauty to the world"; and Dr. Robert Knox who, following Haydon, held that "the

---

[18] Xenophon, *Memor.* III, 8, 7.

[19] J. Ferguson, *An Historical Enquiry into the true principles of Beauty in Art, more especially with reference to Architecture* (London: Longman, Brown, Green and Longmans, 1849), 95f.; 138f.; 149.

[20] Epictetus, *Discourses* III, 1. G. F. Meier, *Anfangsgründe aller schönen Wissenschaften*, §§ 3, 23, 24 (Halle im Magdeburgischen: Hermann Hemmerde, 1748), 6, 38, 40. A. R. Mengs, quoted by William Knight, *op. cit.*, p. 55. Tolstoi, *op. cit.*, p. 113. T. C. Terburg, "The Concept of Beauty," *Modern Sacred Art*, I (January 1938), 133.

[21] Robert Grosseteste, *Comm. in Dion. de div. nom.*, c. 4; Paris, Mazarine Ms. 787; in the "Textes inédits" appendix of H. Pouillon, "La Beauté, propriété transcendentale chez les Scholastiques, (1220–70)," *Archives d'Histoire doctrinale et litteraire du Moyen Ages*, XV (1946), 320f., lines 23 and 3, respectively.

[22] G. Berkeley, *The New Alciphron*, III, 8.

[23] Diderot, quoted by Knight, *op. cit.*, p. 105.

[24] J. F. Herbart, *Schriften zur Einleitung in die Philosophie*, § 89; in *Sämtliche Werke*, I, ed. G. Hartenstein (Leipzig: L. Voss, 1850), 137.

[25] H. Howard, *A Course of Lectures on Painting* (London: Henry G. Bohn, 1848), 71 f.

[26] Avary W. Holmes-Forbes, *The Science of Beauty, An Analytical Inquiry into the Laws of Aesthetics* (London: Trübner, 1881), 41.

absolutely beautiful" was to be found exclusively in the full-grown woman.²⁷

All these monistic theories heretofore listed taken together are far less important and popular than that which maintains that beauty is simply order (τάξις, *ordo*). Some realists holding this view call this sole principle of beauty "order"; others, by some other name. Among the former are Philo of Alexandria, St Augustine, Alexander of Hales, St. Bonaventure, D. Hume, Baumgarten, H. Fuseli, S. T. Coleridge, and Arthur Little.²⁸ About an equal number of aestheticians prefer to call this principle "unity (uniformity) in (amid) variety (diversity)". Among them we find F. Hutcheson, S. Tongiori, Moriz Carrière, E. Grandclaude, David Palmieri, C. Sanseverino, J. C. Murray, G. Baldwin Brown, and George L. Raymond, all of whom interpret this definition completely realistically, whereas J. D. Moore seems to add a neo-Hegelian twist to it.²⁹

There are even some who, in place of both "order" and "unity in variety," prefer other terminology, while still retaining the basic meaning of order, such as "due (apt) disposition" (e.g., John of St. Thomas³⁰); or "harmony of parts"

²⁷ E. Platner, *Neue Anthropology für Ärzte und Weltweise* (Leipzig: S. L. Crusius, 1790), § 814; *Vorlesungen über Ästhetik*, ed. Moriz E. Engel (Zittau and Leipzig: O. M. Nauwerck, 1836), 30-38. B. W. Haydon, *Lectures on Painting and Design*, Lecture 14: "On Beauty" (London: Longmann, Brown, Green, and Longmans, 1846), II, 258. S. Tyler, *Robert Burns, as a Poet and as a Man* (New York: Baker and Scribner, 1848), 13. See also, *ibid.*, pp. 27f. For Dr. R. Knox, see William Knight, *op. cit.*, p. 272. A partial and dialectical version of aesthetic gyneism is advocated by F. Ast: "Die Schönheit ist also die Harmonie zweier Element, gleichsam eines männlichen Prinzips, des Unendlichen, und eines weiblichen, des Endlichen." *System der Kunstlehre oder Lehr- und Handbuch der Ästhetik*, § 45 (Leipzig: J. C. Hinrichs, 1805), 51. The earliest thinker touching on the idea of gyneism seems to be John Scotus Erigena: "Mulierem ... appellans generaliter totius sensibilis creaturae formositatem." (*De divisione naturae*, V, 36; PL 122, 975 D-976 A.)

²⁸ Philo of Alexandria, *De opificio mundi*, VII, 28. Augustine, *De civ. Dei*, XXII, 19, 2 (PL 41, 781); *De ver. rel.* 41, 77, (PL 34, 156). Alexander of Hales, *Summa theol.* II, p. 1, i. 1, tr. 2, q. 3, c. 3, sol. (II, n. 77, p. 100). Bonaventure, *In II. Sent.* d. 1, p. 2, a. 1, q. 1, ad 3 (II, 40b); d. 3, p. 2, a. 1, q. 1, ad 1 (II, 114); d. 9, a. 1, q. 6, ad opp. 3 and ad 3 (II, 252); *ibid.*, q. 8, ad 4 (II, 256b); d. 15, a. 2, a. 3, concl. (II, 387a); and d. 36, a. 2, q. 1, concl. (II, 848b). Hume, *A Treatise of Human Nature*, II, 1, 8. Baumgarten, *Aesthetica*, §§ 19, 14. H. Fuseli, "On Design," *Lectures on Painting by the Royal Academicians, Barry, Opie, and Fuseli*, ed. R. N. Wornum (London: H. G. Bohn, 1848), 490-503. S. T. Coleridge, "On Beauty"; in *Poetry and Prose*, ed. C. Baker (New York: Bantam, 1965), 199. A. Little, *The Nature of Art* (London: Longmans, Green, 1946), 14. Cf. also Thomas of York, *Sapientiale* (of c. 1250-60), Vat. lat. 4301, fol. 41r; Florent. B. Nat. Acad. 6, 437, fol. 51r; in H. Pouillon, "La Beauté, propriété transcendentale chez les Scolastiques, 1220-70," *Archives d'Histoire doctrinale et litteraire du Moyen Age*, XV (1946), 325.

²⁹ F. Hutcheson, *op. cit.*, I, 2, 3; *ed. cit.*, p .17. S. Tongiorgi, *Ontologia* (Paris: Benziger, 1862), 194. Moriz Carrière, *Die Idee des Schönen und ihre Verwirklichung im Leben und in der Kunst* (Leipzig: F. A. Brockhaus, 1885), I, 150. E. Grandclaude, *Metaphysica specialis* (Paris: Lethielleux, 1873), 178. D. Palmieri, *Logica et Ontologia* (Rome: Cuggiani, Santini, 1874), 534. C. Sanseverino, *Ontologia* (Naples: Off. Bibl. Cath., 1885), 89. J. C. Murray, *A Handbook of Psychology*, II, 4, 2 (Boston: D. Wolfe, Fiske, 1890), 233f. G. Baldwin Brown, *The Fine Arts* (New York: C. Scribner's Sons, 1901), 177. George L. Raymond, *Art in Theory* (New York: G. P. Putnam's Sons, 1909), I, 162. Cf. Also Milton C. Nahm, *The Artist as Creator* (Baltimore: The Johns Hopkins Press, 1956), 123, 194; and J. D. Moore, "Beauty as Harmony," *ed. cit.*, pp. 40, 43. An even stronger Hegelian-dialectical interpretation of this difinition is in G. E. Mueller, *op. cit.*, pp. 101-104, especially p. 103.

³⁰ John of St. Thomas, *Naturalis philosophia*, p. IV, q. 4, a. 2, ad 1; *ed. cit.*, p. 120a.

(e.g., L. B. Alberti and G. E. Lessing[81]); "organic unity" or "organization" (e.g., K. C. F. Krause, G. E. Moore, and T. M. Greene[82]); or else "unity of formal relations" (e.g., H. Read[83]).

Finally, there is a special group of aesthetic realists who define beauty in terms of order *and* another principle either added to or listed as the specific difference of order. Among those listing one additional principle besides order is, *e.g.*, Cicero who speaks of "apt disposition," that is, order, and of agreeableness or delicacy (*suavitas*) as aesthetic principles;[34] also A. Comte, who lists order and magnitude as "the first elements of beauty";[35] and John Todhunter, who enumerates order and proportion as the components of beauty.[36]

Of those, on the other hand, who add a specific difference to order, some add to order the adjective "expressive" or "significant" (e.g., S. Alexander[37]); others, that of "lucid" (e.g., Joseph Gredt[38]); whereas most of them employ the phrase "the splendor of (sc. order)." This last group includes M. Liberatore, John Rickaby, A. Rother, L. De Raeymaeker, James K. Feibleman, and Paul Dezza,[39] to mention only a few. Very close to this group stand Albert, Ulrich of Strasbourg, and Mirandola, defining beauty as splendor or clarity of form.[40]

5. With this last version, we have already approached the group of aesthetic realists who define beauty in terms of two co-principles. Characteristically enough, almost everyone of them lists different co-principles. Thus, Plato speaks of measure and proportion; Savonarola, of proportion and correspondence; Richard Price and David R. Hay, of uniformity and (amidst) variety; Richard P. Knight, of balance and proportion; William Hazlitt, of gradation

---

[81] Alberti, *Ten Books on Architecture*, VI, 2; tr. J. Leoni (London: Tiranti, 1955), 113a. G. E. Lessing, *Laokoön*, ch. 20; tr. E. A. McCormick (Indianapolis: Bobbs-Merrill, 1962), 104.

[82] Krause, *Abriss der Ästhetik oder der Philosophie des Schönen und der schönen Kunst*, §§ 22f; ed. J. Leutbecher (Göttingen: Dietrich, 1837), 19, 22; also *Vorlesungen über Ästhetik, oder über die Philosophie des Schönen und der schönen Kunst*, Vorlesung 17, 18, 24; ed. P. Hohlfeld, A. Wünsche (Leipzig: O. Schulze, 1882), 77-79, 83 and 107. G. E. Moore, *op. cit.*, p. 121. T. M. Greene, *The Arts and The Art of Criticism* (Princeton: Princeton University Press, 1940), 7.

[33] H. Read, *The Meaning of Art* (Baltimore, Md.: Penguin Books, 1963), 16.

[34] Cicero, *Tusc. disput.*, IV, 13, 31.

[35] A. Comte, *A General View of Positivism*; tr. J. H. Bridges (London: Trübner and Co., 1865), 301.

[36] J. Todhunter, *The Theory of the Beautiful*; in *Essays*, ed. S. O'Grady (London: Elkin Matthews, 1920), 29.

[37] S. Alexander, *Space, Time and Deity* (London: Macmillan, 1920), II, 293.

[38] J. Gredt, *Metaphysica* (Freiburg in Breisgau: Herder, 1912), 30.

[39] M. Liberatore, *Logica et metaphysica generalis* (Naples: F. Giannini, 1900), 306. J. Rickaby, *General Metaphysics*, p. 151. A. Rother, *Beauty* (St. Louis: B. Herder, 1917), 60. L. De Raeymaeker, *Metaphysica generalis*, I. (Louvain: E. Warny, 1935), 87. J. F. Feibleman, *op. cit.*, p. 31. P. Dezza, *Metaphysica generalis* (Rome: Gregorian University Press, 1952), 104.

[40] Albert, *Opusc. de pulchro*, qq. II and V, sol.; ed. cit., pp. 565, 570. Cf. his *Ethica*, IV, 2, 3 (Borgnet-ed., VII, 299), and *S. theol.* II, 10, 39, 1, 1, 2, obi. 7 and ad 7 (XXXII, 436, 438). Ulrich of Strasbourg, *De pulchro*, ed. cit., p. 74, lines 1-2 and 8-9; and especially p. 76, lines 13-15. Pico della Mirandola, *Heptaplus* (1489), expos. 1, chap. 2, *fin.*; ed. P. J. W. Miller (Indianapolis: The Bobbs-Merrill Co., 1965), 88.

and harmony or symmetry; John G. Macvicar, of unity and harmonious variety; and William B. Scott, of harmony and symmetry.[41]

A further group of realistic definitions is such that each definition includes three principles of beauty. Among them, the variety is even greater than among the dualistic definitions. Thus, Marsilius Ficinus lists arrangement, proportion, and adornment; Alexander Gerard enumerates uniformity, variety, and proportion; Uvedale Price, smoothness, gradual variation, and "idea of youth and freshness"; Jean Francois Marmontel, power, richness, and intelligence (*sic!*); Charles H. deCoster, unity, variety, and order; A. Dupeyrat, integrity, unity in variety, and clarity; Carleton Noyes, design, wholeness, and significance; David Card. Mercier, perfection, order, and brilliance or splendor; H. N. Lee, harmony, proportion, and sensuous charm; and P. Coffey, integrity, size or power, and order.[42]

To these triadic definitions comes an additional version, that has found many followers among modern and contemporary thinkers and aestheticians due to the authority of St. Thomas Aquinas, the author of this theory. According to him, beauty is order[43] in such a way that it has two material principles and one formal principle, viz., integrity or perfection, (due) proportion, and clarity or splendor.[44] Of this doctrine, his modern disciples generally accept the three metaphysical principles of beauty: integrity, proportion, and clarity.[45]

[41] Plato, Phileb. 64e. Savonarola, Sermon for the third Sunday in Lent, in *Prediche Raccolte* (1495); Mss. Bibliotheca Apostolica Vaticana, St. Barbara, BBB. (Microfilm copy in the History of Science Collection, The University of Oklahoma Library.) R. Price, *A Review of the Principal Questions in Morals*, chap. 2; ed. D. D. Raphael (Oxford: Clarendon Press, 1948), 64, 66. D. R. Hay, *First Principles of Symmetrical Beauty* (Edinburgh: Blackwoods, 1846), 20. R. P. Knight, *op. cit.*, pp. 11–12. Wm. Hazlitt, "On Taste"; in *Sketches and Essays* (London: H. Frowde; Oxford University Press, 1936), 170f. J. G. Macvicar, *op. cit.*, p. 152. W. B. Scott, *Half-Hour Lectures on the History and Practice of the Fine and Ornamental Arts* (New York: Scribner, Welford, Armstrong, 1875), 353–55.

[42] M. Ficinus, *Commentary on Plato's Symposium*, Fifth Speech, chap. 6; in *Philosophies of Art and Beauty*, ed. A. Hofstadter, R. Kuhn (New York: The Modern Library, 1964), 213. A. Gerard, *An Essay on Taste*, part I, sect. 3; *ed. cit.*, p. 29. U. Price, *Essay on the Picturesque, as Compared with the Sublime and the Beautiful*, chap. 4 (London: J. Mawman, 1810), I, 68f. J. F. Marmontel, "Beau," in *Éléments de Littérature*, I; *Oeuvres complétes*, XII (Paris: Verdier, 1818), 322. C. Th. H. de Coster, *Éléménts de l'Esthétique générale*; in Wm. Knight, *op. cit.*, p. 134. A. Dupeyrat, *Logica, Ontologia et Cosmologia Generalis* (Paris: V. Lecoffre, 1887), 250. C. Noyes, *The Gate of Appreciation* (Boston, New York: Houghton Mifflin, 1907), 184. D. J. Mercier, *General Metaphysics*, pp. 568f. H. N. Lee, *Perception and Aesthetic Value*, p. 96. P. Coffey, *Ontology* (New York: P. Smith, 1938), 198f.

[43] Thomas, *S. contra gent.* III, 71 and 139; *S. theol.* II–II, 142, 2c; 145, 3c; 183, 2c; *De div. nom.* 4, 21, 554; etc.

[44] *In I. Sent.* 31, 2, 1, sol. and ad 4; *S. theol.* I, 39, 8c.

[45] E.g., T. M. Zigliara, *Summa philosophica* (Lyon: De Briday, 1877), 410. Michael De Maria, *Philosophia Peripatetico-Scholastica*, I (Rome: P. Cuggiani, 1904), 396. James Joyce, *A Portrait of the Artist As A Young Man*, chap. 5; in *The Portable James Joyce*, ed. H. Levin (New York: The Viking Press, 1947), 479. Jacques Maritain, *Art and Scholasticism*, tr. J. F. Scanlan (London: Sheed and Ward, 1932), 24. Carolus Boyer, *Cursus Philosophiae* (Paris: Desclée de Brouwer, 1937), 260. C. Bittle, *op. cit.*, pp. 212–14. V. Remer, *Ontologia* (Rome: Gregorian University Press, 1947), 115.

Before we turn to other genera of realistic definitions of beauty, it may be pointed out that some philosophers have listed in their works a varying number of principles of beauty: in some texts, only one; in others, two or even three. This characterizes some of the greatest philosophers, such as Aristotle and Aquinas. Thus, Aristotle mentions only symmetry in the *Topics*; size and order in the *Poetics*; number and magnitude in the *Politics*; and order, proportion, and definiteness, in the *Metaphysics*.[46] Thomas, on the other hand, mentions only order, the synthetic principle of beauty, in at least six texts; of the three analytical principles (integrity, proportion, and clarity), one only in 11 texts; two principles in six texts, and all three only in three texts.[47] Thereby, the definitions of these and other thinkers (e.g., Augustine and Albert) are, when taken literally, partly monistic, partly dualistic, and partly triadic without, however, being contradictory to each other.

6. Finally, let us briefly consider the realistic definitions that contain more than three principles each.

Some realists have listed four principles of beauty. For instance, Abraham Tucker enumerated composition, succession (i.e., variety), translation, and expression; A. C. Quatremère de Quincey, variety, order (and harmony), truth, and utility; A. Rosmini-Serbati, truth, unity, plurality, and integrity; Sydney Dobell, order, unity, variety, and gradation ("graduation of change"); and Paul Weiss, purity, unification, fulfillment, and encompassment.[48]

Among the aesthetic realists enumerating as much as five principles of beauty, we find Jean Pierre de Crousaz, Charles Lévêque, Abbé Vallet, Albrecht Stöckl, and Eduard Hugon. The first of these thinks that variety, uniformity, regularity, order, and proportion constitute beauty; the second, that unity, variety, harmony, proportion, and propriety (convenance) do so; the third, that variety, integrity, proportion, unity, and splendor do so; the fourth, that beauty has four material principles (goodness, perfection, splendor, and

---

John Fearon, "The Lure of Beauty," *The Thomist*, VIII, 2 (April 1945), 164-69. L. Callahan, *op. cit.*, p. 58. Henry Grenier, *Metaphysics (Thomistic Philosophy*, III), tr. J. P. E. O'Hanley (Charlottetown, Canada: St. Dunstan's University, 1950), 62. G. Esser, *Metaphysica generalis* (Techny, Illinois: St. Mary's Mission Home, 1952), 192. J. S. Hickey, *Theodicaea et Ethica* (Dublin: M. H. Gill and Sons, 1955), 113. D. J. Sullivan, *An Introduction to Philosophy* (Milwaukee: Bruce, 1957), 216.

[46] Aristotle, *Top.* III, 1, 116b 21; *Poet.* VII, 4, 1450b 36; *Pol.* VII, 4, 5, 1326a 34; *Met.* XIII, 3, 11, 1078b 1-2.

[47] See, F. J. Kovach, *Die Aesthetik des Thomas von Aquin*, p. 148, n. 7; p. 149, nn. 18-21; p. 150, n. 25; and p. 105, n. 8.

[48] A. Tucker, *The Light of Nature* I, 22, 5 (London: C. Daly, 1840), 178. A. C. Quatremère de Quincey, "De l'université du Beau, et de la manière de l'entendre"; in Knight, *op. cit.*, p. 109. A. Rosmini-Serbati, *Teosofia* III, 3, 10, § 4 (Milan: Marzorati, 1859), I, 417. (Actually Rosmini lists also a fifth principle, that of "mental approval"—*il plauso intellectuale*; but this "principle" means aesthetic delight and is, thus, evidently the effect rather than the source of beauty.) S. Dobell, *Thoughts on Art, Philosophy, and Religion* (London: Smith, Elder, and Co., 1876), 115. P. Weiss, *The World of Art* (Carbondale: Southern University Press, 1961), 132. Sweeney, p. 161.

variety), and one formal principle, namely, unity; and the fifth maintains, in a somewhat similar manner, that there are four material principles in beauty, viz., variety, proportion, integrity, and unity; and one formal principle, called splendor.[49]

A few aestheticians hold the view that beauty has no less than six intrinsic principles. William Hogarth, for example, listed fitness, variety, uniformity, simplicity, intricacy, and quantity. William Thomson thought that these principles were proportion or fitness, shape, line, color, variety, and smoothness. John Ruskin enumerated six universal qualities of "typical beauty," viz., infinity, unity, repose, symmetry, purity, and moderation, as they are supposedly the types of divine incomprehensibility, comprehensiveness, permanence, justice, energy, and government, respectively. DeWitt H. Parker disagrees with all of them by listing the following principles: organic unity, theme, thematic variation, balance, hierarchy, and evolution.[50]

Edmund Burke has the distinction of having enumerated seven principles of beauty. His exact words on the question are these: "On the whole, the qualities of beauty, as they are merely sensible qualities, are the following: First, to be comparatively small. Secondly, to be smooth. Thirdly, to have a variety in the direction of parts; but, fourthly, to have those parts not angular, but melted as it were into each other. Fifthly, to be of a delicate frame, without any remarkable appearance of strength. Sixthly, to have its colours clear and bright, but not very strong and glaring. Seventhly, or if it should have any glaring colour, to have it diversified with others. These are, I believe, the properties on which beauty depends."[51]

To the mind of J. J. Urráburu, even seven principles are insufficient to make up the total essence of beauty. For this reason, he maintained that beauty is composed of the following *eight* principles: honesty, truth, integrity, just magnitude, variety with unity, order, proportion, and clarity.[52]

There is even at least one philosopher, Béla von Brandenstein, who asserts that beauty has three principles according to each of the three first principles of reality. They are, according to content, purity, sincerity or truthfulness, and

---

[49] J. P. de Crousaz, *Traité du Beau*, chap. 3 (Amsterdam: Francois L'Honoré, 1715), 12–16. C. Lévêque, *La Science du Beau étudiée dans ses principles, dans ses applications et dans son histoire*, I (Paris: August Durand, 1861), 154. Abbé Vallet, *Metaphysica* (Paris: Jouby and Roger, 1880), 52. A. Stöckl, *Lehrbuch der allgemeinen Metaphysik*, II. (Mainz: Kirchheim, 1912), 107f. E. Hugon, *Metaphysica* (Paris: Lethielleux, 1928), 390.

[50] W. Hogarth, *Analysis of Beauty*, ed. Joseph Burke (Oxford: Clarendon Press, 1955), 31. Wm. Thomson, *An Enquiry into the elementary principles of Beauty, in the Works of Nature and Art* (1798); in Knight, *op. cit.*, pp. 192–93. John Ruskin, *Modern Painters*, II, part III, sect. 1, chap. 3, § 17; and chaps. 5–10; *ed. cit.*, pp. 29, 38–85. DeWitt H. Parker, *The Analysis of Art* (1924); reprinted in *A Modern Book of Esthetics*, ed. Melvin Rader (New York: H. Holt, 1952), 357.

[51] E. Burke, *Enquiry into the Origin of our Ideas of The Sublime and the Beautiful*, section 18 (New York: P. F. Collier, 1909), 100.

[52] J. Urráburu, *op. cit.*, p. 530.

attractiveness; according to form, integrity, clarity, and uniformity; and according to "formation," characteristicalness, harmony, and organicalness.[53] This makes nine principles of beauty, and Brandenstein himself an enneadist.

Nevertheless, the largest number of principles of beauty is held not by Brandenstein but by the nineteenth-century Humphry Repton, provided, his "sources of pleasure in landscape gardening," or at least the majority of them, do qualify as genuine principles of beauty. Repton's "sources of pleasure" are as follows: (1) congruity of parts with the whole; (2) utility (that is, convenience, comfort and neatness); (3) order; (4) symmetry; (5) picturesque effect; (6) intricacy; (7) simplicity; (8) variety; (9) novelty; (10) contrast; (11) continuity, as in an avenue; (12) association, historical or personal; (13) grandeur; (14) appropriation, the appearance and display of extent of property; (15) animation, whether of water, vegetation, or animals; (16) seasons and times of day.[54] Even if we omit from this list those "sources" which are obviously particular, namely, Nos. 11 and 14–16, we may still have in him the aesthetician who demands the largest number of necessary principles of beauty: twelve; an appropriate ending, indeed, to this long division of views on the essence of beauty.

[53] B. von Brandenstein, *Muvészetfilozófia* (Philosophy of Art) (Budapest: The Hungarian Academy of Science, 1930), 148–71; and *Der Aufbau des Seins* (Saarbrücken: Minerva-Verlag, 1950), 402–409.
[54] H. Repton, *Sketches and Hints on Landscape Gardening* (London: 1795); in *The Art of Landscape Gardening*, ed. John Nolen (Boston, New York: Houghton Mifflin, 1907), 58–61.

CHAPTER VIII

The Aesthetic Method

HAVING READ ALL THE VARIOUS VIEWS on and all the definitions of beauty listed in the previous chapter, it is indeed very easy for one to wonder whether it is possible for man ever to determine what the essence of beauty is. He may be inclined to agree with Leo Tolstoi who expressed his thoughts on the question in these words: "One of the last books I read on the subject was a not ill-written booklet by Julius Mithalter, called *Rätsel des Schönen* (The Enigma of the Beautiful). And that title precisely expresses the position of the question. What is beauty? After thousands of learned men have discussed it for one hundred and fifty years, the meaning of the word beauty remains an enigma still. The Germans answer the question in their manner, though in a hundred different ways; the physiological aestheticians, especially the Englishmen . . . answer it each in his own way; the French eclectics and the followers of Guyau and Taine, also each in his own way; and all these people know all the preceding solutions. . . . What is this strange conception of 'beauty,' which seems so simple to those who talk without thinking, but in defining which all the philosophers of various tendencies and different nationalities can in a century and a half come to no agreement?"[1] If this doubt becomes genuinely methodological in someone's mind, then he can proceed in this manner. First, he must realize that he must not completely reject the possibility of finding the essential definition of beauty merely because of the great variety of more or less dissenting views, like those listed in the previous chapter. For, after all, there has never been any topic on which philosophers have achieved unanimous agreement. One ought to concede the possibility of finding the essence of beauty, however improbable it may seem to him. The second step follows from the first: admitting the basic possibility one must ask himself in what manner or by what method he might have the best chance of actually finding the essential definition of beauty. To find the answer to this question, one must naturally know what methods could be or have been used and, then, evaluate them.

In the light of these considerations, we will proceed in the present chapter as follows. In article 1, we shall consider and briefly evaluate various methods aestheticians have recommended for use or have actually used to define beauty essentially. In article 2, the conceivably best method will be outlined in terms of its important phases and steps. Thereby the ground will be prepared for defending, in chapter 9, the definition of beauty to be offered there by means of this outlined method.

[1] L. Tolstoi, *op. cit.*, pp. 86f.

ARTICLE 1: *Aesthetic Methods*

1. To achieve our above-mentioned end, it would be entirely superfluous to attempt to compile a more or less complete list or division of methods either suggested or employed by philosophers in connection with determining the essence of beauty. A simple set of such methods gathered in a somewhat arbitrary manner from the last three centuries seems sufficient to show the number and variety of aesthetic methods.

Therefore, let us see first a few suggestions made by various aestheticians in modern history in regard to what methods may successfully be used to define beauty and, next, an admittedly incomplete, yet representative, division of such methods with historical examples of their uses. After these two steps, we will be in the position to evaluate the methods mentioned, and arrive at some conclusion concerning the relative superiority of one over the others.

2. Starting out with eighteenth-century aestheticians and proceeding chronologically, we find, among others, Alexander Gerard advocating a sort of ascending induction, together with a complementary deductive method. "The qualities common to the lower classes," he writes, "will naturally be determined first, by regular induction. But a true critic will not rest satisfied with them. By renewing the induction, and pushing it to a greater degree of subtilty, he will ascertain the less conspicuous properties, which unite several inferior species under the same genus; and will carry on his analysis, till he discovers the highest kinds, and prescribes the most extensive laws of art . . . ." Then he adds, "To complete the criticism, and render it truly philosophical, the common qualities of the several classes, both superior and subordinate, must be compared with the principles of human nature, that we may learn by what means they please or displease, and for what reason."[1] It is easy to see that the inductive first part of this suggested method comes very close to, if it is not identical with, Francis Bacon's suggestion made more than a century earlier out of his distrust for the deductive method: "The understanding must not, however, be allowed to jump and fly from particulars to axioms remote and of almost the highest generality (such as the first principles, as they are called, of arts and things), and taking stand upon them as truths that cannot be shaken, proceed to prove and frame the middle axioms by reference to them; which has been the practice hitherto , . . . But then, and then only, may we hope well of the sciences when in a just scale of ascent [!], and by successive steps not interrupted or broken, we rise from particulars to lesser axioms; and then to middle axioms . . . ; and last of all to the most general."[2] On the other hand, it is equally clear that the deductive second part of Gerard's suggested method

---

[1] A. Gerard, *Essay on Taste*, part 3, sect. 3, pp. 183f.
[2] F. Bacon, *The New Organon*, book I, chap. 104; ed. F. H. Anderson (Indianapolis: Bobbs-Merrill, 1960), 98. See also, *ibid.*, I, 30 and 127; pp. 45, 115f.

anticipates by almost a full century John S. Mill's inverse deductive method.[3]

Three years after Gerard's publication, Lord Kames decided to use the method of ascending induction, just as Gerard suggested it, without the employment of the complementary method of inverse induction, however. "His (sc. the author's) plan is," he wrote, "to ascend gradually to principles, from facts and experiments; instead of beginning with the former, handled abstractedly, and descending to the latter."[4]

In the nineteenth century, Gustav Theodor Fechner is well remembered for his introductory analysis and evaluation of two types of aesthetics to be found in the history of aesthetics in general, and in the nineteenth century in particular. One of these two types of aesthetics is called aesthetics "from above" (*von oben*); and the other, aesthetics "from below" (*von unten*). By the former, he meant aesthetics using the deductive method, moving from the most universal ideas and concepts to the singular; by the latter, aesthetics employing the inductive method of moving from singulars up to the universal.[5] His chosen favorite, of course, is the latter.

In the early twentieth century, David Cardinal Mercier follows in the footsteps of Fechner, urging the employment of the inductive method in aesthetics in three particular forms: "We might begin our study," he declares in the "Method of Procedure," "of the beautiful with a metaphysical definition of it, but to do so would lay us open to the suspicion of starting from a priori concepts. Instead, then, let us begin with observation, and ask ourselves, 'When is it that man, face to face with some object of nature or art, spontaneously says, "That is beautiful"? And ... "That is not beautiful! ..." By so proceeding we may apply to the facts of the aesthetic order the inductive methods, of concordance, of difference and of concomitant variations with a view to discovering what are for the mind the distinctive characteristics of the beautiful. Should we find one or more such characteristics, we may subject them to metaphysical analysis. Thus may we have to reach a definition of the beautiful."[6] The three specific versions of the inductive method suggested here are evidently taken from J. S. Mill's *A System of Logic, Ratiocinative and Inductive*, in which Mill lists and describes altogether four methods of "experimental inquiry": the methods of agreement, difference, residues and concomitant variations, together with a joint method of agreement and difference.[7]

In 1920, DeWitt H. Parker recommended the employment of two methods, of which one is the objective scientific method; and the other, a sort of sub-

[3] J. S. Mill, *A System of Logic, Ratiocinative and Inductive*, II, bk. VI, chaps. 9 and 10, "Of the Physical or Concrete Deductive Method" and "Of the Inverse Deductive, or Historical Method" (London: Parker, Son, and Bourn, 1868), II, 486–528.

[4] Lord Kames, *op. cit.*, Introduction, part II, n. 50; *ed. cit.*, p. 30.

[5] G. T. Fechner, *Vorschule der Aesthetik*, I. (Leipzig: Breitkopf und Härtel, 1897), 1–7.

[6] Mercier, *ed. cit.*, n. 176, p. 564.

[7] J. S. Mill, *A System of Logic, ed. cit.*, I, bk. III, chap. 8, nn. 1, 2, 5 and 6; n. 4; I, 425–29, 436–43, 433–36.

jective method: "How shall we proceed in seeking such an idea of art? We must follow a twofold method: first, the ordinary scientific method of observation, analysis, and experiment; and second, another and very different method, which people of the present day often profess to avoid, but which is equally necessary . . . actually employed by those who reject it. In following the first method we treat beautiful things as objects given to us for study . . . so the student of aesthetics observes works of art and other well-recognized beautiful things, analyzes their elements and the forms of connection of these, arranges experiments to facilitate and guard his observations from error and, as a result, reaches . . . the idea of beauty. . . . Yet a purely objective method will not suffice to give us an adequate idea of beauty. For beautiful things are created by men, not passively discovered, and are made, like other things which men make, in order to realize a purpose . . . We are . . . not always aware of the existence of this purpose when we enjoy a picture or a poem or a bit of landscape; yet it is present none the less . . . . This purpose cannot be understood by the observation and analysis, no matter how careful, of beautiful things; . . . and it cannot be understood by a mere inductive study of aesthetic experiences . . . . No, we must employ a different method of investigation—the Socratic method of self-scrutiny, the conscious attempt to become clear and consistent about our own purposes, the probing and straightening of our aesthetic consciences . . . [For] no one can know the meaning of art except through creating and enjoying and entering into the aesthetic life of other artists and art-lovers."[8]

Seven years after the publication of DeWitt H. Parker's book, Leonard Callahan discusses the same two methods about which Fechner was speaking half a century ago: "The first is an apriori method, usually beginning with . . . a definition . . . The second . . . a posteriori and inductive grounded in the observation of aesthetic phenomena psychical and physical . . . ." However, he deviates from Fechner when he adds to this, "It must not be supposed that a complete aesthetic doctrine . . . can be satisfactorily drawn up by the exclusive use of one of these methods; they are naturally correlative and supplementary . . . ."[9] This last remark is, in fact, an echo of Alexander Gerard's ideas about the proper aesthetic method.

In 1932, there appeared an article by T. E. Jessop in the *Proceedings of the Aristotelian Society*[10] with a rather comprehensive picture of possible and employed aesthetic methods. It speaks of two kinds of objective methods, and two kinds of subjective methods. The first two, as can be expected, are the deductive and the inductive method; the other two are the subjective methods consisting in an analysis of the artist and the beholder, respectively.

[8] Parker, *The Principles of Aesthetics* (New York: Appleton, Century, Crofts, 1946), 2–6.
[9] L. Callahan, *op. cit.*, pp. 15f.
[10] T. E. Jessop, "The Definition of Beauty," *Proceedings of the Aristotelian Society*, XXXIII (1932/33); reprinted in *Art and Philosophy*, W. E. Kennick, ed. (New York: St. Martin's Press, 1965), 524–33. See especially pp. 524–26 and 530.

In a work published in 1957, Walter J. Hipple, Jr., declared that in his opinion, too, the inverse deductive method was the most useful and desirable: "This method is that best adopted to the nature of aesthetic phenomena, where plurality of causes and intermixture of effects often battle attempts at steady ascending induction ... I urge ... that no progress can be made with a purely empirical and inductive method in a derivative science like aesthetics."[11]

Let us conclude this rather random list of suggested aesthetic methods in eighteenth- to twentieth-century literature with the rather novel contribution of M. C. Beardsley to this topic. "But there are," he remarks, "two ways of trying to construct such a definition (sc. of beauty). Of these two ways, the simpler and more convenient one, if it can be carried out, would consist in selecting a set of characteristics that all aesthetic objects possess, though no other objects have them. It may turn out that aesthetic objects have some noteworthy features in common ...." Since he cannot see how this could be accomplished, he concludes, "Therefore, we may consider an alternative type of objective definition. To construct this definition, we must first divide perceptual objects according to their sensory fields: some are seen, some heard. When we review the basic distinctions within the auditory field ..., we shall try to agree on the point at which we shall mark off musical compositions from noises, bird songs, and an orchestra's tuning up .... Again, ... we can distinguish visual aesthetic objects from other visible objects ... And once we have considered the basic elements of language and meaning, we can distinguish literary works from other discourses ... But ... we can then group together disjunctively the class of musical compositions, visual designs, literary works, and all other separately defined classes of objects, and give them the name, 'aesthetic object' to them all. Then an aesthetic object is anything that is either a musical composition, a literary work, and so forth. ... By such a method, then, we can distinguish aesthetic objects from other perceptual objects...."[12]

3. Arranging all these and some additional methods of defining beauty systematically, we can offer the following multiple division:
I. Objective Methods
  A. Deductive Methods
    1. Actually Deductive Method
    2. Apparently Deductive Method
  B. Inductive Methods
    1. Direct Methods of Discovery
      a. Analysis of Objective Principles: Simple or Ascending
      b. Analysis of Differences
      c. Analysis of Meanings (Historic-Genetic Method)
    2. Indirect Methods of Checking the Validity of Discovery

[11] W. J. Hipple, Jr., op. cit., p. 85. Cf. ibid., p. 125.
[12] M. C. Beardsley, Aesthetics, pp. 63f.

a. Method of Agreement
  b. Method of Difference
  c. Method of Residues
  d. Method of Concomitant Variations
 C. Combined Methods
   1. Predominantly or Primarily Deductive Method
   2. Complementary or Inverse Deductive Method
II. Subjective Methods
 A. Method Using Artistic Creation
 B. Method Using Aesthetic Experience

Let us discuss briefly all the methods listed here. Chronologically, the objective methods are prior to the subjective ones; hence the sequence in listing them. The objective methods all have one thing in common: they all use the aesthetic object, natural or artificial, for determining the objective principles or components of beauty.

Deductive and inductive objective methods differ from each other in their respective points of departure and termini. The deductive method goes out from what is postulated to be absolute beauty or absolutely beautiful and the source of all other beauty, i.e., what is the most universal in the aesthetic order, and moves toward the particular or even individual-singular beauty. The inductive method moves the opposite way.

The division of the deductive aesthetic method into actually and apparently deductive is arrived at by asking the question, Who has ever used this deductive method? If one asks Fechner this question, he will say, this method has been advocated among German thinkers by Kant, Schelling, and Hegel; which is to say that, to his mind, the method of the German idealists, both the great masters and their disciples, was generally deductive. On the other hand, if one asks this same question of recent historians of aesthetics, they will tend to assert that medieval aesthetics in general employed the deductive method. However, upon careful consideration of all these listed aesthetic theories, one sooner or later will realize that these opinions are mostly gross generalizations. For, in Kant it is difficult to find any element of his aesthetic theory that is not the result of empirical observation, however incomplete or informal; whereas in Schelling and Hegel the systematic framework may be said to be deductive or postulated, but this certainly does not hold true for the profound insights—necessarily based on observations—they have into the nature of beauty, artistic beauty, natural beauty, and the various kinds of fine artworks.

On the other hand, speaking of medieval aesthetics, it is difficult to see how those schoolmen could possibly postulate or dogmatically assert such propositions as "Beauty is order," or "Beauty demands proportion and clarity," without resorting first to empirical observations, however crude, incomplete, and superficial those observations may have been. Even such dogmatic notions as beauty being light (clarity), although a central idea of Plotinus' metaphysics, demand some empirical basis and do have, as a matter of fact, some experiential justification.

And this is not all. For, if one takes the trouble of carefully weighing the relevant passages in the works of medieval metaphysicians, he will find enough textual evidence for those "deductive" theories of beauty having been based upon or having been subjected to at least some empirical observations and scrutiny. One excellent example is Thomas Aquinas. Although he is often mentioned as one of the medieval thinkers who construed an aesthetic theory aprioristically, he alludes to an empirical basis with respect to each one of the three analytical principles of beauty as well as to his synthetic definition of beauty in terms of order.[13] Needless to say, the same holds true for Plato and Aristotle, who first used in their definitions Thomas' analytic or synthetic principles of beauty.[14] In brief, the exclusive use of the deductive, aprioristic method is almost impossible, although it can be extremely predominant in an aesthetic theory, as in Plotinus'; in most cases, as in that of Thomas, it is simply apparently aprioristic.

Turning next to the inductive methods, one may first differentiate between method of discovery, which is analysis, and method of determining the validity of discovery. To a certain extent, every inductive method contains elements of both. For there is no discovery possible at the empirical level without observing the composite material whole and selecting some parts (components, factors) while ignoring or excluding others; and there is no proof for the correctness of the analytic discovery possible without resorting to the particular method of agreement, or difference, etc. Moreover, there is no need for such particular inductive methods unless there is already some analytically achieved discovery to be checked for validity. The inductive method in general was used, among others, by the British empiricists of the eighteenth century, although not in exactly the same manner. Some, like Hume (surprisingly enough), used it in a rather informal and superficial manner; whereas others, like Archibald Alison, in a very rigorous, technically correct manner.

The specifically analytic method has several versions according to the specific object of analysis. For one may simply analyze the various components

---

[13] See the explicit empirical allusions to integrity, in *De malo*, 2, 4, ad 2; 8, 4; *De regno* I, 3, 9, ad 16; and *De virt. card*. 2, 12a; to proportion, in *In I. Cor*. 11, 4, lect. 2; *In II. Eth*. 7, 320; *In Psalm*. 44, 2; *S. c. gent*. II, 64, 1424; and *In I. Sent*. 31, 2, 1, sol; to clarity, in *In I. Cor*. 11, 4, lect. 2; *In I. Sent*. 31, 2, 1, sol.; *S. theol*. I, 39, 8c; and to order, *S. c. gent*. III, 139, 3142; *De regno*, I, 3; *De malo*, 8, 4c; and *S. theol*. I–II, 54, 1c. Cf. F. J. Kovach, "The Empirical Foundations Thomas Aquinas' Philosophy of Beauty," *Southwestern Journal of Philosophy*, II/3 (Winter 1971), 93–102.

[14] Plato speaks of perfection (integrity) in *Tim*. 30c; of proportion in *Tim*. 31c and *Phileb*. 26ab, 64e. In *Pol*. VII, 4, 5, 1326a 34 and *Poet*. VII, 4, 1450b 36, Aristotle categorically asserts that size (*megethos*) is a principle of beauty; whereas in *Eth. Nic*. IV, 3, 123b 5–8, he empirically justifies this principle by pointing out that "small people may be neat and well-proportioned but not beautiful."

THE AESTHETIC METHOD

common to various kinds of beautiful things; another may instead analyze merely the difference between any given kind of beautiful thing and ugly (non-beautiful) things of the same kind, as suggested by M. C. Beardsley in the above quoted text. It is even possible to analyze not so much beautiful things for their common principles as the various meanings and/or applications of the term "beauty" or "beautiful" from an historical or genetic point of view. This method seems to have appeared first in Richard Payne Knight, and was adopted and elaborated by Dugald Stewart, thus, preparing the way for such contemporary notions of linguistic analysis as those of "family resemblance" and "open texture" terms.

The first of these three versions of inductive analysis, the analysis of objective principles, can itself be twofold: simple and gradually ascending. *The Analysis of Beauty* by William Hogarth and William Gilpin's *Three Essays of Picturesque Beauty* may be cited as instances of the simple analytic method; whereas A. Gerard in *Essay on Taste* employs the more sophisticated ascending version of inductive analysis.

The four versions of the inductive methods—or any number of them—used to determine the validity of analytic discovery have been employed by modern aestheticians beginning with Edmund Burke, who in his essay of 1756 explicitly and carefully listed the rules he set to himself for his inquiry: "But before I proceed further, I hope it will not be thought amiss, if I lay down the rules which governed me in this inquiry, and which have misled me in it, if I have gone astray." Then, having listed four rules, of which the first is what Mill will later call the method of agreement, and the fourth, a version of Mill's joint method of agreement and difference, he continues, "These are the rules which I have chiefly followed, whilst I examined into the power of proportion considered as a natural cause."[15] Before the end of the eighteenth century, Archibald Alison also anticipated quite extensively Mill's canons of induction, such as the method of residues in the second essay of his well-known *Essays on the Nature and Principles of Taste*, 1790.[16] In Germany, under the impact of idealism, it took more than another half-century before the predominance of the deductive method was, in Fechner's opinion, gradually weakened by an ever-increasing employment of the inductive method by such people as Hartsen, Kirchmann, Köstlin, Lotze, Oersted, and Zimmermann, leading ultimately to such exclusively inductive aestheticians as Brücke, Helmholtz, and Oettingen.[17]

The third generic version of aesthetic method is the combined or mixed method made up of both deductive and inductive method. This generic method is either predominantly deductive or equally deductive and inductive. Since,

---

[15] E. Burke, *On the Sublime and Beautiful*. III, 2; *ed. cit.*, p. 79f.
[16] A. Alison, *op. cit.*, Essay II, chap. 1, Introductory; *ed. cit.*, pp. 114–16.
[17] G. T. Fechner, *Vorschule der Aesthetik*, *ed. cit.*, p. 6.

in connection with the deductive aprioristic method we have already seen ancient and modern instances of the predominantly deductive method, let us use here an excellent contemporary instance of it, that in the philosophy of Béla von Brandenstein. In his *Philosophy of Art* of 1930, he argues as follows: Since in other branches of philosophy it has been a fruitful method to look for three components within each of the three first principles of all existent being, viz., content, form, and formation, in aesthetics, too, he will attempt to proceed in this manner, seeking three times three principles of beauty. At the same time, he rejects earlier attempts at determining the components of beauty on the grounds that they are either insignificant or, if significant, not systematic or rich or elaborate enough. He speaks similarly twenty years later in his German principal work, *Der Aufbau des Seins*.[18] The general framework of his approach is unmistakably aprioristic-deductive. However, the nine specific principles, three within each of the three ontological first principles of being, are clearly the results of empirical observation and analysis. Thereby, the total method is truly composite, with the deductive component dominating it.

The second species of the combined inductive-deductive method employs the two pure methods to approximately the same extent: starting out with induction, possibly employing the various canons of induction as described by Mill; then changing to deduction, even to aprioristic argumentation to confirm the empirical findings through the well established or postulated principles of other branches of philosophy, such as metaphysics and psychology. We have already seen how this method has been suggested and used by modern and contemporary thinkers as well.[19]

Finally, in contrast with all the heretofore listed versions of the objective method, there is the so-called subjective method in aesthetics, in use especially for the last one hundred years or so in Germany and France as well as in English-speaking countries. The basic idea with this method is as simple as it is naïve: since there is no artistic beauty without artistic production, and since there is no known artistic or natural beauty without the aesthetic experience of the beholder, the psychological scrutiny of the artist and the beholder, their minds and experiences are the significant and useful, if not the only and necessary, sources of our knowledge of beauty in general and artistic beauty in particular.

4. The evaluation of the above listed and discussed aesthetic methods is a relatively easy task that can be accomplished briefly.

Speaking first of the subjective methods, it is true that there is a necessary,

---

[18] B. von Brandenstein, *Philosophy of Art*, pp. 146f.; *Der Aufbau des Seins*, p. 402.

[19] Aloysius Rother is an additional example for those using both the inductive and the deductive a priori method in proving his thesis, i.e., that beauty is order. *Op. cit.*, nn. 36-38, 43-44; pp. 51-53, 61-62.

causal connection between the work of fine art and its maker, and that no beauty is knowable without the beholder's own, personal aesthetic experience. But it is equally true that studying the maker of a beautiful work is not the same as studying the beautiful work itself, just as the study of a virus in itself, done by a natural scientist, differs from the physician's observation of a person rendered ill by that virus. Similarly, it is quite clear that analyzing the state of mind of a person having an aesthetic experience is not the same as studying the aesthetic object causing that state of mind in the beholder; just as medically observing and measuring the heartbeat of a seriously frightened cardiac patient differs from the observation by a witness of the car accident that caused the fright in the cardiac patient.

On this basis, then, any psychological study of the creative process or the artist himself and of the aesthetic experience or the beholder himself is perfectly valid within the realm of psychology, giving precious information about the causes or the effects of beautiful things; but it is no substitute for the direct study or analysis of the beautiful things that have such causes as the artists and such effects as the beholders' aesthetic experiences.

As far as the objective methods are concerned, the aprioristic-deductive method used alone is, to the limited extent that it is possible at all, totally arbitrary and dogmatic, demanding its acceptance without proof although it needs proof. Such theories of beauty, for this reason, promote our understanding of the psychology of philosophers more than our knowledge of philosophic truths.

As to the inductive method, it is undoubtedly the sole pure method that is reliable and useful for learning about reality in general and its beauty in particular. As long as there is no innate knowledge possible for man, contrary to the ideas of Plato about pre-existence and pre-existent learning or of Augustine about divine illumination, all our knowledge about reality must originate in the senses, and this necessitates the employment of induction in general.

Should this mean that the best method the aesthetician may ever employ is some sort of induction, such as the combination of analysis and Mill's canons of induction? Not at all. For if the solely reliable method can be improved or further supported and perfected by some additional method, then that combined method is clearly superior, consequently, preferable to the pure method of induction. It is for this aprioristic reason that one will sooner or later realize that, if there is any way in which the inductive method can be perfected deductively in some manner, then the aesthetician should use that combined method rather than the inductive method alone. Whether this combined method is what Mill calls the inverse deductive method or a version of the inverse deductive method or something else is, basically, a secondary question. The answer to this will be given in the next article, outlining the method that appears to be most suitable to finding the essence of beauty, and that will actually be used in the next chapter.

ARTICLE 2: *The Aesthetic Method To Be Used in Defining Beauty*

The method that seems to be best for determining the essence of beauty is a combined method—the combination of two others. Accordingly, it comprises two main phases: one at the physical or empirical level, and another at the metaphysical or supra-empirical level. These two main parts of the method will be discussed here in the proper sequence.

1. The physical or empirical phase of inquiry is needed to determine the essence of *material beauty*. The superphysical or metaphysical phase of inquiry aims at finding the essence of *beauty in general*. Since only material beings and, more specifically, material accidents are directly knowable, the only path leading to the metaphysical, i.e., the absolutely universal, definition of beauty is through determining the essence of material beauty in general. This is why the empirical phase necessarily precedes the metaphysical phase in this method.

Taking up the empirical phase of inquiry first, one must realize from the very beginning that this inquiry can be successful only if it includes two stages at the physical or empirical level: one, an analytic-experiential stage; and another, a synthetic-deductive or purely speculative stage.

The analytic-experiential stage consists essentially in making the necessary efforts to find a tentative list of components, factors, or co-principles which, when present, render any and every material thing or object beautiful. The speculative stage, on the other hand, includes all the efforts that are necessary for demonstrating in a deductive manner the tentative list of aesthetic principles which have universal validity in the order of matter. Thus, should one's efforts be successful throughout these two stages, he will be in the possession of a list of principles that render any and every material being or object, that is beautiful at all, beautiful.

The analytic-experiential stage itself comprises three steps. The first of them consists in fulfilling the necessary preconditions of the analytic inquiry in question. The second step lies simply in the analytic inquiry about the universal components of material beauty. The third step is the inductive-experiential confirmation of the tentative list of co-principles of material beauty, which list is the result of the second step. These three crucial steps must be discussed one by one before we can understand the five steps necessary in the purely speculative, deductive stage of this inquiry.

2. The necessary precondition of the successful use of the empirical inquiry in question is the proper selection of beautiful things to be used for aesthetic analysis. However, what selection is proper? One that is both qualitatively and quantitatively suitable to the purpose to be achieved.

What determines the qualitative suitability of the selection of beautiful objects is the fact that each and every thing chosen initially for the inquiry is so obviously or conspicuously beautiful that there will be no doubt about *whether* it is beautiful, but only about *why* it is beautiful. Most philosophers of beauty recognize degrees of beauty within the individuals of any given species, provided, they admit the objective reality of beauty. This means they admit that some individuals are more beautiful in any one species than others, whereas a few constitute the most beautiful individuals. It is such individuals that should be selected from any one species for the analytic inquiry, in order to render the per se very difficult and complex inquiry as easy and successful as possible.

As a matter of fact, there is even a second way in which one can render this extremely complex inquiry somewhat, if not considerably, easier. This method rests on the principle that was well known to such ancient and medieval thinkers as Augustine, Albert, and Thomas; namely, that the juxtaposition of contraries renders the positive extreme more conspicuous and easy to recognize. Accordingly, then, it is highly desirable that, while selecting the most beautiful individuals in any one species for the inquiry, one should also choose one or two quite obviously non-beautiful or ugly individuals from that species, too. Thereby he will have a better chance to recognize what factors are present in the individuals that are beautiful and absent in the individuals that are ugly.

The other specific prerequisite is the quantitative suitability of the individuals chosen for the aesthetic inquiry in question. Concretely, this means that one should choose not only individuals belonging to a few species but rather from a very large number of considerably different genera and species. Many aestheticians who, characteristically enough, despair over the possibility of finding any common quality or qualities in what we call beautiful things or objects, complain also about the enormous variety, heterogeneity, and difference of things that are called beautiful. It is precisely this variety or difference of beautiful things that should be taken advantage of by him who accepts the enormous task of determining the universal principles of beauty in material things.

Concretely, this is to say that he should select at the very beginning both very beautiful and very ugly individuals from natural things as well as artworks; and among the former, from beautiful things as well as beautiful objects (groups of things). Furthermore, among the beautiful natural things, minerals and plants as well as brutes and men should be selected; also, among the beautiful objects, beautiful landscapes as well as seascapes; among the artworks, paintings, statues, and buildings, and poetic, musical, and choreographic works as well as the performances of poetic, musical, and choreographic works. One may argue, of course, that increasing the number of genera and species from which individuals are chosen would only increase the complexity and the difficulty of the task in general. But one must not forget that the purpose of the entire undertaking is to determine not the essence of a more or less specific kind of beauty but rather the essence of material beauty and, ultimately, of beauty in general and, thereby, universality is essential.

It is true, one may still insist that it is better at least to begin with the inquiry of only a few rather than with too many species of beautiful things. However, if one should do so, even initially, and especially if one should begin with the inquiry of beautiful things pertaining to relatively similar genera or species, like this or that kind of flower, this or that kind of music, etc., then he would run the risk of selecting highly specific principles of beauty, not realizing that some of them are not or cannot be the principles of many other kinds of beautiful things. It seems, for instance, that many aestheticians could have avoided quite obvious errors in their theories of beauty had they started out from a broader basis of investigation. When, for instance, one lists color or symmetry as a universal principle of beauty, he has only visible aesthetic objects in mind; when one speaks of life as the essence or a principle of beauty, he thinks only of organisms, etc.,—or else he stretches the meaning of such terms so far as to render them equivocal rather than merely analogous. But, of course, equivocation has no useful place in any theory, in any field of knowledge.

Once one has selected both conspicuously beautiful and conspicuously ugly individuals from as large a number of different genera and species as possible, he has complied with the necessary requirements of the inductive inquiry and is technically ready to begin with the analysis of the principles that are present in each one of the chosen beautiful individuals, and absent in each one of the chosen ugly individuals.

3. The second step is the most arduous and tedious. It consists theoretically in a careful consideration and analysis of each beautiful individual chosen for the inquiry as compared with its aesthetic counterpart; first, within any one species and, later, in comparison with the other species represented by the chosen beautiful individuals. For instance, comparing two human faces or figures, one can notice that the one which is beautiful has symmetrical parts, whereas the one which is ugly, more or less lacks symmetrical parts; or, comparing two musical compositions, one will eventually discover that the one which is melodic or harmonically consonant is beautiful, whereas the one which is unmelodic or dissonant is less beautiful or aesthetically displeasing, disagreeable. From this observation he may reasonably conclude that symmetry in visibly beautiful objects and consonance in audibly beautiful objects are principles of the respective genera of beauty.

Next, he may begin to wonder whether either symmetry or consonance is a principle of beauty in things pertaining to other species, too. Obviously, he will not have too much difficulty in realizing that many beautiful things or objects other than human faces or figures are also symmetrical, and that their aesthetic counterparts lack, at least to some extent, symmetry. He will also make similar discoveries in regard to consonance, or any other specific principle of beauty. On the other hand, as he proceeds in his analysis, he will also find beautiful individuals of certain species or genera that do not have the quality of symmetry or of consonance. In such a case, he will have to conclude that the two principles are either only very specific, i.e., of limited universality, or the species of some higher, and more universal principle that is analogously predicable of the specific principles and other principles as well.

At this point he will have to switch from the heretofore horizontal analysis of basically co-ordinate kinds of beautiful things to a vertical analysis of higher and higher genera of beautiful things. In this manner he may discover that, although both symmetry and consonance are genuine principles of beauty, they are rather particular in validity, and belong to a common genus, such as harmony that is analogously predicable of both visible (and symmetrical) and audible (and consonant) aesthetic objects. This portion of the second step in question is, thus, a genuinely ascending inductive inquiry aiming at discovering the common, i.e., most universal, principles of the beauty of all material beings or things. The desired end result of this both horizontal and vertical (ascending) inductive inquiry thus is a tentative list of a number of generic qualities that seem to the analyst to be present in all chosen beautiful individuals and either conspicuously absent, or present in an obviously smaller degree, in all the chosen ugly individuals and, consequently, seem to be the causes or co-principles of the beauty of all those individuals that have been chosen for the inquiry in question.

4. The third step at the empirical level constitutes, in a way, a complement to the second. At the end of the second step, one would have a tentative list of principles that are supposed to be present in all the selected individuals that are beautiful, and absent from all the chosen individuals that are ugly. This supposition is based on the ascending analysis to which all the selected individual objects have been subjected, while employing Mill's method of agreement and difference or, rather, his joint method of agreement and difference. Having arrived through the analysis of more and more generic and universal principles, at a certain number of most generic principles of beauty, one may reasonably wish to have some experimental or methodological confirmation of each one of the generic principles on his tentative list. The experimental confirmation may simply consist in checking the selected beautiful individuals one by one, or any number of them, in regard to whether, if any one principle of the tentative list is removed from or decreased in the aesthetic object, the object remains beautiful, or has less beauty, or ceases to be beautiful completely.

Let us suppose, for instance, that one of the listed apparent aesthetic principles is integrity or perfection. In that case, one may attempt to remove (if not physically, then cognitively, i.e., cover or render otherwise unnoticeable) one or more integral parts of the various beautiful objects, and compare the objects so isolated with the objects in their original, integral form. Should he notice that the objects are less delightful without than with some of their integral parts, then he would be justified in concluding that integrity or perfection is, indeed, a contributing factor of beauty. He may similarly proceed with regard to each one of the principles on his tentative list. The inductive method of concomitant variations is, of course, not the only method at the most generic level that he may use. In its place, he may contrive some application of the method of residues in its place, or even in addition to the former. At any rate, using inductive method at the highest, generic level, he may eventually satisfy his mind that, at the empirical level, his list of aesthetic principles actually represents the sum total of the qualities which, when present, render things beautiful; when decreased, render things less beautiful; and, when absent, render things ugly.

5. After this experiential level of investigation, that is the most lengthy, complex, and tedious, one may switch to a higher level of scrutiny, namely, the speculative level. Heretofore, he had been using analytic-inductive reasoning; from now on, he will have to employ aprioristic-deductive reasoning.

The reason for needing this second level of reasoning is that, despite all his meticulous efforts at selection and observation, all his careful analysis, and all his rigorous use of the various inductive methods, his conclusion, "Beauty is that quality of things which is the combined result of principles A and B (or, A,B, and C; or, A.B,C, and D; etc.)" is open to several perfectly justified critical questions. One such question is: How does any one of the listed principles contribute to the production of beauty? Another question, that may be raised, is this: Are the listed principles truly necessary for beauty? A third question one may raise is whether or not the listed principles are present in every beautiful material being, or just in those originally selected for investigation. A fourth question may be the following: Are the listed principles truly ultimate, i.e., irreducible to even more universal principles? And finally we may even question whether the listed principles are numerically complete in such a way that there cannot be more principles necessary for beauty than those listed.

Correspondingly, there is a need for five speculative steps to be taken in such a way that, through each one, one of the following theses will be aprioristically demonstrated:

a. Each one of the listed principles actually contributes to the formal constitution of beauty in every material being;

b. Each one of the listed principles is actually necessary for the beauty of every material being;

c. Each one of the listed principles is actually (since necessarily) present in every material being and, thus, in every beautiful material being;

d. Each one of the listed principles is irreducible to a more generic and universal principle of beauty; and,

e. The number of the listed principles is complete.

6. One final question before taking up directly the essential definition of beauty: What kind of aprioristic argument is suitable here for proving the above listed assertions in defense of a list of principles of beauty; or, to rephrase the question, From which specific science or sciences can the premises of the five syllogisms appropriately be taken so as to corroborate in an a priori, deductive manner the empirically found principles of material beauty? It seems that there are only two such sciences: the philosophy of matter and the philosophy of man. The reasons for this are clear. First of all, the object of the entire investigation is the essence of beauty through the essence of material beauty, that is, through the essence of beauty that is to be found in material beings. From this it immediately follows that, if there is something universally true about matter in general that is relevant to the beauty of matter, then the philosophy of matter, the science professionally investigating the ultimate principles of matter, is certainly a science that may render aid to the aesthetician in his investigations about the essence of material beauty, and, through it, of beauty in general. On the other hand, material beauty, just as material accident in general, is directly knowable to man and, as such, directly enjoyable too. If there is any science besides the philosophy of matter that can be of any help in offering aprioristic clues to the essence of material beauty and, through it, of beauty in general, that science is obviously the philosophy of man or philosophic psychology that professionally investigates the mode or manner in which man comes to know things in general. How the philosophy of matter and the philosophy of man can aid in perfecting the method of determining the essence of material beauty and of beauty in general, will be seen in the second article of the next chapter.

7. Let us suppose now that somebody has succeeded in the manner heretofore described or outlined in empirically finding and deductively confirming the ultimate principles of material beauty in general. What such a person would have accomplished is to be in the possession of the essential definition of material beauty in general. However, the ultimate goal is not cosmological but metaphysical, namely, the essential definition not of material beauty but of beauty in general.

For this reason, having worked at the physical level both empirically and speculatively, both inductively and deductively, one must proceed to an even higher level, to a second and complementary stage of investigation, which is metaphysical in character.

At this level, two steps seem to be necessary to move from the essential definition of material beauty to the essential definition of beauty in general. One of these steps is preparatory; the other, demonstrative.

The preparatory step consists in analyzing whether or not the terms signifying the ultimate principles of material beauty are analogous or, at least, capable of assuming analogous meanings. The demonstrative step, on the other hand, lies in proving that the ultimate principles of material beauty, if taken in the analogous sense, are actually and necessarily to be found not only in all beautiful material beings but also in all beautiful beings, material or not. If someone who is in possession of the ultimate principles of material beauty succeeds in taking these two additional steps, he will have found the essence of beauty in general.

The need for the second step is clear: one must not simply assert but demonstrate that a certain definition of an integral part of a whole, like the essential definition of material beauty, does *mutatis mutandis*, analogously hold true also of the whole, which in our case is beauty in general. However, the first of the two steps needs some explanation.

Logically, any one term is either univocal, having one and only one meaning; or equivocal, having two or more entirely different meanings; or analogous, having two or more partly identical and partly different meanings (similar meanings). On the other hand, reality as a whole is characterized by analogy, meaning that any term that is truthfully predicable of reality as a whole or of every being in it is analogous in the sense that this term partly changes its meaning as it is predicable first of one realm, kingdom, or genus in it and later of another. Therefore, unless the terms signifying the ultimate principles of material beauty are analogous, or can partly change their meanings, these terms cannot signify the principles that constitute the beauty of every being that is beautiful, whether material or not, finite or not. This is the reason for the need of the above suggested first methodological step at the metaphysical level.

8. Before ending the characterization of the aesthetic method that seems to be most suitable in finding the essential definition of beauty in general, there is a very fundamental objection we must face. This objection may be briefly formulated as follows. What the philosopher of beauty needs is an essential definition of beauty, whereas the above described method obviously and admittedly leads, if successful at all, to a definition by cause of beauty only. Therefore, the suggested method is anything but suitable for our purpose.

The solution of the problem posed by this objection lies in pointing out the ambiguity of the phrase, "definition by cause." If taken in the strict sense, "cause" means only efficient cause, i.e., that by which something is made or done. If taken in a broader sense, "cause" may mean *any one* of five different kinds of cause: material (that out of which or from which something is made); formal (that which specifically determines the thing made); efficient; exemplary (that according to which as a model a thing is made); and final (that for the sake of which something is made or done). Finally, if taken in the broadest sense, "cause" in the phrase "definition by cause" may mean any one of the five causes just listed or even any two or more of the five causes together. Now, if, in the above objection, one means by "definition by cause" either definition by efficient cause or definition by any one of the other four causes, that definition is generally not an essential definition, and certainly not an essential definition of a material being, since neither one of the five listed causes constitutes by itself the complete essence of material being. But, if the objection means by the phrase, "definition by cause," a definition by two causes, then, inasmuch as the two causes constitute physically the total essence of the thing defined, "definition by cause" is the same as essential definition. For an essential definition consists of the proximate genus and the specific difference of the definitum; and the material cause of a thing is to its formal cause as proximate genus is to its specific difference. From all this it follows that the above described aesthetic method *can* lead to the essential definition of beauty in general.

Chapter IX

The Essential Definition of Beauty

IN THE PRESENT CHAPTER two objectives should be accomplished: the presentation of the essential definition of beauty, and the demonstration of its correctness.

The essential definition will be presented as the end result of an un-detailed inductive investigation of many beautiful and non-beautiful individuals on numerous species of both natural and artificial material things, carried out in the three steps that were described at the experiential level in the second article of the preceding chapter.

Having been explained, the same essential definition of beauty will also be demonstrated speculatively both at the physical and the metaphysical level, following carefully the five physical and the two metaphysical steps described above as being necessary for the proper aesthetic method.

ARTICLE I: *The Presentation of the Essential Definition*

The doctrine to be presented and explained here is twofold in two respects. It deals with beautiful things and beauty, on the one hand, and with both of them at the physical as well as the metaphysical level, on the other. The formal presentation itself will constitute the first of the four paragraphs in this article; the explanation of the presented aesthetic theory, the second paragraph; and two analyses, one of the concrete notion of orderly whole, and another of the abstract notion of order, offered to prove certain parts of the presented aesthetic theory, will make up the third and fourth paragraph of the present article.

1. *Presentation of the Essential Definition of Beauty*

The entire aesthetic theory culminating in the essential definition of beauty in general must be presented, first at the physical level and subsequently at the metaphysical level; and first at both levels in terms of beautiful being, i.e., concretely, and next, in terms of beauty, i.e., abstractly.

a. The Aesthetic Theory at the Physical Level:

(1) Concrete Expression of the Theory:

Every beautiful material being consists of unified, proportionate, integral parts.

Unified, proportionate, integral parts constitute an orderly whole.

Therefore, *every beautiful material being is an orderly whole.*

(2) Abstract Expression of the Theory:

Every material beauty consists of integrity, proportion, and unity.

Integrity, proportion, and unity constitute order.

Therefore, *every material beauty is order, that is, an integral and proportionate unity.*

(3) Combined Expression of the Theory:

Material beauty is the integral unity of a multitude or variety of proportionate parts.

b. The Aesthetic Theory at the Metaphysical Level:

(1) Every beautiful being is an integral whole, with or without proportionate parts.

(2) *Beauty in general is integral unity with or without proportion of parts.*

2. Explanation of This Definition of Beauty

Let us discuss the above presented aesthetic theory both at the physical and the metaphysical level.

The major premise of the syllogism in the concrete expression of the theory is a matter of induction. This is to say, if one takes the trouble of carefully following the previously described aesthetic method at the physical level and with regard to the first or experiential part, he can arrive at the realization that beautiful material beings consist of unified, proportionate, integral parts.

Why are there always parts involved in beautiful material beings? Because there is no material being without parts. What does "integral" mean in the above proposition? Two things: one, the capacity of contributing to the whole of the beautiful material being; two, that these parts, through their presence, actually ensure and constitute the wholeness of the beautiful material being. What does "proportionate" mean? "Suitable to each other and to the whole or capable of being put together with other parts and of being united into the whole of the beautiful material being." What does "unified" signify? The fact that all the proportionate integral parts are actually made to be one and, thereby, actually constitute a whole.

The sequence in which the three adjectives of the parts are listed has doctrinal significance. For just as in the proposition, "Man is a rational animal," "animal" signifies the genus, and "rational" means the specific difference, in stating that "Every beautiful material being consists of unified, proportionate, integral parts," it is indicated that the integrity or completeness of the integral parts is the most basic constituent in beautiful beings, similar to the genus in an essential definition; proportion is the second basic component, and the unity of these parts is the final, completing factor in the beautiful material beings, analogous to the specific difference in an essential definition. Turning now to the minor premise of the same syllogism, "Unified, proportionate integral parts constitute an orderly whole," the all-important single question is this: How is this proposition known to be true? The answer is: analytically. One can take any obviously orderly, well-arranged whole and, upon analysis, he will find in it integrally proportionate, and unified parts. This will be demonstrated to be true in the subsequent paragraph of this article. From this, in turn, it follows that it is an essential definition of orderly whole to have unified, proportionate, integral parts. Inasmuch as the essential definition is convertible with the definitum, it is also true to say that unified, proportionate, integral parts constitute an orderly whole.

Now, insofar as both the discussed major and minor premises are true in an empirically cognoscible and demonstrable manner, the conclusion of this formally valid syllogism is also true, namely, that every beautiful material being is an orderly whole.

Taking up next the abstract formulation of our aesthetic theory, it is easy to see that it is a paraphrase of the first syllogism, employing abstract terms. Thus, inasmuch as the first syllogism is true, so also is the second, using the terms integrity, proportion, and unity on the one hand, and beauty and order on the other. From this one can also recognize immediately the truth of the three versions of the essential definition of material beauty:

(1) Material beauty is order;

(2) Material beauty is an integral and proportionate unity; and

(3) Material beauty is the integral unity of a multitude or variety of (the) proportionate parts (of the material being).

Of these three definitions, the second and the third are analytic in the sense that they list the principles that can always be found in the composite—called material beauty. The first of the three definitions is, on the other hand, synthetic in the sense that it reunites the mentally, analytically separated components of material beauty into one concept, order, that signifies together all three analytic principles of material beauty, viz., integrity, proportion, and unity.

Finally, about the metaphysical definitions of beautiful being and beauty, we may say at this point merely this much. Metaphysics differs from the philosophy of matter inasmuch as it professionally deals with all being rather than only with all material beings. If or inasmuch as there are beings other than material, those beautiful immaterial beings may or may not have really distinct parts, essential or accidental. This is the implication and meaning of the statement that every beautiful being or every beauty is "with or without" proportionate parts or proportion of parts.

In this explanation of the above presented aesthetic theory concerning the essence of beautiful being and beauty, two points need further confirmation or clarification. One is the question whether or not every orderly, arranged whole is, in fact, essentially integral, or has proportionate parts, and is unified and, correspondingly, whether order actually consists, by nature, of integrity, proportion, and unity. The other question flows from the first, and depends on the answer to the first. For, if it is true that every orderly whole consists of integral, proportionate, and unified parts and, accordingly, every material order consists of integrity, proportion, and unity, then we must also find out the exact relations of these three principles within and to material order and material beauty, respectively.

The answer to these two questions necessitates two analyses: one, of orderly material thing; and another, of material order.

3. *Analysis of Orderly Material Whole*

Whichever orderly material thing we may ever consider and analyze, we always and invariably find in it the following three things: parts, a principle of order, and the arranged, orderly whole itself.

a. The parts themselves of any orderly material being have, first of all, a quantitative and a qualitative aspect or principle, namely, number and similarity.

If the orderly thing has only a few parts, it is likely to represent a relatively simple order; if it has many parts, it constitutes a more or less complex order. A brief piece of Gregorian chant sung *a cappella* is an instance of the former; the Milan Cathedral or Wagner's *Parsifal*, an instance of the latter.

If the orderly thing has predominantly or exclusively similar parts it represents a multitude; if it has mainly or considerably dissimilar parts, it constitutes a variety. A dozen building blocks of the same size and color, or a team of male dancers all dressed in the same way and all dancing the same steps represent a multitude; a dozen building blocks, of which every three have a different color and/or size, or the performance of a symphonic orchestra employing dozens of different musical instruments constitute a variety.

Moreover, in the parts of any orderly material thing, one can distinguish two facts in their regard to the material being as a whole. One of them, the more basic and the logically prior, is the actual presence of a certain number of parts, necessary for and contributing to the totality of the orderly material being. The other is the proportion or suitability of the actually present parts directly to each other and indirectly to the whole. This proportion or suitability consists in the presence of at least one specifically identical quality that is to be found, in an individually more or less different manner, in every one of the parts present. Shape is one of the possible qualities that, in a specifically identical manner, is present in all visible material parts in such a way that all parts of a whole have it either in an individually identical or individually different manner. Ten building blocks of the same size, for instance, have the specifically identical shape of a cube in an individually identical manner; the same number of building blocks, the sides of which represent the first ten real numbers in inches, have the specifically identical shape of a cube in individually different manners.

Both of these facts, the presence and the proportion of parts, are necessary for every orderly material being. For, without the presence of parts, there is no composite whole at all: one cannot make a whole out of nothing; and similarly, unless the present parts suit each other as well as the whole, the composite whole cannot come about, cannot be made and, consequently, cannot exist. For instance, without some musical tones, not even the simplest song is possible; and as long as one has only such things present or available that do not suit each other at all, like a piece of rock, a gallon of gasoline, a winter coat, a building block, and a piece of driftwood, he cannot put them together so as to construe an orderly whole rather than a merely haphazard heap of items.

b. Besides the suitable parts, there is also a principle of order belonging to every orderly material being. This principle is a preconceived or imagined individual manner in which the parts, due to their suitability, can be put together so as to constitute a definite real relationship among the parts, within the whole. For instance, if one has ten books of varying sizes, he may decide to arrange them in an ascending manner, having the smallest at the left end and the largest at the right end of the shelf; or he may prefer to arrange them in a both ascending and descending manner, having the largest in the middle, and the two smallest at both ends of the shelf. The size of the books is, in these cases, the specifically identical but individually different quality rendering the books basically suitable to each other and the whole; and the ascending or the both ascending and descending manner of putting them together is, formally, the principle of order. From this, it is clear that the principle of order is an idea in the mind of the one who makes or plans to make an orderly whole by putting together the available suitable parts according to that idea, in that preconceived manner.

c. Finally, a few words about the orderly whole itself. Formally, the whole is the end result of the putting-together, arrangement, or unification of the proportionate parts in a definite manner, according to the preconceived principle of order. In other words, the orderly whole is a composite material being having two intrinsic and at least two extrinsic causes: a material and a formal cause remaining in the whole, and an efficient and an exemplary cause being outside the whole.

The material cause, meaning that out of which the orderly whole is made, is the present proportionate parts. The formal cause, meaning thereby that which specifically or individually determines the whole as to what it is, is the actual arrangement or unity of the available proportionate parts. The efficient cause, i.e., that by which the orderly whole is made, is the agent or the maker of the whole. Finally, the exemplary cause, meaning that according to which the orderly whole is made out of the present proportionate parts, is the preconceived determinate manner of putting those parts together into a whole.

The material cause of the orderly whole is itself twofold or composed. For, for the parts to be present and, consequently, to be available for the production of the whole is one thing; and to be proportionate, i.e., suitable to each other and to the whole to be made from them, is another thing. Of these two things, the presence of parts is both logically and naturally (although not chronologically) prior to the suitability of those parts, since one cannot be suitable to anything unless it is, and is present where needed precisely as suitable to another thing. Thereby, the presence of parts is the necessary precondition of the proportion or suitability of those parts. As a consequence of this, we may also say that the parts, insofar as they are present, constitute the remote or indirect material cause of the orderly whole to be made out of them, whereas the same parts, insofar as they are suitable to each other and also to the whole to be made, constitute the proximate or direct material cause of the whole to be made out of them.

In terms of its intrinsic causes only, any orderly material whole is, thus, a material being, made one out of some present and proportionate parts.

4. *Analysis of Material Order*

Having analyzed the principles or causes of orderly material beings in general, we are now prepared for an analysis of the principles or causes of material order in general.

The first truth to be recognized here is the specific nature of the object of the previous and the present analysis, respectively. "Orderly material whole" or "orderly whole" in general is a concrete concept; "material order," just as "order" in general, an abstract concept. Correspondingly, the principles of the former are themselves concrete; the principles of the latter, to be found in this analysis, are abstract principles. This realization indicates immediately that the method to be employed in the present analysis is simply to find the abstract principles of material order, as they correspond to the various concrete principles of orderly material being or whole.

a. We know from the former analysis that the most fundamental requirement for the production of an orderly whole is that a certain number of parts be present, since, without parts, there is nothing from which the whole could be made. What, then, is the abstract principle in material order in general, corresponding to present parts in regard to orderly material being? This abstract principle is undoubtedly the principle of integrity. For, the presence of parts renders the production of an orderly whole possible only under the following two conditions: (1) that all parts necessary for the orderly whole are present; and (2) that no parts unnecessary (superfluous, unusable) for the orderly whole are present. Having, for instance, all the musicians of a large symphonic orchestra, but not having any solo singers is not enough for the performance of Beethoven's *Ninth Symphony*; nor is it sufficient or proper for that performance to have all the needed musicians and, in place of the four solo singers, four dancers or painters.

On this basis, we may define integrity as the property in virtue of which order has all the parts necessary and no parts unnecessary for it. The presence of all necessary parts is the positive component of integrity; the absence of all unnecessary parts, the negative component in it. The two components are of equal importance to order. For one can no more produce order with unnecessary parts than without necessary parts.

From this analysis it is evident that the principle of order, called integrity, corresponds to the parts present in the orderly material whole. Since, then, the present parts constitute the remote material cause of the orderly material whole, integrity can be clearly recognized as being the remote material cause of order.

b. The previous analysis has shown that proportionate parts are needed for the production of any orderly material whole, for one cannot put together unsuitable parts any more than absent parts. What abstract principle corresponds to the proportionate parts in material order in general? Evidently, proportion or suitability itself. Proportion or suitability means here the quality of the present parts by virtue of which the parts can formally produce order in the whole made from those parts.

Proportion, somewhat like integrity, has two components. One is the proportion of parts with regard to each other; the other, proportion or suitability of parts with respect to the whole. The latter is naturally prior to the former, for if the parts suit the whole as its parts, the parts will suit each other, too. However, in the order of generation and, hence, also chronologically, the proportion of parts with respect to each other is prior to the proportion of parts to the whole.

We can easily see now that the second principle of material order is proportion or suitability, corresponding to the suitable parts in the orderly material whole. Since the suitable parts are the proximate material cause of the orderly whole, correspondingly, proportion is the proximate material cause of material order in general.

c. By now we know two material causes or the generic part of the essence of material order, i.e., the two things out of which material order is made. What we still do not know is the formal cause or the specific essence of material order.

What, then, is the formal cause of material order? Since the present and proportionate parts of orderly material being in general correspond, in material order, to integrity and proportion, respectively, the orderly whole itself made up of the present, proportionate parts can correspond only to the actual unity of the integral and proportionate parts. This is to say, just as the putting-together of the present and proportionate parts results in the orderly material whole, in a similar manner, the actual unification of the parts formally produces order as the actual unity of those parts.

This unity is made possible remotely by integrity, inasmuch as no necessary

ESSENTIAL DEFINITION OF BEAUTY

parts are absent and no unnecessary parts are present; and proximately by proportion, inasmuch as all the present parts are similar and suitable to each other as well as to the order of the material being. As such, the form or formal cause of material order is truly the integral unity that is made of a multitude or variety of proportionate parts, as has been defined in the first paragraph.

Unity, as the formal cause and final or completing principle of order, is either simple or composite. Simple unity is the unity of parts brought about or produced according to an exemplary cause that concerns one specifically identical quality of the parts in one way only. Composite unity, on the other hand, is the unity of parts produced according to an exemplary cause affecting two or more specifically identical qualities of parts in one or more than one manner. When, for example, somebody constructs a spatial order of ten building blocks of the same size and color by means of numerically increasing units:

□
□ □
□ □ □
□ □ □ □

the order so produced is simple. Should he, however, produce from similar building blocks an order by means of both numerically increasing and decreasing units:

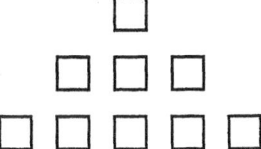

or should he bring about an order from black and white building blocks of the same size, either by means of numerically increasing units of alternating colors:

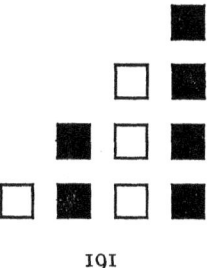

or by means of numerically both increasing and decreasing units of alternating colors:

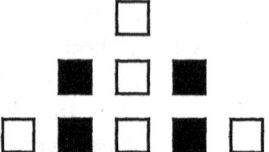

then the material order so produced would be composite. It is easy to see that there is no end to the degree or extent of composite order. Various types of musical compositions, or huge and complex paintings make this quite evident. Similarly, it is also easy to realize that most orders to be found either in natural things or in artworks are quite complex, and very few, if any at all, represent a simple order.

Summing up this analysis, we may conclude that material order, essentially, is a unity having integrity and proportion of parts, or, to put it in a partly different manner, an integral unity of a multitude or variety of proportionate parts. This being the essential definition of material order, and the essential definition always being convertible with the definitum, we may also truthfully state that integrity, proportion, and unity, or the integral unity of proportionate parts is order. Thereby, the minor premise in the syllogism mentioned in the first paragraph of the present article has been proved to be true even in its abstract version.

From this we can validly and rightly conclude that, since, as a matter of experience, every material beauty has integrity, proportion, and unity and, since, as just demonstrated, everything having integrity, proportion, and unity represents an order, every material beauty is an order, that is, a unity having integrity and proportion of parts, or an integral unity (of a multitude or variety) of proportionate parts.

Moreover, through the above two analyses, we have learned not only the analytic identity and the necessity of integrity, proportion, and unity as the principles of material beauty, but also the exact relations which these three aesthetic principles have to beauty. For, from the above said, it is evident that integrity, proportion, and unity constitute material beauty in such a way that integrity is the remote material cause of beauty; proportion, its proximate material cause; and unity, its formal cause, or the specific part of its essence.

There is only one further task to be accomplished: to demonstrate *deductively* that integrity, proportion, and unity are, indeed, the three essential principles of material beauty. For the above conclusion concerning the essence of material beauty is based exclusively on analysis and inductive reasoning.

ARTICLE 2: *Demonstration of the Essential Definition*

While discussing the necessary steps to be taken speculatively for the establishment of the essential definition of material beauty, we have found five such steps. They are as follows:

One. Finding reasons why the analytic principles create beauty in the first place;

Two. Proving the necessity of the analytic principles for the production of beauty;

Three. Proving the presence of the analytic principles in all beautiful material beings;

Four. Proving the completeness of the listed analytic principles of material beauty; and finally,

Five. Proving the ultimacy of the listed analytic principles.

Let us take these five steps now one by one in the same sequence.

1. As the first step, we must investigate what the exact role of each one of the three analytic principles is in beautiful material beings. In other words, we shall inquire about what integrity, proportion, and unity do to beautiful material beings with respect to the beholder. The present inquiry is, thus, clearly psychological in character.

a. It seems that the exact role which integrity plays psychologically in the beautiful material being is to satisfy man's natural desire to know reality in general and individual beings in particular, so as to delight him by the fulfillment of this cognitive desire.

How is this role connected with beauty? By the most basic of all psychological facts, viz., that we call beautiful only and precisely those things which, when they become known to us, and only insofar as they become known to us (in a facile, that is, intuitive manner), delight us.

Our psychological explanation of the role of integrity can be formulated syllogistically as follows:

Integrity renders material things fully knowable; and the fully knowable is delightful to man, as being the fulfillment of his natural cognitive desire. But the cognitively delightful is precisely (what we call) the beautiful. Therefore, integrity renders material things beautiful, and is, as such, a true principle of material beauty.

The crucial question with respect to this syllogism is this: How do we know that it is true that integrity renders material things cognitively delightful? The answer is: empirically. As a matter of fact, our experiences confirm this role of integrity both negatively and positively. Let us suppose, for instance, that somebody walks into the famous Delphi museum of art in Greece, and is suddenly confronted with one of its best known and most precious possessions, the

Charioteer. Upon looking at it, his first impression may well be unpleasant rather than delightful, especially, if he looked forward to seeing this statue, since he had heard its beauty praised. Why, then, is he experiencing displeasure when he finally sees what he wanted? It is because the face of the *Charioteer* is almost completely missing. It is similar to beholding Michelangelo's *Pietá* after a long period of expectation, only to find the face and veil of Mary disfigured. The beholder wants to see, to know, to become completely familiar with an object, and yet he cannot, because the object itself is not complete. Thus, the beholder is naturally frustrated rather than delighted. One experiences such cognitive frustration, to some extent, also upon entering the rooms housing the collection of Greek and Roman sculptural fragments in the Metropolitan Museum of Art: there is not a single statue that satisfies man's desire to know the totality of the original artwork, because each one of them is either a fragment, or reconstructed by later artists. Statues are, of course, not the only kind of artworks that can frustrate the beholder. An interesting novel from which the last few pages are missing; a symphony or opera or drama, from which one misses certain portions because of some noise or, if he watches it on television, because of an electric blackout; all these can frustrate the beholder, and bring about displeasure in him.

On the other hand, there is no such frustration or displeasure in the beholder if the beheld object has integrity, and if he misses no part of it. All this confirms what was said above: integrity, as such, pleases; the lack of it, as such, frustrates and displeases.

It may be noted here that artists seem always to have been well aware of the significance of integrity. One natural sign of this is that artists generally endeavor to complete their works, despite extrinsic or intrinsic difficulties. One needs only to recall the technical difficulties which Michelangelo had to overcome to finish his work on the ceiling of the Sistine Chapel; or to think of Händel, who spent a full seven years correcting and perfecting his compositions despite his total blindness; or of Puccini, who kept working on his *Turandot* despite his diabetic condition and throat cancer; or of Mozart, who forced himself to work on his *Requiem* literally to the last hours of his tragically short life; to see the truth of the universal artistic concern with completion or integrity. There is even another obvious sign of this concern: the fact that many artists have preferred the total destruction by their own hands of their works to leaving those works incomplete, unfinished, imperfect. Vergil, for example, planned to spend three years to correct and improve on his *Aeneid* and, when he realized that he could not carry out this plan, he wanted to destroy all its 9,995 lines because of a mere 150 or so defective hexameters.

b. The psychological role played by proportion is similar to that which integrity plays. This role is to render the material thing intuitively intelligible and, as such, cognitively delightful. Why does proportion play this role? Because, as experience shows, that which is proportionate is intuitively intelligible and, thereby, cognitively delightful; whereas that which is disproportionate is, as such, intuitively puzzling, upsetting, disturbing, even displeasing to the beholder.

To illustrate all this, let us suppose, for example, that one is listening to a lullaby, and suddenly he hears drums sounding fortissimo. There is no need on his part to reason: The lullaby, by its nature, is soft and pleasurably sleep-inducing; but loud drums awaken rather than put one to sleep; therefore, loud drums are unsuitable to any lullaby, including the one presently listened to. Instead, he will instantaneously intuit the unsuitability of the loud sounds of the drums to the soft sounds of the other musical instruments in the lullaby. As a consequence of this intuitive recognition of disproportion, the beholder will be puzzled intellectually, as if to ask, "Why on earth did the composer employ drums in this lullaby?" and this puzzlement will, in turn, cause displeasure in the beholder, replacing the delight he experienced up to the moment that he heard the drums.

This is, of course, a fictitious example; however, it clearly shows the point. We need not, however, rely on imaginary examples. When a person meets another, whose left cheek is swollen, or whose left hand is missing, he will immediately notice the lack of symmetry, i.e., the unsuitability or dissimilarity of the left and the right side of the face or limbs; and, for this reason, he will instantly reject it, and be displeased by it. Or when, during the performance of Mozart's *The Magic Flute*, the soprano misses the high "f" in one of the two brilliant coloratura arias of the Queen of Night, the audience will immediately notice the tonal disproportion (dissonance), and may automatically show, in some manner, its displeasure over it.

All this may be summed up syllogistically as follows: That which is proportionate is cognitively delightful. The cognitively delightful is the beautiful. Therefore, that which is proportionate, or has proportion, is beautiful.

c. What is, finally, the psychological role played by unity? Essentially, it is to render the material being cognitively delightful and, thus, beautiful. How does unity secure the cognitive delightfulness of a material thing? By the fact that unity, as such, is intelligible; multitude, the privation of unity, is not. Inasmuch as the unity of a material being is intuitively, effortlessly intelligible, the knowledge of it is delightful, and the thing itself is cognitively delightful and, as such, beautiful.

How do we know that unity, as such, is intelligible, whereas disunity, multitude, is not? Empirically. Let us take, for example, a multi-million dollar computer. If it is shown, without any explanation, to a non-expert, that person will fail to understand or recognize what it is, whether it is shown him as a whole or taken apart, as a heap of a large number of parts. If it is shown disassembled to an expert, he will probably fail to recognize for what purpose are those parts;

if, however, it is shown him as a whole, the expert will recognize it as being a computer. The explanation is simple: to the layman, that computer is just a heap of many parts, a multitude, and, consequently, unintelligible even if put together; to the expert, the same computer is still not more than a mere multitude if taken apart, and thus unintelligible; but if put together, the computer constituting a unity is intelligible. In general terms, a multitude as multitude is not intelligible; a thing, not considered as a unity, is not intelligible; but as a unity, it is intelligible.

One may point out here that the computer in the above example is, as a unity, merely intelligible but not delightful. The reason for this is the mode of its intelligibility. If something as a unity is discursively intelligible, it is not cognitively delightful; if a thing as a unity is intuitively intelligible, it will delight by the knowledge of it. This, too, is a matter of empirical knowledge.

Let us suppose, for example, that somebody hears successively, without any rhythmic order, definite length, or intensity, fifty-three tones: seven in E flat; five in F; eleven in G; seven in A flat; ten in B flat; six in C; three in D; and four in E flat, one octave higher than the first seven tones. Insofar as there is no order or unity here (except for the fact that the fifty-three tones constitute a complete major scale in E flat), he who listens to this tonal set or heap of tones will not find it either intelligible or delightful. But, if these same fifty-three tones are heard in the sequence, absolute and relative length, and volume in which Brahms composed them as the melody of his famous and well-known *Lullaby*, these tones can easily be recognized as constituting a clear melodic unity of a lullaby and, as such, these tones immediately become cognitively delightful, even to a very young child.

The same applies, naturally, to much longer and much more complex compositions or artworks, with this significant difference: the more parts are recognized instantaneously as constituting a (composite) unity, the greater will be the delight which the parts cause in the mind of the beholder. The average concert- or opera-goer, for instance, generally does not recognize the unity of a symphony or a Wagner opera, or the like, but only the unity of a certain number of parts, such as a theme, a quintet, a unit of a movement, an aria, a choral, etc. For this reason, his enjoyment is normally less intensive than that of a musically educated person beholding the same performance. On the other hand, as that musically uneducated person gradually learns more and more of music, and acquires a more refined taste, he will recognize larger units in such performances and, proportionately, enjoy the music more and more.

Summing up all this syllogistically, the psychological explanation for unity being a principle of material beauty is the following:

That which has unity is intelligible and, if intuitively intelligible, cognitively delightful. That which is cognitively delightful is beautiful. Therefore, that which has unity is beautiful.

2. What we have just accomplished is to explain why integrity, proportion, and unity are aesthetic principles, that is, what role they play psychologically in material beauty. The next logical question is, whether the psychological role of integrity, proportion, and unity, namely, rendering the material being cognitively delightful, is a necessary role, and if so, why? This second inquiry is the more justified because, as we have seen, all three analytic principles play more or less the same psychological role, and thus it may well be true that this role played by any one or any two of the three principles is enough to render material things beautiful.

Are integrity, proportion, and unity all necessary principles of material beauty, and if so, why?

The over-all argument proving the necessity of all three analytic principles in the production of material beauty is as follows:

Unity is necessary for the beauty of any material being because without it the material being is no orderly whole; hence, not intelligible, not cognitively delightful, and, as such, not beautiful. On the other hand, integrity and proportion are necessary for the beauty of any material being because without them there is no unity possible. Therefore, all three analytic principles are necessary, in some manner, for the beauty of any material being.

Let us see this argument in its three parts, step by step.

a. Unity is necessary for the beauty of any and every material being for the following reasons.

Beautiful is that which is cognitively delightful. But that which is cognitively delightful does not delight unless it is, first, known to one. For "cognitively delightful" means exactly delightful precisely in as much as it becomes known to man (intuitively), and no thing is actually known unless it is knowable or intelligible at all. But no thing is intelligible or knowable unless it has unity. Consequently, no thing is beautiful unless it has unity; and this is another way of saying that unity is necessary for the beauty of every material being.

In this argument, the first premise is the first truth concerning beauty that is known to man: everybody calls beautiful that thing which, when becoming known to him, delights him. The last premise, "No thing is intelligible unless it has unity," is also an empirically known truth. For, according to everyone's experience, no heap of many things as a heap or multitude is intelligible; and no whole considered only and precisely as a multitude is intelligible; whereas every whole considered precisely as a unity, is intelligible. The conclusion is thereby true, too, following validly from true premises.

b. Let us ask next whether integrity is necessary for material beauty? We can argue for this necessity on cosmological grounds.

As already proved, there is no material beauty possible without unity, i.e., the unity of the material being. This unity is the order of a material whole composed of parts. But there is no order of a composite whole without integrity. For integrity means the presence of all the parts necessary for the whole to be made from them, and unless all the necessary parts are present and all unnecessary parts are absent, the whole is at best defective, if a whole at all. Therefore, there is no material beauty possible without integrity.

c. Finally, is proportion necessary for material beauty? The proof for this is similar to the proof for the necessity of integrity.

As already demonstrated, there is no material beauty possible without unity, i.e., the unity of the material being or the order of a whole composed of parts. But there is no order of a composite whole possible without proportion, namely, the proportion of parts. For unless the things present and available for the construction of an orderly whole are suitable to each other and to the whole to be made from them, there will be no orderly whole at all but only a heap of unrelated, unsuitable, unconnected things. Consequently, there is no material beauty possible without proportion; or, to put it differently, the proportion of parts is necessary for the beauty of any and every material being.

With this, the necessity of all three analytic principles in question for the production of material beauty has been established.

3. According to the previously outlined aesthetic method, step three consists in demonstrating the presence of integrity, proportion, and unity in all beautiful material beings.

If this demonstration is possible, its logical effect will be the extension of the validity of integrity, proportion, and unity from all the beautiful material individuals that have been initially chosen and analyzed to all beautiful material beings.

To accomplish this task, one can proceed this way. It has already been proved that integrity, proportion, and unity constitute order since order, by its very nature, is the integral unity of proportionate parts. Thus, if we can show that there is order and, hence, integrity, proportion and unity in *every material* being, then we will have proved that there is order, that is, integrity, proportion and unity in *every beautiful material* being. In this manner, the universality of the three analytic principles of material beauty will be properly established.

The question before us, then, is simply this: Is there really an order in every material being? Since material beings include natural things as well as artworks, we shall have to answer this question first with respect to natural things and, later, in regard to the works of fine art.

a. The presence of some order in certain material beings to be found in nature is rather obvious: in crystals, shells, flowers, and, generally, in organisms whose very names indicate a multitude of many definite parts constituting a whole in such a way that each and every part has its own definite place, size, relations, and functions. It is for this reason that even the most superficial consideration reveals an abundance of symmetry (spatial order involving size and shape) and harmony (spatial order of colors; tonal order; and dynamic, functional order) within any organism: the very same orders that are partly missing from what we term monstrosities in nature. Moreover, as we proceed from the lowest to the highest vegetative and sensory organisms, we can easily notice the immense complexity of their static and dynamic orders, composed of a hierarchy of parts (cells, tissues, organs, organ systems) and their functions.

But all this is only a conspicuously visible and, consequently, limited rather than universal order of structure and function in things of nature. It is undoubtedly impressive but not universal at all. For there are many things other than organisms, and many minerals other than crystals or shells. Where, then, is the universality of order in material beings to be found in nature? Modern natural science is ready with the answer: In the atomic and molecular structures upon which, in case of organisms, the cellular structure and the higher biological units are superimposed. Here we actually get a glimpse of the universality of order: every material being represents a structurally or static and, consequently, also a functionally or dynamic order.

At this point one may have this objection: If atomic, molecular, and cellular order had truly aesthetic significance or any aesthetic role to play, it would seem to follow that every material being in nature is beautiful. But this does not seem to correspond to our own experiences. For we call relatively few things in nature beautiful. It seems, therefore, that the structural, static order has little or no aesthetic significance. We can reply to this objection by showing that its general rejection of the aesthetic value of structural or, generally, static orders is contrary to empirical evidence. For what makes an architectural work, like a Gothic cathedral, aesthetically pleasing if not its structure? Also, is it not a matter of common experience that the color harmony as well as the shapes of many flowers and animals are some of the great sources of aesthetic delight for us, just as tonal structures (melody, harmony) are?

We see thus that the objection does not justify a general rejection of the aesthetic significance of static and dynamic orders in natural things. Consequently, we must find an explanation for why, despite the presence of various orders, the majority of natural things are not found beautiful by us. As a matter of fact, there is an easy explanation for this fact. The majority of natural things are neither found nor called beautiful because their orders are at least one of the following kinds:

(1) Not perceivable without special instruments or aids;
(2) Not knowable intuitively, but only discursively;
(3) Relatively inferior and, as such, unimpressive;
(4) Too frequent so that we get used to them and, thus, fail to take delight in them; and, finally,
(5) Conspicuously defective so as to elicit displeasure rather than delight.

The atomic, molecular, and cellular structures belong to the first kind; functional orders must be reasoned out in organisms (as in machines) and are, thus, only discursively knowable; visual (and auditory) orders in some plants and animals are clearly less impressive than others; and, apart from a very few, most individuals in any given species of natural things lack some integral parts, or have disproportionate parts. Hence there are ample reasons why we do not find or call most natural beings beautiful.

With this objection out of our way, we can reaffirm the universality of order in the things of nature. Upon reflection, we are even forced to recognize that the presence of order in every thing in nature is not simply a fact but also a necessary fact. For, if there were absolutely no order in a thing, neither structural, nor spatial, nor functional, hence, neither cellular, nor molecular, nor atomic, it would not be anything specific or determinate and, for this reason, simply could not exist. As St. Thomas puts it, "If all form and order and, consequently, everything that constitutes beauty were completely removed from a body, that body could not remain in existence either."[1] Inasmuch as every material being represents some order, in every material being there is some integrity, some proportion, and some unity. From this, in turn, it evidently follows that every material being that strikes us as being beautiful, has the same three analytic principles in it. For if the universal is true, the particular is also true.

b. With this conclusion the universality of integrity, proportion, and unity in all beautiful things of nature has been cosmologically established. What is still to be done is to extend this universality to all works of fine art.

Why should we separately discuss the presence of the three analytic principles in question in the works of fine arts? Because they, and only they, are by definition supposed to be beautiful enough cognitively to delight the beholder, whereas the works of other arts (the useful arts, such as dressmaking or car making) are beautiful only secondarily and per accident.

While the aprioristic-deductive argument for the presence of order in all things of nature uses solely cosmological premises, the presence of order in all works of fine art can be shown deductively on psychological grounds. For not only do we find order, as a matter of fact, in everything recognized as a work of fine art, but we also find every fine artist to be deeply concerned and preoccupied with properly arranging and ordering the artistic medium or material so as to produce an aesthetic whole in which every part has its proper place, and has definite relations to all other parts as well as the whole. The process of artistic creation in which, first, the main contours of the work appear in the artist's mind, then the details are conceived and worked out in definite relations to the whole, best shows this universal artistic concern with aesthetic order.

---

[1] Thomas, *De div. nom.* 4, 21, 554, in Pseudo- Dionysius, *De div. nom.* 4, 27 (PG 3, 728D). Cf. Thomas, *In VIII. Phys.* 3, 993 in reference to Aristotle, *Phys.* VIII, 1.

Let us listen, for instance, to the famous librettist of Richard Strauss, Hugo von Hofmannsthal, as he describes his own preparations for writing his *Ariadne*. In a letter to R. Strauss, he says, "During the past few days ... I have got through the hardest and most attractive part of the work; namely, to settle the psychological motives of the action, to establish, in my own mind, the relations between the various characters and between the different parts of the whole thing—in short, to sketch a detailed outline of the underlying motives which the poet must have before him (rather as you must have to picture your symphony) if he is to be attracted, roused and held by the work."[2] It would be difficult to make the issue at hand clearer than Hofmannsthal does here. But we can find the same careful preparation in arranging the details of the artwork not only in the playwright but also in the painter, the composer, the choreographer, the conductor, the actor, etc.

Nicolas Poussin, the seventeenth-century French painter warns us, for example, "Beauty does not enter a subject without careful preparation. This preparation includes order, mode, extent or space, and form. Order signifies the distance of the parts; mode treats quantity and number; form relates to contours and colors. It is not enough that all the parts have a suitable order or space, and that all the figures be in their natural places. There must be also 'mode' to keep them within their true limits."[3] Clearly, both Hofmannsthal and Poussin express basically the same artistic concern with that aesthetic order which Aristotle discussed and analyzed in his *Poetics*. Even the surrealists and the artists of the so-called abstract artworks, be they painters or sculptors or whatever else, are genuinely concerned with the arrangement of all the parts of their works, although those works do not represent things as they are found in nature or anything specific in nature at all. Newspaper reporters may joke about an abstract painting being hung upside down in a museum without anybody noticing this fact; but to the artist himself this certainly does make a difference because he knows the reasons for the exact places and relations of every part to every other in his work.

One can, of course, occasionally hear about contemporary painters who leave the final form of their so-called artworks to mere chance. With respect to such "creative" people one must bear in mind two things. One is that such accounts are more often than not exaggerated, because there is still some trace of arranging process involved in the making of such works. The other is that if one has absolutely no preconceived order in mind, and leaves everything up to chance in the production of, let us say, a painting, then he is simply not an artist and, consequently, cannot be used as an instance against the thesis concerning the universal artistic interest in aesthetic order.

[2] Hofmannsthal's letter of July 23, 1911 to R. Strauss, in *A Working Friendship, The Correspondence between Richard Strauss and Hugo von Hofmannsthal*, p. 97.

[3] N. Poussin, *The Outline of a Treatise on Painting*; in *Painters on Painting*, ed. Eric Potter (New York: Grosset and Dunlap, 1963), 70.

Summing up: Every work of fine art represents an order, on the one hand, and is beautiful to some extent, on the other hand. To represent an order means to have integrity, proportion, and unity. Consequently, every work of fine art has integrity, proportion, and unity. Therefore, in works of fine art, the presence of the three analytic principles in question is coextensive with beauty. This, in turn, means that every artwork that is beautiful contains the three analytic principles in question. With this argument, the universal validity of the three analytic principles of beauty has been established in regard to all natural things and all works of fine art.

c. There is only one more kind of aesthetic object in which the presence of integrity, proportion, and unity may be questioned: the aesthetic object representing any group of natural things with or without works of fine art, such as a seascape or a landscape, the latter being with or without a building, a statue, etc. Is it possible deductively to prove the presence of integrity, proportion, and unity in all aesthetic objects of this kind? Unfortunately, it is not. The reason? An aesthetic object taken in the above given sense is, by definition, a spatial whole due to mere chance, and there is nothing universally valid or true in any chance-object. A chance object is subjected neither to any cosmological necessity (physical, chemical, biological laws) nor to any psychologial necessity, such as the artist's concern with order in his work. That the scenery which I am looking at any place in the world includes a blue lake in a valley, surrounded by a pine tree forest on the slopes of a mountain rising high to the sky is a chance combination: the lake and the forest may be there, but not the mountain (e.g., in Minnesota); or the forest and the mountains may be there, but not the lake (e.g., in Upper Bavaria); or the lake may be there, but neither a forest nor a mountain (e.g., in Oklahoma).

With respect to such aesthetic objects, then, the presence of integrity, proportion, and unity is a necessity only with respect to the individual natural things included in that natural scenery, whereas the presence of the three analytic principles in the aesthetic object as a whole is to be determined empirically. But, if all beautiful material beings and all works of fine art contain these 3 principles, it is highly probable that aesthetic objects made up of natural things (and of fine artworks) are also beautiful because of the presence in them of the same three analytic principles. The probability of this is easily shown to be true of any natural scenery that cognitively delights, on the basis of a unity of harmonious or contrasting colors and shapes.

4. As our fourth step, let us attempt to prove the truth of an affirmative reply to this question: Is the list containing integrity, proportion, and unity, certainly complete? For it may happen that these three principles are necessary, and, as such, are always present in every beautiful thing, and yet there is at least one other principle also needed for the beauty of anything material.

The completeness of the list containing integrity, proportion, and unity as the necessary principles of material beauty can be proved aprioristically in this manner.

In every material being, one can find and distinguish nothing more and nothing less than the whole, some parts, and real relations in such a way that the real relations are nothing more or less than that of the parts to the whole, that of the parts to each other, and that of the whole to the parts. In other words, this is a *complete* list of the aspects and components of material being in general.

But, in terms of each one of the not more and not less than three kinds of real relations, the material being poses one demand for its own sake. This means that, in terms of each one of the exactly three kinds of real relations, a certain condition must be fulfilled in order that the material being exist, and be what it is. These three necessary conditions are the following: (1) In terms of the relation of the parts to the whole, it is necessary that all parts needed for the whole be present; (2) In terms of the relation of the parts to each other, it is necessary that all parts present be composable into a whole; and, (3) In terms of the relation of the whole to its parts, it is necessary that the whole be actual, i.e., actually put together from its parts.

Therefore, these three conditions, based on the three real relations to be found in every material being, represent a complete list of necessary conditions.

On the other hand, the first of the three necessary conditions listed above is that of integrity; the second, that of proportion; the third, that of unity.

Consequently, integrity, proportion, and unity represent a complete list of necessary conditions concerning material being in general.

But, it is empirically known that, in virtue of these three conditions or principles, the material being is cognitively delightful, that is, beautiful.

Therefore, integrity, proportion, and unity represent the complete list of the necessary conditions or principles of beauty in the material being.

5. In the fifth and final speculative step at the physical level, we must ask whether each one of the three analytic principles of material beauty, namely, integrity, proportion and unity, is an ultimate principle or rather one reducible to an even higher and more universal principle. The reason for this inquiry is rather obvious. One may be right in holding that the three analytic principles in question are truly necessary for material beauty, are actually present in every beautiful material being, and are the only principles necessary for rendering any material being beautiful. However, it is still conceivable that any one or any two or all three of these three analytic principles be reducible to one higher genus. For, in such a case, each of the three would be necessary and universal but not an ultimate principle of material beauty, although the philosopher always and professionally seeks the ultimate principles of reality or any part or aspect of reality.

Is there a way in which the irreducibility or ultimacy of each of the three analytic principles of material beauty can be demonstrated?

Let us begin with a distinction. It has already been stated that, in one respect, integrity, proportion, and unity are reducible principles of material beauty, viz., inasmuch as they can be synthesized into order. For order is simply unity having integrity and proportion, or the integral unity of (a multitude or variety of) proportionate parts. However, what we are here specifically interested in is not the physical identity of integrity, proportion, and unity with order but rather, whether either any one, any two, or all three of these three principles stand under a more universal genus, or else whether integrity and proportion are logically under the genus of unity.

It seems that there are two kinds of arguments proving the impossibility of so reducing these three analytic principles or, in other words, the ultimacy of the three: one, a deductive or aprioristic; and another, an inductive argument.

a. Arguing deductively or aprioristically, we must prove the irreducibility of any one, any two, or all three analytic principles of material beauty to some higher genus, on the one hand, and the irreducibility of integrity and proportion to unity. Of these two, the latter can be done very briefly and easily; so, let us begin with that part of the task.

If integrity and proportion were reducible to unity, the two would be kinds of or under the genus of unity, rather than the modifiers of it. But, integrity and proportion are modifications rather than kinds or under the genus of unity. This can be seen from the definition of order as being the unity *having* integrity and proportion (or proportionate parts), or as being the integral (modifier) unity (thing modified) of proportionate parts (modifier). Also, from the analysis of order, we know that integrity and proportion are the material causes or physical components rather than the species of order, just as body and soul are the physical parts of man. Therefore, integrity and proportion are not reducible to unity.

Is there a genus to any one or any two or to all three of the analytic principles of material beauty? A cosmological consideration can give us the answer to this question.

Since we are dealing here with the essence and the essential components of *material* beauty, that is, the essence of the beauty of *material being* in general, the logically highest genus related to the question is *material being*. But material being in general is, essentially, a composite being or a being that actually unifies many parts into a more or less complete, perfect, or integral whole. Thus, there is in every material being a more or less actual unity of a multitude of parts. On the other hand, there could not be an actual unity of parts if the parts were not fit to be put together into a whole, or to make up the whole. Thus, in every material being there is a more or less integral, actual unity of a multitude or variety of proportionate parts. What does this mean? It means quite obviously that the very nature of material being directly and immediately contains and necessitates precisely integrity, proportion, and unity. But, if there is nothing between the supreme genus involved in material beauty, namely, material being, and the three analytic principles in question, then these three analytic principles are clearly ultimate and, as such, irreducible.

In brief, the very nature of material being guarantees the ultimacy of integrity, proportion, and unity as the three analytic principles of material beauty.

b. There is also a complementary argument possible to the above outlined cosmological-deductive argument. Although, strictly speaking, it rests on an incomplete induction, this argument may have a greater appeal than the above-outlined cosmological argument, especially to those who are historically minded.

This historical argument is, by its nature, incomplete for two reasons. One is, that no one author of a work on the philosophy of beauty can ever claim to know literally *all* objectivist definitions of material beauty in general ever offered by thinkers. The other reason is that, even if one were in the possession of all essential definitions of beauty ever offered, he would still not be able to foreknow all essential definitions to be offered in the future. Nevertheless, even with these two defects in it, the argument is so forceful, impressive, and amazing that it must be treated here.

The outline of the historical argument for the ultimacy or irreducibility of the three analytic principles of material beauty is the following.

If integrity, proportion, or unity were not an ultimate principle of material beauty, certainly some philosopher would have listed an analytic principle of material beauty or beauty in general that is more universal, or the genus of any one, two, or all three of them. But it seems that this has never happened. Instead, every list of analytic principles ever offered by any philosopher seems to contain only two kinds of aesthetic principles: one, that is a *species* either of integrity, proportion, or unity or else of order; and another, that is a *synonym* either of integrity, proportion, or unity, or else of order. Therefore, it seems that integrity, proportion, and unity are truly ultimate or irreducible analytic principles of material beauty.

In this argument, the major premise is as highly probable as any premise in any historical argument can ever be. What does need proof is the surprising minor premise, which constitutes the crux of the argument. Now, to confirm this premise with any degree of accuracy or completeness, one must first make certain distinctions.

Any list of analytic principles of beauty or material beauty ever offered may contain either subjective principles (principles to be found in the beholder rather than in the aesthetic object) or objective principles (principles to be found actually in the beautiful thing itself). On the other hand, if a list contains only objective principles of beauty or of material beauty, it may include qualities that are evidently *not principles* of beauty at all, (as when the list includes effects rather than causes of beauty, or when it includes species of beauty, or qualities co-extensive with but logically distinct from beauty, or qualities completely unrelated to beauty, or else a quality contradictory to material beauty); or qualities that are evidently *not ultimate* principles of beauty or material beauty (as when the list includes secondary qualities, i.e., qualities growing from order or from other principles of beauty, considered either absolutely or relatively).

Examples for subjective qualities considered or listed to be principles of beauty are Jean Francois Marmontel's "intelligence" and Uvedale Price's "idea of youth and freshness" as well as Humphrey Repton's "novelty." An example for qualities listed as aesthetic principles although they are the effects (principiates) rather than the causes (principles) of beauty is Brandenstein's "attractiveness" (for a thing pleases and attracts because it is beautiful rather than vice versa). Among qualities listed as principles of beauty, although they are, in reality, species of beauty, we find Marsilius Ficinus' "adornment" and H. N. Lee's "sensuous charm." Examples for qualities listed as aesthetic principles despite the fact that they are coextensive with but logically distinct from beauty are de Quincey's and J. J. Urráburu's "truth" and Albert Stöckl's "goodness." An example for qualities listed as aesthetic principles, even though they are completely unrelated to beauty is de Quincey's "utility." Among the qualities listed as ultimate aesthetic principles, although they are only secondary, derivative principles either of order or of some other basic principle of beauty include Richard Price's "variety" (since it means variety of orderly units); the schoolmen's favorite neo-Platonic principle, called "splendor," "clarity," or "brilliance" and A. W. Holmes-Forbes' "suggestiveness" (since they mean properties of order in reference to the beholder); and Abraham Tucker's "expressiveness," Carlton Noyes' "significance" and, perhaps, also Brandenstein' "characteristicalness" (since they mean the orderly whole of the beautiful thing in its relation to other things). An example for a quality listed as an aesthetic principle although clearly contradictory to material beauty is John Ruskin's "infinity" (since no material being is infinite in any respect) or, perhaps, Urráburu's "honesty." Finally, examples for qualities listed as universal aesthetic principles, although evidently limited in their applicability, are William Thomson's "shape and color" (mentioned first as principles of material beauty by Xenophon)[4] as well as Edmund Burke's "comparative smallness' and "clear and bright color."

---

[4] Xenophon, *Memorabilia*, III, 10, 1–2. In due fairness, the following distinctions must be made in this connection:

(1) To hold shape and color to be the first principles of beauty in general is evidently wrong both at the metaphysical and the physical or cosmological level, since neither immaterial beings nor tones have either shape or color.

(2) To hold the same to be the first principles of material beauty in general is still wrong, but only at the physical or cosmological level, since this is to ignore tonal beauty completely.

(3) To consider shape (or proportion) and color to be the first principles of the beauty of the

Now, the reason for listing all these erroneously mentioned principles of beauty is this: each one of these kinds of aesthetics principles must be disregarded in our historical argument for the ultimacy of integrity, proportion, and unity. But, apart from these above listed (or similarly erroneous) subjective or objective qualities ever maintained to be principles of beauty or material beauty, all qualities ever listed by philosophers as being principles of beauty or of material beauty seem to be either the species or the synonyms of integrity, proportion, unity, and order.

Thus, among the ever listed aesthetic principles representing *species of integrity* are: just magnitude, magnitude (meaning proper size or integrity in magnitude), (due) power, quantity (meaning proper size), specific perfection, etc. Among the ever listed aesthetic principles that represent *synonyms of integrity*, we find completeness, fullness, perfection, totality, etc. Moreover, among the principles that have ever been listed about (material) beauty and represent various species of proportion are: consonance, correspondence, due proportion, harmony, measure, relation, etc., whereas the following are clearly *synonyms* of proportion: fitness, propriety, suitability, etc. Furthermore, among the aesthetic principles that have ever been listed, *species* of unity are: coherence, composition, continuity, encompassment (?), form, harmonious co-operation, organic unity, parts melted into each other, uniformity, unity in variety, etc., whereas *synonyms* of unity are: unification, wholeness, etc. Finally, among the aesthetic principles, that are *species* of order we find: balance, composition, contrast, delicate frame, design, evolution, gradation, gradual variation, multiplicity, organicalness, organism, purity, regularity, repose, simplicity, sincerity (or truthfulness, said to be the opposite to artificiality in composition), smoothness (as the formal arrangement of parts in regard to the surface), succession, symmetry, thematic variation, translation, etc., whereas at least these, arrangement and orderliness, are *synonyms* of order.

What does all this prove? Considering the fact that the above-listed over fifty aesthetic principles are taken from almost two hundred lists of aesthetic principles, hence, from almost two hundred aesthetic theories, expounded from

human body (or even any material being) is still wrong, since shape or proportion as well as color is itself reducible to more basic principles. However,

(4) To maintain that shape (or proportion) and color are the two main generic components or integral parts of the total beauty of the human body or even of material being in general, with the implication that both of these two components are reducible to the first or metaphysical principles of beauty in general, is true.

Thus, the mentioned William Thomson is wrong under category (2); whereas ancient and medieval philosophers, like Cicero (*Tusc. disp.*, IV, 13, 31; cf. *De off.*, I, 28, 98); Philo (*De vita Moysis*, III, 140); Plotinus (*Enn.* I, 6, 1); Basil (*Homiliae IX in Hexaemeron*, hom. 2, n. 7; *PG* 29, 48 A); Augustine (*De civ. Dei*, XXII, 19, 2; *PL* 41, 781; and *Epist.* I., ep. ad Nebridium, n. 4; *PL* 33, 65); R. Grosseteste (*In Dion. De div. nom.*, cap. 4; H. Pouillon, "La Beauté . . . ," ed. cit., p. 322); Aquinas (*In I. Sent.* 31, 2, 1, sol.; *In IV. Sent.* 44, 2, 4, 3a; *S. c. gent.*, II, 64, 1424; *De div. nom.* 4, 5, 339); and Dionysius the Carthusian (*op. cit.*, arts. 17 and 22; pp. 242A; 247C) are right, at least inclusively, under category (4).

the fifth century B.C. to the second half of the twentieth century, it is not presumptuous to conclude that, in twenty-five centuries, nobody seems to have found or thought of a single aesthetic principle that would represent the genus (rather than a synonym or species) of either integrity, or proportion, or unity, or, for that matter, order. Thus, it definitely is highly unlikely that these three analytic principles are reducible to higher aesthetic principles. This is another way of saying that the three analytic principles of material beauty, which we have found through analysis, are most probably truly ultimate principles of material beauty.

With this conclusion, we have reached the end of our speculative investigations concerning the essence of material beauty. On this basis, we may repeat here that material beauty is essentially the integral unity of a multitude or variety of proportionate parts or, simply, order.

6. The definition which we have defended above is the definition of the essence of *material beauty* in general. As such, it has universal validity in the realm of matter, that is, with respect to all beautiful material beings, and is thereby truly cosmological in character. This universal validity, however, is plainly relative. For, while it is valid for *all* beautiful material beings, it is valid only for beautiful *material* beings.

At this point the question arises: Is this essential definition of material beauty also metaphysical in character, that is, does it express also the essence of beauty in general?

One may react to this question with a counter-question: Why should we ask this question at all? The answer is, of course, that throughout history, from pre-Socratic to contemporary philosophy, some thinkers have always asserted the beauty of things other than material, such as the human act or virtue (moral beauty), spiritual substances, including the human soul (spiritual beauty), and God (divine beauty).

Upon reflection, one can realize that the above essential definition of material beauty may be truthfully said to be also, in some manner, genuinely metaphysical in character, i.e., to express the essence of beauty in general, if the following three conditions are fulfilled: (1) If there are, in fact, immaterial things in existence in the first place; (2) If the three analytic principles we discussed above and order have analogous meanings; and, (3) If the principles of material beauty can be truthfully predicated of immaterial beings, like the morally good human act or God.

Why are these the necessary conditions of the metaphysical character or metaphysical validity or our essential definition of material beauty?

That the existence of immaterial beings is necessary for our definition to be truly metaphysical is evident. As long as there are only material beings, there is no distinction between the realm of matter and the realm of reality (being as being, as Aristotle puts it) and, thus, no difference between cosmology and metaphysics either.

That the terms signifying the three analytic principles of material beauty and the term "order" must be analogous terms, viz., must have analogous meanings, follows from the fact that, if such things as morality, spirit, or God exist at all, they are beings analogous to material beings and, for this reason, any term, such as "beautiful," when predicated first of material being and later of some immaterial being, partly retains and partly changes its meaning, and is, thereby, analogous by definition.

But how do we know that immaterial things, like God, are analogous to material beings? As long as, for instance, "God" means, as for Aristotle, Augustine, Avicenna, Anselm, Moses Maimonides, Albert, Bonaventure, Thomas Aquinas, Descartes, Spinoza, Leibniz, *et. al.*, an all-perfect being—a being perfect without imperfection, an infinitely perfect being, a pure act, necessarily existent—the term "being" partly changes its meaning while being predicated of God after it was predicated of material things. "Being" retains its meaning in reference to both material being and God insofar as both really and truly exist; but "being" changes its meaning in reference to matter and God insofar as matter is a composite, finite, and mutable being, whereas God is an uncomposed (simple), infinite, and immutable being. But if the most basic of all metaphysical terms predicable of matter and God is analogous, so is necessarily any other term predicable of both material beings and of God, like "good," "capable," "perfect," or "living." For this reason, unless "integrity," "proportion," "unity," and "order" are also capable of analogous predication, the essential definition of material beauty cannot, by its very nature, have metaphysically universal validity.

The third listed necessary condition is readily understandable. One must prove that the three analytic principles of material beauty as well as order can truthfully be predicated of certain immaterial beings, such as the morally good human act or God, in order to claim that, in the analogous sense, these immaterial things are actually beautiful; and, thus, our essential definition of material beauty is, in an analogous manner, truly metaphysical, applying to anything and everything that is beautiful at all.

Let us assume the first necessary condition, namely, that some kinds of immaterial beings and, specifically, God do exist: and let us, on this basis, investigate the other necessary conditions.

7. For the analogous predicability of the three analytic principles of material beauty and of order, we can argue this way.

If the terms "integrity," "proportion," "unity," and "order" can be reasonably and meaningfully predicated of various kinds of beings other than material, then these terms are truly analogous, and it is at least possible for the above-established essential definition of material beauty to be a genuinely metaphysical definition of the essence of beauty in general.

But these four terms can, as a matter of fact, be predicated reasonably and meaningfully of immaterial beings as well as material beings. For integrity means completeness, totality, or perfection, that is, the state in which a being has everything it ought to have according to its nature and, thereby, lacks nothing. This can be the case not only with material beings but also with any being, because a being may have everything and lack nothing whether or not it is composed of integral parts. Consequently, "integrity" is an analogous term.

The same holds true for "proportion," also. For it means suitability of two or more things, be they the integral parts of a material whole or one mental and one real being, as the judgment of the mind may suit, i.e., conform to, the real being judged (mental conformity), or as an artwork may suit an idea which it expresses (artistic conformity), or as the rational, immaterial act of the human will may conform to man's rationally recognized obligation to avoid evil. Clearly, "proportion" does have a meaning in matters of the mind as well as in material beings, and is thereby analogous in character.

Is "unity" also an analogous term? In reference to material beings, it means the result of a physical conjoining of a multitude or variety of integral parts into a whole, or the actual indivision of a material being. But there is also such a thing as unity of views, opinions, intentions, etc., meaning that two or more persons are not divided in their thinking or willing, and this meaning is mental rather than physical. Moreover, it is evident that any being as a being is one, that is, actually undivided, whether it is material or not, real or mental. The only difference between the oneness or unity of the material and that of the immaterial being is this: the material is one as being actually undivided even though divisible; the immaterial is one as being actually undivided *since*, by definition, indivisible. The meaning of unity thus is partly the same and partly different in reference to material and immaterial things, and this, by definition, renders it an analogous term.

The same can be said, finally, of the term "order" signifying the synthetic principle of material beauty. For we speak of spatial and temporal, visible and audible, and, hence, material order as well as mental and moral order. The reason for this is that, whether the parts are material, as in a cathedral, or mental, as in a long, complex sorites, or immaterial powers, as the human intellect and free will in harmonious co-operation, any kind of unity of a multitude or variety of any kind of parts suiting each other and the whole is, by definition, an order.

All the principles in the essential definition of material beauty are, thus, analogous in character; therefore the first condition necessary for our essential definition of material beauty being in some manner also the essential definition of beauty in general is fulfilled.

8. The other and final step in our investigation must consist in determining whether in various immaterial things, like the human act or God, there is necessarily some sort of integrity, some sort of proportion, some sort of unity and, thus, some kind of order. For if so, then those investigated immaterial beings are also beautiful in some manner, and our essential definition of material beauty applies also to immaterial beauty in some manner, and is for that reason truly metaphysical and of universal validity without any qualification.

Before proceeding with this part of the present metaphysical inquiry, there is a methodological question that ought to be answered. One may ask why we should investigate whether or not the principles of material beauty are to be found, with necessity, in immaterial things. Why do we not try, instead, to find out what principles make up the beauty of certain immaterial beings? The answer is obvious. No immaterial being is directly knowable. Consequently, we have no way of directly observing and analyzing the beauty of any immaterial being. Thus the only thing we can do is attempt to find out whether there are principles of beauty, similar to those of material beauty, in immaterial things. For, if there are such, and there are such necessarily, that is, by virtue of the nature of the immaterial being, then we can rightly call such immaterial beings beautiful in the analogous sense, and we can also maintain that our definition is valid analogously for all beautiful material beings, and is for that reason truly metaphysical.

Let us attempt first to determine whether there is some kind of integrity, proportion, and unity, that is, order, in the morally good human act.

Human act is an act done by man knowingly and freely. Morally good human act is a human act that conforms to the norm of morality, viz., human nature (as the objective norm), and one's own moral judgment ("conscience," as the subjective norm). Moreover, every human act comprises the physical reality of its act, namely, the immanent or transient act considered in itself, and a certain number of circumstances connected with it and answering such questions as who? whom? how? where? when? and why? The physical reality of the human act apart from its circumstances has no morality, since it is a mere mental abstraction. What does determine its morality is the circumstances. Furthermore, a human act is morally good only if and when it conforms to the objective or subjective norm of morality in respect to every one of the numerous circumstances connected with it; whereas the human act is morally evil if it fails to conform to the moral norm in respect to one or more circumstances. For instance, if an expectant mother with abdominal cancer undergoes cobalt treatment to save her life, under proper medical supervision, in a properly equipped hospital, and with the sole intention of saving her life, her act of undergoing that treatment is morally good; but, if she does so without proper medical supervision, and/or in a hospital where the equipment is such that her treatment endangers other peoples' lives, her act of undergoing the treatment is morally evil.

With this understanding of the nature of the morally good human act, we are now prepared to answer the following question: Is there any kind of integrity, proportion, and unity or, simply, order in the morally good human act? In the light of the above information, this much is clear. The morally good human act is, first of all, a kind of whole composed of the physical reality and the circumstances of the act, the moral goodness of which is determined by its circumstances. Secondly, this human act is morally good precisely inasmuch as it conforms to the moral norm. Thirdly, the moral goodness of the human act renders that act, in some manner, perfect or complete insofar as its moral goodness consists in the conformity of the human act to the moral norm with respect to not one or two or some, but to all of its circumstances.

In other words, the morally good human act is an integral, composite whole conforming to a norm according to a multitude or, rather, variety of circumstances. All this means that the morally good human act has some kind of integrity, proportion, and unity, and represents thereby some kind of order. But integrity, proportion, and unity—or, generally, order—render material beings beautiful. Consequently, the morally good human act is in some manner, analogously, beautiful; and this is so despite the fact that this kind of beauty is for man not directly knowable and, thus, not cognitively delightful.

Let us next consider the question of divine beauty. On this question we may proceed in two different manners. For while the beauty of the morally good (virtuous) human act cannot be proved deductively, but only through discovering the analogous presence of order and the three analytic principles of material beauty, we can deductively demonstrate that God (if He exists at all) is beautiful without first inquiring about God's having or not having the principles of material beauty; and we can also analytically determine whether God is beautiful.

The deductive method consists in the following reasoning. Inasmuch as God exists at all, or since God's existence is recognized as the necessary condition of the existence of the contingent, mutable world, God is the creative principle (exemplary and efficient cause) of all finite beings with all their perfections, i.e., of everything the finite beings are or have. Beauty is one of the perfections (qualities) of material beings. Therefore God is the creative principle (exemplary and efficient cause) of material beauty. But one cannot communicate any act or perfection to another being without possessing that act or perfection in some manner. Therefore, God must Himself have beauty or be beautiful, in some manner.

After this conclusion the next question is this: In what does divine beauty essentially consist? Since there is no direct knowledge of God possible, we can reason this way. If divine beauty is really and truly beauty, there must be some similarity between material beauty and divine beauty. Material beauty consists of three analytic principles or, simply, of order. Therefore, divine beauty, too, must consist in some manner of these principles. After this conclusion, one must investigate what in God corresponds or can possibly correspond to the principles of material beauty—an investigation that will be carried out step by step below, in connection with the second method.

The other and analytic method is much shorter, and comprises the following logical steps.

Inasmuch as God exists, one can raise the question of whether or not God is beautiful and, in reply to this question, proceed in the following fashion. The beauty of material beings is due to order, that is, integrity, proportion, and unity. Therefore, unless beauty means something completely different in God (in which case the term "beauty" is equivocal, and the question meaningless), God is beautiful if there is some kind of order in Him, that is, some integrity, proportion, and unity, or, since of these three, unity is alone the formal cause or specific essence, if there is at least some unity in God.

Thus, as in the first method, the crucial question is this: Are there, in God, integrity, proportion, and unity, that is, order? Needless to say, in investigating this question we must bear in mind that we must expect the principles of material beauty to be in God not in the same manner as they are in material beings but only in some analogous manner.

Is there unity in God? If by unity we mean unity of composition, i.e., the actual indivision of a composite and, as such, divisible being, as is the unity of the material being, then the answer is no, since a composite God is no God but a contradiction (for every composition means act mixed with potency rather than pure act; and it is the finite being, not God, that is a mixed act). If, on the other hand, by unity we mean unity of simplicity, that is, the actual indivision of the absolutely simple and, as such, indivisible God, then the answer is yes; that is, there *is* unity in God. Furthermore, since the divine unity is the actual indivision of an indivisible being, whereas material unity means the actual undividedness of a divisible being, divine unity is partly the same and partly not the same as, and hence analogous to, material unity.

Is there proportion in God? Many theistic thinkers say there is, arguing this way. God is infinitely perfect and, as such, necessarily has all perfections, since God cannot possibly lack any perfections. Such perfections are life, eternity, omnipresence, omnipotence, omniscience, freedom, etc. All these perfections are perfectly proportionate to the divine essence, since each one of them is as unlimited as the divine essence itself. Consequently, there is some kind of proportion in God. This conclusion, however, is metaphysically false, and has only metaphorical value in asserting proportion of God. For all those specific divine perfections are really identical with the divine essence, and only logically (virtually) distinct from it. But there is no *real* relation of any kind between a being and itself, although there can be a relation between a thing and itself according to the mind's consideration. But the proportion of real (existent) beauty is a kind of real relation. Therefore, there is no real proportion at all in God, not even in the analogous sense.

Is there integrity in God? If integrity means the presence of all integral parts necessary for the whole, as in case of material beauty, the answer is naturally no, on account of God's absolute simplicity; that is, the absence of any kind of parts or components in God. But integrity has also another and similar meaning: perfection. This, in case of composite beings, such as a beautiful material being, consists in having all parts. But, in case of the absolutely simple God, perfection means to be such as not to be limited in any way, or to be such that nothing can be any greater than God. This, of course, is exactly what infinity means, and infinity is one of the traditionally recognized divine attributes in realistic-theistic philosophies. Therefore, there is integrity in God. But God's integrity, as God's unity, is analogous to the integrity of the beautiful material being: the latter has integrity (or is perfect) by not lacking any necessary integral part; God has integrity (or is perfect) by not having any limitation in any way or respect whatsoever.

Is there any order in God? If order means, as in the beautiful material being, the integral unity of proportionate parts, then the answer is no, since, as already stated, there are no parts or composing principles in God and thus no proportion of parts, either. On the other hand, as already shown, God is truly integral or perfect, since infinite; and God is also truly one with a unity of absolute simplicity. Consequently, God is really and truly, although analogously, an integral or perfect unity without proportionate parts. If we compare now the order of the beautiful material being with the order of God, we find the following: the order of the beautiful material being is an integral unity of proportionate parts; God, on the other hand, represents an integral unity without proportionate parts. Order is, thus, partly the same and partly not the same in material beings and God; or, in other words, order in God is analogous to order in material beings.

Summing up, what makes material beings beautiful, viz., order, is also present in God, but analogously. For material beings are beautiful in virtue of an order which consists of integrity, proportion and unity; God is beautiful in virtue of an order that comprises integrity and unity but no proportion.

Combining the results of this investigation concerning the morally good human act and God, we may say the following.

a. Both the morally good human act and God are beautiful; that is, besides material beauty, there is also moral beauty as well as divine beauty.

b. Material beauty is analogous to both moral and divine beauty, but in such a way that, as is to be expected, material and moral beauty are more similar than material and divine beauty. For both material and moral beauty represent, in an analogous manner, integral unity of proportionate parts; divine beauty is, however, integral or perfect unity without proportionate parts.

From all this it follows, finally, that

c. Our essential definition of material beauty is completely valid also for moral beauty, although the principles are to be taken analogously. But our definition is only partly valid for divine beauty since, while integrity, unity, and order are to be taken analogously, proportion is completely absent from divine beauty. Thus a genuinely metaphysical, i.e., universally valid, definition of the essence of beauty in general is partly different from the essential definition of material beauty. On this basis, we can conclude that *beauty in general is order, that is, integral unity, or integral unity with or without proportionate parts.*

Section Three: Consequences of the Essence of Beauty

THE ESSENCE OF BEAUTY, as defined and demonstrated in the previous chapter, has a number of logical consequences both topically and doctrinally.

A topical consequence of the essence of beauty can be defined as any aesthetic topic that is logically posterior to, and is made possible by, the definition of beauty. A doctrinal consequence, on the other hand, can be defined here as any aesthetic doctrine that is logically implied by the above definition of beauty.

Our topical consequence that must be treated here is the question of the division of beauty. For, on the one hand, not only is it historically customary both to define and to divide the subject of any science, but it is actually a logical necessity to clarify the central notion of any science in terms of its comprehension, by means of definition, and also in terms of its extension, by means of division. On the other hand, it is evident that division follows rather than precedes definition, since unless one has the definition of a thing he cannot possibly determine how many kinds or versions that thing may have.

The doctrinal consequences of the definition of beauty are of two kinds: absolute and relative. An absolute doctrinal consequence is a logical implication of the essence of beauty, which implication concerns beauty considered in itself. Correspondingly, a relative doctrinal consequence concerns beauty considered in its relation to man, its beholder. There are two closely related absolute doctrinal consequences of the essence of beauty that ought to be considered here briefly. One is the transcendentality of beauty; and the other, the nature of ugliness. The former is implied in the definition of beauty insofar as beauty is order or unity with or without multitude, and insofar as there is some order or unity to be found in every being. The latter consequence is implied in the definition of beauty inasmuch as beauty, meaning order or unity, is to be found in every being in some manner, and thus there is no such a thing as ugly except in the sense that the beauty of some beings is defective.

Finally, the relative doctrinal consequence that deserves a proportionate treatment is the question of aesthetic experience. This question is truly a doctrinal consequence of the essence of beauty because, being order, beauty delights its knower, that is, causes a cognitive and appetitive experience in him. On the other hand, the treatment of aesthetic experience is truly a relative doctrinal consequence insofar as it shows us not what beauty is in itself but rather what beauty does to man, its beholder.

Of all these topics, the division of beauty will be treated in chapter 10; the transcendentality of beauty and the nature of ugliness in chapter 11; and the aesthetic experience, in chapter 12.

Chapter X
Division of Beauty

THE QUESTION OF THE DIVISION OF BEAUTY can be treated basically in two different ways: historically and doctrinally. This will be done in the subsequent two articles.

ARTICLE 1: *Historical Consideration*

Historically, we find that the question of dividing beauty has been touched upon or treated in various ways.

Methodologically, these treatments are either occasional or professional; either implicit or explicit; either incomplete or complete; and either unsystematic or systematic. According to the basis used, beauty has been divided either (and mostly) on the basis of the natural genera of the things which are beautiful, or else (and less frequently) irrespective of the natural genera of things beautiful, i.e., according to something other than the essences of the beautiful things.

Of the methodological version, the occasional, implicit, and incomplete modes of division usually go together, just as the professional, explicit, and more or less complete divisions do, whereas both the former and the latter modes may be occasionally—but very seldom—of the systematic type.

For instance, Plato speaks sometimes of beautiful colors, figures, and sounds[1] and, at other times, of the beauty of gold and ivory or stone and wood;[2] sometimes of the beauty of animals, like horses and ape[3] and, at other times, of human beauty, like the beauty of boys and girls in general or of individual persons;[4] sometimes of the beauty of human life or human laws and institutions[5] and, at other times, of the beauty of works of art, both fine and useful;[6] sometimes of the beauty of the gods or the beauty of virtue[7] and, at other times, of absolute divine beauty;[8] and, especially, when he occasionally contrasts this perfect, divine beauty (that is eternal and immutable) with relative or imperfect beauty (that is temporal and changeable);[9] or the beauty of the soul

---

[1] Plato, *Gorg.* 474d–e, *Phileb.* 51b–d, *Rep.* V, 400a, etc.

[2] *Hipp. mai.* 289e, *Symp.* 211d, 290c; 292d, etc.

[3] *Tim.* 19b, 87c, *Hipp. mai.* 288c, *Phaed.* 78e, *Hipp. mai.* 289ab.

[4] *Phaed.* 237b, 251c, *Symp.* 211d, *Hipp. mai.* 287e–288a, 289ab; *Charmid.* 154cd, *Phaed.* 278e, etc.

[5] *Epist.* VII, 327d; *Symp.* 210c, 211c; *Hipp. mai.* 292d, etc.

[6] *Meno* 97e, *Hipp. mai.* 298a; *Symp.* 211d, *Phaed.* 18e, *Hipp. mai.* 288ce, etc.

[7] *Hipp. mai.* 289ab; *Leg.* IX, 859d; etc.

[8] E.g., *Hipp. mai.* 289d, *Crat.* 439ce, *Phaed.* 65d, 75d, 78d, 100bc, *Euthyd.* 301a.

[9] E.g., *Symp.* 210d–211c; *Hipp. mai.* 292c.

with the beauty of the body.[10] When he does all this, Plato is in fact offering occasional, implicit, incomplete and unsystematic divisions of beauty. The same can be said of such subsequent ancient philosophers as Cicero, Plotinus, Augustine, and the high-scholastic thinkers in general.

It is easy to see that, if these implicit, occasional and incomplete divisions spread over many of Plato's works are logically put together, they constitute the earliest historical instance of a doctrinal division of beauty based on the genera of beautiful things in an ascending manner,[11] more or less hinted at in one line of the *Greater Hippias*: "[the beauty of] stone and wood and man and god."[12] To show what such a division of beauty looks like, all one needs is to arrange logically the several statements which Thomas Aquinas made on the beauty of various beings, thereby producing an extremely complex and virtually all-inclusive division that represents the culmination of aesthetic thought on the question before the dawn of modern philosophy. Putting it in the form of a diagram, the division is the following:

Beauty
- Ideal Beauty
  - Imaginable
    - Arithmetic Beauty
    - Geometric Beauty
  - Thinkable
    - Beauty of the Form of Thinking
    - Beauty of the Content of Thinking (or Beauty of Truth)
- Real Beauty
  - Divine or Essential Beauty
    - Beauty of God Considered as a Whole
    - Beauty of Divine Attributes
  - Creaturely or Participated Beauty
    - Beauty of Natural Things
    - Beauty of Man-Made or Artificial Things

Taking up first the division of the beauty of natural things,

[10] *Charmid.* 154e; *Phaed.* 91c, *Symp.* 210c, 211c.
[11] *Symp.* 211c.
[12] *Hipp. mai.* 292d.

DIVISION OF BEAUTY

Natural Beauty
- → Essential Beauty
  - → Angelic Beauty
  - → Material Beauty
    - → Partial Beauty
      - → Actual Beauty of Form
      - → Potential Beauty of Prime Matter
    - → Total Beauty
      - → Celestial Beauty
        - → Of Heaven in General
        - → Of Heavenly Bodies
      - → Terrestrial Beauty
        - → Of Minerals
        - → Of Plants
        - → Of Brutes
        - → Of Man
          - → Of Mankind
          - → Of Individual Man
            - → Not as a Whole
              - → Of the Human Soul
              - → Of the Human Body
            - → As a Whole
- → Accidental Beauty
  - → Beauty of Quantity
  - → Beauty of Quality
    - → Of Potency
    - → Of Habit (e.g., Virtue)

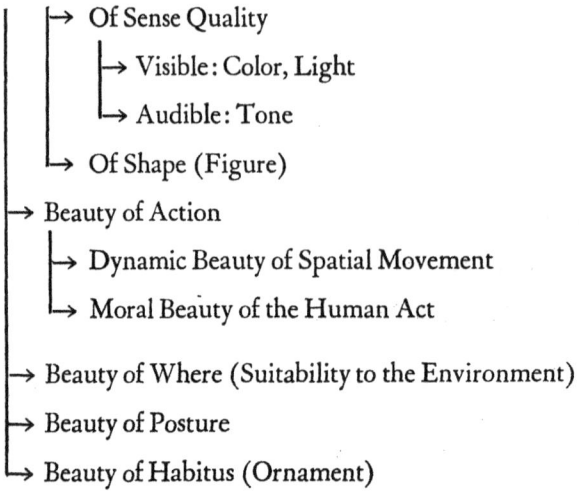

- → Of Sense Quality
  - → Visible: Color, Light
  - → Audible: Tone
- → Of Shape (Figure)
- → Beauty of Action
  - → Dynamic Beauty of Spatial Movement
  - → Moral Beauty of the Human Act
- → Beauty of Where (Suitability to the Environment)
- → Beauty of Posture
- → Beauty of Habitus (Ornament)

Artificial Beauty, in turn, is divided by Thomas in the following way:

Artificial Beauty
- → Beauty of Useful Works
- → Beauty of (what we today call) Fine Artworks.

(To all this may be added a division of supernatural beauty into that of grace, glory, and the Church; but this is a theological division.)[13]

The second type of doctrinal division of beauty that is to be found in ancient and medieval philosophy, is the mere *listing* or mentioning of one or more than one aesthetic species or category, irrespective of the natural genera of the beautiful things. In Aristotle, for instance, we find mention of the tragic and the comic,[14] and the well-proportioned ($σύμμετρον$—*formosum*)[15] and decorated or ornamented ($κόσμος$)[16] as well as the beautiful; in Augustine, of the fit or suitable and the specious[17] as well as the beautiful; in Albert, of the decorous, the honest, the befitting or suitable, the ornamented, the specious, and the shapely[18] besides the beautiful; and in Thomas Aquinas,

---

[13] See all these divisions and the text references to them in F. J. Kovach, *op. cit.*, pp. 93–102.

[14] The tragic: *Poet.* 6, 1449b 24–29; 13, 1425b 32f; 2, 1448a 17f. The comic: *Poet.* 5, 1449a 33f; 2, 1448a 17f.

[15] *Nic. Eth.* IV, 3, 1123b 7–8; see, St. Thomas, *In IV. Eth.* 8, 738.

[16] *Soph. El.* 1, 164b 20.

[17] *Aptum*: *Conf.* IV, 13–15 (PL 32, 701–704); *speciosum*: *De div. quaest. 83*, q. 23 (PL 40, 17).

[18] *Decorum* or *decus*: *Summ. theol.* II, 11, 62, 1, sol. (31, 597); *Opusc. de pulchro*, q. 2, sol. fin.; *ed. cit.*, p. 566. *Honestum*: *Opusc. de pulchro*, q. 2, sol., *ed. cit.*, pp. 565f. *Aptum*: *S. theol.* II, 11, 62, 1, sol. (31, 597); *Ornatum*: *In IV. Sent.* 24 B 7c (30, 40); *Summ. de creat.* I, 4, 71, 2 (32, 727ff.); etc. *Speciosum*: *In I. Sent.* 31, F, 6, 3a (26, 108). *Formosum*: *Eth.* IV, 2, 1 (7, 295f.).

besides the beautiful, of the ornate, the honest, the decorous, the specious, the gracious, the shapely, and the suave.[19]

There must not be any misunderstanding, however, about this matter. Neither the divisions of beauty on the basis of natural genera nor the listing of aesthetic categories irrespective of the genera of things beautiful is confined to ancient and medieval philosophy. On the contrary, both kinds of divisions can be found quite frequently in modern aesthetics. Instances of the former can be found, among others, in K. C. F. Krause (1829), F. T. Vischer (1846), C. Lemcke (1879) and James McCosh (1880). It seems worthwhile to consider their divisions in detail.

Karl C. F. Krause divides beauty in a hierarchical manner according to two bases: Mode of being or modality, and essences. According to modality, his division is the following:

Beauty
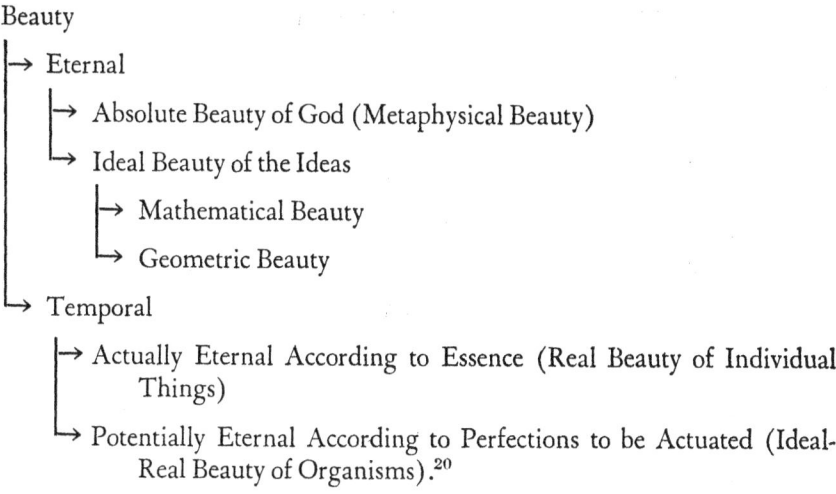

- → Eternal
  - → Absolute Beauty of God (Metaphysical Beauty)
  - → Ideal Beauty of the Ideas
    - → Mathematical Beauty
    - → Geometric Beauty
- → Temporal
  - → Actually Eternal According to Essence (Real Beauty of Individual Things)
  - → Potentially Eternal According to Perfections to be Actuated (Ideal-Real Beauty of Organisms).[20]

According to essences, Krause divides beauty into that of God, that of the world, and that of artworks. Within this three-fold division, his division of the beauty of God is as follows:

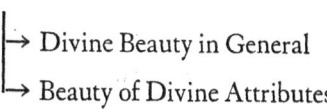

- → Divine Beauty in General
- → Beauty of Divine Attributes

---

[19] *Ornatum*: Thomas, *In II. Sent.* prolog.; *In IV. Sent.* 49, 4, 2, ad 1; etc. *Honestum*: *S. th.* II–II, 145, 2c and 4c; etc. *Decorum*: *In IV. Sent.* 49, 4, 1, ad 5; *S. th.* II–II, 145, 2c. *Speciosum*: *In Is.* 53; *De pot.* 6, 6, 5a; *In Ierem.* 11: 3. *Graciosum*: *In Psalm.* 44: 2; *S. th.* II–II, 177, 1, sed contra; 109, 4c. *Formosum*: *In IV. Eth.* 8, 738; *In I. Sent.* 31, 2, 1, sol; *De pot.* 4, 2c. *Suave*: *In X. Eth.* 6, 2028.

[20] Krause, *Vorlesungen über Ästhetik oder über die Philosophie des Schönen und der schönen Kunst*, Vorl. 34, pp. 143f.

PHILOSOPHY OF BEAUTY

The second main part of his overall division, that of the beauty of the world, includes three parts: the beauty of the spiritual world (pure spirit); of the spiritual and material world (man); and of the material world (nature).

Taking up first the division of the beauty of the spiritual world, he proceeds in this manner:

- Beauty of Thinking
- Beauty of Feeling
- Beauty of Willing or Freedom

After this part comes his division of the spiritual and material world:

Beauty of the Spiritual and Material World (Man)
- Human Beauty in General
  - Spiritualized Bodily Beauty
  - Materialized Spiritual Beauty
- Human Beauty in Particular
  - According to Sex
    - Asexual (apart from sex)
    - Sexually Distinct
      - Male Beauty
      - Female Beauty
    - Sexually United Beauty
      - In the Same Person (Hermaphrodite Beauty)
      - In Different Persons
        - Beauty of Social Contact Between Man and Woman
        - Beauty of Aesthetic Contact Between Man and Woman (e.g. in Dance)
        - Beauty of Biological Contact (in Monogamic Marriage)
  - According to Age

222

DIVISION OF BEAUTY

- Beauty of the Child
- Beauty of the Adolescent Boy and Girl
- Beauty of the Mature Man and Woman
- Beauty of the Aged Man and Woman

The third part of the division of the world is this:

Beauty of the Material World (Nature)
- Its Static Beauty (Spatial Structures)
- Its Dynamic Beauty
  - Of Physical Processes
  - Of Chemical Processes
  - Of Organic Processes
    - Beauty of Plants
    - Beauty of Brutes
    - Beauty of Human Body

The third division of beauty by Krause is that of artworks.[21]

Friedrich Theodor Vischer offers the following division of beauty:

Beauty
- Objective or Natural Beauty
- Subjective Beauty or Beauty of Imagination

F. T. Vischer's Objective Beauty, in turn, is divided thus:

Objective or Natural Beauty
- Inorganic Beauty (of Light, Color, Air, Water, and Earth)
- Organic Beauty
  - Of Plants
  - Of Brutes
  - Of Men
    - General Human Beauty
      - Of General Forms (Shape, Status, Age, Sex, Love, Marriage, and Family)

[21] *Op. cit.*, Vorl. 36–43, pp. 155–83.

- → Of Special Forms (Races, and Ethical, Cultural, and Political Differences)
- → Of Individual Forms (Natural and Moral Determinations, the Character of the Individual)

→ Historical Human Beauty
- → Of Ancient Times
- → Of Medieval Times
- → Of Modern Times.[22]

Carl Lemcke's division is much simpler:

Beauty
- → In Nature
  - → Beauty of Motion, Tone, and Light
  - → Beauty of the Four Elements
  - → Beauty of Vegetation
  - → Beauty of Man
    - → Considered in Himself: Bodily Built, Sex, Age, Race
    - → Considered in His Activities: Manual, Mental
  - → Beauty of States and Nations
- → In Art.[23]

Finally, J. McCosh's division is the following:

Beauty
- → Physical
  - → Sound, Form, Color
  - → Beauty of Physical Objects (Trees, Mountains, Waterfalls, Ocean, and Scenery)
- → Intellectual (= Intellectually Knowable)
  - → Beauty of Sameness

---

[22] F. Th. Vischer, *Aesthetik*, II; *Das Schöne in einseitiger Existenz*, second ed. by R. Vischer (München: Meyer und Jessen, 1922), 3–356.

[23] Carl Lemcke, *op. cit.*, pp. 125–246, 251.

↳ Beauty of Differences
  → Beauty of Whole and Parts
  → Beauty of Means and Ends
  → Beauty of Resemblances
  → Beauty of Spatial Relations
  → Beauty of Relations of Time
  → Beauty of Quantity
  → Beauty of "Active Property"
  ↳ Beauty of Causation.[24]

To confirm the above-mentioned assertion, that the listing of aesthetic categories not based on natural genera is not confined to ancient and medieval philosophy, it will suffice here to point out that such aesthetic notions as the tragic in Aristotle, the befitting in St. Augustine, the specious in Thomas and, above all, the sublime in Longinus reappear in the works of British and German aestheticians of the eighteenth and the nineteenth century over and over again.

Then what, if anything, is novel in modern aesthetics on the question of the division of beauty? Mainly, two things. One is partly novel; the other, completely novel.

The partly novel element, born in eighteenth-century England, is actually twofold. First of all, it is the sudden upsurge in the number of aesthetic categories listed irrespective of the genera of natural things that are beautiful. Secondly, these modern aesthetic categories are, from the very beginning, considered as co-equal with the beautiful or beauty, unlike all the above-listed ancient and medieval aesthetic categories that were considered to be species or versions of the beautiful or beauty.

The completely novel element in modern aesthetics in regard to the division of beauty is the custom born in nineteenth-century Germany to systematize the aesthetic categories that were construed irrespective of the genera of beautiful things. The reason for this modern innovation is both logical and doctrinal. The logical reason is the fact that, from Aristotle to Kant, two or three or more aesthetic categories were simply listed or mentioned by individual thinkers without any explanation as to why precisely so many categories were there or were listed, leaving the reader with the impression of arbitrariness and incompletion. The German systematizations in the nineteenth century

---

[24] J. McCosh, *The Emotions*, pp. 157–68; 192–207.

represent logical attempts to rectify both of these apparent or real defects. The doctrinal reason for this aesthetic systematization was the ever-increasing interest in dialectical systems culminating in Hegel and, under the impact of the Hegelian aesthetics, dominating the field of aesthetics for a number of subsequent decades.

Examples for the partly novel feature in modern aesthetics, namely, the listing or mentioning of some old and some new aesthetic categories, can be found easily in English and German literature. Thus, Joseph Addison and Joseph Warton list three aesthetic categories: the great, the uncommon, and the beautiful.[25] F. Hutcheson and Thomas Reid make only slight changes in this three-fold list by mentioning grandeur, novelty, and beauty;[26] however, Hutcheson also names such additional aesthetic categories in connection with the external beauty of man as sweetness, mildness, majesty, dignity, vivacity, tenderness, etc.[27] Besides beauty and sublimity, E. Burke speaks of grace, elegance, and speciousness;[28] Lord Kames, of grandeur, sublimity, grace, the ridiculous, the burlesque, and beauty;[29] Hugh Blair, in 1790, of the beautiful, the sublime, and the pathetic;[30] F. Schlegel, in 1797, of the beautiful, the characteristic, the piquant, the striking, the daring, the cruel, and the ugly;[31] F. Schleiermacher, of the comic, the beautiful, the sublime, the characteristic, the touching, the lovely, and the tender or delicate, etc.;[32] F. Schiller, of the beautiful, the sublime, the pleasant (pleasurable), the charming, the majestic, the pathetic, the gracious, the tragic, etc.;[33] K. C. F. Krause, of the beautiful, the sublime, the grandiose, the colossal, the tragic, and the tragicomic;[34] Eduard von Hartmann, of the beautiful, the sublime, the charming, the idyllic,

---

[25] J. Addison, *The Spectator*, No. 412, June 23, 1712. J. Warton, *The Adventurer*, No. 80, August 11, 1753; in *The British Classics*, 17 (London: J. Sharpe, 1807), 66.

[26] F. Hutcheson, *An Inquiry into the Original of our Ideas of Beauty and Virtue*, I, 6, esp. §§ 11-13; ed. cit., pp. 81-84. Thomas Reid, *Essays on the Intellectual Powers of Man*, VIII, 2; ed. cit., I, 493a.

[27] Hutcheson, *ibid.*, II, 6, 3; ed. cit., p. 256.

[28] E. Burke, *op. cit.*, III, 1, 22 to 27, ed. cit., pp. 77, 102f., 106f.

[29] Lord Kames, *op. cit.*, chaps. 4, 11, 12; pp. 129-47, 197-207.

[30] H. Blair, *Lectures on Rhetoric and Belles Lettres*, III, lectures 3-5; *A Critical Dissertation on the Poems of Ossian* (London, 1790), reproduced in *The Poems of Ossian*, tr. James Macpherson (Leipzig: B. Tauchnitz, 1847), 111-18.

[31] See F. Schlegel, *Studien des classischen Althertums*, I: *Geschichte der epischen Dichtkunst der Griechen*; in *Sämtliche Werke*, III (Wien: Ignaz Klang, 1846), *passim*; *Studien des classischen Althertums*, II. Essays 1, 2, 5, and 6 (*Sämtliche Werke*, IV; *passim*; and *Vorlesungen über philosophische Kunstlehre*, ed. A. Wünsche (Leipzig: Dietrich, 1911); also, E. von Hartmann, *Die deutsche Ästhetik*, I: *Erster historisch-kritischer Teil* (Leipzig: W. Friedrich, 1886), 363f.

[32] Fr. Schleiermacher, *Vorlesungen über die Ästhetik. Sämtliche Werke*, Abtheilung 3, Bd. VII; ed. Carl Lommetzsch (Berlin: G. Reimer, 1842), 190 ff., and 240-48.

[33] F. Schiller, "Über Anmut und Würde," "Über das Pathetische," "Über das Erhabene," and other philosophic essays.

[34] Krause, *Abriss der Ästhetik oder die Philosophie des Schönen und der schönen Kunst*, §§ 23-30, 36-38, 71-73; pp. 22-25, 29-31, 69-71.

the spectacular, the intriguing, the merry, the touching, the stirring, the sad, the elegic, the comic, the humorous, the tragicomic, etc.[35]

All these aestheticians are surpassed, however, by Karl Köstlin who, while speaking of many aesthetic categories, such as the beautiful, the charming, the gracious, etc., went into so many details about just one aesthetic category, that of the sublime, that he opposed it as the immeasurably great and strong to the minute, that is, the immeasurably small, fine, tender and light, and listed almost twenty aesthetic categories related or "leading up" to the sublime. Among them are: the stately, the complete, the encompassing, the specious, the large, the grand, the impressive, the magnificent, the excellent, the extensive, the majestic, the giant and the gigantic, etc., and also he listed their opposites, such as the lowly, the graceful, the small, the fine, the soft, the mild, the sweet, the tranquil, the pretty, and the dwarfish.[36] In contrast with him, the American James McCosh discusses only the beautiful, the picturesque, the ludicrous, and the sublime.[37]

An outstanding modern instance of the systematization of aesthetic categories, like the ones listed in the above examples, is to be found in Adolf Zeising's *Aesthetic Investigations*. The author recognizes six species of the beautiful as their genus: the purely beautiful, the sublime, the charming, the tragic, the comic, and the humorous. Of these six, three are said to be primary modifications (the purely beautiful, the comic, and the tragic); the other three, to be intermediary modifications, and all this in such a way that the six are arranged in a circular manner analogous to the color circle:

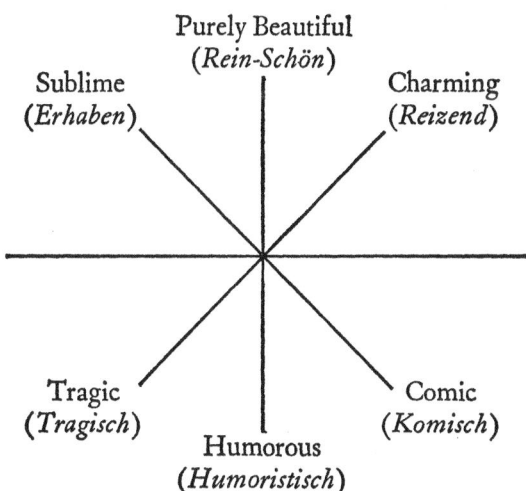

[35] E. von Hartmann, *Die Philosophie des Schönen*, parts IV–V, pp. 298–420.
[36] K. Köstlin, *Aesthetik* (Tübingen: H. Laupp, 1869), I, 141, 147; 107–109; 111; 139; 112–14, 119, 140.
[37] J. McCosh, *The Emotions*, pp. 178f., 181–191.

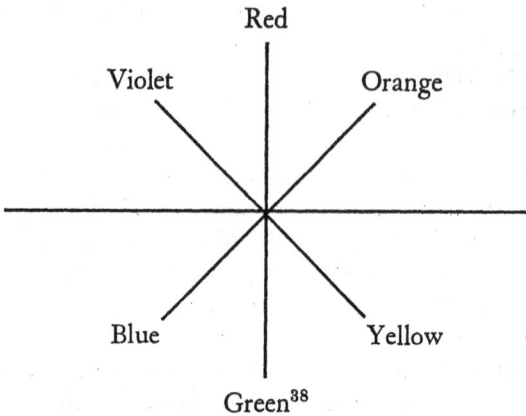

As if this systematization were still not enough, Zeising goes on to say that the three primary modifications of the generically beautiful represent three dialectical species (thetic, antithetic, and synthetic), three corresponding kinds of beauty (subjective, objective, and absolute), and three corresponding phases of development (position, negation, and negation of negation),[39] and that each of the six aesthetic species consists itself of three subspecies of beauty:

(1) The purely beautiful: ("Red")
   Dignified
   Noble
   Pleasurable
(2) The delightful or attractive: ("Orange")
   Graceful
   Interesting
   Piquant (Poignant)
(3) The comic: ("Yellow")
   Droll
   Entertaining
   Burlesque (Vulgar)
(4) The humorous: ("Green")
   Melancholic (Sad)
   Amusing (Capricious)
   Odd (Quaint)
(5) The tragic: ("Blue")
   Demonic (Demoniac)

---

[38] A. Zeising, *Aesthetische Forschungen*, § 429 (Frankfurt am Main: Meidinger's Son and Co., 1855), 413f. For this datum and those in nn. 39–40, see E. von Hartmann, *Die deutsche Aesthetik*, I, 242–44.

[39] A. Zeising, *op. cit.*, pp. 129–31, 133.

Pathetic
Touching
(6) The sublime: ("Violet")
Impressive
Majestic
Glorious[40]

Besides these two innovations of modern aestheticians, there is very little novel contribution of any significance to the question of the division of beauty, except some occasional and genuinely original divisions. Such seems to be Eduard von Hartmann's division of beauty in his *Philosophy of the Beautiful*:

Beauty: A. Unconscious-Formal or Sensuously Pleasant Beauty
      B. Formal Beauty: 1. Mathematically Pleasing Beauty
                       2. Dynamically Pleasing Beauty
                       3. Passively Teleological or Decorative Beauty
                       4. Animate Beauty; and
                       5. Generic (*Gattungsmässige*) Beauty.
      C. Concrete Beauty of the Concretely Beautiful.[41]

ARTICLE 2: *Doctrinal Consideration*

What can we say about all these ancient, medieval, and modern divisions of beauty from the doctrinal point of view?

The answer may be given separately in regard to the divisions based on natural genera and to those not based on natural genera.

1. As to the former divisions, we may assert the following.

First of all, these divisions of beauty are definitely and considerably objective and, as such, much less variable than the listings or divisions made irrespective of natural genera. To see the truth of this statement, it suffices to compare the above detailed divisions by the medieval Aquinas and the nineteenth-century Krause or F. T. Vischer. It is very easy to notice how closely these divisions resemble each other, not only in the main contours (divine vs. finite beauty: immaterial vs. material beauty; etc.), but even in some of the small details.

Secondly, insofar as these kinds of the division of beauty vary with the individual thinkers, the divisions vary mainly and quite understandably with the authors' epistemological principles and their corresponding metaphysical views. For to an empiricist skeptic, nothing immaterial is knowable, and hence he will divide only material beauty while leaving divine or spiritual beauty completely unmentioned. On the other hand, an epistemological realist, who trusts his reason as well as his senses basically, like Aristotle or Hegel,

---

[40] *Op. cit.*, pp. 143, 417.
[41] E. von Hartmann, *Die deutsche Ästhetik*, II: *Philosophie des Schönen*, II, 1–7; pp. 72–208, 328.

will recognize both material and immaterial beings, both finite and absolute beings, and will correspondingly produce a genuinely metaphysical rather than a merely physical or cosmological division of beauty. This, too, can be concretely confirmed by a comparison of Vischer's above-given division with Thomas' or Krause's.

2. Turning next to the divisions of beauty in terms of aesthetic categories irrespective of natural genera, the following points may be made:

First of all, this type of division is considerably more arbitrary in two ways: logically and grammatically. It is more arbitrary *logically* in the comprehension and the extension attributed to the various aesthetic categories listed as species of beauty or "aesthetic value." On the other hand, it is more arbitrary and subjective *grammatically* insofar as old, traditional terms may be used to express either traditional or novel aesthetic categories, or as novel terms may be used to express either traditional or novel aesthetic categories.

To confirm all these assertions, let us find concrete examples of them in both pre-modern and modern aesthetics.

The Latin *ornatus* (decoration, embellishment) means in Augustine a physical thing externally added to another to enhance the latter's sensorily perceivable beauty.[1] The same term is extended by Alexander of Hales so as to mean beauty added to material thing either in virtue of a really distinct, external being, as plants are the ornaments of the earth, or pure spirits, of heaven,[2] or else in virtue of the natural, physical, intrinsic properties of a thing, as luminous perspicuity is the ornament of water, or light, of heaven.[3] But in Thomas its meaning is not only extrinsic and intrinsic physical decoration but also moral decoration.[4] This gradually growing extension in an aesthetic notion is indicative of what changes and variety were to come in modern aesthetics both in the comprehension and the extension of the numerous, partly old and partly new, aesthetic categories.

We may befittingly begin our examples for modern variability and arbitrariness in the meanings of aesthetic categories with the new aesthetic category of the novel (uncommon). To Alexander Gerard, the novel means five things: it is that which causes pleasure, surprise, unity with other emotions, self-gratulation for having recognized it, and sympathy with the original genius that produced it.[5] To Joseph Addison, the conceiver of this aesthetic category, and, implicitly, also to F. Hutcheson, the novel means three things: it is that

---

[1] Cf. Augustine, *De Gen. ad litt.*, II, 13, 26 (PL 34, 273).
[2] Alexander of Hales, *S. theol.* II, p. 1, i. 3, tr. 2, q. 2, tit. 3, chap. 2, sol., vol. II, n. 285, p. 346b; *ibid.*, chap. 1, sol. ad 2; vol. II, n. 284, p. 345.
[3] *Op. cit.*, II, p. 1, i. 3, tr. 2, q. 3, tit. 2, chap. 1, sol. ad 2. vol. II, n. 292, p. 355b. See Alexander's entire treatment of *ornatus* in *S. theol.* lib. II p. 1, i. 3, tr. 2, q. 3; vol. II, nn. 287–310, pp. 348–71.
[4] Extrinsic physical decoration: *De pot.* 4, 2c; *S. th.* I, 70, 1c. Intrinsic physical decoration: *In I. Tim.* 2:11, lect. 2, 116. Moral decoration: *In I. Tim.* 3:2, lect. 1, 100; *S. th.* II–II, 168, 1c.
[5] A. Gerard, *An Essay on Taste* I, 1; *ed. cit.*, pp. 3–11.

which surprises, gratifies our curiosity, and represents constant motion or change.[6] To Lord Kames, the novel does the following three things: it causes wonder, gratifies curiosity, and may aggravate terror (if the novel appears to be harmful); but it does not surprise the knower (unlike the unexpected), nor does it represent motion or change.[7] To Thomas Reid, novelty causes nothing; instead, it represents per se a "relation which the thing has to the knowledge of the person."[8]

The elegant has a similar variety of meanings. To Sir Joshua Reynolds and Dr. Samuel Johnson, it means lower beauty, "beauty without grandeur," as opposed to the higher beauty of the sublime;[9] but to Sir Uvedale Price, it stands for symmetrical beauty,[10] and to E. Burke, for regular beauty.[11]

Similarly, Dr. John Baillie contrasts the pathetic with the sublime;[12] Richard Payne Knight contrasts the two only in real life, and identifies the two in artworks;[13] and Dr. Samuel Johnson simply differentiates, rather than contrasts, the two.[14]

Also, dignity (*Würde*) is identified by Karl W. F. Solger as a species, the finite species of sublimity, just as charm is as the finite species of beauty;[15] but by C. H. Weisse, as a species of beauty, its male species, as opposed to grace, its female species.[16] Furthermore, the picturesque and the beautiful are *opposite* aesthetic species to E. Burke and Sir U. Price;[17] simply *separate* species, to Dugald Stewart;[18] species and its genus, to William Gilpin;[19] and identical as synonyms, to Sir J. Reynolds.[20] Also, Lord Kames, A. Gerard, and K.F.E. Trahndorff agree that sublimity and grandeur differ;[21] but Hugo Blair holds

---

[6] J. Addison, *The Spectator* No. 412, June 23, 1712. F. Hutcheson, *op. cit.*, I, 6, 13; *ed. cit.*, p. 84.

[7] Lord Kames, *Elements of Criticism*, chap. 6, nn. 237, 239; *ed. cit.*, pp. 152f.

[8] Reid, *Essays on the Intellectual Powers of Man*, VIII, 2; *ed. cit.*, I, 493a.

[9] Sir Reynolds, *Discourses*, 4 and 16. Dr. Johnson, "Elegant" and "Sublime" in *A Dictionary of the English Language* (London: J. and P. Knapton, etc., 1755).

[10] See, Hipple, *op. cit.*, p. 210.

[11] E. Burke, *op. cit.*, part III, sect 23.

[12] J. Baillie, *An Essay on the Sublime*. (1747) The Augustan Reprint Society Publication, No. 43. (Los Angeles: University of California, 1953), 32f.

[13] R. P. Knight, *An Analytical Inquiry into the Principles of Taste*, III, 1, 41; *ed. cit.*, p. 361.

[14] Dr. S. Johnson, *op. cit.*, entries "Pathetic" and Sublime."

[15] K. W. F. Solger, *Erwin, vier Gespräche über das Schöne und die Kunst*, part 1, dial. 2 (Berlin: Realschulbuchhandlung, 1815), 238.

[16] C. H. Weisse, *System der Aesthetik als Wissenschaft von der Idee der Schönheit* I, § 24 (Leipzig: E. H. F. Hartmann, 1830), 169.

[17] E. Burke, *op. cit.*, p. III, s. 27. Sir U. Price, *Essays on the Picturesque* (1794), chap. 3 (London: J. Mauman, 1810), I, 49ff.

[18] D. Stewart, *Philosophical Essays*, II, 1, 1, 5, *ed. cit.*, V, 230-32.

[19] W. Gilpin, *Three Essays*, I: "On Picturesque Beauty"; *ed. cit.*, p. IX.

[20] C. R. Leslie and T. Taylor, *Life and Times of Sir Joshua Reynolds* (London: J. Murray, 1865), II, 606.

[21] Lord Kames, *op. cit.*, ch. IV, *ed. cit.*, pp. 129-47. A. Gerard, *op. cit.*, I, 2, *ed. cit.*, pp. 11-28. Trahndorff, *Aesthetik oder Lehre von der Weltanschauung und Kunst*, § 14 (Berlin: Maurer, 1827), 82.

that the two categories do not differ at all.[22] Moreover, as Lord Kames points out, many people think that congruity is a species of beauty; but he differentiates them as two aesthetic categories that never coincide, since beauty is of a single object and pleases; congruity is placed on a plurality of things, and may produce strong displeasure.[23] We could go on and on with this list.

Somebody may say, however, that these listed differences of opinions or definitions concern only insignificant aesthetic categories and, as such, prove very little, if anything. In reply, we may point out that sublimity or the sublime is the most important and most characteristic single aesthetic category in modern aesthetics, and yet the variety and arbitrariness of opinions and definitions are nowhere so great and obvious as in regard to this aesthetic category. To prove this statement, we need to consider only the following *groups* of differences of opinions concerning the sublime.

Considering it first in itself, the sublime is completely in the mind to Archibald Alison and Kant,[24] among others, and completely real to the post-Hegelian German idealists. Also, to A. Zeising, the sublime is completely qualitative in nature;[25] to the majority of the nineteenth-century aestheticians, as to F. T. Vischer,[26] however, it is purely quantitative. Moreover, of the majority of these aestheticians, J. H. von Kirchmann holds the sublime to be a superior but finite power;[27] and R. Zimmermann, to be infinitely great;[28] whereas Kant thinks that the "mathematical sublime" is infinitely great, but the "dynamic sublime" is only immeasurably superior without being infinite,[29] and Karl Köstlin maintains that the same Kantian distinction holds true but only subjectively for the absolute and the relative sublime, respectively.[30] Furthermore, of the German idealists, Schelling, Friedrich G. A. Ast, and Hegel,[31] as well as Trahndorff[32] and F. T. Vischer,[33] taught that, while the infinite idea or ideal and the finite sensory form are well balanced in the beautiful, the infinite idea dominates over the finite form in the sublime. M. Schasler held, instead, that the finite sensory form dominated over the idea in

---

[22] H. Blair, *Lectures on Rhetoric and Belles Lettres* (London: W. Sharpe and Son, 1820), I, 58f.

[23] Lord Kames, *op. cit.*, III, 10; *ed. cit.*, p. 186.

[24] A. Alison, *Essays on the Nature and Principles of Taste*, Essay 1, ch. 2, n. 1 (*ed. cit.*, p. 56). Kant, *Kritik der Urteilskraft*, § 26.

[25] A. Zeising, *op. cit.*, p. 360; as quoted in E. von Hartmann, *op. cit.*, I, 401.

[26] F. T. Vischer, *Aesthetik*, § 90, p. 246.

[27] J. H. von Kirchmann, *Aesthetik auf realistischer Grundlage*, ch. VIII, A, 1, a, § 27 (Berlin: Julius Springer, 1868), II, 9.

[28] R. Zimmermann, *Allgemeine Aesthetik*, II: *Allgemeine Aesthetik als Formwissenschaft*, §§ 97 and 230 (Wien: Braumüller, 1865), 40, 107f.

[29] Kant, *op. cit.*, §§ 26 and 28.

[30] K. Köstlin, *op. cit.*, p. 144 *vs.* p. 141.

[31] E. von Hartmann, *op. cit.*, I, 394, concerning Schelling, Ast and Hegel.

[32] Trahndorff, *op. cit.*, § 13.

[33] F. T. Vischer, *op. cit.*, §§ 83–84; pp. 231–33, especially 233.

the sublime;[34] whereas J. H. Kirchmann thought that there was absolutely no disproportion between the idea and its sensuous expression in the sublime.[35] Moreover, E. Burke maintained that the sublime elicited pain, astonishment, fear, or horror;[36] Kant took the position that the sublime elicited also pleasure, although only indirectly;[37] while G. T. Fechner categorically denied that the sublime elicited any fear in the beholder.[38]

Considering it next relatively, the sublime is held to be the highest degree of beauty by John Ruskin and John M. Anderson;[39] to be a species of beauty, by Sir J. Reynolds and K. C. F. Krause;[40] to differ from beauty in degree only, by Theodor Fechner;[41] to differ from beauty in kind, that is, specifically, by J. Addison, E. Burke, Kant, Schelling, F. Schleiermacher, and F. T. Vischer;[42] to be a species of the beautiful in the broad sense and a co-species of the beautiful in the strict sense, called "the simply beautiful" (*das einfach Schöne*), by J. H. von Kirchmann;[43] and to be both opposed to beauty and to have beauty, in its perfect form, as the mean between the sublime and the imperfectly beautiful, by Solger.[44]

The greatest variety of opinions, however, we find on the question of what is the opposite to the sublime. As a matter of fact, the sublime is considered to be opposed to the beautiful by Edmund Burke, who lists no less than six respects in which the two are opposed to each other; Kant finds at least a fivefold opposition between them; Samuel Tyler, an opposition like that of the male and the female.[45] Moreover, the sublime is opposed to the ridiculous, according to Jean Paul;[46] to the delightful or attractive, in the opinion of Schopenhauer;[47] to the delightful and the pleasant, in the thought of F. G. A. Ast;[48] to the pleasing, the charming, and the gracious, together with the dignified, as the privations of the sublime, according to C. H. Weisse;[49] considered the opposite of—incredibly enough—the formidable (*das Furchtbare*), just as the fright-

[34] M. Schasler, *Kritische Geschichte der Aesthetik*, sect. II, § 541; *ed. cit.* pp. 1067–69.
[35] J. H. Kirchmann, *op. cit., ibid.*, § 32; *ed. cit.*, II, 11.
[36] E. Burke, *op. cit.*, II, 1, 7 and 27.
[37] Kant, *Kritik der Urteilskraft*, § 23.
[38] G. T. Fechner, *Vorschule der Aesthetik, ed. cit.*, II, 175.
[39] John Ruskin, *Modern Painters*, I, p. 1, sect. 2, ch. 3, § 4 (*ed. cit.*, p. 42). J. M. Anderson, *The Realm of Art* (University Park and London: The Pennsylvania State University Press, 1967), 168.
[40] J. Reynolds, *Discourses*, 4 and 15. K. C. F. Krause, *Vorlesungen*, lect. 32, p. 139.
[41] T. Fechner, *Vorschule der Aesthetik, ed. cit.*, II, 172.
[42] J. Addison, *The Spectator*, No. 412, June 23, 1712. E. Burke, *op. cit.*, III, 27. Kant, *Kritik der Urteilskraft*, § 23. Schelling and Schleiermacher, in E. von Hartmann, *op. cit.*, I, 399. F. Th. Vischer, *op. cit.*, § 90, p. 247.
[43] Kirchmann, *op. cit.*, chap. III, C, § 1; *ed. cit.*, I, 73.
[44] K. W. F. Solger, *Erwin*, part I, dial. 2; *ed. cit.*, p. 243.
[45] E. Burke, *op. cit.* III, 27. Kant, *Kritik der Urteilskraft*, § 23. S. Tyler, *op. cit.*, chap. 1, pp. 12f.
[46] Jean Paul, *Vorschule der Aesthetik*, §§ 26f. (Hamburg: Friedrich Perthes, 1804) 152–72.
[47] A. Schopenhauer, *The World as Will and Idea*, I, bk. III, § 40.
[48] F. Ast, *System der Kunstlehre*, §§ 45–46; *ed. cit.*, pp. 51–54.
[49] C. H. Weisse, *System der Aesthetik*, I, § 24; pp. 163, 168.

ful (*das Schreckliche*) is to the grandiose (*das Grosse*), by Trahndorff;[50] to the grandiose and gigantic (*das Kolassale*), by K. C. F. Krause;[51] to the comic, by F. T. Vischer;[52] to the tender or delicate (*das Zarte*) or lowly, by Schleiermacher;[53] to the weak and the powerless, that impresses with its neatness and gracefulness, by A. Zeising;[54] to the pathetic, by Dr. John Baillie;[55] to the lowly, the frightful, and the ridiculous (*das Niedliche, Greuliche und Lächerliche*), by Theodor Fechner;[56] to the charming (as rest is to motion), by Schasler;[57] and to the immeasurably small, tender, fine and light, by Karl Köstlin.[58]

Finally, it may be pointed out that, as the above example of A. Zeising shows quite clearly, any systematization of the various categories that ignores the natural genera of beautiful things is even more subjective and arbitrary than the definitions and interpretations of those aesthetic categories, because such systematization depends almost entirely on the mental habits of the individual aesthetician, his attitude toward an intellectual architectonic, his metaphysical principles or postulates, and his chosen principle of analogy or point of reference.

3. From all these observations, in turn it follows that, if an aesthetician wishes to treat the question of the division of beauty as objectively as possible, he should prefer divisions based on the natural genera of beautiful things, and possibly avoid at least any aprioristic systematization of aesthetic categories not based on natural genera of beautiful things.

On the other hand, setting up his own division of beauty on the basis of natural genera, the aesthetician must endeavor to determine which genera of natural and man-made things conform to his own definition of beauty in general. For him, for instance, who realizes, as we have above, that material beauty is order, that is, an integral unity of a multitude or variety of proportionate parts, and that beauty in general is integral unity with or without a multitude or variety of proportionate parts, this means that he must endeavor to find out in which genera of natural and artificial things there is order or some kind of integral unity to be found. Furthermore, if such an aesthetician is a metaphysical realist recognizing real as well as mental beings and, among the real, both an infinite and finite beings and, among the finite, both material and immaterial beings, then he will eventually arrive at a division basically

---

[50] Trahndorff, *op. cit.*, § 14, p. 82.
[51] K. C. F. Krause, *Vorlesungen*, lect. 32, pp. 137ff.
[52] F. T. Vischer, *op. cit.*, §§ 155–67, pp. 375–403.
[53] F. E. D. Schleiermacher, *Vorlesungen über die Ästhetik*; in *Sämtliche Werke*, ed. cit., VII, 248; and *Ästhetik*, I, 18e, ed. cit., p. 105.
[54] A. Zeising, *op. cit.*, pp. 436, 127; in E. von Hartman, *op. cit.*, I, 402f.
[55] Baillie, *ed. cit.*, p. 33.
[56] Fechner, *op. cit.*, II, 178f.
[57] Schasler, *op. cit.*, section II, § 542; p. 1070.
[58] K. Köstlin, *op. cit.*, p. 147.

similar, at least in its main outline, to those of Krause, Vischer, or Aquinas.[59]

For the sake of completeness, it must be noted here that the above characterized aesthetic realist *may* do one more thing: come up with a trichotomic division of beauty analogous to the age-old, trichotomic division of truth and goodness, viz., the division of beauty into metaphysical, physical, and moral beauty; physical beauty meaning here the order of any individual being due to its conformity to its own natural species, and metaphysical beauty signifying the order of any being simply inasmuch as it exists (or is a being). However, to speak of metaphysical beauty, one must be able to establish the transcendentality of beauty—the topic of the next article.

---

[59] There is an interesting similarity also between the main structure of the divisions by Aquinas and Dionysius the Carthusian (*op. cit.*, art. 4, pp. 229D–230D).

Chapter XI

Extension and Privation of Beauty

IN THE PRESENT CHAPTER the two absolute consequences of the essence of beauty will be considered, namely, the transcendental extension of beauty (Article 1), and ugliness as the privation of beauty (Article 2).

ARTICLE 1: *The Transcendality of Beauty*

1. With regard to the extension of beauty, there are only four possible positions to take. One is, that no being is beautiful; another is, that only one thing is beautiful; a third is, that only some but not all beings are beautiful; and the fourth is, that all beings are beautiful.

The reason why these four are the sole alternatives is easy to see. For either there is or there is not any beautiful thing; in the latter case, there is either only one or more than one beautiful thing in existence; and, if there is more than one beautiful thing existent, either only some or else all beings are beautiful.

The first of the listed four positions is specifically aesthetic subjectivism and, a fortiori, that of the metaphysical nihilist. The second position is taken specifically by the aesthetic monist and, generically, by monists. The third view is held specifically by most aesthetic realists and, generically, by metaphysical pluralists. The fourth alternative is maintained by some aesthetic realists, the so-called aesthetic transcendentalists, and generically, like the third alternative, by metaphysical pluralists.

Which of these positions is right? To the aesthetic realist, i.e., inasmuch as aesthetic realism is properly demonstrated, the first or the subjectivistic-nihilistic view is evidently erroneous. Moreover, inasmuch as the aesthetic realist is also a pluralist, the position of aesthetic monism is untenable, too, since contrary to sense evidence. This leaves the aesthetic realist with only two possible alternatives: one, that some beings are beautiful; and the other, that all beings are beautiful. Which of these two alternatives is actually the case?

In answering this question, it must be pointed out first of all that, in a *non-exclusive* sense, the former alternative is evident. For we do find many things beautiful: natural sceneries, human faces and figures, flowers and animals, paintings and statues, music and dance, buildings and films, poems and plays, etc. On the other hand, we must also realize that, relying on our everyday experiences, it seems false to say that all beings are beautiful. The reason for this is quite obvious. Everybody finds some things non-delightful, that is, non-beautiful, and some other things even displeasing or repulsive, that is, ugly; and, this being so, it seems that the universal proposition, "Every being is beautiful" cannot possibly be true.

From all this, does it follow that the fourth alternative ("Every being is beautiful") is actually false, and that the third alternative ("Some beings are beautiful") is the true one? It does not. As a matter of fact, it will be argued below that the fourth position, that of the aesthetic transcendentalist ("Every being is beautiful"), is the correct one. However, before this demonstration is outlined, it is proper to give a doctrinal and historical background to this question, the doctrinal background consisting in the explanation of the notion of transcendentality or transcendental property; and the historical background consisting in outlining the history of the theories of the transcendentals or transcendental properties in general and of transcendental beauty or the transcendentality of beauty in particular.

2. The notion and the history of the transcendentals and transcendental beauty can briefly be outlined as follows.

a. The theory of the transcental properties of being was first conceived and expounded by Aristotle in connection with the notion of "the one" (τὸ ἕν) considered metaphysically. This theory can be expressed by the following simple proposition, "Every being is one." This is to say that unity is a mode or manner in which every being exists insofar as every being, irrespective of its specific nature, is actually undivided. In other words, unity, as meaning actual indivision, is the necessary consequence of being. But that which necessarily follows from a thing is the property of that thing. Therefore, unity is some kind of property of being, just as risibility, necessarily following from the rationality of man, is a property of man. The basic difference between risibility and unity (as properties) is this: the former is the necessary consequence of the specific nature of a thing; the latter, the necessary consequence of the thing as being. While the former type of property is called logical property, the latter is appropriately named transcendental property. Logical property is confined to a given species or genus; transcendental property transcends all genera and species, and characterizes every kind of being. Aristotle called them the "passions" (πάθη) or "[common] properties" (κοινά),[1] that is, the (first) determinations, of being; and subsequent thinkers, especially the high-scholastic philosophers, did likewise call them by the same name or, mostly, "transcendentals."[2]

---

[1] Aristotle, *Met.* IV, 2, 1004b 6, 11, and 20, respectively. Cf., *De caelo*, I, 1, 268a 3. Aquinas translates these terms by "passiones (entis)" (*In IV. Met.* 4, 571; *In Boetii De Trin.*, I, q. 2, a. 1, ad 3) and "propria (entis)" (*In IV. Met.* 4, 511), respectively.

[2] Some medieval schoolmen after Aquinas still use the name *"passio entis."* Cf. Petrus Joannis Olivi (d. 1297), *In II. Sent.*, q. 14, sol. obi. ad 1; quoted in Günther Schulemann, *Die Lehre von den Transcendentalien in der scholastischen Philosophie* (Leipzig: Felix Meiner, 1929), 50; Duns Scotus, *Op. Oxon.* I, d. 23, q. un., n. 2, in *Opera omnia*, ed. Vivès, X, 259a; F. Toletus, *In Summam Theologiae S. Thomae Aquinatis enarratio*, I, q. 5, a. 1, concl. 1a; and F. Suarez, *Disputationes metaphysicae*, disp. 3, *ed. cit.*, vol. 25. In contrast, one of the earliest schoolmen to use the term "transcendens" or "transcendentia" in the mentioned sense was Roland of Cremona in his *Summa theologica* of 1232; Paris, Mazarine Ms. 795, fol. 7vb; see Henry Pouillon, "Le premier Traité des

Both Aristotle and the medieval schoolmen listed the following characteristics or properties of the transcendental properties of being:

(1) *Convertibility with being*; e.g., every being is one, and every one is a being; every being is good, and every good is a being; every being is beautiful, and every beautiful is a being.[3] This property evidently follows from the coextension of being and of any one of the transcendental properties.

(2) *Convertibility with each other*; e.g., every one is good, and everything good is one; every true is good, and every good is true; every good is beautiful, and every beautiful thing is good.[4] The reason for this property, too, is clear. For, as long as any two things are coextensive with being, like the one, the good, and the beautiful, those two are also coextensive and, consequently, convertible with each other.

(3) *Real identity and a merely logical distinction standing between being and all transcendental properties.* This is to say that a concept, like "the one" is formed by the mind simply by adding a logical note, that of a transcendental mode, to the notion of being; so that "being" and "the one" or "the good" signify one and the same thing and, yet, their meanings are not exactly the

---

Propriétés transcendentales, La 'Summa de bono' du Chancelier Philippe," *Revue néoscholastique de Philosophie*, XLII (1939), 44. So did also Thomas (*De ver.* 21, 4; *S. theol.* I, 30, 3, ad 1; 39, 3, ad 3; *De nat. gen.*, 2, 478; etc.); Duns Scotus (e.g., *Op. Oxon.*, I, d. 8, q. 3, n. 18f., *ed. cit.*, IX,597b–598b) and Thomas Campanella (*Dialectica*, I, c. 4; Paris, 1637; tom. I, p. 32; quoted in G. Schulemann, *op. cit.*, p. 55). Yet, Alexander of Hales (or John of La Rochelle) prefers the name "first determination" (*primae determinationes*; *Summa theol.* I, i. 1, tr. 3, m. 1, cc. 1 and 2; *ed cit.*, I nn. 72f., pp. 113f.); Bonaventure speaks of "properties of being" (*proprietates entis*); e.g., *De mysterio Trinit.*, III, 1, ad 5 (*ed. cit.*, V, 72a); and Albert uses the phrase "universal intentions" (*universales intentiones*); e.g., *De pulchro*, q. 11, ad 5 (*ed. cit.*, p. 583).

[3] For the convertibility of being and the one, see, e.g., Aristotle, *Met.*, X, 2, 1053b 21–24; Boethius, *Liber de persona et duabus naturis*, c. 4 (*PL* 64, 1346 A); Averroes, *In Metaph. Arist.*, XI, c. 1. (Venetiis: apud Junctas, 1562), 279C. Aquinas, *In XI. Met.* 3, 2199 *De ver.* 1, 1c.; *In I. Sent.*, 8, 1, 3; Albert, *Summa de bono*, I, 2, 1, ad 12 (ed. Kühle, Feckes, Geyer, Kübel: Münster: Aschendorff, 1951), 25a; and Duns Scotus, *Op. Oxon.*, I, d. 8, q. 3, n. 19 (*ed. cit.*, IX, 729). For the convertibility of being and the good, see, e.g., Philip the Chancelor, *Summa de bono*, Padoue Antoinne Ms. 156, fol. 1 rb and 1 va, in H. Pouillon, "Le premier Traité des Propriétés transcendentales, La 'Summa de bono' du Chancelier Philippe," *ed. cit.*, p. 50, n. 43; Bonaventure, *In I. Sent.*, d. 1, a. 1, q. 2, 2a (I, 32a); *In II. Sent.*, d. 34, a. 2, q. 3, 4a (II, 814a); Aquinas, *De ver.* 21, 2c.; *Summa theol.*, I, 6, 3, 1a; 16, 3c; and Ulrich of Strasbourg, *De pulchro*, *ed. cit.*, p. 77, lines 11–12. For the convertibility of being and the beautiful, see, e.g., Ulrich of Strasbourg, *ibid.*, and Dionysius the Carthusian, *op. cit.*, art. 3, p. 229A.

[4] For the convertibility of the one and the good, see, e.g., Boethius, *De consol. phil.*, III, prosa 11 (*PL* 63, 772A; 774B). For the convertibility of the true and the good, see, e.g., Philip the Chancellor, *op. cit.*, q. 2, fol. 1 vb; q. 3, fol. 3ra (in H. Pouillon, "La premier Traité, etc.,"*ed. cit.*, pp. 64f.); and Aquinas, *S. theol.* II–II, 109, 2, ad 1. For the convertibility of the good and the beautiful, see, e.g., Thomas Gallus Vercellensis, *Explanatio in Dion. De div. nom.*, c.4 (Vienna, Natl. Bibl. Ms. 695, fol. 50vb; in H. Pouillon, "La Beauté, propriété transcendentale . . .," *ed. cit.*, p. 284); Albert, *S. theol.*, I, 6, 28, sol. (31, 289); I, 6, 26, 1, 2, 3, sol. (31, 242); Thomas Aquinas, *De div. nom.*, 4, 22, 590; Ulrich of Strasbourg, *De pulchro*, *ed. cit.*, p. 76, lines 11–24; and Dionysius the Carthusian, *op. cit.*, art. 1 (*ed. cit.*, p. 227 AB).

same. For "being" means "that which exists (at all, in any way)"; "the one" means "that which is undivided" or "the actually undivided (being)," etc.[5]

b. The history of the theories of the transcendental properties of being can be divided into five periods: the first or pre-Aristotelian, from Heraclitus to Plato; the second, from Aristotle to Avicenna; the third, from Philip the Chancellor to Thomas Aquinas; the fourth, from Duns Scotus to F. Suarez; and the fifth and last period, approximately the last hundred years of neo-scholastic thought. These periods can be briefly characterized as follows.

The pre-Aristotelian period witnesses the occasional recognition and implied expression of the transcendentality of goodness and beauty in Heraclitus, Socrates, and Plato, all three stating that every being is good and beautiful,[6] and Plato maintaining also that whatever is good is beautiful,[7] thereby indicating the convertibility of beauty and goodness.

The second period consists in two important developments. One of them is the birth in Aristotle's *Metaphysics* of an explicit and formal theory of the "passions" of being, among which the Stagirite lists unity, truth, and goodness,[8] but not beauty. The other development is the consequent of the former. It is the many-centuries-long controversy over the exact list of the transcendental properties of being, with one side simply adopting Aristotle's list of the above three transcendental properties, and the other side adding other transcendentals to the Aristotelian list. Thus, Plotinus reverts to Plato in recognizing

---

[5] On the real identity and logical distinction of being and the one, see, e.g., Aristotle, *Met.*, IV, 2, 1054a 13; XI, 3, 1061a 15–16; and Aquinas, *In IV. Met.*, 2, 548–553; *In XI. Met.*, 3, 2199. On the real identity and logical (formal) distinction of the true and the good, see, e.g., Philip the Chancellor, *op. cit.*, q. 2, f. 1vb; q. 3, f. 2vb (*ed. cit.*, p. 64, n. 113 and p. 65, n. 116); Aquinas, *Summa theol.*, II–II, 109, 2, ad 1; and Duns Scotus, *Op. Oxon.*, I, d. 8, q. 4,nn. 18 and 21. On the real identity and the logical distinction of the good and the beautiful, see, e.g., Robert Grosseteste, *Comm. in Dion. De div nom.*, c.4 (in H. Pouillon, "La Beauté, propriété transcendentale chez les Scolastiques," *ed. cit.*, p. 321); Alexander of Hales (John of La Rochelle?), *S. theol.*, I, p. 1, i. 1, tr. 3, q. 3, m. 1, c. 1, a. 2, resp. (I, n.103, p. 162b); Albert, *S. theol.*, I, 6, 26, 1, 2, 3, 4a and sol. (31, 241); II, 11, 62, 1, sol. (32, 597); *Opusc. de pulchro*, q. 2, sol. ad 1. (*ed. cit.*, p. 566); Bonaventure, *In I. Sent.*, d. 31, p. 2, a. 1, q. 3, ad 3 (I, 545 ab); Aquinas, *De div. nom.*, 4, 5, 356; *S. theol.*, I, 5, 4, ad 1; I–II, 27, 1, ad 3; Ulrich of Strasbourg, *op. cit.*, in Grabmann, "Des Ulrich Engelberti von Strassburg O. Pr. († 1277) Abhandlung De pulchro"; *ed. cit.*, p. 76, lines 11–12; and Dionysius the Carthusian, *op. cit.*, a. 3; ed. cit., p. 229 A,C. This common metaphysical doctrine concerning the relation of beauty and goodness has two historical roots. The idea of their real identity comes from Dionysius the Areopagite (*De div. nom.*, 4, 7; PG 3, 704 B); and the idea of their virtual distinction is an application to goodness and beauty by analogy of the virtual distinction standing between being and the one in Aristotle (*Met.*, X, 2, 1054a 13) and Averroes (*In Met. Aristoteles*, XI, c.1; *ed. cit.*, p. 279 C).

[6] Heraclitus, in H. Diels, *Fragmente der Vorsokratiker*, *ed. cit.*, 22 B 102; 1:173. Socrates, in Xenophon, *Memor.* III, 8, 5 and 7. Plato, *Tim.* 53b.

[7] Plato, *Lysis*, 216d; *Tim.* 87c.

[8] Aristotle speaks of transcendental unity in *Met.* IV, 2, 1003b 22–23; and *Top.* IV, 6, 127a 27–28; of transcendental truth, in *Met.* II, 1 993b 31; and of transcendental goodness, in *Eth. Nic.* I, 6, 1096a 23–29.

that every being is beautiful, but omits truth from the Aristotelian list.[9] After him, St. Augustine lends support to this Plotinian theory but reinstates truth.[10] Boethius, on the other hand, prefers to side rather with Aristotle in speaking only of transcendental unity and goodness, and leaving out transcendental beauty.[11] His late contemporary, Dionysius the Areopagite, being a neo-Platonist, naturally sides with the Platonic tradition, and restores the Plotinian list of transcendental unity, truth, goodness, and beauty.[12] A few centuries later, Arabic thinkers, like Avicenna,[13] do something similar to Plotinus: they add novel transcendentals to the Aristotelian list, viz., thing and something, meaning definiteness and otherness, respectively.

The third period is characterized by an endeavor unattempted until the thirteenth century: the systematization, that is, the systematic derivation of the various transcendental properties of being. Thus, in the *Summa de bono* by Philip the Chancellor (c. 1230), three transcendentals are related to three orders of causality;[14] whereas in the *Summa theologiae* attributed to Alexander of Hales (although its first part was authored probably by John of La Rochelle), we find three different systematic listings of the transcendentals,[15] and in the works of Albert the Great, at least two.[16] These attempts, however, all have their own weaknesses, being either incomplete or artificial or even inconsis-

[9] Plotinus, *Enn.* I, 7, 2; II, 9, 3; V, 2, 1; V, 3, 15; VI, 9, 1 (unity); I, 7, 2; V, 5, 12; VI, 2, 17; VI, 7 24 (goodness); V, 8, 9; VI, 6, 18; 7, 31 f. (beauty).

[10] St. Augustine speaks of trancendental unity in *De ver. rel.*, 7, 12 and 36, 66 (*PL* 34, 129, 151); *De Trin.* VI, 10, 12 (*PL* 42, 932); *De moribus Manichaeorum*, II, 6, 8 (*PL* 32, 1348); of transcendental truth: *Conf.* VII, 15, 21 (*PL* 32, 744); *Solil.* II, 5, 8 (*PL* 32, 889); *Enarr. in Psalm.* 4, 3 (*PL* 36, 79); *De vera rel.*, 36, 66 (*PL* 34, 152); of transcendental goodness: *Conf.* VII, 12, 18 (*PL* 32, 743); *Enchiridion*, 10, 3; 12, 4 (*PL* 40, 236); *De ver. rel.* 20, 40 (*PL* 34, 138, 140 f.); and of transcendental beauty: *De civ. Dei*, XI, 4, 2 (*PL* 41, 319); *De ver. rel.* 20, 40 (*PL* 34, 138); *De Trin.* VI, 10, 12 (*PL* 42, 932); *De musica*, VI, 17, 56 (*PL* 32, 1191); *De div. quaest.*, I, 10 (*PL* 40, 14); etc.

[11] Boethius speaks of the transcendentality of unity in *De unitate et uno* (*PL* 63, 1075 A); *De cons. phil.*, III, prosa 11, §§ 237, 239 (*PL* 63, 772 A; 774 B); *Quomodo substantiae in eo quod sint, bonae sint* or *De hebdomadibus*, cap. 9 (*PL* 64, 1311 C); *Liber de persona et duabus naturis contra Euthychen et Nestorium*, c. 4 (*PL* 64, 1346 A); of transcendental goodness: *De cons. phil.* III, prosa 10, § 232 (*PL* 63, 768 B); *Quomodo substantiae* or *De hebdomadibus*, c. 9 (*PL* 64, 1311 D, 1312 A); and of transcendental beauty: *De consol. phil.*, II, prosa 5, § 133 (*PL* 63, 691 A).

[12] Dionysius on transcendental unity: *De div. nom.* 13, 2 (*PG* 3, 977 C); on transcendental truth: *ibid.*, 5, 4 and 5, 7 (*PG* 3, 836 D, 844 C); on transcendental goodness: *ibid.*, 4, 1 (*PG* 3, 694); on transcendental beauty: *ibid.*, 4, 7 and 10 (*PG* 3, 701 C–704 B; 708 A); and *De cael. hier.* 2, 3 (*PG* 3, 141 C).

[13] Avicenna, *Met.*, I, 6. *Opera philosophica* (Venice, 1508; reimpression, Louvain: Bibliothèque, S. J., 1961), 72 A–C. Cf. Thomas, *De ver.* 1. 1c.

[14] Philip the Chancellor, *Summa de bono*, q. 7; Padoue Antoinne Ms., fol. 3vb; in H. Pouillon, "Le premier Traité des Propriétés transcendentales," *ed. cit.*, p. 43.

[15] Alexander of Hales (John of La Rochelle?), *S. theol.* I, i. 1, tr. 3, q. 1, m. 1, c. 2, resp. (I, 114b–115a, n. 73).

[16] Albert, *S. theol.* I, 6, 28 (31, 289); *In I. Sent.* 46, N, 14, sol. (26, 450). Cf. also, *Summa de creat.* I, 4, 38, 2, ad 4–6 (34, 554).

tent.[17] Thomas Aquinas' systematic derivation, unlike the previous ones, excels both in naturalness and simplicity. He begins by pointing out that any given thing can be considered absolutely or in itself and relatively or in its relation to something else; and, that any given being can be judged either affirmatively or negatively. All this may lead to a minimum of four transcendental properties. However, he goes on to say that there are two possible points of reference for every being: a positive and a negative. The latter is Parmenidian, non-being: the former is Aristotelian, the human soul which, in a way, is everything due to its two unique powers, since each of the two has everything for its proper object. For everything is intelligible to the intellect, and desirable to the will. All these principles lead to the following system of transcendental properties:

Considering being absolutely, one can pass this affirmative judgment on it, "Every being has an essence," or "Every being is something definite"—a judgment which leads us to realize the transcendentality of "thing"—"being with a definite essence," and the abstract transcendental of "definiteness." Next, still considering being absolutely, we can pass a negative judgment on it, "No being is actually divided," that corresponds to the judgment, "Every being is actually undivided," and leads the mind to the recognition of the transcendentality of "the one" and its abstract correlative, "unity" or "oneness." In the next steps, one may consider "being" relatively. In so doing, and relating it to non-being, he can realize the truth of this proposition, "Every being is other than non-being," which is the recognition of the transcendentality of "the other" and the abstract "otherness." If, next, somebody relates being to the first unique power of the human soul, the intellect, he can discover the truth of the following proposition, "Every being is intelligible" or "true," and thereby the transcendentality of "the true" and of "truth." If, on the other hand, one relates "being" to the second unique power of the human soul, the will, he may recognize that it is true to say, "Every being is desirable," and, through this judgment, the transcendentality of "the good" and "goodness." Summing up, we may say that there are exactly five transcendental properties of being in such a way that definiteness is an affirmative absolute transcendental; unity, negative absolute; otherness, negative relative; and truth and goodness, affirmative relative.

This system of the transcendentals, as can be readily seen, does not contain transcendental beauty, since this derivation is to be found in a relatively early work of Thomas Aquinas, the *De veritate* (On Truth).[18] Later on, probably while writing his commentary on Pseudo-Dionysius' *On the Divine Names*, Thomas clearly expressed his belief in the transcendentality of beauty, by declaring with Plato that every being is both good and beautiful; also, that the

---

[17] Cf., F. J. Kovach, "The Question of the Authorship of the *Opusculum de pulchro*," *Archiv für Geschichte der Philosophie*, XLIV/3 (Berlin: W. de Gruyter, 1962), 271.

[18] Thomas, *De ver.* 1, 1c. Cf. *De nat. gen.* c. 2; *In I. Sent.* 8, 1, 3, sol.

beautiful is convertible with the good;[19] and that the beautiful and the good are really identical and only logically distinct.[20] But all this leads to the following question: Is there a place in the above Thomistic system for transcendental beauty? Cardinal Mercier categorically denies this and holds instead that it is impossible to add any more transcendental property to the system construed in Thomas' *On Truth*.[21] However, the truth is that there definitely is room for transcendental beauty in Thomas' system. This conclusion can be arrived at by the following reasoning.

Thomas establishes the place of transcendental truth and goodness by considering the two rational powers of the human soul, the intellect and the will, *separately*. (Being, in reference to the intellect becomes, thus, true; in reference to the will, good.) But if this is so, why could not the two powers be considered *jointly*, especially in the light of the fact that the two powers are said to be rooted in the same principle, the human soul?[22] If we do so, we may recognize the following proposition to be true: "Every being is cognitively delightful," and this is a realization resulting from considering "being" affirmatively and relatively, relating it simultaneously to the intellect and to the will. Thereby, we recognize the additional transcendental "the beautiful" and the corresponding abstract transcendental property of "beauty," because we call a thing beautiful precisely if and when it delights us upon becoming known to us. This, in turn, shows that the initial judgment in this last step, "Every being is cognitively delightful" is not one arbitrarily chosen to suit the system but one well-based on reality and conforming to the common meaning of the term in every language and, yet, also one that admirably fits into the Thomistic deduction of the transcendental properties of being.

The fourth period in the history of theories concerning the transcendentals witnesses a shift in emphasis from the metaphysical to the logical order. For Duns Scotus, while accepting the three Aristotelian transcendental properties of unity, truth and goodness,[23] adds an entirely novel second genus or group,

---

[19] Thomas, *De div. nom.* 4, 22, 590.

[20] Thomas, *De div. nom.* 4, 5, 355f.; *S. theol.* I, 5, 4, ad 1; I–II, 27, 1, ad 3. See the same in Bonaventure, *In I. Sent.* d. 31, p. 2, a. 1, q. 3, 3a (I, 543a); d. 46, a. 1, q. 6, 4a (I, 833a); *In II. Sent.* d. 1, p. 1, a. 2, q 1, 4a (II, 26a).

[21] Mercier, *General Metaphysics, ed. cit.*, p. 472.

[22] Thomas, *S. theol.* I–II, 77, 12; *De ver.* 1, 1c; *Quodlib.* X, 3, 1.

[23] Duns Scotus speaks of transcendental unity in *Met. Arist.* IV, 2, 18 (Vivès-ed. VII, 167b); *Op. Oxon.* II, 3, 4, 6 and 10 (XII, 95a and 112a); and *ibid.*, I, 23, 1, 2, (X, 259a); of transcendental truth, in *Op. Oxon.* I, 3, 3, 20 (IX, 145b); of transcendental good, *ibid.*, II, 7, 1, 11 (XII, 386) and *Collatio* 12, 5 (V, 196a). He never calls beauty a transcendental property, although his definition of beauty as the "aggregatio omnium convenientium" in *Ox.* I, q. 17, a. 3, n. 13 implies order; and he explicitly states that every creature is the vestige of the Son precisely in virtue of its participated beauty. For a detailed discussion of this complex issue, see F. J. Kovach, "Divine and Human Beauty in Duns Scotus' Philosophy and Theology"; *Deus et Homo ad mentem I. Duns Scoti*; *Studia Scholastico-Scotistica*, 5; (Romae: Societas Internationalis Scotistica, 1972), 445–59. The Bonaventure-text in question is *De mysterio Trinitatis*, q. 1, a. 1, arg. 11–20 (V, 46f.). Cf. *In Hexaem.* V, 29 (V, 359).

that of the "disjunctive transcendentals" to the traditional genus of "categorical transcendentals."[24] This means that all the transcendentals ever listed prior to Duns Scotus could be used as predicates in categorical propositions with respect to "being" ("Every being is one; definite; other; true; good; beautiful"); whereas the novel transcendentals of Scotus (infinite and finite; necessary and contingent; etc.) could be truthfully predicated of being as being only disjunctively ("Every being is either infinite or finite; either necessary or contingent; etc.). This innovation clearly moves the transcendentals out of the realm of reality and into the realm of thinking, insofar as truth, goodness, beauty, etc., are formally and in themselves "qualities" of being in general, to which transcendental concepts correspond in the mind, whereas a disjunctive predication, like "Being is either finite or infinite," is formally only in the mind, and only fundamentally in things.

In his treatment of the transcendental properties of being, Francis Suarez not only goes along with this Scotistic turn from metaphysics to logic, but he also takes one further step in this direction. For he removes both "definiteness" (*res*) and "otherness" (*aliquid*), the two Avicennian additions, from the list of the transcendental properties of being, and does so on logical grounds. As to the former, he does not question its predicability of all beings (since, indeed, every being is something definite, i.e., of some essence); instead, he asserts only that this term signifies only the essence of a being but not being itself. As to "otherness," he points out that it is *subsequent* to the notion of "unity," since "one" means that which is undivided in itself *and*, as such, divided or distinct from every *other* being.[25] In doing so, Suarez became the leader of those modern and contemporary schoolmen who distinguish between "transcendental" and "property of being."[26] To them, the former means anything truly predicable of every being, i.e., of being as being (as "determinateness" does). The latter term, "property of being," means a concept formed by *directly* adding *one* logical note to the concept "being" so that such a concept expresses a universal aspect of being in general, that is, a "quality" or determination that necessarily follows from being as being just as a logical property does from the essence of a given being. For this reason, a genuine property of being is as predicable of every being as is a transcendental. In brief,

(1) Every "property of being" (like "oneness") is a "transcendental," but not every "transcendental" is a property of being; and

(2) The difference between them lies in the manner in which the mind forms a transcendental on the one hand, and a property of being, on the other hand; and is thereby entirely logical in nature.

---

[24] Scotus, *Op. Oxon.* I, d. 3, q. 2, n. 17; I, 39, 1, 13; II, 1, 4, 15; I, 8, 3, 19 (X, 625a; 11, 111a; IX, 598b).
[25] F. Suarez, *op cit.*, d. 3, sect. 2, nn. 4, 6.
[26] E.g., Henry Grenier, *op. cit.*, § 542, p. 62.

The relevance of this theory of transcendental properties to beauty is the following: Since the concept "beautiful," meaning the cognitively delightful, is formed, (as Aquinas indicates according to Suarez[27]), in such a way that the qualifying note, "cognitively," is added to the concept "good" or "delightful," the concept "beautiful" is not formed by the *direct* addition of one logical note to "being," unlike the "one" (= undivided + being) or the "good" (= desirable + being), but rather by the addition of a logical note to the transcendental concept "good." As a consequence of this logical formation, the concept "beautiful" may be transcendental in the sense that it is truly predicable of all beings, but it is not a genuine "property of being."

In this light, it is no wonder that Suarez does not mention beauty, unlike definiteness and otherness, even as a conceivable transcendental property of being (*passio entis*). Nor is there any doubt about this, that Suarez, like Duns Scotus before him, considerably increased the logical character of Aristotle's completely metaphysical theory of the transcendental properties of being.

The fifth and last (or most recent) period has witnessed a renaissance of scholastic and, especially, Thomistic thought on beauty beginning around the middle of the nineteenth century. This period has contributed no novel doctrines to the theory of transcendentals. However, it has produced an amazing variety of thought especially on the question of the transcendentality or non-transcendentality of beauty.[28] Authors of many nationalities both in Europe and on this continent have been involved in this controversy. This much may be safely said about this period of the last one hundred years. The number of those scholastic thinkers who hold the transcendentality of beauty seems to be ever-growing, thereby representing a reaction to the fourth period that, from Duns Scotus on, tended to move away from the idea of transcendental beauty.[29]

---

[27] Aquinas, *S. theol*. I–II, 27, 1, ad 3; cf., *ibid*., I, 5, 4, ad. 1. For the erroneousness of this kind of interpretation, see F. J. Kovach, "The Transcendentality of Beauty in Thomas Aquinas," *Die Metaphysik im Mittelalter* (*Miscellanea Mediaevalia*, II), ed. Paul Wilpert (Berlin: Walter de Gruyter, 1963), 389f.

[28] See F. J. Kovach, *Die Aesthetik des Thomas von Aquin*, pp. 202f.; "Beauty As A Transcendental," *New Catholic Encyclopedia* (New York: MacGraw-Hill, 1967), II, 207ab; and "The Transcendentality of Beauty in Thomas Aquinas"; *ed cit*., pp. 386–92.

[29] It would be a grave historical mistake to conclude from this brief outline of the history of the theories on the transcendental properties of being in general and on the transcendentality of beauty in particular that, apart from ancient Greek thinkers (Heraclitus, Plato, Plotinus, etc.), patristic authors (Augustine, Pseudo-Denis, etc.), and ancient Indian thought (Jaya Chamara Wadiyar Bakadur: "The Vedanta says that everything is beautiful," in "Indian Aesthetic Speculations"; *The Hibbert Journal*, LV, 238, April 1962, p. 245), only medieval and modern schoolmen considered the problem of the transcendentality of beauty. For one finds quite a number of divergent modern and contemporary aestheticians holding the transcendentality of beauty at least in the way in which Plato did, viz., by affirming that every being is beautiful. (In this context it is irrelevant whether such authors mean by "every being" both God and finite beings, or only material beings and whether they are aesthetic objectivists or subjectivists.) Among such non-scholastic aestheticians are, probably, Lord Shaftesbury ("The Moralists," p. 3, sect. 2; *ed. cit.*, II, pp. 126, 132f., 144); John Ruskin (*op. cit.*, II, p. 3, sect. 1, ch. 6, §§ 5 and especially 6; *ed. cit.*,

3. With all this doctrinal and historical background and explanation in mind, we are finally prepared to answer the following all-important doctrinal question: On what grounds can somebody rightly hold the transcendentality of beauty?

In the light of what has been said about transcendental properties of being heretofore, this is another way of inquiring whether or not one can truthfully say that every being is beautiful. An affirmative answer can be given to this question by the dualistic pluralist, who recognizes the existence of a multitude of things, both infinite and finite, both substantial and accidental, on grounds of the following argument:

"Every being," that is, the totality of reality, includes the infinite being (God) and all finite beings.

Both God and all finite beings are beautiful.

Consequently, every being, that is, the totality of reality, is beautiful; or, in other words, beauty is a transcendental property of being as being.

In this syllogism, the major premise needs no proof provided the existence of God is already recognized; and "God" is being used here in the traditional sense, as in the thought of Aristotle, Augustine, Boethius, Avicenna, Anselm, Hugh and Richard of St. Victor, Moses Maimonides, Bonaventure, Albert, Thomas Aquinas, Duns Scotus, Suarez, Descartes, Locke, Leibniz, Berkeley, Rosmini-Serbati, Maritain, Gilson, and others. The minor of the syllogism, however, is anything but evident, and for this reason demands adequate proof. This proof may be given in two separate steps: proving first the beauty of God; and, next, the beauty of every finite being.

a. The beauty of God can be proved aposterioristically. An aposterioristic argument is one in which the intellect moves from what is naturally or logically posterior to what is naturally or logically prior; an aprioristic argument, on the other hand, is one in which the mind moves from what is naturally or logically prior to what is naturally or logically posterior. If, for instance, one attempts to prove the beauty of God from the beauty of creatures, he concludes from what is naturally posterior, the beauty of the creature or effect, to what is naturally prior, the beauty of the Creator or cause. On the other hand, if one argued from the beauty of God for the beauty of the creature, his argument would be a priori, since the cause is naturally prior to its effect.

Employing an aposterioristic type of argument, one may argue for the beauty of God in this manner:

p. 28); B. van Brandenstein (*Der Aufbau des Seins*, n. 139, pp. 390f.; and *Művészetfilozófia*, §§ 29, 51; pp. 71, 133–35); and Paul Weiss (*op. cit.*, ch. 8, p. 128); and, quite explicitly, A. Schopenhauer (*op. cit.*, bk. III, § 41; *ed. cit.*, p. 271); R. W. Emerson (*Essays*, Essay 12: "Art"; Chicago and New York: Belford, Clarke and Co., n. d., p. 325); G. Santayana (*op. cit.*, § 31; pp. 128, 139); Eric Gill (*Beauty Looks After Herself*, New York: Sheed and Ward, 1933, p. 54); and others. J. Rickaby thinks (*op. cit.*, p. 150, n. 45) that even A. C. Quatremère de Quincey is among those holding the transcendentality of beauty.

If some finite beings are beautiful, God is also beautiful.
As a matter of fact, some finite beings are beautiful.
Therefore, God is also beautiful.

In this argument, the minor premise is empirically known to be true. Therefore, only the major needs a proof, and that can be offered this way:

If an effect has a certain pure perfection, the total or sole cause of that effect also has, by necessity, that pure perfection. The reason for this is, that "effect," by definition, is completely dependent upon its total or sole cause (both as to its existence and to what it is or has), and that one cannot give or impart to another something it itself lacks. The reason for speaking here only of pure perfection is this: the total or sole cause of an effect must possess formally, i.e., actually, and as such, only the pure perfections of its effect, i.e., those perfections the notions of which do not imply or connote any imperfection (like existence, life, knowledge, etc.), but not the mixed perfections of its effect, that is, the perfections the notions of which connote some imperfection (as sense knowledge connotes dependence on the senses; or "coloredness" implies materiality).

But all finite beings are effects of God as their sole and, hence, total cause. The reason for this is that the existence and the whatness of the finite beings are not self-explanatory, and the finite beings thus necessitate the existence of a necessary being, called God. Thus, recognizing that God exists is to realize that the contingent and the mutable beings demand as their necessary condition the existence of God.

Therefore, if finite beings have a certain pure perfection, God must have that pure perfection, too.

But beauty is a pure perfection. As already pointed out, pure perfection is that the notion of which includes no imperfection. Now, beauty has been defined as "integral unity with or without proportionate parts." In this definition, "unity" is certainly a pure perfection because it means "undividedness" or "indivision," and it is not "undividedness" or "indivision" but their opposite, "dividedness" or "division" that signifies imperfection. Similarly "integral" means "complete," "perfect," or "unimpaired," and neither of these means imperfection, whereas their opposites, "incomplete," etc., do. What, then, about the third note in the definition of beauty, "with or without proportionate parts?" Since "part" or "having parts" implies materiality, "with proportionate parts" is an element in the definition that means imperfection. However, the definition reads, beauty is an integral unity "with or without proportionate parts." Thus, this last note in the essence of beauty does not connote imperfection either. We can thus rightly conclude that beauty is, indeed, a pure perfection.

Therefore, if finite beings have beauty (are beautiful), God is also beautiful (and is so formally).

With this reasoning, we have established the truth of the original major premise; therefore we can round up the main argument this way:

As proved, if finite beings are beautiful, God is also beautiful, and is so formally.

As a matter of fact, some finite beings are actually beautiful.

Therefore, God is formally beautiful.

b. The beauty of all finite beings must be proved next.

One may attempt to prove this either empirically, i.e., inductively, or deductively, and if deductively, either in an a posteriori or an a priori manner, and if a priori, either from without or from within the finite being.

The first or empirico-inductive method would conclude from the direct observation of the beauty of some material individuals to the beauty of all material individuals or of finite being in general. This method, however, is patently defective, since it rests on an imperfect induction and moves from a particular to the corresponding universal.

Of the deductive methods, it seems to be impossible to employ some sort of aposterioristic method, because there is no beautiful being that is more directly knowable than the beautiful material being, and because there is no beautiful being that would necessitate as its necessary condition the beauty of all material individuals. This leaves us with only aprioristic arguments for the beauty of all material or finite beings.

Historically speaking, two kinds of a priori arguments have been used in demonstrating or endeavoring to demonstrate that every finite being is beautiful. One is an argument concluding from the beauty of God to the beauty of all creatures or finite beings; the other is an argument concluding from the nature of the finite being to the necessity that there be beauty in every finite being. The former establishes or aims to establish its conclusion from without the finite being; the latter, from within.

The former type of aprioristic argument is conceivable along the following lines: Having established God's beauty aposterioristically, i.e., from the fact that at least some creatures are beautiful, one may reason as follows:

Every effect or that which participates in another is necessarily similar to its own total cause or to that other being in which it participates.

Every finite being is the effect of the beautiful God, or participates in Him.

Consequently, every finite being is similar to the beautiful God, and is, thereby, itself beautiful.

Paul Dezza and George P. Klubertanz argue in such a manner for the proposition, "Every finite being is beautiful."[30] There are, however, two difficulties with this kind of argument.

---

[30] P. Dezza, *Metaphysica generalis*, p. 102. G. P. Klubertanz, *Introduction to the Philosophy of Being* (New York: Appleton, Century, Crofts, 1955), 204.

One difficulty is that, although the effect must be similar to its cause in some respect, it need not be and is not actually similar to it in every respect. Thus, to start out with this major premise dooms this argument to being a fallacy of false generalization. The other defect with this type of reasoning is that its conclusion is true only upon the assumption that every divine perfection or attribute, including beauty, is communicated to every creature; or, at least, that beauty is one of those divine perfections without which God cannot make a thing. But the former assumption is contradicted by facts, since not every finite being is animate, rational, free, etc.; and the latter assumption constitutes the fallacy of begging the question. For to argue that every finite being is beautiful by postulating without a proof that no finite being can be without beauty is to argue that every finite being is beautiful because every finite being is necessarily beautiful. To put this in another way, the only conceivable reason why God should not be able to create a thing without beauty is that beauty is a necessary quality, hence, the property, of being as being. But if you postulate this in an argument aiming to establish the transcendentality of beauty, you patently beg the question.

This leaves one only with an a priori argument for the beauty of every finite being as such taken from the very nature of finite being. Let us consider this argument:

Finite being, by definition, is a being that has its own limitation(s), or is of limited rather than unlimited perfection.

That which is of limited perfection has both act and potency, that is, both perfection and imperfection, the latter limiting the former. And that which has both act and potency, or perfection and imperfection, is composed of them as its (metaphysical) parts. That which is actually composed of its parts is an actual whole made up of its parts and, as such, represents a *unity*.

One empirically-known composition in the finite being is the composition of its essence (what the individual thing most basically is), and of accidents (whatever that individual thing has besides existence). It is for this composition that things in nature can be recognized as belonging to a certain species, such as gold, rose, eagle, or man, because certain accidents, like shape, size, and color, are characteristic of the essence or the species of the individual thing.

Another thing that is empirically known is that the individual finite being may lack some accident which another individual or even the majority of the individuals in that species have: proper size; an integral part, like all the petals of a flower, all organs or limbs, and so on; and the characteristic shape or color. Therefore, while every finite being is a whole or unity, not every finite being is an integral unity in regard to its accidents.

On the other hand, it is equally true that every individual is of a certain kind rather than of no kind. This, in turn, means that every individual finite being has everything belonging to its essence or nature (just as every man has materiality, life, capacity for sense perception, emotions, and reasoning, etc.) and also certain qualities which necessarily flow from its essence (as mortality follows from being an organism, or the capacity for conscious locomotion from being an animal, etc.). Therefore, every finite being is not only a unity but also, at least in terms of its essence (nature) and properties (necessary accidents), an *integral* unity, i.e., a whole so composed of parts that it lacks none of its necessary parts.

Furthermore, that which represents an integral unity is a whole actually composed of many parts. But the parts actually making up the whole are necessarily suitable to each other and the whole as well, since unsuitable units can produce no whole at all but constitute only a heap or plurality of unrelated individuals. From this, however, it follows that, inasmuch as every finite being constitutes an integral unity, every finite being has *proportionate parts*.

Adding up these three findings, we can truthfully say that every finite being, by its nature, is an (essentially) integral whole or unity of proportionate parts. Realizing or recalling, then, that integral unity with or without proportionate parts is beauty, we may finally conclude that every finite being is (at least essentially) beautiful.

Adding up the findings or conclusions of (a) and (b), it is evidently true to say, "Both God and all finite beings are beautiful." But this was the minor premise in our original syllogism, whereas the major needed no proof in respect to one who already realized the existence of God. Therefore, the conclusion of our original syllogism is also true:

Every being, that is, the totality of reality, includes God and all finite beings.
Both God and all finite beings are beautiful.

Therefore, every being is beautiful—which is another way of saying that beauty is, indeed, a transcendental property of being as being.

If someone is epistemologically a skeptic thinker (an empiricist, a positivist, a pragmatist, or a naturalist) or, metaphysically, a materialist, he need not bother, of course, with the metaphysically all-inclusive argumentation. For since to his mind the material world is the whole of reality, "every being," all he must establish is that every material being is beautiful, in order to conclude that, as far as he is concerned, every being is beautiful—that is, beauty is a transcendental property of being.

Furthermore, in his case all that is needed as a proof for the transcendentality of beauty is an empirically-founded brief argument showing that there is some kind and degree of order in every material being, as has been done in the previous chapter, arguing that integrity, proportion, and unity, or simply order, is present in every material being. The outline of the argument of the skeptic or materialist is, thereby, the following:

In every material being, that is, in every being, there is some order. Order is beauty. Therefore, in every material being there is beauty; thus every being is beautiful, and beauty is a transcendental property of being.

4. In concluding the question of the universality or transcendentality of beauty, it is well to point out that there is one serious difficulty with the above outlined or any other kind of arguments for the transcendentality of beauty. This difficulty lies in everybody's everyday experiences. For not only do we experience continuously that some beings are beautiful, i.e., cognitively pleasing, but also that some beings are *not* beautiful, that is, cognitively *not* pleasing at all, and even, that some beings are obviously ugly, that is, cognitively displeasing or repulsive.

Relying on this empirical knowledge, one may construe the following objection to the above conclusion concerning the transcendentality of beauty:

Whenever a theory contradicts or ignores facts, the theory must be rejected as erroneous.

The theory of transcendental beauty contradicts or ignores the fact that we do find non-beautiful and ugly objects as well as beautiful ones in this world.

Therefore, the theory of transcendental beauty must be rejected as erroneous.

In reply it may be pointed out that the minor premise of the above objection is simply not true. For the theory of transcendental beauty neither contradicts nor ignores the fact that we do find non-beautiful and ugly things as well as beautiful ones in this world, in reality.

But does not this answer mean to say on our part that, of all things in existence, some beings are beautiful; others, the rest of them, both beautiful and ugly, so that beauty is truly a transcendental (since all beings are beautiful); and, yet, we understandably find some beings non-beautiful or ugly (since some beings are actually ugly as well as beautiful)? And if this is so, are we not inextricably involved in a patent contradiction?

No, we are not, since nobody asserts here that some beings are both beautiful and non-beautiful or ugly *in the same respect*. The principle of contradiction means only that one cannot both affirm and deny one and the same thing of a being at the same time and in the same respect.

But, then, the opponent may ask, if one and the same being is said to be able to be beautiful in one respect and ugly in another respect, in what respect is a beautiful thing ugly, and what is ugliness at all?

The answers to these questions will be found in the next article dealing explicitly and exclusively with the problem of ugliness.

ARTICLE 2: *Ugliness*

The problem of ugliness will be considered here in two ways: historically and doctrinally. The latter consideration will eventually enable us to resolve the seeming contradiction between the transcendentality of beauty and the fact that some things in this world are ugly.

1. Historically speaking, ugliness has been interpreted in two basically different manners: negatively and positively.

The negative interpretation of ugliness can be found throughout history, beginning with ancient Greek thought. It consists in holding that ugliness is opposed to beauty, and represents a lack, absence, or privation of beauty. Plato expresses this view by defining ugliness as inferiority in beauty, inappropriateness of beauty, and lack of power (beauty being power);[1] and the ugly (αἰσχρόν) as the useless and the shameful (vs. the beautiful being useful).[2] Aristotle speaks of ugliness as the lack of beauty and the lack of the power to delight;[3] and contrasts the beautiful with the non-beautiful as the pleasant with the unpleasant.[4] After them, Longinus,[5] Philo of Alexandria,[6] L. A. Seneca[7] represent this negativist position of ugliness. Plotinus, in a similar vein, suggests that privation of form constitutes ugliness, that the ugly is the contrary of the beautiful, and that the beautiful is to the ugly as the pleasant is to the unpleasant.[8] Proclus defines ugliness both as privation and defect;[9] Augustine, as deformity, and the ugly (*turpe*), as the contrary (*contrarium*) to the beautiful.[10] The disciple of both Plotinus and Augustine, Dionysius the Areopagite, offers a classic definition of ugliness: the defect of form and the privation of order.[11]

When we leave the ancient thinkers and turn to the philosophers of the Middle Ages, we find that even the greatest of them, the high-scholastic philosophers, have little more to say about the topic than reiterate ancient ideas. Thus, Alexander of Hales teaches that there is an opposition between ugliness and beauty, and the ugly and the beautiful; and that ugliness is the defect (imperfection) or the privation of beauty.[12] Similarly, to Bonaventure, ugliness

---

[1] Plato, *Hipp. mai.* 288e–289b; 289e; 290cd; 296a.
[2] *Ibid.*, 295e, 293bc.
[3] Aristotle, *Eth. Nic.* I, 8, 1099b 1–4; cf. *Pol.* IV, 11, 1295b 6–9; *De part. an.* I, 5, 645a 6–7.
[4] Aristotle, *Top.* VI, 7, 146a 24–29.
[5] Longinus, *On the Sublime*, II, 5. Loeb-ed., n. 33.
[6] Philo, *De opif. mundi*, 7, 28; *De ebrietate*, 5, 16, *De agricultura*, 29, 128; *De virt.* 37, 205; *De special. leg.* III, 9, 51; etc.
[7] Seneca, *Epist. ad Lucilium*, ep. 66, 34.
[8] Plotinus, *Enn.* I, 6, 1; I, 6, 6; I, 6, 2; III, 5, 1, 2, and 3.
[9] Proclus, *De malorum subsistentia*, tr. Wm. Moerbecke, in *Procli Opera inedita*, ed. V. Cousin (Paris: A. Durand, 1864), 260. Cf. also, *ibid.*, p. 227. Reprinted in *S. Thomae Aquinatis In libr. B. Dionysii De divinis nominibus expositio*, ed. C. Pera (Taurini: Marietti, 1950), §§ 150, 153, 76; pp. 396, 387.
[10] Augustine, *Epist. ad Marcell.*, n. 5 (PL 33, 527); *De nat. boni c. Manich.*, cap. 15 (PL 42, 556). Cf. also, *De mus.* VI, 13, 38 (PL 32, 391); *De ver. rel.* 40, 74; 41, 78 (PL 34, 147, 149); *De civ. Dei*, XXII, 19, 1 (PL 41, 780f.).
[11] Dionysius: Αἰσχρός ... ἔλλειψις εἴδους καὶ στέρησις τάξεως, *De divin. nom.* 4, 27. Cf. also, *ibid.*, 4, 19; 4, 31; 4, 23 and 4, 7 (PG 3, 728C; 715 C–D; 732B; 724D; 704A).
[12] Alexander, *S. theol.* II, p. 1, i. 1, tr. 2, q. 3, c. 3, a. 1, 2a (II, n. 77, p. 100a); II, p. 1, i. 1, tr. 2, q. 3, c. 3, a. 3, 1a, 2a and resp. (II, n. 79, pp. 101a and 102b); II, p. 1, i. 1, tr. 2, q. 3, c. 3, a. 1, contra 2a (II, n. 77, p. 100a).

is lack of order (*inordinatio*) and privation of form or beauty.[13] Moreover, Albert the Great maintains that the ugly is the opposite of the beautiful; more specifically, its contrary opposite, so that the ugly differs from the beautiful as the evil does from the good; and that ugliness itself is a defect or privation.[14] Finally, Thomas Aquinas teaches that, first, the ugly is opposed to the beautiful, and opposed to it contrarily; and, second, ugliness is a defect of form or privation of order.[15]

This negativist view on ugliness of ancient and medieval thinkers was continued in modern philosophy, too, down to the present century. Thus, among the rationalists, Descartes,[16] Spinoza,[17] and A. G. Baumgarten;[18] among the empiricists, Thomas Hobbes,[19] F. Hutcheson,[20] David Hume,[21] and Edmund Burke;[22] toward the end of the eighteenth century, Kant,[23] the great synthesizer of rationalism and empiricism; in the nineteenth century, John Ruskin,[24] Grant Allen,[25] Joseph Jungmann,[26] and Theodore Lipps;[27] and in the

---

[13] Bonaventure: *turpitudo vel inordinatio* (*In II. Sent.* d. 32, a. 3, q. 1, resp.; II, 770a); *omnis deformitas principaliter dicit privationem formae sive pulchritudinis, ergo speciei* (*In II. Sent.* d. 35, a. 2, q. 2, sed contra 4a; II, 831a).

[14] Albert, *oppositum*: *Opusc. de pulchro*, q. 2, ad opp. (*ed. cit.*, p. 565); *contrarium*: *S. theol.* I, 6, 26, 1, 2, 3, 8a (Borgnet-ed. XXXI, 241); the analogy of *turpe* and *malum*: *S. theol.* II, 11, 62, 1, ad 6; *De laud. B. Mariae Virg.* V, 1, 1 (XXXVI, 274); *De pulchro*, q. 10, obi. 3a–5a (*ed. cit.*, p. 579); *defectus*: *De pulchro*, q. 8, ad 3 (*ed. cit.*, p. 576); *privatum*: *S. theol.* I, 6, 26, 1, 2, 3, 8a (XXXI, 241).

[15] Thomas, *turpe oppositum pulchri*: *Contra impugn.* p. II, c. 6, n. 339; *turpe contrarium*: *In I. Periherm.* 11, 152; *In I. Post. an.* 15, 134; *In VIII. Eth.* 3, 1654c; *In II. De an.* 22, 520; *S. theol.* II–II, 143, 1c.; *turpitudo . . . est defectus alicuius formae aut privatio alicuius ordinis* (*De div. nom.* 4, 21, 554; also, *S. theol.* II–II, 87, 5, ad 4). Cf. *turpitudo* as *inordinatio*, in *S. c. gent.* III, 139, 3142; *macula* as *privatio pulchritudinis*, in *S. theol.* I–II, 89, 2, ad 3; 109, 7c; III, 87, 2, ad 3; *Quodlib.* VII, 5, 2c; and *Symb. Ap.* 4, 914; and moral turpitude as *deformitas*, in *S. theol.* II–II, 144, 2c; 118, 2, ad 4; 187, 5, ad 4; and I–II, 41, 4c.

[16] Descartes, *The Passions of the Soul*, II, 85 and 98f.

[17] Spinoza, *Ethics*, part I, Appendix (*ed. cit.*, p. 76).

[18] A. G. Baumgarten defines beauty (*pulchritudo*) as *perfectio cognitionis sensitivae*; and deformity, as *imperfectio* (*Aesthetica*, § 14; *ed. cit.*, p. 6). See the same in G. F. Meier, *op. cit.*, § 25, p. 42.

[19] Hobbes contrasts the ugly, as the promise of evil, with the beautiful, as the promise of good. (*Leviathan*, I, 6.)

[20] F. Hutcheson: "Deformity is only the absence of Beauty, or deficiency in the Beauty expected in any Species." (*Op. cit.*, I, 6, 1; *ed. cit.*, p. 72.)

[21] Hume: "But beauty . . . gives us a peculiar delight and satisfaction; as deformity produces pain"; "our own beauty becomes an object of pride, and deformity of humility"; "Pleasure and pain, therefore, are not only necessary attendants of beauty and deformity, but constitute their very essence." (*A Treatise of Human Nature*, II, 1, 8. Ed. Green-Grose, II, 95.)

[22] E. Burke, "I imagine it [sc. ugliness] to be in all respects the opposite to those qualities which we have laid down for the constituents of beauty." (*A Philosophical Inquiry into the Origin of Our Ideas of the Sublime and the Beautiful*, III, 21. Ed. *cit.*, p. 102.)

[23] Kant, *Critique of Judgment*, § 48; *ed. cit.*, p. 195.

[24] Ruskin, *Modern Painters*, *passim*, such as, vol. I, sect. 1, ch. 6, § 5 and vol. 2, sect. 1, ch. 4, § 3; *ed. cit.*, I, 28; II, 31.

[25] G. Allen: "The aesthetically beautiful is that which affords the Maximum of Stimulation with the Minimum of Fatigue or Waste . . . The aesthetically ugly is that which conspicuously fails to do

twentieth century, G. E. Moore,[28] John Dewey,[29] E. I. Watkin,[30] DeWitt H. Parker,[31] Thomas Munro,[32] and Paul Weiss,[33] together with many others adopted the negativist view on ugliness.

2. Besides this persistent negativist approach to the question of ugliness, one finds also a positive or, rather, realist position on the issue mainly, if not exclusively, among the nineteenth-and twentieth-century aestheticians. These thinkers can themselves be divided into two groups. Of them, one is motivated by dialectics; the other is guided by modern ideas of value.

Taking up first the dialectical aestheticians, what characterizes them in general is the tendency to attribute some definite, positive role or function to ugliness in a dialectically-conceived world and, thereby, to conclude that ugliness is itself something real and, to that extent, positive. K. W. F. Solger seems to have been the first among those dialectically interpreting the ugly as being the ridiculous and the sad, each of which is, in turn, the synthesis of a certain "contradiction" in beauty. Solger further maintains that the ugly is the humorous; and, as such, the synthesis of the ridiculous and the sad. Inasmuch, then, as each dialectical phase is considered real, the ugly is held here to be real, carrying out some definite and positive role in the origin and development of aesthetic values.[34]

Following Solger, C. H. Weisse teaches that ugliness is positively aesthetic, in a limited manner, since, in the comic and the romantic, the ugly becomes characteristically beautiful.[35] Influenced by both Solger and Weisse, Arnold Ruge considers the ugly as standing between the sublime and the comic, the sublime being the Idea victoriously rising; the ugly, the Idea falling; and the comic, the Idea recovering from the fall.[36] While F. T. Vischer, influenced by Lessing's *Laokoön*, Section 23, confines the ugly to the limited, though positive

---

so; which gives little stimulation, or makes excessive and wasteful demands upon certain portions of the organs." (*Physiological Aesthetics*, chap. 3, *ed. cit.*, p. 39.)

[26] J. Jungmann, *Aesthetik*, nn. 130, 132; pp. 172f., 175ff.

[27] Lipps: "Aesthetics is the study of beauty; implicitly, also the study of the counterpart of beauty, ugliness." (*Aesthetik*, I. section 1, chap. 1; *ed. cit.*, I, 6.)

[28] G. E. Moore: "I shall use the word 'beautiful' to denote that of which the admiring contemplation is good in itself; and 'ugly' to denote that of which the admiring contemplation is evil in itself." (*Principia Ethica*, chap. 6; *ed. cit.*, p. 208.)

[29] J. Dewey, *Art as Experience*, chap. 6; *ed. cit.*, p. 115.

[30] E. I. Watkin: "For ugliness is an undue lack of beauty, of due form." (*A Philosophy of Form*, I, 5; *ed. cit.*, p. 143.)

[31] Parker, *The Principles of Aesthetics*, chap. 12; *ed. cit.*, p. 236.

[32] Munro, *Toward Science in Aesthetics*, p. 33.

[33] Weiss, *The World of Art*, chap. 5, p. 81; chap. 8, p. 126.

[34] K. W. F. Solger, *Erwin*, part 1, dial. 2; *ed. cit.*, pp. 250f.; 257f., 260f.

[35] C. H. Weisse, *System der Ästhetik*, II, §§ 24–26; ed. Rudolf Sender (Leipzig: Findel, 1872), 16f.

[36] A. Ruge, *Neue Vorschule der Ästhetik–Das Komische mit einem komischen Anhange* (Halle: Verlag der Buchhandlung des Waisenhauses, 1837), 58f.

role of the formidable in the sublime,[37] J. K. F. Rosenkranz broadens the positive or realist interpretation of ugliness at three levels. First, he characterizes ugliness as being negative beauty that exists precisely because and insofar as beauty exists,[38] which makes ugliness a dependent or relative existent, as opposed to beauty as an absolute existent; second, he stresses that ugliness, as an ephemeral moment in a comprehensive view of reality can be characteristic and, as such, interesting or aesthetically significant;[39] and, third, he maintains that the ugly stands as a dialectical middle stage between the beautiful or sublime (to which it is the antithesis), and the comic (into which it is resolved).[40]

Faithful to this dialectical thinking, Max Schasler considers the ugly not as a mere privation but, instead, as the negativity in the self-realizing process of the aesthetic idea, so that the beautiful is as impossible without ugliness as the ugly is without the beautiful, and the ugly is the beautiful that has not yet achieved its concrete finiteness.[41] For concrete beauty is born out of abstract beauty, and abstract beauty represents a difference between Idea and appearance that must be overcome, and is eventually overcome through ugliness, the negative reality of beauty, terminating in the synthesis of abstract beauty and ugliness.[42]

Finally, Moriz Carrière, although disagreeing with Schasler that ugliness is a contrast to beauty within beauty (preferring to consider ugliness as outside beauty), agrees with Schasler in holding that ugliness is necessary for the origin of beauty. His reason for this doctrine is that the aesthetic idea, on its way to concrete self-realization, and before overcoming the opposition of ugliness, becomes the ground of the sublime, the tragic, the comic, and the humorous.[43]

This list of dialectical, positive views on ugliness would be defective without mentioning also a very influential late follower of these German aestheticians, namely, Benedetto Croce. He argues that the ugly is a disvalue rather than a non-value, in the sense that value, like beauty, "is activity that unfolds itself freely," whereas disvalue, like ugliness, is an activity "that is embarrassed, impeded, or interrupted," hence, an "unsuccessful expression."[44] That this is a truly dialectical view, although dichotomic rather than trichotomic, can be seen from Croce's view that the *raison d'être* of ugliness is to contradict

---

[37] F. T. Vischer, *op. cit.*, § 98; *ed. cit.*, pp. 261–63.
[38] J. K. F. Rosenkranz, *Ästhetik des Hässlichen* (Königsberg: Gebrüder Bornträger, 1853), III, 7–8.
[39] *Op. cit.*, pp. 38f.
[40] *Op. cit.*, pp. IV, V, VII, 7–10, and 53.
[41] M. Schasler, *Kritische Geschichte der Ästhetik*, section II, §§ 529 and 524; pp. 1035f., 1024.
[42] *Op. cit.*, §§ 526, 529; pp. 1036f., 1028.
[43] M. Carrière, "Das Hässliche und seine Überwindung"; *op. cit.*, I, 3; *ed. cit.*, pp. 147–68.
[44] Croce, *Aesthetic*, part I, 10; *ed. cit.*, p. 78f.

beauty, i.e., a struggle between activity and passivity, freedom and its limitation, success and failure,[45] just as in Ruge, Weisse and others.

It may be mentioned at this point that all these dialectically positive interpretations of ugliness seem to be rooted at least logically, if not also historically, in Plato's sophisticated doctrine in the *Sophist*, asserting non-being as something positive and definite or real.[46] The second version, the non-dialectical version, of the positive interpretations of ugliness, on the other hand, seems to go back to Winckelmann, who ventured to assert that *expressiveness* was one of the primary characteristics of classic art, whereas Lessing held the more traditional view, viz., that *beauty* is the main purpose of classic art.[47] Accordingly, Schlegel, at the end of the eighteenth century (1797), declared that the main concern of *modern* art is not beauty but the characteristic or the interesting, and the characteristic or the interesting may be, among others, the repulsive or hideous, i.e., the ugly.[48]

Beginning with this late eighteenth-century view which, incidentally, saw in ugliness the contrary to and the privation of beauty, we find, as we approach the twentieth century, more and more aestheticians who see in ugliness something positive rather than mere negativity. These aestheticians do so on grounds not of some dialectical metaphysics but of empirical psychology. They consider significant form (expression), rather than beauty, to be the central aesthetic notion. Correspondingly, they are inclined to believe that the ugly is objectively expressive and subjectively significant, interesting and, hence, delightful in its own, unique manner—a view that changed the classic opposition of beauty and ugliness into the synthesis of what they call aesthetic value, under which genus ugliness becomes either a negative or even a positive aesthetic value.

An early advocate, about a hundred years after Schlegel, is George Santayana (1896), who declared, "The values, then, with which we here deal are positive . . . The ugly is hardly an exception, because it is not the cause of any real pain. In itself it is rather a source of amusement."[49] Here we have the key word of this psychologically founded positive view on ugliness: amusement. It rests on the empirical knowledge that, as a matter of fact, many ugly objects cause an emotional response that is more positive (like amusement, fascination, etc.) than negative (like pain).

The contemporary J. L. Jarrett follows in the footsteps of Santayana when stating, "Popularly, 'ugly' is the antonym of 'beautiful,' but it must be noticed that we are unlikely to designate anything as ugly unless it in fact does call

---

[45] *Ibid.*, pp. 77f.
[46] Plato, *Soph.* 257de; cf. *ibid.*, 257c.
[47] Cf. M. Schasler, *op. cit.*, p. 446.
[48] In E. von Hartmann, *op. cit.*, I, 363.
[49] G. Santayana, *The Sense of Beauty*, § 3.

out in us a certain aesthetic response. For instance we might call a gargoyle ugly, or a twisted mass of broken machinery that happened to catch and hold our eye, or such a face as that of Rodin's 'The Old Courtesan'; but in all these cases the response is aesthetic, not non-aesthetic. 'Ugly' seems to indicate a certain kind of negativeness, a sort of antipathy, or aversion—but aversion right along with fascination."[50] Thereby, Jarrett makes it clear that ugliness is not merely the absence of beauty but something positive, i.e., that to which the aesthetic response is partly positive, like intriguing and displeasing. But this is another way of saying that the ugly is, in fact, beautiful—of a certain kind of beauty that does not please without simultaneously displeasing.

Bernard Bosanquet coined—forty-two years before Jarrett's above-quoted work—a new name for this kind of beauty: "difficult beauty," that is, difficult to enjoy, vs. "easy beauty," namely, easy to enjoy.[51] In this manner, the generic identification of beauty and ugliness is an accomplished fact since, as we learn later from Bosanquet, difficult beauty is really apparent ugliness.[52] Incidentally, the idea of ugliness as "difficult beauty" has been adopted by a number of contemporary aestheticians. Samuel Alexander writes, for instance, " 'Ugly' generally means something which displeases . . . But 'beautiful' is used . . . in a special sense, and 'ugly' may be so used, and in that special sense both the beautiful and the ugly are departments of the beautiful in its sense of the aesthetically approved . . . . Otherwise expressed . . . the beautiful is easy aesthetic beauty and the ugly difficult beauty."[53]

3. We have reviewed briefly the negativist and the various positivist or realist views on ugliness. Now the question arises, which generic position should one adopt?

To say merely that the negativist view has been held throughout history, by an overwhelming number of thinkers, would be a merely quantitative argument representing the fallacy of authority. More important is the fact that there is a reason for adopting or rejecting either one of the two generic positions on ugliness. To show this, let us take up both the dialectical and the non-dialectical or psychological version of realist theories.

The cardinal weakness of all dialectical views, as of Hegel's philosophy in general, is the non-evident and unproved postulate that reality is, indeed, dialectical in its origin and nature. Certainly, it is a most intriguing supposition, even fertile in its applications, but still neither is it self-evident nor is there any cogent reason for accepting it as true. The theories of Weisse, Ruge, Rosenkranz, and the rest, all merely postulate that there is an aesthetic Idea that

---

[50] J. L. Jarrett, op. cit., chap. 13; pp. 273f.
[51] B. Bosanquet, *Three Lectures on Aesthetic*, lect. 3; ed. cit., pp. 45-50.
[52] Op. cit., pp. 51f.
[53] S. Alexander, *Beauty and Other Forms of Value*, chap. 9, p. 163f. Cf. H. S. Langfeld, op. cit., p. 34.

undergoes the stages of thesis, antithesis, and synthesis, as Hegel's Idea does; and it is only on the basis of this undemonstrated supposition that they can and do argue for the (negative) reality of ugliness as the antithesis to (abstract) beauty, as the real and transitory stage between abstract and concrete beauty, as the necessary condition of the becoming of all concrete beauty or of any aesthetic synthesis, etc.

One may rejoin here by pointing out that, certainly, these Hegelian aestheticians are right in teaching that the comic, the romantique, the tragic, etc., are aesthetic versions of the characteristic or expressive in which ugliness is resolved into a partly pleasing object and that, consequently, the ugly is truly real and, as cognitively pleasing, an aesthetic value.

This is, of course, basically the line of defense also for all non-dialectically positive interpretations of ugliness. The advocates of this position all stress, although with varying degrees of explicitness, that especially the ugly found in most or all artworks is not simply displeasing but, at least, both pleasing and displeasing. Samuel Alexander, for instance, while arguing for ugliness being simply difficult beauty, points out that, "in natural objects, the toad displeases the eye in itself, but it may be painted beautifully and, ugly and venomous as it is, may enter into beautiful verse." It is for this reason, he adds, that what we call ugly is, in fact, only difficult beauty.[54] Jarrett argues similarly: "A work of art is ugly when, though it attracts and even sustains aesthetic interest, it punishes rather than rewards that attentiveness."[55]

What can we say about this? Is it really true that an ugly object can not only displease but also please us? And does it truly follow from this that ugliness is something real and, at least partly, positive rather that the mere absence or privation of beauty? The premise is undoubtedly true, but the above conclusion does not follow from it.

The premise is true because it is an empirical fact. For, indeed, from ancient tragedies to the gargoyles of medieval cathedrals to Rodin's "The Old Courtesan" to an untold number of contemporary paintings and statues, there have always been artworks that, as such, delighted the beholder while the subjects or topics of such artworks instilled also the element of displeasure into the mind of the beholder, so that he who contemplates such an artwork experiences pleasure and pain simultaneously. This is a truth explicitly stated first by Aristotle, and by aestheticians throughout history. Aristotle himself had this to say on the question: "For we take delight in contemplating the most realistic likeness of things which are in themselves painful to see, as the shapes of the lowest animals and corpses"; and, "every work of skillful imitation is pleasing, . . . even if the object it imitates is not itself delightful."[56]

[54] *Op. cit.*, p. 164.
[55] J. L. Jarrett, *op. cit.*, chap. 13, p. 274.
[56] Aristotle, *Poet.* 4, 1448b 11–13; *Rhet.* I, 11, 137b 6–8.

Similarly, Aquinas pointed out that, although in itself adultery is gravely immoral or evil, one can think up beautiful ways of speaking about it.[57] A. G. Baumgarten declared in a similar vein that ugly things can be thought of beautifully; and beautiful things, in ugly manners.[58] After E. Burke[59] and Boileau,[60] Kant expressed similar thoughts when he remarked, "Beautiful art shows its superiority in this, that it describes as beautiful things which may be in nature ugly or displeasing."[61] DeWitt H. Parker concurs with him,[62] and so do E. I. Watkin[63] and John Dewey. "The artist," writes Dewey, "uses that which is usually found ugly to get aesthetic effect; colors that clash, sounds that are discordant, cacophonies in poetry, seemingly dark and obscure places or even sheer blanks—as in Matisse—in painting."[64]

The premise of the argument is, thus, more or less universally recognized to be true. However, from the fact that artists use ugly objects, and present them beautifully in their works, it does not follow that ugliness, as such, is real and positive, or that it, as such, is pleasurable. Instead, the truth is that the ugly which is employed by artists and spoken of by the aestheticians in question is only a matter of mental abstraction. This is to say that an old courtesan or a toad may, indeed, be ugly as she or it exists in reality; but this really ugly courtesan or toad exists only in nature and not in the artwork. The toad in a poem, or the old courtesan in Rodin's work is, as such, not more ugly than it is a natural thing; instead, it is a beautiful artwork whose object resembles a naturally ugly thing. Insofar, then, as it is an artwork, such a thing causes delight; inasmuch as it resembles an ugly thing in nature, it causes pain; and, consequently, in its totality it is a mixed or limited or difficult beauty, i.e., a beauty that has limitations.

What, then, is real in such an artwork is the beautiful; whereas its ugliness is *real* only insofar as the beautiful thing is really limited in its beauty, but *not real* as an existent thing. In other words, the beautiful is real, and its partial ugliness is the absence of some additional beauty or of some additional factor or degree of beauty. This is exactly what John Dewey is telling us in the

---

[57] Thomas: Sic ergo cogitatio potest cogitari ut delectans prout est cogitatio, et sic non est peccatum; sicut si debeo narrare de fornicatione, et occurrunt pulchrae viae, et delector. (*Quodlib.* XII, 22, 1.)

[58] Baumgarten: Possunt turpia pulcre cogitari, ut talia, et pulcriora turpiter. *Aesthetica*, § 18, *ed. cit.*, p. 8.

[59] E. Burke, *op. cit.*, I, 16; *ed. cit.*, p. 45.

[60] "Il n'est point de serpent ni de monstre odieux,
   Qui, par l'art imité, ve puisse plaire aux yeux.
   D'un pinceau délicat l'artifice agréable
   Du plus affreux object fait un object aimable"
                    Boileau, *L'art poetique*, chant 3.

[61] Kant, *Critique of Judgment*, § 48; *tr. cit.*, p. 195.

[62] DeWitt H. Parker, *The Principles of Aesthetics*, chap. 12, p. 236.

[63] E. I. Watkin *op. cit.*, I, 5, p .143.

[64] J. Dewey, *op. cit.*, chap. 8, p. 173.

following words: "Something which was ugly under other conditions, the usual ones, is extracted from the conditions in which it was repulsive and is transfigured in quality as it becomes a part of an expressive whole. In its new setting, the very contrast with a former ugliness adds piquancy, animation, and, in serious matters, increases depth of meaning in an almost incredible way."[65]

From all this it clearly follows that ugliness, as such, is not real nor anything positive nor delightful (amusing, fascinating, etc.), as the positivist interpretation would want us to believe. Therefore, the realist or positivist theory is wrong, and the negativist interpretation is right.

What, then, is the ugly, and what, ugliness? The ugly is a thing the beauty of which is limited.[66] Insofar as such a thing is beautiful, it may delight; insofar as its beauty is limited, it may fail to delight, and may, instead, succeed in displeasing or causing pain. If the limitation of its beauty is not too great or obvious, the thing may merely fail to delight the beholder and, then, its beholder will probably call it non-beautiful. If, on the other hand, the limitation of its beauty is too extensive or too obvious, the thing may displease us, and then we will call it ugly.

Correspondingly, ugliness is precisely the absence of beauty—the beauty that is not to be found but could be or should be found in a given thing or object. As such, ugliness is properly defined as the absence of beauty. This absence is either a negation or a privation. Accordingly, ugliness is negation of beauty if the absent beauty is not demanded by the nature of the object; and it is privation of beauty if the absent beauty is due to the nature of the object in question. In either case, however, ugliness is the lack of (some) beauty in a beautiful object.

4. With these definitions of the ugly and of ugliness in mind, we are finally in the position to answer a question which we raised at the end of the previous article: insofar as there truly are ugly things or objects, how can beauty still be transcendental?

There have been various attempts made to reconcile ugliness with transcendental beauty. One such attempt was made by George Santayana; another, by B. Bosanquet; and a third, by J. Maritain.

To put Santayana' attempt in the proper light, one must point out first that, in his own pseudo-subjectivist manner, and at the material level, he believed in the transcendentality of beauty. For he stated, "Everything is beautiful be-

---

[65] *Op. cit.*, chap. 5, p. 96.
[66] Albert the Great defines the ugly as being pulchrum secundum quid (*S. theol.* II, 1, 1, 2, 3, 3, 1, ad obi 1–2, vol. II, n. 77, p. 100b); and Aquinas writes in the same spirit when stating, Unde patet quod hoc quod dicitur turpe non est totaliter malum nihil retinens de bono, sed est bonum minoratum a debita proportione. (*De div. nom.* 4, 21, 554). E. I. Watkin simply echoes Thomas' doctrine while stating, "But it [sc. ugliness] is not a total lack of beauty. The ugliest object is beautiful in some respect or seen from a particular point of view." (*Op. cit.*, I, 5, p. 143.)

cause everything is capable in some degree of interesting and charming our attention."[67] But Santayana knew that, if this is so, then he must be able to explain or, rather, explain away ugliness from this material world. So he tried to do two things: one, to reduce ugliness to the genus of positive aesthetic value on the grounds that ugly things amuse us; and two, to identify the type of ugliness that does not amuse us and, instead, causes repulsion in us, with the genus of positive real evil or, more specifically, with practical or moral evil that is apt to elicit a "practical or moral attitude" in the beholder: "When the ugly ceases to be amusing or merely uninteresting and becomes disgusting, it becomes indeed a positive evil: but a moral and practical, not an aesthetic one .... The absence of aesthetic goods is a moral evil."[68] Stephen C. Pepper, incidentally, had adopted this moralistic explaining-away of ugliness from Santayana, by declaring, "Ugliness is moral disapproval of the absence of aesthetic value in a situation. It is an ethical rather than an aesthetic evaluation."[69]

In evaluating this theory, it may be pointed out that Santayana does concede rather than deny or overlook the fact that some objects actually elicit repulsion, that is, strong displeasure, in their beholders. This means that Santayana actually admits the existence of cognitively painful objects which, by the above definition, are ugly. That he *calls* such repulsive objects morally evil rather than ugly, and the human reactions to them moral rather than aesthetic disapproval is within his rights as a thinker and author, but this does not alter the fact that there are, indeed, objects which are *properly* called ugly, and only *untraditionally* and *improperly*, "moral evils." The phrase, "properly," refers to the above reasoned-out definition of ugliness; "untraditionally" and "improperly," to the fact that morality has already been considered to be confined to human acts and persons rather than emotionally displeasing objects of knowledge, so that we can morally disapprove, properly speaking, only of evil human acts but not of cognitively displeasing objects.

Santayana's explanation is, thus, merely nominal, resting on the untraditional employment of the term "moral" or of the phrase "moral evil." That such an attempt to explain away ugliness from this world is inadequate follows from the simple realization that certain kinds of things will not disappear from reality as a result of using novel, unorthodox names for them. If, for instance, somebody were interested in explaining away the presence of tall objects, he might say that there are small and "emotionally impressive" objects; but, from this alleged dichotomy it would not follow that there are actually no tall objects to be found in this world. Since, then, Santayana's attempt amounts to nothing more than such unorthodoxy in terminology, San-

[67] G. Santayana, *op. cit.*, § 31; *ed. cit.*, p. 128.
[68] *Op. cit.*, § 11, *ed. cit.*, p. 50; cf., § 3, p. 25.
[69] S. C. Pepper, *The Basis of Criticism in the Arts* (Cambridge, Mass.: Harvard University Press, 1946), 58.

tayana cannot be said to have succeeded in explaining away ugliness from this world.

Bernard Bosanquet's attempt is much more intricate and elaborate. The point of departure in his theory is the question whether there is in this world such a thing as "true ugliness," that is, "invincible ugliness, such as no sane imagination can see as beauty," so that it is not simply "difficult beauty."[70] Bosanquet employs two arguments to show that, apparently, there is no such a thing as true ugliness but only difficult beauty in this world.

The first argument consists of a "general paradox," described as follows. "Beauty is feeling become plastic," that is, an expressive feeling. Correspondingly, ugliness either is or is not expressive. If it is not, ugliness is aesthetically nothing. If it is expressive, ugliness is beautiful. Consequently, there is no invincible or true ugliness in reality.[71]

The second argument employs a disjunctive major, and runs like this. True ugliness is either (a) the perfectly formless, or (b) a conflict between beautiful parts within a whole, or (c) the purely inexpressive, or (d) an appearance that both arouses and frustrates our feelings, or else (e) "the pretension to pure expression." But, (a) the perfectly formless is either a totally unexpected form or the sublime and the humorous; and each of these three alternatives is expressive. Similarly, (b) conflict between beautiful parts within a whole is "beauty in the wrong place," and the conflict may be said to be "a part of the whole beauty." Moreover, (c) the purely inexpressive is a contradiction aiming to justify "our want of insight and sympathy." Furthermore, (d) an appearance that both arouses and frustrates our feelings is, as such, "not the merely inexpressive," since the merely inexpressive cannot either arouse or frustrate feelings. Finally, (e) our pretense to pure expression, representing a clear and positive failure, i.e., ugliness, is never nature's but always man's own product. Therefore, there is no true ugliness in reality.

In reply to the first of these two arguments, we may point out that the conclusion follows only if it is true that the inexpressive is aesthetically *nothing*. However, while ugliness is, truly, the absence (lack) of beauty, this absence means concretely that there is, indeed, a thing in reality whose beauty is more or less limited. This actual limitation is actual ugliness, and the thing actually limited in its beauty is what we properly call the ugly. For this reason, the conclusion of Bosanquet's first argument does not follow. Unsuccessful expression is *not* nothing aesthetically but, instead, something, namely, the truly ugly.

As to the second argument, at least the first and the fifth alternatives apparently fail to lead to the asserted conclusion. For, "the perfectly formless" can be not only the totally unexpected form or the sublime and the humorous

---

[70] B. Bosanquet, *Three Lectures on Aesthetic*, lect. 3, p. 51 f.
[71] *Op. cit.*, p. 52f.

but also some serious defect in the expressive form; and insofar as pretension is true ugliness (as Bosanquet presumes it), and is to be found in artworks, there is true ugliness in the realm of fine art, which realm is, after all, a part of reality. Thus, Bosanquet's conclusion, "There is no true ugliness in reality" simply does not follow from the premises.

Finally, let us consider Jacques Maritain's surprising position in one of his more recent works. Having repeatedly asserted the transcendentality of beauty explicitly and unequivocally,[72] and recognizing that there are ugly material beings, Maritain attempts to reconcile his theory of transcendental beauty with ugliness in this world by the following explanation. There are two kinds of beauty: transcendental and aesthetic. The former is rooted in the act of existence and, as such, can be found in every existent being. This is not the beauty that our senses perceive in things but that which "God beholds." Aesthetic beauty, on the other hand, belongs not to the realm of existence but to "a province of beauty in which senses and sense perception play an essential part, and in which, as a result, not all things are beautiful." This aesthetic beauty, Maritain goes on to say, is a "particular determination of transcendental beauty," that confronts "not simply the intellect, but the intellect and the sense acting together in one single act." The result of this is that "things divide into beautiful and ugly" according to whether they do or do not "fit human senses" permeated by intelligence. At the level of aesthetic beauty, then, "we meet the category of the Ugly," which category "has no sense for a pure spirit, and no sense for God. Because (*sic*) a pure spirit sees everything in a merely intellectual, not sensitive manner."[73]

What this view really means is that there is ugliness only insofar as some beings do not suit or please the senses: "Ugly is what, being seen, displeases: where there are no senses, there is no category of ugliness."[74] Since all things have "number, measure, and position" (these being the suitable objects of the pure intellect), "all (beings) are beautiful and there is nothing ugly in nature."[75] One must admit that this view, if its premises are true, does successfully explain away ugliness and, thus, successfully defends the transcendentality of beauty. But it is also true that, in this passage, at least in the way it sounds, Maritain comes dangerously close to an anti-objectivist aesthetic position. For, clearly, things are not ugly because they do not suit the senses; instead, at least some of them do not suit the senses because they are ugly.

But does the neo-Thomist Maritain really mean to deny that there are ugly

---

[72] J. Maritain, *Art and Scholasticism and The Frontiers of Poetry*; English tr. of the original French edition of 1927 by Joseph W. Evans (New York: C. Scribner's Sons, 1962), 30 ff.; "An Essay on Art," *ibid.*, pp. 172f., n. 66; *Creative Intuition in Art and Poetry*, chap. 2, n. 7 and chap. 5, n. 3 (Cleveland-New York: The World Publishing Co., 1961), 41, 125f.

[73] J. Maritain, *Creative Intuition*, chap. 5, p. 125f.

[74] *Op. cit.*, p. 126.

[75] *Ibid.*

objects perceivable in this world? Not really, because he admits in the same context, "There are things deprived in some respect of due proportion, radiance, or integrity."[76] Thus, he escapes from the charge of aesthetic subjectivism, and does even conform, implicitly, to the traditional idea of the ugly being a thing of limited beauty. Yet, by the same token, his above-expounded view is inconsistent. For either it is true that, apart from the senses, there is no ugliness and, then, it is false that some things are deprived of the principles of beauty; or, it is true that some things are deprived of principles of beauty and, then, it is false that, apart from the senses, there is no ugliness in the world. In the light of these facts, we can only conclude that this attempt of Maritain does not succeed in explaining away ugliness from the world and, consequently, in defending the transcendentality of beauty.

This failure is the more strange because the very text from which we have been quoting contains all the principles that are needed for a successful defense of the transcendentality of beauty despite the presence of ugliness in some things. These doctrinal principles are two in number. One is that aesthetic beauty is a particular determination of transcendental beauty. The other is stated as follows: "There are things deprived in some respect of due proportion, radiance, or integrity, but in which Being still abounds, and which keep on pleasing the sight to that very extent."[77] How these ideas are the very ingredients of a satisfactory reconciliation of ugliness with transcendental beauty is the last task before us in this chapter.

5. All one needs for reconciling ugliness in things with the transcendentality of beauty is the proper and clear understanding of what each of these two notions, "ugliness" and "transcendentality of beauty," mean.

The transcendentality of beauty means simply that there is beauty in every being. He who understands beauty as being integral unity with or without proportionate parts understands also that both the integrity of any given thing and the proportion of its parts, if it has any at all, admit of various degrees, and so does, then, also its order. In other words, beauty does not necessarily mean perfect, unimpaired unity with perfect, unimpaired proportion or, simply, perfect, unimpaired order, as Benedetto Croce would have it.[78] For he considers only the simply successful expression to be beautiful, and any more or less successful expression to be more or less ugly. That Croce is wrong, and the opposite notion of beauty is right follows from the most fundamental of all human knowledge of beauty, namely, that we call beautiful that which, when becoming known, delights us, and that, as a matter of fact, this cognitive delight can be of more or less intensity or degree according to whether the beauty of the object in question is perfect or imperfect, unimpaired or impaired

[76] *Ibid.*
[77] *Ibid.*
[78] Croce, *Aesthetic*, p. 79.

and, if imperfect or impaired, more or less imperfect or impaired. In other words, not only the perfectly but also the imperfectly beautiful things can and do delight us.

Insofar, then, as there is some order or some integral unity in a thing, there is at least a minimal capacity in it cognitively to delight its beholder and, to that extent, the thing is beautiful. But, as a matter of fact, there is some integral unity or order in every being. For every being is actually one, undivided, and lacks nothing of what it should have in terms of its essence (since essence admits no variation in degree: a thing either has everything essential and, then, it is of a certain essence; or it does not, and then it is not of that but of another essence); and any being can lack something only of its accidents. Consequently, every being is *more or less* beautiful, or has *more or less* beauty in it. If it has all the accidental perfections of its species, it is completely or perfectly beautiful; if it lacks some of its accidental perfections, it is imperfectly or incompletely beautiful at the accidental level, while it is still completely beautiful at the essential level. In the former case, the thing is more beautiful, or has more beauty; in the latter case, it is less beautiful, or has less beauty. In either case, however, the thing is beautiful (since it is necessarily beautiful at the level of essences). All this means that beauty is truly a transcendental property of being even though the individuals within any given species can be and are *more or less* beautiful.

We must also properly understand what it means that some things are ugly. As already stated, the ugliness of things means that some beings have defective or impaired unity, proportion, and/or integrity. When this imperfection or impairment in either the material or the formal component(s) of beauty is such that we do notice it, but do not notice its beauty, that is, its limited beauty, then our knowledge of that object results only in pain but no pleasure, and consequently we call that object ugly instead of beautiful, despite the presence of the (limited) beauty in it. Such objects are aesthetically ugly since of defective accidental or aesthetic beauty; and yet, they are still beautiful at least at the essential level (as well as, in some other respects, at the accidental level).

There is, then, no need really to deny ugliness in things or to explain away ugliness in order to be able to say that every being is beautiful. For a thing is either perfectly or imperfectly beautiful, and an ugly thing is, in reality, a thing of limited beauty or an imperfectly beautiful thing. If we wish to be accurate in talking about the beauty of reality, in the light of the presence of ugliness in some things we should not simply say, "Every being is beautiful," but, more accurately, "Every being is *more or less* beautiful." Since, however, the latter sentence, while qualifying the former in degree, is equally universal, preferring the latter to the former sentence is by no means giving up but only specifying the transcendentality of beauty.

Chapter XII

The Aesthetic Experience

IN THE FIRST SECTION of this work dealing with the philosophy of beauty, the existence of beauty was discussed and affirmed; in the second section, the essence of beauty was determined; and in the first two chapters of the present third section, the entitative implications of the essence of beauty have been considered, namely, the division, the extension, and the privation of beauty. In the remaining last chapter of this section and of this work, we may attempt to complement these entitative implications with an operative implication of the nature of beauty, viz., with what beauty causes in man. Nowadays, this question is most frequently called the question of the aesthetic experience. Thus the question, What does beauty do to man? can be rephrased as, What is the aesthetic experience?

In answering this question, one must bear in mind that the question is anything but novel; it is one that has been touched upon or formally treated in various contexts, for various purposes, and to various extents, from Plato to contemporary aestheticians. For this reason, as we did before dealing with the existence and the essence of beauty or even any lesser question, we shall give an outline of the variety of philosophic thought on this issue— an outline of various views, positions, and theories. This outline, although fairly lengthy, is not meant to be comprehensive; yet, it will be rich enough in its details to be representative of the variety of thoughts that characterizes the history of aesthetics on this question.

After this historical treatment, taking up the first article of the present chapter, we shall endeavor to answer directly the question at hand by outlining the inner structure of the aesthetic experience and discussing its various components one by one in article 2.

ARTICLE I: *An Historical Review*

As all the previous historical reviews in this work, the present one, too, although genuinely historical in nature, will follow not the chronological order of the various theories listed but a logical order. The reason for this is readily seen: the purpose of this review is not to serve as an historical monograph on the theories concerning the nature of the aesthetic experience but, instead, to give the reader an insight into the variety of thoughts on the topic in question; and this can be achieved better by a logical division of views than by a list of theories mentioned in the chronological order.

1. We can begin this historical review by pointing out that there has been no

consensus among philosophers even on the question of whether or not there is such a thing as aesthetic experience that is unique or, at least, basically different from other experiences. This basic difference of opinions should not be interpreted as if it consisted only in disagreeing on the relative intensity of aesthetic and non-aesthetic experiences, although this, too, is a point of disagreement. For, while some, like Ethel D. Puffer, go so far as to reduce the experience of mystic ecstasy, supposedly one of the most soul-shattering experiences man may ever have, and the experience of the beholder of beauty to one common denominator; others, like Emmanuel Chapman, unhesitatingly underplay the intensity of the aesthetic experience, as when stating, "Though the question of what constitutes the aesthetic emotion has certainly been given too much attention at the expense of eclipsing more important aspects—indeed, anyone who is honest with himself will admit that the amount of pleasure one gets from art has been greatly exaggerated (does not a cup of tea at the Metropolitan Museum of Art often give more pleasure than looking at some of the masterpieces?)."[1]

Indeed, the disagreement among some aestheticians goes much, much deeper than intensity: it is with them a matter of affirming or categorically denying that the aesthetic experience is an experience *sui generis*, of its own kind. At least two reasons have been given for denying that there is such a thing as aesthetic experience. One, given by William E. Kennick, is that what we call aesthetic experience includes many experiences that are so dissimilar that aesthetic experience is not really their common genus.[2] The other reason has been given by I. A. Richards who, in his *Principles of Literary Criticism*, boldly dedicates an entire chapter to "The Phantom Aesthetic State," asserting that experiences of beauty are "not in the least a new and different kind of thing" from many other experiences,[3] and that it is only the unfounded assumption of modern aesthetics "that there is a distinct *kind* of mental activity present in what are called aesthetic experiences," whereby "the phantom problem of the aesthetic mode or aesthetic state" arose.[4] In reality, however, "[when] we look at a picture, or read a poem, or listen to music, we are not doing something quite unlike what we were doing on our way to the Gallery or when we dressed in the morning," and certainly not something "of a fundamentally different kind."[5]

More recent aestheticians, like Marshall Cohen and George Dickie, each for

---

[1] Compare E. D. Puffer, *The Psychology of Beauty*, pp. 60 ff. with E. Chapman, "The Perennial Theme of Beauty and Art," *Essays in Thomism*, ed. Robert E. Brennan (New York: Sheed and Ward, 1942), 341 f.

[2] Wm. E. Kennick, "Does Traditional Aesthetics Rest On A Mistake?" *Mind*, 67 (July 1958), 323.

[3] I. A. Richards, *Principles of Literary Criticism*, (New York: Harcourt, Brace, 1925; Harvest Book, Sixth impression), 16.

[4] *Op. cit.*, p. 11.

[5] *Op. cit.*, p. 16f.

his own reasons, wholeheartedly agree with the above two authors on the non-existence of aesthetic experience or the impropriety of talking about this as a separate kind of experience.[6] Other aestheticians, like Roger Fry and S. K. Langer, take the opposite view. "Now I hope to show certain reasons," declares Fry, "why we should regard our responses to works of art as distinct from our responses to other situations."[7] S. K. Langer argues for the same position on introspective grounds: "The true connoisseurs of art, however, feel at once ... that aesthetic experience is different from any other, the attitude toward works of art is a highly special one, the characteristic response is an entirely separate emotion .... They feel a different emotion, and in a different way."[8]

Between these two positions, one of them denying and the other affirming an essential difference between aesthetic and non-aesthetic experience, there is to be found a compromise view holding that the difference in question is not one in kind but only one in degree. John Dewey is one of its advocates when he writes, "I have tried to show in these chapters that the esthetic is no intruder in experience from without ..., but that it is the clarified and intensified development of traits that belong to every normally complete experience."[9] With this view, Dewey almost verbatim echoes the position taken by I. A. Richards himself, who maintained that the experiences of beauty are "only a further development, a finer organization of ordinary experiences," and that the question is plainly "a question as to degree of likeness."[10]

This list may seem to have exhausted all the conceivable alternative positions on the question. Yet, there is to be found at least one more position taken by those aestheticians who seem to be unable to take a stand on whether the aesthetic experience is *sui generis* (I. A. Richards' favorite expression) and unique, or not. Morris Weitz, for instance, in one context calls the aesthetic experience categorically "a unique experience," but soon afterward he characterizes it as a "rather unique affair."[11]

2. Turning next to those authors who do find at least some characteristic difference or differences between aesthetic and other experiences, one can differentiate between theories attempting some sort of, what may be termed, phenomenological characterization of the aesthetic experience and theories

---

[6] M. Cohen, "Aesthetic Essence," *Philosophy in America*, ed. Max Black (Ithaca, New York: Cornell University Press, 1965) 116f. George Dickie, "The Myth of the Aesthetic Attitude," *American Philosophical Quarterly*, I, 1 (January 1964), 56–65, and "Beardsley's Phantom Aesthetic Experience," *The Journal of Philosophy*, LXII (1965), 129–136.

[7] R. Fry, *Transformations* (London: Chatto and Windus, 1926; reprinted: New York: Doubleday, Anchor, 1956), 3.

[8] S. K. Langer, *Feeling and Form*, pp. 36f. It is interesting that the medieval Bonaventure already clearly distinguished between aesthetic delight or experience and formal reasoning about why the experienced beauty delights us. (*Itiner.* II, 5–6; *ed. cit.* V, 301a.)

[9] J. Dewey, *Art as Experience*, chap. 3, p. 46.

[10] I. A. Richards, *Principles of Literary Criticism*, pp. 16, 44.

[11] M. Weitz, *Philosophy of the Arts* (Cambridge, Mass.: Harvard University Press, 1950), 189.

characterizing the aesthetic experience in terms of the various human powers or faculties involved in the aesthetic experience or playing some role in it.

Taking up first the phenomenological characterization, we find that some authors at least question, if not categorically deny, that the aesthetic experience can be analyzed or become known and, as such, can be characterized in terms of some qualities; whereas most aestheticians do believe that such an analysis or characterization is possible. Victorino Tejera speaks of authors holding the former view;[12] and, according to one of his statements, E. I. Watkin might be listed among them, although he himself qualifies his denial of the impossibility of analyzing the aesthetic experience and himself gives quite a characterization of it. His skeptic statement is this: "The greater obscurity . . . of aesthetic intuition . . . makes it impossible to formulate adequately an aesthetic insight . . . ."[13] For the latter and much, much larger group of thinkers, Arthur Berndtson could be quoted as an example who clearly states, "Since the aesthetic experience may be understood in general terms, aesthetics is possible."[14]

Some of those who, like Berndtson, hold the phenomenological characterization of the aesthetic experience possible, attempt to characterize this experience in terms of one single dominating feature; others prefer other ways of characterization. Among the former, in turn, two views are represented: the intellectualist view and the voluntarist view. According to the former, the aesthetic experience is, as a whole, an experience in which contemplation or knowledge dominates; according to the latter, emotion is the main characteristic of this experience. To these is added a third and compromise view, according to which the aesthetic experience is both intellectualist or contemplative and voluntarist or appetitive in nature. The intellectualist or contemplativist view is advocated, among others, by the brothers John and Michael Menichini,[15] E. Bullough,[16] Roger Fry,[17] H. N. Lee,[18] E. I. Watkin,[19] Curt J. Ducasse,[20] E. Gilson (who declares, "we mean to say that this [sc. aesthetic] experience is essentially distinct from intellectual knowledge, but we also maintain its essentially cognitive nature"[21]), Jerome Stolniz,[22] etc. On the other hand, the voluntaristic or

---

[12] V. Tejera, *Art and Human Intelligence*, p. 20.

[13] E. I. Watkin, *A Philosophy of Form*, part 2, chap. 4, p. 325.

[14] A. Berndtson, *Art, Expression, and Beauty* (New York: Holt, Rinehart and Winston, 1969), 5.

[15] J. and M. Menichini, "Del vero, del buono e del bello secondo san Tommaso," in the Neopolitan journal *La scienza e la fede*, 1878/79, vol. 110, p. 448; as quoted by J. Jungmann, *op. cit.*, p. 311 and n. 267 on pp. 914f.

[16] E. Bullough, *art. cit.*, in *ed. cit.*, p. 402.

[17] R. Fry, *Transformations*, p. 8.

[18] H. N. Lee, *Perception and Aesthetic Value* (New York: Prentice Hall, 1938) 36–37.

[19] E. I. Watkin, *op. cit.*, part 2, chap. 4, esp. pp. 318–21.

[20] C. J. Ducasse, *Art, The Critics and You*, chap. 3, pp. 72–73.

[21] E. Gilson, *Painting and Reality*, chap. 6, sect. 1, p. 180.

[22] J. Stolnitz, *op. cit.*, chap. 2, pp. 34f.

emotionalist view is maintained by such authors as Leo Tolstoi,[23] Yrjö Hirn,[24] S. Freud,[25] DeWitt H. Parker (who stated, "If the question were raised, which is more fundamental in the aesthetic experience, idea or emotion? the answer would have to be emotion"[26]), A. Berndtson,[27] et al.

A third group of aestheticians strike a balance between the above two positions in maintaining that the over-all character of the aesthetic experience is as much cognitive-contemplative as emotional-appetitive. Early advocates of this view include Augustine,[28] three Franciscan schoolmen: William of Auvergne, Alexander of Hales, and Bonaventure,[29] as well as Thomas Aquinas,[30] whereas, among contemporary authors, D. W. Prall[31] and S. K. Langer[32] seem to be inclined toward this view.

3. In contrast with the above-discussed aestheticians, others prefer to characterize the aesthetic experience not in terms of one, over-all, or dominating feature but, instead, in terms of similarity or contrast.

Those employing the former method endeavor to show the similarity standing between the aesthetic experience and some other experience or experiences, thereby offering a generic characterization of the aesthetic experience. Among these thinkers, some compare the aesthetic experience with play as an activity; others, with religious ecstasy or contemplation.

Undoubtedly following the ideas of Friedrich Schiller,[33] Karl Groos stands out as the advocate of the theory interpreting aesthetic experience in terms of

---

[23] L. Tolstoi, *What Is Art?*, chap. 5, p. 121.

[24] Y. Hirn. *The Origins of Art* (New York: MacMillan, 1900), 102–110.

[25] S. Freud, *A General Introduction to Psycho-Analysis*; tr. Joan Riviere (Garden City, N. Y.: Garden City Publishing Co., 1943), 327f.

[26] D. H. Parker, *The Principles of Aesthetics*, chap. 4, p. 56. See also B. von Brandenstein, *Művészetfilozófia* § 76, p. 189.

[27] A. Berndtson, *op. cit.*, chap. 1, p. 12 and part 2, chaps. 8–9.

[28] Augustine: ideo delectare quia pulchra sunt (*De ver. rel.* c. 32; *PL* 34, 148); beate contemplari (*De ord.* II, 12, 35; *PL* 32, 1011); Contemplans illustratur, inhaerens iucundatur; est, videt, amat (*De civ. Dei* XI, 24; *PL* 41, 338). Cf. *ibid.*, XIX, 13, 1; *PL* 41, 640.

[29] William of Auvergne, *De bono et malo* (Balliol Ms. 207, fol. 206v); *ed. cit.*, p. 268. Alexander of Hales (John of La Rochelle?): (Pulcrum) est placitum apprehensione (*Summ. theol.* I, p. 1, i. 1, tr. 3, q. 3, m. 1, c. 1, a. 2, resp.; *ed. cit.*, II, n. 103, p. 162); solebamus enim pulcrum dicere quod in se habebat unde conveniens esset in aspectu (*ibid.*, II, p. 1, i. 1, tr. 2, q. 3, c. 1, resp.; *ed. cit.*, II, n. 75, p. 99); and, pulcrum est delectabile intellectui (*ibid.*). Bonaventure, *In IV. Sent.* d. 18, p. 2, dub. 4, resp. (IV, 497); cf. *In II. Sent.* d. 38, a. 1, q. 3, sed contra 4 (II, 886a).

[30] Thomas: ad rationem pulchri pertinet quod in eius aspectu seu cognitione quietetur appetitus ... Et sic patet, quod ... pulchrum ... dicatur id cuius ipsa apprehensio placet. *Summ. theol.* I–II, 27, 1, ad 3. See also, *ibid.*, I, 5, 4, ad 1.

[31] D. W. Prall, *Aesthetic Analysis*, chap. 1, pp. 9–10, and especially p. 19.

[32] S. K. Langer, *Feeling and Form*, chap. 21, p. 397.

[33] F. Schiller, *Über die ästhetische Erziehung des Menschen, in einer Reihe von Briefen* (1793–94), esp. letters 14 and 15; in *Schillers Werke*, VIII, ed. L. Bellermann (Leipzig und Wien: Bibliographisches Institut.), 217–225.

play,³⁴ whereas E. D. Puffer stresses the similarity between religious ecstasy and aesthetic experience.³⁵

A much larger number of thinkers employ the method of characterizing the aesthetic experience by way of contrasting it with various non-aesthetic experiences. Yet, they themselves differ in respect to the generic or specific nature and the number of non-aesthetic experiences with which they contrast the aesthetic experience. Grant Allen, for example, contrasts the aesthetic experience with vital or life-serving experiences generically, and with play specifically: "What is common to these two classes [sc. play and aesthetic pleasure] is their remoteness from life-serving functions," and, "In this primordial distinction [sc. of the active and the passive] we see the root of the difference which we recognize between Play and the Aesthetic Feelings."³⁶ Hyppolite Taine, on the other hand, confines himself simply to contrasting science with art or speculative with aesthetic contemplation.³⁷ A recent author, E. Chapman, deviates partly from both in pointing out the opposite or different characteristics of philosophic, theological, mystic, and aesthetic contemplation or knowledge.³⁸

4. Finally, there are a number of authors who try to do something different either from those who offer some over-all characterization of the aesthetic experience or from those who prefer to contrast aesthetic with non-aesthetic experience.

Those employing the former method all have one thing in common: they list several characteristics of the aesthetic experience; those using the latter method resort in their characterization to a combination of a list of properties and contrasts.

The aestheticians listing several characteristic properties of the aesthetic experience themselves differ in at least one respect. They see in this experience either homogeneous or heterogeneous qualities. Thus, Herbert Sidney Langfeld lists two negative characteristics (absence of utility or purpose and psychic distance) and three positive characteristics (concentration by detachment or isolation; complete participation, and feeling of unreality);³⁹ John Dewey, only one negative and two positive qualities (no absence of desire; completeness and unity or integrity);⁴⁰ and M. C. Beardsley, four positive and no negative characteristics (attention, intensity, coherence, and completeness, the last two meaning simply unity).⁴¹ Despite all these specific differences, all the above

---

[34] K. Groos, *Der aesthetische Genuss*, chap. 1: "Der aesthetische Genuss als Spiel," pp. 13–24.
[35] E. D. Puffer, *The Psychology of Beauty*, chap. 3, pp. 60–86.
[36] G. Allen, *Physiological Aesthetics*, chap. 3, §§ 1, 2, pp. 33, 34.
[37] H. Taine, *Lectures on Art*, part I, § 7; tr. J. Durand (New York: H. Holt, 1875), 83.
[38] E. Chapman, *art. cit.*, pp. 343–44.
[39] H. S. Langfeld, *The Aesthetic Attitude*, chap. 3, §§ 2–7 (New York: Harcourt, Brace, 1920), 45–69.
[40] J. Dewey, *Art As Experience*, chap. 3, pp. 37–41; chap. 11, pp. 254, 258; and chap. 12, p. 274.
[41] M. C. Beardsley, *Aesthetics*, pp. 527–29.

positive and negative qualities are homogeneous insofar as they are co-ordinate, i.e., properties of equal significance. Morris Weitz, however, deviates from all three views in characterizing the aesthetic experience both in terms of a primary or dominant and several secondary or subordinate qualities: unity being the former, and emotional effect, disinterestedness, unpredictability, hedonic quality, and voluntariness being the latter features.[42]

Finally, as already mentioned, there are some thinkers who find in the aesthetic experience both absolute and relative (comparative) characteristics, and use for this reason both a list of absolute qualities and a list of contrasts. Among these is, for instance, E. I. Watkin. He contrasts aesthetic and speculative contemplation in terms of inner form without or with matter, without or with abstraction, and for or not for its own sake, and then he lists one positive and one negative characteristic of the aesthetic knowledge, viz., objectivity and non-discursiveness.[43] Another such aesthetician is James L. Jarrett, who finds in aesthetic experience one absolute quality, namely, openness to the aesthetic object, and also contrasts it with four non-aesthetic attitudes, the practical, the personal, the common-sense, and the analytic attitude.[44] A third author of similar views or method, D. W. Gotshalk, finds two absolute characteristics in the aesthetic experience, attention and interest,[45] and also discusses differences between aesthetic, practical, and scientific activity.[46] Needless to say, all these listed differences in the chosen method of characterizing the aesthetic experience rest on different views and interpretations of the elusive nature of the aesthetic experience.

5. In addition to the phenomenological interpretations and characterizations, one finds at least an equal if not an even larger number of theories endeavoring to explain the aesthetic experience in terms of the various human powers involved and the respective roles they play in that experience.

While attempting to classify such operative or functional views, one must first of all distinguish between skeptic and nonskeptic positions. In the skeptic view, in the present context, there are no really distinguishable human powers or faculties, and consequently, no operative or functional characterization is possible. Such a position is implied by statements like the following by Dewey: "There is, therefore, no such thing in perception as seeing or hearing *plus* emotion. The perceived object or scene is emotionally pervaded throughout." and "[No experience is] either merely physical or merely mental, no matter how much one factor or the other predominates"; and, especially, "There are no intrinsic psychological divisions between the intellectual and the sensory

---

[42] M. Weitz, *Philosophy of the Arts*, chap. 9, pp. 188, 190 f.
[43] E. I. Watkin, *op. cit.*, part 2, chap. 4, pp. 321 f., 324f., 332.
[44] J. L. Jarrett, *The Quest for Beauty*, chap. 7, pp. 106–111.
[45] D. W. Gotshalk, "Aesthetics, Perception Theory," in *Dictionary of World Literature*; ed. Joseph T. Shipley (Paterson, N. J.: Littlefield, Adams, 1960), 8.
[46] D. W. Gotshalk, *Art and The Social Order*, chap. 1, pp. 6–8.

aspects; the emotional and ideational; the imaginative and the practical phases of human nature."⁴⁷

Turning next to the non-skeptic views on the question of an operative or functional analysis of the aesthetic experience, we may distinguish first of all between theories speaking and not speaking of a special faculty. Promoters of the former type of theories, among whom the first was not, as B. Croce claims, Baltazar Gracian (1647),⁴⁸ but Plotinus ("and the Soul includes a faculty peculiarly concerned with Beauty"⁴⁹), maintain that man has a specific power with the sole function of recognizing or judging the beauty or the lack of beauty of the perceived objects. Holders of the latter theories, on the other hand, think that man has no special faculty for beauty; instead, he uses a number of general cognitive powers for this purpose.

The methodological, if not epistemological, reason for holding the special-faculty view is, as V. Tejera⁵⁰ and others pointed out, rather obvious. With its advocates, it is a matter of taking the attitude: "I do not really know how beauty is recognized; consequently, let us simply postulate a special power for this function." Despite this *"je ne sais quoi"* attitude as the generic basis of the special faculty theory, the advocates of this kind of view display an impressive variety of thought on the related details.

The first difference is the less important one: some aestheticians express their beliefs in the existence of a special aesthetic faculty quite explicitly and unequivocally; others do so only implicitly and obscurely, by indicating rather than clearly stating their opinion about the issue. Francis Hutcheson is one of those who could not be more explicit about his position: "I should rather choose to call our Power of perceiving these Ideas [sc. of Beauty and Harmony] an Internal Sense, were it only for the Convenience of distinguishing them from other Sensations of Seeing and Hearing, which Men may have without Perception of Beauty and Harmony."⁵¹ Hugh Blair also speaks rather clearly when stating in a lecture on the standard of taste, "Taste . . . is ultimately founded on an internal sense of beauty, which is natural to man, and which, in its application to particular objects, is capable of being guided and enlightened by reason."⁵² C. W. Opzoomer calls this *"Schoonheidsgevoel"* an innate sense, and J. K. Feibleman, "the special ability to feel the qualitative aspect" of proportion or harmony, that is, beauty;⁵³ whereas John Ruskin declares that the

---

⁴⁷ J. Dewey, *Art As Experience*, chap. 3, p. 53; chap. 11, pp. 246, 247.

⁴⁸ Baltasar Gracian, *Agudeza y arte de ingenio* (Madrid: V. J. Lastanosa, 1642; enlarged, *ibid.*, Huesca, 1649) 39–54; in Croce, *Aesthetic*, p. 190, n. 4; p. 191, n. 2.

⁴⁹ Plotinus, *Enn.* I, 6, 3; V, 5, 12.

⁵⁰ V. Tejera, *op. cit.*, chap. 2, pp. 20–21.

⁵¹ F. Hutcheson, *op. cit.*, I, 1, 10; *ed. cit.*, p. 8. See also *ibid.*, p. 9 and I, 1, 12, p. 11.

⁵² H. Blair, "On the Standard of Taste," included as chapter 26 in the James R. Boyd-ed. of Lord Kames (Henry Home), *Elements of Criticism* (New York and Chicago: A. S. Barnes and Co., 1883), 481.

faculty of beauty is neither intellectual nor sensual but moral, which he names the "theoretical faculty."[54] J. B. DuBos, however, matches Hutcheson and surpasses the other two above-quoted thinkers in explicitness when calling the creative and critical power of beauty "a sixth sense" (*sixième sense*).[55]

Other authors, like Dominique Bouhours, calling taste "an instinct of right reason,"[56] or J. Ulrich König, defining taste as "a power of the intellect ... which makes one able to feel the true, good and beautiful,"[57] or Dr. Thomas Reid, explaining the nature of taste as "that power of the mind by which we are capable of descerning and relishing natural and artistic beauty,"[58] do not make it quite clear that, or whether, to their minds, taste is a specific human power or just one of many functions of the intellect.

A more significant disagreement or difference among the advocates of the special-faculty theory concerns the question whether this power is sensory or suprasensory (rational). The classification of authors on this basis is not easy, since most of them are not interested enough in this per se very important distinction to make their views clear on this question. Nevertheless, it seems fairly reasonable to say that such modern aestheticians as F. Hutcheson, A. G. Baumgarten, and Richard Payne Knight held the alleged special faculty of beauty to be sensory in nature. Hutcheson explicitly endeavors to prove this faculty to be sensory when pointing out that, while it differs only in degree from the external senses, "[this] superior Power of Perception is justly called a Sense, because ... the Pleasure is different from any Knowledge of Principles, Proportions, Causes, or of the Usefulness of the Object: nor does the most accurate knowledge increase this Pleasure of Beauty, however it may superadd a distinct rational Pleasure from Prospects of Advantage, or may bring along that peculiar kind of Pleasure, which attends the Increase of Knowledge."[59] Baumgarten's position is obvious from his defining aesthetics as the science of sensory cognition (*cognitio sensitiva*) and assigning the perfection of sense cognition as the purpose of aesthetics.[60] R. P. Knight's position can be seen from these

[53] C. W. Opzoomer, *Het Wezen der Kennis*, ed. cit., part I, § 12, pp. 77f. J. K. Feibleman, *op. cit.*, p. 155.

[54] J. Ruskin, *Modern Painters*, I, part 1, sect. 1, chap. 6, § 3–4. (I, 26); part 3, sect. 1, chap. 1, § 10, and chap. 2, § 1 (II, 10, 12); and especially part 3, sect. 1, chap. 2, § 8 (II, 17).

[55] J. B. DuBos, *Réflexions critiques sur la poésie et la peinture*, (Paris: J. Mariette, 1770), §§ 1, 23, 26, 28, 33, 34; in Croce, *Aesthetic*, pp. 196f.

[56] D. Bouhours, *La manière de bien penser dans les ouvrages d'esprit*. Paris: V. de S. Mabre-Cramoisy, 1687.

[57] J. U. König, *Untersuchung von dem guten Geschmack in der Dicht-und Redekunst* (Leipzig, 1727); in Croce, *Aesthetic*, p. 199.

[58] Dr. Reid, *Essays on the Intellectual Powers of Man*, Essay 8: "Of Taste," chap. 1; ed. cit., I, 490a. Cf. *ibid.*, I, 491v.

[59] F. Hutcheson, *op. cit.*, I, 1, 12; *ed. cit.*, p. 10f.

[60] A. G. Baumgarten, *Aesthetica*, §§ 1, 14. Croce holds a somewhat different view on this issue since, according to some texts, such as *Aesthetica*, §§ 12, 424, 433f., and 483, he thinks that Baumgarten's special aesthetic sense stands in between the senses and reason; and thus, follows Leibniz' law of continuity. (*Aesthetic*, pp. 215–17.)

words: "Reason, in the strict sense of the word, has little or nothing to do with taste; for taste depends upon feeling and sentiment, and not upon demonstration or argument."[61]

Unlike these and many other authors, some others at least seem to talk about a suprasensory special faculty or to be completely unaware of their failure to specify their supposed special faculty of beauty as being sensory or rational. Among the former seems to be Eric Newton, who describes good taste as a "receptive attitude of mind" and "the capacity to understand the work of art, and, by understanding it, to share the particular kind of love that was responsible for its creation."[62] For, if words have any special meaning at all, "understanding" is the act of the rational intellect, as we never talk about the understanding of the senses. On the other hand, those who leave their position ambiguous on this question include, so it seems, Joseph Addison and J. K. Feibleman. For the former calls "fine taste" a "faculty of the mind" or "of the soul," and, on the other hand, considers all aesthetic pleasures to be those of the imagination; whereas Feibleman considers the sense of beauty "a true sense" which, however, is "higher than touch, smell, or even sight (the "most cognitive" sense in aesthetic tradition), without specifying whether it is higher in degree or kind.[63]

6. Many authors are, of course, strongly opposed to the special faculty theory. Among them, some explicitly state their rejection of it, either giving some reason for it, as Antonio Conti does by accusing F. Hutcheson of a superfluous multiplication of faculties;[64] or, as Francis Jeffrey does, by stating that, declaring beauty to be no inherent property of the objects, "we get rid of all the mystery of a peculiar sense or faculty, imagined for the express purpose of perceiving beauty";[65] or, as J. G. Herder and Paul Weiss do, on empirical and methodological grounds respectively;[66] or else without offering any specific reason of their opposition to the special-faculty theory. Among the latter are Dugald Stewart simply stating, "taste is not a simple and original faculty,"[67] and also Alexander Gerard, who points out that "taste is not one simple power

---

[61] R. P. Knight, *An Analytical Inquiry into the Principles of Taste*, part II, chap. 3, n. 1; *ed. cit.*, p. 263. Cf. part 1, chap. 5, n. 35, p. 95; and part 2, chap. 1, n. 1, p. 99. It must be admitted, however, that there are texts in this work that render this classification questionable. Such is the following text: "Beauty . . . is pleasing either to the sense, the imagination, or the understanding." (*Op. cit.*, Introduction, n. 6, p. 9.)

[62] E. Newton, *The Meaning of Beauty*, chap. 9, p. 162.

[63] J. Addison, *Essays on the Pleasures of the Imagination*, in *The Spectator*, nos. 409 and 411–21, June 19 and June 21 to July 3, 1712. J. K. Feibleman, *op. cit.*, p. 156.

[64] A. Conti, *Prose e poesie* (Venice, 1756), II, 171–77; as quoted by Croce, *Aesthetic*, p. 237.

[65] F. Jeffrey, *op. cit.*, pp. 4b, 5a.

[66] J. G. Herder, *Kritische Wälder, oder Betrachtungen über die Wissenschaft und Kunst des Schönen* (1769), Fourth Forest. *Sämtliche Werke*, I, 6 (Hildesheim: Georg Olms, 1967), 33–42. Paul Weiss, *op. cit.*, p. 127.

[67] D. Stewart, *Elements of the Philosophy of the Human Mind*, I, ch. 5, part 2, sect. 2 (Albany: E. and E. Hosford, 1822), 181.

but an aggregate of many."[68] Some among all these authors explicitly reject the special-faculty theory of an individual author rather than the theory in general. Such is M. Mendelssohn who, as Croce reports, expressly rejected Hutcheson's theory of a special aesthetic faculty.[69]

Another and much larger group of aestheticians express their opposition to the special-faculty theory simply by listing a number of conventional human powers involved in aesthetic experience.

According to the mode of listing such powers, we can differentiate between those aestheticians who name only two or more generic human faculties or one or more groups of faculties as being involved in the aesthetic experience; those who list a number of quite specific powers; and those who list both generic and specific powers. G. E. Moore[70] and Matthew Lipman[71] are among those listing two generic faculties (cognition and emotion); Roger Fry speaks of two groups of powers (mental faculties and aptitudes);[72] again others mention three groups of generic powers. In this third group we find H. Taine, mentioning the senses, reason, and "heart";[73] Karl Groos, speaking of pleasure, senses, and intellectual powers;[74] E. D. Puffer, listing the soul, sense, and motor impulses;[75] and S. Alexander, who enumerates understanding, imagination, and emotions.[76]

Another group of aestheticians, in contrast, prefer to name a number of quite specific human powers involved in the aesthetic experience. Thus, Luigi Taparelli names these cognitive powers: visual and auditory sense, commune sense, imagination, and intellect, and adds to all these the power of delight.[77] Joseph Jungmann accepts this detailed list in its entirety, but adds one more sense to it, the estimative power.[78] Similarly, E. Chapman enumerates about the same specific human powers as playing some aesthetic role, viz. conscious and unconscious sense powers, the imagination, the intellect, and the sensory and the rational will.[79]

An additional group of aestheticians speak of both generic and specific human powers involved in the aesthetic experience. Richard Payne Knight, for

[68] A. Gerard, *An Essay on Taste*, II, 7; *ed. cit.*, p. 148.
[69] M. Mendelssohn, *Abhandlungen über die Hauptgrundsätze der schönen Wissenschaften und Künste* (1761); quoted in Croce, *Aesthetic*, p. 257, n. 2.
[70] G. E. Moore, *Principia Ethica*, § 114; p. 189.
[71] M. Lipman, *What Happens in Art?* (New York: Appleton, Century, Crofts, 1967), 51, 119.
[72] R. Fry, *Transformations*, p. 7.
[73] H. Taine, *Lectures on Art*, part I, § 7, p. 83.
[74] K. Groos, *op. cit.*, chap. 1, p. 14; chap. 2, p. 27.
[75] E. D. Puffer, *op. cit.*, chap. 3, p. 77.
[76] S. Alexander, *Beauty and Other Forms of Value*, chap. 2, pp. 28, 33f. and chap. 7, p. 130.
[77] L. Taparelli, *Delle Ragioni del bello secondo la dottrina di san Tommaso d'Aquino*, § 9, nn. 3–6, in *La Civiltà cattolica*, 1859–60, ser. 4, vol. 7 (Neapoli, 1859–60), 556f.; discussed by Jungmann, *op. cit.*, pp. 296–98.
[78] J. Jungmann, *op. cit.*, p. 296, n. XXX.
[79] E. Chapman, *art. cit.*, pp. 343–45.

instance, talks about the powers of sensation, association (with the latter involving the powers of perception), imagination, and judgment, and also the powers of contemplation and pleasure.[80] D. W. Gotshalk divided the aesthetic faculties into mechanical and telic groups, the former including sensation, intuition, imagination, intellect, memory and feeling, whereas the telic components are "cravings, needs, interests, purposes, aims, drives, desires, conations, impulses, strivings."[81] Kant himself lists sensory powers (vision and hearing), and the internal powers of imagination, understanding, and emotionality.[82] Somewhat similarly, Béla von Brandenstein enumerates the senses, among them vision and hearing as "higher senses" and smell and taste as "lower senses," and also the emotional evaluative power and emotionality as being involved in the experience of the beholder.[83] Stolnitz' list is also similar: sensory powers (including vision, hearing, etc.), perceptual, intellectual, imaginative, and emotional powers.[84]

7. A more important classification of theories concerning aesthetic faculties is the one on the basis of the specific faculty by which beauty as such is formally recognized. In this respect, we find two generically opposed views and two compromise positions. The two generically opposed views are the sensualist and the intellectualist view.

According to the sensualist position, the senses themselves or powers related to them recognize beauty as such, thereby implying that there are no suprasensory faculties involved in the experience of beauty. Among the representatives of this theory there are some who consider certain external senses to be the powers of formal aesthetic recognition; others maintain that the central nervous system connected with the senses enable man formally to recognize beauty; again others think that the imagination plays this specific role.

Among those maintaining that the external senses do formally recognize beauty, we find Johann August Eberhard, who considers the beautiful as "that which pleases the more distinct senses," namely, the eye and the ear;[85] Charles Darwin, who stated, "The senses of man and of the lower animals seem to be so constituted that brilliant colours and certain forms, as well as harmonious and rhythmical sounds, give pleasure and are called beautiful";[86] his disciple, H. Berg, who completely identifies the brute's and man's knowledge and pleasure of beauty;[87] also, apparently, D. W. Prall, who speaks only of sensory

---

[80] R. P. Knight, *An Analytical Inquiry into the Principles of Taste*, part 1, chap. 5, nn. 33-35, pp. 94f.

[81] D. W. Gotshalk, *art. cit.*, p. 8; and *Art and the Social Order*, chap. 1, pp. 18-21.

[82] Kant, *Critique of Judgment*, §§ 34, 42.

[83] B. von Brandenstein, *Művészetfilozófia*, §§ 76, 50; pp. 189, 128f.

[84] J. Stolnitz, *op. cit.*, pp. 63, 70f.

[85] J. A. Eberhard, *Theorie der schönen Künste und Wissenschaften*, § 6. (Halle: Waisenhaus, 1790), 3-4.

[86] C. Darwin, *The Descent of Man and Selection in Relation to Sex*; in *The Origin of Species and The Descent of Man*. (New York: The Modern Library), p. 890; cf. also chap. 3, p. 467.

apprehension and delight as well as various sense powers "of the brain" in connection with the aesthetic experience;[88] surprisingly enough, Étienne Gilson, since he speaks of the "aptitude of human sense powers to perceive intelligible relations under the form of sensible qualities";[89] and C. Lemcke, to whose mind aesthetics is simply the science of sense perception and sense pleasure, and the faculty of taste completely independent of and separate from the intellect.[90]

Those who ascribe the formal recognition of beauty to something related to the senses include Spinoza, holding that what we call beautiful is anything that soothes our nerves;[91] Grant Allen, who declared the "nervous organization" to be the faculty of aesthetic taste;[92] and Hugo Münsterberg, who seems to be a faithful disciple of Grant Allen in his physiological analysis of the aesthetic experience.[93]

Among the aestheticians who consider the imagination to be the formal cognitive faculty of beauty, we find Pietro Sforza Pallavicino,[94] J. Addison,[95] Baumgarten,[96] G. F. Meier,[97] and many others.

The intellectualist view started out in ancient times with Plato who, in the *Major Hippias*, refuted the idea that the eye and ear recognized beauty,[98] and with Aristotle, who also, although obliquely, proves the impossibility of sensorily recognizing beauty as such.[99] In the patristic period, Augustine[100] was among those who held this view; in medieval times, Bonaventure and Thomas Aquinas[101] did so. In modern philosophy, Lord Shaftesbury,[102] Boileau (in his *Art poétique*); J. P. de Crousaz (in his *Traité du Beau* of 1715); J. G. Her-

---

[87] H. Berg, *Die Lust an der Musik* (Berlin: Behr, 1879), V, VI, 12, 18, 20; in Jungmann, *op. cit.*, pp. 290 f.

[88] D. W. Prall, *Aesthetic Judgment*, (New York: T. Y. Crowell, 1967), 19, 23, 26, 38, 64f.; *Aesthetic Analysis*, chap. 1, pp. 10, 19.

[89] E. Gilson, *Painting and Reality*, chap. 6, sect. 1, p. 180.

[90] C. Lemcke, *Populäre Ästhetik*, chap. 1, p. 1; chap. 2, p. 42.

[91] Spinoza, *Ethics*, I, Appendix, *ed. cit.*, p. 76.

[92] G. Allen, *op. cit.*, chap. 3, § 4, p. 48.

[93] H. Münsterberg, *The Principles of Art Education* (New York: Prang, 1905), 77–102, 107.

[94] P. S. Pallavicino, *Del bene* (Naples, 1681), Bk. 1, part 1, chaps. 49–53; in Croce, *Aesthetic*, p. 201.

[95] J. Addison, *The Pleasures of the Imagination*, esp. the essay in *The Spectator*, No. 411, June 21, 1712.

[96] A. G. Baumgarten, *Aesthetica*, §§ 424, 443, 483f., etc.

[97] G. F. Meier, *op. cit.*, §§ 5, 23, 92; pp. 8–9, 39, 189f.

[98] *Hipp. mai*, 299e ff.

[99] Aristotle, *Top.* VI, 7, 6, 146a 20–30.

[100] Augustine, *De ver. rel.* 30, 56 (*PL* 34, 146).

[101] Bonaventure, *In I. Sent.* d. 1, a. 3, q. 2, concl. (I, 41a); *In II. Sent.* d. 38, a. 1, q. 3, sed contra 4 (II, 886a); *In IV. Sent.* d. 30, dub. 6 (IV, 713b). Thomas, *S. theol.* I, 91, 3, ad 3; I–II, 27, 1, ad 3; also *De div. nom.* 4, 5, 339; and *S. contra gent.*, II, 64, 1424 to be read in the light of *S. theol.* II–II, 58, 4c. and *In I. Eth.* L.1, n.1 Cf. F. Toletus, *In Summam theologiae S. Thomae Aquinatis Enarratio*, I, q. 5, a. 4, fin.; ed. J. Paria. (Romae, Taurini, Parisiis, 1869), I, 101 f.

[102] Shaftesbury, *Characteristics*, II, treatise 5: "The Moralists," part 3, sect. 2; *ed. cit.*, pp. 141–44. Cf. Treatise 6: "Miscellaneous Reflections," V, chap. 3; *ed. cit.*, p. 344.

der;[103] J. F. Herbart, who declared, "No true beauty is sensible";[104] J. Jungmann who, seeking support from Cicero and Augustine, sharply argues for the exclusively suprasensory knowability of beauty;[105] James McCosh who, criticizing Grant Allen's sensualist position, declares that for the perception of relations in which beauty consists the rational intellect is always needed;[106] E. I. Watkin, teaching that "aesthetic intuition is an exercise of the intellect,"[107] and many others represent this view.

In between these two extreme views, many compromise positions have been devised by aestheticians. Croce suggests one by maintaining that even F. Hutcheson's "inner sense" of beauty and A. G. Baumgarten's imagination were meant to be faculties higher than the senses.[108] But even apart from this interpretation, many genuinely compromise theories can be found in the writings of aestheticians. One such comes from J. and M. Menichini, who held that sensory beauty is recognized by the senses and spiritual beauty by the intellect.[109] Another compromise view is Cardinal Pallavicino's, who taught that beauty pleases either the eye or the intellect (*o nell' occhio o nel intelletto*).[110] A third such view was expounded by C. Ettori to the effect that imagination was considered to play an inferior role and the intellect the dominating role in the aesthetic experience and judgment,[111]—a position reduced to a more generic form by J. G. Sulzer who simply contended that beauty aroused both the imagination and the intellect.[112]

8. Closely connected with and dependent upon the above question is another one that concerns the specific nature of the beholder of beauty. Is it man alone who can recognize and enjoy beauty as such, or can the brute also do so? Holding the first alternative to be true are, among others, Cicero,[113] Plotinus,[114] Augustine,[115] Aquinas,[116] Lord Shaftesbury,[117] I. Kant,[118] J. Jungmann,[119]

[103] J. G. Herder, *Kritische Wälder*, IV, ed. cit., I, 6, pp. 35-39.
[104] J. F. Herbart, *Einleitung in die Philosophie*, I, 49.
[105] Jungmann, *op. cit.*, nn. 109f., pp. 148f.; nn. 15-17, pp. 26-29.
[106] J. McCosh, *The Emotions*, bk. 2, chap. 3, sect. 2, p. 157.
[107] E. I. Watkin, *op. cit.*, part 2, chap. 4, p. 333.
[108] Croce, *Aesthetic*, pp. 206f., 215-217.
[109] J. and M. Menichini, *op. cit.*, in *La scienza e la fede*, vol. 110, p. 448; as quoted by Jungmann, *op. cit.*, pp. 914f., n. 267.
[110] P. S. Pallavicino, *Del bene*, II, part 1, cap. 11; quoted in Jungmann, *op. cit.*, p. 295 and 914f., n. 267.
[111] C. Ettori, *Il buon gusto ne componimenti rettorici* (Bologna, 1696); in Croce, *Aesthetic*, pp. 192, 202.
[112] J. G. Sulzer, entries "Schön" and "Schönheit" in *Allgemeine Theorie der schönen Künste*.
[113] Cicero, *De off.* I, 4, 14.
[114] Plotinus, *Enn.* I, 6, 2 and 3.
[115] Augustine, *De ver. rel.* 30, 55f. (*PL* 34, 146); *De quaest. 83*, quaestio 30 (*PL* 40, 19).
[116] Aquinas: solus homo delectatur in ipsa pulchritudine sensibilium. (*Summa theol.* I, 91, 3, ad 3.) For the analysis of this text, see F. J. Kovach, *Die Aesthetik des Thomas von Aquin*, pp. 232-37.
[117] Shaftesbury, "The Moralists," part 3, sect. 2, in *Characteristics*, vol. II, ed. cit., pp. 141-44.
[118] Kant, *Critique of Judgment*, § 5.

et al. Among those believing that brutes, too, know beauty as such, are Charles Darwin, H. Berg, and Willi Nef. Thus Darwin speaks of the "taste for the beautiful" in birds,[120] and of the "sense of beauty" he remarks, "This sense has been declared to be peculiar to man. I refer here only to the pleasure given [sc. to brutes] by certain colours, forms, and sounds, and which may fairly be called a sense of the beautiful,"[121] and, "man and many of the lower animals are alike pleased by the same colours, graceful shading and forms, and the same sounds"; from which he then concludes, "The taste for the beautiful, at least as far as female beauty is concerned, is not of a special nature in the human mind."[122] The only qualification that Darwin recognizes on this issue is the following: "With the great majority of animals, however, the taste for the beautiful is confined as far as we can judge, to the attractions of the opposite sex."[123] At the same time, however, he also believes that, "[judging] from the hideous ornaments, and the equally hideous music admired by most savages, ... their aesthetic faculty was not so highly developed as in certain animals, for instance, as in birds."[124] In a similar vein, H. Berg, Darwin's follower, speaks of the aesthetic sense, among other animals, of crickets and frogs,[125] whereas Willi Nef attributes the "intuitive knowledge" of beauty to man and brutes as well.[126]

In addition to these two opposite camps of aestheticians, there is a third, small group holding some kind of compromise view on the question. Francis Hutcheson, for instance, states that we conceive "few or no" animals with the internal power of beauty, or, "if some have them," it is in a much inferior degree than in man.[127] Richard Payne Knight's position, contrary to Hutcheson's, can be called a compromise view only insofar as he admits that what later became Charles Darwin's position is empirically justified only in reference to man: "[There] can be little doubt that all male animals think the females of their own species the most beautiful productions of Nature. At least, we know this to be the case among the different varieties of men ...."[128] He makes, however, no secret of his own personal view, and endeavors to support it with empirical facts: "If, however, a boar can think a sow the sweetest and most lovely of living creatures, we can have no difficulty in believing that he also thinks her the most beautiful: for the sense of smell is much more impartial ... than that of sight."[129]

9. Another question closely connected with the problem of the formal cog-

---

[119] J. Jungmann, *op. cit.*, p. 29, n. 17.
[120] C. Darwin, *The Descent of Man*, chap. 14, *ed. cit.*, pp. 741-44; also, chap. 16, p. 814.
[121] *Op. cit.*, chap. 3, *ed. cit.*, p. 467.
[122] *Op. cit.*, p. 468.
[123] *Op. cit.*, p. 467.
[124] *Op. cit.*, p. 468. See also, chap. 19, p. 890 and chap. 21, p. 923.
[125] H. Berg, *op. cit.*, p. 20; quoted in Jungmann, *op. cit.*, p. 291.
[126] W. Nef, *Die Aesthetik als Wissenschaft der anschaulichen Erkenntnis* (Leipzig: Herman Haacke, 1898), 40 ff.
[127] F. Hutcheson, *op. cit.*, I, 1, 11, *ed. cit.*, p. 9.
[128] R. P. Knight, *An Analytical Inquiry into the Principles of Taste*, Introduction; *ed. cit.*, p. 9.
[129] *Op. cit.*, n. 11, p. 18.

nitive aesthetic faculty concerns the specific nature of the aesthetic delight stemming from aesthetic knowledge. The reason for the connection is readily seen: there must be a specific similarity between knowledge and the pleasure caused by the knowledge in the sense that sensory knowledge will cause sensory pleasure; rational knowledge, rational delight.

Just as there have been two fundamentally opposed schools of thought on the specific nature of the formal cognitive power of beauty together with a certain compromise position, there have been also two basically opposite positions on the specific nature of aesthetic delight together with certain compromise views.

According to one of these views, aesthetic pleasure is sensory; according to the other, it is suprasensory or rational. The former, sensualist view was held first by Hippias, a pupil of Aristippus, in Plato's *Hippias Major*.[130] Among the modern aestheticians, the sensualist view was defended by Grant Allen, who considers aesthetic delight the soothing effect of non-life-serving processes of the nervous organization;[131] by S. Freud, to whom aesthetic pleasure is the satisfaction of the libido through the beholding of artworks;[132] by H. N. Lee ("[Aesthetic pleasure is] pleasure in the data of perceptual intuition"[133]); by R. G. Collingwood, who takes the position that a simple color or tone gives purely sensual pleasure; artworks, imaginative (and, thus, essentially also sensory) pleasure;[134] and by H. D. Waley, to whom aesthetic pleasure is simply "an excited condition" of the brain.[135]

At the other end of the scale are the intellectualists, among them: Plato,[136] Philo of Alexandria,[137] Plotinus,[138] Augustine,[139] Thomas Aquinas,[140] St Francis de Sales,[141] Baron de Montesquieu,[142] Jacques Maritain,[143] *et al*.

[130] The position of Theodore the Atheist, as to be found in *Diog. Laert.* II, 8, 99, is considered by Jungmann to be a sensualist view (*op. cit.*, p. 292), but this is a completely unfounded interpretation.

[131] G. Allen, *op. cit.*, chap. 3, §§ 2, 3, 4; pp. 34, 39, 42.

[132] S. Freud. *op. cit.*, twenty-third lecture, pp. 327f.

[133] H. N. Lee, *Perception and Aesthetic Value*, chap. 3, § 7, p. 38. Cf. *ibid.*, p. 36f.

[134] R. G. Collingwood, *The Principles of Art* (New York: Oxford University Press, 1958), 141, 148.

[135] H. D. Waley, "Low Level Approaches to Aesthetic Problems," *The Hibbert Journal*, LIX (October 1960), 65f.

[136] Plato, *Laws*, II, 655cd; *Phaedr.* 250e; *Phileb.* 66b, *Rep.* 401e.

[137] Philo, *Leg. alleg.* III, 4, 16.

[138] Plotinus, *Enn.* I, 6, 2 and 3.

[139] Augustine, *De ver. rel.* 30, 56 (PL 34, 146); *De civ. Dei*, VIII, 6 (PL 41, 231); *De div. quaest. 83*, q. 30 (PL 40, 19); *De ord.* II, 12, 35, (PL 32, 1011); *Contra Academ.*, II, 3, 7, (PL 32, 922).

[140] Thomas, *Summa theol.*, I, 5, 4, ad 1; I–II, 27, 1, ad 3.

[141] "Le beau ce qui plaist à l'entendement et à la cognoissance." St. Francis de Sales, *Traité de l'amour de Dieu* (of 1616), I, 1. English translation by John K. Ryan (Garden City, N. Y.: Doubleday, 1963), I, 53.

[142] Montesquieu, fragmentary essay "On Taste" (of c. 1755), in *Diderot, d'Alembert, and Others, Encyclopedia.* tr. N. S. Hoyt and T. Cassierer (Indianapolis: Bobbs-Merrill, 1965), 341, 364.

[143] J. Maritain, *Art and Scholasticism*, chap. 5, p. 24.

Of the compromise views, one is that of William of Auvergne and P. S. Pallavicino, who maintain that sensory beauty elicits sensory pleasure, whereas intellectual beauty causes intellectual delight.[144] Another view is Taparelli's, which is that beauty elicits intellectual *and* sensory pleasure.[145] In a third compromise view, maintained by E. Burke and similar to Taparelli's, aesthetic pleasure is primarily sensory and secondarily that of the imagination and reason.[146] A fourth compromise theory held by Richard P. Knight, represents an extension of Pallavicino's, and resembles also Taparelli's. In this view, beauty is "pleasing either to the sense, the imagination or the understanding."[147] In conclusion, two additional positions deserve mentioning in this context: those of Santayana and Marshall Cohen. Trying to avoid or, at least, belittle the issue of the dilemma of sensory *vs.* suprasensory pleasure, Santayana declared that the difference between aesthetic and physical pleasure is that the former has "greater dignity and range" than do the others, implying thereby a difference merely in degree, not in kind; whereas Cohen goes so far as to question whether pleasure "is, truly, an essential feature of aesthetic experience," with the obvious implication that the entire controversy may be quite superfluous.[148]

10. Just as the question of the sensory or suprasensory nature of the aesthetic delight is closely connected with the question of the sensory or suprasensory character of the formal power of recognizing beauty, there is an additional question intimately related to the question of the sensory or suprasensory nature of the aesthetic delight. This question concerns the specific difference of aesthetic delight or, as many aestheticians put it, what constitutes the *"differentia"* of aesthetic *vs.* non-aesthetic delight.

As is to be expected, there have been several answers given also to this question. The quality of the aesthetic delight most frequently mentioned is disinterestedness, i.e., the absence of any consideration of usefulness or existence. The one who made this popular was Immanuel Kant, by remarking, "The satisfaction which determines the judgment of taste is disinterested."[149] He, in turn, took this idea from eighteenth-century British aestheticians, like F. Hutcheson ("the Pleasure does not arise from any knowledge of Principles, Proportions, Causes, or of the Usefulness of the Object; but strikes us at first with the Idea of Beauty"[150]), Lord Kames (who contrasted fine arts with useful

---

[144] Wm. of Auvergne, *op. cit.*, c. XV; O'Donnell-ed., p. 297. P. S. Pallavicino, *De bene*, II, part 1, c. 11; in Jungmann, *op. cit.*, p. 295 and 914, n. 267.
[145] L. Taparelli, *op. cit.*, in *ed. cit.*, ser. IV, vol. 7, pp. 556f., as quoted by Jungmann, *op. cit.*, p. 298.
[146] E. Burke, *op. cit.*, part IV, sect. 25; *ed. cit.*, p. 23.
[147] R. P. Knight, *An Analytical Inquiry into the Principles of Taste*, p. 9.
[148] Santayana, *op. cit.*, § 7, p. 36. M. Cohen, "Aesthetic Essence," p. 118.
[149] Kant, *Critique of Judgment*, § 2, p. 46. See also §§ 5, 6, 13, 29; pp. 55, 56, 72, 134, 139.
[150] F. Hutcheson, *op. cit.*, I, 1, 12; p. 11.

arts[151]), and E. Burke ("Beauty and the passion caused by beauty which I call love, is different from desire"[152]), as well as from non-British sources, like Moses Mendelssohn,[153] *et al.* This, however, does not mean, as has been suggested erroneously by some, like J. Stolnitz[154] and Gilbert-Kuhn,[155] that the idea of aesthetic disinterestedness is *the* modern contribution to aesthetics, for as much as five hundred years before them Thomas Aquinas expressed this idea ("Man takes delight in the beauty of sensible beings for its own sake"[156]); and there are good reasons to believe that his doctrine was rooted in the thoughts of ancient patristic and even pre-Christian Greek philosophers, with most of them stressing at least this much, that beauty delights of and by itself—that is, for its own sake. Such thinkers are, prior to Aquinas, Albert;[157] Franciscans like Bonaventure, Alexander of Hales, and William of Auvergne;[158] John Scotus Erigena,[159] Augustine,[160] Plotinus,[161] Philo,[162] Cicero,[163] Aristotle,[164] and even

[151] Lord Kames, *op. cit.*, chap. 25, p. 463.
[152] E. Burke, *op. cit.*, part 3, sect. 1; p. 77.
[153] M. Mendelssohn, *Morgenstunden oder Vorlesungen über das Daseyn Gottes*, I, 7. (Frankfurt and Leipzig, 1790), 118f.
[154] J. Stolnitz, "On the Origins of 'Aesthetic Disinterestedness,'" *The Journal of Aesthetics and Art Criticism*, XX/2 (Winter 1961), 131-143; "A Third Note on Eighteenth-Century 'Disinterestedness,'" *ibid.*, XXII, 1 (Fall, 1963), 69; "Some Stages in the History of an Idea," *The Journal of the History of Ideas*, XXII/2 (April-June 1961), 189.
[155] Gilbert-Kuhn, *A History of Esthetics*, chap. 11, p. 322.
[156] Homo delectatur in ipsa pulchritudine sensibilium secundum seipsum (*S. theol.* I, 91, 3, ad 3); ad rationem pulchri pertinet quod in eius aspectu seu cognitione quietetur appetitus (*S. theol.* I-II, 27, 1, ad 3); sensibilia aliorum sensuum sunt delectabilia propter sui convenientiam, sicut cum delectatur homo in sono bene harmonizato (*ibid.*, II-II, 141, 4, ad 3). See *In VI. Eth.* L. 10, n. 1259; L. 19, nn. 604-11; and *In V. Met.* L. 20, nn. 1080f. in the light of *In I. Eth.* L. 12, n. 142 and *S. theol.* I-II, 4, 5c. For the entire question, see F. J. Kovach, "Esthetic Disinterestedness in Thomas Aquinas," *Actes du Cinquième Congrès International d'Esthétique*, Amsterdam, 1964; Jan Aler, ed. (Paris: Mouton, 1968), 768-73. This doctrine was adopted from Aquinas by some early modern schoolmen, such as F. Suarez (*Disputationes metaphysicae*, disp. 30, sect. 16, n. 40; *ed. cit.*, vol. 26, 196b).
[157] Albert: Liberales autem artes dico, *quas propter* se et *non propter aliud volumus*, sicut musicorum artem (*Met.* I, 1, 6; *ed. cit.* V, 12); Pulchrum enim est, quod propter se expetendum est (*De bono, ed. cit.*, tract. 1, q. 2, a. 2, sol. 8, n. 48, p. 27, line 52); Pictura . . . per se delectabilis (*Pol.* VIII, 4, g; VIII, 784); [Pulchrum] propter se appetatur (*Summa theol.* II, tr. 10, q. 39, m. 1, a. 1, part. 2, obi. 7; *ed. cit.*, XXXII, 436). Cf. also, *ibid.*, tr. 11, q. 62, m. 1, sol. and ad 1, 2, and 3; pp. 597f.; *ibid.*, m. 2, q. 4, sol., pp. 601 f.
[158] Bonaventure: (Homo) appetit scire occulta, videre pulcra et habere cara. (*De triplici via*, I, 1, 5; VIII, 4b.) Cf. his *Reductio artium ad theologiam*, n. 14 (V, 323). Alexander of Hales (John of La Rochelle?): "[Pulcrum est] placitum apprehensioni" (*S. theol.* I, p. 1, i. 1, tr. 3, q. 3, m. 1, c. 1, a. 2, resp.; I, n. 103, p. 162); [Solebamus] enim pulcrum dicere quod in se habebat unde conveniens esset in aspectu. (*Ibid.*, II, p. 1, i. 1, tr. 2, q. 3, c. 1, resp.; II, n. 75, p. 99). William of Auvergne: [Pulchrum] visu dicimus quod natum est per se ipsum placere spectantibus et delectare secundum visum (*De bono et malo*, Codex Balliol 207, f. 206v; *ed. cit.*, p. 268.) Hugh of St. Victor: Gratum est eiusmodi, quod ad usum quidem habile non est, et tamen ad spectandum delectabile. (*Didascalicon*, VII, 14; *PL* 176, 822 B. See also VII, 15, 823 A-B.)
[159] John Scotus Erigena, *De divisione naturae*, IV, n. 16; V, n. 36 (*PL* 122, 828 C-D; 975 C-D).
[160] Augustine: Delectationis enim causa . . . scribunt poetae, non utilitatis (*De civ. Dei*, VI, 6, 3. *PL* 41, 184); propter se expectandum (*De div. quaest. 83*, q. 30. *PL* 40, 19). Cf. Conf. X, 34, 53 (*PL* 32, 801); *De ver. rel.* 30, 55f. (*PL* 34, 146); and *De doctr. Christ.*, I, 4, 4 (*PL* 34, 20).

Plato himself.[165] Thus, it is little wonder that, after Kant, aesthetic disinterestedness becomes a common doctrine held, among others, by S. T. Coleridge and A. Schopenhauer,[166] Theodore Jouffroy,[167] Herbert Spencer,[168] Alexander Bain,[169] Gustav Theodor Fechner,[170] G. Allen,[171] Roger Fry,[172] D. W. Prall,[173] H. S. Langfeld,[174] S. Alexander,[175] E. I. Watkin,[176] E. Gilson,[177] H. Mead,[178] J. Stolnitz,[179] et al.

In contrast, a few aestheticians reject the idea that disinterestedness is the specific difference of aesthetic pleasure. So does, for instance, Alexander Bain, who claims that disinterestedness characterizes the entire intellectual life: scientific and moral as well as aesthetic, and is thereby not the specifying difference of the aesthetic delight.[180] Leo Tolstoi implies a similar denial by teaching that the delight which the artist evokes in the beholder must serve humanity or religion.[181] Santayana, too, denies that disinterestedness is a specific difference, and he does so quite explicitly,[182] although he admits that it is a "not

---

[161] Plotinus, *Enn.* I, 6, 4; VI, 5, 10; III, 5, 1; V, 5, 12.

[162] Philo declares, for instance, that the most beautiful things in nature are the objects of vision, not of possession (κτητά) (*De migratione Abrahami*, 9, 46). Cf. *ibid.*, 30, 165; *Legum allegoria*, III, 4, 16; 26, 99.

[163] Cicero: quid est cur non recte pulchritudo etiam ipsa propter se expetenda ducatur? Nam si pravitatem imminutionemque corporis propter se fugiendam putamus, cur non etiam, ac fortasse magis, propter se formae dignitatem sequamur? (*De finibus bonorum et malorum*, V, 17, 47.) Cf. *ibid.*, III, 5, 18; II, 33, 107; *De off.* I, 4, 14.

[164] Aristotle: "The beautiful is desirable for its own sake" (δι' αὐτὸ αἱρετόν) (*Rhet.* I, 9, 3, 1366a 33); "But the beautiful and that which is in itself desirable are in the same series" (*Met.* XII, 7, 1072a 34f.). Cf. *Eth. Eudem.* VIII, 3, 3, 1248b 19–20 and *Eth. Nic.* III, 13, 1176b 29 – 1118a 23.

[165] Plato, *Hipp. mai.* 297e; *Phileb.* 51b–e; *Leg.* II, 655cd; *Rep.* 401e; *Phileb.* 66b; *Phaedr.* 250e; *Gorg.* 474d.

[166] S. T. Coleridge, "General Principles (The Agreeable and the Beautiful Distinguished)" (1814); in *Coleridge, Selected Poetry and Prose*, ed. Stephen Potter (New York: Random House, 1933), 311, 313. A. Schopenhauer, *op. cit.*, III, 41.

[167] T. Jouffroy, *Cours d'Esthétique*, lesson 32, pp. 242–46.

[168] H. Spencer, "Use and Beauty"; (of 1852); in *Essays Scientific, Political and Speculative* (New York: D. Appleton, 1892), II, 370–74.

[169] A. Bain, *Mental and Moral Science*, (London: Longmans, Green, 1868), 290.

[170] G. T. Fechner, *Vorschule der Aesthetik*, I, chap. 15, pp. 203–09.

[171] G. Allen, *op. cit.*, chap. 3, § 7, p. 41.

[172] R. Fry, *Vision and Design*, Essay 2, p. 29.

[173] D. W. Prall, *Aesthetic Judgment*, chap. 1, pp. 12f.; chap. 11, p. 221.

[174] H. S. Langfeld, *The Aesthetic Attitude*, chap. 3, § 2, pp. 44–47.

[175] S. Alexander, *Beauty and Other Forms of Value*, chap. 3, p. 35.

[176] E. I. Watkin, *op. cit.*, part 2, chap. 4, p. 323.

[177] E. Gilson, *Painting and Reality*, chap. 6, sect. 1, p. 175.

[178] H. Mead, *op. cit.*, chap. 2, pp. 13, 17–18.

[179] J. Stolnitz, *Aesthetics*, p. 35. Cf. Konrad Lange, *Das Wesen der Kunst*, II, (Berlin: G. Grote, 1901), 353, 180; and Milton C. Nahm, *Aesthetic Experience and Its Presuppositions* (New York: Harper and Brothers, 1946), 218–20.

[180] Wm. Knight, *op. cit.*, p. 233.

[181] L. Tolstoi, *op. cit.*, chaps. 16, 17; pp. 230, 251.

[182] G. Santayana, *op. cit.*, § 8, p. 37.

very fundamental" characteristic of aesthetic delight.[183] H. N. Lee and M. Weitz hold similar views by listing disinterestedness only among the secondary qualities of aesthetic delight.[184] On the other hand, John Dewey denies the specificity of disinterestedness in aesthetic delight on the grounds that "disinterestedness" means not "absence of desire" in aesthetic delight but, instead, "thorough incorporation into [the] perceptual experience" of the beholder's desire; whereas Jerome Schiller urges making a distinction between "interested" [personal] approach to beauty and "disinterested" [impersonal] delight in beauty.[185] These last two views, and especially Dewey's, may already be considered as a sort of compromise position on the question at hand. Arthur Berndtson represents an obvious compromise position.[186] For, to him, it is not the aesthetic emotion itself but the contemplation of the aesthetic emotion that is disinterested: "the [aesthetic] experience reveals its special virtue in the disinterested contemplation of emotions." Paul Weiss and James K. Feibleman also hold some modified or compromise positions of the disinterestedness of the aesthetic experience; whereas Paul J. Olscamp goes so far as to admit only that disinterestedness, "when conjoined with several other properties," suffices to distinguish "*some* aesthetic experiences from any other kind."[187]

One may ask now what those who deny disinterestedness to be the specifying difference of aesthetic delight hold to be the true *differentia* between aesthetic and non-aesthetic delight. Santayana replies, it is its objectification, whereby the beholder invariably ascribes the aesthetic delight to the beheld object in such a way as to call it beautiful.[188] H. R. Marshall, on the other hand, takes the position that the aesthetic pleasure is "permanently pleasurable in revival," i.e., that the capacity of aesthetic pleasure for being recalled and remembered with a great degree of facility is the specifying difference of the aesthetic delight.[189] While H. N. Lee rejects Marshall's above view, just as Santayana does both "disinterestedness" and the Kantian "universality," Lee offers a specific difference on his own, namely, communicability to others, which is another name for universality: "Some pleasure is internal and subjective .... Therefore, it is not strictly common to others or even communicable. Beauty, on the other hand, is felt to be more or less common or universal."[190] Strangely enough, Lee

---

[183] *Op. cit.,* p. 38.
[184] H. N. Lee, *op. cit.,* chap. 2, § 8, p. 19. M. Weitz, *op. cit.,* chap. 9, p. 190.
[185] J. Dewey, *op. cit.,* chap. 11, p. 254. J. Schiller, "An Alternative to 'Aesthetic Disinterestedness,' " *The Journal of Aesthetics and Art Criticism,* XXII, 3, (Spring 1964), 296.
[186] A. Berndtson, *Art, Emotion and Beauty,* chap. 5, p. 87.
[187] P. Weiss, *The World of Art,* chap. 8 (Arcturus Books edition, 1964), 130. J. K. Feibleman, *op. cit.,* pp. 150 f. Cf. P. J. Olscamp, "Some Remarks about the Nature of Aesthetic Perception and Appreciation," *The Journal of Aesthetics and Art Criticism,* XXIV/2 (Winter 1965), 251.
[188] Santayana, *op. cit.,* § 10, pp. 44f.
[189] H. Marshall, *Pain, Pleasure and Aesthetics* (London-New York: Macmillan, 1894), 110, 151–53.
[190] H. N. Lee, *op. cit.,* chap. 3, § 7, p. 37.

concludes ultimately that this communicability, as a sign of objectivity, is what Santayana meant by the ability to be objectified,[191] which seems to be a rather questionable interpretation. When, however, he goes on to say that "aesthetic pleasure is not pleasure in sensation alone, but pleasure in perception,"[192] Lee comes close not only to Gilson's view[193] but, in a way, even to Aquinas,' to whom the specific difference between the good and the beautiful was this, that the good is that which simply delights, whereas the beautiful is that which cognitively, "by its apprehension," delights.[194]

11. One more area of disagreement is so important and widespread that it cannot be left unmentioned. It concerns the generic question of the extension of sense powers involved in the aesthetic experience or, more specifically, it is the question whether only some senses, the so-called "higher senses" play some role in the aesthetic experience or else the so-called "lower senses."

Historically, this question is rooted, on the one hand, in Plato's *Laws*,[195] where vision and hearing are called the "noblest of the senses"; and, on the other hand, in the *Major Hippias*, in which vision and hearing are listed as the only two senses through which beauty can be recognized.[196] Aristotle adopted from Plato the doctrine of the nobility of vision, meaning that vision is the most cognitive,[197] and also the doctrine that vision and hearing are the aesthetic senses. Augustine, synthesizing Plato and Aristotle, teaches that vision and hearing are the noblest senses since they are the only ones containing "traces of reason" and, as such, able to grasp their objects as wholes.[198] Thomas, like Alan of Lille and Alexander of Hales before him, simply extends Aristotle's reason by declaring that the eye and the ear are the superior senses as being the "most knowing" of all.[199] St. Francis de Sales simply echoes Thomas on this question.[200]

Using this distinction between higher and lower senses as a basis, one can divide the various theories concerning the involvement of the senses in the

---

[191] *Op. cit.*, p. 38.
[192] *Ibid.*
[193] Gilson, *Painting and Reality*, p. 180.
[194] Thomas, *Summa theol.* I, 5, 4, ad 1; I–II, 27, 1, ad 3; *De div. nom.* 4, 5, 356.
[195] Plato, *Leg.* XII, 961d.
[196] Plato, *Hipp. mai.* 298a. Cf. *Gorg.*, 474d.
[197] Aristotle, *De an.* III, 3, 429a 3; *Top.* VI, 7, 146a 22.
[198] Augustine, *De ord.* II, 11, 32–33 (PL 32, 1010); *De lib. arb.* II, 7, 16–19; 14, 38 (PL 32, 1249–51; 1261f.).
[199] Thomas: illi sensus . . . respiciunt pulchrum, qui maxime cognoscitivi sunt, scilicet visus et auditus rationi deservientes (*Summa theol.* I–II, 27, 1, ad 3); [Visus] est altior inter omnes sensus et universalior (*De an.* 13c. Also, *In Psalm.* 44, 2; *In II. De an.* L. 14, nn. 417f.; *In III. De an.* L. 6, n. 668; *S. c. gent.* III, 53, 2302; *S. theol.* I, 91, 3, ad 3). For this doctrine in Alan de Lille, see *Anticlaudianus*, IV, 2 (PL 210, 521C–522A); in Alexander of Hales, *S. theol.*, I–II, i. 4, tr. 3, q. 2, c. 2, 5a and ad 5 (II, 702a and 703b, n. 496); and in Witelo, *Liber de intelligentiis*, prop. XII; (*ed. cit.*, p. 16.).
[200] *Op. cit.*, I, 54.

aesthetic experience into two main groups. One of them consists in holding that only the so-called higher senses, that is, the eye and the ear, are involved in aesthetic experience; the other major position is, on the other hand, that both higher and lower senses play some role in the experience of the beholder.

The former position, although quite rigid, has found many advocates throughout history. Among them are Plato,[201] Philo of Alexandria,[202] Demetrius,[203] Plotinus,[204] Augustine,[205] Albert the Great,[206] St. Francis de Sales,[207] Kant,[208] Santayana,[209] Roger Fry,[210] and J. Maritain.[211]

Another large number of mainly modern aestheticians are less rigid in their views, insofar as they attribute some aesthetic role also to the lower senses. This is a position that was taken in the Middle Ages already by Thomas Gallus and Bonaventure.[212] Yet, these aestheticians themselves disagree in at least three respects: in the number of the lower senses thought to be involved in this experience, in the identity of those lower senses, and in the precise role those lower senses are said to play.

Since there are only three so-called "lower senses" among the five external senses ("exteroceptors"), there can be no more than three alternative views. And, indeed, we find that some like J. Addison and E. I. Watkin ascribe some role in the aesthetic experience to only one lower sense; others, like R. P. Knight and B. von Brandenstein, to two lower senses; and again some others, like E. Burke, J. M. Guyau, John Ruskin, H. N. Lee, DeWitt H. Parker, D. W. Prall, and J. L. Jarrett, to all three lower senses.[213]

According to the identity of the lower senses to which some aesthetic role is ascribed, we find the following theories. In J. Addison's and E. I. Watkin's

[201] Plato, *Hipp. mai.* 298a; 299a. It is safe to say this despite the fact that, in *Phileb.* 51e, Plato calls pleasures caused by smells to be cognate with the pleasures caused by beautiful colors, forms, and sounds; because, in the latter text, the emphasis is on some other issue.
[202] Cf. Philo, *De migratione Abrahami*, 39, 218.
[203] Demetrius, *On Style*, 3, 173.
[204] Plotinus, *Enn.* I, 6, 3.
[205] Augustine, *De ord.* II, 11, 32 (PL 32, 1010); *Conf.* X, 33–34, nn. 49–51 (PL 32, 799f.); *De mus.* 6, 13, 38 (PL 32, 1184); *De lib. arb.* II, 7, 16–19; 14, 38 (PL 32, 1249–51; 1261f.)
[206] Albert: "[pulchrum] in aliis sensibilibus non est, tactus scilicet, odoratus et gustus: sed id solum in visu et auditu." (*Pol.* VIII, 4 g; *ed. cit.*, VIII, 784.)
[207] St. Francis de Sales, I, 1; *ed. cit.*, pp. 53f.
[208] Kant, *Critique of Judgment*, I, §§ 42, 51, 8, 14; *ed. cit.*, pp. 181f., 212f., 61, 73f., 76.
[209] G. Santayana, *op. cit.*, §§ 15, 17.
[210] R. Fry, *Transformations*, p. 5.
[211] J. Maritain, *Art and Scholasticism*, pp. 23, 25.
[212] Thomas Gallus, *Expositio in Dion. De div. nom.*, c. 4; Rev. ed., pp. 506, 512, 646; de Bruyne, *Études*, III, 61, 63 and 66. Bonaventure, *Itinerarium*, II, 5 (V, 300b–301a). On this issue these thinkers might have been influenced by the fact that some earlier authors had not distinguished between the aesthetic and the non-aesthetic pleasures of the senses. Cf. Cassiodorus, *De anima*, cap. 2 and 12 (PL 70, 1284 A; 1304 B); Alcuin, *Dialogus de rhetorica et virtutibus* (PL 101, 946 A); and Hugh of St. Victor, *Expositio in Hierarchiam coelestem S. Dionysii*, II, 1 (PL 176, 950 A–B).
[213] See the text references in nn. 214–224 below.

opinion, smell is the only lower sense joining the eye and the ear in the aesthetic experience.[214] On the other hand, Richard P. Knight[215] and Brandenstein[216] hold that both smells and tastes are the companions of the two higher senses. In the third group of aestheticians attributing some aesthetic role to all three lower senses we find, among others, E. Burke,[217] G. Allen,[218] J. M. Guyau,[219] D. W. Prall, [220] DeWitt H. Parker, [221] H. N. Lee,[222] J. L. Jarrett,[223] and E. Chapman.[224]

On the specific roles attributed to the lower senses, the opinions of the aestheticians are even more varied. These opinions can be divided into simple and composite opinions.

The simple opinions on the aesthetic role of the senses can be divided into two main versions. One of them is that the so-called lower senses play the same role as the higher senses. The other version is that they play different roles, and, in the latter case, they are held to play either essentially different roles from the eye or the ear, or roles that are different only in degree from the roles of the higher senses.

The philosophers maintaining that there is no difference between the roles of the higher and the lower senses include, to mention only a few, E. Burke, to whom the objects of all the lower senses as well as the objects of vision and hearing please the beholder by soothing his nerves;[225] B. Croce, who declares that all impressions can enter into aesthetic expressions or formations and, for this reason, the distinction between the higher and lower senses is "altogether arbitrary";[226] and E. Chapman, according to whom not only sight but "all the other senses" enter into the aesthetic experience.[227]

An early representative of the position that, while both the higher and the lower senses may be involved in aesthetic experience, the lower senses play different roles from the higher senses is Thomas Aquinas, declaring that the higher senses do "mainly" delight us in the aesthetic experience (a position that

---

[214] J. Addison, *The Pleasures of the Imagination*, in *The Spectator*, No. 412, June 23, 1712. E. I. Watkin, *op. cit.*, part 2, ch. 4, p. 318.
[215] R. P. Knight, *An Analytical Inquiry into the Principles of Taste*, p. 9.
[216] B. von Brandenstein, *Művészetfilozófia*, § 50, p. 128.
[217] E. Burke, *op. cit.*, part 4, sect. 20–22, pp. 127–30.
[218] G. Allen, *op. cit.*, chap. 4, §§ 2–3, and chap. 5, § 2, pp. 76f., 83f., 92.
[219] J. M. Guyau, *Les Problèmes de l'Esthétique Contemporaine* (Paris: F. Alcan, 1884); quoted by Groos, *op. cit.*, chap. 2, n. 1, p. 31.
[220] D. W. Prall, *Aesthetic Judgment*, pp. 64f.
[221] D. H. Parker, *The Principles of Aesthetics*, chap. 4, pp. 46f.
[222] H. N. Lee, *op. cit.*, chap. 2, pp. 27f.
[223] J. L. Jarrett, *op. cit.*, chap. 2, p. 15.
[224] E. Chapman, *art. cit.*, p. 343.
[225] E. Burke, *op. cit.*, part 4, sect. 20, 23, 25; pp. 127–30, 134–35.
[226] B. Croce, *Aesthetic*, pp. 18f.
[227] E. Chapman, *art. cit.*, p. 343.

seems very similar to that held later by Roger Bacon).[228] That Thomas meant thereby an essentially rather than a merely quantitatively different role can be seen from a text in which Thomas points out that we do not use the term "beauty" in reference to the objects of the lower senses.[229] Alexander Bain puts the same view in this way: the eye and the ear play the properly aesthetic role in the beholder's mind; but the objects of the other senses act similarly if "contemplated in the *idea* in place of being enjoyed in reality," i.e., only as objects of artistic representation.[230] D. W. Prall, on the other hand, expresses the view that the lower senses simply enhance and enrich the delight caused by vision and hearing, with the obvious implication that the pleasure which the lower senses cause is non-aesthetic, although it adds to the beholder's aesthetic delight.[231] And Jarrett thinks that the lower senses have a strong imagistic appeal to the higher senses, although the beholder does not literally taste or smell or move.[232]

Among the aestheticians holding a quantitative difference between the roles of the higher and the lower senses, we find Brandenstein,[233] who speaks of a difference in intensity between the roles in question; R. P. Knight, who opines that we do not so often speak of beautiful smells or flavors as of beautiful forms, colours, and sounds,"[234] thereby stressing a difference not in intensity but in frequence; and H. N. Lee, who emphasizes a quantitative difference both in terms of intensity and frequency between the aesthetic roles of the higher and the lower senses.[235]

Taking up finally that selected group of thinkers who give much more than a simple answer to the question concerning the aesthetic role of the lower senses, it seems to be worthwhile to enumerate the distinctions of at least three aestheticians: DeWitt H. Parker, G. Allen, and Karl Groos.

The relatively least complicated among these three positions is that of Parker. He holds that all the external senses, including the lower senses, can enter into the aesthetic experience, provided, that (1) they act in a disinterested manner, i.e., "free from practical ends"; (2) their objects are expressive of feel-

---

[228] Aquinas: Illi sensus praecipue respiciunt pulchrum, qui maxime cognoscitivi sunt, scilicet visus et auditus (*S. theol.* I–II, 27, 1, ad 3); Duo sensus vigent in homine principaliter, scilicet visus et auditus: unde per haec duo aliquis gratiosus apparet; per pulchritudinem visui, per gratiosum verbum auditui (*In Psalm.* 44, 2). Cf. *Compend. theol.*, c. 165, on "suaves sapores." For a similar view, see *The Opus Maius of Roger Bacon*, VII, p. 3, ch. 5; tr. Robert B. Burke (Philadelphia: University of Philadelphia Press, 1928), 680.

[229] Aquinas: In sensibilibus autem aliorum sensuum non utimur nomine pulchritudinis, non enim dicimus pulchros sapores aut odores. (*S. theol.* I–II, 27, 1, ad 3.)

[230] A. Bain, *The Emotions and the Will*, (of 1859), part 1, chap. 14, n. 3. (New York: Appleton, 1899), 226.

[231] D. W. Prall, *Aesthetic Judgment*, pp. 64f.

[232] Jarrett, *op. cit.*, chap. 2, p. 15.

[233] Brandenstein, *op. cit.*, § 50, p. 129.

[234] R. P. Knight, *op. cit.*, p. 9.

[235] H. N. Lee, *op. cit.*, chap. 3, pp. 26f.

ings, as the odor of incense in a cathedral is of devotion; and (3) except rare instances, their objects are objects of nature rather than works of fine arts.[236] Grant Allen's doctrine is more detailed and complicated, but it is such at the empirical or practical level. For he does not generalize about the lower senses; instead, he discusses the non-aesthetic or aesthetic functions of taste, smell, and touch separately. About the first he holds this: "Properly speaking, no sensation of taste can be classed as aesthetic," although some tastes, that are only remotely connected with digestion, approach the aesthetic level more nearly; and others, that are "strongly in sympathy with the stomach," recede very far from it. Nevertheless, there is one way in which the former type of tastes can play some aesthetic role, if, namely, it is "idealized and surrounded by other aesthetic objects" by the painter or the poet.[237] About smell, he has this to say. Since its object is in itself the least intellectual and most purely emotional, some smells are completely "inadmissable into Poetry, even in the ideal form"; yet, some others, like sweet smells, "are in almost every respect raised into the aesthetic class," and, more specifically, "we cannot doubt that some part in the poetical effectiveness of fragrant flowers must be attributed to the sense of smell."[238] In regard to touch, Allen takes the position that "the purely disinterested pleasures and pains of smoothness and roughness belong entirely to the aesthetic group.... Accordingly, elements derived from the sense of Touch enter freely into the various arts, both in the actuality and in the idea."[239] Thus, even though touch in general is a "very little aesthetic" sense, "out of the emotional feelings which it yields a considerable proportion belong to the strictly aesthetic class, and that it is accordingly entitled to rank with sight and hearing as forming part of the basis for the fine arts and for Poetry."[240]

In contrast with G. Allen's numerous concrete distinctions, Karl Groos' theory is eminently theoretical, distinguishing between dependent (*unselbständig*) and independent (*selbständig*) roles, as well as indirect and direct roles, and discussing them in various combinations. Accordingly, he recognizes (1) some dependent and indirect role, (2) some dependent and direct role, and also (3) some independent and direct role, this third being considered in reference to aesthetic delight taken both in the broad and in the strict sense. Of all these roles, Groos admits that the lower senses can play (1) a dependent and indirect role, in so far as the reproductions of the objects of such senses are perceived together with actually given optic or acoustic qualities; and (2) a possibly very important dependent and direct role, in as much as real smells, tastes, or tactile qualities together with acoustic and visual qualities are being perceived in the aesthetic experience. As to the question whether the lower senses play

---

[236] DeWitt H. Parker, *The Principles of Aesthetics*, chap. 4, pp. 46f.
[237] G. Allen, *op. cit.*, chap. 4, § 2, pp. 76f.
[238] *Op. cit.*, pp. 83f.
[239] *Op. cit.*, p. 93.
[240] *Op. cit.*, p. 96.

also some direct and independent role in the aesthetic experience, that is, whether something like the fragrance of a rose or the sweetness of sugar can ever be the formal source of aesthetic delight, Groos replies with a distinction again. In so far as such odoriferous or olfactory qualities are enjoyed in themselves for their own sake and not as serving some biological purpose, the one who perceives such qualities has aesthetic experience taken in the broad sense. Yet, the same experience is non-aesthetic, Groos goes on to say, if by aesthetic experience we mean, in the strict sense, an experience in which a sensory quality is not only enjoyed in itself but also as the "carrier" or expression of some intellectual content (*ein geistiger Inhalt*). The reason for this is the intrinsic inability (colorfully called "*die geistige Armut*") of the proper objects of the lower senses to express or signify anything intellectual.[241]

The above outline, however limited, is apt to give the reader some idea of the wealth and divergence of thought among aestheticians concerning a number of more or less important and more or less specific questions connected with the aesthetic experience. Against this broad historical background, let us attempt now to express what and how much can be safely and truthfully said about the inner structure and the components of the aesthetic experience.

ARTICLE 2: *The Structure and Components of the Aesthetic Experience*

In this concluding article we face two correlated questions. The first is forced upon us especially by the contemporary skeptic aestheticians, and concerns the very possibility of a philosophic analysis of the structure and the components (human powers and their functions) of the aesthetic experience. The second question is concerned directly with the inner structure of the aesthetic experience in terms of the human powers involved in that experience and of the roles these powers play in that experience.

1. A careful study of skeptic objections to the type of philosophic analysis of the aesthetic experience that is planned here reveals that there are altogether three specific questions the realistic philosopher of beauty must face and answer. One is, whether it is necessary and, as such, reasonable at all to break down the organic unity of the aesthetic experience into various powers and functions. Another question is, whether any breakdown of human faculties and functions can ever be more than an arbitrary proliferation or multiplication of human nature and human experience. The third question is whether, even if such breakdown is both necessary and objectively limited rather than unreasonable and arbitrary, any list of really distinct powers and functions is intelligible or useful in the light of the bewildering differences of meanings attributed by

---

[241] K. Groos, *op. cit.*, ch. 2, n. 1, pp. 32–34. John Ruskin makes this aesthetic role of the lower senses dependent on a different condition, viz., whether the proper objects of these senses are sought and received not "in the abstract and ardently," but "with thankfulness and with reference to God's glory"—a truly unique position. (*Op. cit.*, II, part 3, sect. 1, chap. 2, § 7; p. 16.)

philosophic psychologists and epistemologists to terms signifying various human powers or functions.

In answering the first of these three questions, one can argue this way. According to his own self-consciousness, the beholder as such undergoes certain changes during the aesthetic experience by doing certain things like acquiring knowledge of beauty and enjoying that knowledge. But, evidently, he who does something *can* do that thing; for, otherwise, it would be true that one does what he cannot do. Furthermore, he who can do something has a potency or power for that thing. Thus, the beholder himself obviously has and uses certain powers during the aesthetic experience. On the other hand, there is evidently a real (not mind-made or logical) distinction between a power and the use of that power. For the natural explanation of the fact that a person occasionally has aesthetic experience is that he possesses certain powers for such an experience, which powers he only occasionally uses; just as one may have the moral power, i.e., the right of ownership to a house, although he makes only occasional use of it. Another way of demonstrating the real distinction between power and its use or function is this. If power and its use were the same thing, one should always do what he ever does since, as already shown, there is no action possible without the capacity for that action. But, of course, no one beholder does constantly act as a beholder although he has the constant capacity for acting as a beholder at any time.

Next, one may ask whether, even if it is true that the beholder has some potencies or powers that are really distinct from their actual use in the aesthetic experience, it is necessary and objectively justified to attribute a number of really distinct powers to the beholder except, for the sake of accounting for every component of the aesthetic experience. In reply to this question, we may point out first of all the fact well known from self-consciousness that, in the aesthetic experience, the beholder does several generically or specifically distinct things. Thus, he sees and hears; he unifies different sets of sense data (visual and audible, even tactile data); he imagines and associates; he takes delight in what he recognizes; he judges and remembers what he beheld and enjoyed; etc. Now, it is only reasonable and also empirically justified that one should attribute generically or specifically distinct functions to generically or specifically distinct powers. For it is both absurd and contrary to experience to say that, for instance, one both sees and hears with his eye, or that he sees with his ear and hears with his eye. What is indeed reasonable is to hold that for every generically or specifically distinct function to be found in the beholder as such there must be a really distinct human power, potency, or faculty, such as the external senses of vision and hearing, the internal senses of unifying external sense data and of imagination, and the rational intellect and will. On these grounds, the real question to be answered in the next part of this article is not *whether* there are really distinct powers and functions involved in the aesthetic experience but, instead, *which* human powers and functions constitute the structure and the components of this experience.

With the answers to the first two questions given, we may turn our attention to the remaining third question raised by the skeptic aesthetician, viz., whether in the light of the chaotic situation in epistemological and psychological terminology, it is not a hopeless task to attempt to discuss the roles the various human faculties play in the aesthetic experience. It was, among others, John Dewey who pointed out the fact that "each one of these terms [sc. those signifying the powers and functions involved in the aesthetic experience] has different meanings given to it by different schools of psychology."[1]

One needs only a little random sampling of the terminology of thinkers of certain periods in the history of philosophy to realize the truth of this remark. The most frequent form of confusing terminology consists in ascribing the traditionally recognized role of one faculty to an entirely different faculty. From Aristotle throughout the Middle Ages to modern rationalists it had been a tradition, for instance, to differentiate between the cognitive and the appetitive (emotional) powers of man, with the understanding that a knowing power can feel as little as an emotional power can know. Yet, Carl Lemcke asserts that sentiment (*Empfindung*), when it works actively, becomes an idea, "the life of phantasm."[2] This amounts to speaking of a cognitive feeling, somewhat similar to Kant's "feeling of the beautiful" in his youthful *Observations on the Feeling of the Beautiful and Sublime*[3] and, even more so, to John Ruskin's "theoretical faculty" characterized as a particular feeling.[4] Conversely, D. W. Prall talks about the apprehension of sensuous elements as relational structures and being, thereby, "in its very nature feeling."[5]

Another confusion in terminology tends to ignore the difference, recognized since Plato and Aristotle, not between cognitive and appetitive but between sensory and rational cognitive powers in man. Sir Joshua Reynolds, for example, talks about taste as a faculty of the mind judging not only painting and music but also geometric demonstrations,[6] a function that is to ancient, medieval, and modern rationalist thinkers essentially rational.

But the most arbitrary, most unconventional and, consequently, most confusing terminology is probably that of Dugald Stewart. He defines "conception" as being "simple apprehension," both Aristotelian terms referring to the first act of the rational intellect; and yet, he characterizes "conception" as Aristotle does imagination, a sensory power (representing an absent object

---

[1] Dewey, *Art as Experience*, chap. 11, p. 245.
[2] C. Lemcke, *Populäre Ästhetik*, chap. 1, p. 1.
[3] Kant, *Observations on the Feeling of the Beautiful and Sublime*, chap. 1. Tr. John T. Goldthwait (Berkeley and Los Angeles: University of California Press, 1960), 47.
[4] J. Ruskin, *Modern Painters*, vol. 2, part 3, sect. 1, chap. 1, § 9, and chap. 2, § 8; pp. 11, 17.
[5] D. W. Prall, *Aesthetic Analysis*, chap. 1, p. 19.
[6] Sir J. Reynolds, *op. cit.*, discourses 7 and 13, pp. 109, 202.

previously perceived),[7] while he explicitly differentiates "conception" from "imagination."[8] Moreover, he distinguishes between "imagination" (as the power of modifying or rearranging our "concepts") and "fancy" (as the power of association)[9] as well as between "imagination" and "wit" (as the power of recalling the ideas it combines),[10] even though all these functions used to be attributed in the Aristotelian and scholastic tradition to the imagination itself. To top all this, in a later chapter he declares that "conception or simple apprehension," together with "fancy," "abstraction" and "judgment or taste," are simply the four elements of the imagination as a "complex power,"[11]—a statement that not only confuses his own terminology but also ignores the traditional distinction between powers that were formerly distinguished as being sensory and suprasensory, respectively.

These examples more than suffice to show that the terminology of the various epistemological and psychological schools produces, indeed, confusion. However, this possible danger of confusion does not render the analysis of the various powers and functions involved in the aesthetic experience futile. For there is a simple remedy for avoiding any terminological confusion: precise definition of terms. If we take the trouble of exactly defining every faculty and function involved in the aesthetic experience, our subsequent analysis can be quite intelligible and useful.

2. Reflecting on the structure and the composing parts of the aesthetic experience, one can easily realize that there is a twofold as well as a threefold structure in that experience. Of these two, the former may appropriately be characterized as a vertical structure; the latter, as a horizontal structure.

The twofold structure entails the two basic generic potencies of man and brute as well, namely, the cognitive and the appetitive faculties, from which the two basic components of the aesthetic experience, viz., knowledge and delight, directly follow. This structure may well be called vertical for the obvious psychological reason that the acts of the appetitive (emotional) powers depend upon and, to this extent, are inferior to the acts of the cognitive faculties; thus, the proper place of the appetitive functions in the diagram of the inner structure of the aesthetic experience is *under* the place of the cognitive functions.

The threefold structure comprises the three generic factors which any human experience naturally has, namely, the preconditions, the essential parts, and the consequences or effects of the aesthetic experience. That they are listed vertically in the diagram is understandable from the chronological point of view. For unless certain conditions are first fulfilled, the aesthetic experience itself cannot easily take place or will not take place at all; whereas, once a person really and

[7] D. Stewart, *Elements of the Philosophy of the Human Mind*, I, chap. 3, p. 70.
[8] *Op. cit.*, chap. 3, p. 71.
[9] *Op. cit.*, chap. 5, part 1, sect. 4, III, p. 155.
[10] *Op. cit.*, chap. 5, part 1, sect. 4, I, p. 149.
[11] *Op. cit.*, chap. 7, sect. 1, p. 237.

truly has an aesthetic experience, there will be in his mind certain effects following that experience and proceeding from it. Thus, the preconditions of the aesthetic experience are truly the first components in a hierarchical sequence, whereas the effects of the same experience constitute the third and last component.

Putting the vertical and the horizontal components together, we arrive at the following basic structure of the aesthetic experience:

A. *Pre-Conditions*
  1. Cognitive Conditions
  2. Appetitive Consequences of These Pre-Conditions

B. *Essential Parts*
  1. Cognitive Essential Part
  2. Appetitive Essential Part

C. *Effects*
  1. Cognitive Effects
  2. Appetitive Effects

Now the question is, what specifically are these six structural components of the aesthetic experience?

The easiest to identify are the two essential parts. For, according to the testimony of every beholder's self-consciousness, he who becomes a contemplator of beauty experiences basically and invariably two things within himself: recognition of beauty and delight caused by that recognition. It is, however, not so easy to determine either the preconditions or the effects of the aesthetic experience. Reflection upon this matter will, however, lead one sooner or later to the realization that there are both necessary and contingent preconditions as well as necessary and contingent effects to this experience. A condition of the aesthetic experience is necessary if without it the aesthetic experience cannot take place at all; whereas a condition is contingent if without it the experience is possible but not so easily as when this condition is fulfilled. Correspondingly, an effect of the aesthetic experience is necessary if there cannot be any aesthetic experience without such an effect flowing from it; otherwise, the effect is contingent. Furthermore, any necessary precondition is proximate, i.e., one directly rendering the essence of the aesthetic experience (namely, aesthetic cognition and delight) possible. On the other hand, any contingent precondition is remote; that is, one indirectly rendering the aesthetic cognition and delight possible by promoting the necessary preconditions of the aesthetic experience. In an analogous manner, the necessary effects flow directly from the aesthetic cognition and delight; the contingent effects only indirectly, through the necessary effects.

With these distinctions in mind, one will sooner or later realize the following points. First, the necessary or proximate precondition consists of sense perception: the perception, through some sense organ or organs, of the aesthetic object, with the consequence that the perceived object, being proportionate with its beauty to those senses, pleases those senses and causes, therefore, sensory pleasure in the beholder. Secondly, the contingent or remote preconditions comprise, first of all, some mental state that is favorable to the perception of the aesthetic object. This is, clearly, the cognitive part of what is usually called the "aesthetic attitude." It consists in the mental concentration solely on what is expected to happen, namely, the coming-to-know and the enjoyment of the beauty of some object. Corresponding to this cognitive factor is an appetitive factor flowing from the above-characterized mental concentration. This is, of course, nothing else than the emotional expectation of the pleasurable aesthetic knowledge. Thirdly, the necessary or direct cognitive effect of the aesthetic cognition is the aesthetic judgment and the memory of the recognized and enjoyed beauty, the latter meaning an habitual knowledge of the fact that the beheld object is beautiful. From this habitual aesthetic memory, in turn, there follows an appetitive component, namely, aesthetic love in the form of a deep, lingering desire to relive that memorable and delightful aesthetic cognition. Fourthly and finally, there may be several contingent effects stemming from the aesthetic experience, such as refinement of taste as a cognitive component and enrichment of the beholder's emotional life as an appetitive component of this class of aesthetic effects.

Thereby, the inner structure of the aesthetic experience can be said to be the following:

	Preconditions:		*Essential Parts*:	*Effects*:	
	Contingent:	Necessary:		Necessary:	Contingent:
Cognitive Components	Aesthetic Attention,	Sensory Perception,	Aesthetic Cognition	Aesthetic Judgment and Knowledge	Refined Taste, etc.
Appetitive Components	Aesthetic Expectation	Sensory Pleasure,	Aesthetic Delight	Aesthetic Desire	Emotionally Enriched Life, etc.

Now let us discuss each one of these components separately.

3. The so-called contingent cognitive pre-condition, as already stated, is contingent in the sense that it is favorable to but not necessary for aesthetic experience. For there are basically two ways in which this experience can take place: unexpectedly and expectedly. If somebody walks into the home of a friend, and suddenly finds himself looking at a beautiful painting, or suddenly hears somebody playing a Beethoven sonata; or if somebody is driving along a highway and, upon making a sharp turn, is all of a sudden confronted with a breathtaking scene, then he has a completely unexpected aesthetic experience at that moment. But when we go to the Metropolitan Opera for a performance

of the *Götterdämmerung* under the baton of Herbert von Karajan and with Birgit Nilsson in the leading role, or to a concert to hear Mozart's *Jupiter Symphony* and, let us say, Beethoven's *Emperor Concerto*, both directed by L. Bernstein, then we expect and foresee the aesthetic experience which that opera or concert may cause in us. Now, whenever one has an unexpected aesthetic experience, it is not preceded by any aesthetic attention that would act as a precondition favorable to and promoting his aesthetic experience, although the very moment that the aesthetic object strikes him with its beauty quite unexpectedly, his attention will be captured and kept focused on that beautiful object for a while.

On this basis, it is safe to say that there is always some kind of attention involved in the aesthetic experience. It is involuntary whenever the experience is unexpected; and voluntary whenever the experience is expected. Of these two kinds of attention, the former is the characteristic feature of the aesthetic cognition in particular; the latter, the dispensable but favorable precondition of the aesthetic experience in general.

But what specifically is the nature of this voluntary aesthetic attention? It has been variously called and characterized as attention,[12] openness,[13] or attention and interest,[14] or detachment,[15] etc. It seems, however, that none of these characterizations is sufficient in itself. For as far as attention or even voluntary attention is concerned, it is certainly nothing unique but only the necessary condition of every successful intellectual activity, be it of aesthetic or scientific or practical or any other character. Furthermore, interest as a habit of wanting to know something specific is simply the cause of attention, and is therefore no less unique than attention itself. Little different is the case with the idea of detachment. For if it means isolation from its environment of the beheld object, then detachment is simply the negative and objective component of attention in general (attention meaning the concentration of one's cognitive power upon an object present to the mind while ignoring other objects) and, consequently, as Langfeld properly pointed out,[16] it characterizes every act of attention, not only aesthetic attention. If, on the other hand, detachment means subjectively the isolation of the aesthetic object from one's own personality, then it is simply questionably true since, as again Langfeld correctly remarked, without "the appeal to one's underlying tendencies, there would be the cold intellectual judgment" rather than the warm, enriching, and personally delightful experience with beauty.[17]

---

[12] D. W. Gotshalk, *Art and the Social Order*, chap. 1, p. 3.
[13] J. L. Jarrett, *op. cit.*, chap. 7, p. 106. Cf. Ducasse, *Art, the Critics and You*, chap. 5, p. 73.
[14] C. J. Ducasse, *op. cit.*, p. 72.
[15] H. Münsterberg, *The Principles of Art Education*, part 1, p. 20. Cf. E. D. Puffer, *op. cit.*, chap. 3, p. 79.
[16] Langfeld, *The Aesthetic Attitude*, chap. 3, § 2, pp. 49, 51.
[17] *Op. cit.*, p. 49.

Thus, the aesthetic attention may, perhaps, be characterized more properly in both positive and negative terms, together with an all-important understanding in mind. The positive aspect of aesthetic attention is a cognitive openness to whatever the aesthetic object has to offer us. In aesthetic attention we deliberately turn to the aesthetic object in order to recognize its beauty as fully as possible and, thereby, to enjoy it as much as possible. At the same time, this cognitive openness is evidently a selective one. For, while we turn our attention toward the aesthetic object, or, at least, keep our attention in readiness to recognize the beauty of the object the very moment it appears before us, we endeavor at the same time to turn away from every other object that might interfere with our aesthetic experience.

Thus, in terms of the former and positive aspect, the aesthetic attention is cognitive openness; in terms of the latter and negative aspect, aesthetic attention is a concentrated openness of the would-be beholder's mind to the upcoming aesthetic object. Insofar as the aesthetic attention means, positively, cognitive openness, aesthetic attention is an interested attitude: interested in whatever the aesthetice object has to offer to the rational mind. Insofar, however, as aesthetic attention means, negatively, a concentrated openness, a restriction in cognitive openness, aesthetic attention is a disinterested attitude. Being aesthetically interested and, at the same time, non-aesthetically disinterested, the aesthetic attention differs in its specific object from every other kind of attention or attitude, the speculative, the practical, etc. From this, however, it does not follow that aesthetic attention is unique in every respect, or that it is a generically unique precondition of the aesthetic experience. What many critics of the various characterizations of the favorable pre-conditions of the aesthetic experience overlook is that the contingent precondition of the aesthetic experience *need not* be unique, except in its specific object, since the uniqueness of the aesthetic experience stems not from its contingent precondition but from its essential constituents.

Closely connected with aesthetic attention or concentrated openness to the aesthetic object as the *cognitive* contingent precondition of the aesthetic experience is an *appetitive* counterpart. This is aesthetic expectation: not the cognitive readiness for beauty, but, instead, the emotional effect of this readiness. It is a sort of hopefulness with respect to being delighted by the recognition of the expected beauty.

The cognitive and the appetitive contingent preconditions are experienced together, and work together in such a way as to properly predispose both the intellect and the appetite of the would-be beholder for the aesthetic experience. Besides this teleological tie, there is another tie, too, holding the two contingent preconditions in question together. It is the causal relation between them. For, psychologically, it is precisely the concentrated openness as a cognitive attitude that elicits in the will the appetitive reaction to it, the emotional expectation of beauty.

4. Whether the aesthetic experience is preceded by some aesthetic attention and expectation, there is no formal aesthetic experience possible without some kind of sense perception which, in turn, is invariably accompanied by a certain amount and degree of sensory pleasure caused by the sense perception of the aesthetic object. This is to say that sensory perception is the necessary precondition of what constitutes the essence of the aesthetic experience.

Someone may rejoin here immediately by saying that this is a misinterpretation of the aesthetic experience, since the perception of the beautiful object is an integral part rather than merely the necessary condition of the aesthetic experience. The aesthetic experience can be taken in the broad sense, as it includes everything that normally takes place in the mind of the beholder; or else in the strict sense, as it is confined solely to what is the very essence of the aesthetic experience, exclusive of its preconditions and effects. Taking this experience in the broad sense, the sense perception that leads to aesthetic recognition is indeed an integral part of the aesthetic experience; but taking the same in the strict sense, the sense perception in question is only the necessary precondition of the essence of this experience, that is, of the aesthetic recognition and delight.

A more important and more difficult question concerns the identity of the senses involved in the perception of the aesthetic object. In reply, one may divide the external senses in this manner. Some of them are aesthetic, that is, such as to play some aesthetic role; others are non-aesthetic, playing no aesthetic role at all. Moreover, among the aesthetic senses, some are primarily and perfectly aesthetic; one other is only secondarily and imperfectly aesthetic. Furthermore, among the non-aesthetic senses, one can play a non-aesthetic contributive role in the aesthetic experience; another can play no role at all, neither aesthetic nor contributive role.

The primarily aesthetic senses are those of vision and hearing; the secondarily aesthetic sense is touch; fragrance can play the non-aesthetic contributive role; and taste plays no role of any kind. Let us elaborate on these facts one by one.

Firstly, the beautiful object must be either seen or heard or both seen and heard in order to be formally recognized and enjoyed as being beautiful. Secondly, the aesthetic object may be formally perceived, perfectly or imperfectly, with the help of the imagination, by way of touch, as when a person who became blind touches the entire surface of a statue or a face, or when a seeing person touches a statue to receive additional information about its texture or shape. Thirdly, certain smells, such as the fragrance of a flower, while they cannot contribute anything to our knowledge of the beauty of that flower, can contribute to the total delightfulness of the aesthetic experience, by adding non-aesthetic, olfactory pleasure derived from the fragrance to the aesthetic sense pleasure stemming from seeing that flower and also to the formally aesthetic delight flowing from the formal aesthetic intuition. Fourthly, taste adds neither aesthetic nor non-aesthetic pleasure to the total delightfulness of the aesthetic experience.

The next related question concerns the basic reasons behind the roles played by the various senses in general, and by vision and hearing in particular. There have been many answers given to these questions by a number of aestheticians, some of them listed by Karl Groos. One conceivable reason which he correctly rejects is that only in the realm of visible and audible objects is there enough variety to delight us.[18] This is patently false since there are innumerable tastes and smells. Another conceivable reason is mentioned by J. L. Jarrett: the peculiar transitoriness of the objects of smell and taste. But, even if this quality be granted, one can immediately see, as Jarrett points out, the weakness of this reason; for, after all, tones are also transitory and still the objects of aesthetic delight.[19] Jarrett obliquely mentions also a third conceivable reason, namely, that hearing is an aesthetic sense because its objects, unlike smells and tastes, can be "notated on a score." Jarrett's own reason for rejecting this explanation, namely, the analogy of a recipe book,[20] is unsatisfactory both on account of the weakness of the analogy and because the inexpressibleness in writing of combinations of smells and tastes is irrelevant to the aesthetic character of smells and tastes. A further reason, suggested by Grant Allen, viz., that the objects of taste, unlike those of the other senses, become destroyed in being perceived,[21] is again unsatisfactorily criticized by Jarrett (pointing out that "it is not the actual eating and digesting of food but the tasting and savoring of food" that delights[22]), because not being destroyed has nothing to do with aesthetic delightfulness, and mainly because every tasting and savoring is, indeed, a process of destruction. Thus, the explanation must be sought in a different direction, itself suggested by Jarrett, viz., that taste and smell too are internal.[23] For at the root of the facts that the objects of vision and hearing are undestroyed and extrinsic there lies a truly significant circumstance which is recognized by such different authors as Grant Allen and DeWitt H. Parker. Allen calls this circumstance the "remoteness from life-saving function" of the objects of vision and hearing;[24] Parker, the lack of the "practical" functions of the lower senses, whereby taste and smell are "bound up with instincts and actions."[25] What both mean here is the presence of physical distance and the lack of biological usefulness in

---

[18] K. Groos, *op. cit.*, chap. 2, p. 35.
[19] J. L. Jarrett, *op. cit.*, chap. 2, pp. 16f.
[20] *Op. cit.*, p. 17.
[21] G. Allen, *op. cit.*, chap. 4, § 3, p. 84.
[22] Jarrett, *op. cit.*, p. 17.
[23] *Ibid.*
[24] Allen, *op. cit.*, chap. 3, § 1, p. 33.
[25] DeWitt H. Parker, *The Principles of Aesthetics*, chap. 4, p. 45.

the objects of the higher senses, as against the presence of this usefulness and the absence of physical distance in smells and tastes.[26]

This explanation is in complete harmony with what we have recognized already in the argument for the objective reality of beauty, namely, that the aesthetic delight is due to knowledge or mental possession alone. Indeed, for tasting and smelling some physical possession or physical union is needed; for seeing or hearing, only mental possession rather than physical union is necessary. Should one object here that, if only mental possession could cause aesthetic delight, touch could never lead to aesthetic experience, even in the blind, which is obviously false; we can answer this way. In such cases, touch is merely a means whereby something per se visible, namely, shape itself, becomes imagined by the beholder; thus, what delights the blind beholder is not the touched surface but the shape made known to him by touch. Another objection to the above distance theory concerning the higher senses comes from Karl Groos on the basis that smell also involves distance and, yet, we do not consider it a higher sense, and it does not play any aesthetic role in the proper sense.[27] However, his criticism breaks down at the empirical level. For there is no smelling possible without actual, direct contact between odoriferous molecules coming from the smelled object and the olfactory sense organ—a circumstance which does not hold true for either visible or audible objects.

One certain reason, then, for the aesthetic role of the two higher senses and the lack of that role in the lower senses is cognitive distance or solely cognitive delightfulness to be found only or mainly in the objects of vision and hearing. This judgment is expressed in more or less similar terms by such contemporaries as DeWitt H. Parker and H. S. Langfeld.[28]

Is there yet another reason for the same? We can find the answer through some additional explanations suggested by various authors. Thus, Grant Allen points to the resistance of smell to "rapid and distinct succession of impressions in time or space."[29] Roger Fry, on his part, thinks that different smells cannot be perceived "in relation one to another," resulting in the impossibility of an art of smells.[30] The same thought is expressed by H. N. Lee: the objects of the lower senses "tend to be amorphous" and the organs themselves are less discriminative.[31] Almost the same reason is cited by St. Francis de Sales, echoing Aristotle, Augustine, and Aquinas: the objects of the higher senses have "the greatest capacity for knowledge and best serve the intellect."[32] Brandenstein's

[26] Cf. Brandenstein, *op. cit.*, § 50, p. 129. For a specific objection to this view, see Milton C. Nahm, *Aesthetic Experience and Its Presuppositions*, p. 307n.

[27] K. Groos, *op. cit.*, chap. 2, n. 1, p. 35.

[28] Cf. Parker, *op. cit.*, chap. 4, p. 45; and H. S. Langfeld, *The Aesthetic Attitude*, chap. 3, § 9, p. 74.

[29] G. Allen, *op. cit.*, chap. 3, § 4, p. 87.

[30] R. Fry, *Transformations*, p. 5.

[31] H. N. Lee, *Perception and Aesthetic Value*, chap. 3, n. 3, p. 27.

[32] St. Francis de Sales, *op. cit.*, p. 53.

way of putting this reason is the following: the lower senses have "less purely intellectual significance."[33] Here one could even quote Augustine himself, who made the keen observation that the difference between the higher senses and the lower senses is the fact that only with the former can several people come to know the whole of any given object.[34]

What is behind all these suggested reasons? A very obvious and basic metaphysical fact: that only the orderly, the well-arranged, the properly structured or organized whole is beautiful. The most fundamental reason for the aesthetic role of the higher senses and the lack of such a role of the lower senses is simply this: the objects of the former senses are organizable and properly structured; those of the latter are not. This is, incidentally, the conclusion of such aestheticians as James McCosh, DeWitt H. Parker and Jarrett,[35] although not each one of them would accept this as the main reason for the different roles the higher and the lower senses play in the aesthetic experience. Thus, following Groos in this respect (who considers the eye and the ear the only "speech senses," *Sprachsinne*),[36] Parker contends, for example, that vision and hearing are aesthetic mainly because "they are the natural media of communication: sounds in speech and music; visual shapes in writing, gesture and facial expressions . . . ."[37] To this the best remark is not what Jarrett makes, namely, that Parker's reason is poor since "all senses can be employed for communicative purposes"[38] (because it is difficult to see how this can seriously be maintained), but rather this: the eye and the ear are the senses of communication precisely because of the unparalleled capacity or aptitude of colors, shapes, and tones, i.e., the proper objects of vision and hearing, to form orderly structures and, consequently, to be properly expressive of human ideas and thoughts.

In brief, there are two reasons for vision and hearing playing the primary aesthetic role: a subjective, affecting the beholder; and an objective, involving the aesthetic object. The former lies in the fact that only visible and audible objects secure disinterestedness through physical distance; the latter, in the fact that only visible and audible objects are properly structured, i.e., discernibly and expressively orderly.

5. Speaking of the role of the external senses in the aesthetic experience, several additional issues must also be discussed.

One concerns the usual psychological distinction between sensation and perception, which is so strongly stressed, for instance, by H. N. Lee. He defines the former as "the conscious response to the stimulation of a sense organ, or nerve

---

[33] Brandenstein, *op. cit.*, p. 129.
[34] Augustine, *De lib. arb.* II, 7, 17f. (*PL* 32, 1249f.)
[35] J. McCosh, *The Emotions*, bk. 2, chap. 3, sect. 3, p. 158. Parker, *The Principles of Aesthetics*, chap. 4, p. 45. Jarrett, *op. cit.*, pp. 17, 106.
[36] Groos, *op. cit.*, chap. 2, n. 1, p. 36.
[37] Parker, *op. cit.*, chap. 4, p. 45.
[38] Jarrett, *op. cit.*, chap. 2, p. 17.

receptor," whereas perception, to him, "involves selection among sensations, combination, organization, and sometimes supplementations from the imagination."[39] The significance of this distinction in his opinion lies in the fact that it is never sensation but always perception that is aesthetic or "the material of the aesthetic experience,"[40] even though sensations are the "content" or the material of perception.[41] Now, the distinction between sensation and perception is sound, and conforms to the testimony of our self-consciousness. For, in our consciousness, we do not have an unrelated heap of isolated sensations but, rather, more or less correlated and organic wholes, although the single external senses clearly receive only the isolated sense data. Nevertheless, the real distinction between sensation and perception does not justify the assertion that the data of pure sensations cannot be aesthetic at all. For even such pure "sensations" as that of a single tone or even color, despite its seeming simplicity, is in fact a composite, composed of static and/or dynamic, qualitative or quantitative parts and, as such, constitute a more or less well-organized whole, thus fulfilling the requirements of beauty, viz., unity in multitude (if not in variety).

Closely related to this is a more important psychological question which H. N. Lee almost completely ignores, namely, which sense or senses are the ones that change the sensations into perceptions. For, as already mentioned above, it is obvious that the eye cannot hear, nor the ear see, each sense organ having its own specific proper object; and yet, we are conscious not of isolated, fragmentary sense data but of objects composed of different sets of sense data. Since, then, none of the five external sense organs is capable of dealing with any but its own proper kind of sense data, there must be an internal sense whose proper object is the sense data of the external senses, and whose proper function (or at least one of its proper functions) is the unification of those sense data.[42] Whether we call this sense by an ancient and medieval name, common or commune sense, thus indicating its primary role, or by another name, it is certain that such an internal sense does exist, and is involved in the aesthetic experience as well as in every other experience of sense knowledge. If this were not so, we would be conscious only of certain colors, shapes, sizes, etc., but never of things like a beautiful face or tree or flower, etc.

It is to be noted here that this internal sense is really distinct from what has at least traditionally been called "imagination" or "phantasy," to which the above-discussed internal sense passes on all unified sense data for preservation. Indeed, the former is to the latter sense as the maker and giver of unified sense data is to the receiver and preserver of the same data. The imagination, in turn, does more than merely receive and store the images: it recalls them in either a positive or a negative or a creative manner. By positive recall is meant the

[39] H. N. Lee, *op. cit.*, chap. 3, n. 2, p. 25.
[40] *Op. cit.*, n. 3, p. 26.
[41] *Op. cit.*, p. 28.
[42] Cf. Aristotle, *De an.* III, 2, 426b 9–29; and, for another role, *ibid.*, 425b 11–18.

"reactualization" of the stored-up phantasm or image without changing it in any way; i.e., without either leaving out any detail from it or adding any to it. Negative recall, on the other hand, is one that leaves out certain individual aspects from any given image so as to produce a "general image," which is one that more or less represents and resembles many rather than only one object of sense perception. The creative recall, finally, is the aesthetically significant recall. It alters significantly the original image by freely substituting certain parts of it with parts of other images or by connecting, associating it with other images for reasons of similarity, dissimilarity, or else simply in a completely arbitrary manner. It is at this point that the personality of the beholder has the greatest impact on the manner in which the beholder actually sees and/or hears the perceived aesthetic object, altering, enriching or impoverishing it according to his cognitive and/or emotional habits, dispositions, etc. It is like imposing a layer on the objective content of the image, changing that image into a mixture of a partly objective and partly subjective mental representation of the perceived aesthetic object. This is why any two beholders, considering one and the same object, may have considerably different, if not aesthetically opposite, intuitions and emotional reactions to that object.

Briefly, in addition to the external aesthetic senses, there are at least two internal senses playing significant roles in the aesthetic experience. The external senses (eye, ear, and, partly, touch) acquire the pure sense data; the first internal sense unifies them into some definite units or wholes; and the imagination may partly alter them. This third and last role causes, thus, what we may call the (partial) subjectification of the phantasm or image with the result that the image may become thereby either more or less delightful, but only for the individual beholder himself.

Just as there is an appetitive concomitant or effect to aesthetic attention, namely, the aesthetic expectation, there is an appetitive effect also to sensation, the cognitive role of the external senses, and to the reception and favorable subjectification of the aesthetic phantasm by the imagination. This appetitive reaction to sense cognition is proportionate to the knowledge that causes it and is, therefore, itself a specifically sensory pleasure flowing from the attainment by the external and internal senses of their proper, connatural object. The metaphysical reason for this sensory pleasure is mentioned as early as in the fifth century B.C. by Plato, who put it this way: "Like likes like."[43] Whereas too much light causes pain in the eye, and too loud a tone pains the ear,[44] the perception of the beautiful is the cognitive fulfillment of the proper and proportionate object at least of the eye, ear, and imagination, and for this reason causes, understandably, some pleasure in the sensory will. This pleasure is not the specifically and formally aesthetic delight in the beholder's rational will, but only the

[43] See Plato, *Lys.* 214b. Cf., *Gorg.* 510c.
[44] Cf. Aristotle, *De an.* III, 2, 426a 30–b 8.

generically epistemological, non-aesthetic pleasure stemming from the sensory cognition of any object proportionate to the senses.

As far as the imagination is concerned, however, there is a difference between the sensory pleasure stemming from the mere reception of the aesthetic image and the additional sense pleasure that originates from the subjectification of that image, provided, or to the extent that the subjectification is favorable or individually suitable to the beholder. If, however, this subjectification happens to render the aesthetic object unsuitable to the beholder, then the emotional reaction will be painful rather than pleasurable—completely destroying the beholder's chances for enjoying the aesthetic object in its pure, unsubjectified form. If this pain lingers, it may even decrease or destroy the delightfulness of the subsequent aesthetic intuition itself.

This is the picture of the necessary and the contingent preconditions of the aesthetic experience. Every additional element is either a part of the essence or an effect of this experience.

6. Like its preconditions, the essence of the aesthetic experience, too, has a cognitive and an appetitive component, namely, aesthetic cognition and aesthetic delight. Let us discuss each of these two at some length.

As far as the cognitive component of the essence of the aesthetic experience is concerned, there are several specific questions to be clarified. The most fundamental is this: By which specific cognitive power does the beholder formally recognize the beauty of the beheld object?

There are, of course, two basic alternatives conceivable: by the senses or by the rational, suprasensory intellect. Each alternative has found, we have seen, numerous advocates in the history of aesthetics. Which, then, of the two alternatives is the true subject of aesthetic cognition?

There is at least one kind of artwork whose beauty does not leave any doubt about which of the two genera of man's cognitive powers is needed for the formal recognition of beauty. This artwork is, obviously, the work of poetry, be it a brief poem or a lengthy epic, an ancient tragedy or a contemporary novel. For, while the words as articulate sounds or groups of sounds can be heard, if spoken, and seen, if written, their meanings are concepts that transcend the realm of matter, and so do the various logical relations of those concepts, the judgments expressed by sentences. The simplest way of recognizing the immateriality of concepts is to recognize that, while every image received into the imagination is the more or less exact mental representation of one individual object and is, thereby, singular, every concept is basically the mental representation of many individuals (actually, of all individuals of a species or class), and is thereby universal. Insofar as the image, due to its sensory origin, is sensory or material, the concept, being essentially dissimilar and opposite in its basic universality to the singular image, is *not* sensory but suprasensory, *not* material but immaterial.

But this is another way of saying that the concept is the act or product of a cognitive faculty that is itself, by necessity, suprasensory or immaterial, called the intellect. For the essentially less perfect can never produce something essentially more perfect, and that which is sensory or material, like the singular image, *is* essentially less perfect than the universal concept. Inasmuch then as we grasp the meanings and logical relations of the words which poetry uses in its works, the beauty or, at least, the full beauty of the poetic work is knowable only by the intellect in cooperation with some external and some internal senses.

A similar conclusion can be reached, analogously, with respect to every kind of artwork in which meaningful words are naturally employed, such as songs that have texts, and operas, for their librettos. But all the other artworks as well as the beautiful things in nature are essentially material. Thus, the question arises whether the senses suffice to recognize their beauty, or whether we need the suprasensory intellect for the recognition of their beauty, too.

The answer to this question lies in the nature of material beauty in general. We have learned that material beauty, that is the only possible object of man's aesthetic experience, is the integral unity of a multitude or variety of proportionate parts. In other words, what makes something beautiful is the fact that, in it, there is a multitude of parts, components, factors, or aspects, and, at the same time, also a unity made up of those parts, components or whatever. The aesthetic object represents for this reason both a multitude and a unity. But, of these two aspects of beauty, only multitude is as such sensorily knowable: the various colors and shapes, their various places, the various tones, the various movements, etc. of the visible and/or audible object. For what we actually perceive is all the colors, all the shapes, all the movements, all the tones of the aesthetic object; but all these constitute, evidently, a multitude or variety, but certainly not unity. The unity in the beautiful object is due to the *relations* which all those directly perceivable colors, shapes, movements, and tones have to each other and to the whole, whereas those colors, shapes, movements, etc., are not themselves relations but only the principles and terms of relations. Therefore, material beauty, that is formally a unity, the unity of a multitude or variety, is sensorily incognoscible; instead, it necessitates the act of a suprasensory intellect to be formally recognized.

It is on these or similar grounds that the defenders, great and not so great, of the suprasensory cognoscibility of beauty, argued for their position. Thus, St. Thomas stated simply that sensory cognition does not extend to the cognition of the proportion of one thing to the other, the latter being the sovereign act of the rational intellect.[45] In contrast, the neo-Thomist Jungmann gave a some-

---

[45] Thomas: apprehensio sensitiva non se extendit ad hoc quod cognoscere possit proportionem unius ad alterum, sed hoc est proprium rationis. (*Sum. theol.* II–II, 58, 4c.) Cf. Sapientia est potissima perfectio rationis, cuius proprium est cognoscere ordinem. Nam etsi vires sensitivae cognoscant res aliquas absolute, ordinem tamen unius rei ad aliam cognoscere est solius intellectus aut rationis. (*In I. Eth.* L. 1, n. 1.)

what Platonic[46] twist to the argument: One perceives beautiful things with his eye or ear. But, if the eye as such could perceive beauty itself, it should be able to perceive also audible beauty, whereas the ear should be able to recognize visible beauty, too. But this is patently not the case. Therefore, neither of the two higher senses can recognize beauty as such. And since these are the most cognitive senses, the lower senses cannot formally recognize beauty—a fact confirmed by common linguistic usage. Consequently, beauty is sensorily not cognoscible.[47]

But one may argue for the suprasensory knowability of beauty also in a radically different fashion. The major premise here is not the essence of beauty as being unity in multitude, i.e., order, but the empirical realization that the non-poetic artworks, too, have a suprasensory principle of beauty, namely, the artistic idea, manifested, expressed, or symbolized by the artwork in such a way that the entire arrangement of all its parts is made according to that idea as the exemplary cause of the artistic order. Whether one takes this symbolic function of artistic beauty in Hegelian terms ("Beauty is matter through which the Idea shines"), or in the curious combination of neo-Hegelianism and neo-Thomism, as E. I. Watkin does ("Distinctively aesthetic contemplation always apprehends ... the idea as expressed in an outer form, a corporeal form"),[48] or as Clive Bell, S. K. Langer or Herbert Read does, all three of them calling beauty "significant form," that is, a material form expressive of an idea, one thing is clear: the idea as such, of which material beauty is expressive, is sensorily not knowable. But to recognize an order or arrangement without recognizing the principle of that order or arrangement is certainly impossible. Consequently, insofar as any material beauty is symbolic, i.e., expressive of an idea, it is not cognoscible unless a suprasensory cognitive power, called the intellect, is formally engaged in the aesthetic experience.

7. Another question concerning aesthetic cognition is that if beauty is formally recognized by the suprasensory intellect of the beholder, how does this aesthetic recognition exactly take place?

Before we have any idea of the answer to this question, this much is undoubtedly clear: since aesthetic cognition is the cognitive part of the *essence* of the aesthetic experience, the manner in which the rational intellect recognizes beauty as beauty must be *unique*, or else aesthetic experience is not specifically different from other human experiences, just as I. A. Richards or Hugo Münsterberg claimed it.

Generally, there are two ways in which man can come to know something by conceptualization. One is by abstracting the universal concept from the image of the concrete object. The other consists in applying the universal concept

---

[46] Cf. Plato, *Hipp. mai.* 299a ff. and Aristotle, *Top.* VI, 7, 6, 146a 20–31.
[47] Jungmann, *op. cit.*, n. 15, pp. 25f.
[48] E. I. Watkin, *op. cit.*, part 2, chap. 4, p. 321.

already formed to the perceived material singular. The former is being used, for instance, when one forms the universal concept "dog" from one or several images of individual dogs; the latter method is being used, for instance, when one recognizes that a perceived object is a dog, that is, that the concept "dog" is predicable of that material singular, the individual dog, thereby forming the singular concept "this dog."

The former manner of conceptualization is clearly abstractive and pre-judicatory (formed before judgment); the latter is applicative and judicatory (formed in judgment). Thus, both have two things in common: they are both connected with concepts either producing universals or deriving from universal concepts some singular concepts; and they are both connected with judgment, either making judgments possible or using judgments for the formation of a new and singular concept.

But neither of these really happens in the aesthetic experience. Not the former, because, as reflection testifies to every beholder, the beholder as such does not form a universal concept, such as that of "beauty in general" by contemplating a given beautiful object; nor does the beholder form a singular concept of the contemplated object. The reason for saying the former is a fact known from self-reflection, viz., that by coming to know and enjoy the beauty of this object, we do not as yet know what is beauty in general. Instead, we recognize the object in its intelligibility, i.e., as a concrete unity in the concrete multitude or, simply, as a concrete. The reason for saying that, in the aesthetic experience, the beholder forms no singular concept, such as "this beauty," is the equally well-known fact that the aesthetic judgment, "This is beautiful," in which the singular concept "this beauty" is formed, is passed on the beheld object normally and naturally only *after* the beholder recovers from the aesthetic bliss of contemplating the beautiful object.

Hence the recognition of beauty in the aesthetic experience must be other than abstractive or applicative, other than prejudicatory or judicatory. What, then, is this cognitive act of beauty as beauty? If it is not abstractive, it leads to no universal concept; if it is not applicative, it uses no universal concept. Thus, it is completely non-conceptual. Moreover, if it is neither pre-judicatory nor judicatory, it must be either post-judicatory or non-judicatory, that is, either a cognitive act that derives a concept from judgments already formed (as is the case with the so-called "transcendental concepts" in neo-scholastic philosophy, all described as judicatory in neo-scholastic works on metaphysics; including the concept "beautiful"[49]); or else a cognitive act that has nothing to do with judgment either as its principle or as its principiate, that is, either as something from which judgment is formed or something that is formed in or from a judgment. But, as already pointed out, in the aesthetic contemplation itself no

[49] G. Klubertanz, *op. cit.*, p. 40. R. J. Kreyche, *First Philosophy* (New York: Holt, Rinehart, Winston, 1964), 153.

concept is formed at all, at least not per se, according to the nature of the aesthetic contemplation. Therefore, neither is a concept formed that is derived from or in judgment, nor one from which a judgment is formed.

How are we to understand this non-abstractive and non-judicatory act of recognizing beauty? Even if one does not accept the Aristotelian doctrine of the agent and passive intellect, or the partly changed version of it in Aquinas' epistemology and psychology, this theory can well serve as a workable, graphic model for the unique nature of the aesthetic cognition. For, in this Aristotelian-Thomistic theory, the agent intellect, i.e., the active part of the rational intellect, the one which actually abstracts the concept from the phantasm, is described in its *abstractive* role as a cognitive power that turns to the image, derives from it a universal concept, and passes it on to the "passive" intellect, the receptive part of man's suprasensory cognitive power, for conservation and two subsequent uses, judgment and reasoning; and, in its *applicative* second role as borrowing a universal concept from the passive intellect, turning with it to the phantasm, and applying the universal concept to the thing of which the phantasm is a sensory representation in the imagination. Thus, the intentional direction of the movement of the agent intellect in its first and abstractive role is from the suprasensory level of the intellect down to the sensory level of the imagination and phantasm, and from that sensory level back to the suprasensory level of the passive intellect and universal concept. On the other hand, the intentional direction of the movement of the agent intellect in its second and applicative role is from the suprasensory level of the *passive* intellect and universal concept down to the sensory level of the imagination and phantasm. If, then, the aesthetic cognition is unlike both of these cognitive acts or roles, its intentional direction itself must also be unlike that of either of the two other cognitive acts or roles. But this can be only that from the suprasensory level of the *agent* intellect down to the sensory level of the imagination and phantasm. Thereby, this cognitive movement of the agent intellect in the aesthetic experience is only the first half of the one it makes in its abstractive role; and the precise opposite of the movement the agent intellect makes in its applicative role.

This graphic explanation is completely supported by everyone's own reflection upon what was happening to him while beholding a beautiful object: his mind turned to the contemplation of the aesthetic object (of which the senses produced a phantasm in the imagination), and then stayed with that contemplated object. It is as if the rational intellect were so engulfed, overwhelmed, or even awed by the intelligible unity of the composite aesthetic object, that is, by its order or beauty, that it could not tear itself away from its vision and, instead, stays with it for a while, and takes it in with the full openness of cognitive capacity. In doing so, the intellect of the beholder is both passive and active, both static and dynamic (although, of course, not in the same respect) in an ideally balanced manner. This contemplation is active and dynamic, since the intellect notices or discovers in its own light the integral parts with their relations to each other and the whole; and this contemplation is also passive or static insofar as it does nothing with the blissful vision of the beautiful object in a discursive manner. This is to say, the intellect does not even attempt to transform the phantasm into a concept, nor does it move away from the phantasm of the aesthetic object so as to turn back with a newly formed concept to the suprasensory level, nor does it bring down a universal concept from the suprasensory level to apply it to that aesthetic phantasm.

If this characterization of the aesthetic cognition is correct as it shows us the uniqueness of aesthetic cognition, then the knowledge so acquired of beauty must specifically differ from every other kind of knowledge. It obviously does, for the following reasons. Being non-abstractive, it differs from speculative or scientific knowledge in general, including the aesthetic knowledge of the art critic and the philosopher of beauty, since speculative knowledge is per se knowledge through universal concepts and universally valid judgments made up of those concepts. Secondly, being suprasensory and non-applicative, even though nonconceptual, it differs from the completely empirical knowledge of the artisan, since the artisan, unlike the beholder, relies heavily on his sense experience in his work, and applies universal concepts to the material singulars with which he works. And, since the non-conceptual and non-applicative aesthetic knowledge is achieved solely by the intellect, this aesthetic knowledge differs also from theological and (if there is such a thing) mystic knowledge, insofar as the theologian's primary source is faith, and the mystic's, both faith and his senses, especially his imagination. However, all this is true only insofar as we mean here by aesthetic knowledge the beholder's knowledge of the beauty of the contemplated object, but not the beholder's knowledge that the contemplated object is beautiful. For these are two separate and different kinds of knowledge, of which the latter is the result of the former—a truth to be discussed later.

8. Having thus seen the specific nature of aesthetic cognition or knowledge in negative terms, that is, as it is specifically unlike other acts of cognition, let us discuss now aesthetic cognition in positive terms, i.e., in terms of what positive properties it has. It seems that it has two positive qualities, both of which render aesthetic cognition unique, and thus both do invariably characterize it in every instance of the aesthetic experience. One of these is intuitiveness; the other, cognitive delightfulness.

The intuitiveness of the aesthetic cognition consists simply in these two characteristics closely correlated: instantaneity and non-discursiveness. In terms of the former, aesthetic cognition is an immediate, yet full grasp by the intellect of the beauty of the contemplated object; in terms of the second characteristic that follows from the first, the aesthetic cognition is not the result of any syllogistic reasoning. The instantaneousness of the aesthetic cognition is empirically known to every beholder. One need not even expect an encounter with beauty at all and, yet, the very moment that he looks at an aesthetic object or suddenly hears a few bars of a composition, he can recognize the beauty of that object, and take delight in it, too. The non-discursiveness of the aesthetic cognition, on the other hand, can be proved this way. One might have already recognized and enjoyed the beauty of an object; he might even have judged the object beautiful, and, yet, if asked why he thinks that the object is beautiful, he may have great difficulty in giving reasons, especially sufficient reasons, for his aesthetic delight and judgment—a difficulty that is quite distinct from that of *verbalizing* the reasons one may have discovered for his aesthetic delight and favorable aesthetic judgment. Now, it is obvious that all this would not be so if aesthetic delight and the subsequent aesthetic judgment were based upon and flowed from discursive reasoning. It is clear, then, that holding aesthetic cognition to be intuitive in the sense of both instantaneousness and non-discursiveness is empirically well founded. Thereby, one does not deny, of course, that recognizing every element or detail or part of the beauty of an object may take much time not only in case of artworks that are knowable in a chronologically successive manner but also in case of completely spatial artworks or aesthetic objects. For the instantaneousness of aesthetic cognition means merely that however much of the whole aesthetic object may become known to the beholder at any given moment, the beauty of that object or of that part of the object is instantly grasped, without needing any thinking or reasoning; although, especially if the chronologically successive aesthetic object is lengthy, the recognition of the total beauty of the aesthetic object may take by necessity quite a while.

Does this intuitiveness render the aesthetic cognition unique? It certainly does, and it does so for the following reasons. First of all, by virtue of this intuitiveness, the aesthetic cognition of the beholder differs from the knowledge of the art critic and the philosopher of art, as the latter two come to know what they know professionally about an artwork and beauty in general, respectively, gradually and discursively. Secondly, aesthetic cognition differs from both knowledge by sense perception and the recognition of self-evident principles of thinking and being, despite the fact that both of the latter two are themselves intuitive in terms of instantaneousness and non-discursiveness. For aesthetic cognition is intuitive knowledge by the rational intellect as shown above; sensory perception (sensation) is intuitive knowledge by sensory powers. Their difference is, thus, a difference in their subject or knowing power. Conversely, aesthetic cognition is intuitive knowledge about a sensory object; whereas the intuition of the first principles of thinking and of being is intuition of suprasensory objects. Their difference is, thus, a difference in their object or the thing known. What all this amounts to is that the uniqueness of the intuitiveness of the aesthetic cognition lies in the sensoriliness of its object and in the suprasensoriliness of its subject. In other words, whereas sense perception is an intuition with a sensory subject and object, and the grasp of self-evident principles is an intuition with a suprasensory subject and object, aesthetic cognition is an intuition sensory in its object and suprasensory in its subject.

9. The second property of aesthetic cognition is its intrinsic delightfulness, causing the second part of the essence of the aesthetic experience, viz., aesthetic delight. Like the first property, intuitiveness, this second property is also universally and empirically known. For every beholder knows from his own experience that, the very moment he looked at and/or listened to certain objects, he experienced delight. Moreover, like intuitiveness, this aesthetic delightfulness renders aesthetic cognition unlike every other knowledge: sense perception, discursive knowledge, recognition of self-evident principles, practical knowledge, and theological knowledge.

Firstly, aesthetic cognition differs in its delightfulness from sense perception in two respects: one, that sense perception is only per accident delightful, i.e., only if its object is proportionate to the sense organ's capacity; the other, that, even if it happens to be delightful, sense perception is delightful at the sensory level both in terms of its object, which is always a material accident, and of its subject, which is the sense. In contrast, aesthetic cognition is, firstly, per se delightful; and, secondly, delightful at the sensory level in terms of its object, the beautiful, but delightful at the suprasensory level in terms of its subject, the rational will as it rests in the mental possession of the intuited beauty.

Secondly, aesthetic cognition differs from discursive knowledge in its delightfulness. For, while aesthetic knowledge is per se delightful, discursive knowledge is per se non-delightful, and only per accident delightful on account either of its object, some abstract truth, and/or the little effort it took to recognize that truth. Moreover, while aesthetic knowledge is delightful on account of its sensory object, a concrete, material and beautiful object, discursive knowledge is delightful, if at all, on account of its suprasensory object, a universal and abstract truth.

Thirdly, aesthetic knowledge differs in its delightfulness from practical knowledge in two respects. For aesthetic knowledge is delightful both for its effortlessness and for its exclusively speculative character, i.e., solely on the basis of the beauty of its object considered in itself as an end rather than a means; practical knowledge is not delightful because of the effort needed in acquiring it, except relatively and per accident; and even insofar as it is delightful, it is delightful only as a means to an end, hence, in terms of some interest or practical use of it. This latter characteristic is the famous disinterestedness of the aesthetic knowledge, made famous but not discovered by Immanuel Kant.

Finally, aesthetic knowledge differs in its delightfulness from theological knowledge. For, while aesthetic knowledge is per se delightful because of both its object and effortlessness, theological knowledge is per se not delightful either on account of its object, (which is abstract and suprasensory) or on account of the discursive manner in which it is acquired. Instead, if it is delightful, theological knowledge is such only per accident, due to its object, i.e., the all-perfect God; and relatively, in respect to the possible ease of its acquisition.

In brief, aesthetic cognition is unique both in its nature as a cognitive act and in its properties, the cognitive intuitiveness and the appetitive delightfulness. With this in mind, we may turn now to the effect of the aesthetic experience.

10. Taking up first the necessary effects, we must discuss two cognitive effects before considering the appetitive effect. One of the two cognitive necessary effects of the aesthetic experience is actual, the aesthetic judgment; the other is habitual, namely, a certain kind of aesthetic knowledge.

The actual effect that flows from the essence of the aesthetic experience with psychological necessity is the formal aesthetic judgment "This is beautiful" (or something analogous to this) in reference to the intuited and enjoyed aesthetic object. It follows from the essence of the aesthetic experience with psychological necessity. For, on the one hand, it follows aesthetic contemplation invariably; on the other hand, we cannot help forming this judgment once we recovered from the attraction which tied our intellect to the aesthetic object, and prompted the will to rest in the mental possession of that object.

The aesthetic judgment is formally passed on the contemplated object as follows. Once the aesthetic experience has ended (either because the aesthetic object itself ceases to be, like the performance of a play or music, or else because the intellect manages to turn away from the contemplation of the object after a while), the intellect turns back to the intellectual level, and recognizes that the concept "beautiful" applies to the beheld object since "the beautiful" subjectively means "that which, simply by becoming known, delights," and since the aesthetic object did actually delight the beholder once it became known to him. This is to say, the formal aesthetic judgment is post-conceptual, utilizing as the predicate the previously acquired universal concept "beautiful."

Both the fact that we pass aesthetic judgment on the beheld object and the manner in which we do so are empirically known from self-reflection. Yet, one may still question the assertion that the formal aesthetic judgment is passed *after* the aesthetic experience is all over. For we often find ourselves *during* the performance of a play, symphony, opera, or film, or *during* the reading of a novel or drama, judging that artwork or a certain part of it as being beautiful or less beautiful, more or less interesting, fascinating or boring, etc. (The additional alternative, that the aesthetic judgment precedes and causes the aesthetic experience, listed by Étienne Gilson,[50] need not be considered here since it seems to disregard the relevant data of self-consciousness.)

In answering this question, one may readily concede that the judging of the

[50] E. Gilson, *The Arts of the Beautiful* (New York: C. Scribner's Sons, 1965), 39.

artwork during the aesthetic experience happens quite frequently. Nevertheless, this does not contradict the above statement that the formal aesthetic judgment succeeds the aesthetic experience proper. Instead, all that is needed is a more specific statement on the question. Since the intellect is simply incapable of judgment or reasoning during aesthetic contemplation, the aesthetic judgment is per se subsequent to the aesthetic experience. However, since especially lengthier artworks have less fascinating and even boring parts (e.g., certain scenes in a play), and since during the contemplation of such parts the beholder's attitude easily changes from the aesthetic to the non-aesthetic precisely because the less beautiful part of the artwork fails to tie the beholder's intellect to itself, one may say either one of these two things: that the formal aesthetic judgment may per accident be pronounced during the aesthetic experience itself; or, that the very moment that the artwork fails to attract our intellect, the aesthetic experience is, at least momentarily, over, and for this reason it is still true that the aesthetic judgment is passed *after* that experience.

11. The second necessary cognitive effect of the aesthetic experience raises two questions: What is its specific object? and What is its specific cause?

As to the first question, the answer is rather simple and obvious, although it is often misunderstood or misinterpreted. This necessary cognitive effect is not the knowledge of the intuited and enjoyed beauty of the beheld object but the beholder's habitual knowledge that the beheld object is beautiful and the approximate greatness of its beauty.

We know this twofold character of the aesthetic knowledge through self-reflection. We can clearly remember that an object we beheld in the past is beautiful simply by recalling that we intuited that object and, while doing so, we experienced great aesthetic delight. This we can remember, significantly, without needing to recall in our imagination the phantasm of the previously beheld aesthetic object. In contrast, if we wish to consider and enjoy again that aesthetic object, we must recall its image in our imagination, and intellectually contemplate and intuit its beauty. On this basis, we may even say that the beholder's knowledge that a beheld object is beautiful lingers in his intellectual memory as habitual knowledge, which can be changed into actual knowledge by simple recall either voluntarily or involuntarily. In contrast, the intuited and enjoyed beauty itself remains in the beholder as the object neither of habitual nor actual intellectual knowledge. Instead, only the sensory material of this knowledge, namely the visual and/or audible image of the previously beheld aesthetic object, remains in the imagination as the beholder's habitual sense knowledge of the beautiful thing (but not of its beauty).

The answer to the second question is somewhat more difficult and controversial. There are four conceivable reasons why one knows or remembers that an object is beautiful. The first reason is that he remembers the beauty itself of the previously beheld object. Another is that he remembers having intuited or beheld the beauty of the object in question. The third conceivable reason is that he remembers how much he enjoyed the object while he beheld it. Finally, the fourth reason is that the beholder remembers either the beheld beauty or the act of beholding that beauty *and* the enjoyment derived from beholding the same. Now, of these alternatives the first reason, as well as the first part of the fourth reason, is untenable. For, as already shown, what one habitually knows at the suprasensory level after an aesthetic experience is not the beauty itself of the beheld object but that it is beautiful. On the other hand, the formally aesthetic intuition as well as the formally aesthetic enjoyment of the intuited beauty may be a long-lasting, memorable experience. Therefore, of the above-listed four alternatives, the second and the third, taken separately, are only partly true. Thus, we are left with the second part of the fourth explanation, viz., that we remember an object is beautiful because we recall having intuited and enjoyed its beauty. This conclusion is supported by an appeal to everyone's own self-consciousness. Secondarily, of course, the reason for remembering that an object is beautiful may be another thing, viz., the formal aesthetic judgment. In this manner, the beholder may remember that an object that he previously contemplated is beautiful because he remembers having judged it so after the aesthetic experience itself.

12. The necessary appetitive effect of the aesthetic experience is the aesthetic desire that flows directly from either one or both the actual and the habitual aesthetic knowledge of the beholder, and indirectly from the aesthetic intuition and delight.

This aesthetic desire follows directly from the formal aesthetic judgment and/or from the beholder's habitual knowledge that the beheld object is beautiful. For it is the very nature of the delightful to be lovable in general and desirable in particular in such a way as to make us want to encounter it again.

Consequently, the very moment that the favorable aesthetic judgment is passed on the contemplated object, the aesthetic desire is born in the mind of the beholder—a desire that lingers either as long as he remembers how delightful was the intuition of that aesthetic object or until the moment that his desire finds its fulfillment in a subsequent aesthetic encounter with the beauty that he longed to behold again.

At this point we may ask, What is the relation of this aesthetic desire to the aesthetic delight of the beholder? For the answer, we must know the difference between love, desire, and delight (joy). The three are by no means identical; instead, the latter two are the two species of love. For love in general is the appetitive or emotional reaction to the cognition of the good, irrespective of the presence or absence of that good; thus, the proper object of love in general is the (present or absent) good in general. In turn, desire is love for the good that is absent; and joy, love specifically for the good that is present or possessed.

With these distinctions in mind, we may say that the very moment the beholder intuits the beauty of an object, aesthetic love is born in his mind—a love that assumes the specific character of aesthetic joy or delight, since the object of this love, beauty itself, is present as being mentally possessed by the beholder. This love ceases, however, to be aesthetic joy the very moment that the aesthetic experience comes to an end, which is normally the moment that the beholder formally passes the favorable aesthetic judgment on the beheld object. From that moment on, beauty itself is not known or mentally possessed by the person, since the aesthetic contemplation itself has ended, and the only knowledge he retains is the knowledge that the contemplated object is beautiful. In other words, the beauty of that object is no longer present to the beholder's mind, and aesthetic delight is replaced by aesthetic desire—love of the absent beauty. This desire is basically proportionate in intensity to the greatness of the previously contemplated beauty and, also, to the depth of delight the beholder took in that beauty. The effect of this desire is that the beholder will suffer as long as he remembers how beautiful and delightful was the previously contemplated object, or to the very moment that this aesthetic yearning comes to an end through either a secondary or a second aesthetic experience with the desired beauty. *Secondary* aesthetic experience means here one resulting from the return of the beholder's intellect to the aesthetic image in his own imagination and producing fainter aesthetic delight than the original. *Second* aesthetic experience, on the other hand, means here a subsequent real aesthetic experience with the aesthetic object previously beheld and enjoyed.

A last question: What is the formal object of the above-characterized aesthetic desire? Is it the intuition, the enjoyment, or both the intuition and the enjoyment of the previously beheld beauty? Aristotle seems to hold implicitly the second alternative, speaking repeatedly of the intellectual enjoyment while he discusses the purpose of studying music;[51] whereas R. W. Emerson and a twentieth-century schoolman, Joseph Donat, are among those who hold, at least by implication, the first alternative by showing that seeking beauty only for the delight which it causes degrades the beholder and beauty itself.[52] The cognition seems to be the true alternative, but only normatively. This is to say that many beholders, probably the majority of them, yearn for the repetition of aesthetic experience precisely and formally because of its delightfulness. Gilson had them in mind when he remarked, "The art lover loves a work of art for the joy it brings him."[53] Yet, this aesthetic yearning seems to dethrone beauty as an intrinsic, objective value, and degrade it from the level of an end to the hedonistic and pragmatic level of a means, so that the entire realm of aesthetic experience is brought close to the subjective realm of extrinsic values.[54] There-

[51] Aristotle, *Pol.* VIII, 3, 1338a 22; *ibid.*, chap. 5, 1339b 13.
[52] R. W. Emerson, *Essays*, Essay 12: "Art"; *ed. cit.*, p. 324. J. Donat, *Ontologia* n. 493 (Innsbruck: F. Rauch, 1940), 280 f.
[53] Gilson, *The Arts of the Beautiful*, p. 40.
[54] Cf. the implication of Plato, *Leg.* II, 655d.

fore the ideal form of aesthetic desire is the *eros* of which Plato speaks in the *Symposium*—the formal desire to behold beauty face to face.[55] For if this truly Platonic desire is ever to be fulfilled, one attains anyway, by psychological (if not metaphysical) necessity, also the secondary and intellectually hedonistic component of the essence of the aesthetic experience, which is the aesthetic delight.

13. In the last step of this analysis of the components of the aesthetic experience, we may consider briefly the possible contingent effects of the aesthetic experience.

Since, by definition, neither of these effects necessarily stems from the aesthetic intuition and/or the aesthetic delight, no definitive or certainly complete list can be written up of these effects. As a matter of fact, opinions on the number of such effects vary at least as much as opinions on the number of contingent preconditions. Some authors, for instance, like E. Burke, mention no contingent effect at all, but only love as the necessary effect of the aesthetic experience.[56] Other thinkers would list either one or a few only. Plato, for instance, speaks only of the educational benefits of beauty that enrich the mind and refine one's taste,[57] whereas Aristotle discusses amusement as a mode of relaxation, refinement of taste, and conduciveness to virtue or moral character.[58] Others come up with an impressive list of possible effects the aesthetic experience may have on the beholder. D. W. Gotshalk, for example, lists among "the major uses" of the aesthetic response, besides the intrinsic value of the aesthetic delight itself as a "terminal good," three "instrumental values," namely, "refreshment, as escape, as pastime, as emotional release"; furthermore, "a means of self-growth" by fostering "an affection for appreciation and contemplation as against possessiveness"; and also the "great use" of the aesthetic experience as a "preparation for the creation of works of fine art."[59] Monroe C. Beardsley, on the other hand, goes so far as to list seven effects of the aesthetic experience: "that aesthetic experience relieves tensions and quiets destructive impulses"; "resolves lesser conflicts within the self, and helps to create an integration, or harmony"; "refines perception and discrimination"; "develops the imagination"; "[is] an aid to mental health"; "fosters mutual sympathy and understanding" by drawing "men together"; and, finally, "offers an ideal for human life."[60]

There is no doubt that all the above-listed effects *can* result from aesthetic experience, however varied these single lists of effects may be. Consequently, as

[55] Plato, *Symp.* 211e.
[56] E. Burke, *A Philosophical Inquiry into the Origin of our Ideas of the Sublime and Beautiful*, part 4, sect 25, p. 135.
[57] Plato, *Rep.* III, 401cd.
[58] Aristotle, *Pol.* VIII, chaps. 3–5.
[59] D. W. Gotshalk, *Art and the Social Order*, pp. 25–27.
[60] M. C. Beardsley, *Aesthetics*, pp. 574f.

already mentioned, it would be futile to attempt to draw up a comprehensive list of the contingent effects of the aesthetic experience. Instead, we may, in conclusion, confine ourselves to a fairly comprehensive division of the various genera of possible aesthetic effects.

The contingent effects of the aesthetic experience can be either cognitive or appetitive in nature; the cognitive effects may be either speculative or practical in character; the speculative ones as well as the appetitive ones, either of sensory or of suprasensory nature; and the practical effects, either of aesthetic or social or moral nature.

In confronting man with the glorious beauties of this world, in producing in him the uniquely subtle and noble (since liberal and disinterested) aesthetic delight and desire, and in enriching his mind and his character with all the above-mentioned values of the contingent effects, aesthetic experience is not only a truly unique and profoundly rewarding experience but also one that is, as Plato saw,[61] comparable to mystic experience and, as Thomas Aquinas hinted,[62] the mundane analogate of what theologians call "beatific vision." For in both the mystic experience and the "beatific vision" man is said to see Beauty itself, and to see it not through the glass darkly but directly, face to face.

[61] Plato, *Symp.* 211d–212a.
[62] Thomas, *Comp. theol.* II, c. 9, n. 591.

Bibliography

(The date listed in parentheses after the title of any book is the date of the first publication.)

Addison, J. *The Pleasures of the Imagination*; in *The Spectator*, nos. 411–21, June 21–July 3, 1712. *The British Classics*, X (London: J. Sharpe, 1803) 71–124.

———. "Observations on the Odyssey continued"; in *The Spectator*, No. 80, August 11, 1753. *The British Classics*, XVII (London: J. Sharpe, 1807) 66–71.

Alan of Lille (d. 1202). *Anticlaudianus*; in Migne, *Patrologia Latina* (hereafter: *PL*) 210, 487–576.

Albert the Great, St. *Opera omnia*. 38 vols. Borgnet, A., ed. Paris: L. Vivès, 1890–99.

———. *De pulchro et bono*, in *S. Thomae Aquinatis Opuscula philosophica et theologica*, III. Maria, M. de, ed. (Tiferni Tiberini, 1886) 561–88.

———. *Metaphysica*, in *Opera omnia*, 16, Geyer, B., ed., Münster: Aschendorff, 1960.

———. *Sumna de bono*, in *Opera omnia*, 18; *ed. cit.*, 1951.

Alberti, L. B. *Ten Books on Architecture*. (1651) Leoni, J., tr. London: Tiranti, 1955.

Alcuin of York (730–804). *Dialogus de rhetorica et virtutibus*; in Migne, *PL* 101, 919–50.

Aldrich, V. C. *Philosophy of Art*. Englewood Cliffs, N. Y.: Prentice Hall, 1963.

———. "Back to Aesthetic Experience," *The Journal of Aesthetics and Art Criticism*, XXIV/3 (Spring 1966) 365–71.

Alexander of Hales (and others?). *Summa theologica*. 5 vols. Quaracchi: Collegium S. Bonaventurae, 1924–48.

Alexander, S. *Beauty and Other Forms of Value*. London: Macmillan, 1933.

———. *Space, Time and Diety*. London: Macmillan, 1920.

Alison, A. *Essays on the Nature and Principles of Taste*. (1790) Corrected and improved edition by Mills, A. New York: Harper and Brothers, 1858.

Allen, G. *Physiological Aesthetics*. London: H. S. King, 1877.

Ambrose, St. *De Isaac et anima*; in Migne, *PL* 14, 527–60.

Ames, Van M., *Introduction to Beauty*. New York: Harper, 1931.

Anderson, J. M. *The Realm of Art*. University Park and London: The Pennsylvania State University Press, 1967.

André, Le P. Y. ("Père"). *Essai sur le Beau*. Paris: H. L. Guérin et J. Guérin, 1741.

Antisthenes. Diogenes Laertius, VI, 1. The Loeb Classical Library edition (London: Wm. Heinemann; New York: G. P. Putnam, 1925) II, 3–23.

Aquinas—*see*: Thomas Aquinas, St.

Aristotle. *Opera*. Bekker, I., ed. 5 vols. Berlin, 1831–70. *The Basic Works of Aristotle*. McKeon, R., ed. New York: Random House, 1941.

Aristoxenus. *The Harmonies of Aristoxenus*, Macran, H. S., ed. Oxford University Press, 1902.

Ast, F. G. A. *System der Kunstlehre oder Lehr-und Handbuch der Aesthetik.* Leipzig; J. C. Hinrichs, 1805.
Augustine, St. *Opera,* in Migne, *PL,* vols. 32–47.
Averroes. *Aristotelis Metaphysicorum libri XIV, cum Averrois Cordubensis in phica,* Venice, 1508; reprinted: Louvain: Edition de la bibliothèque S. J., 1961.
Avicenna. *Philosophia prima* (often referred to as *Metaphysica*), in *Opera philosoeosdem commentariis, et epitome (Aristotelis omnia opera, cum Averrois in ea opera commentariis, VIII).* Venetiis: apud Iunctas, 1562. Reprinted: Frankfurt am Main: Minerva, 1962. German translation of *Epitome in librum Metaphysicae Aristotelis: Die Metaphysik des Averroes (Abhandlungen zur Philosophie und ihrer Geschichte,* Erdman, B., ed., vol. 36). Frankfurt am Main: Minerva, 1960.
Bacon, F. *The New Organon.* (1620) Anderson, F. H., ed. Indianapolis: Bobbs & Merrill, 1960.
Bacon, R. *Opus maius.* 2 vols. Burke, R. B., tr. Philadelphia: University of Pennsylvania Press, 1928.
Baeumker, C. *Witelo, ein Philosoph und Naturforscher des XIII. Jahrhunderts.* Münster: Aschendorffscher Verlag, 1908.
Baillie, J. *An Essay on the Sublime.* Monk, S. H., ed. London, 1747. The Augustan Reprint Society Publication, No. 43, Los Angeles: The University of California Press, 1953.
Bain, A. *The Emotions and the Will.* (1859) Fourth edition. New York: Appleton, 1899.
———. *Mental and Moral Science.* London: Longmans, Green, 1868.
Bakadur, J. C. W. "Indian Aesthetic Speculation," *The Hibbert Journal,* LX, No 238 (April 1962) 243–51.
Barns, W. "Thoughts on Beauty and Art"; in *Macmillan's Magazine,* Masson, D., ed., London: Macmillan; June, 1861.
Bartók, Béla. *Levelei* (Letters). Ed. J. Demény. Budapest: Zeneműkiadó Vállalat, 1955.
Bascom, J. *Aesthetics, or the Science of Beauty.* Revised edition. New York: G. P. Putnam, 1881.
Basilius, St. *Homiliae IX in Hexaemeron;* in Migne, *Patrologia Graeca* (hereafter: *PG*) 29, 4–208.
———. *Homiliae in Psalmos;* in *PG* 29, 209–493.
Baumgarten, A. G. *Aesthetica.* Francofurti cis Viadrum: J. C. Kleyb, 1750.
———. *Aestheticorum pars altera.* Francofurti cis Viadrum: J. C. Kleyb, 1758.
———. *Meditationes philosophicae de nonnullis ad poema pertinentibus.* Halle: J. H. Grunertus, 1735. *Reflections on Poetry.* Aschenbrenner–Holther, trs. Berkeley and Los Angeles: University of California Press, 1954.
———. *Metaphysica.* (1739) Seventh edition. Halae Magdeburgicae: C. H. Hemmerde, 1779.
Bayer, R. "Esthétique," in *Grand Larousse Encyclopedique,* Haminault, H., ed. (Paris, 1961) XIV, 715.
Beardsley, M. *Aesthetics.* New York: Harcourt, Brace, and World, 1958.
———. "Aesthetics"; in *New Catholic Encyclopedia.* (New York: McGraw–Hill, 1967) I, 160–64.

Bell, C. *Art.* (1913) New York: G. P. Putnam's Sons, 1958.
Bell, Sir C. *The Anatomy and Philosophy of Expression as connected with the Fine Arts.* London: J. Murray, 1806. Third edition *ibid.*, 1844.
Berg, H. *Die Lust an der Musik erklärt.* Berlin: Behr's Verlag, 1879.
Berkeley, G. *The New Alciphron,* (1732) *The Works of G. Berkeley, III.* Jessop, T. E., ed. London: Th. Nelson and Sons, 1950.
———. *Three Dialogues between Hylas and Philonous.* (1713) Cleveland–New York: The World Publishing Company, 1963.
Berndtson, A. *Art, Expression, and Beauty.* New York: Holt, Rinehart & Winston, 1969.
Bittle, C. N. *The Domain of Being, Ontology.* Milwaukee: Bruce, 1939.
Black, M., ed. *Philosophy in America.* Ithaca, N. Y.: Cornell University Press, 1965.
Blair, H. *A Critical Dissertation of Ossian, II* (1790); in *The Poems of Ossian,* Macpherson, J., tr., Leipzig: B. Tauchnitz, 1847.
———. *Lectures on Rhetoric and Belles Lettres,* III (1783) New edition. London: W. Sharpe and Son, 1820.
———. "On the Standard of Taste"; included as Chapter 26 in Home, H., *Elements of Criticism,* Boyd, J. R., ed., New York and Chicago: A. S. Barner, 1883.
Blunt, Sir A. *Artistic Theory in Italy 1450–1600.* Oxford: Clarendon, 1962.
Boas, G. "The Mona Lisa in the History of Taste," *Journal of the History of Ideas,* I, No. 2 (April 1940) 207–24.
Boethius. *Opera*; in Migne, *PL* 63–64.
Boileau, N. *Art poétique.* Batteaux, M., ed. Paris: Saillant et Nyon, 1771. Berthou, H. E., ed. Paris: Hachette, 1923.
Bonaventure, St. *Opera omnia.* 11 vols. Quaracchi: Collegium St. Bonaventurae, 1882–1901.
Bosanquet, B. *A History of Aesthetic.* Cleveland–New York: The World Publishing Co., 1961.
———. *Three Lectures on Aesthetic.* (1915) Ross, R., ed. Indianapolis: The Bobbs-Merrill Company, 1962.
Bouhours, D. *La manière de bien penser dans les ouvrages d'esprit.* Paris: V. de S. Mabre-Cramoisy, 1687.
Boyer, C. *Cursus Philosophiae.* Paris: D. de Brouwer, 1937.
Bradley, A. C. "The Sublime"; in *Oxford Lectures on Poetry,* London: Macmillan, 1926.
Brandenstein, B. von. *Der Aufbau des Seins.* Saarbrücken: Minerva-Verlag, 1950.
———. *Művészetfilozófia.* Budapest: The Hungarian Academy of Science, 1930.
Brown, G. B. *The Fine Arts.* New York: C. Scribner's Sons, 1901.
Brown, T. *Lectures on the Philosophy of the Human Mind.* (1828) Hallowell: Glazier, Masters and Smith. 1842.
Bruyne, E. de. *Études d'Esthétique Médievale.* 3 vols. Brugge: De Tempel, 1946.
———. *L'Esthétique du Moyen Age.* Louvain: L'Institute Supérieur de Philosophie, 1947. *The Esthetics of the Middle Ages.* Hennesey, E. B., tr. New York: F. Ungar, 1969.
Buffier, Père C. *Traité des Vérités premières et de la source de nos jugements.* Paris:

V. Monge, 1724. English tr.: *First Truths, and the Origin of Our Opinions.* London: J. Johnson, 1780.

Bullough, E. " 'Psychical Distance' as a Factor in Art and An Esthetic Principle," *British Journal of Psychology,* V (1913) 87–118. Reprinted in *A Modern Book of Esthetics,* Rader, M., ed. (New York: Henry Holt, 1952) 401–28.

Burke, E. *A Philosophical Enquiry into the Origin of our Ideas of the Sublime and Beautiful.* (1757) Boulton, J. T., ed. London: Routledge and K. Paul; New York: Columbia University Press, 1958.

Caffin, C. H. *Art for Life's Sake.* Chicago: Pranz, 1913.

Cajetan, Cardinal. *Commentaria,* II, ad *S. Thomae Summam Theologiae*; in *St. Thomae Opera Omnia,* Leonine-edition, vol. VI.

Callahan, L. *A Theory of Esthetic according to the Principles of St. Thomas Aquinas.* (1927) Second edition. Washington D. C.: The Catholic University of America Press, 1947.

Calugero, G. "Estetica," in *Encyclopedia Italiana,* (1932) XIV, 402–408.

Carrière, M. *Die Idee des Schönen und ihre Verwirklichung im Leben und in der Kunst.* (1859) Third edition. Leipzig: F. A. Brockhaus, 1885.

Carritt, E. F. *An Introduction to Aesthetics.* London: Hutchinson's University Library, 1949.

———. *The Theory of Beauty.* New York: Macmillan, 1914.

Cassiodorus. *De anima*; in Migne, *PL* 70, 1279–1308.

Chapman, E. "The Perennial Theme of Beauty and Art"; in *Essays in Thomism,* Brennan, R. E., ed. (New York: Sheed and Ward, 1942) 333–46.

Chrysippus. In Diogenes Laertius, VII, 1. The Loeb Classical Library. (London: Wm. Heinemann; New York: G. P. Putnam's Sons, 1925) II, 287–319.

Chrysostom, J., St. *In Epistulam II. ad Corinthios*; in Migne, *PG* 61, 381–610.

Cicero, M. T. *De finibus bonorum et malorum.*

———. *De natura deorum.*

———. *De officiis.*

———. *Tusculanae disputationes.*

Cleanthes. In Diogenes Laertius, VII, 5. The Loeb Classical Library (London: Wm. Heinemann; New York: G. P. Putnam's Sons, 1925) II, 273–85.

Clement of Alexandria, St. *Paedagogus*; in Migne, *PG* 8, 247–684.

Coffey, P. *Ontology,* New York: P. Smith, 1938.

Cohen, M. "Aesthetic Essence"; in *Philosophy in America,* Black, M., ed., Ithaca, N. Y.: Cornell University Press, 1965.

Cohn, J. *Allgemeine Aesthetik.* Leipzig: W. Engelmann, 1901.

Coleridge, S. T. "On Beauty"; in *Poetry and Prose,* Baker, C., ed., New York: Bantam, 1965.

———. "General Principles (The Agreeable and the Beautiful Distinguished)" (1814); in *Coleridge, Selected Poetry and Prose,* Potter, S., ed., New York: Random House, 1933.

———. "On the Principles of Genial Criticism Concerning the Fine Arts," Essay 2; in *Biographia literaria,* Oxford: Clarendon, 1907.

Collingwood, R. G. *The Principles of Art.* New York: Oxford University Press, 1958.

Comte, A. *A General View of Positivism.* (1848) Bridges, J. H., tr. London: G. Routledge and Sons, 1908.
Cooper, C. W. *The Arts and Humanity.* New York: Philosophical Library, 1952.
Copland, A. *Music and Interpretation.* New York: The New American Library, 1952.
Cory, H. E. *The Significance of Beauty in Nature and Art.* Milwaukee: Bruce, 1947.
Cotton, J. *De musica;* in Migne, *PL* 150, 1381-92.
Crane, L. *Art and the Formation of Taste.* (1882) Boston and New York: Educational Publishing Co., 1889.
Croce, B. *Aesthetic.* (1909) Ainslie, D., tr. New York: The Noonday Press, 1956.
———. *The Philosophy of Giambattista Vico.* Collingwood, R. G., tr. London: H. Latimer, 1913.
Crousaz, J. P. de. *Traité du Beau.* Amsterdam: F. L'Honover, 1712.
Damjanovich, M. "Das Problem des Hässlichen in der Ästhetik"; in *Actes du IV Congrès International,* Michelis, P. A., ed. (Athens, Greece, 1960) 454-57.
Darwin, C. R. *The Descent of Man and Selection in Relation to Sex* (1871); in *The Origin of Species and The Descent of Man,* New York: The Modern Library, 1936.
Demetrius of Phaleron (?). *On Style;* in *Aristotle: The Poetics, "Longinus": On the Sublime, Demetrius: On Style.* New York: G. P. Putnam's Sons, 1932.
Descartes, R. *Compendium of Music.* (1618) Robert, W., tr. Rome: American Institute of Musicology, 1961.
———. *Les Passions de l'Ame* (1649); in *Oeuvres et letters* (*Bibliothèque de la Pleiade,* 40), Bridoux, A., ed. (Paris: Gallimard, 1953) 691-802. Partial English tr. in *The Philosophical Works of Descartes,* Haldane-Ross, trs. (Cambridge: The University Press, 1968) I, 329-427.
———. Letters to Père Mersenne; in *Oeuvres et letters* (as above).
Dewey, J. *Art as Experience.* (1934) New York: G. P. Putnam's Sons, 1958.
Dezza, P. *Metaphysica generalis.* Third edition. Romae: Universitas Gregoriana, 1952.
Dickie, G. "Beardsley's Phantom Aesthetic Experience," *The Journal of Philosophy,* LXII (1965) 129-36.
———. "The Myth of the Aesthetic Attitude," *American Philosophical Quarterly,* I, 1 (January 1964) 56-65.
Diels, H. *Die Fragmente der Vorsokratiker.* Fourth edition. Berlin: Weidmann, 1922.
Diez, M. *Allgemeine Ästhetik.* Berlin-Leipzig: Göschen, 1912.
Diogenes Laertius. *Lives of Eminent Philosophers.* Loeb Classical Library, Greek, 184-85. 2 vols. London: Wm. Heinemann; New York: G. P. Putnam's Sons, 1925.
Dionysius the Areopagite (Pseudo-Denis). *De coelesti hierarchia;* in Migne, *PG* 3, 187-370.
———. *De divinis nominibus;* in Migne, *PG* 3, 585-996. English translation by C. E. Rolt. London-New York: Macmillan, 1920. Reprinted, 1966.
Dionysius Ryckel, the Carthusian. *De venustate mundi et pulchritudine Dei;* in *Opera omnia,* 34 (Tornaci: Cartusiae S. M. de Pratis, 1901) 223-53.

Dobell, S. T. *Thoughts on Art, Philosophy, and Religion,* Nichol, J., ed. London: Smith and E., 1876.
Donat, J. *Ontologia.* Ninth edition. Innsbruck: F. Rauch, 1940.
Dubos, J. B. *Reflexions critiques sur la poésie et sur la peinture.* Paris: J. Mariette, 1719.
Ducasse, C. J. *Art, the Critics, and You.* (1944) Indianapolis–New York: The Bobbs-Merrill Co., 1955.
Duns Scotus. *Opera omnia.* 26 vols. Paris: L. Vivès, 1891–95.
Dupeyrat, A. *Logica, Ontologia et Cosmologia Generalis.* Paris: V. Lecoffre, 1887.
Dürer, A. *The Literary Remains of Albrecht Dürer.* Conway, Wm., ed. Cambridge, 1889.
Eberhard, J. A. *Theorie der schönen Künste und Wissenschaften.* Halle: Waisenhaus, 1790.
Eidlitz, L. *The Nature and Function of Art, more especially of Architecture.* London: Sampson Low, Manston, Searle, and Rivington, 1881.
Emerson, R. W. "Art"; in *Essays,* Essay 12, Chicago–New York: Belfore, Clarke, and Co., n.d.
———. "Beauty"; in *Conduct of Life,* Essay VIII. Boston–New York: Houghton Mifflin, 1904.
———. *Nature.* Boston–New York: Houghton Mifflin, 1903.
Epictetus. *Discourses.* 2 vols. Oldfather, W. A., tr. New York: G. P. Putnam's Sons, 1926–28.
Epicurus. Fragments; in *The Stoic and Epicurean Philosophers, The Complete Extant Writings of Epicurus, Epictetus, Lucretius, Marcus Aurelius,* Oatis, W. J., ed., New York: The Modern Library, 1940.
Erigena, J. S. *De divisione naturae;* in Migne, *PL* 122, 439–1022.
Esser, G. *Metaphysica generalis.* Second edition. Techny, Illinois: St. Mary's Mission Home, 1952.
Faulkner, Ziegfield, Hill, eds. *Art Today.* New York: H. Holt, 1959.
Fearon, J. "The Lure of Beauty"; *The Thomist,* VIII, 2 (April 1945) 164–69.
Fechner, G. T. *Vorschule der Aesthetik,* I. (1876) Second edition. Leipzig: Breitkopf and Härtel, 1897.
Feibleman, J. K. *Aesthetics.* New York: Buell, Sloan, and Pearce, 1949.
Ferguson, J. *An Historical Enquiry into the true principles of Beauty in Art, more especially with reference to Architecture.* London: Longman, Brown, Breen and Longman, 1849.
Ficinus, M. *Commentary on Plato's Symposium.* (1496) Jayne, S. R., tr. Columbia University Press, 1944. Reprint in part in *Philosophies of Art and Beauty,* Hofstadter, A., Kuhn, eds., New York: The Modern Library, 1964.
Flaccus, L. W. *The Spirit and Substance of Art.* New York: F. S. Grofts, 1926.
Francis de Sales, St. *Traité de l'amour de Dieu.* Lyon: P. Rigaud, 1616. *On the Love of God.* Ryan, J. K., tr. Garden City, N. Y.: Doubleday, 1963.
Freud, S. *A General Introduction to Psycho-Analysis.* Riviere, J., tr. Garden City, N. Y.: Garden City Publishing Co., 1943.
Friedländer, M. J. *On Art and Connoisseurship.* Boston: Beacon Press, 1960.

Fry, R. *Transformations*. (1926) New York: Doubleday, Anchor, 1956.
———. *Vision and Design*. New York: Brentano, 1925.
Fuseli. "On Design"; in *Lectures on Painting by the Royal Academicians, Barry, Opic and Fuseli*. Warnum, R. N., ed. London: H. G. Bohn, 1848.
Gerard, A. *An Essay on Taste*. (1759) Third edition. Edinburgh: Bell, W. Creech, 1780. A facsimile reproduction. Hipple, Jr. W. J., ed. Gainesville, Florida: Facsimiles Scholars, 1963.
Ghiselin, B., ed. *The Creative Process*. New York: The New American Library, 1964.
Gietmann, G. "Aesthetics"; in *Catholic Encyclopedia* (New York: The Gilmary Society, 1913) I, 174–76.
Gilbert, K. E. "Aesthetics, Historical Survey," in *Dictionary of World Literature*, Shipley, J. T., ed. (Paterson, N. J.: Littlefield and Adams, 1960) 4–7.
Gilbert, K. E., Kuhn, H. *A History of Esthetics*. London: Thomas and Hudson, 1956.
Gill, E. *Beauty Looks After Herself*. New York: Sheed and Ward, 1933.
Gilpin, Wm. *Three Essayss On Picturesque Beauty; On Picturesque Travel; and On Sketching Landscape*. (1792) Third edition. London: Cadell, Davies, 1808.
Gilson, E. *The Arts of the Beautiful*. New York: C. Scribner's Sons, 1965.
———. *Painting and Reality*. Cleveland–New York: The World Publishing Co., 1959.
Gioberti, V. *"Del buono e del bello."* (1857) *Essay on the Beautiful*. Thomas, E., ed. London: Simpkin, 1860.
Goethe, J. W. *Letters from Goethe*. Herzfeld, M., Sym, C. J., trs. Edinburgh: The University Press, 1957.
Gotshalk, D. W. *Art and Social Order*. (1947) Second edition. New York: Dover, 1962.
———. "Aesthetics, Perception Theory," in *Dictionary of World Literature*, Shipley, J. T., ed. (Paterson, N. J.: Littlefield, Adams, 1960) 8.
Grabmann, M. "Des Ulrich Engelberti von Strassburg, O. Pr. (+ 1277) Abhandlung De pulchro"; in *Sitzungsberichte der Bayerischen Akademie der Wissenschaften*, Philosophisch–philologische und historische Klasse, Jahrgang 1925, 5. Abhandlung. München: Verlag der Bayerischen Akademie der Wissenschaften, 1926.
Gracian, B. *Agudeza y arte de ingenio*. Madrid: V. J. Lastanosa, 1642.
Grandclaude, E. *Metaphysica specialis*. Fourth edition. Paris: Lethielleux, 1873.
Gredt, J. *Metaphysica*. Second edition. Freiburg in Breisgau: Herder, 1912.
Greene, T. M. *The Arts and the Art of Criticism*. Princeton: The University Press, 1940.
Gregory, St., Nazianzen, *Orationes*, I-XXVI; in Migne, *PG* 35, 986–1044.
Grenier, H. *Metaphysics (Thomistic Philosophy, III)*. O'Hanley, P. E., tr. Charlottetown, Canada: St. Dunstan's University, 1950.
Griggs, E. H. *The Philosophy of Art*. New York: B. W. Huebeck, 1913.
Groos, K. *Der ästhetische Genuss*. Giessen: J. Ricker, 1902.
Guyau, J. M. *Les Problèmes de l'Esthétique Contemporaine*. Paris: F. Alcan, 1884.

Hartmann, E. von. *Die deutsche Aesthetik seit Kant*, I: *Erster historisch-kritischer Teil*. Leipzig: W. Friedrich, 1886.
———. *Die deutsche Aesthetik seit Kant*, II: *Die Philosophie des Schönen*. Leipzig: H. Haacke, 1890.
Hartmann, N. *Aesthetik*. Berlin: W. de Gruyter, 1953.
Hay, D. R. *First Principles of Symmetrical Beauty*. Edinburgh, Blackwoods, 1846.
Haydon, B. W. *Lectures on Painting and Design*. London: Longmann, Brown, Green, and Longmans, 1846.
Hazlitt, W. "On Criticism"; in *The Complete Works of William Hazlitt*, VIII. Howe, P. P., ed., London: J. M. Dent, 1931.
———. "On Taste" (1819); in *Sketches and Essays,* London: H. Frowde; Oxford University Press, 1836.
Hegel, G. W. F. *Vorlesungen über die Äesthetik*. (1835) *Sämtliche Werke*. Jubiläumsausgabe, XII. Stuttgart: F. Frommans, 1927.
Hemsterhuis, F. "Alexis"; in *Philosophische Schriften*. (1782), Hilss, J., ed., Karlsruhe and Leipzig: Dreililien Verlag, 1912.
Herbart, J. F. *Schriften zur Einleitung in die Philosophie* (1813); in *Sämtliche Werke*, I., Hartenstein, G., ed., Leipzig: L. Voss, 1850.
Herder, J. G. *Kritische Wälder*; in *Sämtliche Werke*, IV, Hildesheim: G. Olms, 1967.
Hermann, C. *Die Ästhetik in ihrer Geschichte und als wissenschaftliches System*. Leipzig: F. Fleischer, 1875.
Heyl, B. C. *New Bearings in Esthetics and Art Criticism*. Yale University Press, 1943.
Hickey, J. S. *Theodicaea et Ethica*. Eighth edition. Dublin: M. H. Gill and Sons, 1955.
Hilary of Poitiers, St. *De Trinitate*; in Migne, *PL* 10, 9-472.
Hipple, W. J., Jr. *The Beautiful, the Sublime and the Picturesque in Eighteenth-Century British Aesthetic Theory*. Carbondale: Southern Illinois University Press, 1957.
Hirn, Y. *The Origin of Art*. New York: Macmillan, 1900.
Hobbes, Th. *De homine (Opera philosophica*, II) (1658).
———. Leviathan (1659).
Hofmannsthal, H. *A Working Friendship, The Correspondence between Richard Strauss and Hugo von Hofmannstahl*. Hammelmann, H. and Osers, E., trs. New York: Random House, 1961.
Hogarth, Wm. *Analysis of Beauty*. (1753) Burke, J., ed. Oxford: Clarendon Press, 1955.
Holmes-Forbes, A. W. *The Science of Beauty, An Analytical Inquiry into the Laws of Aesthetics,* London: Trübner, 1881.
Hopkins, G. M. *Further Letters of G. M. Hopkins, Including His Correspondence with Coventry Patmore*. Abbott, C. C., ed. London: Oxford University Press, 1938.
Horatius, F., Q. *Ars Poetica*.
———. *Satirae*.
Hospers, J. "Problems of Aesthetics"; in *The Encyclopedia of Philosophy*, Edwards, P., ed. (New York: Macmillan, 1967) I, 35-56.

Howard, H. *A Course of Lectures on Painting.* London: H. G. Bohn, 1848.
Hugh of St. Victor, *Didascalicon*; in Migne, *PL* 176, 739–838.
———. *Expositio in Hierarchiam coelestem S. Dionysii*; in Migne, *PL* 175, 923–1154.
Hugon, E. *Metaphysica.* Paris: Lethielleux, 1928.
Hume, D. *A Treatise of Human Nature.* (1739) 2 vols. Green, T. H., and Grose, T. H., eds. London–New York: Longmans, Green, 1898.
———. "Of the Standard of Taste" (1757); in *Essays, Moral, Political, and Literary,* Green and Grose, eds., London: Logmans, Green, 1898.
Hungerland, I. C. Review article on Mueller, G. E., *The World as Spectacle*; in *The Journal of Aesthetics and Art Criticism,* IV, 4, (June 1946) 251.
Hutcheson, F. *Enquiry into the Original of Our Ideas of Beauty and Virtue.* (1725) Fifth edition. London: Ware, Knapton, Longman, 1753.
Iamblichus. *De vita Pythagorica liber.* Kiessling, T., ed. Leipzig: W. Vogel, 1815–16.
Jarrett, J. L. *The Quest for Beauty.* Englewood Cliffs, N. J.: Prentice-Hall, 1957.
Jean Paul (Richter, F.). *Vorschule der Aesthetik.* Hamburg: F. Perthes, 1804.
Jeffrey, Lord F. "Beauty"; in *Encyclopedia Britannica* (1824), reprinted in *Contributions to the Edinburgh Review,* London: Longman, Brown, Green, and Longmans, 1855.
Jerome, St. (Hieronymus), *In Osee Commentariorum libri tres*; in Migne, *PL* 25, 815–946.
Jessop, T. E. "The Definition of Beauty," *Proceedings of the Aristotelian Society,* XXXIII (1932/33). Reprinted in *Art and Philosophy,* Kennick, W. E., ed., New York: St. Martin's Press, 1965, pp. 524–33.
Joad, C. E. M. *Guide to Philosophy.* New York: Dover, 1936.
———. "The Objectivity of Beauty"; in *Matter, Life and Value,* London: Oxford University Press, 1929. Reprinted in *The Problems of Aesthetics,* Vivas and Krieger, eds., New York: Holt, Rinehart, and Winston, 1962.
John Cotton (Joannes Cottonis). *De musica*; in Migne, *PL* 150, 1391–1430.
John of St. Thomas. *Naturalis philosophia (Cursus Philosophicus Thomisticus,* III). Second edition. Taurini: Marietti, 1948.
Johnson, Dr. S. *A Dictionary of the English Language.* 2 vols. London: J. and P. Knapton, 1755. Reprinted, New York: AMS Press, 1967.
Jouffroy, Th. *Cours d'Esthétique.* Damiron, ed. Paris: Librairie de L. Hachette, 1843.
Joyce, J. *A Portrait of the Artist As A Young Man.* (1916) *The Portable James Joyce.* Levin, H., ed. New York: The Viking Press, 1947.
———. *Ulysses.* New York: Random House, 1946.
Jungmann, J. *Aesthetik.* Freiburg in Breisgau: Herder, 1884.
Kames, Lord (Home, H.). *Elements of Criticism.* (1761) Boyd, R., ed. New York: A. S. Barnes, 1883.
Kant, I. *Critique of Pure Reason.* Smith, N. K., tr. London: Macmillan, 1963.
———. *Critique of Judgment.* Bernard, J. H., tr. Second edition. London: Macmillan, 1914.
———. *Observations on the Feeling of the Beautiful and Sublime.* (1764) Goldthwait, J. T., tr. Berkeley: University of California Press, 1960.

Kennick, W. E. "Does Traditional Aesthetics Rest On a Mistake?", *Mind*, 67 (July 1958) 317–334.
———, ed. *Art and Philosophy*. New York: St. Martin's Press, 1965.
Kirchmann, J. H. von. *Aesthetik auf realistischer Grundlage*. Berlin: J. Springer, 1868.
Kirk, G. S. and Raven, J. E. *The Presocratic Philosophers*. Cambridge University Press, 1963.
Klubertanz, G. P. *Introduction to the Philosophy of Being*. New York: Appleton, Century, Crofts, 1955.
Knight, R. P. *An Analytical Enquiry into the Principles of Taste*. (1805) Fourth edition. London: T. Payne and J. White, 1808.
Knight, Wm. *The Philosophy of the Beautiful*, I: *Its History*. London: J. Murray, 1968.
Koestenbaum, P. *Philosophy: A General Introduction*. New York: American Book Company, 1968.
König, J. U. *Untersuchung von dem guten Geschmack in der Dicht-und Redekunst*. Leipzig, 1727.
Köstlin, K. *Aesthetik*. Tübingen: H. Laupp, 1869.
Koren, H. J. *An Introduction to the Science of Metaphysics*. St. Louis: B. Herder, 1955.
Kovach, F. J. *Die Aesthetik des Thomas von Aquin, eine genetische und systematische Analyse*. Berlin: W. de Gruyter, 1961.
———. "Beauty as a Transcendental," in *New Catholic Encyclopedia* (New York: McGraw-Hill, 1967) II, 205–207.
———. "Divine and Human Beauty in Duns Scotus' Philosophy and Theology," in *Deus et Homo ad mentem I. Duns Scoti* (Romae: Societas Internationalis Scotistica, 1972) 445–59.
———. "The Empirical Foundations of Thomas Aquinas' Philosophy of Beauty," *Southwestern Journal of Philosophy*, II/3 (Winter 1971) 93–102.
———. "Esthetic Disinterestedness in Thomas Aquinas," in *Actes du Cinquième Congrès International d'Esthétique, Amsterdam 1964*. Aler, J., ed. (Paris: Mouton, 1968) 768–73.
———. "The Question of the Authorship of the *Opusculum de pulchro*," in *Archiv für Geschichte der Philosophie*, Wilpert, P. and Morrow, G., eds. 44/3 (Berlin: W. de Gruyter, 1962) 245–77.
———. "The Transcendentality of Beauty in Thomas Aquinas," in *Die Metaphysik im Mittelalter* (*Miscellanea Mediaevalia*, II), Wilpert, P., ed. (Berlin: W. de Gruyter, 1963) 386–92.
Krause, K. C. F. *Abriss der Aesthetik oder der Philosophie des Schönen und der schönen Kunst*. Leutbecher, J., ed. Göttingen: Dietrich, 1837.
———. *Vorlesungen über Aesthetik, oder über die Philosophie des Schönen und der schönen Kunst*. Hohlfeld, P., and Wünsche, A., eds. Leipzig: O. Schulze, 1882.
Kreyche, R. J. *First Philosophy*. New York: Holt, Rinehart, Winston, 1964.
Krieger, M., ed.—*see*: Vivas, E.
Lachelier, J. E. N. *Du fondement de l'induction* (1872); in *Oeuvres*, 2 vols., Paris:

F. Alcan, 1933. *The Philosophy of Jules Lachelier.* Ballard, E. G., tr. The Hague: M. Nijhoff, 1960.
Lange, K. *Das Wesen der Kunst,* II. Berlin: G. Grote, 1901.
Langer, S. K. *Feeling and Form.* New York: C. Scribner's Sons, 1953.
———. *Philosophy in a New Key.* New York: The New American Library, 1962.
———. *Problems of Art.* New York: C. Scribner's Sons, 1957.
Langfeld, H. S. *The Aesthetic Attitude.* New York: Harcourt, Brace, 1920.
Lechner, R. *The Aesthetic Experience.* Chicago: H. Regnery, 1953.
Lee, H. N. *Perception and Aesthetic Value.* New York: Prentice-Hall, 1938.
Lee, V., Anstruther-Thompson, C. *Beauty and Ugliness and Other Studies in Psychological Aesthetics.* New York and London: J. Lane, 1912.
Lehmann, A. G. *The Symbolist Aesthetic in France 1885–1895.* Oxford: B. Blackwell, 1950.
Leibniz, G. W. *Opera mathematica;* in *Opera omnia,* Dutens, L., ed., Geneva: Fratres de Tournes, 1768.
Lemcke, C. *Populäre Ästhetik.* (1864) Fifth edition. Leipzig: E. A. Seemann, 1879.
Lepore, G. *Lectiones Aesthetices seu philosophia puchri et artium.* Viterbii: Agnesotti, 1905.
Leslie, C. and Taylor, T. *Life and Times of Sir Joshua Reynolds.* London: J. Murray, 1865.
Lessing, G. E. *Laokoon.* (1766) McCormick, E. A., tr. Indianapolis: Bobbs-Merrill, 1962.
Lévêque, C. *La Science du Beau, étudiée dans ses principes, dans ses applications et dans son histoire.* Paris: A. Durand, 1861.
Lewis, C. I. *An Analysis of Knowledge and Valuation.* La Salle, Illinois: Open Court, 1946.
Liberatore, M. *Logica et metaphysica generalis.* (1840) Fifth edition. Naples: F. Giannini, 1900.
Lipman, M. *What Happens in Art?* New York: Appleton, Century, Crofts, 1967.
Lipps, Th. *Ästhetik: Psychologie des Schönen und der Kunst.* Hamburg-Leipzig: L. Voss, 1903.
Little, A. *The Nature of Art.* London: Longmans, Green, 1946.
Locke, J. *An Essay Concerning Human Understanding.* (1690)
Longinus (?). *On the Sublime; see:* Demetrius.
Mackenzie, G. S. *Essay on some subjects connected with Taste.* Edinburgh: Oliphant, Waugh and Innes, 1817.
Macrobius, A. T. *Commentary on the Dream of Scipio.* Stahl, Wm. H., tr. New York: Columbia University Press, 1952.
Macvicar, J. G. *On the Beautiful, the Picturesque, the Sublime.* London: Scott, Webster, and Geary, 1837.
Maria, M. de. *Philosophia Peripatetica-Scholastica,* I. Third edition. Rome: P. Cuggiani, 1904.
Maritain, J. *Art and Scholasticism and The Frontiers of Poetry.* Evans, J. E., tr. New York: C. Scribner's Sons, 1962.
———. *Creative Intuition in Art and Poetry.* Cleveland–New York: The World Publishing Company, 1961.

Marmontel, J. F. "Beau"; in *Elements de Litterature*, I (1807), *Oeuvres completes*, XII, Paris: Verdier, 1818.
Marsden, Wm. *The History of Sumatra*. (1783) Reprint of the third edition. Kuala Lumpur–New York: Oxford University Press, 1966.
Marshall, H. R. *Aesthetic Principles*. New York: Macmillan, 1895.
———. *The Beautiful*. London: Macmillan, 1924.
———. *Pain, Pleasure, and Aesthetics*. London–New York: Macmillan, 1894.
McCosh, J. *The Emotions*. New York: C. Scribner's Sons, 1880.
———. *Psychology, The Motive Powers*. New York: C. Scribner's Sons, 1887.
Mead, H. *Introduction to Aesthetics*. New York: The Ronald Press Co., 1952.
Mehlis, G. "The Aesthetic Problem of Distance," *Logos*, VI (1916–17) 173–84. Reprinted in *Reflections on Art*, Langer, S. K., ed., New York: Oxford University Press, 1961.
Meier, G. F. *Anfangsgründe aller schönen Wissenschaften*. Halle im Magdeburgischen: C. H. Hemmerde, 1748.
Mendelssohn, M. *Betrachtungen über die Quellen der schönen Wissenschaften und Kunst*. Leipzig, 1757. Later entitled, *Über die Hauptgrundsätze der Künste und Wissenschaften*. Erlangen: Palm, 1777.
———. *Morgenstunden oder Vorlesungen über das Daseyn Gottes*. Berlin: Voss, 1786. Revised edition, Frankfurt und Leipzig, 1790.
Menichini, J. and M. "Del vero, del buono e del bello secondo san Tommaso"; in the Neopolitan journal *La Scienza e la fede*, CX (1878–79) 110–449.
Mercier, D. F. F. Cardinal. *A Manual of Modern Scholastic Philosophy*, Parker, T. L., and Parker, S. A., trs. St Louis: Herder, 1932.
Michelangelo. "To Cavalieri" (1536–42); in Blunt, Sir A., *Artistic Theory in Italy 1450–1600* (Oxford: Clarendon, 1962) 69.
———. *I, Michelangelo, Sculptor*. Stone, I. and J., trs. New York: The New American Library, 1964.
Mill, J. S. *A System of Logic, Ratiocinative and Inductive* II. (1843) Fifth edition. London: Parker, Son, and Bourn, 1868.
Mirandola—*see*: Pico della Mirandola.
Montesquieu, Baron de. "On Taste" (1755); in *Diderot, d'Alembert, and Others, Encyclopedia*. Hoyt-Cassierer, trs. Indianapolis: Bobbs-Merrill, 1965.
Moore, G. E. *Principia Ethica*. (1903) Cambridge: Harvard University Press, 1962.
Moore, J. S. "Beauty as Harmony," *The Journal of Aesthetics and Art Criticism*, II, 1 (Winter 1962/63) 40–50.
Morris, B. *The Aesthetic Process*. Evanston: Northwestern University Press, 1943.
Mozart, W. A. *The Letters of Mozart and His Family*. 2 vols. E. Anderson, tr. London: Macmillan, 1938.
Mueller, G. E. "Style," *The Journal of Aesthetics and Art Criticism*. I, 2/3 (Fall 1941) 105–122.
———. *The World as Spectacle*. New York: Philosophical Library, 1944.
Müller-Freienfels, R. *Allgemeine Grundlegung und Psychologie des Kunstgeniessens (Psychologie der Kunst*, I). (1912) Second edition. Leipzig-Berlin: R. G. Teubner, 1923.

Munro, Th. *Toward Science in Aesthetics*. Indianapolis: The Bobbs and Merrill Co., 1956.
Münsterberg, H. *The Principles of Art Education*. New York: Prang, 1905.
Murray, J. C., *A Handbook of Psychology*. (1885) Second edition. Boston: De Wolfe, Fiske, 1890.
Nahm, M. C. *Aesthetic Experience and Its Presuppositions*. New York: Harper and Brothers, 1946.
———. *The Artist as Creator*. Baltimore: The Johns Hopkins Press, 1956.
Nef, W. *Die Aesthetik als Wissenschaft der anschaulichen Erkenntnis*. Leipzig: H. Haacke, 1898.
Newman, J. H., Cardinal *The Idea of a University*. (1852) Garden City, N.Y.: Doubleday, 1959.
Newton, E. *The Meaning of Beauty*. London: Longmans, Green, 1959. Penguin Books, 1962.
Nicole, P. *Traité de la Vraye et de la Fausse Beauté*. (1698) *An Essay on True and Apparent Beauty*. Cunningham, J. F., tr. The Augustan Reprint Society, No. 24. Los Angeles: University of California Press, 1950.
Noyes, C. *The Gate of Appreciation*. Boston, N. Y.: Houghton Mifflin, 1907.
O'Donnell, J. R., ed. "*Tractatus Magistri Guillelmi Alverniensis De bono et malo*"; in *Mediaeval Studies*, VIII (Toronto: Pontifical Institute of Mediaeval Studies, 1946) 245–99.
Ogden, C. K., Richards, I. A., *The Meaning of Meaning*. (1923) Tenth edition. New York: Harcourt, Brace, 1952. *See also*: Richards, I. A.
Ogden, R. M. *The Psychology of Art*. New York: C. Scribner's Sons, 1938.
Olscamp, P. J. "Some Remarks about the Nature of Aesthetic Perception and Appreciation," *The Journal of Aesthetics and Art Criticism*, XXIV/2 (Winter 1965) 251–58.
Opzoomer, C. W. *Het Wezen der Kennis, een Leesboek der Logika*. Amsterdam: J. H. Gebhard, 1867.
Origen. *Libellus de oratione*; in Migne, *PG* 17, 415–563.
Osborn, H. *Aesthetics and Criticism*. New York: The Philosophical Library, 1955.
———. *Theory of Beauty*. London: Routledge and Kegan Paul, 1952.
Paccioli, Luca. *De divina proportione*. Venice: per Paganinum de Brixia, 1509.
Pallavicino, P. S., Cardinal *Del bene*, Libri IV. Rome, 1644.
Palmieri, D. *Logica et Ontologia*. Rome: Cuggiani, Santini, 1874.
Parker, D. H. *The Principles of Aesthetics*. Boston–New York: Silver, Burdett and Company, 1920. Second edition, New York: Appleton, Century, Crofts, 1946.
———. "The Analysis of Art" (1924); reprinted in Rader, M., ed., *A Modern Book of Esthetics*, revised edition, New York: H. Holt, 1952.
Pellegrini, M. *Delle Acutezze, che altrimenti spiriti, vivezze, e concetti si appellano trattato*. Second edition. Genova and Bologna: C. Ferroni, 1639.
Pepper, S. C. *The Basis of Criticism in the Arts*. (1945) Second edition. Harvard University Press, 1946.
———. *Principles of Art Appreciation*. New York: Harcourt, Brace, 1949.
Perry, R. B. *General Theory of Value*. New York: Longmans, Green, 1926.
Pesch, T. *Ontologia*. Second edition. Freiburg in Breisgau: B. Herder, 1919.

Petavius, D. *De Deo Deique proprietatibus* (*Dogmata theologica*, I.). (1700) Editio nova. Fournialis, J. B., ed. Paris: L. Vivès, 1865.
Petrus Johannis Olivi (d. 1298). *Quaestiones in II. librum Sententiarum.* Quaracchi: Collegium S. Bonaventurae, 1924.
Philip the Chancellor (d. 1236). *Summa de bono.* Padoue Antonienne MS. 156. H. Pouillon, "Le premier Traité des Propriétés transcendentales, La 'Summa de bono' du Chancelier Philippe," *Revue néoscolastique de Philosophie*, XLII (1939) 40–77.
Philo of Alexandria. *Works.* The Loeb Classical Library, 12 vols. New York: G. P. Putnam's Sons, 1929–62.
Pico della Mirandola. *Heptaplus.* (1489) Miller, P. J. W., ed. Indianapolis: The Bobbs-Merrill Co., 1965.
Piero della Francesca. *De prospectiva pingendi.* (c. 1480) Fasola, G. N., ed. Firenze: Vallecchi, 1942. Selections in Potter, E., ed., *Painters on Painting* (New York: Grosset and Dunlap, 1963) 16–19.
Platner, E. *Neue Anthropologie für Ärzte und Weltweise.* Leipzig: S. L. Crusius, 1790.
———. *Vorlesungen über Aesthetik.* Engel, M. E., ed. Zittan und Leipzig: O. M. Nauwerck, 1836.
Plato. *Collected Dialogues*, Hamilton, E., Cairns, H., eds. Bollingen Series LXXI. New York: Pantheon Books, 1961.
Plinius, S. C. *Historia naturalis.* 10 vols. Rackham, H., tr. Cambridge: Harvard University Press, 1938–63.
Plotinus. *The Enneades.* Mackenna, S., tr. Second edition. London: Faber and Faber, 1956.
Porphyrius, P. O. *Vita Pythagorae* (1630); in *Opuscula selecta*, Bibliotheca Scriptorum Graecorum et Romanorum Teubneriana. (Lipsiae, 1886.) Reprint, Hildesheim: G. Olms, 1963.
Potter, E. *Painters on Painting.* New York: Grosset and Dunlap, 1963.
———. *Quaestionum Homericarum ad Iliadem pertinentium reliquiae.* Schrader, H. ed. 2 fasc. Leipzig: Teubner, 1882.
Pouillon, H. "La Beauté, propriété transcendentale chez les Scolastiques (1220–1270)"; in *Archives d'Histoire doctrinale et litteraire du Moyen Age*, XV (1946) 263–327.
———. "Le premier Traité . . ."; see: Philip the Chancellor.
Poussin, N. *Mesures de la célèbre statue d'Antinous suivies de quelques observations sur la peinture.* (1672) Paris: Perlet, 1803. Selections in Potter, E., *ed. cit.* pp. 69–70.
Prall, D. W. *Aesthetic Analysis.* New York: T. Y. Crowell, 1936. New York: Apollo Editions, 1967.
———. *Aesthetic Judgment.* New York: T. Y. Crowell, 1967.
Pratt, C. C. "The Stability of Aesthetic Judgments," *The Journal of Aesthetics and Art Criticism* XV/1 (September 1956) 1–11.
Price, R. *Review of the Principal Questions of Morals.* (1757) Raphael, D. D., ed. Oxford: Clarendon Press, 1948.

Price, U. *A Dialogue on the Distinct Characters of the Picturesque and the Beautiful.* London: Hereford, 1801.

———. *An Essay on the Picturesque, as Compared with the Sublime and the Beautiful.* London: Hereford, 1794. London: J. Mauman, 1810.

Proclus. *Commentarium in Platonis Alcibiadem priorem*, in Cousin, V., ed. *Procli Opera inedita.* Paris: A. Durand, 1864. O'Neill, Wm., tr. *Alcibiades I, A Translation and Commentary.* The Hague: M. Nijhoff, 1965.

———. *De malorum subsistentia.* Moerbecke, Wm. tr. Cousin, V. ed. (as above). Reprinted in *S. Thomas Aquinatis in librum B. Dionysii De divinis nominibus expositio.* Pera, C., ed. Taurini: Marietti, 1950.

Puffer, E. D. *The Psychology of Beauty.* Boston: Houghton Mifflin, 1906.

Pyrrhon of Elis. In Diogenes Laertius, IX, ii (New York: G. P. Putnam, 1925) II, 474–518.

Pythagoras. Diogenes Laertius, VIII, 1; Loeb-edition II, 320–66.

Quintilian, M. F. *Institutio Oratoria.* English tr. by Watson, J. S. 2 vols. London: G. Bell and Sons, 1891.

Raeymaeker, L. de. *Metaphysica generalis*, I. Louvain: E. Warny, 1935.

Ram, F. "Beauty in the eyes of an evolutionist," *The Journal of Science* (London: Horse-Shoe Court, Ludgake Hill, February and March, 1882) 76–81.

Ramsay, G. *Analysis and Theory of the Emotions, with Dissertations on Beauty, Sublimity, and the Ludicrous.* London: Longman, 1848.

Raymond, G. L. *Art in Theory.* New York: G. P. Putnam's Sons, 1909.

Read, H. *The Meaning of Art.* Baltimore, Md.: Penguin Books, 1963.

Reid, L. A. *A Study in Aesthetics.* London: George Allen, and Unwin, 1931.

Reid, Th. *Essays on the Intellectual Powers of Man.* (1785) *Works.* Hamilton, Sir Wm., ed. 2 vols. Sixth edition. (Edinburgh: Maclachlan and Stewart, 1863) I, 213–508.

———. *An Inquiry into the Human Mind on the Principles of Common Sense.* (1764) Same edition, I, 93–211.

———. "Of Taste"; in *Essays on the Intellectual Powers of Man*, Essay VIII (same edition I, 490–508), with chapter IV, "Of Beauty," *ibid.* pp. 498–508.

Remer, V. *Ontologia.* (1895) Ninth edition. Rome: Gregorian University Press, 1947.

Repton, H. *Sketches and Hints on Landscape Gardening.* (1795) London: H. Bohn, 1849.

Reynolds, Sir J. *Discourses on Art.* (1778) New York: Crowell-Collier, 1961.

———. Essay on the true idea of beauty; in *The Idler*, No. 82, Nov. 10, 1759. *The British Classics,* XXIV. (London: W. Suttaby, 1810) 110–14.

———. *Letters.* Hilles, F. W., ed. Cambridge: The University Press, 1929.

Richards, I. A., *Principles of Literary Criticism.* New York: Harcourt, Bruce, 1925.

———, and Ogden, C. K.: *see* Ogden, C. K.

———, Ogden, C. K. and Wood, J., *The Foundations of Aesthetics.* New York: Lear, 1925.

Rickaby, J. *General Metaphysics.* (1898) London: Longmans, Green, 1902.

Robert, G. *The Borzoi Book of Ballets.* New York: A. A. Knopf, 1949.

Robert Grosseteste. *Commentarius in Dionysii De divinis nominibus*, c. 4. Paris.

Mazarine MS. 787. See the "Textes inédits" appendix of Puillon, H., "La Beauté, propriété transcendentale..." (*see*: Pouillon, H.) pp. 319–22.
Roland of Cremona. *Summa theologica* (of c. 1230). Paris, Mazarine Ms. 795.
Rosenkranz, J. K. F. *Die Ästhetik des Hässlichen.* Königsberg: Gebrüder Bornträger, 1853.
Rosmini-Serbati, A. *Sistema filosofico.* (1853) Torino: Unione tipografico, 1886. English tr. by T. Davidson. London: Kegan Paul and C., 1882.
———. *Teosofia.* 2 vols. Torino: Marzorati, 1859.
Ross, W. D. *The Right and the Good.* Oxford: Clarendon Press, 1930.
Rother, A. *Beauty.* St. Louis: Herder, 1917.
Ruckstull, F. W. *Great Works of Art.* Garden City, N. Y.: Garden City Publishing Company, 1925.
Ruge, A. *Neue Vorschule der Aesthetik – Das Komische mit einem komischen Anhang.* Halle: Verlag der Buchhandlung des Waisenhauses, 1837.
Ruskin, J. *Modern Painters.* (1846) Third edition. New York: Merrill and Baker, n. d.
———. *The True and the Beautiful in Nature, Art, Morals, and Religion.* Selected by Tuthill, L. C. Second edition. New York: Merrill and Zatzen, 1886.
Samson, G. W. *Elements of Art Criticism.* Philadelphia: J. B. Lippincott, 1867.
Sanseverino, C. *Ontologia.* Naples: Officium Bibliothecae Catholicae, 1885.
Santayana, G. *The Sense of Beauty.* (1896) New York: Dover, 1955.
Sartre, J. P. "Francois Mauriac and Freedom"; in *Literary Essays*, New York: Philosophical Library, 1957.
Savonarola. *Prediche Raccolte* (1495). Mss. Bibliotheca Apostolica Vaticana, St. Barbara, BBB. Microfilm copy in the History of Science Collection, The University of Oklahoma Library, Norman, Oklahoma.
Schasler, M. *Kritische Geschichte der Aesthetik. Grundlegung für die Aesthetik als Philosophie des Schönen und der Kunst.* Berlin: Nicolai, 1872.
Schelling, F. W. *Philosophie der Kunst.* (1802–83) *Sämtliche Werke*, V. Stuttgart-Augsburg: J. G. Cotta, 1859.
———. *System des transcendentalen Idealismus.* (1800) Ed. cit. vol. III (1858) pp. 327–634.
Schiller, F. *On the Aesthetic Education of Man.* (1793–94) Snell, R., tr. New Haven: Yale University Press, 1954.
———. *Aesthetical and Philosophical Essays;* in *Complete Works*, VIII, New York: P. F. Collier and Son, 1902.
Schiller, J. "An Alternative to 'Aesthetic Disinterestedness," *The Journal of Aesthetics and Art Criticism*, XXII/3 (Spring 1964) 295–302.
Schlegel, F. *Geschichte der epischen Dichtkunst der Griechen (Studien des classischen Althertums*, I), (1798) *Sämtliche Werke*, III. Second edition. Wien: I. Klang, 1846.
———. *Vorlesungen über philosophische Kunstlehre.* Wünsche, A., ed. Leipzig: Dietrich, 1911.
Schleiermacher, F., *Aesthetik.* Odebrecht, R., ed. Berlin-Leipzig: W. de Gruyter, 1931.

———. *Vorlesungen über die Aesthetik*; in *Sämtliche Werke*, VII, Berlin: G. Reimer, 1842.
Schneider, E. *Aesthetic Motive.* New York: Macmillan, 1939.
Schoen, M. *The Enjoyment of the Arts.* New York: The Philosophical Library, 1944.
Schopenhauer, A. *The World as Will and Idea.* (1818) Haldane-Kemp, trs. Seventh edition. London: Kegan Paul, Trench, Trübner and Co., n.d.
Schulemann, G. *Die Lehre von der Transcendentalien in der scholastischen Philosophie.* Leipzig: F. Meiner, 1929.
Scott, W. B. *Half-Hour Lectures on the History and Practice of the Fine and Ornamental Arts.* (1861) Third edition. New York: Scribner, Welford, Armstrong, 1875.
Seneca, L. A. *Ad Aebutium Liberalem de beneficiis.*
———. *Dialogi morales de consolatione.*
———. *Epistulae morales ad Lucilium.*
Sextus Empiricus. *Adversus Mathematicos*; in *Opera*, vols. 2–4, Loeb-edition, London: Heinemann; Cambridge: Harvard University Press, 1961–69.
Shaftesbury, Lord. *Characteristics.* (1711) Robertson, J. M., ed. Indianapolis: The Bobbs-Merrill Co., 1964.
Shipley, J. T., ed. *Dictionary of World Literature.* Paterson, N. J.: Littlefield, Adams, 1960.
Siebeck, H. *Das Wesen der aesthetischen Anschauung, Psychologische Untersuchungen zur Theorie des Schönen und der Kunst.* Berlin: F. Dummler, 1875.
Simplicius of Cilicia. *Commentarii in octo Aristotelis Physicae libros.* (1551) *Commentaria in Aristotelem Graeca*, vols. 9–10, Diels, H., ed. Berolini: G. Reimer, 1882, 1895.
Small, H. A. *Form and Function, Remarks on Art by Horatio Greenough.* Berkeley: University of California Press, 1947.
Socrates—*see* Xenophon.
Solger, K. W. F., *Erwin. Vier Gespräche über das Schöne und die Kunst.* Berlin: Realschulbuchhandlang, 1815.
———. *Vorlesungen über Aesthetik.* Heyse, K. W. L., ed. Leipzig: F. A. Brockhaus, 1829.
Spencer, H. "Use and Beauty" (1852); in *Essays Scientific, Political and Speculative*, Library edition (New York: D. Appleton, 1892) 370–74.
Spinoza. *Ethics* (1677); in *Philosophy of Benedict de Spinoza*, Elwes, R. H. M., tr. New York: Tudor, 1934.
Stace, W. T. *The Meaning of Beauty.* London: G. Richards, H. Toulmin, 1929.
Steiss, A. J. "Outline of a Philosophy of Art," *The Thomist*, II (January 1940) 14–58.
Stewart, D. *Elements of the Philosophy of the Human Mind.* (1972) 2 vols. Albany: E. and E. Hosford, 1822.
———. *Philosophical Essays* (1810); in *Collected Works*, V. Edinburgh: Th. Constable; London: Hamilton, Adams, 1855.
Stöckl, A. *Lehrbuch der allgemeinen Metaphysik*, II. Eighth edition. Mainz: Kirchheim, 1912.

Stolnitz, J. *Aesthetics and Philosophy of Art Criticism*. Boston: Houghton Mifflin, 1960.

———. "On the Origins of 'Aesthetic Disinterestedness,'" *The Journal of Aesthetics and Art Criticism*, XX/2 (Winter 1961) 481–82.

———. "A Third Note on Eighteenth-Century 'Disinterestedness,'" *ibid*. XXII/6 (Fall 1963) 69–70.

———. "Some Stages in the History of an Idea," *Journal of the History of Ideas*, XXII/2 (April–June 1961) 481–82.

Strauss, R. *A Working Friendship, The Correspondence between Richard Strauss and Hugo von Hofmannsthal*. Hammelman and Osers, trs. New York: Random House, 1961.

Suarez, F. *Disputationes metaphysicae*. (1597) *Opera omnia*, vols. 25–26. Paris: Vivès, 1861.

Sullivan, D. J. *An Introduction to Philosophy*. Milwaukee: Bruce, 1957.

Sully, J., "Aesthetics"; in the eleventh edition of the *Encyclopedia Britannica* (1910) I, 277–89.

———. "On the Possibility of a Science of Aesthetics"; in *Sensation and Intuition, Studies in Psychology and Aesthetics*, London: H. S. King, 1874.

Sully-Proudhomme, R. T. *L'Epression dans le beaux arts, application de la psychologie à l'etude de l'artiste et des beaux-arts*. Paris: A. Lemerre, 1883.

Sulzer, J. G. *Allgemeine Theorie der schönen Künste*. Leipzig: Weidmann, 1792.

Sweeney, L. *A Metaphysic of Authentic Existentialism*. Englewood Cliffs, N. J.: Prentice Hall, 1965.

Taine, H. *Lectures on Art*. Durand, J. tr. New York: H. Holt, 1875.

Taparelli, L. d'Azeglio, "Delle ragioni del bello secondo la dottrina san Tommaso d' Aquino"; 19 articles in *La Civiltà Cattolica*, IV, 5–7, Naples, December 1859–September 1860.

Tatianus. *Address to the Greeks*; in Migne, *PG* 6, 803–88. English tr. by Ryland, J. E. *The Anti-Nicene Fathers*, II., New York: C. Scribner's Sons, 1926.

Taylor, T.—*see*: Leslie, C.

Tejera, V. *Art and Human Intelligence*. New York: Appleton, Century, Crofts, 1965.

Thomas Aquinas, St. *Opera omnia*. (The paragraph numbering, wherever it is used in the text references, is taken from the Marietti edition of his works.)

Thomas Gallus Vercellensis. *Explanatio in Dionysii De divinis nominibus*. (1242) Edited by Pez, in *Thesaurus anecdotorum novissimus, seu veterum monumentorum*, tom II, 1 (Augusta Vindelicorum et Graecii, 1721) col. 503–690.

Thomas of York. *Sapientiale* (of 1250–60). Florence, Bibl. Natl. Conv. sopp. A, 6, 437 and Vat. Lat. 4301. See Puillon, H., "La Beauté, propriété...," (see: Pouillon, H.) pp. 323–27.

Thomson, Wm. *An Enquiry into the elementary principles of Beauty, in the Works of Nature and Art*. London, 1798.

Todhunter, J. *The Theory of the Beautiful* (1872); in *Essays*, O'Grady, S., ed., London: E. Mathews, 1920.

Toletus, F. Cardinal *In Summam Theologiae S. Thomae Aquinatis Enarratio*, I. Paria, J., ed. Romae, Taurini, Parisiis, 1869.

Tolstoi, L. *What is Art?* (1898) Maude, A., tr. New York: Oxford University Press, 1962.
Tongiorgi, S. *Ontologia*. Brussels: H. Goemaere; Paris: Benziger, 1862.
Töpffer, R. *Réflexions et Menus-Propos d'un Peintre Genevois, ou Essai sur le Beau dans les art.* (1848) Second edition. Paris: Hachette, 1872.
Torossian, A. *A Guide to Aesthetics*. Stanford University Press, 1937.
Trahndorff, K. F. E. *Aesthetik oder Lehre von der Weltanschauung und Kunst*. Berlin: Maurer, 1827.
Tucker, A. *The Light of Nature*. (1768) Fifth edition. London: C. Daly, 1840.
Turburg, T. C. "The Concept of Beauty," in *Modern Sacred Art*, I. (January, 1938) 133–36.
Tyler, S. *Robert Burns as a Poet and as a Man*. New York: Baker and Scribner, 1848.
Ulrich Engelbert of Strasburg. "De pulchro"; *Summa de bono*, II, tract. 3, cap. 3. Grabman, M., "Des Ulrich Engelberti von Strassburg, O. Pr. (+ 1277) Abhandlung De pulchro," *Sitzungsberichte der Bayerischen Akademie der Wissenschaften, Philosophisch–philologische und historische Klasse*. Jahrgang 1925, 5. Abhandlung. München: Verlag der Bayerischen Akademie der Wissenschaften, 1926.
Urráburu, J. J. *Ontologia*. Vallisoleti: Cuesta, Lutetiae Parisiorum et Romae, 1891.
Vallet, Abbé C. P. *Metaphysica et ethica (Praelectiones philosophicae ad mentem S. Thomae Aquinatis,* II) Parisiis: A. Roger et F. Chernoviz, 1879. Second edition. Paris: Jouby et Roger, 1880.
Vico, G. B. *La scienza nuova e opere scelte*. (1721) Abbagnano, N., ed. Torino: Temporelli, 1966.
Vischer, F. T. *Aesthetik oder Wissenschaft des Schönen*. (1846–57) Zweite Ausgabe. München: Meyer und Jessen, 1922.
Vitruvius, M. F. P. *De architectura* (of 20–11 B.C.) English translation by Morgan, M. H. Cambridge: Harvard University Press, 1914.
Vivas, E., and Krieger, M., eds. *The Problems of Aesthetics*. New York: Holt, Rinehart, Winston, 1962.
Volkelt, J. *Grundlegung der Aesthetik (System der Aesthetik,* I). (1905) Zweite Ausgabe. München: C. H. Bech, 1927.
Waley, H. D. "Low Level Approaches to Aesthetic Problems," *The Hibbert Journal*, LIX (October 1960) 59–66.
Warton, J. Article in *The Adventurer*, No. 80, August 11, 1753. *The British Classics*, XVII (London: T. Sharpe, 1807) 66–71.
Watkin, E. I. *A Philosophy of Form*. (1938) Third edition. London: Sheed and Ward, 1950.
Weiss, P. *The World of Art*. Carbondale and Edwardsville: Southern University Press, 1961. Arcturus Books edition, 1966.
Weisse, C. H. *System der Aesthetik als Wissenschaft von der Idee der Schönheit*. Leipzig: E. H. F. Hartmann, 1830. *System der Aesthetik nach dem Collegienhefte letzter Hand*. Seydel, R., ed. Leipzig: Findel, 1872.
Weitz, M. *Philosophy of the Arts*. Cambridge: Harvard University Press, 1950.
Wiener, N. "Aesthetics," in *Encyclopedia Americana* (New York: Americana Corporation, 1966) I, 198–203.

BIBLIOGRAPHY

Wilde, O. *The Picture of Dorian Grey.* (1891) New York: The Modern Library, n. d.

William of Auvergne. *Tractatus de bono et malo* (of 1228). O'Donnell, J. R., ed. *Mediaeval Studies,* VIII (1946) 245-299.

Winckelmann, J. J. *Geschichte der Kunst des Altertums.* (1764) Zweite Ausgabe. Lessing, J., ed. Leipzig: Dürr, 1882.

Witelo. *Liber de intelligentiis* (of 1260). Baeumker, C., ed., *Witelo, ein Philosoph und Naturforscher des XIII. Jahrhunderts* (Münster: Aschendorffscher Verlag, 1908) 1-71.

———. *Perspectiva* (of 1260). Baeumker, *op. cit.*, pp. 127-79.

Wood, J.—*see*: Richards, I. A.

Wulf, M. M. de, *L'Oeuvre d'art et la beauté.* Louvain: Institute Superieur de Philosophie, 1920. English tr. by Udell, M. G. St. Louis: Herder, 1950.

Xenophon. *Memorabilia*; in *The Anabasis, or Expedition of Cyrus, and the Memorabilia of Socrates.* Watson, J. S., tr. New York: Harper and Brothers, 1855.

Zeising, A. *Aesthetische Forschungen.* Frankfurt am Main: Meidinger Sohn und Co., 1855.

Zeno of Citium. Diogenes Laertius, VII, 1. The Loeb Classical Library edition (London: Wm. Heinemann; New York: G. P. Putnam's Sons, 1925) II, 111-263.

Ziff, P. "The Task of Defining A Work of Art"; *The Philosophical Review,* LXII (January 1953) 58-78.

Zigliara, T. M. *Summa philosophica.* Lyon: De Briday, 1877.

Zimmermann, R. *Allgemeine Aesthetik.* 2 vols. Wien: Braumüller, 1858-65.

Index of Names

Adam, C.: 23
Addison, J.: 5, 15, 19, 21, 29, 108, 109, 226, 230, 231, 233, 274, 277, 286, 287
Alan of Lille: 285
Albert the Great, St.: 5, 13, 14, 17, 18, 28, 49, 85, 112, 157, 161, 163, 177, 209, 220, 238, 239, 240, 245, 252, 259, 282, 286
Alberti, L. B.: 13, 15, 161
Alcuin of York: 286
Aldrich, V. C.: 118
Aler, J.: 282
Alexander of Hales: 5, 18, 28, 160, 230, 238, 239, 240, 251, 269, 282, 285
Alexander, S.: 144, 145, 161, 256, 257, 275, 283
Algazel: 92
Alison, A.: 15, 17, 19, 120, 121, 172, 173, 232
Allen, G.: 16, 23, 148, 252, 270, 276, 277, 278, 280, 283, 287, 288, 289, 299, 300
Ambrose (Ambrosius), St.: 14
Ames, Van M.: 144
Anaxagoras: 12
Anderson, E.: 60
Anderson, J. M.: 233
André, (Père) Le P. Y.: 21, 145
Anselm of Canterbury, St.: 209, 245
Ansermet, E.: 133
Anstruther-Thomson, C.: 22, 148
Antisthenes: 12
Antigonos of Karystos: 13
Aquinas: *see* Thomas Aquinas, St.
Aristippus: 280
Aristophanes: 130
Aristotle: 5, 6, 7, 12, 13, 17, 18, 25, 27, 28, 49, 58, 84, 85, 108, 112, 115, 117, 130, 139, 163, 172, 201, 209, 220, 225, 229, 237, 238, 239, 240, 241, 244, 245, 251, 257, 277, 282, 283, 285, 292, 293, 300, 302, 303, 308, 315, 316
Aristoxenus: 5, 13
Ast, F. G. A.: 15, 160, 232, 233
Augustine, St.: 5, 7, 10, 13, 14, 17, 18, 28, 62, 75, 85, 106, 108, 109, 112, 113, 115, 116, 120, 128, 129, 139, 146, 160, 163, 175, 177, 207, 209, 218, 220, 225, 230, 240, 244, 245, 251, 269, 277, 278, 280, 282, 285, 286, 300, 301
Averroes: 238, 239
Avicenna: 209, 239, 240, 243, 245

Bach, J. S.: 88, 112

Bacon, F.: 167
Bacon, R.: 288
Baeumker, C.: 115
Baillie, J.: 231, 234
Bain, A.: 283, 288
Bakadur, J. C. W.: 244
Balbi, G.: 14
Baldwin, J. M.: 15
Barns, W.: 146
Bartók, Béla: 29, 107, 127, 130
Bascom, J.: 149
Basil, St. (Basilius): 14, 114, 207
Batteux, Abbé: 15
Baumgarten, A. C.: 5, 6, 7, 8, 9, 15, 17, 22, 23, 146, 147, 160, 252, 258, 273, 277, 278
Bayer, R.: 22
Beardsley, M. C.: 21, 23, 29, 83, 106, 142, 170, 173, 270, 316
Beattie, J.: 70
Beethoven, L. von: 59, 60, 86, 113, 124, 127, 131, 134, 189, 295, 296
Bell, Sir Charles: 143
Bell, Clive: 158, 306
Bellini, J.: 127
Berg, H.: 276, 277, 279
Bergman, I.: 86
Berkeley, G.: 79, 80, 92, 146, 159, 245
Berlioz, H.: 127
Berndtson, A.: 268, 269, 284
Bernstein, L.: 296
Biese, A.: 16
Bittle, C. N.: 138, 162
Bizet, G.: 127
Black, M.: 267
Blair, D.: 16
Blair, H.: 19, 226, 231, 232, 272
Blunt, Sir A.: 145
Boas, G.: 69, 72, 73
Boccaccio, G.: 15
Boethius, M. S.: 13, 62, 85, 238, 240, 245
Boileau, N.: 157, 258, 277
Bonaventure, St.: 5, 13, 14, 17, 28, 85, 109, 115, 160, 209, 238, 239, 242, 245, 251, 252, 267, 269, 277, 282, 286
Bosanquet, B.: 20, 21, 117, 130, 154, 256, 259, 261 f.
Bouhours, D.: 273
Bouterwek, F.: 21
Boyd, J. R.: 272

INDEX OF NAMES

Boyer, C.: 162
Bradley, A. C.: 153
Brahms, J.: 113, 121, 133, 196
Brandenstein, B. von: 164, 165, 174, 206, 245, 269, 276, 286, 287, 288, 300
Bratranek, F. T.: 16
Brennan, R. E.: 266
Bridge, R.: 134
Brown, G. B.: 160
Brown, T.: 108, 118, 119, 151
Bruyne, E. de: *see* De Bruyne, E.
Buffier, (Père) C.: 145
Bullough, E.: 124, 125, 268
Burke, E.: 18, 19, 105, 146, 164, 173, 206, 226, 231, 233, 252, 258, 281, 282, 286, 287, 316
Burton, R.: 111

Caffin, C. H.: 148
Cajetan, Cardinal (Thomas de Vio): 146
Callahan, L.: 53, 54, 99, 163, 169
Callas, M.: 113
Calliades: 110
Callistratus: 110
Calmetta, G.: 110
Calugero, G.: 22
Campanella, T.: 238
Carrière, M.: 16, 154, 160, 254
Carritt, E. F.: 23, 155
Caruso, E.: 60
Cassierer, T.: 280
Cassiodorus: 286
Cassirer, E.: 16
Castelvetro, L.: 15
Caufield, D.: 60
Cellini, B.: 116
Chapman, E.: 266, 270, 275, 287
Chopin, F.: 116, 127
Chrysippus: 13
Chrysostom, St. John: 13
Cicero, M. T.: 5, 7, 10, 13, 108, 118, 123, 139, 146, 161, 207, 218, 278, 282, 283
Clement of Alexandria, St.: 14
Cocteau, J.: 60
Coffey, P.: 162
Cohen, M.: 266f., 281
Cohn, J.: 143f.
Coleridge, S. T.: 60, 61, 160, 283
Collingwood, R. G.: 8, 280
Comte, A.: 15, 161
Condillac, E. B. de: 15
Conti, A.: 274
Cooper, C. W.: 144, 151 f.
Copland, A.: 60
Corneille, P.: 15
Cory, H. E.: 123
Coster, C. H. de: 162

Cotton, J.: *see* John Cotton (Joannes Cottonis)
Cousin, V.: 21, 251
Crane, L.: 141
Croce, B.: 5, 8, 23, 52, 53, 151, 254, 263, 272, 273, 274, 275, 276, 278, 287
Croesus: 130
Crousaz, J. P. de: 21, 163, 164, 277

Damjanovich, M.: 20
Darwin, C. R.: 276, 277, 279
D'Alembert, J.: 15, 16
D'Alverny, M. T.: 146
De Bruyne, E.: 54, 146, 286
Demény, J.: 107
De Maria, M.: 18, 162
Demetrius of Phaleron: 13, 286
De Quincey, A. C. Quatremère: 21, 163, 206, 245
Descartes, R.: 5, 7, 15, 52, 124, 209, 245, 252
Dessoir, M.: 16
Deutinger, M.: 154
Dewey, J.: 28, 87, 88, 151, 253, 258f., 267, 270, 271 f., 284, 292
De Wulf, M.: *see* Wulf, M. de
Dezza, P.: 161, 247
Dickie, G.: 266f.
Diderot, D.: 15, 159
Diels, H.: 84
Diez, M.: 16, 22, 23
Diodorus of Sicily: 10
Diogenes Laërtius: 12, 13, 17, 130, 280
Dionysius the Areopagite: 5, 13, 17, 26, 84, 139, 200, 239, 240, 241, 244, 251
Dionysius Ryckel, the Carthusian: 5, 14, 17, 28, 146, 207, 235, 238, 239
Dobell, S. T.: 163
Donat, J.: 315
Downes, O.: 134
Dryden, J.: 60
DuBos, (Abbé) J. B.: 15, 273
Ducasse, C. J.: 83, 94, 106, 135, 136, 147, 268, 296
Duns Scotus: 237, 238, 239, 242, 243, 244, 245
Dupeyrat, A.: 162
Dürer, A.: 15, 141
Duris of Samos: 13

Eberhard, J. A.: 15, 276, 277
Eidlitz, L.: 155
Emerson, R. W.: 144, 157, 245, 315
Empedocles: 85
Engel, G.: 15
Ennius: 123
Epictetus: 13, 112, 139, 159
Epicurus: 118
Erigena, Joh Scotus: 160, 282

Eschenburg, J. J.: 15
Esser, G.: 163
Ettori, C.: 278
Euripides: 59
Eustachius, Fr., O. F. M.: 14
Euthycrates: 110

Faulkner, R.: 148
Fearon, J.: 163
Fechner, G. T.: 16, 168, 169, 171, 173, 233, 234, 283
Feibleman, J. K.: 23, 161, 272, 274, 284
Ferguson, J.: 159
Ficino, Marsilio: *see* Marsilius Ficinus
Fiedler, K.: 15
Flaccus, L. W.: 105
Fokin, M.: 133
Forster, E. M.: 130 f.
Francis de Sales, St.: 280, 285, 286, 300
Freud, S.: 269, 280
Friedländer, M. J.: 148
Fry, R.: 158, 267, 268, 275, 283, 286, 300
Fuselli (Fuseli), H.: 160

Galli-Curci, A.: 113
Galton, F.: 16
Gautier, Th.: 133
Gerard, A.: 15, 19, 162, 167, 168, 169, 173, 230, 231, 274, 275
Gershwin, J.: 107
Ghiselin, B.: 60
Giddings, F. H.: 15
Gietmann, G.: 221
Gigli, B.: 113
Gilbert, K. E.: 21, 22, 282
Gill, E.: 245
Gilpin, Wm.: 19, 142, 173, 231
Gilson, E.: 23, 245, 268, 276, 277, 283, 285, 312, 315
Gioberti, V.: 155
Goethe, J. W.: 128, 143
Gorgias of Leontini: 92, 141
Gotshalk, D. W.: 147, 148, 271, 276, 296, 316
Grabmann, M.: 13, 14, 239
Gracian, B.: 272
Grandclaude, E.: 160
Gredt, J.: 161
Greene, T. M.: 161
Greenough, H.: 144
Gregory Nazianzen, St.: 14
Grenier, H.: 163, 243
Grieg, E.: 127
Griggs, E. H.: 119, 149
Groos, K.: 16, 22, 23, 269, 270, 275, 288, 289, 290, 299, 300, 301

Grosse, E.: 15
Grünewald, M.: 29
Guyau, J. M.: 15, 166, 286, 287

Hamilton, Sir Wm.: 19, 67, 68
Hammelmann, H.: 128
Händel, G. F.: 194
Hanslick, E.: 15
Harris, J.: 15
Hartmann, E. von: 15, 20, 154, 226, 227, 228, 229, 232, 233, 255
Hartmann, N.: 22
Hay, D. R.: 161, 162
Haydon, B. W.: 159, 160
Hazlitt, W.: 130, 161, 162
Hegel, G. W. F.: 5, 15, 16, 20, 21, 153, 154, 171, 226, 229, 232, 256, 257, 306
Heifetz, J.: 113
Heliodorus of Athens: 13
Helmholtz, H. L. F.: 16, 173
Hemsterhuis, F.: 147
Hennessy, E. B.: 54
Heraclitus: 5, 12, 84, 85, 112, 113, 239, 244
Herbart, J. F.: 16, 21, 158, 159, 278
Herder, J. G.: 15, 274, 277
Hermann, C.: 23
Herodotus: 6
Hesiod: 139
Heyl, B. C.: 107
Hickey, J. S.: 163
Hilary of Poitiers, St.: 14
Hill, G.: 148
Hippias: 145, 280
Hipple, Jr., W. J.: 68, 170, 231
Hirn, Y.: 269
Hirt, G: 16
Hobbes, Th.: 146, 252
Hofmannsthal, H. von: 128, 201
Hogarth, Wm.: 15, 164, 173
Holmes-Forbes, A. W.: 159, 206
Home, H.: *see* Kames, Lord
Homer: 68, 114, 130, 139
Hopkins, G. M.: 131, 132, 134
Horace (Quintus Horatius Flaccus): 13, 118, 126, 132
Hospers, J.: 22
Housman, A. E.: 60
Howard, H.: 159
Hoyt, N. S.: 280
Hugh of St. Victor: 245, 282, 286
Hugon, E.: 163, 164
Humboldt, W. von: 15, 21
Hume, D.: 15, 17, 57, 65, 66, 67, 68, 69, 75, 82, 89, 91, 92, 105, 113, 121, 126, 127, 128, 129, 130, 132, 160, 172, 252
Hungerland, I. C.: 145

INDEX OF NAMES

Hutcheson, F.: 15, 17, 123, 160, 226, 230, 231, 252, 272, 273, 274, 275, 278, 279, 281

Iamblichus: 12

Jacob (Iacobus) de Voragine, O. P.: 14
Jarrett, J. L.: 22, 23, 30, 54, 96, 97, 98, 99, 130, 152, 255, 256, 257, 271, 286, 287, 288, 296, 299, 301
Jean Paul (Richter, F.): 233
Jeffrey, Lord F.: 53, 76f., 82, 83, 91, 93, 94, 95, 96, 274
Jerome, St. (Hieronymus): 118, 131
Jessop, T. E.: 169
Joad, C. E. M.: 93, 106, 110
John Chrysostom, St.: *see* Chrysostom, St. John
John Cotton (Johannes Cottonis): 13, 130
John of La Rochelle: 5, 238, 239, 240, 269, 282
John of St. Thomas: 146, 160
Johnson, Dr. S.: 15, 231
Jouffroy, Th.: 21, 153, 283
Joyce, J.: 130, 131, 162
Jungmann, J.: 9, 10, 22, 23, 157, 252, 253, 268, 275, 276, 278, 279, 280, 281, 305f.

Kames, Lord (Henry Home): 15, 17, 19, 20, 54, 78, 80, 86, 108, 109, 114, 129, 152, 168, 226, 231, 232, 272, 281, 282
Kant, I.: 5, 6, 15, 17, 19, 52, 75, 78, 87, 88, 92, 108, 115, 157, 158, 171, 225, 232, 233, 252, 258, 276, 278, 281, 283, 284, 286, 292, 311
Karajan, H. von: 296
Karsavina, T.: 133
Kazan, E.: 86
Kemény, J.: 107
Kennick, W. E.: 169, 266
Kirchmann, J. H. von: 173, 232, 233
Kirk, G. S.: 5, 12
Klubertanz, G. P.: 247, 307
Knight, R. P.: 17, 20, 29, 120, 146, 147, 161, 162, 173, 231, 273, 274, 275, 276, 279, 281, 286, 287, 288
Knight, Wm.: 143, 159, 160, 162, 163, 164, 283
Knox, R.: 159, 160
Koestenbaum, P.: 23
König, J. U.: 273
Köstlin, K.: 173, 227, 232, 234
Koren, H. J.: 108, 109, 110
Kovach, F. J.: 17, 163, 172, 220, 241, 242, 244, 278, 282
Krause, K. C. F.: 21, 154, 161, 221–23, 226, 229, 230, 233, 234, 235
Kreyche, R. J.: 307
Krieger, M.: 93
Kuhn, H.: 282

Lachelier, J. E. N.: 157
Lalo, C.: 15, 16
Laminault, H.: 22
Lange, K.: 16, 283
Langer, S. K.: 16, 21, 22, 109, 125, 131, 158, 267, 269, 306
Langfeld, H. S.: 22, 96, 97, 98, 99, 270, 283, 296, 300
Lawrence, D. H.: 60
Lechner, R.: 23
Lee, H. N.: 20, 22, 23, 162, 206, 268, 280, 284f., 286, 287, 288, 300, 301 f.
Lee, V.: 22, 148
Lehmann, A. G.: 23
Leibniz, G. W.: 8, 15, 209, 245, 273
Lemcke, C.: 22, 117, 221, 224, 276, 277, 292
Leoncavallo, R.: 127
Lepore, G.: 10
Leslie, C.: 231
Lessing, G. E.: 15, 161, 253, 255
Lévêque, C.: 21, 163, 164
Lewis, C. I.: 98, 116
Liberatore, M.: 161
Lipman, M.: 275
Lipps, T.: 16, 22, 148, 252, 253
Liszt, F.: 121, 127
Little, A.: 160
Locke, J.: 53, 77f., 79, 80, 81, 90, 245
Lomazzo, G. P.: 15
Longinus: 13, 17, 18, 225, 251
Lotze, R. H.: 15, 16, 21, 154, 173
Lowell, A.: 60

Mackenzie, G. S.: 147
Macran, H. S.: 13
Macvicar, J. G.: 19, 162
Maimonides, Moses: 209, 245
Mair, B. Y.: 16
Manet, E.: 110
Maria, M. de: *see* De Maria, M.
Maritain, J.: 5, 75, 162, 245, 259, 262f., 280, 286
Marmontel, J. F.: 162, 206
Marsden, Wm.: 108
Marshall, H. R.: 22, 151, 284
Marsilius Ficinus (Marsilio Ficino): 162, 206
Massine, L.: 133
Matisse, H.: 258
Mauriac, F.: 134
McCosh, J.: 10, 142, 150, 221, 224f., 227, 278, 301
Mead, H.: 55, 78, 80, 82, 283
Mehlis, G.: 125
Meier, G. F.: 6, 15, 22, 23, 159, 252, 277
Meising: 154
Mendelssohn, M.: 15, 19, 20, 127, 275, 282

Mengs, A. R.: 143, 159
Menichini, J. and M.: 268, 278
Menuhin, Y.: 113
Mercier, D. J. Cardinal: 123, 167, 168, 242
Mersenne, Père: 52, 124
Merz, C.: 16
Michelangelo: 59, 116, 144, 145, 194
Milhaud, D.: 118
Mill, J. S.: 167, 168, 173, 174, 175, 179
Miller, D. C.: 16
Miller, H.: 60
Mirandola: *see* Pico della Mirandola
Mithalter, J.: 166
Montesquieu, Baron de: 280
Moore, G. E.: 147, 161, 253, 275
Moore, J. S.: 140, 160
Morris, B.: 155
Moussorgsky, M. P.: 127
Mozart, W. A.: 29, 60, 121, 133, 194, 195, 296
Mueller, G. E.: 114, 145, 160
Müller-Freienfels, R.: 151
Munro, Th.: 5, 21, 23, 30, 83, 141, 143, 253
Münsterberg, H.: 276, 277, 296, 306
Muratori, L. A.: 15
Murray, J. C.: 160

Nahm, M. C.: 160, 283, 300
Nancydes: 110
Nef, W.: 279
Nepos, C.: 13
Neumberg, M.: 16
Newman, E.: 133
Newman, J. H. Cardinal: 134
Newton, E.: 147, 274
Nicole, P.: 156, 157
Nietzsche, F.: 5
Nijinska, B.: 116
Nijinsky, V.: 110, 113, 133
Nilsson, B.: 296
Nordau, M.: 15
Noyes, C.: 162, 206

Oatis, W. J.: 118
O'Donnell, J. R.: 54
Oersted, H. C.: 154, 173
Oettingen, V.: 173
Offenbach, J.: 112
Ogden, C. K.: 16, 150, 152
Ogden, R. M.: 22, 152
Olivi, P. J.: 237
Olscamp, P. J.: 284
Opzoomer, C. W.: 158, 272, 273
Origen: 14
Osborn, H.: 22, 23, 144, 155
Osers, E.: 128
Ovid (Publius Ovidius Naso): 126, 132

Pacioli, L.: 15
Palestrina, G.: 88, 112
Pallavicino, P. S., Cardinal: 276, 277, 278, 281
Palmieri, D.: 160
Panofsky, E.: 16
Parker, D. H.: 22, 164, 168, 169, 253, 258, 269, 286, 287, 288, 289, 299, 300, 301
Parmenides: 92, 241
Patmore, C.: 131, 132, 134
Pavlova, A.: 113
Pellegrini, M.: 18
Pepper, S. C.: 148, 260
Perry, R. B.: 111, 128
Pesch, T.: 157
Petavius, D.: 146, 158
Petrus Joannis Olivi: *see* Olivi, P. J.
Philip the Chancellor: 238, 239, 240
Philo of Alexandria: 5, 12, 13, 139, 160, 207, 251, 280, 282, 283, 286
Philo the Sculptor: 110
Pico della Mirandola: 161
Pictet, A.: 21
Piero della Francesca: 15
Platner, E.: 159, 160
Plato: 5, 6, 7, 12, 13, 17, 26, 61, 84, 85, 106, 112, 113, 114, 128, 138, 139, 140, 145, 153, 157, 161, 162, 172, 175, 217, 218, 239, 241, 244, 251, 255, 277, 280, 283, 285, 286, 292, 303, 306, 315, 316, 317
Pliny the Elder (Plinius, S. C.): 13
Plotinus: 5, 7, 12, 13, 17, 28, 84, 85, 108, 109, 112, 114, 115, 131, 139, 146, 153, 157, 172, 207, 218, 239, 240, 244, 251, 272, 278, 280, 282, 283, 286
Pope, A.: 15
Porphyry: 5, 12
Potter, E.: 201
Pouillon, H.: 159, 160, 207, 237, 239, 240
Poussin, N.: 201
Prall, D. W.: 21, 22, 23, 143, 269, 276, 277, 283, 286, 287, 288, 292
Pratt, C. C.: 107
Preminger, O.: 125
Price, R.: 15, 161, 162, 206
Price, U.: 19, 162, 206, 231
Proclus: 146, 251
Proudhon, P. J.: 15
Pseudo-Dionysius: *see* Dionysius the Areopagite
Puccini, G.: 127, 194
Puffer, E. D.: 148, 149, 266, 270, 275
Pyrrhon of Elis: 17, 81
Pythagoras: 12, 110
Pythagoreans: 5, 12

Quintilian, M. F.: 118

INDEX OF NAMES

Rabelais, F.: 130
Rader, M.: 124, 164
Raeymaeker, L. De: 161
Ram, F.: 148
Rameau, J. P.: 16
Ramsay, G.: 19
Ravel, M. J.: 127
Raven, J. E.: 5, 12
Raymond, G. L.: 160
Read, H.: 5, 161, 306
Reid, L. A.: 154
Reid, Th.: 15, 19, 29, 67, 68, 142, 226, 231, 273
Remer, V.: 162
Renoir, P.: 29, 60
Repton, H.: 165, 206
Reynolds, Sir J.: 15, 52, 64, 70, 71, 72, 128, 129, 231, 233, 292
Richard of St. Victor: 245
Richards, I. A.: 16, 150, 152, 266, 267, 306
Rickaby, J.: 106, 161, 245
Riemann, H.: 15
Rimsky-Korsakov, N.: 133
Robert, G.: 111, 117, 133
Robert Grosseteste: 159, 207, 239
Rodin, A.: 86, 105, 111, 256, 257, 258
Roeber, F. G.: 16
Roland of Cremona: 237
Rosenkranz, J. K. F.: 20, 21, 25, 254, 256
Rosmini-Serbati, A.: 9, 10, 163, 245
Ross, W. D.: 144, 145
Rother, A.: 161, 174
Rubens, P. P.: 29, 61, 86
Ruckstull, F. W.: 147
Ruge, A.: 253, 255, 256
Ruskin, J.: 15, 112, 146, 164, 206, 233, 244, 252, 272, 273, 286, 290, 292

Samson, G. W.: 141
Sanseverino, C.: 160
Santayana, G.: 5, 20, 23, 51, 88, 151, 245, 255, 259–61, 281, 283f., 285, 286
Sappho: 110
Sartre, J. P.: 134
Savonarola: 161, 162
Schasler, M.: 16, 20, 25, 154, 232, 233, 234, 254, 255
Schelling, F. W. J.: 15, 153, 154, 171, 232, 233
Schiller, F.: 20, 128, 146, 226, 269
Schiller, J.: 284
Schlegel, F.: 20, 21, 226, 255
Schleiermacher, F. E. D.: 23, 154, 155, 226, 233, 234
Schnaase, K.: 15
Schneider, E.: 148
Schoen, M.: 144
Schönberg, A.: 133

Schopenhauer, A.: 5, 153, 154, 233, 245, 283
Schubert, F.: 29
Schulemann, G.: 237, 238
Schumann, R.: 127
Schütz, C. G.: 6
Scott, W. B.: 162
Sender, R.: 253
Seneca, L. A.: 13, 251
Sextus Empiricus: 81
Shaefer-Simmern, H.: 16
Shaftesbury, Lord: 15, 117, 127, 156, 244, 277, 278
Shakespeare: 110, 130
Shaliapin, F.: 60, 113
Shipley, J. T.: 21, 150, 271
Siebeck, H. G.: 16, 158
Simplicius of Silicia: 12
Slawska, O.: 116
Small, H. A.: 144
Socrates: 12, 17, 138, 139, 145, 159, 239
Solger, K. W. F.: 20, 23, 25, 153, 154, 231, 233, 253
Solon: 130
Sorel, G.: 15
Sourian: 148
Spencer, H.: 15, 16, 283
Spender, S.: 16, 60
Spinoza, B.: 7, 8, 17, 49, 53, 74, 75, 76, 82, 121, 209, 252, 276, 277
Stace, W. T.: 155
Stein, H. von: 15
Steiss, A. J.: 157
Stern, P.: 161
Stewart, D.: 18, 19, 29, 77, 105, 173, 231, 274, 292f.
Stewart, G. W.: 16
Stöckl, A.: 163, 164, 206
Stolnitz, J.: 82, 93, 98, 129, 130, 131, 141, 142, 268, 276, 282, 283
Stone, E. and J.: 116
Strauss, R.: 128, 201
Stravinsky, I.: 127
Stumpf, C.: 16
Suarez, F.: 146, 237, 239, 243, 244, 245, 282
Sullivan, D. J.: 163
Sully, J.: 21, 141
Sully-Proudhomme, R. T.: 123
Sulzer, J. G.: 15, 20, 278
Sweeney, L.: 163, 335

Tacitus, C.: 126, 132
Taine, H.: 15, 166, 270, 275
Taparelli, L.: 275, 281
Tari, A.: 16
Tartini, G.: 16
Tatian: 110

Taylor, E.: 111
Taylor, T.: 231
Tchaikovsky, P. I.: 113
Tejera, V.: 23, 268, 272
Terburg, T. C.: 159
Theodore the Atheist: 280
Thomas Aquinas, St.: 5, 7, 13, 14, 15, 17, 18, 26, 27, 28, 49, 54, 58, 61, 62, 65, 66, 67, 75, 84, 85, 108, 111, 112, 114, 115, 118, 119, 120, 121, 122, 124, 126, 129, 131, 132, 146, 157, 162, 163, 172, 177, 200, 207, 209, 218–20, 221 f., 225, 229, 230, 235, 237, 238, 239, 240, 241, 242, 244, 245, 251, 252, 258, 259, 269, 277, 278, 280, 282, 285, 287, 288, 300, 305, 308, 317
Thomas Campanella: 238
Thomas Gallus Vercellensis: 146, 238, 286
Thomas of York: 5, 160
Thomson, Wm.: 164, 206, 207
Thucydides: 10
Tieck, L.: 143
Tintoretto, I. L.: 29
Todhunter, J.: 161
Toletus, F. Cardinal: 237, 277
Tolstoi, L.: 5, 22, 110, 134, 142, 159, 166, 269, 283
Tongiorgi, S.: 160
Töpffer, R.: 157
Torossian, A.: 21, 22, 152
Toscanini, A.: 113
Trahndorff, K. F. E.: 154, 231, 232, 234
Tryon, T.: 125
Tucker, A.: 163, 206
Tyler, S.: 159, 160, 233

Ulrich Engelbert of Strasbourg: 13, 14, 18, 28, 161, 238, 239
Urráburu, J. J.: 138, 164, 206

Vallet, (Abbé) C. P.: 163, 164
Varro, M. T.: 13
Vasari, G.: 13
Verdi, G.: 86, 121, 127
Vergil (Virgil), P. M.: 114, 130, 194
Vico, G. B.: 8, 15

Vischer, F. T.: 15, 16, 153, 154, 223f., 229, 230, 232, 233, 234, 235, 253, 254
Vischer, R.: 16, 221
Vitruvius Pollio: 13, 139
Vivas, E.: 93
Volkelt, J.: 16, 22, 23
Vollert, C.: 120

Wagner, R.: 115, 127, 187, 196
Waley, H. D.: 280
Walter, B.: 113
Warton, J.: 226
Watkin, E. I.: 107, 158, 253, 258, 259, 268, 271, 278, 283, 286, 287, 306
Weber, C. M. von: 133
Weiss, P.: 163, 245, 253, 274, 284
Weisse, C. H.: 20, 21, 25, 154, 231, 233, 253, 255, 256
Weitz, M.: 267, 271, 284
Wiener, N.: 22
Wigman, M.: 60
Wilde, O.: 109
William of Auvergne: 54, 114, 146, 269, 281, 282
Wilpert, P.: 244
Winckelmann, J. J.: 13, 15, 21, 138, 143, 255
Wirth: 154
Witelo: 115, 116, 120, 285
Wittgenstein, L.: 77
Wolfe, T.: 60
Wolff, C.: 5, 8
Wood, J.: 16, 150, 152
Worsworth, W.: 132
Wortis, P.: 16
Wulf, M. de: 54, 99, 100, 152

Xenocrates of Sikyon: 13
Xenophon: 19, 139, 159, 206, 239

Zeising, A.: 154, 227–29, 232, 234
Zeno of Citium: 13
Ziegfield, E.: 148
Ziff, P.: 77
Zigliara, T. M.: 162
Zimmermann, R.: 15, 16, 173, 232

Index of Topics

Act and potency: 248
Aesthetic association: 93, 94, 95, 96, 104, 105, 119, 122–24; *see also* Reasons for real aesthetic disagreement (22) and (26)
Aesthetic attention: 295–97, 299, 303
Aesthetic beholder: 37, 55f., 58, 59, 60, 61, 62, 63, 85–88, 100, 106, 108, 112, 114, 116, 117, 118, 119, 121, 124, 125, 126, 132, 297, 301, 303, 304, 307, 309, 311, 313, 314, 315, 316
Aesthetic categories: 225, 230; (1) the attractive, 233; (2) the bizarre, 28; (3) the burlesque, 226, 228; (4) the charming, 226, 227, 233, 234; (5) the colossal, 226; (6) the comic, 20, 29, 130, 220, 226, 227, 234; (7) the congruous, 20, 232; (8) the decorous, 18, 220, 221; (9) the demonic, 228; (10) the dignified (dignity), 20, 228, 231, 233; (11) the elegant, 226, 231; (12) the elegic, 227; (13) *formositas*, 18, 220; (14) the gigantic, 227, 234; (15) the glorious, 228; (16) the gracious (grace), 18, 20, 28, 221, 226, 227, 228, 231, 233, 234; (17) the grandiose (grandeur), 19, 226, 227, 234; (18) the great, 225; (19) the humorous, 227, 228; (20) the idyllic, 226; (21) the ludicrous (ridiculous, risible), 19, 20, 226, 227, 233, 234; (22) the magnificent, 227; (23) the majestic, 226, 227, 228; (24) the naïve, 20; (25) the noble, 18, 228; (26) the novel, 19, 226, 230 f.; (27) the pathetic, 20, 226, 228, 231, 234; (28) the picturesque, 19, 28, 93, 227, 231; (29) the piquant, 226, 228; (30) the pleasant, 20; (31) the proper (propriety), 20; (32) the satirical, 130; (33) the sentimental, 20; (34) the specious, 220, 221, 225f.; (35) the suave, 18, 221, 226; (36) the sublime, *see* sublime; (37) the suitable, 18, 220, 225; (38) the tragic, 20, 29, 130, 220, 226, 227; (39) the tragicomic, 226, 227; (40) the trivial, 20; (41) the uncommon, 226; (42) *venustas*, 18; (43) reasons for systematizing the aesthetic categories, 225f.
Aesthetic channelization: 129
Aesthetic cognition: (1) as the act of the intellect, 304–306; (2) intrinsic delightfulness of, 311 f.; (3) intuitiveness of, 309–11; (4) nature of, 306–309; (5) object and cause of, 313f.; (6) properties of, 309–12; (7) uniqueness of, 306, 309, 310 f., 311 f., 317

Aesthetic delight: 37, 55f., 66, 81, 88, 93, 94, 95, 96, 310 f., 312, 315; (1) cause of, 55, 57–61, 62, 63, 67, 89, 120, 300, 303; (2) conditions of, 88f.; (3) disinterestedness of, 59, 281–84, 311, 317; (4) nature and properties of, 279–81, 311; (5) difference between non-aesthetic and, 281–85
Aesthetic defects: 102f., 107–14
Aesthetic deformity: 89
Aesthetic desire: (1) effect of, 315; (2) object of, 315f.; (3) principle of, 314; (4) relation of, to aesthetic delight, 314f.
Aesthetic dichotomy: 19
Aesthetic disagreement: 81–84, 89, 90, 91, 92, 101; (1) apparent, 101 f., 105–107; (2) division of reasons for, 101–105; (3) known to premodern thinkers, 84; (4) real, 102–105, 107–36; (5) reasons for, *see* separate entry; (6) use of, as a subjectivist argument, 82f.; *see also*, reasons for apparent aesthetic disagreement, Reasons for real aesthetic disagreement, and Reasons for aesthetic disagreement
Aesthetic disinterestedness: *see* Aesthetic delight (3), and Aesthetic experience (9)
Aesthetic distance: 105, 124f.
Aesthetic distraction: 105, 121 f.
Aesthetic encyclopedia: 20
Aesthetic *eros*: 316
Aesthetic experience: 60, 66, 95, 217, 265–317; (1) characterization by human powers of, 271–79; (2) cognitive and appetitive conditions of, 293, 294, 307; (3) compromise views on, 267, 269, 270 f., 278, 279, 281; (4) conditions of, 60 f., 97 f.; (5) contingent effects of, 316f.; (6) contingent preconditions of, 293, 294, 295–99, 303; (7) difference from non-aesthetic experience of, 266f.; (8) disagreements on, 266f., 269f., 270, 270 f., 271–76, 276–78, 278f., 279–81, 281–84, 285–90, 292f., 299–301, 301; (9) Disinterested delightfulness of, 281–84; (10) dissimilarities to other experiences of, 270; (11) elements of, 57; (12) essence of, 294f., 304–12; (13) historical consideration of views on, 265–90; (14) human powers involved in, 271–76; (15) intellectualist and voluntarist characterization of, 268f.; (16) intelligibility of the powers involved in, 292f.; (17) nature, number and roles of the senses involved in, 285–

345

90, 299–301; (18) nature of the cognitive powers involved in, 276–78; (19) nature of the delight in, 279–81; (20) nature of the subject of, 278f.; (21) necessary effects of, 312–16; (22) necessary preconditions of, 298–301, 302–304, 308, 313; (23) phenomenological characterization of, 267–71; (24) properties of, 270f.; (25) role of the agent intellect in, 308f.; (26) second and secondary, 315; (27) sensation and perception in, 301f.; (28) similarities to other experiences of, 269f.; (29)—and beatific vision, 317; (30)—and mystic experience, 317

Aesthetic expectation: 105, 132f., 297, 298, 299

Aesthetic fact: (1) negative, 55, 62, 68, 90; (2) positive, 55, 56, 58, 62, 81f., 89, 90, 99

Aesthetic gyneism: 159f.

Aesthetic hierarchies: 93, 103, 112f.

Aesthetic idealism: (1) abstract and concrete, 154; (2) emotionalist, 155; (3) German, 153–55; (4) immanent, 154f.; (5) intellectualist, 155; (6) platonic, 153; (7) transcendentalist, 152–54; (8) vitalist, 155

Aesthetic ignorance: 103, 111

Aesthetic inattention: 105, 121f.

Aesthetic intuition: 309–12

Aesthetic judgment: 312–14; see also art critic (1)

Aesthetic knowledge: (1) cause of, 55, 57–61, 66, 313f.; (2) object of, 313, 315f.

Aesthetic method(s): 72, 137, 167–83; (1) division of the, 170–74; (2) evaluation of the, 174–76; (3) historical review of the, 167–70; (4) proposed, 176–81, 181f.

Aesthetic objectivism: 17, 55–64, 80, 86, 99, 100, 101, 236; (1) clarification of, 63f.; (2) direct argument for, defended, 62f.; (3) direct argument for, detailed, 56–61; (4) direct argument for, outlined, 55f.

Aesthetic objectivists: 17, 56, 61, 63f., 77, 85, 86, 89, 99

Aesthetic pluralism: 20

Aesthetic powers: 271–76, 292f., 293–316

Aesthetic prejudice: (1) favorable, 104f., 118f.; (2) unfavorable, 105, 125f.

Aesthetic realism: (1) dualistic, 161f.; (2) formalist, 156, 157f.; (3) gyneist, 159f.; (4) monistic, 159f.; (5) ordinist, 160f.; (6) pluralistic, 163–65; (7) totalist, 156, 158–65; (8) transcendentalist, 156f.; (9) triadic, 161f.

Aesthetic relationism: 53f.

Aesthetic relativism: 52, 68–73

Aesthetic roles: 37, 43f., 59

Aesthetic senses: 285–90

Aesthetic skepticism: (1) explicit, 140f., 141f.; (2) immoderate, 140f.; (3) implicit, 141, 142–49; (4) moderate, 141–49; (5) partly objective, 149; (6) partial, 149

Aesthetic sophistication: 112f.

Aesthetic standards: 105, 133f.

Aesthetic subjectivism: 17, 99, 100, 101, 236; (1) (alleged) misinterpretations of, 67f., 88f.; (2) apparent, 65–68; (3) arguments for, 67f.; (4) associationist, 93–96; (5) cosmological, 77–81; (6) division of, 51–53, 65–100; (7) evaluation of, 54, 65–100; (8) explicit, 73; (9) implicit, 68; (10) metaphysical, 73–77; (11) psychological, 81–93; (12) relationist, 96–100; (13) relativist, 68–73

Aesthetic subjectivists: 17f., 51–53, 86, 88, 89

Aesthetic taste: 68f., 105, 127–32

Aesthetically educated, uneducated: 129, 196

Aesthetics: (1) auxiliary sciences of, 32, 44–47; (2) branches of, see separate entry; (3) definition of, see separate entry; (4) difficulties with definitions of, 3; (5) division of, 32–47; (6) essential definition of, see separate entry; (7) etymological definition of, 5–10; (8) gradual development of, 12–16; (9) independent and propedeutic science, 8; (10) international congresses of, 11; (11) name of, see separate entry; (12) opposite to logic, 8; (13) paradox of, 5; (14) premodern and modern treatment of, 17–21; (15) scope of, 11f., 12–16, 25; (16) subject matter and object matter of, 7, 25f.; (17) two kinds of definitions of, 3

Analysis of material order: 189–92

Analysis of orderly whole: 187–89

Analogy of the Principles of Material Beauty: 209f.

Arguments against: (1) apparent aesthetic subjectivism, 67f.; (2) aesthetic associationism, 93–96; (3) aesthetic relationism, 98–100; (4) aesthetic relativism, 68–73; (5) aesthetic subjectivism in general, 102–36, especially 135f.; (6) cosmological aesthetic subjectivism, 79f.; (7) dialectical interpretation of ugliness, 256–59; (8) metaphysical aesthetic subjectivism, 74–76; (9) negative psychological subjectivism, 83–93; (10) perception as the necessary condition of aesthetic experience, 298; (11) proposed aesthetic method, 182; (12) Thomas' system of the transcendentals, 242; (13) transcendentality of beauty, 250; (14) transcendentalist theories explaining away ugliness, 260f., 261f., 262f.; (15) universality of material order, 199

Arguments for: (1) aesthetic associationism, 93; (2) aesthetic knowledge being due to the intellect, 304–306; (3) aesthetic relationism,

INDEX OF TOPICS

96–98; (4) aesthetic relativism, 68, 69f., 72f.; (5) alternative scopes of beauty, 236; (6) analogy of the principles of material beauty, 209f.; (7) analytic and synthetic definitions of material beauty, 187–92; (8) analytic principles of material beauty, 193–96; (9) attributing specific human powers to aesthetic experience, 290, 291 f.; (10) beauty of all finite beings, 247–49; (11) beauty of all finite beings despite ugliness, 259–63, 263f.; (12) beauty of God, 245–47; (13) completeness of the list of analytic principles of beauty, 202f.; (14) correctness of the proposed essential definition of aesthetics, 25–31; (15) cosmological aesthetic subjectivism, 77f.; (16) difficulty with changing the name of aesthetics, 10; (17) difficulty with defining aesthetics, 11–16, 16–21; (18) elusiveness of the essence of beauty, 139f.; (19) existence of beauty, 55f., 56–63; (20) intelligibility of the human powers involved in aesthetic experience, 290 f., 292f.; (21) metaphysical aesthetic subjectivism, 73f., 76, 77; (22) negative psychological subjectivism, 82, 83; (23) necessity of the analytic principles of material beauty, 197f.; (24) object and specific cause of aesthetic knowledge, 313f.; (25) perception being the necessary condition of aesthetic experience, 298; (26) presence of the principles of material beauty in God, 212–14; (27) presence of the principles of material beauty in the morally good act, 211 f., 214; (28) proposed essential definition of beauty, 208–15; (29) proposed essential definition of material beauty, 193–208; (30) structure in aesthetic experience, 290 f.; (31) time of passing aesthetic judgment, 312f.; (32) Thomas' system of the transcendentals being complete, 242; (33) transcendentality of beauty, 245–50; (34) ultimateness of the analytic principles of material beauty, 203–208; (35) universal presence of the principles of material beauty, 198–202

Art: (1) applied, decorative, and mixed, 40; (2) fine, divided, 34f.; (3) Philosophy of, 34f.

Artist: (1) creative, 59, 60, 88; (2) reproductive, 88

Artistic: (1) activity, 85; (2) concern with completing the art-work, 194; (3) concern with order, 200 f.; (4) creation (production), 37, 86, 88, 132; (5) frustration, 88; (6) knowledge, 59; (7) training, 85f.

Artwork(s): (1) fine, 60f., 88, 107f., 109, 110, 111, 112, 113, 115, 116, 117, 118, 119, 121, 124, 125, 127, 129, 131, 132f., 133, 134, 187, 189, 194, 195, 196, 201, 295f.; (2) contemporary fine, 26; (3) medieval fine, 25, 114; (4) modern fine, 25f., 114, 130; (5) mutilated fine, 109f., 194; (6) novelty of fine, 108f.; (7) parts and whole of fine, 109f., 111, 117; (8) Renaissance fine, 25f.; (9) subject matter of fine, 110; (10) and taste, 68f.; (11) and ugliness, 28f.

Art Critic: (1) judging the artwork, 105f., 107; (2) limitation of the, 129; (3) prejudice of the, 134f.; (4) and art historian, 43f.; (5) and moralist, 43f., 110 f.

Art criticism: 38, 42–44

Bases of dividing beauty: 221, 229f.; (1) arbitrariness of some, 230–35; (2) objective and subjective, 229f.

Beautiful, objective and subjective sense of the: 106f.

Beauty: (1) causes of, 192; (2) definitions of, *see* separate entry; (3) definition of material, 185, 186, 208; (4) degrees of, 264; (5) divisions of, *see* separate entry; (6) essence of, *see* separate entry; (7) essential definition of, *see* separate entry; (8) existence of, *see* separate entry; (9) extension of, 236f., 265; *see also* transcendentality of beauty; (10) generic (central) aesthetic value, 18, 29; (11) gradually dethroned, 18–21; (12) in the broad and strict sense, 29; (13) kinds of, *see* separate entry; (14) known through the senses and the intellect, 7, 8; (15) premodern and modern treatment of, 18–21; (16) principles of, *see* separate entry; (17) privation of, 236, 251–53; *see also* ugliness; (18) pure perfection, 246; (19) suprasensory knowability of, 304–306; (20) transcendentality of, *see* transcendentality of (1); (21) unknowableness of, 76, 77; (22) variety of, 76, 94; (23) where born, 99f.; *see also*, bases of dividing beauty

Beauty, kinds of: (1) accidental, 219, 264; (2) actual, 99, 221, 223; (3) adherent, 87; (4) aesthetic, 262; (5) angelic, 219; (6) arithmetic, 218; (7) artistic, 34, 37, 88, 218, 220, 223, 224; (8) asexual, 222; (9) audible, 81, 220, 224; (10) of action, 220, 225; (11) of body, 36, 87, 123, 218, 219, 222, 223; (12) of content, 218; (13) of form, 218, 219; (14) of habit, 219; (15) of mind (soul), 36, 217, 219, 222; (16) of music, 8, 111, 112; (17) of ornament (decor), 220, 229, 230; (18) of poem, 109, 111; (19) of posture, 220; (20) of prime matter, 219; (21) of quality, 219, 225; (22) of quantity, 219, 225; (23) of relation, 225; (24) of shape, 220, 223; (25) of society, 37; (26) of where, 220; (27)

347

celestial beauty, 219; (28) corporeal, 34; (29) creaturely, 218; (30) difficult, 256; (31) divine, 34, 208, 212–14, 217, 218, 221, 229, 245–47, 249; (32) dynamic, 223, 229; (33) easy, 256; (34) essential, 219, 264; (35) eternal, 221; (36) formal, 229; (37) geometric, 218, 221; (38) hermaphrodite, 222; (39) human, 36, 87, 93, 217, 219, 222, 223, 224; (40) ideal, 218, 221; (41) imaginary, 218; (42) immaterial, 229; (43) imperfect, 264; (44) intrinsic, 87; (45) material, 219, 222, 223, 229; (46) mathematical, 221, 229; (47) metaphysical, 235; (48) moral, 221 f., 223, 224, 235; (49) natural, 87, 88, 93, 108, 112, 113, 114, 118f., 130, 202, 217, 218, 223, 224; (50) objective, 30, 85, 228; (51) partial, 219, 225; (52) perfect, 264; (53) physical, 37, 224, 235; (54) potential, 99, 221; (55) real, 218; (56) sexual, 222; (57) social, 222, 223; (58) spiritual, 34, 222; (59) static, 223; (60) subjective, 30, 85, 228; (61) supernatural, 220; (62) symmetrical, 231; (63) temporal, 221; (64) terrestrial, 219; (65) thinkable, 218, 222; (66) total, 219, 225; (67) visible, 81, 87, 220, 224

Beauty and: (1) association, 119, 122–24; (2) distraction, 121 f.; (3) expectation, 132f.; (4) frequency of form, 69–72; (5) inattention, 121 f.; (6) individual standard, 133–35; (7) its interpretation, 72f., 83; (8) light, 116f.; (9) love, 66, 118f.; (10) maturity, 131 f.; (11) mood, 120 f.; (12) pain, 120; (13) prejudice, 125f.; (14) psychical distance, 124f.; (15) sense, 114f., 120, 122; (16) sensory pleasure, 122; (17) taste, 68f., 94, 127–31; (18) temperament, 126f.

Branches of aesthetics: (1) acoustical (tonal) aesthetics, 16, 36; (2) aesthetics of symbols, 16; (3) angelological aesthetics, 13; (4) architectural aesthetics, 13; (5) art appreciation, 16, 38, 41; (6) art criticism, see separate entry; (7) art pedagogy, 38–40; (8) biological aesthetics, 36; (9) botanical aesthetics, 16, 36; (10) charismatic aesthetics, 14, 38; (11) chemical aesthetics, 36; (12) Christological aesthetics, 14, 38; (13) cosmological aesthetics, 12, 34; (14) cultural aesthetics, 16; (15) dogmatic theological aesthetics, 14, 37f.; (16) dynamic aesthetics, 36; (17) ecclesiological aesthetics, 14, 38; (18) eschatological aesthetics, 14, 38; (19) ethical aesthetics, 12; (20) geometrical aesthetics, 12, 35; (21) history of aesthetics, 44f.; (22) history of art, 13, 15, 45f.; (23) liturgical aesthetics, 38, 39, 40 f.; (24) logical aesthetics, 14; (25) Mariological aesthetics, 14, 38; (26) mathematical aesthetics, 12, 15, 35; (27) metaphysical aesthetics, 12, 33f., 49; (28) moral theological aesthetics, 14, 37f.; (29) musical aesthetics, 13, 15, 35; (30) optical aesthetics, 16, 36; (31) philosophical aesthetics, 15, 33–35, 38; (32) philosophy of art, see art (3); (33) philosophy of beauty, 49; (34) philosophy of fine art, 15, 34; (35) philosophy of historical beauty, 16; (36) philosophy of material beauty, 34; (37) philosophy of natural beauty, 15f., 34; (38) philosophy of social beauty, 16; (39) philosophy of the history of aesthetics, 16, 47; (40) philosophy of the history of art, 46; (41) phenomenological aesthetics, 16; (42) physical aesthetics, 16, 36; (43) physiological aesthetics, 16; (44) pictorial aesthetics, 13, 15, 35; (45) pneumatological aesthetics, 34; (46) Poetical aesthetics, 13, 14, 35; (47) practical aesthetics, 32, 38–44; (48) psychoanalytical aesthetics, 16; (49) psychological aesthetics, 12, 15, 16, 36f.; (50) scientific aesthetics, 15, 35–37, 38; (51) sculptural aesthetics, 13, 35; (52) sociological aesthetics, 15, 36f.; (53) spatial aesthetics, 36; (54) speculative aesthetics, 32, 33–38; (55) technological aesthetics, 38f.; (56) theistic aesthetics, 34; (57) theological aesthetics, 13, 14, 37f.; (58) therapeutic aesthetics, 16, 38–40; (59) trinitarian aesthetics, 14, 38; (60) zoological aesthetics, 16, 36

Cause: (1) and effect, 246, 247, 248, 297; (2) the four, of the whole, 188–90; (3) five genera of, 182f.

Comparison of: (1) apparent and real aesthetic subjectivism, 65–68; (2) Aquinas' and Hume's aesthetic theories, 65–67

Definition of aesthetics: (1) essential, see separate entry; (2) etymological, 5–10; see also arguments for (17)

Definition(s) of beauty: 66, 137; (1) circular, 144f.; (2) essential, 137, 215, 246, 263; (3) inconvertible, 144; (4) logically correct, 145–49; (5) logically incorrect, 143–45; (6) metaphysical, 143; (7) negative, 143f.; (8) nominal, 143; (9) non-essential, 143–49; (10) obscure, 144; (11) partly skeptic, 149; (12) Pseudo-definitions of, 145; (13) by accident, 145; (14) by efficient cause, 145f.; (15) by effect, 24, 146–49.

Delight, aesthetic and non-aesthetic: 96, 279–81, 303f.

Delightful: (1) Non-aesthetically, 29f., 62, 95;

INDEX OF TOPICS

(2) and beautiful, 233; (3) by usefulness, 30; (4) knowledge, 197

Division(s) of Beauty: 215, 217–35, 265; (1) bases of the, *see* separate entry; (2) dichotomic, 217, 218; (3) historical consideration of the, 217–29; (4) trichotomic, 225

Essence of Beauty: 137–215; (1) absolute consequence of the, 215–36; (2) consequences of the, 215f., 217–35, 236–64, 265–317; (3) elusiveness of the, 138–40; (4) idealist views on the, 152–56; (5) implication of the, 265; (6) realist views on the, 149–65; (7) relative consequence of the, 215; (8) skeptic views on the, 141–49; (9) subjectivist views on the, 149–52; (10) topical and doctrinal consequences of the, 215; (11) views on the, 138–65

Essential Definition(s) of Aesthetics: 11–31; (1) difficulty with finding the, 11–12; (2) axiological objection to the proposed, 29f.; (3) Doctrinal, historical objection to the proposed, 25–28; (4) explanation of the proposed, 23–25; (5) historical objection to the proposed, 28f.; (6) logical objection to the proposed, 25; (7) metaphysical objection to the proposed, 30 f.; (8) proposed, 23, 31; (9) variety of, 21–23

Essential definition of beauty: 184–215; (1) demonstrated at the material level, 193–208; (2) demonstrated at the metaphysical level, 208–15; (3) explained, 185f.; (4) presented, 184f.; (5) recognized through the analysis of material order, 189–92; (6) recognized through an analysis of orderly material whole, 187–89; (7) restated, 185f., 192, 208, 215, 263; (8) necessary conditions of, 208f.

Existence of Beauty: 51–64, 65–100, 101–36, 137, 265; (1) direct argument for the, 55f., 56–64; (2) indirect arguments for the, 64–100, 101–36

God: 34, 74, 75, 76, 85, 89, 111, 145, 208, 209, 211, 248, 262, 263, 290; (1) beauty of, 209, 212–14, 245–47, 249; (2) effects of the beauty of, 247; (3) existence of, 89, 209, 213; (4) methods of establishing the beauty of, 212f., 245–47; (5) nature of, 245; (6) relation of moral beauty to the beauty of, 214f.

Good, the: (1) delights, 93, 285; (2) transcendentality of, 239, 240, 241, 242; (3) and the beautiful, 285

Historical consideration of: (1) aesthetic objectivism as compared with apparent aesthetic subjectivism, 65–68; (2) aesthetic subjectivism, 51–54; (3) aesthetic methods, 167–70; (4) aesthetics as a science, 5; (5) attempts at explaining away ugliness, 259–63; (6) employment of ugliness in the fine arts, 25f.; (7) gradual development of aesthetics, 12–16; (8) name "aesthetics," 5–8; (9) names for aesthetics, 9–10; (10) notion of ugliness, 251–56; (11) premodern and modern aesthetics, 17–21; *see also* views

"Like likes like": 303

Method(s) of: (1) Demonstrating God's beauty, 245f.; (2) Demonstrating the beauty of all finite beings, 247–49; (3) Dividing beauty; *see*: Bases of the Division(s) of Beauty; (4) Socratic, 169

Name(s) of aesthetics: (1) evaluation of the, 8–9; (2) irreplaceable, 10; (3) meaning of the, 6, 7; (4) other, 9–10; (5) reasons for the, 7–8, 9; (6) weakness of the, 9

Order: 26, 87, 185–215, 249, 263; (1) Causes of, 190 f.; (2) kinds of, 199; (3) parts of, 187–90; (4) principles of, 187, 188; (5) requirements of producing, 189

Participation: 247, 248
"Passions" of being: 237, 238
Perfection: (1) accidental, 264; (2) divine, 248; (3) finite, 248; (4) pure and mixed, 246
Possession: 55–58
Primary and secondary qualities: 53, 78–81, 90
Principle of causality: 57
Principles of beauty: 76f., 87, 127, 133; (1) analytic, 65, 184–215; (2) clarity (radiance), 66, 263; (3) integrity, 65, 184–215 (especially 190), 249, 264; (4) material and formal, 264; (5) objective and subjective, 205f.; (6) order, *see* separate entry; (7) presence of, in God, 212–15; (8) presence of, in the morally good act, 211 f., 214; (9) proportion, 65, 66, 87, 184–215 (especially 190), 249, 263, 264; (10) relation of other principles to the synthetic and analytic, 207f.; (11) relation of the synthetic and analytic, 188f., 190 f., 192, 203; (12) synthetic, 65, 66, 184–215; *see also* order; (13) unity, 184–215, 249, 263, 264; *and* analogy of the principles of material beauty
Property, logical and transcendental: 237

Reasons for aesthetic disagreement: 101–36; (1) comparison of, 135f.; (2) reasons for apparent, *see* separate entry; (3) reasons for real, 102–105, 107–35; *see also* separate entry

Reasons for apparent aesthetic disagreement: 101 f., 105–107; (1) analogous uses of "beautiful," 102, 105f.; (2) analogous use of "ugly," 102, 107; (3) equivocal uses of "beautiful," 102, 106f.; (4) subjective use of "beautiful," 102, 106

Reasons for real aesthetic disagreement: (1) aesthetic defects, *see* separate entry; (2) aesthetic hierarchies, *see* separate entry; (3) aesthetic ignorance, *see* separate entry; (4) completely subjective, 104f., 119–35; (5) complexity of the aesthetic order, 104, 117f.; (6) disproportion of mental capacity to the artwork, 104, 117f.; (7) disproportionate mood, 104, 120 f.; (8) distraction, *see* aesthetic distraction; (9) excessive familiarity, 103, 107f.; (10) extreme length of the artwork, 104, 117; (11) favorable prejudice, *see* aesthetic prejudice (1); (12) habitual expectation, *see* aesthetic expectation; (13) illness or pain, 104, 120; (14) inattention, *see* aesthetic inattention; (15) individual standard, *see* aesthetic standards; (16) lack of aesthetic distance, *see* aesthetic distance; (17) lack of familiarity, 103, 108f.; (18) lack of suitable distance, 104, 115f.; (19) lack of suitable light, 104, 116f.; (20) lack of suitable size and volume, 104, 114f.; (21) large size of the artwork, 104, 117; (22) pleasant association, 104, 119; (23) sensory malfunction, 104f., 119f., 122; (24) taste, *see* aesthetic taste; (25) unfavorable prejudice, *see* aesthetic prejudice (2); (26) unpleasant association, 105, 122–24; (27) unsuitable temperament, 105, 126f.

Senses: (1) aesthetic and non-aesthetic, 286–90, 298–301, 302–304; (2) external and internal, 298–304; (3) higher and lower, 285–90; (4) primary and secondary aesthetic, 298f., 301

Sublime: 18, 19, 20, 29, 93, 130, 226, 227, 228, 231; (1) nature and properties of the, 232f.; (2) opposite of the, 233f.; (3) relation of, to aesthetics, 28; (4) relation of, to beauty, 18, 19; (5) relation of, to grandeur, 19, 231

Substance and accident: 248

Transcendentality of: (1) beauty, 215, 235, 236–50, 259–64; (2) definiteness, 241, 243, 244; (3) goodness, *see* good (2), (3); (4) otherness, 240, 241, 243, 244; (5) truth, 241, 242; (6) unity, 237, 240

Transcendental(s): (1) Aristotle's theory of, 237f.; (2) categorical and disjunctive, 243; (3) convertibility of, 238, 242; (4) demonstration of, 245–50, 263f.; (5) distinction between properties of being and, 243f.; (6) history of the theories of, 237, 239–44; (7) list of, 239f.; (8) logical *vs.* metaphysical, 242–44; (9) medieval theories of, 238; (10) real identity of, 238f., 242; (11) systematization of, 240–43

Ugliness: (1) as absence (privation) of beauty, 251–53, 259; (2) as amusing, 255; (3) as both pleasing and displeasing, 255, 257f., 261; (4) as a conflict, 261; (5) as difficult beauty, 256; (6) as formless, 261 f.; (7) as inexpressive, 261; (8) as limited beauty, 258, 259, 264; (9) as moral evil, 260; (10) as negation or privation, 259; (11) as pretension, 261, 262; (12) as subject of aesthetics, 27f.; (13) aesthetic and metaphysical, 262; (14) alleged subjectivity of, 262f.; (15) dialectical interpretations of, 253–55, 256–59; (16) division of, 26f.; (17) essence of, 20 f., 27, 215; (18) hierarchy of, 20; (19) historical consideration of, 251–56; (20) kinds of, 20, 26, 262; (21) nature of, 250–64; (22) negative interpretations of, 251–53; (23) non-dialectical positive interpretations of, 255f.; (24) positive interpretations of, 253–56; (25) question of the reality of, 258f., 262f.; (26) relation of, to aesthetic value (beauty), 20f., 28; (27) role of, in beauty, 28; (28) theories explaining away, 260, 261, 262; (29) in modern art, 25f.; (30) in tragedy and comedy, 25; (31) represented beautifully, 28, 257, 258

Ugly, the: 112, 113, 114, 122f., 226, 250

Views on: (1) aesthetic experience, 265–90; (2) the contingent effects of aesthetic experience, 316; (3) the division of beauty, 217–29, 230–34; (4) the essence of beauty, 138–65; (5) the essential definition of aesthetics, 21–23; (6) the intelligibility of the aesthetic powers, 292f.; (7) the role of the senses in aesthetic experience, 299–302; (8) the transcendentals and the transcendentality of beauty, 237–44; *see also* historical considerations

"Weakness of the spectator": 130

Woman (Women): 66, 85, 86, 93, 95, 112, 113, 122, 131, 145, 159f.

www.ingramcontent.com/pod-product-compliance
Lightning Source LLC
Chambersburg PA
CBHW071650160426
43195CB00012B/1416